DYNAMIC MACROECONOMIC ANALYSIS

Dynamic stochastic general equilibrium (DSGE) models have begun to dominate the field of macroeconomic theory and policy-making. These models describe the evolution of macroeconomic activity as a recursive sequence of outcomes based upon the optimal decision rules of rational households, firms and policy-makers. While posing a micro-founded dynamic optimisation problem for agents under uncertainty, such models have been shown to be both analytically tractable and sufficiently rich for meaningful policy analysis in a wide class of macroeconomic problems, for example, monetary and fiscal policy, economic cycles and growth and capital flows. This volume collects specially commissioned papers from leading researchers, which pull together some of the key recent results in diverse areas. This book promotes research using optimising models and will inform researchers, postgraduate students and economists in policy-oriented organisations of some of the key findings and policy implications.

Sumru Altug is Professor at Koc University, Turkey. She is the joint author of *Dynamic Choice and Asset Markets* (with Pamela Labadie) (1995).

Jagjit S. Chadha is Professor of Economics at the University of St Andrews. Formerly fellow of Clare College, Cambridge and lecturer at Cambridge University.

Charles Nolan is Reader in Economics at the University of Durham.

D1470700

DYNAMIC MACROECONOMIC ANALYSIS

Theory and Policy in General Equilibrium

EDITED BY

SUMRU ALTUG, JAGJIT S. CHADHA

AND

CHARLES NOLAN

CAMBRIDGE
UNIVERSITY PRESS

PUBLISHED BY THE PRESS SYNDICATE OF THE UNIVERSITY OF CAMBRIDGE
The Pitt Building, Trumpington Street, Cambridge, United Kingdom

CAMBRIDGE UNIVERSITY PRESS
The Edinburgh Building, Cambridge, CB2 2RU, UK
40 West 20th Street, New York, NY 10011–4211, USA
477 Williamstown Road, Port Melbourne, VIC 3207, Australia
Ruiz de Alarcón 13, 28014 Madrid, Spain
Dock House, The Waterfront, Cape Town 8001, South Africa

http://www.cambridge.org

First published 2003

Printed in the United Kingdom at the University Press, Cambridge

Typeface Adobe Garamond 11/12.5 pt.   *System* LaTeX 2$_\varepsilon$ [TB]

A catalogue record for this book is available from the British Library

Library of Congress Cataloging in Publication data
Dynamic macroeconomic analysis : theory and policy in general equilibrium / edited by
Sumru Altug, Jagjit S. Chadha, Charles Nolan.
p. cm
ISBN 0 521 82668 3 – ISBN 0 521 53403 8 (pb.)
1. Macroeconomics.   2. Equilibrium (Economics)   I. Altug, Sumru.   II. Chadha, Jagjit.
III. Nolan, Charles.
HB172.5.D96 2003   339.5 – dc21   2003043589

ISBN 0 521 82668 3 hardback
ISBN 0 521 53403 8 paperback

The publisher has used its best endeavours to ensure that the URLs for external
websites referred to in this book are correct and active at the time of going to press.
However, the publisher has no responsibility for the websites and can make no guarantee
that a site will remain live or that the content is or will remain appropriate.

Contents

v

Contributors

SUMRU ALTUG is currently a Professor of Economics at Koç University in Istanbul, Turkey. She received her BA in Economics from the University of Pittsburgh in 1978 and her PhD from Carnegie-Mellon University in 1985. She has held professorial appointments at the University of Durham and the University of York from 1999 to 2002. She was on the faculty at the Department of Economics at the University of Minnesota between 1984 and 1994 and has held visiting appointments at the University of Wisconsin, Duke University, and Virginia Polytechnic Institute and State University. Formerly a visiting scholar at the National Bureau of Economic Research (NBER) and the Federal Reserve Bank of Minneapolis, she is a past member of the ESRC Politics, Economics, and Geography (PEG) College at the Economic and Social Research Council (ESRC) in the UK, an Associate Editor at the *Economic Journal*, and a Research Fellow at the Centre for Economic Policy Research (CEPR).

CRISTINA ARELLANO is a PhD economics graduate student at Duke University. She is from Ecuador and received a BS in Economics (1998) from Indiana University with honours. Her areas of specialization are macroeconomics and international economics. Her current research focuses on economic fluctuations, financial frictions in emerging markets and sovereign debt.

MATTHEW B. CANZONERI has been a Professor of Economics at Georgetown University since 1985. He was Chair of the Economics Department from 1991 to 1994. He has served on the staff of the Board of Governors of the Federal Reserve System and as a consultant at the International Monetary Fund, the Bank of England, and the Bank of Spain. He has published extensively on monetary policy and on the coordination of policy between countries. He has also testified before the US House Subcommittee on Domestic Monetary Policy on the implications of European monetary integration for US economic interests. He received a PhD in Economics from the University of Minnesota in 1975 and a BS in Mathematics from Stanford University in 1967.

JAGJIT S. CHADHA is Professor of Economics at the University of St Andrews. He was educated at University College, London and the London School of Economics. He has held appointments at the London School of Economics, Southampton University and the Bank of England and most recently, Cambridge University. He is Secretary of the ESRC-funded Money, Macro Finance Group and has acted as Consultant to the European Commission and to BNP Paribas. His research interests are monetary and macroeconomic quantitative theory.

ROBERT E. CUMBY is Professor of Economics in the School of Foreign Service of Georgetown University. He received his BA in economics from the College of William and Mary and his PhD in economics from the Massachusetts Institute of Technology. At Georgetown, he teaches international trade and finance in the undergraduate and in the masters of science in foreign service programs. Prior to joining the faculty of Georgetown University in 1994, he was on the faculty of the Stern School of Business of New York University between 1982 and 1994. Prior to that, he was an economist at the International Monetary Fund. During the 1993–4 academic year, he served as senior economist on the Council of Economic Advisers, and between 1998 and 2000 as Deputy Assistant Secretary for Economic Policy at the United States Department of Treasury. His primary research interests are in international finance, macroeconomics, and applied econometrics. He has served as an associate editor and co-editor of the *Journal of International Economics* and is a research associate of the National Bureau of Economic Research.

FANNY S. DEMERS holds a PhD from The Johns Hopkins University and is Associate Professor at Carleton University, Ottawa, Canada. She has published in the areas of investment, macroeconomics and the economics of uncertainty.

MICHEL DEMERS has a PhD from The Johns Hopkins University and is Associate Professor at Carleton University, Ottawa, Canada. He has published in the areas of investment, economics of uncertainty and economic integration.

BEHZAD T. DIBA is Professor of Economics at Georgetown University. He received his PhD in economics from Brown University in 1984. He has taught courses on macroeconomics, financial markets, international finance and applications of mathematical methods. His research interests are in macroeconomics and international finance.

GIOVANNI GANELLI is a research fellow at Trinity College, Dublin. He holds a PhD and a Masters degree in Economics from the University of Warwick and an undergraduate degree in Economics and Statistics from the University of Rome 'La Sapienza'. His current research focuses on open economy macroeconomic models with imperfect competition and nominal rigidities.

PHILIP R. LANE is the Director of the Institute for International Integration Studies (IIIS) at Trinity College, Dublin, where he is Associate Professor of Economics and a College Fellow. He received a doctorate in Economics at Harvard University in 1995 and was an Assistant Professor of Economics and International Affairs at Columbia University during 1995–1997. He is scientific leader of an EU research network 'Analysis of International Capital Markets: Understanding Europe's Role in the World Economy.' He is a research fellow at the Centre for Economic Policy Research (CEPR) and has been a visiting scholar at the International Monetary Fund and the Federal Reserve Bank of New York and a consultant to the European Commission. His research interests include international macroeconomics, economic growth, European Monetary Union and Irish economic performance. He is an *Economic Policy* panel member and is on the editorial boards of the *European Economic Review*, *Economics and Politics*, *Economic and Social Review*, *Open Economies Review* and *International Tax and Public Finance*. In November 2001, he received the German Bernacer Award in Monetary Economics as most outstanding young monetary economist among Eurozone member countries.

ENRIQUE G. MENDOZA is a Professor of International Economics and Finance at the University of Maryland and a Faculty Research Fellow of the NBER. He is co-editor of the *Journal of International Economics* and member of the editorial board of the *American Economic Review*. He held associate professor and professor appointments at Duke University (1997–2001) and worked as an Economist in the Division of International Finance of the Board of Governors of the Federal Reserve System (1994–7) and in the Research Department of the International Fund (1989–94). He holds PhD and MA degrees from the University of Western Ontario and an Hons BA degree from Anahuac University in Mexico City. His research focuses on international capital flows, stabilization policy and business cycles.

CHARLES NOLAN was educated at the University of Strathclyde and Birkbeck College, University of London. He worked for eight years as an economist at the Bank of England. He has taught at the University of Reading, UK and is currently reader in Economics at the University of Durham, UK. He is a member of the European Monetary Forum. His research interests are quantitative general equilibrium macroeconomics and monetary theory, international finance and business cycles analysis.

JAMES PEMBERTON is Professor of Economics and Head of the Business School at the University of Reading. He has researched and published in many areas of macroeconomics, including consumption and saving behaviour, decision-making under uncertainty, unemployment, inflation, and macroeconomic policy-making.

PAUL SÖDERLIND has been Professor of Finance at the University of St Gallen (Switzerland) since 2003. He has been Associate Professor 1998–2002 at the Stockholm School of Economics and holds a PhD from Princeton University (1993). He has published in scholarly journals on asset pricing, monetary economics and business cycles. He is a Centre for Economic Policy Research (CEPR) research fellow and a member of the scientific advisory board of Norges Bank (the central bank of Norway) and a former member of the Swedish Economic Council.

GABRIEL TALMAIN is Professor of Economics at York University. He was educated at Université Pierre and Marie Curie, Ecole Nationale de la Statistique et de l'Administration Economique, at the Sorbonne and Columbia University. He has held academic appointments at Columbia University, State University of New York and Visiting Appointments at University of British Columbia and Banco de Portugal. His research interests lie in the area of real business cycles, in particular on monopolistic competitive models of the RBC with heterogenous firms. He is a Research Fellow of the Centre for Economic Policy Research (CEPR).

STEPHEN J. TURNOVSKY is the Castor Professor of Economics at the University of Washington, a position to which he was appointed in 1993. For the period 1990–5 he was the Chairman of the Department of Economics. Prior to coming to the University of Washington in 1987 he was IBE Distinguished Professor of Economics at the University of Illinois, and before that was Professor of Economics at the Australian

National University. He obtained his PhD from Harvard University in 1968. He was elected a Fellow of the Econometric Society in 1981 and was President of the Society of Economic Dynamics and Control from 1982–84. He is a past Editor of the *Journal of Economic Dynamics and Control* and remains on its Advisory Board. He has served, or is currently serving on, the editorial boards of several other journals, including the *International Economic Review*, the *Journal of International Economics*, the *Journal of Public Economics*, the *Journal of Public Economic Theory*, the *Journal of Money, Credit, and Banking*, and *Macroeconomic Dynamics*. His main area of research is in intertemporal macroeconomics and international macroeconomics. He has published several books in this area, the most recent being *Methods of Macroeconomic Dynamics*, 2nd edn. (MIT Press, 2000), as well as many articles in a wide range of journals.

CARL E. WALSH is a Professor of Economics at the University of California, Santa Cruz. He has held faculty appointments at the University of Auckland, New Zealand, and Princeton University and served as a senior economist at the Federal Reserve Bank of San Francisco, where he is currently a visiting scholar. He has held visiting appointments at UC Berkeley and Stanford and has been a visiting scholar at the Federal Reserve Banks of Kansas City and Philadelphia. His research focuses on issues in monetary economics and monetary policy. In addition to numerous journal articles, he is the author of *Monetary Theory and Policy*, a graduate level text on monetary economics. He is a past member of the board of editors of the *American Economic Review*, an associate editor of the *Journal of Money, Credit, and Banking* and the *Journal of Economics and Business,* and a member of the editorial board of the *Journal of Macroeconomics*.

Foreword

William A. Brock

In *Dynamic Macroeconomic Analysis: Theory and Policy in General Equilibrium*, Altug, Chadha and Nolan, hereafter 'ACN', have undertaken the extremely difficult task of bringing the reader up to date on the vast literature that has developed in this key area of economics since such seminal books as Cooley's *Frontiers Of Business Cycle Research* (1995).

ACN tackle this formidable assignment by recruiting top scholars to write individual chapters. Each individual chapter is of exceptionally high quality because each scholar is a first-rate expert in the chapter's area.

The approach of the book is 'quantitative theorising', in the sense that each chapter presents not only recent developments in theory but also recent developments in compilation of the facts that confront the theory. Discrepancies between facts and theories are carefully discussed. Many of the chapters offer modifications to the baseline theory that make it do a better job of matching the facts.

I give the reader a quick overview of the contents of this book in a brief introduction to each of the chapters. Three chapters are discussed in more detail than the others in order to keep my foreword within standard space limits. But all of the chapters are equally exciting and have equal command on the reader's attention. I hope this somewhat unusual approach to writing a foreword will entice more readers to add this important book to their libraries. In addition to saying a few words about the chapters, I shall use the discussion of some of them to give some reflections about the field they cover as well as give some speculations and opinions about potentially fruitful future research.

Jim Pemberton (chapter 1) reviews dynamic life cycle consumption/ savings models, the facts they are designed to explain, the struggles in attempting to modify the basic core model to fit these facts and other uses to which they are put. Particularly interesting is discussion of how minor modifications can lead to big and rather counterfactual predictions by some of the models. For example, adding a small safety net in one model caused the model's consumer to borrow too large an amount of money early on to be consistent with fact.

Fanny and Michel Demers and Sumru Altug (hereafter, DDA; chapter 2) review investment theory, adjustment cost models, the Q-theory of investment, new developments on the effects of irreversibility and uncertainty upon investment, recent work in the impact of temporary and permanent changes in taxes and other policy instruments on investments and weave a connecting fabric between the facts one needs to explain and the theory available to do it. Not only that, the chapter gives the reader a guided tour through the impacts of increases in uncertainty through various channels upon investment with an especially thorough treatment of the interaction between increases in uncertainty and irreversibilities upon today's investment rate. It also treats simultaneous learning while investing and the influence of this channel upon the investment rate.

Let me offer some speculations about potentially fruitful future directions for investment theory research that are stimulated by the work reviewed in this chapter.

First, there is a substantial discussion in the chapter on the impact that learning has upon investment. Learning in DDA is Bayesian. The impact on investment can be dramatic. For example DDA show that 'Adopting a uniform prior...the impact of uncertainty about the permanent component of the price of capital is to induce a dramatic decline in investment expenditures, and a much greater frequency with which firms prefer to delay current investment...Even with an informative prior, the decline in total investment is still very substantial...the results...suggest that policies that are aimed at reducing uncertainty about the unknown costs of investing will have a greater impact in increasing investment than policies that are aimed at reducing the cyclical variation in the price of capital or other components of the costs of investing.' I quote DDA at length here because replacing 'uncertainty' in their treatment by 'ambiguity' and extending recent work on optimization under 'ambiguity' (e.g. Epstein and Wang 1994; Hansen and Sargent 2001) may strengthen this effect found by DDA. Furthermore 'ambiguity' seems particularly appropriate to their treatment of 'political risk' since, here, it seems particularly difficult to attach probabilities in a Bayesian manner. Indeed, one might even view the elimination of 'political risk' in monetary policy as a major impetus behind the recent spurt of research on rule-based approaches to monetary policy (e.g. discussion of Taylor rules, in Taylor and Woodford 1999). After all a transparent rule-based approach to monetary policy should allow economic agents to do a much better job of attaching precise probabilities to how the monetary authorities will act conditional on each state of the economy. However, 'political risk' seems to lie more in the domain of imprecise probabilities which are modelled by sets of probability measures with updating modelled by sets of likelihoods (e.g. Epstein and Schneider 2002 and references to workers in the area of imprecise probabilities such as Peter Whalley). Imprecise probabilities are one way of modelling 'Knightian Uncertainty' in the original spirit of Frank Knight. I expand on the theme of modelling 'ambiguity' via tools from the area of imprecise probabilities below. The end result of extending DDA's work in this direction is likely to be a general strengthening of their findings on the dampening effects upon investment induced by uncertainty increases including increases in 'Knightian Uncertainty.'

The recent burst of interest in robust control (e.g. Hansen and Sargent 2001) suggests an extension of received investment theory to a setting where the information that firms must act upon is not precise enough to assign probabilities (Epstein 1999). This theory is motivated by phenomena such as 'ambiguity' avoidance (e.g. Epstein and Wang 1994, and their discussion of Ellsberg's covered urn). If investment theory were generalised to include investing under ambiguity, one might be able to locate a set of sufficient conditions for an increase in ambiguity to depress investment and/or employment. If so, this would lead to an interesting empirical problem: How does one use data to distinguish between 'ambiguity' aversion, risk aversion and aversion to irreversible investments? While Epstein (1999) provides some results on using data to investigate a market counterpart to the Ellsberg paradox, it will be more difficult to design a test that separates increases in ambiguity from increases in risk or, perhaps, increases in amount of irreversibility.

An adaptation of Epstein and Schneider (2002) seems promising. Consider, for example, their differentiation between responses to signals of a firm making investment decisions who models the future using a Bayesian model with known precision in contrast to a firm who models the future using an ambiguity model. The ambiguity modeller takes bad news especially seriously, so one would conjecture that such a firm would be slow to make an investment commitment in contrast to the Bayesian. In the case of asset markets studied by Epstein and Schneider (2002), they show that patterns of 'over reaction' to seemingly 'small' news about fundamentals that are implausible in a Bayesian context emerge easily in an ambiguous context. It seems promising to investigate whether ambiguity models might help explain 'anomalies' in investment theory. This should be a fruitful area of future research.

This brings us to the issue of modelling the act of learning. Much robust control literature uses a stationary infinite horizon setup with a 'shroud' (i.e. a neighborhood of misspecifications around a baseline model) of constant size which one wishes to 'robustify' against. One looks at the maximin and solves for it using methods from zero-sum two-player infinite horizon games with the planner maximising against a malevolent player who minimises against her (e.g. Hansen and Sargent 2001). The malevolent player is constrained in his action set. This setup would probably need modification to include non-stationary settings before application to investment theory problems, many of which take place in a non-stationary setting where 'learning' takes the form of chasing a moving structure.

Much ambiguity modelling uses a family of priors which could be updated into a family of posteriors, unlike usual Bayesian learning where one prior is updated into one posterior. Under stationary conditions, one can locate sufficient conditions for convergence (i.e. 'merging') of beliefs that are quite general. The same conditions could be applied to a family of priors (Epstein and Schneider 2002). So this suggests that continued injection of 'new' risk and/or new 'ambiguity' is needed to keep a neighbourhood of constant size logically plausible in a robust control setting applied to economics. Epstein and Schneider (2002) inject new ambiguity with a family of likelihoods against each prior in a family of priors and give a nice motivation for this way of doing it. They also discuss generalizations of Laws of Large Numbers to this setting which should be relevant for study of which of these micro-level phenomena survive aggregation (a type of cross-sectional Law of Large Numbers) to matter at the macro level. I have discussed this type of modelling in detail because it seems relevant for extension of investment theory to economic settings where the economic environment is constantly changing and changing in ways where assignment of probabilities as a Bayesian would do does not seem natural and where full learning and merging of opinions does not seem natural either.

For example one might believe that during 'normal times' when markets are operating well, economic agents would have less trouble assigning precise probabilities than in 'abnormal times'. If I am allowed to speculate, 'normal times' could be modelled by separating shocks to the system into a category of small and frequent shocks and 'abnormal times' modelled by a category of rare but large shocks. The level of imprecision of probabilities could be modelled by the size of the support over which the minimizing measure is taken in the Epstein and Wang (1994) framework.

Stephen J. Turnovsky (chapter 3) shows how to compute equilibria in continuous time recursive intertemporal general equilibrium stochastic macroeconomic models, especially those with externalities common in new growth theory. The chapter reviews applications of continuous time stochastic methods, then sets out a basic model which extends AK growth models, investigates fiscal policy effects on the equilibrium growth rate and studies optimal fiscal policy. The chapter makes extensions of the basic model by adding money, adjustment costs, elastic labour supply, productive government spending, puts forth a theory of the optimal size of government in this context and studies risk and international tax policy. This chapter also extends the model to recursive preferences and shows how this makes a difference.

Matt Canzoneri, Bob Cumby and Behzad Diba (chapter 4) review a subset of papers in the 'New Neo-classical Synthesis' (NNS) literature that is particularly relevant to a recent debate on the question 'Is price stability a good strategy for macroeconomic stabilisation?' Much of the current debate over stabilisation policy is concerned about asymmetries in what might be called 'welfare-damaging inertias' and what monetary policy might do to counteract these welfare-damaging inertias. Examples include inertias in price and wage setting, inertias in response abilities of individual economic sectors to outside shocks and the like. Inertias in response to outside shocks might be due, for example, to endogenous constraints on borrowing (due to incentive compatibility constraints, perhaps). Much of this chapter focuses on wedges due to monopolistically competitive price and wage setting with nominal inertia.

Jagjit Chadha and Charles Nolan (chapter 5) review the large literature on joint interaction of monetary and fiscal policy including such controversial subjects as the Fiscal Theory of the Price Level (FTPL). It gives a precise formulation of FTPL and then uses this precise formulation to discuss the controversies unleashed by this approach. Not only that, it reviews recent work on the design of jointly optimal 'simple rules' (e.g. Taylor-type rules) when monetary and fiscal policy are jointly determined.

It is interesting to contrast this chapter with much of the recent literature on 'Taylor' rules. Much if not most of the recent literature on Taylor-type rules abstracts away from fiscal policy and concentrates on the 'tradeoff' between inflation and unemployment. It emphasizes the 'Taylor Principle' that rules with coefficients on inflation bigger than unity with relatively smaller coefficients on unemployment have good stabilisation properties. The usual abstraction away from fiscal policy in the 'rules literature' may arise from the specialised concerns of Central Banks with managing price stability. Chadha and Nolan discuss joint design of simple rules. I will take the liberty here of using the discussion of jointly optimal rules in this chapter to make some speculative remarks about potentially fruitful future research in this area.

Since monetary policy is typically managed by a professionalized Central Bank staff which is highly trained in thinking about tradeoffs in the overall public interest, this management group contrasts with the 'management group' that manages fiscal policy. Fiscal policy is typically determined by a political–authoritative allocation of value process whose properties not only draw the negative attention of scholarly commentators, but also the derision of late-night show comedians. The descriptions of the efficiency and predictability of this process are not always favourable. I am leading up to the following issue. As I said above, there has been much recent activity in applying methods from robust control and ambiguity modelling to economics. This is especially so in recent works in the 'Taylor rules' literature (e.g. Onatski and Stock 2000; Onatski and Williams 2002; Orphanides and Williams 2002). The main posture of these papers is that there is a neighbourhood N of possible departure models from a 'baseline' model that one wishes to robustify against. So one first allows 'Nature' to minimise the policy-maker's objective over N, then the policy-maker maximises over Nature's worst within N. This is a 'local' approach in the sense that there is one basic baseline model with a neighbourhood N (which could be quite large) around it.

A main difficulty with the existing treatments of robustification is modelling the formation of N itself. The managers of fiscal policy would seem to be a good source of 'ambiguity production' in the sense that one needs continuous injections of 'new ambiguities' to prevent plausible learning mechanisms from collapsing the 'width' of the ambiguity, i.e. collapsing the size of N down towards zero. (See Epstein and Schneider 2002, where they model 'ambiguity production' as a family of likelihoods at each date t, conditional on data received at date $t-1$. They argue that this mechanism can prevent the usual 'merging-of-opinions' results from collapsing the 'width' of the ambiguity as time passes on.) In the USA the mere change of one Senator from the Republican Party to an Independent dramatically changed the direction and momentum of policy – i.e. fiscal policy dynamics would appear to be a good place for the devotees of imprecise probabilities to find sources of phenomena that are 'ambiguous' enough that one can not convincingly assign probabilities to them. Furthermore the structure and balances of the House and the Senate are constantly changing with each election in the USA. The structure of pressures upon these congresspeople are also constantly changing due to outside shocks as well as internal pressures.

Hence a Central Bank which is attempting to design jointly optimal monetary and fiscal rules is likely to face a lot of 'technical ambiguity' on the fiscal side because it is difficult for it to formulate an agreed-upon 'baseline model' of the fiscal policy implementation and effect process. It is difficult enough to formulate a baseline model of the monetary policy implementation and effect process, much less the fiscal policy counterpart.

In a different but related growth policy-making context, Durlauf and myself (Brock and Durlauf 2001) took the posture that we needed more than one baseline model that we need to robustify against. We have a similar project underway for the design of 'Taylor-type' rules. Extension of this chapter's work on the joint determination of monetary and fiscal policy in a 'Taylor-type' rule framework to a setting where the degree of ambiguities differs between the fiscal part and the monetary part would seem to be a very promising area for future research.

Philip Lane and Giovanni Ganelli (chapter 6) review the recent literature on 'new open economy macroeconomics' (NOEM). Since these models have explicitly stochastic frameworks with explicit micro-foundations and precisely defined wage- and price-setting rules they can directly highlight the role of uncertainty embodied in wages and prices. Several contentious issues must be dealt with in constructing useful abstractions in this area.

A major issue that must be dealt with is where (and in which currency) to put the sticky prices and sticky wages. Sticky wages are not as controversial as sticky prices because economists are used to differentiating labour markets with all their institutional detail and the 'commodities' being traded (e.g. human time accompanied by all those feelings of 'fairness', 'self-esteem', etc. that are not present when trading bushels of soybeans) and commodity markets where 'things without feelings' are traded. (See Bewley 1999 for a strongly argued case for the behaviour of labour markets.)

Even in the commodity markets, controversies lurk concerning on which commodity markets to put the sticky prices. When shocks hit the system, the markets that are 'temporarily' free end up momentarily adjusting to absorb the whole shock before the other markets 'loosen up.' This effect of a shock hitting the momentarily small sliver of 'free-price' markets can cause embarrassing conflicts with data if these models are not set up carefully. No one believes soybean prices are 'sticky' but what about house prices, automobile prices, and the like? But even here high intertemporal substitutability between a car delivered at date t and the same car delivered at date $t + 1$ can generate an illusion of a fixed price when they may actually be flexible.

Another major issue is the impact of openness on the conduct of monetary policy. For example, what is the proper measure of inflation in 'Taylor rule'-type exercises? What is the role of the current account and net foreign assets in adjustment processes? For example, net external liabilities can loom large in open economy settings. As pointed out by Cristina Arellano and Enrique Mendoza's chapter 7, external liabilities can interact with credit constraints in such a way as to expose a country to risk of a 'Sudden Stop' disaster. So we are in a difficult area here. This chapter handles this touchy area by walking the reader through the different predictions generated by different models as well as empirical evidence for or against those predictions.

Arellano and Mendoza start out by listing the empirical regularities associated with the 'Sudden Stop' phenomenon of emerging market crises. Empirical regularities of 'Sudden Stop' include sudden loss of access to world capital markets, large reversal of the current account deficit, collapse of domestic production and demand, big 'corrections' in asset prices and sharp increase in prices of tradeables relative to non-tradeables. The authors review recent work on recursive infinite horizon stochastic small open economy models with constraints on borrowing from world capital markets. The borrowing constraints are formulated using recent work on incentive compatibility constraints; there must be willingness to pay in most or all states of the world, and ability to pay. Extensive discussion is given of the ability of these types of advances in theory-building to mimic the empirical regularities of 'Sudden Stops' as well as the ability of such theories to enhance our understanding of the forces that deepen welfare losses caused by 'Sudden Stops'.

Paul Söderlind in chapter 8 reviews the large literature on consumption-based asset pricing models and shows how these models miss not only well-known facts such as the equity premium puzzle and the risk-free rate puzzle, but also cross-sectional facts. The chapter also discusses other recent models of the stochastic discount factor that attempt to fix the data mismatches of earlier models.

Let me use this chapter to launch a few speculations about promising future directions of research on asset pricing. There are two main directions that one might go to improve the match between fact and theory: (i) relatively minor modifications of existing theory, (ii) relatively drastic modifications of existing theory.

In the first category, Akdeniz and Dechert (2002) have shown that they can produce equity premia closer to fact with much smaller risk aversion using a rather conventional production-based asset pricing model with heterogeneous firms and depreciating capital. They have developed a very fast computational algorithm that solves the model with heterogeneous firms where capital that is invested in a sector must remain fixed there for one period before it can be moved. The interaction between (*A*) diminishing returns in the individual sectoral technologies, (*B*) depreciation of the capital used, and (*C*) tastes of the consumers appears to be key. Economic forces *A* and *B* are not available in usual endowment-based models of asset pricing. For example Basu and Samanta (2001) are able to produce the well-known 'Constant Elasticity of Variance' (CEV) relationship between volatility and stock prices by exploiting the relationship between marginal product of capital value of the firm's claims on the income stream from that capital and decreasing returns to that capital. I believe one reason that production-based asset pricing models have not been used as much as endowment-based asset pricing models is because of the lack of rapid computational algorithms and of the lack of very fast computers make them difficult to solve.

Another reason for lack of use of production-based models may be the many puzzles and the grave difficulties that received models have in matching facts that are surveyed in Campbell's chapter in Taylor and Woodford (1999). For example, Campbell suggests the simplest versions of production-based models will generate very stable movements in asset prices because the real interest rate equals the marginal product of capital, which in turn is perturbed by technology shocks. Capital is also costlessly transformable into consumption in the basic model. Hence, Campbell states that modifications such as adjustment costs will be needed to generate realistically volatile asset returns.

Of course other modifications will be needed to the simple Real Business Cycle (RBC)-type model like that used by Akdeniz and Dechert (2002) to study the equity premium in order to avoid conflict with other facts. Adding ingredients such as heterogeneity, more realistic treatments of labour markets and incomplete markets is sure to be a major route to improvement (Calvet, Grandmont and Lemaire 2002; Browning, Hansen and Heckman's chapter 8 in Taylor and Woodford 1999; King and Rebelo's chapter 14 in Taylor and Woodford 1999). Browning, Hansen, and Heckman study both infinite horizon models and overlapping generations models with agent heterogeneity. They give a strong argument that macroeconomic model-building must treat heterogeneity much more seriously than the current literature in order to do a better job in matching and explaining facts.

I believe that as computational methods like Akdeniz and Dechert's become more popular we will see more movement in the asset pricing literature away from the general equilibrium endowment-based models towards general equilibrium production-based models with more heterogeneity, not only on the firm side, but also on the consumer side, as argued by Brown, Hansen, and Heckman. The investment theory work surveyed in this chapter will be a major input.

In the second category one might include theories that depend upon non-stationarities such as Rational Belief Equilibrium (RBE) theory to replace Rational Expectations Equilibrium theories (REE) as in Kurz (1997). Kurz (1997) argues that many asset pricing puzzles including the equity premium puzzle vanish in RBE theory. Another line of theory is 'ambiguity aversion theory' also called 'Knightian Uncertainty' (Epstein and Wang 1994). Epstein and Schneider (2002) argue that this type of theory can explain intertemporal patterns of asset price behaviour like that immediately following the 9–11 attacks more easily than conventional theories. Situations where it is difficult to argue that one can attach probabilities (or satisfy axioms for existence of probabilities) would seem natural for applications of Knightian Uncertainty in finance. But in pure finance theory only 'undiversifiable' risk and 'undiversifiable' Knightian Uncertainty should be priced at any point in time as in the derivations of the Capital Asset Pricing Model (CAPM) and the APT. In intertemporal settings, Epstein and Schneider (2002) discuss Laws of Large Numbers (LLNs) in ambiguity settings as well as mechanisms that prevent the ambiguity from collapsing asymptotically under learning mechanisms. Future research in this area would seem promising for finance.

One might use this theory to argue that the US government itself is currently (26 September 2002) injecting extra Knightian Uncertainty into the environment, that this contribution is at the 'macro' level (it cannot be 'diversified away'), and hence, the stock market seems unable to rebound even though interest rates are at an extremely low level and the fundamentals do not look that bad. Of course a serious study of this possible effect would require a whole paper, not just a speculative comment.

Carl Walsh in chapter 9 reviews empirical facts such as the large and persistent hump-shaped real responses of real output to monetary shocks and the difficulties that models based upon nominal rigidities have in matching these facts. The chapter reviews models based upon a unification of aggregate matching functions in labour economics with optimising models of price rigidities and of monopolistic competition. The chapter treats some of the most difficult facts for DSGE models (even after they are augmented with sticky prices and other bells and whistles). As in Talmain's chapter 11, the problem again is the fact of real persistence. Walsh goes after this challenging problem by combining 'a Mortensen–Pissarides aggregate matching function with an optimising model of price rigidity'. Since relationships between firms and employers are a type of real rigidity this route to producing persistence seems promising. The chapter mentions other routes to persistence such as the Cooley–Quadrini model where money is introduced into a DSGE model, a matching model of the labour market is present, but prices are flexible while nominal portfolio adjustment is sticky. This device gets proper propagation of monetary shocks. Walsh uses a model with wholesale and retail sectors where wholesale production requires matching with retail firms having sticky prices with a fraction optimally adjusting each period. He linearises this model, calibrates it and simulates it to produce many interesting results which he compares to other models.

Stephen Turnovsky in chapter 10 studies the impact of distortions such as taxes in continuous time intertemporal general equilibrium macroeconomic models of Romer type where there are externalities. Many comparative dynamics results are derived. Both chapters by Turnovsky give the reader a nice guide to methods for computing equilibria and doing comparative dynamics in these kinds of models.

Gabriel Talmain in chapter 11 reviews recent literature on RBC models and their mismatches with facts. There is also a short discussion of endogenous business cycle models. There is useful material on computing approximate solutions for a class of RBC models; the chapter then discusses how a more systematic treatment of aggregation across different sectors in multi-sectoral models can lead to models that are more consistent with the facts, e.g., persistence.

Indeed, the chapter argues that once that part of measured persistence due to aggregation of the individual component time series that make up macroaggregates is partialled out of total measured persistence, many 'puzzles' in macro and macrofinance vanish. After a discussion of sources of measured persistence from aggregation that might confuse the unsuspecting researcher, Talmain uses an example (apparently originating from Griliches) of a time series regression of a 'dependent variable' y_t upon its lag, and another 'independent variable' x_t that is AR(1). With an AR(1) error in the y-equation and shows how bad the bias is in the estimates of the constant term and the slope term in the y-equation. He then uses this regression as an expository vehicle to contend, for example, that 'paradoxes such as the well-known uncovered interest parity (UIP) puzzle are purely an artifact of persistence'.

Regardless of one's position on Talmain's arguments, careful investigation of the relationship between properties of component series making up macroaggregates used in empirical work in macro and in macrofinance and the use of these macroaggregate series in attempting to resolve empirical puzzles and anomalies seems a promising area for future research. For example, writers in empirical finance put a lot of stress on how properties of individual firm return series which, in turn, are caused by institutional details in the market settings in which those individual securities are traded, can cause behaviour in index returns series that is difficult to understand without breaking out the individual components of the index. It is surely in the profession's interest to follow a similar research programme in macro, especially when apparent 'puzzles' emerge.

It is natural to launch some speculations prompted by this chapter. First recent work on aggregation of heterogeneous beliefs by Calvet, Grandmont and Lemaire (2002) suggests that puzzles such as the equity premium puzzle may be explained under plausible assumptions on heterogeneity, e.g. 'It is shown further that an upward adjustment of the market portfolio due to the heterogeneity of beliefs, may contribute to explaining such challenges as the so-called "equity premium puzzle" whenever aggregate relative risk aversion is decreasing with aggregate income' (Calvet, Grandmont, and Lemaire 2002: 2).

Second, aggregation theory is closely related to cross-sectional Laws of Large Numbers. Methods from statistical mechanics have been applied to deliver tractable models where cross-sectional LLNs break down (cf. papers in Arthur, Durlauf and Lane 1997). The interaction between cross-sectional LLNs and temporal properties of macroaggregates seems to still need further research.

This ends my short description of each chapter and my musings about several specific chapters. Much of the book is centred around extensions of DSGE models and how they must be modified in order to fit the facts. A fundamental problem that must be faced in macroeconomics (and many other branches of economics) is this. Think of matching facts with a core baseline model with modifications of that baseline model as a mapping M from a domain subspace of Model Space into a subset of Fact Space. Even if we can get macroeconomists to agree on the facts that need to be explained, the set of competing 'core baseline' models equally consistent with these commonly agreed upon facts is likely to be large. This set of equally consistent competing models can be further narrowed by comparing impulse response behaviour with observations and sensibility as in, for example, Christiano, Eichenbaum and Evans's chapter in Taylor and Woodford (1999). But there still will be competing models left after this screening process. This raises the issue of which baseline model serves as the best one on which to erect a research programme. The analogy with multi-armed bandit theory suggests that it may be socially optimal to encourage several competing core baseline models to erect modifications upon.

Even more difficult is the task of getting structural models like DSGE models to do a better job of predicting out of sample than naive and simple models with little economic structure. This problem is well known in the exchange rate area. See Obstfeld and Rogoff's discussion (1996, chapter 9) of the early work of Meese and Rogoff on the inability of 'structural' models to predict out of sample better than naive models such as random walk models and the work that followed. They discuss later work that is consistent with statistically significant superior performance of structural models at very long horizons. They point out that the problem of getting superior performance over naive models on out of sample prediction with structural models is 'shared with virtually any other field that attempts to explain asset price data'. Of course out of sample prediction is not the only criterion. Reasonable Impulse Response Functions (IRFs) is another. Whatever the case, however, this performance problem is likely to lead to enduring controversies since the class of models that do equally well on several reasonable performance criteria is likely to be large and quite varied in their normative implications.

Let me now cut to the chase. This book provides an extremely important service to the economics community. It gets readers to the frontiers of the subject, giving them central theories and central facts that the theories must match and explain. It shows the reader where the baseline theories fail and gives good advice on what must be done to fix them. One can not ask more of a book than that. This book belongs on every economist's bookshelf.

BIBLIOGRAPHY

Akdeniz, L. and Dechert, W. (2002). 'The Equity Premium in Brock's Asset Pricing Model', Department of Economics, Bilkent University and University of Houston

Arthur, W., Durlauf, S. and Lane, D. (eds.) (1997). *The Economy as an Evolving Complex System II*, Reading, Mass.: Addison-Wesley for the Santa Fe Institute

Basu, P. and Samanta, P. (2001). 'Volatility and Stock Prices: Implications from a Production Model of Asset Pricing', *Economics Letters*, 70, 229–35

Bewley, T. (1999). *Why Wages don't Fall during a Recession*, Cambridge, Mass.: Harvard University Press

Brock, W. and Durlauf, S. (2001). 'Growth Empirics and Reality', *The World Bank Economic Review*, 15(2), 229–72

Calvet, L., Grandmont, J. and Lemaire, I. (2002). 'Aggregation of Heterogeneous Beliefs and Asset Pricing in Complete Markets', Harvard University, CNRS-CREST, University of Venice and INSEE

Epstein, L. (1999). 'Are Probabilities Used in Markets?', Department of Economics, University of Rochester

Epstein, L. and Schneider, M. (2002). 'Learning Under Ambiguity', Department of Economics, University of Rochester and UCLA

Epstein, L. and Wang, T. (1994). 'Intertemporal Asset Pricing Behavior under Knightian Uncertainty', *Econometrica*, 62, 283–322

Hansen, L. and Sargent, T. (2001). 'Robust Control and Model Uncertainty', *American Economic Review*, 91(2), 60–6

Kurz, M. (ed.) (1997). *Endogenous Economic Fluctuations*, Berlin: Springer-Verlag

Marimon, R. (1989). 'Stochastic Turnpike Property and Stationary Equilibrium', *Journal of Economic Theory*, 47, 282–306

Obstfeld, M. and Rogoff, K. (1996), *Foundations of International Macroeconomics*, Cambridge, MA: MIT Press

Onatski, A. and Stock, J. (2000). 'Robust Monetary Policy Under Model Uncertainty in a Small Model of the US Economy', NBER Working Paper, 7490

Onatski, A. and Williams, N. (2002). 'Modeling Model Uncertainty', European Central Bank, Working Paper, 169

Orphanides, A. and Williams, J. (2002). 'Robust Monetary Policy Rules with Unknown Natural Rates', Federal Reserve Board, Washington, DC, 30 August

Taylor, J. and Woodford, M. (1999). *Handbook of Macroeconomics, Volumes IA, IB, IC*, Amsterdam: North Holland

Preface

The aim of this volume is simple: to demonstrate how quantitative general equilibrium theory can be fruitfully applied to a variety of specific macroeconomic and monetary issues. There is, by now, no shortage of high-quality advanced macroeconomic and monetary economics texts available – indeed two of the contributors to the present volume (Stephen Turnovsky and Carl Walsh) have recently written first-rate graduate texts in just these areas. However, there is often rarely space in a text book to develop models much past their basic setup, and there is similarly little scope for a detailed discussion of a model's policy implications. This volume, then, aims to bridge some of that gap.

To that end, we asked leading researchers in various areas to explain what they were up to, and where they thought the literature was headed. The result, we think, bears testimony to the richness of aggregate economic modelling that has grown out of the real business cycle (RBC) approach to growth and business cycle fluctuations. We treat this book as both a mark of the tremendous progress in this field and a staging post to even further progress subsequently.

We would like to thank colleagues who have taken the trouble to read parts of this book and provided useful comments: Anthony Garratt, Sean Holly, Campbell Leith, Paul Levine, David Miles, Ed Nelson, Sheilagh Ogilvie, Argia Sbordone, Frank Smets, Alan Sutherland, Peter Tinsley, Marcelo Veracierto, Simon Wren-Lewis, Mike Wickens. Ashwin Rattan and Chris Harrison at Cambridge University Press have provided constant support. Finally, we would like to thank Anne Mason and Gill Smith without whose efficiency this book would not have been so expertly completed.

January 2003

SUMRU ALTUG
JAGJIT S. CHADHA
CHARLES NOLAN

The application of stochastic dynamic programming methods to household consumption and saving decisions: a critical survey

James Pemberton

1 INTRODUCTION

This chapter discusses work which applies the methods of stochastic dynamic programming (SDP) to the explanation of consumption and saving behaviour. The emphasis is on the intertemporal consumption and saving choices of individual decision-makers, which I will normally label as 'households'. There are at least two reasons why it is important to try to explain such choices: first, it is intrinsically interesting; and, second, it is useful as a means of understanding, and potentially forecasting, movements in aggregate consumption, and thus contributing to understanding and/or forecasts of aggregate economic fluctuations. The latter motivation needs no further justification, given the priority which policy-makers attach to trying to prevent fluctuations in economic activity. The former motivation – intrinsic interest – is less often stressed by economists, but it is hard to see why: it is surely worthwhile for humankind to improve its understanding of human behaviour, and economists, along with other social scientists, have much to contribute here.

The application of SDP to household consumption behaviour is very recent, with the first published papers appearing only at the end of the 1980s. Young though it is, this research programme has already changed significantly the way in which economists now analyse consumption choice, and has overturned a number of previously widely held views about consumption behaviour. Any research programme which achieves such outcomes so quickly would normally be judged a success, and in many respects this is an appropriate judgement here. The judgement needs to be qualified, however, on at least two counts. First, some of the ideas which the SDP research programme has overturned, although previously widely believed by mainstream economists, were never subscribed to by those working outside the mainstream. Non-mainstream economists might argue that the SDP programme has simply allowed the mainstream to catch up with their own thinking. Second, there is room for doubt that SDP methods really capture at all well the ways in which humans actually make decisions.

These issues are considered in the rest of this chapter. Section 2 reviews the development of economists' thinking about consumption behaviour since the time of Keynes, and places the SDP programme in this longer term context. Section 3 looks in more detail at some of the most prominent contributions to the SDP research programme. Section 4 considers criticisms of the SDP programme, and looks at other possible approaches to modelling consumption behaviour. Section 5 draws some conclusions.

2 THE DEVELOPMENT OF HOUSEHOLD CONSUMPTION MODELLING

2.1 Keynes, Modigliani and Friedman

Modern interest in consumption and saving behaviour started with Keynes (1936). Keynes' emphasis on aggregate demand as a short-run determinant of the level of economic activity required him to consider the major components of aggregate demand, of which aggregate private consumption is easily the largest in typical market-based economies. In order to model consumption behaviour, Keynes introduced a theoretical concept – the marginal propensity to consume (MPC) – which has remained central to all subsequent work on consumption and saving behaviour. The basis of Keynes' modelling of the MPC was his 'fundamental psychological law. . . . that men are disposed, as a rule and on the average, to increase their consumption as their income increases, but not by as much as the increase in their income' (Keynes 1936: 96). In the context of modern perspectives on consumption behaviour, a difficulty with this statement is that it does not define the 'income' concept: e.g. is it current, or permanent, income which matters? And does it make any difference whether or not the increase in income was previously anticipated? On the other hand, it is interesting to note that Keynes' accompanying discussion of the MPC (1936: chapters 8 and 9) anticipated a number of issues which have become central to more recent work on consumption: e.g. he allows for windfalls, changes in time preference, changes in expected future income relative to current income, precautionary motives, changing family needs over the life cycle and inter-generational bequests.

It soon became evident that Keynes' model of an MPC between zero and one was at odds with time series evidence showing a roughly constant ratio of aggregate consumption to aggregate income despite persistent growth in the latter. This issue was addressed by the life cycle hypothesis (LCH) and the permanent income hypothesis (PIH) associated, respectively, with Modigliani (Modigliani and Brumberg 1954) and with Friedman (1957). Virtually all economists since then have accepted the basic idea of both the LCH and the PIH, namely that households are *forward-looking*: they are concerned about future as well as current consumption, and they take account of expected future income as well as current income.

Friedman's original (1957, 1963) statement of the PIH implied a very flexible framework. For example, he argued that (i) when calculating permanent income, the discount rate used to obtain the present value of future income is a highly subjective concept, not necessarily bearing any relation to market interest rates (e.g. Friedman 1963 argued for an annual discount rate of around 33 per cent, implying a time horizon of around three years); (ii) different discount rates may be applied to different types of income; and (iii) permanent income may be expected to vary over the future, as new information is acquired (Friedman 1957, figure 1.2:24). Such a framework allows uncertainty (about future income in general, or about particular sources of income, or about future preferences) to have a large influence on behaviour. The short time horizon implied by point (i) is one possible way in which the framework permits households to respond to such uncertainty. By contrast Modigliani's LCH, as retrospectively summarised in his Nobel Lecture (Modigliani 1986) is more closely circumscribed: the time horizon is the remaining expected life cycle, and choice is governed by 'the self-evident proposition that the representative consumer will choose to consume at a reasonably stable rate, close to his anticipated average life consumption' (1986: 301). This leads to the simple, but very influential, diagrammatic representation of life cycle behaviour in figure 1.1, henceforth the 'Modigliani diagram'. The household's income, OY, is constant throughout working life (OR) and falls to zero in retirement (RN); its 'self-evident' desire to maintain constant consumption leads to the steady consumption level OC and the pattern of asset accumulation and decumulation OAN. Of course, numerous complications (e.g. variable working income, variable household size, etc.) are ignored, but many of these would not alter the basic idea.

The simplified life cycle behaviour illustrated in figure 1.1 became the received orthodoxy of mainstream economics as the LCH became the standard framework. To illustrate its influence and durability, it has survived unchanged through all eight editions of one of the leading international student textbooks on intermediate macroeconomics (Dornbusch, Fischer and

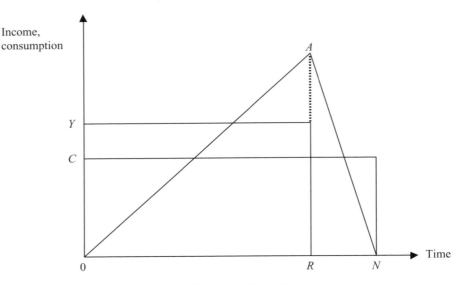

Figure 1.1 The 'Modigliani' diagram

Startz 2001). The only change in successive editions has been the gradual inclusion of more material discussing ideas from SDP models – which contest the whole basis of figure 1.1 – though this is given less prominence than the basic Modigliani diagram. Thus, many world-wide cohorts of economics students have absorbed the ideas of figure 1.1 as the basis of mainstream economics views about consumption and saving behaviour.

Figure 1.1's basic idea can easily be derived from the following LCH set-up:

$$V(t) = E_t \sum_{i=0}^{N} (1+d)^{-i} u[c(t+i)] \qquad (1.1)$$

$$E_t \sum_{i=0}^{N} (1+r)^{-i} c(t+i) = F(t) + H(t) \qquad (1.2)$$

$$H(t) = E_t \sum_{i=0}^{N} (1+r)^{-i} w(t+i). \qquad (1.3)$$

$V(t)$ is the lifetime objective function at time t, $c(n)$ is consumption at time n, $u(c(n))$ is the one-period utility function at time n, and $d > 0$ is the per period rate of time discounting. N is the number of remaining lifetime periods after the present period. E_t is the expectations operator as at time t. Equation (1.1) thus says that the household maximises expected discounted lifetime utility. Equations (1.2) and (1.3) specify the lifetime budget constraint, with $F(t)$ and $H(t)$ denoting accumulated non-human wealth and human wealth, respectively at time t, $w(t)$ denoting labour income at time t,[1] and r being the per period real interest rate. (Following much, though not all, of the literature, I assume that both r and d are constant throughout this chapter.) (1.1)–(1.3) provide a reasonably general statement of the lifetime maximising problem. They generate the Modigliani diagram with the following restrictions: no uncertainty about the future; and interest and time preference rates which are equal to one another ($r = d$). The latter is a convenient simplification which affects details rather than fundamental principles,[2] but ruling out uncertainty is a critical assumption, whose effect is that an increase of X in current income has exactly the same impact on current consumption as an increase of $(1 + r)^N X$ which will occur N periods in the future, no matter how large is N. This simple, but striking, proposition, together with the Modigliani diagram and the model of (1.1)–(1.3) with uncertainty excluded, became the received mainstream economics view about consumption and saving behaviour in the 1960s and 1970s. Note that, as emphasised above, it is very different from Friedman's original version of the PIH model. Thus, the frequent references in the literature to the 'LCH/PIH framework' are quite misleading in their implication that the two models are virtually identical. Friedman's approach is more sophisticated than Modigliani's, but it is not so easily reduced to a simple framework such as (1.1)–(1.3) and figure 1.1. Thus, many of Friedman's sophisticated complications were lost sight of in the 1960s and 1970s as mainstream economics adopted the simplified LCH model.

2.2 Hall and random walks

Hall (1978) started from the model of (1.1)–(1.3), including the assumptions of constant r and d (not necessarily $r = d$), and focused on the implications of uncertainty about future labour income. The centrepiece of Hall's paper was the then relatively unfamiliar, but now standard, first-order intertemporal optimising equation, now usually termed the Euler equation:

$$E_t u'(c(t+1)) = [(1 + d)/(1 + r)]u'(c(t)). \qquad (1.4)$$

[1] Equation (1.3) allows labour income to continue right to the end of the life cycle, but a retirement phase can be allowed by setting $w = 0$ for later periods.
[2] If r is more (less) than d, then in figure 1.1 consumption rises (falls) over the life cycle rather than remaining constant.

Equation (1.4) indicates that the marginal utility of consumption evolves as a random walk, with a trend if r and d are not equal, and trendless if $r = d$. An important special case occurs if utility is quadratic, i.e.

$$u(c(t)) = Ac(t) - Bc(t)^2, \quad A > 0, \quad B > 0. \qquad (1.5)$$

Then marginal utility is linear in consumption, and (1.4) implies:

$$E_t c(t + 1) = a_0 + a_1 c(t) + e(t + 1). \qquad (1.6)$$

When $r = d$, $a_0 = 0$ and $a_1 = 1$; a_0 is increasing, and a_1 is decreasing, in $(r - d)$. $e(.)$ is a random shock, with $E_t e(t + 1) = 0$. Thus, consumption itself follows a random walk. This case has become known as the *certainty equivalent* (CEQ) model, because its implications for intertemporal consumption and saving choices are equivalent to those in the basic Modigliani model, despite the presence of uncertainty. In particular, (1.6) implies exactly the same propensity to consume out of (expected) lifetime resources as is implied by (1.1)–(1.3) with perfect certainty. It also implies, exactly as in the Modigliani model, that an increase in current income of X or an increase in expected income N periods in the future of $(1 + r)X^N$ have identical effects on current consumption.

Where (1.6) differs is in the random walk response to income shocks, which by assumption do not occur in the Modigliani framework. The basic idea is most easily understood if $r = d$ is assumed, so that $a_0 = 0$ and $a_1 = 1$ in (1.6). Then, if there were no shocks so that $e(.) = 0$ in every period, consumption would be constant over life, equal to permanent income, exactly as in the Modigliani diagram. Under uncertainty it is still optimal to plan for consumption to be constant and equal to permanent income, but now any income shock causes calculated permanent income to be revised upwards or downwards, and planned consumption is likewise revised so as to be constant at the new permanent income level. Thus, consumption's random walk derives from the random walk followed by permanent income. Notice the similarity to Friedman's earlier emphasis on the fact that permanent income is typically revised over time.

This model triggered a large empirical research programme, aimed at testing the prediction that households revise their consumption by an amount equal to the permanent income value of any unexpected income change. The income process is critical here. If unexpected changes in income are quickly reversed, their permanent income value is tiny and consumption should hardly alter. Conversely, if unexpected changes are long-lasting, then consumption should alter roughly in line with the current income shock. Early tests of Hall's model (e.g. Flavin 1981) concluded that consumption is excessively sensitive to income (i.e. consumption alters by more than the permanent income value of shocks), but later work (e.g. Campbell and Deaton 1989) suggests the reverse, i.e. that consumption is too smooth in relation to income. The difference reflects different estimated models of the income process: Flavin's work suggested that income levels follow an autoregressive process, whereby a rise of X in current income implies a rise of less than X in permanent income; by contrast, Campbell and Deaton's work suggested that the growth rate – not the level – of income is autoregressive, whereby a rise of X in current income implies a rise of more than X in permanent income.

2.3 Beyond the certainty equivalent model

The CEQ model of (1.5) and (1.6) is a special case of (1.4). Quadratic utility is less plausible as an assumption about preferences than a constant relative risk aversion (CRRA) utility function:

$$u(c(t)) = \begin{cases} \dfrac{c(t)^{1-\sigma} - 1}{1 - \sigma} & (\sigma \neq 1) \\ \ln c(t) & (\sigma = 1). \end{cases} \tag{1.7}$$

The CRRA assumption is now routinely used in most SDP treatments of consumption, and is adopted in most of the rest of this chapter. To see its implications, substitute (1.7) into (1.4) and rearrange:

$$c(t)^{-\sigma} = [(1 + r)/(1 + d)]E_t c(t + 1)^{-\sigma}. \tag{1.8}$$

Unlike in the CEQ case, the Euler equation is now no longer linear in consumption. This fundamentally alters both the economic implications, and the technical treatment, of the model. The modern SDP analysis of consumption focuses on these economic and technical issues.

Looking first at the basic economic implications, note that the third derivative of the utility function is zero with quadratic utility, as in (1.5), but is positive with CRRA utility, as in (1.7). Consider a simplified context in which the life cycle consists of just two periods – the importance of this simplification is considered shortly – and in which second-period income can be either 'high' or 'low' with equal probability. Then second-period consumption takes either the 'high' value $c(2H)$, or the 'low' value $c(2L) < c(2H)$, with equal probability. These two possible second-period outcomes are depicted on the horizontal axis of figure 1.2, and $E_1 c(2)$ denotes mean expected second period consumption, viewed from the vantage

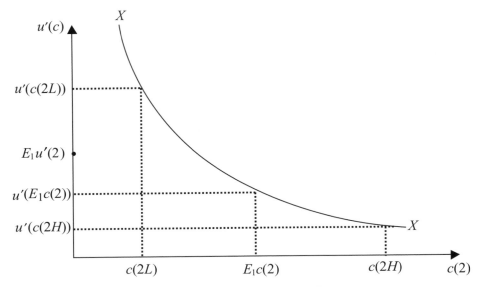

Figure 1.2 Second-period marginal utility of consumption

point of period 1. The vertical axis measures the marginal utility of second-period consumption, and the curve XX depicts the relationship between consumption and marginal utility when utility is CRRA. The marginal utilities associated with $c(2L)$, $c(2H)$ and $E_1c(2)$ are shown on the vertical axis. The expected marginal utility is

$$E_1u'(2) = [u'(c(2H)) + u'(c(2L))]/2, \qquad (1.9)$$

and is also shown on the vertical axis. The key point is that $E_1u'(2)$ is more than $u'(E_1c(2))$: expected future marginal utility is more than the marginal utility of expected future consumption. This inequality must always hold if the third derivative of the utility function is positive. By contrast, in the CEQ model with a zero third derivative, the curve XX in figure 1.2 is replaced by a straight line, and the inequality is converted into an equality.

Contrasting the linear and non-linear versions of XX in figure 1.2 illustrates why most economists believe CRRA (the non-linear case) to be more plausible than quadratic utility (the linear case). The non-linear case drawn in figure 1.2 implies that as consumption goes towards zero, so the marginal utility of consumption goes towards infinity – implying, surely plausibly, that a destitute individual places enormous value on a small consumption gain – whereas linearity implies that marginal utility is no higher at zero consumption than at any positive consumption level (so that, seemingly implausibly, someone who is destitute does not value extra consumption specially highly). This is why most economists place greater trust in the results of models using CRRA utility than in results from CEQ models.

2.4 Precautionary saving

The implications of replacing (1.5) with (1.7) can be seen by looking again at the Euler equation (1.4). For a given pattern of uncertainty about future income, there is a particular time path of present and future consumption which satisfies the Euler equation (1.4) under CEQ preferences. With CRRA preferences, this time path cannot satisfy (1.4) because the non-linearity in figure 1.2 raises expected future marginal utility relative to current marginal utility. To restore equality requires a different consumption time path: present consumption has to be lower (which increases current marginal utility), and planned future consumption has to be higher (so as to lower expected future marginal utility), compared with the optimal CEQ time path. Thus, for a given pattern of future income uncertainty CRRA preferences yield lower current consumption, and more saving, than CEQ preferences. This extra saving compared with the CEQ case results from *any* utility function with a positive third derivative: CRRA is simply a convenient special case. The extra saving is often labelled *precautionary saving*. Kimball (1990) provides a framework for analysis. He distinguishes between risk aversion and what he terms 'prudence'. The standard measurement of the degree of absolute risk aversion is $-u''(c)/u'(c)$; Kimball proposes an analogous measure of the degree of absolute prudence, $-u'''(c)/u''(c)$. The conceptual distinction is that '[the] term "prudence" is meant to suggest the propensity to prepare and forearm oneself in the face of uncertainty, in contrast to "risk aversion", which is how much one dislikes uncertainty and would turn away from uncertainty if possible' (Kimball 1990: 54).

The idea of precautionary saving predates the recent literature – see, e.g., Leland (1968) – but until relatively recently, no systematic work had been done. This reflected substantial technical difficulties in extending the two-period example in figure 1.1 to a multi-period context. The Euler equation (1.4) relates marginal utility in the current period and the next period, but it does not provide a self-contained solution unless the second-period is also the last period, since otherwise the second-period solution depends on a further Euler equation relating periods two and three; the period-three solution in turn depends on period four, and so on. SDP is the standard means of solving this sort of problem, but until relatively recently the computing power needed to solve multi-period SDP problems was not available to most researchers.

3 RECENT RESEARCH ON CONSUMPTION

3.1 SDP solutions of life cycle problems

SDP is applied to multi-period life cycle consumption problems by defining a final period of life, T, in which all remaining resources are consumed. This defines a two-period problem between periods T and $(T - 1)$, the solution to which implicitly defines optimal $c(T - 1)$. The latter is in turn inserted into another two-period problem between $(T - 1)$ and $(T - 2)$, from which optimal $c(T - 2)$ emerges, and so on. The appendix (p. 31) enlarges on the methods used; here the focus is on the underlying economic issues.

The first application of this backward induction procedure to a multi-period life cycle problem was by Zeldes (1989), and his computing techniques have been followed by others, albeit with more complicated problems becoming feasible as computing power expanded rapidly during the 1990s. The problem of computing power is well illustrated by Zeldes' own description of the difficulties of simulating a version of his model involving both permanent and transitory shocks to income. He was unable to solve this model over more than fifteen periods because it required 'creating two matrices with about 625,000 elements each. The optimal consumption (and value function) then had to be determined for each of the 625,000 possible nodes, for each of the fifteen periods' (Zeldes 1989, n. 22: 286). This exhausted available computer memory. Earlier researchers lacked the computing power to attempt even this; subsequent researchers have solved progressively more complex problems. Thus, research progress during the 1990s was triggered by the availability of greater computing power rather than by new theoretical ideas. The use of this power, however, has itself generated a number of new ideas and insights, which are outlined in the rest of this section. At the same time the sheer complexity of the problem constitutes a potential objection to SDP methods; this issue is taken up in section 1.4.

3.2 Basic SDP life cycle results

Recall some basic propositions of the Modigliani/Hall LCH framework: (1) the present value of lifetime consumption cannot exceed that of lifetime income, but other than this there is no connection between the two. In particular, the pattern of lifetime consumption is divorced from that of lifetime income (cf. figure 1.1); (2) the MPC for a current-period increase in income of X is the same as that for an increase of $(1 + r)^N X$ expected to occur N periods in the future; and (3) a household changes its current consumption by the permanent income equivalent of any unexpected change in current income.

SDP analysis using CRRA utility comprehensively overturns these results. Instead, what emerges is the following:

(1) The MPC is generally larger, often much larger, out of an increase in current income than out of an increase of equal present value in expected future income.

(2) This disparity is especially important for households whose current accumulated financial wealth is low relative to normal income. Conversely, households with high levels of financial resources relative to normal income behave more like Modigliani consumers.

(3) A household's planned rate of growth of future consumption is negatively related to its current asset holdings.

(4) There is no systematic relationship between the MPC out of a current unexpected income change, and the latter's permanent income equivalent.

(5) The pattern of lifetime consumption is not divorced from that of lifetime income. Instead, consumption closely tracks income, at least for households below the age of around 45–50.

3.3 The buffer stock model

I focus first on Carroll (1997), who provides an interesting and fully developed application of SDP to consumption and saving issues. I then look more briefly at other influential SDP models.

Carroll assumes that the household maximises an objective function of the form of (1.1) (with the horizon N sometimes allowed to go to infinity) assuming CRRA utility as in (1.4). He specifies the relevant budget constraints and income processes as follows:

$$x(t + 1) = (1 + r)[x(t) - c(t)] + E_t w(t + 1); \qquad (1.10)$$

$$E_t w(t + 1) = E_t[p(t + 1)v(t + 1)]; \qquad (1.11)$$

$$E_t p(t + 1) = (1 + g)p(t)E_t n(t + 1); \qquad (1.12)$$

$$v(t) = \begin{cases} 0 & \text{with probability } q \\ Z & \text{with probability } 1 - q; \end{cases} \qquad (1.13)$$

$$\ln Z \approx N\big(-\sigma_{\ln Z}^2/2, \sigma_{\ln Z}^2\big); \qquad (1.14)$$

$$\ln n \approx N\big(-\sigma_{\ln n}^2/2, \sigma_{\ln n}^2\big). \qquad (1.15)$$

$x(t)$ is 'cash on hand' at time t, defined as:

$$x(t) = F(t) + w(t). \tag{1.16}$$

Labour income $w(t)$ has both a persistent component, $p(t)$, and a transitory component, $v(t)$. The persistent component grows at a trend rate of g per period, and is also subject to shocks, n, specified in (1.15) such that $E_t n(t+1) = 1$. Carroll designates the trend path of the persistent income component as 'permanent income', but this is potentially confusing because it is by no means the same as the usually understood definition of 'permanent income', which is based on the notion of a constant annuity. I therefore label it as 'normal income' in what follows.

Disturbances to the persistent income component lead to persistent changes in income. Labour income in any period is also subject to transitory shocks $v(.)$. These are of two types. With probability q they cause labour income to be zero (e.g. unemployment), and with probability $(1-q)$ they have less dramatic effects, causing income to vary around its 'normal' level (e.g. variations in bonuses, overtime payments, etc.).

Before considering the model further, some limitations of it and of most of the other work considered in this chapter should be mentioned. First, it assumes perfect capital markets, whereas many economists might consider it more reasonable to focus on the implications of market imperfections, especially limitations on the ability to borrow against expected future income. This is briefly discussed later in the chapter. A second limitation is that the model assumes only one type of saving asset, whose returns are themselves not subject to uncertainty. Although this assumption is often made in the literature, it is oversimplified in two respects: there are many potential savings vehicles, and most of these are subject to at least some uncertainty of return. Thus, consumers have to contend not only with labour income uncertainty, but also with choices among different saving assets with different risk–return patterns. In practice, focusing only on labour income uncertainty is a sensible strategy in analysing life cycle behaviour at least for consumers in the first half to two-thirds of their working lives. Few such consumers have significant amounts of discretionary financial wealth, so that for them, labour income uncertainty is overwhelmingly the most important source of uncertainty. Introducing capital as well as labour income uncertainty would substantially complicate the model without adding much insight for consumers in this age range. A third simplification is that consumers are assumed to have no source of insurance against future income uncertainty other than self-insurance. Thus, markets offering insurance contracts against such contingencies are assumed absent, as of course is the case in reality. The obvious reason for this is the problem of moral hazard. Some of these insurance possibilities are, however, provided in many countries by the state, and later in the chapter I look at the importance of such social safety nets: they have an important impact on SDP models. The chapter does not discuss other possible sources of insurance against adverse income contingencies such as intra-family transfers.

Many of Carroll's results are based on the log linearised Euler equation, which takes the form:

$$\Delta \log c(t+1) \cong \sigma^{-1}(r-d) + 0.5(1+\sigma)E_t s^2(t+1) + e(t+1)$$

$$(1.17)$$

$s(t+1)$ is implicitly defined by $c(t+1) = [1 + s(t+1)]c(t)$. The implications of (1.17) can most easily be understood in combination with what Carroll labels the 'impatience condition', which determines whether or not the optimal consumption rule derived from the model of (1.10)–(1.15) by SDP-type backward induction converges. Optimal consumption in any period t is defined by normalising both consumption and cash on hand by 'normal' labour income $p(t)$ for that period, and specifying the optimal consumption rule for period t in terms of these normalised variables:

$$[c(t)/p(t)] = f[x(t)/p(t)]. \qquad (1.18)$$

Carroll shows that the function $f(.)$ converges if the following 'impatience condition' holds:

$$\sigma^{-1}(r-d) + \left(\frac{\sigma}{2}\right)\sigma^2_{\ln n} < g - \sigma^2_{\ln n}/2. \qquad (1.19)$$

To interpret (1.19), note that if there is no income uncertainty, so that $\sigma^2_{\ln N} = 0$, then this condition simplifies to $\sigma^{-1}(r-d) < g$, which is the condition in a Modigliani life cycle model with no uncertainty for consumption to grow more slowly than income over life. This in turn means that, since the present value of lifetime consumption and of lifetime income must be equal, initial consumption exceeds initial income; in other words, consumers are impatient, and choose to boost current consumption by borrowing against future income growth. Thus, (1.19) indicates impatience in the no uncertainty case; the $\sigma^2_{\ln N}$ terms in (1.19) reflect the impact of income uncertainty on planned consumption growth (left-hand side) and on income growth (right-hand side). Note that (1.19) can hold even if $r = d$; in practice, however, Carroll focuses in much of his work on the case in which $d > r$.

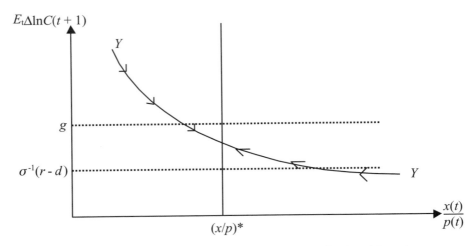

Figure 1.3 Expected consumption growth and the ratio of cash to labour income

The implications can be seen in figure 1.3, where the curve YY plots expected consumption growth from (1.17) against the ratio of cash on hand to normal labour income. The horizontal lines $\sigma^{-1}(r-d)$ and g indicate, respectively, planned consumption growth in a CEQ Modigliani model, and normal labour income growth. The vertical line $(x/p)^*$ indicates the target ratio of cash on hand to normal labour income, such that if $(x/p)^*$ is attained, households thereafter seek to maintain it constant. $(x/p)^*$ is stable in Carroll's model; thus, the arrows on YY indicate the direction of planned movement.

Figure 1.3 and (1.17) can best be understood together, (1.17) indicates that planned consumption growth varies positively with the variance of future consumption growth. The size of the latter is partly determined by the variance of future labour income, but it is also determined by the quantitative importance of future labour income relative to financial wealth: since financial wealth is not subject to uncertainty, the larger the stock of such wealth relative to uncertain labour income, the greater its ability to cushion consumption from labour income shocks, and hence the smaller the expected variance of future consumption growth. Thus, the variance of future consumption growth is an endogenous variable because it depends on the household's saving and wealth accumulation decisions. Figure 1.3 and (1.17) both indicate that when wealth is low relative to normal income, households seek to accumulate wealth – planned consumption growth is high, indicating that the current consumption level is low – in order to increase their future cushioning ability. Thus, Carroll-type models are often labelled *buffer stock models*: wealth acts as a buffer against income shocks.

3.4 Impatience versus prudence

As noted above, Carroll mostly focuses on cases in which $d > r$, and invariably $g > 0$ (i.e. growth in normal income). In a CEQ model this parameter combination would generate initial borrowing against future income, and subsequently falling consumption over the lifetime. Why does this not happen in Carroll's framework? Here the specification of the income process is critical. In the model of (1.10)–(1.15) there is a positive probability, q, of zero income in any individual period, so that in a remaining lifetime of N periods, there is a positive probability q^N that income will be zero in all N future periods. Thus, if the household chose to accumulate no buffer stock of financial wealth – or *a fortiori* if it chose to borrow (i.e. negative wealth) – it would face the probability q^N of complete destitution (i.e. $c = 0$) for its remaining lifetime. Because CRRA utility implies infinite marginal utility at $c = 0$, the household will always choose to hold some positive wealth in order to insure against the possibility of destitution. Note the importance here of the assumption, emphasised earlier, that self-insurance is the only option available for countering this threat. I return to this later when the role of social safety nets is considered.

The household's impatience is at war with its prudence. The impatient strand in preferences provides a temptation to overspend now; the prudent strand focuses on the future consequences of overspending in the event of a sequence of extremely unlucky income outcomes. The result is a compromise: the household chooses to accumulate some – but not much – wealth. This produces a now standard finding in the buffer stock literature. Looking at the pattern of life cycle behaviour, saving and wealth accumulation decisions over working life fall into two distinct phases. For typical households up to around age 45–50, buffering behaviour dominates: they choose to accumulate small amounts of wealth as a cushion against income shocks. For typical households from age 45–50 up to retirement, more traditional life cycle motives – saving for retirement – dominate, leading to the accumulation of significantly larger amounts of assets. Thus, all saving choices are ultimately driven by consumption smoothing motives, but for younger working age households it is high frequency smoothing which matters, while for working age households approaching retirement low frequency smoothing is more important. Similar results have been obtained in other recent work using similar frameworks (e.g. Gourinchas and Parker

2001, 2002; Gourinchas 2000). This same argument also generates the 'consumption tracks income' phenomenon: once a household has attained its target stock of financial wealth relative to normal income, further growth in normal income leads to approximately equal proportionate growth in consumption, allowing the wealth–income ratio to remain at its target level. Similarly, the CEQ proposition that households consume the permanent income value of any change in either present or future income does not hold. In general, a change in expected future income has little impact on current consumption in the buffer stock model, since it does not affect the ratio x/p which is what drives behaviour. Conversely, a change in current income (and thus in x) can have a large impact on current consumption, depending on the value of x/p relative to the target value.

3.5 The HSZ framework

The foregoing discussion focused on Carroll's (1997) framework. A partly similar, and partly contrasting, framework which has also been influential in the SDP literature is that of Hubbard, Skinner and Zeldes (HSZ) (1994, 1995). The HSZ model differs from Carroll's in the following ways: (1) As well as labour income uncertainty, HSZ also incorporate uncertainty about the remaining length of life, and about the possibility of medical spending in the event of future ill health; (2) HSZ also incorporate social security, the effect of which is to introduce a consumption floor, c(min), which is underwritten by the government; i.e. if the household experiences income draws which are sufficiently unlucky that its total available resources fall below the amount needed to consume at c(min), then the government provides transfer income sufficient to meet the difference; (3) HSZ focus on different baseline parameter combinations from Carroll; in particular, their baseline case sets $r = d$ whereas Carroll assumes $r < d$, and HSZ also assume significantly slower growth of labour income than in Carroll's model; (4) HSZ assume the existence of borrowing constraints, such that the household's total wealth can never be negative, i.e.

$$F(t) \geq 0 \quad \text{all } t. \tag{1.20}$$

HSZ simulate lifetime consumption and wealth accumulation profiles for households with different levels of education, and therefore different absolute levels, and lifetime patterns, of labour income. They show that all groups have hump-shaped wealth profiles, but that the presence of the consumption floor has a proportionately large effect on households with low education attainments, and therefore relatively low lifetime income. For these households, the incentive to accumulate wealth is much reduced – and in some cases disappears altogether – because the guaranteed consumption floor $c(\min)$ is a relatively high proportion of their normal annual income. Thus, for such low-income households it is sensible to save little or nothing, relying on the social security safety net in the event of unfavourable contingencies. By contrast, for households with higher education attainments and therefore higher income levels, it is not attractive to rely on social security because the consumption floor $c(\min)$ is very low relative to their normal income levels, and would therefore involve too large a drop in consumption. Thus, private precautionary saving is relatively more important for high-education than for low-education households. It follows that the presence of social security is a key part of the HSZ model. Of the other differences between the HSZ model and the Carroll framework, the presence of medical uncertainty and length of life uncertainty turns out to have quantitatively small effects, as does the existence of borrowing constraints for some, though not all, parameter combinations.

The final difference between the HSZ and Carroll frameworks concerns the choice of baseline values for the parameters which govern 'impatience', i.e. the choice of the time preference rate, d, relative to the interest rate, and also the assumed rate of lifetime income growth. As noted above, compared with Carroll, HSZ assume lower values both for d, and for average lifetime income growth; thus, they assume significantly lower degrees of impatience. Having simulated their model with their own preferred parameter values, HSZ then rework it using typical Carroll-type values; and in his own work Carroll returns the compliment by using HSZ-type parameter values in his framework. What emerges from these exercises is that (surely unsurprisingly) neither framework can easily be made consistent with all features of observed behaviour. For example, (1) HSZ argue (1994: 86) that using Carroll-type parameter values in their framework generates counterfactually small levels of pre-retirement wealth accumulation (because greater impatience reduces the willingness to accumulate pre-retirement savings to supplement guaranteed pension income); but conversely (2) Carroll and Samwick (1997: section 5) argue that using HSZ-type parameter values in their framework causes the sensitivity of the level of accumulated wealth to changes in the degree of uncertainty of future labour income to be counterfactually high (because lower time preference means that unfavourable contingencies relatively far into the future still exert a significant impact on current behaviour).

3.6 Discussion

There are other difficulties with both the Carroll and the HSZ model. The most important concerns the validity, or otherwise, of the entire SDP-type approach which is common to both; I consider this in section 1.4 below. Here, I consider further aspects of the two sets of models within the SDP approach.

Carroll's model hinges critically upon his assumption that at any given time there is a positive probability of zero income over the whole of the remaining lifetime. If this assumption is correct, any household with zero net wealth risks being left destitute for the rest of life, and all households choose to keep assets positive at all times to insure against such an outcome. Because they are also impatient, however, households keep only small amounts of precautionary wealth, at least until near to retirement. This is the mechanism by which Carroll explains the observation that many households hold small positive wealth stocks. Carroll justifies it as follows. He observes that a small fraction of households has zero incomes in any one year in the PSID data, and *assumes* that there is no social security safety net which would catch such households in the event that they were to suffer repeated zero incomes over a run of years. He provides no direct evidence in support of this assumption. Thus, his entire model is driven by an extreme contingency for which no direct supporting evidence is available (Deaton 1992: 192; Pemberton 1998). One could just as easily assume the opposite, i.e. that although events can cause some households *temporarily* to have zero income, any set of circumstances which threatened to cause *prolonged* zero incomes would be caught by a safety net.

Suppose that one assumes the existence of a safety net such that the household can obtain a fraction $Q > 0$ of its 'normal' income in the event of any persistently unfavourable contingency (continued unemployment, chronic ill health, etc.), while otherwise using the Carroll framework unchanged (Q is analogous to HSZ's $c(\min)$). How would this change the model's predictions? We can see at least an approximate answer to this easily, without formally simulating and solving the full model. In Carroll's setup, $Q = 0$ and the typical household in the first part of its life cycle chooses to hold small (near zero) levels of wealth. Thus, in the event that the lifetime destitution contingency were to materialise, this household would be able to consume at fractionally above zero in each year thereafter. Now let Q be positive. Normalise current normal income equal to unity, and, following Carroll, let the annual growth rate of normal income be g and the annual interest rate be r. Taking an infinite horizon for simplicity, the present value of normal income is:

$$P = (1 + r)/(r - g). \tag{1.21}$$

The present value of the safety net is simply QP.[3] Since households are impatient by assumption, they want to spend as much as possible immediately, consistent with being able to consume at just above zero if disaster strikes. Thus, they wish to borrow an amount just short of QP. Since current income is normalised at unity, the ratio of desired borrowing to current income is (slightly less than) QP. Taking typically assumed values for r and g of 0.04 and 0.02, respectively, and taking a safety net value of $Q = 0.2$, implies that the typical household will choose to borrow 10.4 times its current annual income. Thus, a household with current annual income of 40,000 Euros will choose to go into debt to the tune of 416,000 Euros![4] Modifying the parameter values or the framework (e.g. finite rather than infinite life) alters the numbers, but so long as Q is positive the inevitable outcome is a large amount of desired borrowing. Pemberton (1998) provides a more formal analysis of this, albeit within the context of a bounded rationality model (see section 1.4) rather than an SDP model, and shows that with Carroll-type parameter assumptions, typical households choose to build up huge amounts of indebtedness over the first few periods of the life cycle, and then pay them off gradually over the rest of life.

Thus, Carroll's model delivers plausible predictions for wealth accumulation only if it assumes $Q = 0$, i.e. no safety net. If instead $Q > 0$, the model delivers non-sensical results, predicting absurdly counterfactual levels of desired borrowing. Since safety nets have been a widespread feature of post-1945 societies in much of Western Europe and North America, it is not clear that the model provides a robust explanation of observed behaviour. Pemberton (1998) argues that this applies more generally, and that even if one assumes much less household impatience than implied by Carroll's benchmark parameter values, households will still desire to accumulate implausibly large amounts of debt.

There are two ways in which the model can be rescued. The first is to assume borrowing constraints, as in HSZ and also as in Deaton (1991, 1992) who combines such constraints with a model otherwise similar to the Carroll framework. Then, no matter how great is the household's impatience, it is unable to incur any net indebtedness. However, there must be some doubt about the underlying plausibility of such a framework. Do

---

[3] Q grows at an annual rate of g, so as to keep in line with normal income.
[4] To be precise, slightly less than 416,000 Euros.

we really believe that households would ideally choose to go into debt to
the tune of many times their current annual income, and are prevented
from doing so only by binding borrowing constraints?

An alternative way to rescue the model is to modify the utility function.
Suppose that, instead of (1.7), the utility function is as follows:

$$u(c(t)) = \begin{cases} \dfrac{[c(t) - c_0(t)]^{1-\sigma} - 1}{1 - \sigma} & (\sigma \neq 1); \\ \ln[c(t) - c_0(t)] & (\sigma = 1). \end{cases} \qquad (1.22)$$

With preferences as in (1.22), marginal utility approaches infinity as $c(t)$
approaches $c_0(t)$, rather than zero. $c_0(t)$ can be interpreted as a 'minimum
acceptable' level of consumption, which in the context of low-income countries might be the subsistence level required for physical survival, and in
richer countries might instead carry 'keeping up with the Joneses' connota-
tions. Suppose now that we equate $c_0(t)$ with $Q(t)$. Then all Carroll's results
still go through, because households always choose to accumulate at least
small amounts of wealth, no matter how large is $Q(t)$. This is the approach
taken by Zeldes (1989). There are still problems, however, stemming from
the requirement that the model should be able to explain observed wealth
holdings across different countries and time periods if it is to be convincing.
The difficulty is that the value of $Q(t)$ reflects policy decisions made by
national governments, and as such it varies across both countries and time
periods. Some countries at some times have provided much more generous
safety nets than other countries at other times, where 'generosity' is measured in the context by the proportion of one's 'normal' earnings which can
be replaced by social security if unfavourable contingencies occur. Thus, unless the value of $c_0(t)$ happens to vary across countries and time periods precisely in line with the corresponding variations in $Q(t)$ – unlikely, given that
Q is policy-driven whereas c_0 reflects underlying consumer preferences –
the model cannot provide a universal explanation of behaviour.

A similar point applies to the HSZ explanation of differences in saving behaviour as between high-education and low-education households.
As seen above, this also rests on the role of the safety net, which has a
proportionately much larger impact on low-education (and thus relatively
low-income) households than on high-education (high-income) households. An implication is that there should be no significant differences in
saving and wealth accumulation as between different education and income
groups in contexts in which there is no safety net: in such contexts, *ceteris
paribus*, the ratio of wealth to permanent income should be independent
of the level of permanent income. James, Palumbo and Thomas (JPT)

(1997) examine saving data in the pre-1914 USA. They find evidence that a substantial fraction of relatively low-income households saved nothing over their lifetimes, while higher-income households typically saved considerable amounts. Indeed, JPT draw the striking conclusion that the cross-sectional patterns of saving pre-1914 and post-1945 are remarkably similar, despite the vast differences in social security provisions and safety net arrangements in the two eras. Such a finding poses awkward questions for the HSZ model's emphasis on social security as an explanation of cross-sectional saving differences.

3.7 Conclusion

SDP models are potentially capable of explaining various features of observed intertemporal household choices which are anomalous from the perspective of the Modigliani–Hall LCH framework. On the other hand, there is room for doubt about the robustness of their explanations across different times and different countries. A critical issue is (the presence or absence of) social security safety nets, and their impact on household choices. To date it is not obvious that this issue has been satisfactorily resolved within the SDP framework. On this and other issues it is clear that there is scope for much further research. At the same time there are deeper questions about whether SDP, or some other framework, is the appropriate vehicle for such research. This is the subject matter of the next section.

4 IS SDP THE RIGHT WAY TO MODEL INTERTEMPORAL CONSUMPTION PLANNING?

4.1 Decision-making complexity

The application of SDP techniques to intertemporal consumption choice has undoubtedly changed the way in which many mainstream economists view consumption and saving behaviour. For example, the presence of large numbers of consumers who accumulate only small amounts of discretionary wealth in the first half of their working lives is now seen as consistent with optimising behaviour, rather than as a paradox which core models cannot explain.

At the same time there are grounds for scepticism. The most basic cause for concern is that the SDP approach is based upon what seems to be an impossibly complex decision-making process. As noted earlier, solving SDP models is computationally very difficult. Until around 1985, the computing power did not exist to solve even fairly simple SDP models. Even now there are various problems which economists would like to solve but for which there is no computer sufficiently powerful. Yet if we take the SDP model literally, these are the problems that ordinary inexpert consumers routinely solve in order to work out how much to save each year.

Of course this argument is not conclusive. There is nothing about SDP problems which makes them intrinsically impossible for human calculation. On the contrary, humans routinely solve SDP problems on an almost daily basis. For example, working out what time to leave home in order to catch a train which will get one to a planned meeting at the right time is an SDP-type (i.e. backward induction) problem involving several sources of uncertainty (the road to the station may have a traffic hold up, the train may be delayed, etc.). Trying formally to model even this relatively simple SDP problem would be quite difficult, yet most people do get to meetings (approximately) on time. On the other hand, this problem is clearly several orders of magnitude less complicated than using SDP to solve one's lifetime consumption problem. Some introspection is surely in order in assessing the plausibility of the SDP approach in this context. Try answering the following question for various values of N:

What proportion of the cash on hand which you expect to have available N years from now do you plan to spend in that year in the event that your N-year-ahead labour income turns out to be one standard deviation below its expected normal level?

The point of the question, of course, is that if we take SDP seriously as a description of how people behave, then the typical consumer should be able to answer it routinely for any value of N up to the maximum possible length of remaining life, because he/she should already have worked out the answer to it (and should have recalculated it every time any new information about future income prospects arrives). In practice, my guess is that most people could probably answer it for $N = 1$ and some people for $N = 2$, but that no-one could answer it for, say, $N = 30$. Not only that, but I surmise that if this question were put to a random sample of consumers (or even to a sample of professional economists) almost all would respond by saying, not merely that they could not answer for any moderately sized N, but that the question itself is non-sensical because the implicit assumption of detailed planning for annual consumption patterns far into the future bears no relation to reality.

A defender of SDP might invoke Friedman's (1953) argument in response. Friedman used the analogy of billiards. A mathematician can 'solve' a billiards game by producing formulae for the speed, direction and spin needed for each shot in a winning sequence of shots, but a professional billiards player capable of executing such a sequence would almost certainly not recognise the formulae as a description of his/her actions. Similarly, Friedman argued, decision-makers in economic contexts may not recognise mathematical statements of optimising solutions as describing how they solve problems, but may nonetheless still replicate these solutions by more intuitive means.

The extent to which the billiards example generalises to all types of economic problems is a matter for debate. A champion billiards player has rare intrinsic ability, builds upon this with long hours of practice and receives coaching/advice from assistants. None of these features applies to the use of SDP in intertemporal consumption choices. *All* households – not just rare mathematical geniuses – have to make such choices, and there is no scope for practice. Whether or not one household can be 'coached' by others depends on the scope for social learning, discussed later. Thus, while the billiards player may be able intuitively to replicate the mathematician's formulae, it is less clear that the household can do so. Such doubts are strengthened by the inability of economists to find any short-cut procedure for obtaining backward induction solutions. Conlisk (1996) argues that whether or not optimising solutions can be replicated by decision-makers depends on the degree of complication relative to the degree of expertise. He specifically cites multi-period life cycle problems as ones in which the complication:expertise ratio is too high for unbounded optimisation to make sense.

This poses the question of whether or not one can validly adopt SDP as a basis for analysis when there is no obvious way in which decision-makers can use such techniques in practice. It seems unlikely that there will ever be a consensus about this methodological issue among economists. On the one hand, a believer in Friedman's arguments might dismiss such difficulties as unimportant, implicitly assuming that the human brain can always find a way of cutting through complexities when there is an incentive to do so. On the other hand, sceptics are likely to insist on a demonstration of how, in practice, decision-makers can either learn about or simplify SDP techniques before accepting the SDP framework. Thus, neither group really believes the other's research agenda to be legitimate.

4.2 Learning and rules of thumb

Allen and Carroll (2001) (hereafter AC) seek to specify a learning mechanism. Using Carroll-type SDP models of the sort described earlier, they

show that the SDP solution can be approximated by a simple rule of thumb
of the following form:

$$c(t)/p(t) = \min[x(t)/p(t), \quad (x/p)^* + h(x(t)/p(t) - (x/p)^*)],$$
$$0 < h < 1. \tag{1.23}$$

This is a simple two-parameter rule with a sensible intuition – save something when times are good, spend everything when times are bad – but for it
to work well requires a suitable choice of parameter values for h and $(x/p)^*$.
Thus, the problem for consumers is to identify 'sensible' values (where
'sensible' in this context signifies a reasonable approximation to the 'true'
SDP parameters). AC specify a learning procedure – select initial parameter
values, observe the results, update the values and observe again, etc. – and
conclude that for an individual consumer to be confident of identifying
sensible parameter values would require at least one million years of observations! At first sight this seems implausible, but the intuition is actually
straightforward. The effects of even a single chosen parameter set can be
observed only over a number of years rather than instantaneously, and even
then there is a 'signal to noise' problem in disentangling the effects of the
parameter values from those of income shocks occurring over the trial years.
(It might be argued that the problem is overstated because of an arbitrary
assumption that periods are annual rather than, say, weekly, daily, etc. However, specifying the 'period' as a year is not arbitrary because the assumed
stochastic income process is calibrated using annual data, and meaningful
income shocks do not occur over substantially shorter periods.) Thus, to
select a sensible parameter set from the many candidate sets with confidence
requires an immense number of annual observations. AC conclude that it
is impossible for individual consumers, acting in isolation, to learn enough
to be able to approximate SDP optimisation by rules of thumb.

Since AC's underlying assumption is that SDP provides the appropriate
basis for analysis, they argue that consumers must use some other learning
method. They speculate that 'social learning' might be the answer (e.g.
instead of one consumer taking a million years to learn, consider one million
consumers who each experiment for a year and then pool their information).
This seems to be a key issue – see the earlier discussion of Friedman's
methodology based on his billiards analogy – but to date it does not appear
to have been addressed at all. If proponents of SDP consumption models
are to convince the sceptics, some serious theoretical and empirical work
on the scope for social learning in this context appears to be essential. For
example, can parents pass on accumulated wisdom about such matters to

their children? Are there other ways (schools? mass media?)? In principle it is obviously possible to impart considerable information in a variety of ways. On the other hand, an important part of the SDP consumption literature is its emphasis on *idiosyncratic* income shocks, and this emphasises a difficulty with social learning in this context: it may be relatively easy to provide general information but it is harder to see how social learning can tell individuals all that they need to know, or find out, about their own individual circumstances. In this context the idea of intergenerational parental knowledge transfer may be particularly problematic, since it is quite unlikely that one generation's experience of income trends, fluctuations, safety nets, etc. will be a good guide to the next generation's prospects. Thus, what is a sensible set of parameter choices in (1.23) may well change across generations.

AC specify 'learning' as a process of moving closer to the 'true' SDP model. Other work on learning and rules of thumb permits the possibility that households may select some other rule of thumb in preference to the 'true' SDP model. For example, Lettau and Uhlig (1999) (henceforth LU) compare two rules. One is SDP; the other involves a weighted average of SDP and 'break even' (i.e. $c = x$) behaviour. Households stick with one rule or switch to the other according to what they learn from repeated outcomes. LU show that the non-SDP rule can plausibly dominate SDP.

Both the AC and the LU papers exemplify a growing interest in rules of thumb, motivated by the view that SDP is too complex to be a plausible decision-making process. Both papers, and much of the literature, share two features. First, they take SDP as the true, or ideal, model and typically calculate the loss from using any non-SDP method (in terms of less smooth consumption over time). Second, they do not model the cost (in time, effort, or money) of learning about and implementing alternative decision rules. This seems to be an internally contradictory procedure. That there are learning and operating costs is implicit in the approach: if learning were costless, all households would instantly acquire all the information needed to operate the SDP procedure, given that this is known to provide the best outcomes. But given that there are learning and operating costs, there then appears to be no basis for taking SDP as the ideal model, to be used as the yardstick against which others are measured. Rather, there is an array of possible decision-making models, each offering *benefits*, in terms of a stream of consumption outcomes, but each also involving *costs*, in terms of the time and effort needed to learn about and operate them. The optimal model is the one with the most favourable benefit/cost ratio. SDP may, or may not, be optimal: we know that it offers higher benefits than any alternative, but we might plausibly suppose that it also involves higher costs. To date, however, most researchers in the area have not even acknowledged the issue of costs, let alone made any effort to model or quantify them.

4.3 Bounded rationality

This criticism applies as much to SDP critics as to SDP advocates, the difference being that the critics start from the opposite implicit assumption to that of the advocates, namely that the learning and operating costs of SDP are prohibitively high. On the basis of this implicit assumption, the critics have then formulated various non-SDP decision-making models. I briefly review two such approaches.

Mental accounting methods (Shefrin and Thaler 1988; Thaler 1990)
This literature predates the Carroll–Deaton–Kimball emphasis on the conflicting pressures of prudence and of impatience, and offers an alternative view of the same ideas. It focuses upon methods by which households use 'self-control' to keep impatience at bay. The key assumption is that households keep separate notional 'accounts' – current spending, precautionary saving, long-run life cycle saving – which they discipline themselves to treat as non-fungible. Self-control is reinforced by use of longer-term saving instruments which cannot be 'raided' (or at least only with a penalty) such as Christmas clubs and pension funds. Thus, households guard against the danger that their future selves may be excessively impatient by locking away their current savings in inaccessible forms. Such behavioural models are capable of explaining many of the same features of household behaviour that the SDP buffer stock models address. The models are inconsistent with most of the propositions of the Modigliani–Hall LCH. For example, extra income of X now does not generate the same consumption response as $(1 + r)^N X$ in N periods' time, because the latter is in a different mental account. Thus, as noted earlier, many behavioural economists are not overly impressed by the SDP research agenda, given that they never believed in the first place in the Modigliani–Hall propositions whose overturning is the main contribution claimed by SDP modellers.

The behavioural models' emphasis on self-control has been addressed from a perspective closer to the SDP approach by Laibson (1997). His model resembles a standard SDP-type life cycle framework except that he replaces the standard assumption of a fixed time preference rate with *hyperbolic* time preference. The latter applies a much higher discount rate to the near future than to the farther distant future. Thus, consider the choice from today's perspective between booking a holiday in exactly one year's time, or in thirteen months' time. A typical consumer may be virtually indifferent between the two options. In twelve months' time, however, the choice will be between an immediate holiday, or one delayed by a month, and the same consumer may then substantially prefer immediate gratification to a one-month delay. Laibson argues that from today's perspective, households have an incentive to lock savings into long-term accounts in order to protect their future selves from impatience and consequent overspending. This echoes 'mental accounting' behavioural models, but within an SDP framework. Thus, it is possible to integrate behavioural insights into an SDP model.

Present–future tradeoff models (Hey 1983; Pemberton 1993, 1998)

All economic problems ultimately involve tradeoffs, and every human being makes many decisions involving tradeoffs every day. Most are trivial in their ultimate impact (e.g. whether to buy a CD or a book on a shopping trip), some relatively infrequent ones are more quantitatively significant (e.g. whether or not to move to a more expensive house), and a few are potentially life-changing (e.g. whether or not to have children). Generally, the more significant tradeoffs require the decision-maker to weigh up a wider range of issues, but ultimately all tradeoffs are conceptually straightforward because they are *self-contained*: a better outcome in one dimension has an opportunity cost in terms of some other dimension, and information about relative prices and about the relative importance in the preference function of each dimension is all that is needed. Friedman's billiards analogy is appealing when applied to almost any self-contained tradeoff: decision-makers who have never heard of the term 'opportunity cost' can nonetheless make good decisions based on an intuitive understanding of the concept.

In principle consumption and saving decisions can be fitted into this framework, as a tradeoff between present and future consumption, with an extra Euro of saving raising future consumption at the expense of current consumption. This tradeoff is simple enough to be a plausible basis for household decisions provided that 'future consumption' is treated as a single entity. Pemberton (1993) argues that this is precisely the way in which saving decisions are made. He proposes a framework in which in each period households choose between current consumption and *sustainable future consumption* (SFC), the latter defined as that consumption level which, for given expected lifetime resources, can be maintained constant over all future periods until the expected end of life. Thus, SFC is identical to permanent income (Friedman's, not Carroll's, definition): it is the constant

annuity equivalent of the expected lifetime resources remaining at the end
of the current period. The objective function is thus no longer (1.1), but
instead as follows:

$$V(t) = \frac{c(t)^{1-\sigma} - 1}{1 - \sigma} + \frac{1}{1 - \sigma} E_t \sum_{i=1}^{N} (1 + d)^{-i} c_p(t + 1)^{1-\sigma} \quad (1.24)$$

$$c_p(t) = \left(\frac{r}{1 + r}\right) \left[\frac{1}{1 - (1 + r)^{-(1+N)}}\right] [F(t) + H(t)]. \quad (1.25)$$

$F(t)$ and $H(t)$ are as defined in (1.2). $c_p(t + 1)$ denotes SFC as at time
$(t + 1)$. Its definition in (1.25) indicates that it is equivalent to permanent
income as usually defined. The model of (1.24)–(1.25) converts the multi-
period life cycle problem into a *two-period* problem. This is because SFC
is notionally assigned to *every* future period, which is appropriate given
the definition of SFC. If the household allocates an extra Euro to current consumption its current-period utility increases, but its future utility
decreases because its sustainable future consumption decreases. This is a
self-contained tradeoff whose optimal solution is surely within the computational capacity of most households in a way which SDP solutions are
not. Note that uncertainty about future income is incorporated (because
permanent income and therefore SFC depends on uncertain future labour
income), and that although the problem is a two-period one there is no
myopia (the time horizon is the same as in multi-period SDP models).
Pemberton (1993) provides a fuller discussion.

There are (at least) two possible objections to such an approach. The
first involves the possibility of especially bad outcomes such as Carroll's zero
income path. If there is a positive probability of such a path, then it will both
reduce the mean expected value of SFC, and increase its variance and higher
moments. It will thus raise the amount of precautionary saving generated by
the model. However, it can be argued that this gives insufficient weight in
the decision-making process to such extremely unfavourable outcomes. In
Pemberton (1998) I adapt the model to deal with this. I model an income
process in which each year there is a probability $(1 - h)$ of continuing
along a normal income path for a further year ('normal' in Carroll's sense,
and defined similarly) and a probability h of an adverse shock such as
long-term disability which deflects the household *permanently* away from
this normal path, and forces it instead to rely on a social security safety
net which provides drastically lower income for the rest of life. This is
more severe than the corresponding shock in Carroll's model (which is
a transitory rather than a persistent shock). Following the discussion in

the previous section, I assume that in general the social security safety net guarantees (low) income in such circumstances, though I also allow the Carroll extreme of zero income as a special case. The resulting objective function is as follows:

$$V(t) = \frac{c(t)^{1-\sigma} - 1}{1 - \sigma} + \left(\frac{1-h}{1-\sigma}\right) E_t \sum_{i=1}^{N} (1+d)^{-i} c_p(t+1)^{1-\sigma}$$
$$+ h D(t+1). \tag{1.26}$$

$c_p(.)$ has the same interpretation as before, except that now it is contingent on normal rather than abnormal circumstances. The latter are captured by the final right-hand side term, with $D(t+1)$ measuring lifetime utility from period $(t+1)$ onwards conditional on being reduced to the safety net from then on. $D(.)$ is fully determined by the safety net rules.[5]

The second possible criticism of the model is that it is potentially time inconsistent: at time t the household assigns SFC to each future period $t+1, t+2\ldots$ in deciding how much to save at time t, but it does not necessarily plan to consume SFC in each of these future periods. While time inconsistency in this sense is certainly present in the model, however, a possible response is 'so what?'. Essentially, the household uses SFC as a calculating device – somewhat analogous to the mental accounting devices discussed earlier – to enable it to make decisions about its present–future tradeoff, with the subsequent allocation of the 'future' part of its resources being determined period by period as that future unfolds. There is no obvious sense in which such behaviour is foolish, or leaves the household ripe for exploitation; thus, it is not clear what problem is posed by such time inconsistency.

The present–future tradeoff model has no difficulty with the thought-experiment question about N-period-ahead plans posed earlier. It offers the following answer:

I will not determine precisely how much to spend in N periods' time until I get there, but my current plans take account of the need to preserve resources up to (and if necessary beyond) N periods ahead.

Thus, it says that households take 'the future' seriously, but that they do not attempt the (seemingly impossible) task of formulating precise plans for each individual subperiod of that future. By contrast, the SDP approach formulates such precise plans, but has so far been unsuccessful in demonstrating that households can behave in such a way.

---

[5] If there is uncertainty about the future specification of these rules, then $D(.)$ likewise incorporates uncertainty.

5 CONCLUSION

I have reviewed leading SDP models of consumption behaviour. I have
also discussed objections to the SDP approach, and various non-SDP
models. As should be clear from the discussion, there is considerable dis-
agreement among economists. SDP advocates argue that they have significantly advanced knowledge about how households make intertemporal
consumption and saving decisions. SDP critics argue that the models have
merely overturned results that the critics never believed in anyway, and
that the models are too complex to be taken seriously as representations of
behaviour.

I believe that there is considerable research potential in efforts to find
common ground between these conflicting viewpoints. Such research might
start from the proposition that in choosing among possible methods of
making intertemporal decisions, households face a tradeoff: more complex
methods such as SDP yield better outcomes, but are also more costly to
implement. Thus, in choosing among decision-making processes a dynamic
consumption–leisure tradeoff is involved: SDP yields better consumption
outcomes, but worse leisure outcomes, than simpler rival methods. The key
analytical issues which this raises are, first, how to model households' initial
levels of knowledge (or ignorance) and, secondly, how to model the costs of
learning. It seems inevitable that convincing models of these issues will need
to incorporate insights and empirical results from psychology research. That
is, we need to model knowledge and learning in ways which correspond
to actual human behaviour and mental capacities, rather than according
to preconceived axioms. In many ways this suggested research programme
is more intellectually challenging than the current SDP programme. The
latter is technically complex, but it sidesteps the truly difficult conceptual
issues of knowledge and learning. SDP households never learn because they
are somehow endowed with perfect understanding.

How one judges the SDP research agenda in the context of household
behaviour ultimately rests on what one thinks that economic theory is, or
ought to be, trying to achieve.[6] If the aim is to model the decision processes
which would be followed by an idealised decision-maker who satisfies preconceived axioms and who is endowed with unbounded computational
ability, then SDP has achieved impressive advances in knowledge since the
1990s though, as noted at the end of section 1.4, there is still much to

---

[6] I emphasise the phrase 'in the context of household behaviour'. The complexities of SDP might
be more easily surmountable in other contexts, e.g. large firms or government agencies might use
supercomputers programmed by experts in order to solve their intertemporal problems.

do. If, instead, the aim is to model the ways in which decisions are actually made by real live human beings, then it is not clear what has been achieved, or could ever be achieved, by the SDP research programme.

APPENDIX: NUMERICAL SOLUTIONS OF SDP CONSUMPTION MODELS

This appendix enlarges a little on the summary of solution methods given at the start of section 1.3. It does not seek to provide a detailed exposition. Carroll (2002) provides a much fuller description of solution methods.

The basic aim is to find a function $c(t) = f[x(t)]$ which determines optimal consumption, c, as a function of cash on hand, x. Starting with the final period T, since all remaining resources must be consumed, the optimal function is simply $c(T) = x(T)$. Now consider period $T - 1$. For simplicity suppose that the interest and time preference rates are equal ($r = d$) and that utility is logarithmic. Then the Euler equation is:

$$c(T - 1)^{-1} = E_{T-1} c(T)^{-1}. \tag{A.1}$$

Substituting for $c(T)$ using the one-period budget constraint in (1.10):

$$c(T - 1)^{-1} = E_{T-1}[(1 + r)(x(T - 1) - c(T - 1)) + w(T)]^{-1}$$
$$= \sum_i [(1 + r)(x(T - 1) - c(T - 1)) + w_i(T)]^{-1}. \tag{A.2}$$

The second line of (A.2) emphasises that the source of uncertainty is future labour income, $w(T)$. In general (A.2) cannot be solved analytically. Instead numerical solutions are required. These are based on formulating a grid of discrete values for $x(T)$, based on distributions of possible values for next period's uncertain labour income $w(T)$ and for current cash on hand $x(T - 1)$. For each point on the grid, the value of $c(T - 1)$ which solves (A.2) can be calculated numerically. The entire grid of points gives the function $c(T - 1) = f[x(T - 1)]$ which defines optimal consumption as a function of current cash on hand. Proceeding to period $T - 2$, repeating (A.2) and substituting $c(T - 2) = f[x(T - 2)]$ and $c(T - 1) = f[x(T - 1)]$:

$$f[x(T - 2)]^{-1} = \sum_i f[(1 + r)(x(T - 2) - f[x(T - 2)])$$
$$+ w_i(T - 1)]^{-1}. \tag{A.3}$$

This equation can again be solved numerically over a grid of values. It is more complex than (A.2) because the right-hand side now depends on

$f[T - 2]$ as well as $f[T - 1]$. Similar solutions for earlier periods, and eventually back to the first period of the life cycle, can be obtained by repeating the process the required number of times.

The main computational burden is the numerical solution for each period, utilising the grid procedure. For any income process with a reasonable range of possible stochastic outcomes, and for a life cycle of a significant number of periods, the total size of grid rapidly becomes extremely large, requiring a huge amount of computing memory. It is this which, until recently, prevented the solution of any but the simplest such problems. The decision-making complexity involved also illustrates why there is debate about whether ordinary consumers can plausibly mimic the solution method; this is discussed in section 1.4.

BIBLIOGRAPHY

Allen, T. W. and Carroll, C. D. (2001). 'Individual Learning about Consumption', Johns Hopkins University, mimeo, and at http://www.econ.jhu.edu/People/Carroll

Campbell, J. Y. and Deaton, A. (1989). 'Why is Consumption so Smooth?,' *Review of Economic Studies*, 56, 357–74

Carroll, C. D. (1997). 'Buffer Stock Saving and the Life Cycle/Permanent Income Hypothesis', *Quarterly Journal of Economics*, 107(1), 1–56

Carroll, C. D. (2002). 'Lecture Notes on Solution Methods for Microeconomic Dynamic Stochastic Optimisation Problems', Johns Hopkins, mimeo, and at http://www.econ.jhu.edu/People/Carroll

Carroll, C. D. and Samwick, A. A. (1997). 'The Nature of Precautionary Wealth,' *Journal of Monetary Economics*, 40(1)

Conlisk, J. (1996). 'Why Bounded Rationality?', *Journal of Economic Literature*, 34, 669–700

Deaton, A. (1991). 'Saving and Liquidity Constraints', *Econometrica*, 59, 1121–42
  (1992). *Understanding Consumption*, Oxford: Clarendon Press

Dornbusch, R., Fischer, S. and Startz, R. (2001). *Macroeconomics*, 8th edn, New York: Mc-Graw Hill

Flavin, M. (1981). 'The Adjustment of Consumption to Changing Expectations about Future Income', *Journal of Political Economy*, 89, 974–1009

Friedman, M. (1953). *Essays in Positive Economics*, Chicago: Chicago University Press
  (1957). *A Theory of the Consumption Function*, Princeton: Princeton University Press
  (1963). 'Windfalls, the 'Horizon', and Related Concepts in the Permanent Income Hypothesis', in C. F. Christ (ed.), *Measurement in Economics*, Stanford: Stanford University Press

Gourinchas, P. O. (2000). 'Precautionary Saving, Life Cycle and Macroeconomics', Princeton University, mimeo

Gourinchas, P. O. and Parker, J. A. (2001). 'The Empirical Importance of Precautionary Saving', *American Economic Review*, Papers and Proceedings, 91, 406–12

(2002). 'Consumption Over the Life Cycle', *Econometrica*, 70, 47–89

Hall, R. E. (1978). 'Stochastic Implications of the Life Cycle–Permanent Income Hypothesis: Theory and Evidence', *Journal of Political Economy*, 86, 971–86

Hey, J. D. (1983). 'Whither Uncertainty?,' *Economic Journal*, 93, 129–38

Hubbard, G., Skinner, J. S. and Zeldes, S. P. (1994). 'The Importance of Precautionary Motives for Explaining Individual and Aggregate Saving', *in Carnegie-Rochester Conference Series on Public Policy*, A. H. Meltzer and C. I. Plosser (eds.), 40, 59–125

(1995). 'Precautionary Saving and Social Insurance,' *Journal of Political Economy*, 103, 360–397

James, J. A., Palumbo, M. G. and Thomas, M. (1997). 'Have Working Class Americans Always been Low Savers? Saving and Accumulation before the Advent of Social Insurance: The United States, 1885–1910', University of Virginia, mimeo

Keynes, J. M. (1936). *The General Theory of Employment, Interest and Money*, London: Macmillan

Kimball, M. S. (1990). 'Precautionary Saving in the Small and the Large', *Econometrica*, 58, 53–73

Laibson, D. A. (1997). 'Golden Eggs and Hyperbolic Discounting', *Quarterly Journal of Economics*, 112, 443–77

Leland, H. E. (1968). 'Saving and Uncertainty: The Precautionary Demand for Saving', *Quarterly Journal of Economics*, 82, 465–73

Lettau, M. and Uhlig, H. (1999). 'Rules of Thumb versus Dynamic Programming', *American Economic Review*, 89, 148–74

Modigliani, F. (1986). 'Life Cycle, Individual Thrift and the Wealth of Nations', *American Economic Review*, 76, 297–313

Modigliani, F. and Brumberg, R. (1954). 'Utility Analysis and Aggregate Consumption Functions: An Interpretation of Cross-Section Data', in K. K. Kurihara (ed.), *Post-Keynesian Economics*, New Brunswick: Rutgers University Press

Pemberton, J. (1993). 'Attainable Non-Optimality or Unattainable Optimality: A New Approach to Stochastic Life Cycle Problems', *Economic Journal*, 103, 1–20

(1998). 'Income Catastrophes and Precautionary Saving', Reading, UK, mimeo

Shefrin, H. M. and Thaler, R. H. (1988). 'The Behavioural Life-Cycle Hypothesis', *Economic Inquiry*, 26, 609–43

Thaler, R. H. (1990). 'Saving, Fungibility, and Mental Accounts', *Journal of Economic Perspectives*, 4, 193–205

Zeldes, S. P. (1989). 'Optimal Consumption with Stochastic Income: Deviations from Certainty Equivalence', *Quarterly Journal of Economics*, 104, 275–98

2

Investment dynamics

Fanny S. Demers, Michael Demers and Sumru Altug

1 INTRODUCTION

Investment decisions occupy a central role among the determinants of growth. As empirical studies such as Levine and Renelt (1992) have revealed, fixed investment as a share of gross domestic product (GDP) is the most robust explanatory variable of a country's growth. DeLong and Summers (1991) also provides evidence emphasizing the correlation of investment in equipment and machinery with growth. Investment is also the most variable component of GDP, and therefore an understanding of its determinants may shed light on the source of cyclical fluctuations. Policy-makers are typically concerned about the ultimate impact of alternative policy measures on investment and its variability. Several theories of investment have emerged since the 1960s in an attempt to explain the determinants of investment. The most notable of these have been the neoclassical model of investment, the cost-of-adjustment-Q-theory model, the time-to-build model, the irreversibility model under uncertainty and the fixed-cost (S, s) model of lumpy investment.

Beginning with the neoclassical model developed by Jorgenson and his collaborators (see for example, Hall and Jorgenson 1967; Jorgenson 1963), investment theory distinguishes between the actual capital stock and the desired or optimal capital stock, where the latter is determined by factors such as output and input prices, technology and interest rates. In the neoclassical model of investment, an exogenous partial adjustment mechanism is postulated to yield a gradual adjustment of the actual capital stock to its desired level as is observed in the data. An alternative way of obtaining a determinate rate of investment is to assume the existence of convex costs of adjustment, as has been proposed by Eisner and Strotz (1963), Gould (1967), Lucas (1976) and Treadway (1968). Abel (1979) and Hayashi (1982) have shown that the standard adjustment cost model leads to a Tobin's Q-theory of investment under perfect competition and a constant returns to scale production technology. A complementary explanation assumes that it takes time to build productive capacity. (See Altug 1989, 1993; Kydland and Prescott 1982.)

A number of authors have emphasised irreversibility and uncertainty as important factors underlying the gradual adjustment of the capital stock. The notion of irreversibility, which can be traced back to Marschak (1949) and subsequently to Arrow (1968), was initially applied in the context of environmental economics where economic decisions, such as the destruction of a rain forest to build a highway, often entail actions that cannot be 'undone.'[1] In the presence of uncertainty, the decision-maker may wish to reverse the decision in view of new information received after the fact, but will not be able to do so if the investment decision is irreversible.

The notion of irreversibility was also applied more recently to the investment decisions of firms. Contributions to this literature include Abel and Eberly (1994, 1996b), Bernanke (1983), Bertola (1988), Bertola and Caballero (1994), Caballero and Pindyck (1996), M. Demers (1985, 1991), Dixit and Pindyck (1994), McDonald and Siegel (1985, 1986), Nickell (1977, 1978) and Pindyck (1988). In fact, as documented by several empirical studies, firms in a variety of industries face substantial irreversibility, and firms may lose an important percentage of their initial investment should they wish to disinvest. Firm-level investment also tends to be intermittent, with periods of investment alternating with periods of inaction, a fact that can be explained by the theory of irreversible investment under uncertainty. Another observation revealed by data is that firm-level investment tends to be lumpy, so that firms invest sporadically but undertake large investments whenever they decide to invest.[2] The (S, s) models of investment address this issue and are able to explain the lumpy nature of investment by the presence of fixed costs of investing (see Caballero and Engel 1999; Caballero and Leahy 1996).[3]

There have been relatively few studies that have analysed the dynamic general equilibrium models with irreversible or lumpy investment. One

[1] See also Arrow and Fisher (1974) and Henry (1974) for early contributions to this literature.

[2] For empirical evidence on irreversibility, intermittence and lumpiness of investment see, for example, Caballero, Engel and Haltiwanger (1995), Cooper, Haltiwanger and Power (1999), Doms and Dunne (1998) and Ramey and Shapiro (2001). Doms and Dunne and Caballero, Engel and Haltiwanger both use a large sample of manufacturing plants from the LRD and find very significant spikes in investment at the plant level. In the context of the aerospace industry, Ramey and Shapiro find that, after accounting for depreciation, machine tools lose 69 per cent of their purchase value while structural equipment loses 95 per cent of its value at resale.

[3] See Abel (1990), Caballero (1999), Carruth, Dickerson and Henley (2000), Chirinko (1993), Dixit and Pindyck (1994), Hassett and Hubbard (2002), Hubbard (1998), Nickell (1978) and Pindyck (1991) for surveys on different aspects of investment theory.

notable seminal contribution is Sargent (1980), which shows the existence of a competitive equilibrium with irreversible investment under uncertainty.[4] More recently, multi-sector general equilibrium models with irreversibility and lumpy investment have been used to examine the effects of irreversible investment on the propagation of sectoral shocks, and on the evolution of the long-run capital stock. (See Caplin and Leahy 1993; Coleman 1997; Dow and Olson 1992; Faig 2001; Ramey and Shapiro 1998; Thomas 2002 and Veracierto 2002.)

In this chapter, we provide an overview of the alternative approaches underlying modern investment theory. Sections 2 and 3 present the neoclassical theory of investment and the cost of adjustment model as well as the Q-theory of investment. Empirical evidence is also discussed. Section 4 discusses a model of partial irreversibility and expandability and extensively presents the irreversibility model of investment under uncertainty.[5] We discuss the impact of demand uncertainty, cost uncertainty, tax policy and of liquidity constraints and imperfect capital markets on the level of irreversible investment. We show that features of the firm's economic environment such as time-to-build, regime shifts and subjective uncertainty and learning, lead to a richer set of dynamic relationships. Finally, we discuss the behaviour of the capital stock in the long run as well as empirical evidence on irreversibility models. Section 5 is devoted to the aggregation of individual investment decisions. We first examine Caballero and Engel's generalised (S, s) model of lumpy investment (1999). We then survey empirical evidence on the aggregation of lumpy and irreversible investment. Finally, we draw the implications of fixed costs for Q theory. Section 6 reviews the extensions to general equilibrium of investment theory. The central question that is addressed is whether the intermittence and lumpiness observed at the firm level also affects investment at the aggregate level once general equilibrium effects are taken into account. Section 7 draws some general conclusions from our survey.

2 THE HALL–JORGENSON NEOCLASSICAL MODEL

The modern economic theory of investment was launched by the pioneering work of Hall and Jorgenson (1967) and Jorgenson (1963). In the Hall–Jorgenson 'neoclassical' theory of investment, the firm faces an optimisation problem involving its choice of capital stock and variable factors of production.

---

[4] Olson (1989) also proves the existence of a competitive equilibrium with irreversible investment.
[5] Our discussion derives in part from Altug, Demers, and Demers (1999, 2000, 2001, 2002a, 2002b, 2002c), Demers (1985, 1991) and Demers, Demers and Schaller (1994).

At time t the firm produces output, Y_t, using capital, K_t, and labour, L_t.[6] The firm's production function $F(A_t, K_t, L_t)$ is twice continuously differentiable, increasing, concave, and satisfies the Inada conditions. In this expression, A_t is a stochastic shock to technology and the function F displays constant returns to scale (CRS) with respect to L_t and K_t. Firms are assumed to own the physical stock of capital, and to make optimal investment decisions to maximise the value of owners' equity, which is equivalent to maximising the present value of cash flows subject to the law of motion of the capital stock. The output and input markets are perfectly competitive. Let p_t, w_t, p_t^k denote the output price, wage rate and price of each unit of investment respectively at time t.

In the usual formulation adopted by Jorgenson and his collaborators, the neoclassical firm is modelled as choosing its capital stock under conditions of certainty with respect to the marginal value product of capital. In Jorgenson's model K_t^* and L_t^* solve:

$$p_t F_K(A_t, L_t, K_t) = c_t \qquad (2.1)$$

$$p_t F_L(A_t, L_t, K_t) = w_t, \qquad (2.2)$$

where F_K and F_L are the partial derivatives of F with respect to K and L and K and L and c_t is the firm's cost of capital.

2.1 The cost of capital

The cost of capital or 'user cost', introduced forty years ago by Jorgenson (1963), permits us to incorporate the effects of changes in tax policy, technological or market-based changes that affect the price of capital, changes in interest rates and changes in depreciation rates on firms' optimal capital accumulation decisions.[7] Thus, firms choose the level of their desired capital stock for time t, K_t^*, by setting the marginal revenue product of capital, $p_t F_K(A_t, L_t, K_t)$, equal to the cost of capital (or 'user cost') c_t, where

$$c_t \equiv (1 + r)p_t^k - (1 - \delta)p_{t+1}^k$$

$$= p_t^k \left\{ r + \delta - (1 - \delta)\left[\frac{p_{t+1}^k - p_t^k}{p_t^k} \right] \right\}. \qquad (2.3)$$

---

[6] More generally, L_t could represent a vector of variable factors (such as labour and material inputs) in which case w_t also denotes a vector.

[7] In other applications, Jorgenson and his collaborators have also introduced the concept of 'marginal effective tax rates'. See Jorgenson and Auerbach (1980). This has been used to study the general equilibrium effects of alternative tax policies. (See, for example, Jorgenson and Yun 1990.)

If the price of capital is constant $p_t^k = p_{t+1}^k$ for all t, then the user cost simplifies to $p_k(r + \delta)$. Since the marginal revenue product of capital is decreasing in K_t, a higher price of capital p_t^k, a higher interest rate, r, or a higher depreciation rate of the capital stock, δ, would induce firms to lower their desired stock of capital. If the price of capital is not constant, the term $[p_{t+1}^k - p_t^k]/p_t^k$ represents the (percentage) capital gain (or loss) on investment goods. Thus, for example, when firms expect an increase in the future price of investment, they will choose to purchase more capital goods today.

If there is a corporate income tax rate (denoted by τ_t) and an investment tax credit (denoted by γ_t), (2.1) becomes:

$$p_t(1 - \tau_t)F_K(A_t, L_t, K_t) = c_t^\tau, \qquad (2.4)$$

where the cost of capital with taxes, c_t^τ, is:

$$c_t^\tau \equiv (1 - \gamma_t)p_t^k \left\{ r + \delta - (1 - \delta)\left[\frac{(1 - \gamma_{t+1})p_{t+1}^k - (1 - \gamma_t)p_t^k}{(1 - \gamma_t)p_t^k} \right] \right\}. \qquad (2.5)$$

In this case, cost of capital includes current and future investment tax credits, and the corporate income tax affects the future (after-tax) marginal revenue product of capital.

2.2 The dynamics of investment and empirical evidence

In the neoclassical model of investment firms do not choose the rate of investment. Instead, they choose the level of the capital stock. Thus, this model predicts that as the cost of capital changes, firms should instantaneously adjust their capital stock to the 'desired' level. In practice, numerous studies have found that investment responds slowly to changes in the cost of capital. To account for this empirical phenomenon, a partial adjustment mechanism is added to the theory of the choice of capital stock to yield a model of investment. This has been called the 'flexible accelerator model'. Empirical studies first specify a desired stock of capital, K_t^* which is obtained from the first-order condition (2.1).[8] Assuming a Cobb–Douglas production function, K_t^* is obtained as:

$$K_t^* = \eta Y_t/(c_t)^{-\sigma}, \qquad (2.6)$$

where $0 < \eta < 1$ is the share of capital with constant returns to scale (CRS)

---

[8] See Jorgenson (1963) and Hall and Jorgenson (1967).

and σ is the elasticity of substitution.[9] Secondly, a lag structure is assumed. Let K_t be a rational distributed lag function of desired capital stocks:

$$K_t = \frac{u(L)}{v(L)} K_t^*, \qquad (2.7)$$

where $u(L)$ and $v(L)$ are polynominals in the lag operator, L. If $u(L) = \varphi$ and $v(L) = 1 - (1 - \varphi)L$ then we have the geometric lag so that

$$K_t - K_{t-1} = \varphi(K_t^* - K_{t-1}), \qquad (2.8)$$

with $0 < \varphi < 1$ denoting the speed of adjustment of the current capital stock K_t to its desired level K_t^*. Replacement investment is added to net investment to obtain gross investment. In empirical work, Jorgenson assumes $\sigma = 1$. Cross-section studies have found estimates of σ close to unity while time series studies have revealed lower values.[10]

An extensive literature has documented the impact of the cost of capital on investment.[11] Although the 'flexible accelerator' performs relatively well empirically, it is not fully satisfactory at the theoretical level. First, no theoretical justification is provided for the existence of such a partial adjustment of the capital stock. Secondly, there is no reason to expect the adjustment parameter φ to be constant over time. It may change as the cost of capital itself changes, due, for example, to changes in the interest rate or to changes in the price of investment p_t^k. Since the cost of capital is in general a function of tax parameters, any changes in tax policy will also cause the speed of adjustment to change.[12]

---

[9] Note that K_t^* is determinate when there are decreasing returns to scale but not when there are constant returns to scale. However, Jorgenson (1972: 246) argues that, in the presence of CRS, K_t^* 'should be interpreted as a moving target rather than a long-run equilibrium value'. Jorgenson's interpretation is consistent with a cost of adjustment model where K_t^* is a moving target along the adjustment path.

[10] The importance of the cost of capital has also been addressed in long-run estimation which avoids the difficulties involved with the specification of K_t^* and with the adjustment mechanism. Caballero (1994) assumes that differences between $\ln K_t$ and $\ln K_t^*$ are only transitory. After taking logarithms in (2.6), and substituting $\ln K_t = \ln K_t^* + \epsilon_t$ where ϵ_t is a residual and dropping the constant we have:

$$\ln K_t - \ln Y_t = \sigma \ln c_t + \epsilon_t$$

which he estimates by OLS for US quarterly data from NIPA from 1957 to 1987. Caballero uses Monte Carlo simulations to correct for the small-sample bias and finds an estimate $\hat{\sigma}$ close to 1 as predicted by the neoclassical model. Bertola and Caballero (1994) and Caballero, Engel and Haltiwanger (1995) find similar values.

[11] See Chirinko (1993) for a review of the literature and Auerbach and Hassett (1991, 1992) for more recent studies.

[12] Thus, it is subject to the Lucas (1976) critique. As we discuss below, this last feature is also shared by cost-of-adjustment models in which the adjustment cost parameter is specified exogenously. See Chirinko (1988, 1993) for a discussion of the theoretical and empirical importance of the Lucas critique in this context.

3 COSTS OF ADJUSTMENT AND Q-THEORY

One way to overcome some of the theoretical problems with respect to the adjustment mechanism in the neoclassical model is to make it endogenous. This can be accomplished by introducing convex costs of adjustment into the firm's optimisation problem. The proponents of this approach (Eisner and Strotz 1963), argue that it takes time to put new machinery into place, to integrate it into the production process and to train workers to use the new machinery.

3.1 The model with adjustment costs

Convex costs of adjustment are often represented by a quadratic function such as

$$G(I_t, K_t) = \left(\frac{b}{2}\right)\left(\frac{I_t}{K_t}\right)^2 K_t, \qquad (2.9)$$

where $b > 0$. Let subscripts on G denote derivatives with respect to its arguments $G_I > 0$, $G_{II} > 0$, $G_K < 0$ and $G_{KK} > 0$. Thus, the marginal cost of investing is positive and increasing. Furthermore, the larger the capital stock K_t that the firm starts with at the beginning of time t, the lower will be the costs of adjusting its capital stock. To simplify the notation let $h_t \equiv (p_t, w_t, A_t)$. We can now write the short-run profit function to incorporate costs of adjustment.

$$\Pi(K_t, h_t) = \{p_t F(A_t, K_t, L_t^*) - w_t L_t^* - G(I_t, K_t)\}, \qquad (2.10)$$

where $L_t^* \equiv L^*(K_t, h_t)$ denotes the maximised value of the variable input. Thus, marginal short-run profits are given by

$$\Pi_K(K_t, h_t) = \{p_t F_K(A_t, K_t, L_t^*) - G_K(I_t, K_t)\}. \qquad (2.11)$$

We can now rewrite the optimisation problem of the firm in the presence of adjustment costs as:

$$V\left(K_t, h_t, p_t^k\right) = \max_{I_t} \left\{ p_t F(A_t, K_t, L_t^*) - w_t L_t^* - G(I_t, K_t) \right.$$
$$\left. - p_t^k I_t + \beta E_t V\left(K_{t+1}, h_{t+1}, p_{t+1}^k\right)\right\}$$
$$\text{subject to } K_{t+1} = (1 - \delta)K_t + I_t. \qquad (2.12)$$

Let E_t denote expectations conditional on information available at time t. Taking a Lagrangian we can express the problem as follows:

$$\mathcal{L}(K^*_{t+1}, I^*_t, \lambda^*_{t+1}) = \max_{I_t, K_{t+1}} \left\{ p_t F(A_t, K_t, L^*_t) - w_t L^*_t - G(I_t, K_t) \right.$$

$$- p^k_t I_t + \beta E_t V\left(K_{t+1}, h_{t+1}, p^k_{t+1}\right)$$

$$\left. + E_t \lambda_{t+1}[(1-\delta)K_t + I_t - K_{t+1}] \right\}. \qquad (2.13)$$

The first-order conditions with respect to I_t, K_{t+1} and $E_t \lambda_{t+1}$ are given by:

$$\frac{\partial \mathcal{L}}{\partial I_t} = -G_I(I_t, K_t) - p^k_t + E_t \lambda_{t+1} = 0. \qquad (2.14)$$

$$\frac{\partial \mathcal{L}}{\partial K_{t+1}} = \beta E_t V_K\left(K_{t+1}, h_{t+1}, p^k_{t+1}\right) - E_t \lambda_{t+1} = 0 \qquad (2.15)$$

$$\frac{\partial \mathcal{L}}{\partial E_t \lambda_{t+1}} = (1-\delta)K_t + I_t - K_{t+1} = 0. \qquad (2.16)$$

Now, using the envelope condition, we find that

$$V_K\left(K_{t+1}, h_{t+1}, p^k_{t+1}\right) = \Pi_K(K_{t+1}, h_{t+1}) + (1-\delta) E_t \lambda_{t+2} \qquad (2.17)$$

so that we can rewrite (2.15) as follows:

$$\frac{\partial \mathcal{L}}{\partial K_{t+1}} = \beta E_t \Pi_K(K_{t+1}, h_{t+1}) - E_t \lambda_{t+1} + \beta (1-\delta) E_t \lambda_{t+2} = 0. \qquad (2.18)$$

Solving this first-order difference equation, we obtain:

$$E_t \lambda_{t+1} = E_t \left\{ \sum_{j=1}^{\infty} \beta^j (1-\delta)^j \Pi_K(K_{t+j}, h_{t+j}) \right\}. \qquad (2.19)$$

First remember that the Lagrange multiplier represents the 'shadow value' of a unit of capital, since it tells us by how much the maximised value of the firm would increase if we were to have one extra unit of capital. This 'shadow value' is equal to the expected discounted value of the stream of future marginal short-run profits that would accrue to the firm if it started period $t + 1$ with an extra unit of capital (taking into account its depreciation through time at the rate of δ per period).

Considering again the first-order condition for investment, and substituting for $E_t \lambda_{t+1}$, from (2.19) and rearranging we have:

$$p_t^k + G_I(I_t, K_t) = \sum_{j=1}^{\infty} \beta^j (1 - \delta)^j E_t \Pi_K(K_{t+j}, h_{t+j}). \quad (2.20)$$

From (2.20),[13] we see that in the presence of adjustment costs, the investment decision of the firm is forward looking since expectations of all future marginal profits enter explicitly in the optimality condition for this decision. The firm chooses the optimal investment level as that level of I_t^* at which the cost of purchasing an extra unit of investment *plus* the adjustment costs on this extra unit are just equal to the expected discounted sum of all future marginal short-run profits generated by this extra unit of investment.

3.2 The Q-theory of investment

One of the most influential ideas in the modern theory of investment derives from the notion of Tobin's Q, developed by Tobin (1969). According to this view, investment should be an increasing function of the ratio of the firm's market value to the replacement cost of its capital stock. That is, letting Q^A denote 'average Q':

$$Q_t^A = \frac{\beta E_t V\left(K_{t+1}, h_{t+1}, p_{t+1}^k\right)}{p_t^k K_{t+1}}. \quad (2.21)$$

Thus, Tobin's Q-theory of investment states that firms will invest if Q_t^A exceeds unity, and will disinvest if Q_t^A falls below unity. The main insight of Tobin's model lies in its reliance on stock market data in order to capture firms' expectations with respect to future profitability.

Abel (1979) and Hayashi (1982) modified Tobin's concept and defined marginal Q as the ratio of the marginal value of an additional unit of capital (or its shadow value) to the price of a unit of capital:

$$Q_t^M = \left(\frac{\beta d E_t V\left(K_{t+1}, h_{t+1}, p_{t+1}^k\right)}{d K_{t+1}}\right) \frac{1}{p_t^k}. \quad (2.22)$$

Noting that $(\beta d E_t V(K_{t+1}, h_{t+1}, p_{t+1}^k)/d K_{t+1}) = E_t \lambda_{t+1}$, using (2.19) and (2.20) Q_t^M can be related to the firm's costs of adjusting its capital

---

[13] Note that here investment I_t can be positive or negative. That is, if the firm has too much capital K_t, then the firm can choose $I_t < 0$ so that the above first-order condition may be satisfied.

stock as follows:

$$G_I(K_t, I_t) + p_t^k = p_t^k Q_t^M. \tag{2.23}$$

3.3 Empirical applications of the cost-of-adjustment model

Empirical applications of the cost-of-adjustment model require that we have a measure of the 'shadow value' of capital. If stock markets are efficient, then the value of an extra unit of capital or the 'shadow value' of capital would be given by the stock market value of that extra unit. While Q^M cannot be directly observed, Q^A can be observed and is given by the stock market value of the firm divided by its capital stock. As demonstrated by Hayashi, if the firm is perfectly competitive, has a constant returns to scale technology and has a linearly homogeneous cost-of-adjustment function, $Q_t^M = Q_t^A$, that is, marginal Q equals average Q. More generally, this will hold as long as cash flow is a linearly homogeneous function of K, L and I.[14] Substituting for G_I and re-arranging, we can derive the empirical equation

$$\frac{I_t}{K_t} = \frac{p_t^k}{b} \left[Q_t^M - 1 \right] + \varepsilon_t, \tag{2.24}$$

where ε_t is an error term.

Empirical studies have attempted to estimate the value of the adjustment cost parameter b. However, these studies often found that the 'adjustment cost with Tobin's Q' model did not perform satisfactorily.[15] Whereas Q theory implies that all relevant information is captured in market valuation, other variables such as cash flow and profitability are statistically significant.[16] Lagged values of I_t/K_t and of Q_t are usually statistically significant and estimated adjustment costs are implausibly large even in panel studies. For example, Summers (1981) finds an estimated value of $b = 32$ which implies that 'a 10 per cent increase in the value of the stock market raises $\frac{I_t}{K_t}$ by about 0.009'.[17] Although panel studies have not led to more realistic estimates of b, the use of natural experiments with panel studies has helped. In two panel studies, one for US firms and another for 3,000 firms in fourteen countries, Cummins, Hassett and Hubbard (1994, 1996) have

---

[14] See Abel (1990).
[15] See in particular, Abel and Blanchard (1986). See also Oliner, Rudebusch and Sichel (1995) who demonstrate that an ad hoc accelerator model performs better than a Q-theoretic model.
[16] See Chirinko (1993) for a detailed discussion and review of the evidence.
[17] See Summers (1981: 95).

made use of tax reforms as natural experiments to estimate the coefficient of Q. They have found substantially lower estimates of the cost-of-adjustment parameter. For example, when tax reforms are used as instruments, the estimated adjustment cost parameter for international data falls from a range of 8 to 59 to a range from 0.67 to 16 (excluding two countries where the results were insignificant). For US data, it falls from 20 to 1.5.[18]

In a panel study which uses three different estimation techniques to forecast marginal Q, namely the Euler equation with a parameterised production function, a Q-theoretic model, and a linear projection method, Demers, Demers and Schaller (1994) show that the cost-of-adjustment parameter is varying through time, an element that is not present in the theory and that seems to be more in line with an irreversibility and learning explanation of investment. A further problem in Q-theory is that stock prices may not always reflect fundamentals. Thus, even average Q may be mis-measured.[19]

Some theoretical criticism was also directed by Rothschild (1971), among others, who argued that there was no compelling reason why adjustment costs should be convex; they could well be concave if there is learning-by-doing, and workers get better at adapting to new machinery as time goes on. As we will discuss later in Section 2.5, Caballero and Leahy (1996) explain the failure of the above Q-theory by the presence of a fixed cost of investing which produces increasing returns in the adjustment cost function thus causing lumpy investment.

4 THE IRREVERSIBILITY MODEL OF INVESTMENT UNDER UNCERTAINTY

An alternative theory of investment that takes into account some of the criticisms directed towards the adjustment cost model is the theory of 'irreversible' investment. 'Irreversibility' refers to the fact that many firms may not be able to sell their capital stock. Their capital stock may be highly firm-specific. Alternatively, the capital stock may be industry-specific, but industry-level uncertainty may affect all firms similarly. Hence, if firms wish to sell their excess capital in response to an adverse demand shock, they

---

[18] Using the traditional method the lowest estimate of the adjustment cost parameter (which is for Denmark) yields adjustment costs in the order of 70 per cent per unit of investment expenditures. When tax reforms are used as instruments, estimated adjustment costs amount to 5–10 per cent of investment expenditures.

[19] See Chirinko and Schaller (1996, 2001) for empirical investigations of the implications of speculative bubbles for investment.

may not be able to find buyers willing to purchase it. Even for less firm- or industry-specific capital goods, there may exist a 'lemons' problem of adverse selection in the market for used capital that may similarly prevent firms from disinvesting. They may have to let their capital stock depreciate or else sell it for its scrap value, incurring very high costs of disinvesting in both instances.

Arrow (1968) was among the first to emphasise the importance of irreversibility. Arrow and Fisher (1974) and Henry (1974) also demonstrated that under uncertainty there exists an option value to waiting before undertaking an irreversible action. A number of authors have examined the *timing* of irreversible investment decisions in the context of project selection, for example, Baldwin (1982), Bernanke (1983), Brennan and Schwartz (1985), Cukierman (1980) and McDonald and Siegel (1985, 1986). Among these papers, Baldwin (1982), Brennan and Schwartz (1985) and McDonald and Siegel (1985, 1986) apply financial options pricing to the analysis of irreversible investment decisions.[20] Bernanke (1983) and Cukierman (1980) examine the timing of an investment decision when information about the value of the project arrives over time. Bernanke emphasises 'the bad news principle' and the option value that is generated by the irreversibility of investment projects together with the opportunity to acquire new information in the future. In Baldwin (1982), Brennan and Schwartz (1985) and McDonald and Siegel (1985, 1986), the firm's option to delay investment is akin to holding a call option to invest now or in the future to meet expansion needs. The firm has the right, but not the obligation, to invest in a project at some time in the future.

The literature on the timing of project selection does not address the sequential determination of the amount invested. In what follows, we focus not only on the timing of investment decisions but also on the sequential determination of the amount invested. We are interested in whether or not the firm invests, and if so how much: in other words, we are interested in both the extensive and intensive margins.

A number of authors have examined the latter question when investment is irreversible; that is, they have emphasised irreversibility and uncertainty as important factors underlying the gradual adjustment of the capital stock. In particular, Nickell (1977, 1978) focuses on delivery lags and timing uncertainty as an explanation of the gradual adjustment of the capital stock and shows that the irreversibility constraint strengthens

---

[20] This approach to the analysis of corporate investment has been dubbed the 'real options' approach. See, for example, Brennan and Trigeorgis (2000) for applications.

the need for caution, M. Demers (1985, 1991) introduces the learning behaviour of a firm, and shows how output price uncertainty reduces the investment of a Bayesian firm facing irreversibility, while Abel and Eberly (1994, 1996b), Bertola (1988), Bertola and Caballero (1994), Caballero and Pindyck (1996), Dixit and Pindyck (1994) and Pindyck (1988) characterise the optimal investment decision with Brownian motions for the relevant stochastic variables.[21] Finally, Abel *et al.* (1996) develop a two-period model of imperfect resale markets and limited expandability.

In the sequel, we first present a model of *partial irreversibility and expandability*. Abstracting from resale markets altogether (i.e. assuming complete irreversibility) permits a simpler framework within which to analyse the impact of different sources of uncertainty in the context of irreversibility. Then, taking the special case of complete irreversibility, we examine, in turn, the implications of demand uncertainty, cost uncertainty, tax policy, regime shifts, time-to-build and imperfect capital markets. We also investigate the long-run impact of irreversibility and uncertainty and the implications of learning. Finally, we address the empirical evidence.

4.1 A model of partial irreversibility and expandability

We now develop a model where investment is partially irreversible and expandable. 'Expandability' refers to the possibility for the firm to put off its investment decision. The cost of delaying its investment decision is the price differential it may have to pay to acquire the same capital stock in the future. The firm also faces irreversibility in the sense that the resale price for its excess capital stock is lower than the price at which the stock was purchased. The lower the resale price, the greater the degree of irreversibility faced by the firm.

Perfect expandability occurs when the future purchase price is equal to the current purchase price of capital. However, the higher the future purchase price of capital, the lesser the expandability of the firm. An infinite future purchase price for the capital stock implies the total lack of expandability. In this case the firm faces a 'now or never' situation *vis-à-vis* its current investment decision. By contrast, the firm faces total irreversibility when

---

[21] Bertola (1988) develops a dynamic programming model of irreversible investment and shows the equivalence with the contingent claims solution. Pindyck (1988) develops a model of incremental capacity choice where the firm's value is the sum of the firm's capital in place and of its growth options. Abel and Eberly (1996b) explore the implications of limited reversibility and expandability while Abel and Eberly (1994) introduce costs of adjustment in a model with imperfect resale markets. Bertola and Caballero (1994) investigate aggregation of individual irreversible investment decisions while Caballero and Pindyck (1996) examine industry equilibrium with sunk costs of entry.

resale markets are absent, which is equivalent to assuming that the resale price is zero. In this case, once the firm invests, it cannot get rid of the additional capital stock even if economic conditions warrant a lower desired capital stock. Because it cannot access resale markets, it can only allow its excess capital stock to depreciate through time. Thus, the firm can always adjust its capital stock upward ($I_t \geq 0$) but it cannot adjust it downward, in other words, it cannot disinvest.

We consider a monopolistic risk neutral firm. Each period, it makes variable input and investment decisions. At time t it produces output Y_t using capital K_t (which is predetermined at t), and labour, L_t. The firm's production function $F(A_t, K_t, L_t)$ is twice continuously differentiable, increasing, concave, and satisfies the Inada conditions. In this expression, A_t is a shock to technology and the function F may display decreasing, constant or even increasing returns with respect to L_t and K_t. Let p_t denote the stochastic output price. We assume a constant elasticity demand function. The inverse market demand function is given by:

$$p_t = (\alpha_t)^{-\frac{1}{\varepsilon}} (Y_t)^{\frac{1}{\varepsilon}}, \qquad (2.25)$$

where $\varepsilon < -1$ is the price elasticity of demand and α_t is a stochastic parameter representing the state of demand.[22]

The optimal choice of variable factors involves static optimisation under certainty. We can define the short-run profit function at time t, $\Pi(K_t, \alpha_t, A_t, w_t)$, as

$$\Pi(K_t, \alpha_t, A_t, w_t) \equiv \max_{L_t > 0}\{p_t F(A_t, K_t, L_t) - w_t \cdot L_t\}. \qquad (2.26)$$

The short-run profit function Π is continuous in K_t, α_t, A_t, w_t, increasing in K_t, α_t and A_t, decreasing in w_t, and strictly concave in K_t.[23] We assume that Π is bounded for finite K_t, α_t, w_t and A_t. Let $h_t \equiv (\alpha_t, A_t, w_t)$. The

---

[22] This market structure is monopoly. In many investment studies it is loosely referred to as 'monopolistically competitive'. More formally, a monopolistically competitive industry would be characterised by the following demand function:

$$\frac{p_t}{\overline{p}_t} = (\alpha_t)^{-\frac{1}{\varepsilon}} (Y_t)^{\frac{1}{\varepsilon}}$$

where $\overline{p}_t$ is the average price charged by competitors and is taken as given by each individual firm. The analysis of investment which follows carries through to monopolistic competition provided that the investing firm takes $\overline{p}_t$ as given, that is, provided the firm is myopic with respect to the actions of its competitors and assumes that its relative price is solely determined by its own output and by the exogenous shock, α_t. In other words, provided that the firm has static expectations with respect to the industry-wide capital stock. See Leahy (1993) for an analysis of the perfectly competitive industry.

[23] The strict concavity of Π is necessary in a model of irreversible investment in order to ensure the uniqueness of the investment policy.

firm's after-tax cash flow at time t, R_t, is defined as

$$R\left(K_t, h_t, p_t^{kH}, p_t^{kL}\right) = \Pi(K_t, h_t) - p_t^{kH} \max\{I_t, 0\} - p_t^{kL} \min\{I_t, 0\},$$
(2.27)

where I_t is the firm's rate of gross investment measured (in physical units) if $I_t > 0$ and sales of capital goods if $I_t < 0$. p_t^{kH} is the purchase price of capital goods and p_t^{kL} is the resale price of capital goods. We assume:

$$p_t^{kH} \geq p_t^{kL}.$$
(2.28)

Let $h_t^k \equiv (p_t^{kH}, p_t^{kL})$. Let δ be the deterministic depreciation rate, with $0 < \delta < 1$. The law of motion of the capital stock is

$$K_{t+1} = (1 - \delta) K_t + I_t.$$
(2.29)

Let $G^\alpha(\alpha_{t+1}|\alpha_t)$ be the distribution function of α_{t+1} conditional on α_t. The optimisation problem of the firm now becomes

$$V\left(K_t, h_t, h_t^k\right) = \max_{I_t} \left\{ R\left(K_t, h_t, h_t^k\right) + \beta E_t V\left(K_{t+1}, h_{t+1}, h_{t+1}^k\right)\right\}$$

subject to (2.28) and (2.29).
(2.30)

If resale markets were perfect the model would be identical to the neo-classical model since there are no costs of adjustment. However, when we assume partial irreversibility, the investment decision of the firm becomes dynamic, contrary to the neoclassical model. The first-order conditions are given by

$$-p_t^{kH} + \beta E_t V_K\left(K_{t+1}, h_{t+1}, h_{t+1}^k\right) = 0$$
(2.31)
$$\text{if } \beta E_t V_K\left((1-\delta)K_t, h_{t+1}, h_{t+1}^k\right) > p_t^{kH}$$

$$-p_t^{kL} + \beta E_t V_K\left(K_{t+1}, h_{t+1}, h_{t+1}^k\right) = 0$$
(2.32)
$$\text{if } \beta E_t V_K\left((1-\delta)K_t, h_{t+1}, h_{t+1}^k\right) < p_t^{kL}$$

$$K_{t+1} = (1 - \delta)K_t$$
$$\text{if } p_t^{kL} \leq \beta E_t V_K\left((1-\delta)K_t, h_{t+1}, h_{t+1}^k\right) \leq p_t^{kH}.$$
(2.33)

Also, define α_t^H and α_t^L, respectively, by:

$$p_t^{kH} = \beta \int_0^\infty V_K\left((1-\delta)K_t, h_{t+1}, h_{t+1}^k\right) dG^\alpha\left(\alpha_{t+1}|\alpha_t^H\right)$$
(2.34)

$$p_t^{kL} = \beta \int_0^\infty V_K\left((1-\delta)K_t, h_{t+1}, h_{t+1}^k\right) dG^\alpha\left(\alpha_{t+1}|\alpha_t^L\right)$$
(2.35)

For any given value of the inherited capital stock, K_t, for any given distribution function $G^\alpha(\alpha_{t+1}|\alpha_t)$ and for any pair of capital goods prices, p_t^{kL} and p_t^{kH}, there are critical values of α_t^H and α_t^L such that the expected marginal value of capital conditional on α_t^H is equal to p_t^{kH} with zero investment and the expected marginal value of capital conditional on α_t^L is equal to p_t^{kL} with zero capital sales. The first-order conditions indicate that if $p_t^{kH} < \beta E_t V_K((1-\delta)K_t, h_{t+1}, h_{t+1}^k)$, the firm chooses a positive level of investment, $I_t^* > 0$, and the first-order condition (2.31) will hold with equality. In other words, for high states of demand, that is, for $\alpha_t \geq \alpha_t^H$, the firm invests. If $p_t^{kL} > \beta E_t V_K((1-\delta)K_t, h_{t+1}, h_{t+1}^k)$ the firm chooses $I_t^* < 0$, that is, to sell capital and (2.32) holds with equality. For low states of demand, that is, for $\alpha_t \leq \alpha_t^L$, the firm sells used capital. However, for intermediate states of demand $\alpha_t^L \leq \alpha_t \leq \alpha_t^H$ the firm finds itself in a zone of inaction where it neither invests nor disposes of its used capital.

Define $C_t(K_{t+1}, p_{t+1}^{kH})$ and $P_t(K_{t+1}, p_{t+1}^{kL})$ as, respectively, the call and put options of investing an additional unit of capital at time $t + 1$:

$$C_t(K_{t+1}, p_{t+1}^{kH})$$
$$= -\int_{\alpha_{t+1}^H}^{\infty} \{\beta E_{t+1}[V((1-\delta)K_{t+1} + I_{t+1}(\alpha_{t+1}), h_{t+2}, h_{t+2}^k)$$
$$- V((1-\delta)K_{t+1}, h_{t+2}, h_{t+2}^k)] - p_{t+1}^{kH} I_{t+1}(\alpha_{t+1})\} dG^\alpha(\alpha_{t+1}|\alpha_t)$$
$$(2.36)$$

$$P_t(K_{t+1}, p_{t+1}^{kL})$$
$$= \int_0^{\alpha_{t+1}^L} \{\beta E_{t+1}[V((1-\delta)K_{t+1} + I_{t+1}(\alpha_{t+1}), h_{t+2}, h_{t+2}^k)$$
$$- V((1-\delta)K_{t+1}, h_{t+2}, h_{t+2}^k)] - p_{t+1}^{kL} I_{t+1}(\alpha_{t+1})\} dG^\alpha(\alpha_{t+1}|\alpha_t).$$
$$(2.37)$$

The call option is the discounted value of making a positive investment at $t + 1$ while the put option is the discounted value of selling capital goods at $t + 1$. Referring to (2.36), note that the expression on the right-hand side captures expandability, that is, the firm's option to invest and adjust its capital stock upward in the future should the state of demand warrant it ($\alpha_{t+1} \geq \alpha_{t+1}^H$). It is the firm's value of waiting to invest or alternatively the value of the call option to invest at $t + 1$. Higher values of p_{t+1}^{kH}, that is higher values of the future purchase price of capital lower the value of waiting, and as will be shown, induce the firm to invest at t. Referring to (2.37), the expression on the right-hand side is the value of the option to sell capital at $t+1$ at a price of p_{t+1}^{kL}. The firm will choose to exercise this option if $\alpha_{t+1} \leq \alpha_{t+1}^{L}$. Using the call and put options, $E_t V(K_{t+1}, h_{t+1}, h_{t+1}^k)$ can be expressed as:

$$E_t V\big(K_{t+1}, h_{t+1}, h_{t+1}^k\big)$$
$$= E_t\big\{\Pi(K_{t+1}, h_{t+1}) + \beta E_{t+1} V\big((1-\delta)K_{t+1}, h_{t+2}, h_{t+2}^k\big)\big\}$$
$$+ P_t\big(K_{t+1}, p_{t+1}^{kL}\big) - C_t\big(K_{t+1}, p_{t+1}^{kH}\big). \tag{2.38}$$

$E_t V(K_{t+1}, h_{t+1}, h_{t+1}^k)$ is the sum of next period's expected profit, the discounted future value assuming the firm does not invest next period, a put and call option. From (2.38) after differentiating with respect to K_{t+1} we obtain

$$E_t V_K\big(K_{t+1}, h_{t+1}, h_{t+1}^k\big)$$
$$= E_t\big\{\Pi_K(K_{t+1}, h_{t+1}) + \beta(1-\delta)E_{t+1} V_K\big((1-\delta)K_{t+1}, h_{t+2}, h_{t+2}^k\big)\big\}$$
$$+ P_{Kt}\big(K_{t+1}, p_{t+1}^{kL}\big) - C_{Kt}\big(K_{t+1}, p_{t+1}^{kH}\big). \tag{2.39}$$

where C_{Kt} and P_{Kt} are the marginal call and put options, respectively,

$$C_{Kt}\big(K_{t+1}, p_{t+1}^{kH}\big)$$
$$= -\int_{\alpha_{t+1}^H}^{\infty} \beta(1-\delta)\big\{E_{t+1}\big[V_K\big((1-\delta)K_{t+1} + I_{t+1}(\alpha_{t+1}), h_{t+2}, h_{t+2}^k\big)$$
$$- V_K\big((1-\delta)K_{t+1}, h_{t+2}, h_{t+2}^k\big)\big]\big\}dG^{\alpha}(\alpha_{t+1}|\alpha_t)$$
$$= \int_{\alpha_{t+1}^H}^{\infty} (1-\delta)\big[-p_{t+1}^{kH} + E_{t+1}\beta V_K\big((1-\delta)K_{t+1}, h_{t+2}, h_{t+2}^k\big)\big]$$
$$\times dG^{\alpha}(\alpha_{t+1}|\alpha_t)$$
$$= (1-\delta)E_t \max\big\{0, \beta E_{t+1} V_K\big((1-\delta)K_{t+1}, h_{t+2}, h_{t+2}^k\big) - p_{t+1}^{kH}\big\} \geq 0. \tag{2.40}$$

Using the optimality conditions for optimal purchases and sales of capital equipment[24] at $t+1$ we find that the marginal call option is positive since for $\alpha_{t+1} \geq \alpha_{t+1}^H$ it is optimal to invest. That is, $C_{Kt} \geq 0$ provided

[24] For $\alpha_{t+1} \geq \alpha_{t+1}^H$, the firm invests and purchases machinery and equipment. That is, $p_{t+1}^{kH} = \beta E_{t+1} V_K((1-\delta)K_t + I_{t+1}, h_{t+1}, h_{t+1}^k)$.

that $G^\alpha(\alpha_{t+1}^H|\alpha_t) < 1$. Furthermore, since $\partial C_{Kt}(K_{t+1}, p_{t+1}^{kH})/\partial p_{t+1}^{kH} = -(1-\delta)[1 - G^\alpha(\alpha_{t+1}|\alpha_t)] \leq 0$ a higher future purchase price for machinery and equipment which limits the firm's expandability options lowers the marginal call option. We can obtain P_{Kt} similarly as:

$$P_{Kt}(K_{t+1}, p_{t+1}^{kL})$$

$$= \int_{0,t}^{\alpha_{t+1}^L} \left\{ \beta(1-\delta)E_{t+1}\left[V_K((1-\delta)K_{t+1} + I_{t+1}(\alpha_{t+1}), h_{t+2}, h_{t+2}^k)\right. \right.$$

$$\left. \left. - V_K((1-\delta)K_{t+1}, h_{t+2}, h_{t+2}^k)\right]\right\} dG^\alpha(\alpha_{t+1}|\alpha_t)$$

$$= \int_0^{\alpha_{t+1}^L} (1-\delta)\left[p_{t+1}^{kL} - \beta E_{t+1} V_K((1-\delta)K_{t+1}, h_{t+2}, h_{t+2}^k)\right]$$

$$\times dG^\alpha(\alpha_{t+1}|\alpha_t)$$

$$= (1-\delta)E_t \max\left\{0, p_{t+1}^{kL} - \beta E_{t+1} V_K((1-\delta)K_{t+1}, h_{t+2}, h_{t+2}^k)\right\} \geq 0.$$

$$(2.41)$$

Using the optimality conditions for optimal sales of capital equipment[25] at $t+1$ we find that the marginal put option is positive since for $\alpha_{t+1} \leq \alpha_{t+1}^L$ it is optimal to sell capital goods at $t+1$. In addition, noting that $\partial P_{Kt}(K_{t+1}, p_{t+1}^{kL})/\partial p_{t+1}^{kL} = (1-\delta)G^\alpha(\alpha_{t+1}|\alpha_t) \geq 0$, a higher future resale price for capital goods raises the marginal put option.

Assuming $\alpha_t \geq \alpha_t^H$ so that it is optimal to invest at time t and substituting for $E_t V_K$ from (2.39) we can express the optimality condition (2.31) as:

$$p_t^{kH} + \beta C_{Kt}(K_{t+1}, p_{t+1}^{kH}) - \beta P_{Kt}(K_{t+1}, p_{t+1}^{kL})$$

$$= \beta E_t\left\{\Pi_K(K_{t+1}, h_{t+1})\right.$$

$$\left. + \beta(1-\delta)E_{t+1} V_K((1-\delta)K_{t+1}, h_{t+2}, h_{t+2}^k)\right\}. \quad (2.42)$$

The cost of investing consists of the market price for capital goods and the discounted marginal call option. By investing one additional unit at t, the firm loses the opportunity to invest that unit in the future and incurs a loss of a call option. That is, the firm 'kills' the option to wait. This additional cost tends to discourage investment. On the other hand, the marginal put option lowers the current cost of investing. That is, the marginal put option stimulates investment since an additional unit of investment raises the value

---

[25] For $\alpha_{t+1} \leq \alpha_{t+1}^L$, the firm sells machinery and equipment. That is, $p_{t+1}^{kL} = \beta E_{t+1} V_K((1-\delta)K_t + I_{t+1}, h_{t+1}, h_{t+1}^k)$.

of the put option. Similarly, assume $\alpha_t \leq \alpha_t^L$ so that it is optimal to sell capital at time t and substituting for $E_t V_K(K_{t+1}, h_{t+1}, h_{t+1}^k)$ from (2.39), we can write (2.32) as:

$$p_t^{kL} + \beta C_{Kt}(K_{t+1}, p_{t+1}^{kH}) - \beta P_{Kt}(K_{t+1}, p_{t+1}^{kL})$$
$$= \beta E_t\{\Pi_K(K_{t+1}, h_{t+1})$$
$$+ \beta(1 - \delta)E_{t+1} V_K((1 - \delta)K_{t+1}, h_{t+2}, h_{t+2}^k)\}. \quad (2.43)$$

We can relate optimal investment to Q-theory as follows. On the right-hand side of (2.43) add and subtract $\beta E_t \sum_{j=1}^{\infty} \beta^j (1 - \delta)^j \Pi_K((1 - \delta)^j K_{t+1}, h_{t+j+1})$. We obtain:

$$p_t^{kL} + \beta C_{Kt}(K_{t+1}, p_{t+1}^{kH}) - \beta P_{Kt}(K_{t+1}, p_{t+1}^{kL}) = Q_t + \Upsilon_t, \quad (2.44)$$

where:

$$Q_t = \beta E_t \sum_{j=0}^{\infty} \beta^j (1 - \delta)^j \Pi_K((1 - \delta)^j K_{t+1}, h_{t+j+1}). \quad (2.45)$$

$$\Upsilon_t = \beta^2(1 - \delta)E_{t+1} V_K((1 - \delta)K_{t+1}, h_{t+2}, h_{t+2}^k)$$
$$- E_t \sum_{j=1}^{\infty} \beta^j (1 - \delta)^j \Pi_K((1 - \delta)^j K_{t+1}, h_{t+j+1}). \quad (2.46)$$

The first term on the right-hand side of (2.46) represents the expected marginal value of capital from time $t + 2$ onward given that the firm does not invest at time $t + 1$, but may invest or disinvest in future periods. The second term represents the expected marginal value of capital if the firm never invests or disinvests from $t + 2$ onward. Thus, Υ_t represents the increase in the expected marginal value of capital due to *future* marginal call and put options available to the firm. Q_t in (2.45) is Tobin's Q, and represents the expected marginal value of capital if the firm never invests or disinvests from $t + 1$ onward and simply allows its capital stock to depreciate. The right-hand side of (2.45) thus represents the 'naive net present value' (NPV) of an additional unit of capital. It is clear from the first-order condition above that firms that make their investment decisions according to the naive NPV rule would be behaving sub-optimally since they would be ignoring the availability of the future marginal call and put options that is captured by the term Υ_t.

We can now derive a modified cost of capital for the partial irreversibility model. Let Λ_t denote next period's shadow value of a marginal unit of capital:

$$\Lambda_{t+1} = \int_{\alpha_{t+1}^L}^{\alpha_{t+1}^H} E_{t+1} V_K\big((1-\delta)K_{t+1}, h_{t+2}, h_{t+2}^k\big) dG^\alpha(\alpha_{t+1}|\alpha_t)$$

$$+ p_{t+1}^{kH}\big[1 - G^\alpha(\alpha_{t+1}^H|\alpha_t)\big] + p_{t+1}^{kL} G^\alpha(\alpha_{t+1}^L|\alpha_t), \qquad (2.47)$$

where the right-hand side captures the three possible situations that the firm may face at $t+1$, weighted by the respective probabilities, namely, inaction, investment and disinvestment. Let $\widehat{c}_t^i = p_t^{ki}(r+\delta)$ denote the opportunity cost of funds when the price of capital is p_t^{ki}, $i = H, L$. Let c_t^H and c_t^L denote the cost of capital when there are purchases and sales of capital at time t, respectively:

$$c_t^H = \widehat{c}_t^H - (1-\delta)\big(E_t\Lambda_{t+1} - p_t^{kH}\big)$$

$$= \widehat{c}_t^H - (1-\delta)E_t\big\{\big(p_{t+1}^{kH} - p_t^{kH}\big)\big[1 - G^\alpha(\alpha_{t+1}^H|\alpha_t)\big]$$

$$+ \big(p_{t+1}^{kL} - p_t^{kH}\big)G^\alpha(\alpha_{t+1}^L|\alpha_t)\big\} + (1-\delta)$$

$$\times \left\{\int_{\alpha_{t+1}^L}^{\alpha_{t+1}^H} \big[p_t^{kH} - E_{t+1} V_K\big((1-\delta)K_{t+1}, h_{t+2}, h_{t+2}^k\big)\big] dG^\alpha(\alpha_{t+1}|\alpha_t)\right\}$$

$$(2.48)$$

$$c_t^L = \widehat{c}_t^L - (1-\delta)\big(E_t\Lambda_{t+1} - p_t^{kL}\big). \qquad (2.49)$$

We observe that in (2.48) the first term captures the opportunity cost of funds.[26] The second term is the expected differential cost of future instead of current expansion. This term which is positive when expandability is costly (that is, when $p_{t+1}^{kH} > p_t^{kH}$) contributes to lowering the cost of capital and to raise K_{t+1}. The third term arises from the expected capital loss on the sale of capital equipment. It is positive when reversibility is costly (that is, when $p_{t+1}^{kL} < p_t^{kH}$) and it raises the cost of capital. Finally, the fourth term results from a mismatch between the current purchase price and the expected shadow value when the realisation of future states of demand makes inaction optimal. An analogous interpretation can be made of c_t^L. Using the cost of capital we can reinterpret the firm's optimal decision at

---

[26] The first term in (4.24) is similar to the first term in Jorgenson's cost of capital. In the Hall–Jorgenson (1967) neoclassical model with fully reversible investment, the cost of capital is $c_t \equiv (r+\delta)p_t^k - (1-\delta)(p_{t+1}^k - p_t^k)$ where p_t^k is the unique value of the purchase and resale price for machinery and equipment.

time t as:

$$c_t^H = E_t \Pi_K(K_{t+1}, h_{t+1}) \quad \text{for } \alpha_t \geq \alpha_t^H$$
$$c_t^L = E_t \Pi_K(K_{t+1}, h_{t+1}) \quad \text{for } \alpha_t \leq \alpha_t^L$$
$$K_{t+1} = (1 - \delta)K_t \quad \text{for } \alpha_t^H \geq \alpha_t \geq \alpha_t^L. \quad (2.50)$$

When the current state of demand is high, the firm invests so as to equate the relevant cost of capital, c_t^H to the expected marginal revenue product of capital. When it is low, it sells capital so as to bring c_t^L to equality with $E_t \Pi_K$. Finally, when the state of demand is neither high nor low the firm is inactive.

Consider two special cases. First, if investment were completely irreversible (there were no resale markets) and if there were complete expandability c_t^H would exceed the Jorgensonian cost of capital, $\widehat{c}_t^H$, due to an expected capital loss on the part of the firm making irreversible investments.[27] Thus, investment would be lower under irreversibility. Alternatively, suppose there were no possibility for the firm to expand in the future, but that there existed resale markets with a constant resale price for all t, then the cost of capital, c_t^L, would be lower than the Jorgensonian cost of capital, $\widehat{c}_t^L$ one to an unexpected capital gain.[28] This leads to a higher capital stock at time t.[29]

Note that, in the case of partially expandable and irreversible investment, the decision to invest, disinvest or remain inactive at t is affected by the probability of high values $[1 - G^\alpha(\alpha_{t+1}^H | \alpha_t)]$ and by the probability of low values, $G^\alpha(\alpha_{t+1}^L | \alpha_t)$, but not by the shape of G^α in these ranges of high and

---

[27] Assume complete expandability as in the Jorgenson model, that is:

$p_t^{kH} = p_{t+1}^{kH} \equiv p^{kH}$. It can be shown that

$$c_t^H = \widehat{c}_t^H + \int_{\alpha_{t+1}^L}^{\alpha_{t+1}^H} \left[p^{kH} - E_{t+1} V_K\big((1 - \delta)K_{t+1}, h_{t+2}, h_{t+2}^k\big) \right] dG^\alpha(\alpha_{t+1} | \alpha_t) > \widehat{c}_t^H.$$

[28] In view of complete expandability, $p_t^{kH} = p_{t+1}^{kH} \equiv p^{kH}$. Assume a constant resale price, $p_t^{kL} = p_{t+1}^{kL} \equiv p^{kL}$. We have:

$$c_t^L = \widehat{c}_t^L + \int_{\alpha_{t+1}^L}^{\alpha_{t+1}^H} \left[p^{kL} - E_{t+1} V_K\big((1 - \delta)K_{t+1}, h_{t+2}, h_{t+2}^k\big) \right] dG^\alpha(\alpha_{t+1} | \alpha_t) < c_t.$$

Since the second term is negative.

[29] Abel and Eberly (1996) consider a model of limited irreversibility and expandability. Assuming a geometric Brownian motion for α_t they solve for V_K. They show that $c_t^H > \widehat{c}_t^H$ and $c_t^L < \widehat{c}_t^L$ because conditional on p_t^{kH} the firm faces an expected capital loss whereas conditional on p_t^{kH} the firm faces an expected capital gain. They also find through simulations that even small differences between p^{kH} and and p^{kL} can cause the investment triggers to be closer to the ones that would prevail under irreversibility.

low values. Thus, for example, an increase in the probability of very high values of α_{t+1}, i.e. in the range $\alpha_{t+1} > \alpha_{t+1}^H$ will not affect the decision of the firm since these are values of α for which the firm intended to invest even before the shift in distribution occurred. Similarly an increase in the probability of very low values will not affect the decision of the firm since these are values of α for which the firm intended to disinvest even before the shift in distribution occurred. It is only for the interval $\alpha_{t+1}^L \leq \alpha_{t+1} \leq \alpha_{t+1}^H$ that a shift in the distribution function, $G^\alpha(\alpha_{t+1} | \alpha_t)$ may affect investment. This has been called the 'Goldilocks principle' by Abel *et al*. (1996). When investment is totally irreversible but completely expandable, then there are only two ranges of α_{t+1} values, namely those less than and those greater than α_{t+1}^H. In this case, an increase in the probability of values of α_{t+1} greater than α_{t+1}^H will not affect the decision to invest since those are values for which the firm intended to invest in any case. However, a shift in the distribution in the range $0 < \alpha \leq \alpha^H$ may affect the decision as to whether to invest or not. This is Bernanke's 'bad news principle.'

A model of irreversible investment
In the sequel, we will focus on irreversible investment. In this case, the constraint

$$I_t \geq 0 \tag{2.51}$$

needs to be imposed. Complete irreversibility eliminates the put option. In this case, assuming $\alpha_t \geq \alpha_t^H$ (2.42) becomes:

$$
\begin{aligned}
p_t^{kH} &+ \beta C_{Kt}\left(K_{t+1}, p_{t+1}^{kH}\right) \\
&= \beta E_t\left\{\Pi_K(K_{t+1}, h_{t+1}) + \beta(1 - \delta)E_{t+1}V_K\left((1 - \delta)K_{t+1}, h_{t+2}, h_{t+2}^k\right)\right\} \\
&\equiv Q_t + \Upsilon_t.
\end{aligned}
\tag{2.52}
$$

On the right-hand side of (2.52) the marginal benefit of investing an additional unit appears as the sum of next period's discounted expected marginal value of capital and of the expected value of the unused portion of the capital stock assuming the firm does not invest in the next period. The sum of these benefits can alternatively be expressed as the sum of $Q_t + \Upsilon_t$ as discussed above, except that Υ_t captures the increase in value due to only future call options. On the left-hand side is the total cost of investing which is the sum of the purchase price of investment and of the discounted marginal loss of the option value of waiting when the firm invests an additional unit. This additional cost of investing must be taken into account when investment is irreversible. The option to invest will be exercised when α_t is sufficiently high. If, on the other hand, $\alpha_t \leq \alpha_t^H$ the firm finds itself in the inaction zone so that $K_{t+1} = (1 - \delta)K_t$. Hence, irreversibility, uncertainty and expandability lead to a zone of inaction.

When investment is irreversible and firms face uncertainty about future demand and productivity, firms are cautious; rather than being stuck with too much capital, they prefer to invest less than they would if they could sell their excess capital. As we discuss in detail in the next section, greater uncertainty increases the value of the call option and thus reduces the incentive to invest. Furthermore, C_{Kt} reflects expectations of the firms about future economic conditions and whether they are likely to have too much capital in the future. Thus, C_{Kt} will vary whenever these expectations change. We can also interpret C_{Kt} as a time-varying risk premium or 'cost-of-adjustment' term, and we note that it arises *endogenously*, whereas the existence of adjustment costs is postulated in the cost-of-adjustment model. Thus, the irreversibility model provides an explanation as to why adjustment costs are varying through time, as has been shown in empirical studies. Note that C_{Kt} is entirely due to irreversibility and expandability.

Altug, Demers, and Demers (1999) and M. Demers (1985, 1991) derive an alternative optimality condition for irreversible investment. They find the envelope condition for the irreversibility model as:

$$
\begin{aligned}
V_K\left(K_{t+1}, h_{t+1}, p_{t+1}^k\right) \\
= \Pi_K(K_{t+1}, h_{t+1}) + (1 - \delta) \min\left[p_{t+1}^{kH}, \beta E_{t+1} V_K\right. \\
\left. \times \left((1 - \delta)K_{t+1}, h_{t+2}, p_{t+2}^{kH}\right)\right].
\end{aligned}
\tag{2.53}
$$

They express the optimality condition for irreversible investment as:

$$
E_t \Pi_K(K_{t+1}, h_{t+1}) = c_t + \Phi_t,
\tag{2.54}
$$

where $c_t \equiv (r + \delta)p_t^{kH} - (1 - \delta)(E_t p_{t+1}^{kH} - p_t^{kH})$ is the traditional Jorgensonian cost of capital and Φ_t is an endogenous risk premium (or endogenous cost of adjustment) due to irreversibility and is given by

$$
\begin{aligned}
\Phi_t = (1 - \delta)\left\{E_t p_{t+1}^{kH} - E_t \min\left[p_{t+1}^{kH},\right.\right. \\
\left.\left. \times \beta E_{t+1} V_K\left((1 - \delta)K_{t+1}, h_{t+2}, p_{t+2}^{kH}\right)\right]\right\}.
\end{aligned}
\tag{2.55}
$$

If investment were reversible, (2.53) or (2.54) would reduce to:

$$
p_t^{kh} = \beta E_t \Pi_K(K_{t+1}, h_{t+1}) + \beta(1 - \delta)E_t p_{t+1}^{kH}
\tag{2.56}
$$

just as in the frictionless neoclassical model.

We define the firm's desired stock of capital, $K_{t+1}^* \leq K_{t+1}$ such that $K_{t+1} = K_{t+1}^*$ if $I_t^* > 0$ and $K_{t+1}^* < K_{t+1} = (1 - \delta)K_t$ if $I_t^* = 0$ where

K^*_{t+1} solves (2.52) or (2.54). The desired capital stock with irreversibility, K^*_{t+1}, is smaller than the desired stock without any frictions, K^f_{t+1}, which solves (2.56). Nevertheless, if low values of α_t are realised the firm may find itself with excess capital because it cannot disinvest. Therefore, the actual capital stock of a firm facing irreversible investment may be larger than when investment is reversible.[30]

The short-run impact on irreversible investment of different sources of uncertainty – demand, productivity, costs and tax policy – will be clarified in the next sections. The long-run impact of uncertainty and the issue of whether the firm accumulates more capital with or without irreversibility will be investigated in Subsection 4.9.

4.2 Demand uncertainty and productivity shocks

The impact of demand uncertainty on investment has been a topic of considerable importance since Hartman's (1972) contribution. In a cost-of-adjustment model with a constant returns to scale production function (CRS) and perfect competition, Hartman showed that greater variability of the output price around a constant mean, that is, a mean-preserving spread (MPS) will increase investment. Hartman's conclusion stems from the convexity of the profit function in the output price, the latter being the result of the firm's ability to adjust some factors of production after the realisation of the price. In the absence of CRS the impact of a MPS depends on the properties of the marginal revenue of capital with respect to the price. (See Hartman 1973.)

When investment is irreversible and there are no costs of adjustment, the investment policy exists and is well defined provided one of the following conditions holds: the firm is perfectly competitive in the output market and the production function has decreasing returns to scale (DRS); or if the firm is monopolist (for example with a constant elasticity demand function) and

---

[30] If investment is both irreversible and lumpy, the desired stock of capital will correspond to the one prevailing under irreversibility. However, the firm will not invest as frequently due to the presence of a fixed cost. Assume that the firm faces a fixed cost of investing, f_t which is proportional to the firm's stock of capital. As a result, the total cost of investing becomes $f_t K_t + p^k_t I_t$. Assuming $\alpha_t \geq \alpha^H_t$ the firm's desired stock of capital given irreversibility will be determined by the first-order condition as before. That is, $p^k_t = \beta E_t V_K(K_{t+1}, h_{t+1}, p^k_{t+1})$ where V_K takes into account the future fixed costs which an additional unit of capital entails. However, the firm will invest only when another condition is satisfied. Investment will take place and the firm will adjust its capital stock if the difference in the expected value of the firm achieved by investing exceeds the total cost of investing including the fixed cost: $\beta E_t V((1 - \delta)K_t + I^*_t, h_{t+1}, p^k_{t+1}) - \beta E_t V((1 - \delta)K_t, h_{t+1}, p^k_{t+1}) > f_t K_t + p^k_t I^*_t$. Hence, if this latter condition does not hold the firm will not invest even though positive investment would be warranted by the first-order condition. That is, a positive investment level will be chosen only if the net expected total benefits exceed the benefits of not investing.

the production function has constant or increasing returns (provided that the latter are not too large).

What is the impact of greater demand uncertainty or alternatively greater uncertainty with respect to productivity shocks when investment is irreversible? To answer this question we need to distinguish between the type of uncertainty faced by firms (idiosyncratic versus market-wide uncertainty) and the degree of competition (perfect competition or monopoly). We consider each of these factors in turn.

Firm-specific uncertainty for a monopolist

Demand uncertainty   We focus on firm-level uncertainty for a monopolist. In the McDonald and Siegel (1985, 1986) model of project selection greater demand uncertainty raises the value of waiting and lowers a monopolist's investment. In the irreversibility model that we have described, the timing and the quantity invested are determined simultaneously and there is also the choice of variable inputs. Once the capital stock is in place, the firm benefits from additional flexibility by adjusting variable factors of production. As in the McDonald and Siegel model, greater uncertainty raises the value of the option to invest and thus the threshold or hurdle rate, thereby discouraging investment. However, an additional channel arises which depends on the concavity of the shadow value of capital, V_K, in the price or the state of demand, α. In turn, the latter depends on the convexity of Π_K in α. In what follows we explore these issues.

We assume a Cobb–Douglas production function:

$$Y_t = A_t L_t^{\eta_1} K_t^{\eta_2}, \tag{2.57}$$

where $\eta_1 + \eta_2 \geq 1$ to allow for the possibility of increasing returns to scale. Given the inverse market demand function specified in (2.25), the profit function can be found as:

$$\Pi(K_t, h_t) \equiv v \alpha_t^{\mu_1} K_t^{\mu_2} A_t^{\mu_3} w_t^{\mu_4}, \tag{2.58}$$

where $\mu_1 > 0$, $\mu_2 > 0$, $\mu_3 > 0$, $\mu_4 < 0$, and $v > 0$.[31] Hence, Π is

---

[31] Let $\widehat{\eta}_1 = \eta_1(1 + \varepsilon)$ and $\widehat{\eta}_2 = \eta_2(1 + \varepsilon)$, with $\widehat{\eta}_1 < 0$, $\widehat{\eta}_2 < 0$. Note that if $\eta_2 < \varepsilon/(1 + \varepsilon)$, $\mu_1 = 1/[\eta_2(1 + \varepsilon) - \varepsilon] > 0$,

$$\mu_2 = -\eta_1(1 + \varepsilon)/[\eta_2(1 + \varepsilon) - \varepsilon] > 0,$$
$$\mu_3 = -(1 + \varepsilon)/[\eta_2(1 + \varepsilon) - \varepsilon] > 0 \text{ and}$$
$$\mu_4 = \eta_2(1 + \varepsilon)/[\eta_2(1 + \varepsilon) - \varepsilon] < 0.$$

We also have $v = [-\widehat{\eta}_2/(\widehat{\eta}_2 - \varepsilon)]^{-\widehat{\eta}_2/(\widehat{\eta}_2-\varepsilon)} [1 - \widehat{\eta}_2/\varepsilon]^{1-\widehat{\eta}_2/\varepsilon} > 0.$

increasing in α_t, K_t, A_t and decreasing in w_t, and is concave in K_t, α_t and A_t.[32]

Since $\Pi_{K\alpha} > 0$ it can be shown that $V_{K\alpha} > 0$, and so stochastically larger future demand in the sense of first-order stochastic dominance (FSD)[33] will raise the expected marginal value of capital and investment if α_{t+1} is IID or is positively serially correlated.

It can also be shown that the concavity of Π_K in α implies the concavity of V_K in α when α is IID. As a result, we can conclude that greater variability in future demand (for example caused by changes in fashion for a particular type of product) around a constant mean (a MPS)[34] increases the marginal call option thereby lowering irreversible investment today. Furthermore, the size of the inaction zone rises.[35]

Bertola (1988) and Bertola and Caballero (1994) show that demand uncertainty lowers irreversible investment when it follows a geometric Brownian motion (GBM).[36] To see the implications of positive serial correlation in our discrete time setup, we assume that α_{t+1} follows a random walk. It can be shown that V_K is concave in α_t so that a MPS (or a higher conditional variance) will reduce current investment. Thus, if we focus on firm-specific uncertainty, greater variability in demand increases the value of waiting and raises the threshold at which positive investment takes place, increases the inaction zone and lowers irreversible investment.

Productivity shocks Since $\Pi_{KA} > 0$, $V_{KA} > 0$, a stochastically larger future productivity level in the sense of FSD will raise investment. By a similar reasoning, we can conclude that greater variability in productivity will also have an adverse effect on investment since V_K is concave in A_t

---

[32] $\partial^2 \Pi_t / \partial K_t^2 < 0$ if $(\eta_1 + \eta_2) < \epsilon/(1+\epsilon)$, $\partial^2 \Pi_t / \partial \alpha_t^2 < 0$ if $\eta_2 < 1$ and $\partial^2 \Pi_t / \partial A_t^2 < 0$ if $\eta_2 < -1/(1+\varepsilon)$.

[33] A cdf $\widehat{G^\alpha}(\alpha_{t+1})$ dominates $G^\alpha(\alpha_{t+1})$ in the sense of FSD (First-Order Stochastic Dominance) if and only if $\widehat{G^\alpha}(\alpha_{t+1}) \leq G^\alpha(\alpha_{t+1})$ for all α_{t+1}.

[34] A cdf $\widehat{G^\alpha}(\alpha_{t+1})$ is a MPS (Mean-Preserving Spread) of $G^\alpha(\alpha_{t+1})$ if and only if, for all y

$$\int_{\alpha^L}^{y} [G^\alpha(\alpha_{t+1}) d\alpha_{t+1} - \widehat{G^\alpha}(\alpha_{t+1})] d\alpha_{t+1} \leq 0$$

and $= 0$ for $y = \alpha^H$.

[35] When α_t is IID, different realisations of α_t do not affect the expected value of f V_K. When a MPS occurs, if the firm's desired stock of capital is lower than the actual stock then the firm will refrain from investing until the firm's actual capital stock reaches its desired level. If $K_{t+1}^* > (1-\delta)K_t$ the firm immediately adjusts its capital stock. If there are no other sources of uncertainty the firm will maintain its capital stock at the desired level. Thus, the capital stock will not vary from period to period in the absence of other shocks.

[36] See also Pindyck (1988). In Pindyck's model greater volatility increases the firm's operating options (from its existing capacity) but since its opportunity costs of investing rises even more, optimal capacity is lower.

both in the IID and positively serially correlated case, for example when A_t follows a random walk.

Monopoly

Two critical factors determine the impact of firm-specific demand uncertainty: how Π_K changes as the firm's capital stock changes over time; and how Π_K is affected by the response of competitors.

Caballero (1991) inquires as to whether the negative impact of firm-specific uncertainty on investment is due to imperfect competition or to irreversibility. Caballero considers the following demand function: $p_t = \alpha_t(Y_t)^{1/\epsilon}$ with a CRS technology. For a monopolist, Π_K is a strictly decreasing function of K_t. As demand becomes less elastic the convexity of Π_K in α_t is reduced and furthermore, as the markup rises, Π_K decreases more with a given increase in capital (in other words $\partial \Pi_{KK}/\partial markup < 0$). By contrast, Caballero (1991) suggests that for a CRS production function as the elasticity of demand becomes infinite ($\epsilon \rightarrow -\infty$), Π_K is independent of K_t and the irreversibility constraint becomes irrelevant so that an increase in firm-level uncertainty raises investment in a perfectly competitive environment.[37] Hence, imperfect competition when the technology is CRS is the critical factor in explaining the negative relationship between firm-level (or idiosyncratic) uncertainty and irreversible investment.

Furthermore, the monopolist is not threatened by entry so that there is no upper barrier on the output price. However, there is a positive value of waiting. Irreversibility renders the monopolist's distribution of Π_K asymmetric because the firm cannot disinvest in the future if negative shocks are realised. Thus the monopolist invests less today so as to reduce exposure to negative shocks.

Idiosyncratic (firm-level) and industry-wide uncertainty in industry equilibrium

Although the firm's Π_K is independent of the firm's investment, in a competitive industry with CRS, the distribution of Π_K depends on industry-wide (or market-wide) investment if the elasticity of demand faced by the industry is less than infinite. Thus, inferences with respect to the impact of uncertainty require the development of a full model of market equilibrium. Caballero and Pindyck (1996), Dixit (1989), Hopenhayn (1992) and Leahy (1993), analyse investment in a competitive market equilibrium

---

[37] Alternatively, a DRS production function for a perfectly competitive firm would make Π_K depend on the firm's capital stock so that uncertainty would matter.

with entry and exit.[38] Dixit (1989) analyses industry evolution in the presence of aggregate shocks while Leahy (1993) considers industry equilibrium with an endogenous price. Lambson (1991) develops a discrete time model of technology choice under market-wide and firm-specific uncertainty. Hopenhayn examines the steady-state properties of a discrete time competitive equilibrium model of entry and exit with firm specific uncertainty.

Leahy (1993) compares the behaviour of two types of firms. The first type correctly anticipates how the decisions of its competitors interact with prices and exogenous shocks. The second type assumes that the capital stock in the industry remains fixed forever so that it expects that future prices will be driven solely by exogenous shocks. Thus, the second type of firm has 'static expectations regarding industry output, but rational expectations regarding other shocks that influence price in the market'. Leahy exploits the connection between a competitive equilibrium and the resource allocation of a social planner to demonstrate that the output prices which trigger investment are the same for both types of firms. Thus, the competitive firm may optimally invest assuming that the price follows an exogenous log normal random walk.

Caballero and Pindyck (1996) examine the impact of idiosyncratic and aggregate uncertainty when firms face a sunk cost of entry and have a CRS production function. They assume a continuum of risk neutral firms where each firm produces one unit of output. There are no variable factors of production. Aggregate and individual productivity are both stochastic. The industry demand curve is iso-elastic and is subject to an aggregate shock. In this context irreversibility affects the equilibrium distribution of the price, which in turn affects entry. In turn, the entry of firms changes the stochastic process for the equilibrium price from a Brownian motion to a regulated Brownian motion.

In the case of firm-specific uncertainty, each firm will compare the benefits of investment with the value of waiting. By postponing investment the firm can reduce its exposure to bad shocks. The downside of the shock to profit is cushioned by the possibility of waiting. Greater uncertainty makes waiting more valuable and discourages investment. However, the idiosyncratic shocks lead to a symmetric distribution for Π_K. The shocks faced by different firms are IID so that through the Law of Large Numbers, industry aggregates are non-random, although they are affected by the parameters of

---

[38] Lucas and Prescott (1971) analyse a rational expectations equilibrium in a competitive industry with adjustment costs. They also demonstrate the equivalence between the social optimum and the equilibrium.

the distribution function of firm-specific uncertainty. Furthermore, aggregate certainty hides considerable variation at the micro level as some firms enter, invest and exit in response to firm-specific shocks.

Leahy (1993) and Pindyck (1993a) and Caballero and Pindyck (1996) show that aggregate, i.e. market-wide, uncertainty reduces irreversible investment. Consider an increase in market-wide uncertainty with respect to productivity. Each period if demand increases, the expansion of existing firms and entry of new firms will limit the extent of the price rise. However, when demand falls there is no analogous mechanism which prevents the price from falling. The distribution is truncated as negative shocks reduce profits more than positive shocks raise them. Thus, the trigger at which investment takes place increases and irreversible investment falls. Once one takes into account the market feedback, uncertainty and irreversibility have the same adverse impact on investment as monopoly. Unlike the case of monopoly, investment in the perfectly competitive industry does not fall due to an increase in the option value of waiting. The latter is zero for aggregate uncertainty since free entry eliminates all profits.

4.3 Cost uncertainty

One motivation for studying the impact of cost uncertainty on investment decisions derives from Jones' finding of a strong negative relationship between growth and machinery price (1994). Furthermore, there are substantial innovations in the development of new machinery and equipment which induce a high degree of uncertainty for p_t^k.[39] This uncertainty may be partly non-diversifiable since changes in input costs are likely to be correlated with the state of the economy. For the adjustment cost model, Hartman (1973) concludes that a mean-preserving spread has no impact while Abel (1983) examines randomness in the cost-of-adjustment function, and shows that if the third derivative of the cost-of-adjustment function is positive, investment increases as a result of greater risk.

In this section, we examine the impact of FSD shifts as well as increases in risk in the price of capital on irreversible investment. Our analysis of the latter issue derives from Altug, Demers and Demers (1999). When the firm faces both demand and cost uncertainty its decision to invest will depend on α_t and p_t^k. The firm will invest when α_t is high and p_t^k is low. Given α_t, the firm will decide to invest when p_t^k is sufficiently low. For simplicity,

---

[39] Henceforth we drop the superscript H on the purchase price of capital goods and we simply use p_t^k.

in the remainder of this section we assume that p_t^k is the only source of uncertainty.

We begin by considering the case when p_t^k is independently distributed. Following Altug, Demers and Demers (1999), it can be shown that V_K is concave in p_t^k and thus, a MPS in p_{t+1}^k depresses the expected future marginal value of capital. Hence, when investment is irreversible, a riskier price of capital goods (in the sense of a MPS) reduces current investment and increases the size of the inaction zone.[40]

We next consider that p_t^k is positively serially correlated. Let $G^p(p_{t+1}^k \mid p_t^k)$ denote the distribution of p_{t+1}^k conditional on p_t^k. We can re-write the shadow price of capital as

$$V_K\left(K_{t+1}, h_{t+1}, p_{t+1}^k\right)$$
$$= \Pi_K(K_{t+1}, h_{t+1}) + (1 - \delta)$$
$$\times \min\left[p_{t+1}^k, \beta \int V_K\left((1 - \delta)K_{t+1}, h_{t+2}, p_{t+2}^k\right)dG^p\left(p_{t+2}^k \mid p_{t+1}^k\right)\right].$$

$$(2.59)$$

First, consider FSD shifts in the conditional distributions. If the future resembles the present when prices are serially correlated, then a FSD shift in $G^p(p_{t+1}^k \mid p_t^k)$ lowers the probability of low values of p_{t+1}^k and indicates the prospect of facing higher purchase prices for investment goods in the future. In this case, expandability becomes more costly, thereby lowering the value of waiting so that the firm raises investment. Turning to a MPS in the serially correlated case, suppose that p_{t+1}^k is a stochastic linear (or concave) and increasing function of p_t^k then more volatile costs for machinery and equipment (a MPS in $G^p(p_{t+1}^k \mid p_t^k)$) will depress the expected shadow value of capital, V_K, and increase the inaction zone.[41] Altug, Demers and Demers (1999) perform simulations and show that if p_{t+1}^k is log normally distributed an increase in the conditional variance will depress current investment.

In a model of project selection, Pindyck (1993b) shows that the impact of cost uncertainty on the decision to invest can be quantitatively large. Furthermore, the impact of input cost uncertainty with a large systematic component can be even larger. In particular, if the correlation between

---

[40] Then, for any given value of the inherited capital stock, K_t, and any given distribution function $G^p(p_{t+1}^k \mid p_t^k)$, there is a critical value of p_t^k, say $\hat{p}^k$, such that for $p_t^k > \hat{p}^k$, $I_t^* = 0$. In the absence of other sources of uncertainty, this is the zone of inaction.

[41] Alternative sufficient conditions can be found for a MPS in the conditional distribution to lower investment. For example, if $G^p(p_{t+1}^k \mid p_t^k)$ is convex in p_t^k.

input costs and the market is 0.3, investment is depressed since the threshold such that investment is positive falls by 25 per cent compared to the no-correlation case. Finally, another type of cost uncertainty arises when investment occurs in stages, for example when there is time-to-build. For example, costs may become fully known only when the project is implemented. We will discuss this issue below.

4.4 The discount factor

So far, we have assumed that the firm discounts future cash flows at the rate β without specifying the exact form of the discount factor. Here we discuss different methods of discounting. First, the firm may discount its cash flows with the risk-free rate, for example the rate of return on government bonds. That is, letting r denote the risk-free rate, $\beta = (1 + r)^{-1}$. However, since typically the firm's assets are risky, this riskiness should be taken into account when discounting cash flows.

What is the appropriate discount factor that the firm should use in calculating the present value of its cash flow? To the extent that ultimately firms are owned by consumers, its goal is to maximise its value to its shareholders. Thus, from the point of view of the consumer, the firm is an asset with a risky return given by

$$(1 + \xi_{t+1}) = \frac{V_{t+1} + R_{t+1}}{V_t}, \tag{2.60}$$

where ξ_{t+1} denotes the return on the risky asset, V_t[42] denotes the value of the firm at time t and R_{t+1} denotes the cash flow at time $t + 1$. From the consumer's optimal portfolio choice, we know that the following conditions must be satisfied for each asset included in the portfolio:

$$u'(c_t) = E_t \left[\beta^c u'(c_{t+1}) \left(\frac{V_{t+1} + R_{t+1}}{V_t} \right) \right], \tag{2.61}$$

where β^c is the representative consumer-investor's subjective discount factor. Alternatively, letting $M_{t+1} \equiv \beta^c u'(C_{t+1}) / u'(C_t)$ denote the marginal rate of intertemporal substitution, we can rewrite the above expression as

$$1 = E_t[M_{t+1}(1 + \xi_{t+1})]. \tag{2.62}$$

---

[42] The subscripts t and $t + 1$ on V are used here to distinguish the value of the firm at time t versus time $t + 1$, but is not meant to imply any time dependence of the value function itself.

For the risk-free rate which is known with certainty this expression specialises to

$$(1 + r) = [E_t M_{t+1}]^{-1}. \tag{2.63}$$

Equation (2.61) is a difference equation in V_t. Solving it forward we obtain the value of the firm at time t as:[43]

$$V_t = E_t \left\{ \sum_{i=1}^{\infty} M_{t+i} R_{t+i} \right\}. \tag{2.64}$$

Hence we can see that the discount factor that should be used by the firm in this context is the time-varying intertemporal MRS of the representative consumer. Note also that a firm whose cash flow is pro-cyclical and varies positively with consumption (and hence negatively with the marginal utility of consumption) will discount its future cash flow more heavily and will have a lower value than one whose cash flow varies counter-cyclically and is therefore viewed as a hedge against cyclical risks. To see this, we can use (2.62) and (2.63) to obtain

$$E_t \xi_{t+1} - r = \frac{-Cov_t(\xi_{t+1}, M_{t+1})}{[E_t M_{t+1}]}. \tag{2.65}$$

The left-hand side of this expression represents the excess return (or risk premium) on the risky firm (over and above the risk-free rate) that is required by consumers in order to hold the asset. Again we see that a firm whose return or cash flow is pro-cyclical and varies positively with consumption (and hence negatively with the marginal utility of consumption) will have a positive risk premium while one whose cash flow varies negatively with consumption is seen as a hedge and therefore will have a negative premium.

The above expression for $E_t \xi_{t+1}$ is very similar to the required rate of return derived from the CAPM model. In fact, since the CAPM is a special case of the consumption CAPM[44] we can obtain the required rate of return as follows.[45] Let the utility function be quadratic (so that marginal utility is linear in consumption) and assume that consumption is perfectly positively

---

[43] This solution of the expectational difference equation assumes that there are no bubbles. See Blanchard and Fischer (1989).

[44] See Cochrane (2001, chapter 9) for details. The CAPM can be obtained from the consumption CAPM by making any one of the following assumptions: (*a*) a quadratic utility function with IID returns; (*b*) a logarithmic utility function with normal returns; (*c*) an exponential utility function with normally distributed returns.

[45] For simplicity, we follow Blanchard and Fischer (1989: 508) to illustrate this point.

correlated with the return on the market portfolio. Then, (2.65) becomes

$$E_t \xi_{t+1} = r + \beta^{CAPM} \left(E_t \xi_{t+1}^M - r \right). \qquad (2.66)$$

where $\beta^{CAPM} = Cov_t(\xi_{t+1}, \xi_{t+1}^M) / Var_t(\xi_{t+1}^M)$ and ξ_{t+1}^M denotes the return on the market portfolio. Now, note that $Cov_t(\xi_{t+1}, \xi_{t+1}^M) = \rho_t^{\xi,M} \sigma_t^M \sigma_t^\xi$, where $\rho_t^{\xi,M}$ denotes the correlation coefficient between the market return and the return on the risky asset, σ_t^M and σ_t^ξ denote, respectively, the standard deviation of the market return and of the return on the risky asset. Letting $\theta_t \equiv E_t \xi_{t+1}$ be the required rate of return at time t we can write (2.66) as:

$$\theta_t = r + \omega_t \rho_t^{\xi,M} \sigma_t^\xi, \qquad (2.67)$$

where $\omega_t \equiv (E_t \xi_{t+1}^M - r)/\sigma_t^M$ is the market price of risk. According to the CAPM, θ_t reflects the asset's systematic or non-diversifiable risk. Thus θ_t is the risk-adjusted expected rate of return which investors would require to hold the asset.[46] Thus, the firm's discount factor should be $\beta_t = (1 + \theta_t)^{-1}$. We will also study a specialisation of this rate of return in subsection 4.8 when the differential taxation of equity, debt and dividends is considered.

4.5 Tax policy

There are numerous tax provisions that affect corporate investment, three of the most noteworthy being the statutory corporate profits tax rate, the investment tax credit (ITC) first introduced in the USA in 1962, and accelerated depreciation allowances introduced in 1954.[47] These tax instruments have been altered frequently. For example, in the USA there were thirteen important changes in the corporate tax code between 1962 and 1988. A specific ITC lasted on average 3.67 years, while on average the tax credit was abolished for three years. These observations indicate that tax

---

[46] This analysis has used the representative consumer assumption. If there are heterogeneous consumers, the same analysis would be valid provided that existing assets span the different states of nature. Then the marginal rates of substitution of different agents will be equated across states of nature as they will equal the state-contingent prices. (See Altug and Labadie 1994.) If spanning does not hold then the discount factor indicated by the CAPM will still be appropriate provided that the firm (or the risky projects it is evaluating) is in the space spanned by existing assets. If it is not, then the CAPM (or consumption CAPM) cannot be used to obtain the firm's appropriate discount factor. One would have to assume an arbitrary discount factor. This, for example, is the case for R&D projects. (See Dixit and Pindyck 1994 on this point.)

[47] For an extensive survey on tax policy and investment, see Hassett and Hubbard (2002). See Cummins, Hassett and Hubbard (1994), who document post-war tax changes in the US.

policy uncertainty is an important factor that may affect firms' investment decisions.

The impact of alternative tax policies on investment behaviour under certainty has been the topic of numerous studies beginning with Hall and Jorgenson's (1967) pioneering work within the neoclassical framework. Abel (1979, 1982), Alvarez, Kanniainen and Sodersten (1998), Auerbach (1989), Auerbach and Hines (1988) and Summers (1981), analyse changes in corporate tax rates and in the ITC using a cost-of-adjustment model based on Q-theory. The analysis of tax changes in theoretical and empirical cost-of-adjustment models with Q proceeds in two steps. First, the impact of tax changes on Q is determined. This requires an assessment of how stock markets react to these changes, and in turn, the latter necessitates a market expectation of how future investment will be affected by tax changes. Second, the impact of changes in Q on investment is analysed. The differential impact of temporary and permanent incentives of the same magnitude is of special interest. With convex costs of adjustment it is optimal for the firm to spread the impact of a tax change or of an ITC over time.

According to conventional wisdom a temporary ITC has a larger impact on investment than a permanent ITC since it induces an intertemporal reallocation of investment. When $\Pi_{KK} < 0$ (DRS technology) a temporary increase in the ITC provides greater stimulus than a permanent one.[48] However, with a CRS technology, Abel (1982) shows that a temporary ITC will not have a more stimulating impact on investment than a permanent one since the marginal value of capital is constant. When the tax wedge[49] is positive, an unanticipated permanent increase in the ITC, a fall in the tax rate or an increase in depreciation allowances increase investment. Abel also shows that the impact of unexpected changes in the corporate tax rate depends on the scheme for depreciation allowances. Nevertheless, a permanent corporate tax cut has a larger impact on investment than a temporary one. Making use of numerical simulations, Summers (1981) also investigates the impact of taxes on investment taking into account the firm's financial policy. He stresses the importance of the announcement and timing effects of tax changes. For example, an announced permanent reduction in the corporate tax rate will have a greater impact on investment due to accelerated depreciation. Auerbach (1989) adopts an alternative approach

---

[48] A permanent ITC leads to a higher time path of the capital stock and a lower time path of discounted Π_K. The more long-lived is the ITC the smaller the stimulus to investment.

[49] The tax wedge is $(1 - \gamma_t - z_t)$ where γ_t is the ITC and z_t is the present value of depreciation allowances.

to Abel and Summers. He obtains an analytical solution by linearising the firm's capital stock and Q_t around the steady state. He then examines the impact of anticipated tax reforms in a cost-of-adjustment model with a concave production function. Anticipated tax changes will affect the firm's investment and Q separately. Along the adjustment path the firm's desired capital stock deviates from its long-run value due to future tax changes and adjustment costs. An anticipated corporate tax cut affects investment in two ways, first through the smoothing of investment to the new desired long-run capital stock and second, through the anticipated capital gains or losses due to changes in the relative treatment of new and old capital goods. When a tax cut is imminent and there is accelerated depreciation a delayed tax cut may increase investment if initial depreciation allowances are large enough. In the case of an ITC, an anticipated (either permanent or tempo-rary) increase in the ITC has two opposing effects on investment. On the one hand, it leads to higher current investment to smooth the accumulation of capital stock. On the other hand, it depresses the value of old capital which does not qualify for the ITC and thus discourages investment. The net effect is a reduction of current investment if the unstable root of the differential equation for the adjustment of the capital stock is sufficiently large, a case which is empirically relevant according to Auerbach.

Alvarez, Kanniainen and Sodersten (1998) and Auerbach and Hines (1988) extend this analysis by introducing uncertainty with respect to the timing of reforms. Auerbach and Hines argue that investors form expectations of tax reforms under uncertainty. Even without any policy action, the *ex ante* value of depreciation allowances change yearly due to changes in expected inflation and real interest rates. Furthermore, although tax parameters change infrequently, proposed tax changes are debated for years and may or may not be adopted. Thus, firms operate under uncer-tainty. Auerbach and Hines assume that the probability of a new tax law is exogenous.[50] With high adjustment costs (which conform to typical esti-mates in empirical studies), they find that anticipated tax policy has little impact on investment whereas with low costs of adjustment anticipated tax changes affect investment. Alvarez, Kanniainen and Sodersten (1998) analyse the impact of uncertainty with respect to the size and the timing

[50] They use a variable tax reform probability which is set equal to the fraction of the previous five years in which a tax change occurred. Alternatively, they use a constant probability of 0.5, which is the fraction of years in the sample (from 1953 to 1985) in which tax changes occurred. They also regress the tax adjusted cost of capital on the unemployment rate, output growth, the real interest rate and investment as a share of GNP. All variables are significant at the 90 per cent significance level, providing evidence for the endogeneity of tax policy. This regression predicts out of sample a tax reform in 1986 similar to the one adopted by Congress.

of tax changes.[51] The expectation of a tax cut induces firms to accelerate investment so as to spread the adjustment to a new desired stock of capital. They show that the investment response is inversely related to the convexity of the cost-of-adjustment function. Increased uncertainty about the magnitude of the tax cut has no impact on investment while increased uncertainty about the timing has an ambiguous impact under a CRS technology but will accelerate investment under DRS.

On the empirical front, Auerbach and Hassett (1992) and Cummins, Hassett and Hubbard (1994, 1996) provide empirical evidence regarding the impact of tax policy and tax reform in cost-of-adjustment models with Q-theory. In particular, using reduced form estimation Auerbach and Hassett (1992) examine investment at the level of individual industries and assets and reconcile the predicted effects of the tax reform of 1986 with the pattern of investment in the years 1987–9. Their results indicate that investment performance would have been stronger were it not for the removal of the ITC. Auerbach and Hassett (1991) adopt a structural model and estimate the impact of tax policy on investment for the USA from 1956 to 1988 and consider endogenous policy. They relate investment directly to the determinants of Q, a procedure which allows them to capture the effect of anticipated tax changes. In particular, the cost of capital term which captures the anticipation of future tax changes has a stronger impact on investment than a cost of capital term which ignores tax changes. According to their model, greater instability in the sum of future costs of capital will make investment more unstable. Their empirical results lend support to the view that investment policy has had a destabilising (rather than a stabilising) impact on investment. Cummins, Hassett and Hubbard (1994, 1996) also obtain evidence of significant effects of tax parameters on investment. These studies provide evidence of the depressing impact on investment of the removal of the ITC as part of the tax reform of 1986.

There have been few analyses of tax policy in a context of uncertainty and irreversibility of investment. In a general equilibrium model with an AK technology Aizenman and Marion (1993) consider the impact of randomness in the corporate tax rate while in a model of the firm Faig and Shum (1999) and MacKie-Mason (1990) analyse the impact of the corporate tax on the firm's investment decisions in view of the asymmetry in the corporate income tax such that firms' gains and losses are treated

---

[51] They assume, in contrast to the literature, that costs of adjustment depend only on gross investment. However, they argue that their results would extend to a cost-of-adjustment function which depends on the investment to capital ratio.

differently.[52] Hassett and Metcalf (1999) study the impact of increases in risk in the ITC when firms must optimally choose the time to undertake an irreversible investment project while Altug, Demers and Demers (2002a, 2002b), respectively, analyse the impact of changes in the ITC and in the corporate tax rate on both the extensive and intensive margin.[53] We review this literature below.

We proceed by first analysing some results regarding changes in the level and in the distribution of the future corporate tax rate and of the ITC, more specifically with respect to their impact on the volatility of investment. First, we introduce some notation. The firm's after-tax cash flow at time t, R_t, is defined as

$$R_t = (1 - \tau_t) \, \Pi(K_t, \alpha_t, A_t, w_t)$$

$$+ \tau_t \sum_{x=1}^{T} D_{x,t-x} \, p_{t-x}^{k} \, I_{t-x} - (1 - \gamma_t) \, p_t^{k} I_t, \qquad (2.68)$$

where I_t is the firm's rate of gross investment measured in physical units, and p_t^{k} the non-stochastic purchase price of investment goods, τ_t is the corporate tax rate at time t, γ_t is the investment tax credit at time t as a percentage of the price of the investment good, $D_{x,t-x}$ is the depreciation allowance per dollar invested for tax purposes for capital equipment of age x on the basis of the tax law effective at time $t - x$ and T is the life of the equipment. Let r denote the real rate of interest. For future reference, define z_t as the present value of tax deductions on new investment and p_t^{I} as the tax-adjusted price of investment goods, where

$$z_t = \sum_{n=1}^{T} \tau_{t+n} D_{n,t} \, (1 + i)^{-n}, \qquad (2.69)$$

where i_t is the nominal interest rate and

$$p_t^{I} = (1 - \gamma_t - z_t) \, p_t^{k}. \qquad (2.70)$$

The corporate tax rate
Assume that the firm faces a random corporate tax rate, τ_{t+1}, while the time paths of all prices and productivity are known to the firm. For simplicity, initially assume that there are no depreciation allowances, that is $z_t = 0$.

---

[52] Since they consider imperfect capital markets, Faig and Shum's contribution will be reviewed below.
[53] See also MacKie-Mason (1990).

Let $G^\tau(\tau_{t+1} \mid \tau_t)$ denote the conditional distribution function of τ_{t+1}. We examine the impact of changes in the current value of the tax rate as well as of changes in the distribution function of the future tax rate conditional on the current value of τ_t. First focusing on the impact of changes in τ_t, holding $G^\tau(\tau_{t+1} \mid \tau_t)$ constant and assuming an interior solution, we obtain from the first-order conditions after integrating the numerator by parts

$$\frac{\partial I_t}{\partial \tau_t} = \frac{\int V_{K\tau}(K_{t+1}, h_{t+1}, \tau_{t+1}) G^\tau_{\tau_t}(\tau_{t+1}|\tau_t) d\tau_{t+1}}{\int V_{KK}(K_{t+1}, h_{t+1}, \tau_{t+1}) dG^\tau(\tau_{t+1}|\tau_t)}, \qquad (2.71)$$

where $G^\tau_{\tau_t}$ denotes the derivative of G^τ with respect to τ_t and $h_t \equiv (\alpha_t, A_t, w_t)$. The current corporate tax rate affects investment through an information effect. It affects $G^\tau(\tau_{t+1} \mid \tau_t)$ and the expectation of the future marginal value of capital (V_K). Hence, unless the corporate tax rate is serially correlated, the current tax rate does not have any impact on current investment. When there is positive serial correlation ($G^\tau_{\tau_t} < 0$), a higher current corporate tax rate signals higher future tax rates. It can be shown that $V_{K\tau} < 0$ so that current investment is depressed by a higher corporate tax rate.[54]

Turning now to changes in future tax rates, assume that the tax rate is positively serially correlated. Suppose that $\widehat{G^\tau}(\tau_{t+1} \mid \tau_t)$ dominates $G^\tau(\tau_{t+1} \mid \tau_t)$ by FSD so that the probability of a higher future tax rate is higher under $\widehat{G^\tau}$. Since $V_{K\tau} < 0$, then I_t^* is lower under $\widehat{G^\tau}$. In other words, if there is a change in policy (possibly caused by a change in government) such that higher values of the tax rates are more probable, the expected marginal value of capital is reduced so that investment conditional on τ_t will be depressed.

Policy-makers can increase the variability of the tax rate around a constant mean (a MPS). First consider τ_{t+1} to be serially uncorrelated. We observe that $V_{K\tau\tau} = 0$. Hence, we find, as Aizenman and Marion (1993), that greater tax randomness (an increase in risk) has no impact on investment unless there is persistence in policy. Second, we turn to a positively serially correlated case. If τ_{t+1} is an increasing concave or linear function of τ_t, Altug, Demers and Demers (2002b) show that a MPS will lower current investment. Under this condition, when a higher tax rate today signals a higher tax rate in the future, greater volatility around a constant mean increases the opportunity cost of investing due to the loss of option value of waiting and lowers investment.

---

[54] This result follows since $V_{KK} > 0$ and since an application of Hadar and Russell's (1971) FSD theorem yields:

$$\int V_{K\tau}(K_{t+1}, h_{t+1}, \tau_{t+1}) G_\tau d\tau > 0 \text{ as } V_{K\tau} < 0.$$

Policy-makers can also affect the degree of persistence or predictability of policy, that is, the extent to which high tax rates today are likely to be followed by high rates in the future. Since $\partial I_t / \partial \tau_t < 0$ it can be shown that greater policy persistence will increase the variability of investment. Under the less persistent policy if the realised tax rate is low (high) investment is high (low); under the more persistent policy even more (less) is invested when the tax rate is low (high). Thus, in the absence of accelerated depreciation, the variability of investment is enhanced with a more predictable corporate tax rate policy.

One may also investigate the impact of changes in the corporate tax rate in the presence of accelerated depreciation allowances, that is when $z_t > 0$. Consider a special case where depreciation deductions are proportional to physical depreciation. Let τ_{t+1} be positively serially correlated. A higher current value of τ_t will now have a cost reduction effect as it implies greater tax savings which will work in the opposite direction to the information effect thereby rendering the sign of $\frac{\partial I_t}{\partial \tau_t}$ ambiguous. If the cost reduction effect dominates, $\frac{\partial I_t}{\partial \tau_t} > 0$ which implies that greater policy persistence leads to lower variability in investment. Furthermore, greater variability in future tax rates will lower irreversible investment even when tax rates are IID. These results point to the important role played by depreciation allowances in the analysis of corporate tax policy on investment.

Finally, MacKie-Mason (1990) examines tax non-linearities such as depreciation allowances under two rules for corporate income taxation: full-loss refunds and no-loss refunds when firms face output price uncertainty. He shows that raising depreciation allowances may deter investment when the interaction of uncertainty and tax non-linearities is taken into account. Furthermore, a higher corporate tax rate can stimulate investment by lowering the threshold at which investment takes place since a higher corporate tax rate increases the government's share of the value of waiting and reduces the firm's willingness to wait. In the absence of uncertainty a tax rate increase lowers investment, thus the tax non-linearities do not suffice to discourage investment when the tax rate rises.

The ITC

We now assume the firm faces a random tax credit, γ_t, while τ_t, all prices and productivity are non-stochastic. Let $G^\gamma (\gamma_{t+1} \mid \gamma_t)$ denote the distribution function of $\tilde{\gamma}_{t+1}$, conditional on γ_t. Hassett and Metcalf (1999) study the impact of increases in risk in the ITC when firms must optimally choose the timing of an irreversible investment project. They show that when policy uncertainty is in the form of a continuous geometric Brownian motion, a mean-preserving spread increases the median time to investing. Hassett and Metcalf attribute their finding to the non-stationarity of the process driving the ITC.

Hassett and Metcalf also argue that changes in the ITC are better characterised by a Poisson process, since they are infrequent. They point out that policy changes tend to occur at discrete time intervals and to involve large changes, with the timing of the change being uncertain. Assuming that the ITC is generated by means of a two-state stationary Poisson process, they find that an increase in risk leads to a decline in both the median time to investing and the *ex post* average hurdle price ratio, that is, a MPS in the ITC raises investment. Hassett and Metcalf also make tax policy endogenous by letting the arrival rate of the low and high values of the ITC depend on the firm's profitability. More specifically, they assume that as profitability increases the probability of encountering a high ITC falls. They find that greater variability in the ITC slightly increases median time to investing, and thus lowers investment, when policy is endogenous. Thus, endogenous policy mitigates the positive impact of variability in the ITC on investment.

Altug, Demers and Demers (2002a) investigate analytically and numerically the impact of changes in the current ITC as well as changes in the distribution of the future ITC in the sense of stochastic dominance, persistence and mean-preserving spreads (MPS) on the level of irreversible investment and on the incidence of the binding constraint. In particular, Altug, Demers and Demers examine the consequences of a government policy which increases the variability of the ITC around a known mean. When the ITC is independently distributed, they show that greater volatility in the ITC reduces investment. Furthermore, they show that greater mean-preserving risk lowers irreversible investment and increases the probability of a binding constraint when the tax process follows a stationary mean reverting Markovian process such as an AR(1) log-normal process.

Next, they use a Poisson process and generalise Hassett and Metcalf's approach by confronting the firm with greater uncertainty. When the firm faces uncertainty both with respect to the timing and the direction of the change in the ITC, an increase in risk unambiguously reduces the amount invested and raises the incidence of the binding irreversibility constraint. They also examine endogenous policy and they investigate the impact of temporary and permanent increases in volatility.

The argument that a more predictable (i.e. more persistent) and less variable ITC leads to lower variability of investment is also made by some general equilibrium models that address the issue of the variability of the corporate tax rate and of the ITC. Bizer and Judd (1989) consider a general equilibrium stochastic growth framework with uncertain taxation and which ignores any costs of adjustment. They demonstrate that randomness in the capital income tax raises revenues at a small welfare cost relative to a stable rate whereas a random ITC generates substantial fluctuations in investment at a large welfare cost. They further argue that it is not useful to summarise the impact of taxes on investment by an 'effective tax rate' because it does not recognise the differential effects of uncertainty with respect to the capital income tax and the ITC.

Finally, Chang (1995) uses a Kydland–Prescott (1982) time-to-build RBC framework to investigate the impact of exogenously specified distortionary corporate and personal income taxes on the variability of investment in the presence of productivity shocks and uncertainty with respect to tax parameters which are assumed to follow a random walk. The model is calibrated to fit key aggregates of the US economy between 1962 and 1980. Chang's results indicate that a higher corporate income tax reduces investment and the capital stock in the steady state and has a smoothing effect on output, on hours worked and on inventories, but increases the variability of investment in both structures and equipment. While a constant ITC stimulates the steady-state level of investment and has a stabilising effect on investment, a random ITC, on the contrary, has a destabilising impact on investment. In particular, the variability of both equipment and structures investment, increases by 23 per cent and 40 per cent, respectively. The ITC for equipment also has a tendency to delay investment in structures. A combined corporate income tax–ITC policy package increases the variability of aggregate investment, equipment investment and structures investment by, respectively, 44, 56 and 53 per cent. Thus, Chang's analysis emphasises that variability in exogenous tax policy can have a substantial impact on the variability of investment.

4.6 Regime shifts

There are many situations in which one may think of the economy transiting to a state that is characterised by different distributions for the underlying stochastic variables than the original one. For example, real interest rates or productivity may change from one decade to the next. Policy reforms in matters of taxation, trade, financial markets or various regulations may be envisaged. Alternatively, the firm may be exposed to the threat of expropriation, disruptions in market access, unfavourable government regulations, unsustainable exchange rates, debt crises, fiscal crises, policy reversals, risk of political disintegration, or other shock. However, there may be uncertainty with respect to the timing and magnitude of changes.[55]

One way of modelling such situations is in terms of 'regime shifts'. Let us assume that there are two regimes $s_t = 0$ and $s_t = 1$ and that the regime shift is governed by a two-state Markov chain with time-varying transition probabilities which depend on a vector $\mathbf{x}_t$ of economic and political indicators that may affect the transition probability to next period's regime.[56] Suppose that the current regime, $s_t = 0$, is observed by firms, but the future regime, s_{t+1}, is not known with certainty. For example, suppose that a policy reform (such as trade liberalisation) is in effect, $s_t = 0$, but there may be a positive probability of collapse of the reform process. That is, a deterioration of economic and political conditions could provoke a shift to protectionism to $s_{t+1} = 1$.[57] To describe the two-state Markov process governing the regime shift, let P_t denote the matrix of transition probabilities at time t where

$$P_t = \begin{bmatrix} \chi_t^0 & 1 - \chi_t^0 \\ 1 - \chi_t^1 & \chi_t^1 \end{bmatrix}, \tag{2.72}$$

where

$$\chi_t^0 = Pr(s_{t+1} = 0 \mid s_t = 0, \mathbf{x}_t) \tag{2.73}$$

$$\chi_t^1 = Pr(s_{t+1} = 1 \mid s_t = 1, \mathbf{x}_t). \tag{2.74}$$

To simplify the notation, we suppress $\mathbf{x}_t$ as an argument of χ. Note, however, that χ is a time-independent function of $\mathbf{x}_t$.[58] This specification admits the possibility that should a policy shift to regime 1 occur at some time $j < t$, there is a possibility of returning to the status quo ante. In other words, the regime shift is not perceived as being itself totally irreversible. Even though firms observe the realisation of $\mathbf{x}_t$ at time t, they do not know the future realisations of this random variable which is governed by a

---

[55] For example, several studies document the importance of political risk in the unsuccessful recovery of private investment following the adoption of IMF stabilisation packages in various countries. See, for example, Serven and Solimano (1993).

[56] Another example of a situation where the probability of a regime shift depends on economic and political variables is the case of an economy which is currently functioning under a policy of trade liberalisation, but where a deterioration of economic and political conditions could provoke a shift to protectionism.

[57] See Rodrik (1991) for a model of the impact of policy reversal on the timing of investment decisions.

[58] In principle, any functional form that maps $\mathbf{x}_t$ into the unit interval can be used to obtain the transition probabilities. Of these, the logit and probit among others yield a well-defined log-likelihood function and are compatible with maximum likelihood estimation.

stationary first-order Markov process and has the conditional distribution function $G^{\mathbf{x}}(\mathbf{x}_t|\mathbf{x}_{t-1})$. For simplicity, we assume that the regimes differ only with respect to the state of demand and productivity. Let $G^{\alpha_s}(\alpha_{t+1}|\alpha_t)$ and $G^{A_s}(A_{t+1}|A_t)$ denote the distribution functions of the state of demand and productivity in regime s_t. $G^{\alpha_0}(\alpha_{t+1}|\alpha_t)$ and $G^{\alpha_1}(\alpha_{t+1}|\alpha_t)$ (and $G^{A_0}(A_{t+1}|A_t)$ and $G^{A_1}(A_{t+1}|A_t)$) can be ranked according to FSD, MPS, or second-order stochastic dominance (SSD). Thus, for example, regime 1, 'protectionism', is worse than regime 0, 'policy reform', in the sense of FSD or may be riskier in the sense of MPS.

We can express the firm's problem recursively using a dynamic programming approach. The state variables of the problem consist of the current-period capital stock K_t, the state variables $h_t^s = (\alpha_t^s, A_t^s, w_t, p_t^k, \mathbf{x}_t)$ and the current regime s_t. We can express the firm's problem given that regime 0 is in effect at t as

$$V\big(K_t, h_t^0, s_t = 0\big) = \max_{I_t}\{(1 - \tau_t)\,\Pi\,\big(K_t, \alpha_t^0, w_t, A_t^0\big) - p_t^k I_t$$

$$+ \beta\chi_t^0 \int V\big(K_{t+1}, h_{t+1}^0, s_{t+1} = 0\big)dG^{\mathbf{x}}(\mathbf{x}_{t+1}|\mathbf{x}_t)$$

$$\times\, dG^{\alpha_0}(\alpha_{t+1}|\alpha_t)dG^{A_0}(A_{t+1}|A_t) + \beta\big(1 - \chi_t^0\big)$$

$$\times \int V\big(K_{t+1}, h_{t+1}^1, s_{t+1} = 1\big)dG^{\mathbf{x}}(\mathbf{x}_{t+1}|\mathbf{x}_t)$$

$$\times\, dG^{\alpha_1}(\alpha_{t+1}|\alpha_t)dG^{A_1}(A_{t+1}|A_t)\} \qquad (2.75)$$

subject to (2.29), (2.51), K_t given, and where $V(K_t, h_t, \mathbf{x}_t, s_t = i)$ denotes the value function, conditional on regime i at time t.

If demand and productivity are stochastically lower in the protectionist regime or, if they are expected to be more variable in the protectionist regime, then even a small probability that a regime shift may occur will lower the expected marginal value of capital and raise the marginal loss of the option value of waiting when the firm invests an additional unit. As a result, irreversible investment falls and the size of the inaction zone increases. This will be the case even if the bad regime has never been observed to date, as is true of our application to the risk of separation of Quebec. (See Altug, Demers and Demers (2000).)

Altug, Demers and Demers (2000) show that the significant declines that occurred in investment in Quebec in the 1990s can be accounted for in a model of irreversible investment with regime shifts. Their results are based on a simulation analysis of a structural model of irreversible investment that allows for stochastic shocks to wages, technology and demand, and that features learning.

4.7 Time-to-build

The cost-of-adjustment model and the irreversible investment model under uncertainty ignore the effects of time lags in the investment process on the optimal capital stock and investment decisions of firms. However, in most investment projects the capital stock must be installed in sequence and remains unproductive until the project is finished. The source of the time lags lies directly in the production technology. Investment lags in power-generating plants, aerospace and pharmaceuticals can be between six and ten years. The lead times in other industries are shorter but are nevertheless important. The implications of time-to-build has been examined in general equilibrium models which abstract from the irreversibility of investment and from option values by Kydland and Prescott (1982) and Altug (1989, 1993). In particular, Kydland and Prescott introduced this feature of investment in RBC models in order to explain the propagation of shocks.[59] The firm's optimal investment reflects the multiple periods required to build the capital stock. Altug (1989) performs maximum likelihood estimation of the Kydland–Prescott model. In a general equilibrium model with time-varying real interest rates, Altug (1993) shows that the cost of capital is a weighted average of real interest rates having maturities at least as long as the production lags, the weights reflecting the fraction of resources allocated to the incomplete projects. She also derives the implications of time-to-build for Q-theory.

In what follows we introduce time-to build in our model of the firm with irreversible investment and we explore the implications for the option value of waiting. To describe the time-to-build model, we replace the assumption that investment expenditures at time t yield productive capital in period $t + 1$. Instead, we assume that a unit of investment in period t yields productive capital with a lag of J periods, where J is exogenously specified. Let $s_{J,t}$ denote the number of new projects initiated at time t. Also let $s_{j,t}$ for $j = 1, \ldots, J - 1$ denote the investment projects j periods from completion in period t. The laws of motions that describe the evolution of the incomplete investment projects are given by

$$s_{j,t+1} = s_{j+1,t}, \quad j = 1, \ldots, J - 1. \tag{2.76}$$

---

[59] Zhou (2000) provides a recent empirical study while Chang (1995) uses this framework to analyse the impact of tax variability on investment.

It is also assumed that a fraction ϕ_j of resources are expended in each period for the different incomplete projects, which implies that total investment expenditures in period t are given by

$$I_t = \sum_{j=1}^{J} \phi_j s_{j,t}, \qquad (2.77)$$

where $0 \le \phi_j \le 1$ and $\sum_{j=1}^{J} \phi_j = 1$. Hence, when it invests the firm is viewed as being committed to investing a specific amount over J periods. With these assumptions, the law of motion for the capital stock becomes

$$K_{t+1} = (1 - \delta)K_t + s_{1,t}. \qquad (2.78)$$

We assume that investment is irreversible, which for the time-to-build model requires that[60]

$$s_{J,t} \ge 0. \qquad (2.79)$$

We assume that the firm faces mutually independent demand uncertainty and cost uncertainty. The state of demand α_t is positively serially correlated. To formulate the problem of the firm as a dynamic programming problem, we note that the state variables at time t include the capital stock which is productive at time t, K_t, and the sequence of unfinished projects which are inherited from past decisions, namely $s_{J-1,t}, \ldots, s_{1,t}$. Define $\kappa_t \equiv (K_t, s_{J-1,t}, \ldots, s_{1,t})$ and $\widehat{\kappa}_t \equiv ((1-\delta)K_t, s_{J-1,t}, \ldots, s_{1,t})$. Let $h_t \equiv (\alpha_t, A_t, w_t)$. Thus, the optimisation problem of the firm is now given by

$$V(\kappa_t, h_t, p_t^k) = \max_{s_{J,t}} \left\{ \Pi(K_t, h_t) - p_t^k I_t + \beta E_t V(\kappa_{t+1}, h_{t+1}, p_{t+1}^k) \right\}$$
$$(2.80)$$

subject to (2.76), (2.77), (2.78) and (2.79). To derive the first-order condition with respect to investment in new projects $s_{J,t}$, we note that $s_{J-1,t+1} = s_{J,t}, \; s_{J-2,t+2} = s_{J-1,t+1} = s_{J,t}$ and continuing in a similar manner, $s_{1,t+J-1} = s_{2,t+J-2} = \cdots = s_{J,t}$. Furthermore, new investment at date t affects only the productive capital stock at date $t + J$.

---

[60] In Altug (1993), it is assumed that there exist perfect markets for used capital such that the price of new and used capital goods are equal. Thus, while the aggregate capital stock can be increased only through new investment, an individual firm can alter its own capital stock through purchases or sales of existing capital.

Thus, the first-order condition with respect to new investment at date t becomes

$$-\phi_J p_t^k + \beta E_t \left[\frac{\partial V}{\partial s_{J-1,t+1}} \left(\kappa_{t+1}, h_{t+1}, p_{t+1}^k \right) \right] \leq 0. \quad (2.81)$$

Next, we evaluate the shadow value of projects with $J-1, J-2, \ldots, 1$ stages to completion at time $t+1$ as:

$$\frac{\partial V \left(\kappa_{t+1}, h_{t+1}, p_{t+1}^k \right)}{\partial s_{J-1,t+1}}$$
$$= -p_{t+1}^k \phi_{J-1} + \beta E_t \left[\frac{\partial V}{\partial s_{J-2,t+2}} \left(\kappa_{t+2}, h_{t+2}, p_{t+2}^k \right) \right] \quad (2.82)$$
$$\cdots$$
$$\frac{\partial V \left(\kappa_{t+J-1}, h_{t+J-1}, p_{t+J-1}^k \right)}{\partial s_{1,t+J-1}}$$
$$= -p_{t+J-1}^k \phi_1 + \beta E_t \left[\frac{\partial V}{\partial K_{t+J}} \left(\kappa_{t+J}, h_{t+J}, p_{t+J}^k \right) \right].$$

After substituting (2.82) in (2.81), we obtain

$$-\phi_J p_t^k - \beta \phi_{J-1} E_t \left(p_{t+1}^k \right) - \cdots - \beta^{J-1} \phi_1 E_t \left(p_{t+J-1}^k \right)$$
$$+ \beta^J E_t \left[\frac{\partial V}{\partial K_{t+J}} \left(\kappa_{t+J}, h_{t+J}, p_{t+J}^k \right) \right] \leq 0, \quad (2.83)$$

where $\phi_J p_t^k + \beta \phi_{J-1} E_t(p_{t+1}^k) + \cdots + \beta^{J-1} \phi_1 E_t(p_{t+J-1}^k) \equiv MC_t^k$ is the expected marginal cost of investing at time t which depends on outlays to be disbursed over time and which are therefore not known with certainty at time t. In the above model the firm is committed to a stream of expenditures which are predetermined once s_{Jt}^* is chosen.[61] In other words, the firm chooses at t how much it will invest in all stages of the project but it does not know the realised costs in all future periods nor the state of future demand J periods ahead. As we discussed in subsection 4.3 input cost uncertainty raises the value of waiting and lowers investment. With time-to-build the firm needs to anticipate the price of these inputs over several future periods. Thus, the adverse impact of input cost uncertainty is magnified. The marginal benefit of investing an additional unit is obtained after J periods when the capital stock becomes productive. Hence, the firm needs to forecast the state of demand over a longer time horizon.

---

[61] This is consistent with the Kydland–Prescott and Altug formulations of time-to build.

It is more uncertain about the state of demand, the value of waiting is larger, thereby depressing investment. Thus, with time-to-build the firm is exposed to greater uncertainty: first, the marginal costs which must be incurred over time are uncertain; second, the marginal benefits of investing occur J periods in the future when the state of demand is less certain. These two factors will act so as to lower irreversible investment and increase the incidence of the binding constraint relative to the basic model without time-to-build.[62] However, the opportunity cost of waiting is also larger with time-to-build since there are lags between the beginning of an investment project and the increased capacity. This latter effect will act in the opposite direction to the value of waiting effect. Thus, the net effect on irreversible investment and the incidence of the binding constraint is ambiguous and needs to be determined empirically.

We now need to evaluate $\frac{\partial V}{\partial K_{t+J}}$. According to the envelope condition, the shadow price of capital which is expected at time t is given by:

$$\frac{\partial V}{\partial K_{t+J}} \left(\kappa_{t+J}, h_{t+J}, p_{t+J}^k \right)$$

$$= \begin{cases} \Pi_K(K_{t+J}, h_{t+J}) + (1-\delta)MC_{t+1}^k & \text{if } s_{J,t+1}^* > 0 \\ \Pi_K(K_{t+J}, h_{t+J}) + (1-\delta)\beta E_{t+1} \\ \quad \times \left[V_K \left(\widehat{\kappa}_{t+J+1}, h_{t+J+1}, p_{t+J+1}^k \right) \right] & \text{if } s_{J,t+1}^* = 0. \end{cases}$$

Let C_{Kt}^{TTB} denote the loss of option value incurred by investing an additional unit in the presence of time to build and irreversibility:

$$C_{Kt}^{TTB} \left(K_{t+J}, MC_{t+1}^k \right)$$
$$= \int_{\alpha_{t+1}^H}^{\infty} (1-\delta) \left[-E_t MC_{t+1}^k + E_{t+1}\beta^J V_K \left(\widehat{\kappa}_{t+J+1}, h_{t+J+1}, p_{t+J+1}^k \right) \right]$$
$$\times dG^\alpha(\alpha_{t+1} | \alpha_t)$$
$$= (1-\delta)E_t \max \left\{ 0, \beta^J E_{t+1} V_K \left(\widehat{\kappa}_{t+J+1}, h_{t+J+1}, p_{t+J+1}^k \right) \right.$$
$$\left. - MC_{t+1}^k \right\} \geq 0. \tag{2.84}$$

---

[62] Consider only demand uncertainty for the moment, and assume that α_t is positively serially correlated. Then, for any given value of the inherited capital stock, K_t, and any given distribution function, $G^\alpha(\alpha_{t+J} | \alpha_t)$, the critical value of α_t, say α_t^H, such that for $\alpha_t < \alpha_t^H$, $s_{Jt}^* = 0$ will, *ceteris paribus*, be larger when there is time-to-build. The inaction zone where the option to invest will not be exercised will be larger with time-to-build. By a parallel argument, in the presence of cost uncertainty and abstracting from demand uncertainty, for any given value of the inherited capital stock, K_t, and any given distribution functions $G^p(p_{t+j}^k | p_t^k)$, for $j = 1, \ldots, J-1$ the critical value of p_t^k, say $\widehat{p}^k$, such that for $p_t^k > \widehat{p}^k$, $I_t^* = 0$, will be lower with time-to-build. Thus, the inaction zone will be larger on account of both demand uncertainty and cost uncertainty.

Assuming an interior solution obtains at time t and using the envelope condition for the capital stock, we can express (2.83) as follows:

$$
MC_t^k + \beta C_{Kt}^{TTB} = \beta^J E_t \{\Pi_K(K_{t+J}, h_{t+J}) + \beta(1 - \delta) \\
\times E_{t+1} V_K(\widehat{\kappa}_{t+J+1}, h_{t+J+1}, p_{t+J+1}^k)\}. \quad (2.85)
$$

Hence, optimal investment is chosen so as to equate the sum of the expected marginal cost of investing (given the time lags), MC_t^k, and the discounted marginal loss of option value, βC_{Kt}^{TTB}, to the discounted future marginal benefit which is the sum of the discounted expected marginal value of capital, $\beta^J E_t \Pi_K$, and of the expected marginal value of the unused portion of the capital stock (assuming that a corner solution prevails at $t + 1$).[63] We can alternatively express (2.83) in terms of the cost of capital given irreversibility, c_t^H, as:

$$
c_t^H = E_t \Pi_K(K_{t+J}, h_{t+J}) \quad for \; \alpha_t \geq \alpha_t^H, \quad (2.86)
$$

where

$$
c_t^H = \widehat{c}_t^H - (1 - \delta)\{(E_t MC_{t+1}^k - MC_t^k)[1 - G^\alpha(\alpha_{t+1}^H | \alpha_t)]\} \\
+ (1 - \delta) \left\{ \int_{\alpha_{t+1}^L}^{\alpha_{t+1}^H} [MC_t^k - E_{t+1} V_K(\widehat{\kappa}_{t+J+1}, h_{t+J+1}, p_{t+J+1}^k)] \right. \\
\left. \times dG^\alpha(\alpha_{t+1} | \alpha_t) \right\}. \quad (2.87)
$$

Finally, let Φ_t^{TTB} denote the loss of risk premium incurred by investing an additional unit in the presence of time to build and irreversibility. Φ_t^{TTB} is given by:

$$
\Phi_t^{TTB} = (1 - \delta)\{E_t MC_{t+1}^k - E_t \min[MC_{t+1}^k, \beta^J E_{t+1} V_K \\
\times (\widehat{\kappa}_{t+J+1}, h_{t+J+1}, p_{t+J+1}^k)]\}. \quad (2.88)
$$

Assuming that the firm discounts at the risk-free rate, that is, $\beta = (1 + r)^{-1}$, we can alternatively express (2.83) in terms of the marginal risk premium as

$$
\beta^{J-1} E_t \Pi_K(K_{t+J}, p_{t+J}, w_{t+J}) = c_t^{TTB} + \Phi_t^{TTB}, \quad (2.89)
$$

---

[63] As we noted above, the right-hand side may be expressed as the sum of Q_t which reflects the expected marginal value of capital if the firm never invests or disinvests from $t + 1$ onward and simply allows its capital stock to depreciate and Υ_t which represents the increase in the expected marginal value of capital due to *future* marginal call options (or growth options) available to the firm.

where c_t^{TTB} is the cost of capital applicable to time-to-build which reflects the weighted average of the percentage change in the price of capital goods between periods $t + 1$ and $t + J$ but which abstracts from irreversibility.[64]

In this model the firm does not have the option to suspend its investment plan. In general, in a project that spans several periods, the firm will choose sequentially how much to invest at each stage and furthermore will determine whether or not it is worth continuing the project on the basis of sequential option values. For example, the firm may invest in the first stage but when the second stage arrives the marginal cost of investing may exceed the threshold in which case the firm delays investment. The implications are explored by Dixit and Pindyck (1994), Majd and Pindyck (1987) and Pindyck (1993a) and in models of the firm.

Majd and Pindyck (1987) analyse investment in a project which involves a series of expenditures made sequentially, each of which cannot exceed k per period. The total cost is known to be C. The market value at completion, V, is unknown. It evolves according to a log-normal process. Although investment is completely irreversible, the project may be costlessly suspended. The investment project is a compound option since each unit invested buys an option on the next unit. Majd and Pindyck obtain a number of interesting results. First, they find that greater uncertainty raises the threshold (V^*) and delays investment. Second, the investment threshold is also higher for projects with time-to-build. Third, increasing the opportunity cost of delay reduces the threshold when it is low but raises it when it is high, the reason being that time-to-build reduces the present value of the payoff (received upon completion) by more when the opportunity cost of delay is large. Fourth, they show that increasing time-to-build has little impact on the threshold and the option value when the opportunity cost is low, but it deters investment when it is high.[65] Thus, the opportunity cost of delaying is critical in determining how investment is affected by time-to-build. However, the opportunity cost of delay in Majd and Pindyck is independent of uncertainty.[66] When the latter is made to

64        $c_t^{TTB} = \phi_J \{(r + \delta) p_t^k - (1 - \delta) [E_t(p_{t+1}^k) - p_t^k]\} \cdots +$
$$+ \beta^{J-1} \phi_1 \{(r + \delta) E_t(p_{t+J-1}^k) - (1 - \delta) [E_t(p_{t+J}^k) - E_t(p_{t+J-1}^k)]\}.$$

65   Time-to-build (TTB) is equal to C/k. Thus, by raising k, TTB falls. Projects can be built with technologies that differ with respect to flexibility. More flexible technologies imply a higher k and shorter TTB, C/k. However, more flexible technologies may be accompanied with a higher total cost, C.

66   In Majd and Pindyck's (1987) model the opportunity cost of delaying investment is $\delta = \theta - \varsigma$ where ς is the growth rate of V and θ is the firm's required rate of return according to the static CAPM. (See 2.28.) When the standard deviation of V, σ, increases there are two possibilities. First, ς may be treated as a fundamental constant in which case when σ increases, θ and δ increase

depend on uncertainty, the net effect of greater uncertainty on investment may be an increase in investment since it will depend on the extent to which the value of waiting has risen in relation to the opportunity cost.[67]

Bar-Ilan and Strange (1996) consider the timing of an irreversible investment project with an abandonment option. The output price is stochastic and follows a geometric Brownian motion. The study demonstrates that uncertainty has a smaller deterrent effect when there are investment lags. The ability to abandon softens the irreversibility constraint because it truncates the downside risk of investment. Furthermore, as variability rises greater uncertainty speeds up investment.[68] The fundamental reasons underlying this reversal of the impact of uncertainty on investment stem from two facts: uncertainty affects the opportunity cost as well as the option value of waiting and the option to abandon the project once it has begun. Costly abandonment weakens the reversal result. In the absence of abandonment, greater uncertainty unambiguously delays investment.[69] Bar-Ilan, Sulem and Zanallo (2002) find similar results to Bar-Ilan and Strange even though there is no abandonment option in their model. In the market for electricity they assume the existence of costs of insufficient capacity in addition to costs of excess capacity. Delaying investment increases the likelihood of lacking capacity to meet demand. Greater uncertainty can increase the cost of delay more than the benefit. Thus, with investment lags, uncertainty does not necessarily adversely affect the timing and size of investment.

Finally, another type of input cost uncertainty has been analysed in the literature in the context of time-to-build. The latter, dubbed 'technical uncertainty' by Pindyck (1993b), stems from the physical difficulty of completing the project. Even if the costs of the inputs needed to build the capital equipment were known with certainty the firm may not know how

---

pari passu so that the threshold at which investment occurs is affected. Second, δ may be treated as a fundamental constant so that, when σ increases, ς adjusts to offset the effect of σ on θ. As a result, the threshold for investment is not affected. Majd and Pindyck (1987) adopt the second approach.

[67] Milne and Whalley (2000) add an optimality condition to Majd and Pindyck's model, namely at the investment threshold the marginal benefit of investing should be equal to the marginal cost. When costless suspension is possible, Milne and Whalley find that, as a consequence, the effect of uncertainty in raising investment thresholds is significantly lower with TTB. Finally, when TTB is long and the opportunity cost of forgone cash flows is high, the effect of the option value of waiting on investment may be offset by TTB because the option to suspend lowers the investment threshold.

[68] When it reaches its minimum, the trigger is lower than the certainty trigger (assuming an annual standard deviation of 12.6 per cent).

[69] With a longer lag the trigger price for investment is less affected by uncertainty. On the one hand, a longer lag means that the return on investment has a larger variance. Thus, the option value of waiting rises. On the other hand, the opportunity cost of waiting rises with the lag. Bar-Ilan and Strange's (1996) simulation results show that the opportunity-cost effect dominates.

much time, effort and materials will be required to complete the project.[70] This type of uncertainty is diversifiable. The information effect reduces the full cost of investing and thus leads to higher investment.[71] Pindyck assumes that the cost of completion of a project, C is unknown while the value of the project upon completion, V, is non-stochastic. There is time-to-build and the firm may invest a maximum of k per period. Assuming that the risk-free rate is zero, the value of the investment can be obtained as the value if there were no abandonment and a put option (the option to abandon the project if costs are higher than expected). Pindyck's simulations reveal that the effect of technical uncertainty on investment is significant but is less than that of input cost uncertainty such as the price of machinery and equipment.

4.8 Liquidity constraints and imperfect capital markets

The Modigliani–Miller Theorem states that in the absence of transaction costs, bankruptcy costs, taxes and agency costs between shareholders and managers and between creditors and managers, there is no optimal capital structure. Thus, the firm's cost of capital is unaffected by changes in the proportion of debt and equity, the value of the firm is unaffected by the amount of leverage and the firm's investment decision is made independently of its financing decision. Thus, firms' financing decisions are irrelevant for investment decisions. In all of the investment models which we have presented thus far, the Modigliani–Miller Theorem is implicitly assumed. The supply of funds is a horizontal line at the market real rate of interest adjusted for risk. The capital stock is determined by the intersection of the downward-sloping demand curve for capital and the horizontal supply curve of capital.[72] Firms can borrow and lend unlimited amounts of funds at the market interest rate. In this framework firms undertaking investment decisions and suppliers of funds have the same information about the firm's investment projects and opportunities so that internal funds do not have any role in influencing investment.

However, typically, firms face transaction costs, taxes matter, there are bankruptcy costs and financial markets are characterised by imperfections

---

[70] For example the development of a new model of aircraft necessitates engineering studies, the production of a prototype and further testing.

[71] This is similar to the effect of learning by doing or the learning curve. See below for other examples of this type of effect.

[72] This implication is true for all the models described so far, with the exception that the characterisation of investment or the demand for funds changes depending on the model we consider.

due to problems of asymmetric information and incentives. Thus, in practice, the conditions underlying the Modigliani–Miller Theorem are violated. There is an optimal capital structure and firms adopt a financing hierarchy. The firm will first resort to retained earnings at the expense of equity financing because managers value flexibility and control. To the extent that external financing reduces flexibility for future financing and control, managers prefer retained earnings as a source of capital for investment. The cost of external finance may also exceed the cost of internal finance due to taxes and transaction costs. Second, the firm will resort to debt financing which involves a higher cost of funds. However, there are tax advantages to the use of debt rather than equity financing since interest payments are tax-deductible whereas dividends are paid out of after-tax cash flows and are thus subject to double taxation. Finally, it will rely on equity finance at an even higher cost in view of the implied loss of control.

In a context of asymmetric information firms may issue dividends as a signal to indicate that the firm believes it has the capacity to generate these cash flows in the future, thereby inducing confidence in the stock. Thus, the use of dividends as a signalling device limits the firm's reliance on internal funds.

Early work by Meyer and Kuh (1957) emphasised the importance of financial constraints for investment. In the past decades, a very large theoretical and empirical literature has developed. See, for example, Bernanke, Gertler and Gilchrist (1996), Bond and Meghir (1994) and Fazzari, Hubbard and Petersen (1988).[73] Empirical studies reveal that investment is significantly correlated with proxies for changes in net worth or internal funds and that the correlation is more important for firms facing informational problems in capital markets. In what follows we discuss debt finance and equity finance in turn. Then, we present a model of irreversible investment with financial constraints and we discuss empirical evidence.

Debt finance

The firm may borrow by seeking a loan from banks or it may issue corporate bonds. From the point of view of small firms, bank debt has several advantages over bond financing. First, it can be used to borrow small amounts whereas bond issues are characterised by economies of scale. Second, it may be easier to convey information to a bank if the firm is small and not well known. Third, firms only have to transact with the lending bank whereas with bond issues they have to contend with rating agencies that

---

[73] See Chirinko (1993) and Hubbard (1998) for surveys.

have stricter requirements. Bond issues offer advantages to larger publicly traded firms. For example, financing terms are cheaper since the financing costs are spread across a large number of investors.

The first cost of debt is the increase in the risk of bankruptcy if the firm were to be incapable of meeting its principal and interest obligations. The second cost of debt stems from agency costs owing to the conflict of interest between creditors and managers who act in the interest of shareholders. The conflict over investment projects, financing and dividends will also be exacerbated as the debt–equity ratio rises.[74] For example, managers may issue new debt which raises the riskiness of the firm. Managers may also perversely choose projects with a negative NPV which will raise the value of equity due to their impact in depressing the market value of existing debt. These incentive problems are compounded when there is imperfect information. If the monitoring of actions is costly and imperfect, external suppliers of funds require a premium to compensate them for these monitoring costs and the moral hazard problem linked with managers' control. Alternatively, creditors typically obtain covenants which restrict the firm's ability to make investment, financing and dividend decisions, for example by specifying target debt–equity ratios. Debt covenants may specify working capital requirements which may lower the supply of internal funds available for investment. As a result, the firm suffers from additional costs, the cost of monitoring the covenants and the loss of financial flexibility.

Furthermore, when information about the quality or riskiness of the borrowers' investment projects is imperfect, adverse selection creates an additional gap between the cost of external and internal finance as lenders require a premium, and credit rationing may even arise.[75] As Fazzari, Hubbard and Petersen (1988) stress, only *Fortune 500* firms face a smoothly rising loan interest rate in debt markets. The vast majority of firms outside the *Fortune 500* rely on private placement. When credit tightens in the economy small and medium-size firms may lose access to private placements as well as to bank loans and lines of credit.

Equity finance
Equity takes many forms: owner's equity, venture capital, common stock, warrants and contingent value rights. Most firms start as small businesses funded by the owners themselves who reinvest the retained earnings. As small businesses grow they often face shortages of funds. Smaller and riskier

---

[74] For a good discussion see Damodaran (1999).   [75] See Stiglitz and Weiss (1981).

firms resort to venture capital and have to give up, in return, a dispropor-
tionate share of the value of the firm. Then, after a certain stage of growth
and maturity the firm can become public and issue common stock at a
market determined price. When the firm is newly listed the price of the
stock is estimated by an investment banker. For an existing firm it is based
on the market price. Each share may receive dividends and voting rights.
Alternatively, there may be different classes of stocks assigning different
dividend and voting privileges.[76]

New share issues involve substantial transaction costs such as underwrit-
ing which may vary considerably depending on the size of the offering. In
addition, new equity issues may be associated with adverse selection problems owing to the fact that potential investors cannot distinguish perfectly
the quality of firms and will value them at the average.[77] Thus, investors
will request a premium to purchase the shares of good firms to offset the
risk of investing in 'lemons'.

A model of irreversible investment with financial constraints
In a cost-of-adjustment model which abstracts from irreversibility, Fazzari,
Hubbard and Petersen (1988) and Hubbard, Kashyap and Whited (1995)
analyse the impact of financial constraints on investment. In what follows
we introduce financial constraints in our model of the firm with irreversible
investment and we explore the implications for the option value of waiting
as well as for the interrelationships between financing and investment decisions. We assume that the firm faces demand uncertainty (with positive
serial correlation) but all other prices and productivity are non-stochastic.
We first introduce some notation. Let D_t be the dividends paid at t, V_t the
value of the firm's equity and V_{t+1}^N the value of new share issues at $t + 1$.
Ω_{t+1} is a 'lemons' premium, B_t the real stock of debt outstanding at
t, τ^c is the capital gains tax, s is the tax on dividends and θ_t is the investors' required rate of return on stocks. Arbitrage in the stock markets
yields:

$$\frac{(1 - \tau^c)\left[E_t\left(V_{t+1} - (1 + \Omega_{t+1})V_{t+1}^N\right) - V_t\right] + (1 - s)E_t D_{t+1}}{V_t} = \theta_t.$$

$$(2.90)$$

[76] Warrants may also be issued. They assign the rights to the holders to buy shares at a fixed price
in return for purchasing the warrants upfront. Since warrants create no immediate obligations nor
dilution this method of financing is sought by high-growth firms when cash-flows are non-existent.
Finally, contingent value rights give the right to the holder to sell a share of stock at a fixed price
during a specified time period.

[77] See Myers and Majluf (1984).

The right-hand side of (2.90) is the opportunity cost for investors of holding shares which must be equal to the after-tax rate of return on stocks. The latter is equal to the expected appreciation of stock value net of new stock issues adjusted for the 'lemons' premium plus expected after-tax dividend payments. After solving (2.90) forward and ruling out speculative bubbles we find the value of the firm as of time t:

$$V_t = E_t \sum_{i=0}^{\infty} \left[\prod_{j=0}^{i-1} \beta_{t+j} \right] \left(m D_{t+i} - (1 + \Omega_{t+i}) V_{t+i}^N \right), \qquad (2.91)$$

where $m \equiv (1 - s)/(1 - \tau^c)$ and the firm discounts at the (risk-adjusted) required rate of return, taking into account the tax rate on capital gains. That is, $\beta_t = (1 + \theta_t(1 - \tau^c)^{-1})^{-1}$ is the discount factor at time t. Since the sources of funds must equal the uses of funds, we find the firm's dividends at time t as after-tax profits net of interest payments on the debt less investment expenditures plus new share issues and net borrowing

$$D_t = (1 - \tau_t)(\Pi(K_t, h_t) - i_{t-1}B_{t-1} - \Gamma(B_{t-1}, K_t))$$
$$- p_t^I I_t + (1 - e_t)V_t^N + B_t - (1 - \pi_t^e)B_{t-1}, \qquad (2.92)$$

where e_t is the transaction cost per unit of new share issues, i_t is the nominal interest rate paid on corporate bonds, π_t^e is the expected rate of inflation, p_t^I is the tax-adjusted price of investment goods and Γ is an agency–financial distress cost function which captures the premium on external borrowing due to asymmetric information and enforcement problems. Γ is an increasing function of the stock of debt and a decreasing function of the physical capital stock since a larger K_t implies larger collateralised assets. We assume that the firm maximises its value subject to the law of motion of the capital stock, the irreversibility constraint and three additional constraints: a constraint on dividends, on new issues and on indebtedness. First, firms need to pay a minimum amount of dividends, $\overline{D}$:

$$D_t \geq \overline{D}. \qquad (2.93)$$

Second, in view of tax incentives the firm could raise its value by reducing dividends and distributing cash to shareholders as share repurchases. To limit such activities on the part of the firm we impose the restriction that

$$V_t^N \geq \underline{V}, \qquad (2.94)$$

where $\underline{V}$ is a finite negative value. Third, the firm may face imperfect markets for corporate debt so that the outstanding debt as a ratio of the value of the capital stock must be lower than a ceiling, $\overline{B}_t$, a maximum debt to capital ratio which may depend on measures of the firm's financial health:[78]

$$\frac{B_t}{p_t^I K_{t+1}} \geq \overline{B}_t. \tag{2.95}$$

In addition, a transversality condition is imposed to prevent the firm from borrowing an infinite amount in order to make dividend payouts:

$$\lim_{T \to \infty} \left[\prod_{j=t}^{T-1} \beta_j \right] B_{t+T} = 0 \quad \forall t. \tag{2.96}$$

Also, let $h_t^F \equiv (\alpha_t, A_t, w_t, p_t^I, \Omega_t, e_t, i_{t-1}, \pi_t^e)$. We can express the Lagrangian as:

$$\mathcal{L}(K_t^*, I_t^*, \lambda_t^*, B_t^*)$$

$$= \max_{I_t, B_t, V_t^N} \left\{ m D_t - (1 + \Omega_t) V_t^N + \beta_t E_t V\big((1 - \delta)K_t + I_t, B_t, h_{t+1}^F\big) \right.$$

$$\left. + \lambda_t^D [D_t - \overline{D}] + \lambda_t^B \left[\overline{B}_t - \frac{B_t}{p_t^I K_{t+1}} \right] + \lambda_t^N [V_t^N - \underline{V}], \quad (2.97) \right.$$

where D_t is defined in (2.92), $\lambda_t^D, \lambda_t^B, \lambda_t^N$ are the shadow prices attached to the dividend, bond and new equity issues constraints, respectively. The optimality conditions are obtained as:

$$\frac{\partial \mathcal{L}}{\partial I_t} = -m p_t^I + \beta_t E_t V_K\big((1 - \delta)K_t + I_t, B_t, h_{t+1}^F\big) - \lambda_t^D p_t^I \leq 0, \tag{2.98}$$

$$\frac{\partial \mathcal{L}}{\partial B_t} = 1 + \lambda_t^D - \frac{\lambda_t^B}{p_t^I K_t} + \beta_t E_t V_B\big((1 - \delta)K_t + I_t, B_t, h_{t+1}^F\big) \leq 0, \tag{2.99}$$

$$\frac{\partial \mathcal{L}}{\partial V_t^N} = -(1 + \Omega_t) + \lambda_t^N + \big(m + \lambda_t^D\big)(1 - e_t) \leq 0, \tag{2.100}$$

$$\frac{\partial \mathcal{L}}{\partial \lambda_t^B} = \left[\overline{B}_t - \frac{B_t}{p_t^I K_{t+1}} \right] \geq 0, \tag{2.101}$$

---

[78] See Whited (1992). We could also formally introduce bankruptcy costs as well as a probability of default. However, in the event of bankruptcy the ownership of the firm would be transferred to creditors. See Bond and Meghir (1994).

$$\frac{\partial \mathcal{L}}{\partial \lambda_t^D} = (1 - \tau_t)(\Pi(K_t, h_t) - i_{t-1} B_{t-1} - \Gamma(B_{t-1}, K_t)) - p_t^I I_t$$

$$+ (1 - e_t) V_t^N + B_t - \left(1 - \pi_t^e\right) B_{t-1} - \overline{D} \geq 0, \qquad (2.102)$$

$$\frac{\partial \mathcal{L}}{\partial \lambda_t^N} = \left[V_t^N - \underline{V} \right] \geq 0, \qquad (2.103)$$

and $I_t \geq 0$, $B_t \geq 0$, $V_t^N \geq 0$, $\lambda_t^B \geq 0$, $\lambda_t^D \geq 0$, $\lambda_t^N \geq 0$, and $\frac{\partial \mathcal{L}}{\partial X_t} X_t = 0$ for $X_t = I_t, B_t, V_t^N, \lambda_t^B, \lambda_t^D, \lambda_t^N$. Using the envelope theorem we find the marginal value of debt, V_B, and of capital, V_K, respectively, as

$$V_B\left(K_t, B_{t-1}, h_{t+1}^F\right) = -\left(m + \lambda_t^D\right)\left[(1 - \tau_t)(i_{t-1} + \Gamma_B(B_{t-1}, K_t))\right.$$
$$\left. + \left(1 - \pi_t^e\right)\right] \qquad (2.104)$$

$$V_K\left(K_{t+1}, B_t, h_{t+1}^F\right) = \left(m + \lambda_{t+1}^D\right)(1 - \tau_{t+1})[\Pi_K(K_{t+1}, h_{t+1})$$
$$- \Gamma_K(B_t, K_{t+1})] + (1 - \delta) E_t \min \left[\left(m + \lambda_{t+1}^D\right)\right.$$
$$\left. \times p_{t+1}^I, \beta_{t+1} E_{t+1} V_K\left((1 - \delta)K_{t+1}, B_{t+1}, h_{t+2}^F\right)\right]. \qquad (2.105)$$

Assume that $\alpha_t \geq \alpha_t^H$ so that it is optimal to invest at t,[79] that is, $I_t > 0$, then

$$\left(m + \lambda_t^D\right) p_t^I = \beta_t E_t\left(m + \lambda_{t+1}^D\right)(1 - \tau_{t+1})(\Pi_K(K_{t+1}, h_{t+1})$$
$$- \Gamma_K(B_t, K_{t+1})) + \beta_t (1 - \delta) E_t \min \left[\left(m + \lambda_{t+1}^D\right)\right.$$
$$\left. \times p_{t+1}^I, \beta_{t+1} E_{t+1} V_K\left((1 - \delta)K_{t+1}, B_{t+1}, h_{t+2}^F\right)\right]. \qquad (2.106)$$

Let C_{Kt}^F be the marginal call option when there are financial constraints.

$$C_{Kt}^F\left(K_{t+1}, p_{t+1}^I\right) = \int_{\alpha_{t+1}^H}^{\infty} (1 - \delta)\left[-p_{t+1}^I\left(m + \lambda_{t+1}^D\right) + E_{t+1}\beta_{t+1}\right.$$
$$\left. \times V_K\left((1 - \delta)K_{t+1}, B_{t+1}, h_{t+2}^F\right)\right] dG^\alpha(\alpha_{t+1} \mid \alpha_t)$$
$$= (1 - \delta) E_t \max \left\{0, \beta E_{t+1} V_K((1 - \delta)K_{t+1}, h_{t+2}, h_{t+2}^k)\right.$$
$$\left. - p_{t+1}^I\left(m + \lambda_{t+1}^D\right)\right\} \geq 0. \qquad (2.107)$$

---

[79] In the model with financial constraints α_t^H is defined by

$$p_t^I = \beta \int_0^\infty V_K\left((1 - \delta)K_t, B_t, h_{t+1}^F\right) dG^\alpha\left(\alpha_{t+1} \mid \alpha_t^H\right).$$

However, α_t^H will depend not only on K_t but also on B_t and all other financial variables.

We can express (2.106) in terms of C_{Kt}^F as follows:

$$\left(m + \lambda_t^D\right)p_t^I + \beta_t C_{Kt}^F = \beta_t \left\{ E_t\left(m + \lambda_{t+1}^D\right)(1 - \tau_{t+1})(\Pi_K(K_{t+1}, h_{t+1})\right.$$
$$- \Gamma_K(B_t, K_{t+1})) + (1 - \delta)\beta_{t+1}E_{t+1}$$
$$\left. \times V_K\left((1 - \delta)K_{t+1}, B_{t+1}, h_{t+2}^F\right)\right\}. \quad (2.108)$$

Confronted by irreversibility and financial constraints, the firm chooses a level of investment so as to equate the marginal cost of investing including the loss of option value to the marginal value of an additional unit of capital. We observe that the firm's financial constraints need to be taken into account in the determination of the optimal level of investment. On the one hand, the presence of a constraint on the issuing of dividends at t increases the marginal cost of investing at t since it constrains the cash flows available for retained earnings which is the cheapest source of investment financing. *Ceteris paribus*, irreversible investment is lower as a result. Furthermore, the expectation of facing a binding constraint on dividends at $t + 1$ (that is, $E_t\lambda_{t+1}^D > 0$) will increase the likelihood of facing a corner solution at $t + 1$. The anticipation of more costly expandability will thus lower the value of waiting and the marginal loss of option value, C_{Kt}^F thus raising investment, *ceteris paribus*. The anticipation of being dividend constrained at $t + 1$ will also raise the expected marginal value of an additional unit of capital thus stimulating investment. Finally, investing has an additional benefit: it lowers the risk premium, Γ.[80]

To gain some further insight on the effect of imperfect capital markets on irreversible investment, we examine the optimality conditions for corporate

---

[80] The right-hand side may equivalently be expressed as the sum of Q_t which reflects the expected marginal value of capital if the firm never invests or disinvests from $t + 1$ onward and simply allows its capital stock to depreciate, and Υ_t which represents the increase in the expected marginal value of capital due to *future* marginal call options (or growth options) available to the firm. Both will reflect financial constraints. Alternatively, the optimality condition for investment can be expressed as:

$$\left(m + \lambda_t^D\right)p_t^I + \beta_t\Phi_t^F = \beta_t E_t\left(m + \lambda_{t+1}^D\right)(1 - \tau_{t+1})$$
$$\times (\Pi_K(K_{t+1}, \alpha_{t+1}, A_{t+1}, w_{t+1})$$
$$- \Gamma_K(B_t, K_{t+1})) + \beta_t(1 - \delta)E_t\left(m + \lambda_{t+1}^D\right)p_{t+1}^I,$$

where Φ_t^F, is a marginal risk premium due to an additional unit of investment under financial constraints. Φ_t^F is given by:

$$\Phi_t^F = (1 - \delta)E_t\left(m + \lambda_{t+1}^D\right)p_{t+1}^I - (1 - \delta)E_t \min\left[\left(m + \lambda_{t+1}^D\right)p_{t+1}^I,\right.$$
$$\left.\beta_{t+1}E_{t+1}V_K\left((1 - \delta)K_{t+1}, B_{t+1}, h_{t+2}^F\right)\right].$$

debt and share issues. Using (2.104) we can rewrite (2.99) for $B_t > 0$ as:

$$
\begin{aligned}
\frac{\partial \mathcal{L}}{\partial B_t} &= m + \lambda_t^D - \frac{\lambda_t^B}{p_t^I K_{t+1}} - \beta E_t\left(m + \lambda_{t+1}^D\right) \\
&\quad \times \left[(1 - \tau_{t+1})(i_t + \Gamma_B(B_t, K_{t+1})) + \left(1 - \pi_{t+1}^e\right)\right] \\
&= 0.
\end{aligned}
\tag{2.109}
$$

Furthermore, iff $V_t^N > 0$

$$
\lambda_t^N = -\left(m + \lambda_t^D\right)(1 - e_t) + (1 + \Omega_t).
\tag{2.110}
$$

We can identify several financial regimes in which the firm will find itself. First, there may be enough retained earnings to finance investment and for dividends to exceed the minimum ($D_t > \overline{D}$, $B_t = 0$, $V_t^N = 0$). Second, retained earnings may not suffice to finance investment and pay floor dividends. Investment is constrained by internal funds, but it is not optimal to issue new shares nor increase the debt. Firms are liquidity constrained so that a 'windfall increase' in retained earnings will raise investment ($D_t = \overline{D}$, $B_t = 0$, $V_t^N = 0$). Third, in view of its investment opportunities the firm's financial needs are larger so that investment is partly financed by borrowing up to the point where the firm is indifferent between one additional unit of debt and one additional unit of retention ($D_t = \overline{D}$, $B_t > 0$, $V_t^N = 0$). Fourth, if the firm's investment opportunities are greater still, funding by borrowing may become exhausted but it may still not be optimal to issue new equity. In this case the firm may become liquidity constrained so that a windfall increase in earnings will raise investment. Fifth, if the cost of borrowing rises sufficiently the firm may issue stocks to finance part of the increase in investment ($D_t = \overline{D}$, $B_t > 0$, $V_t^N > 0$). Typically, the firm will often use several modes of financing.

In this model, we observe that the firm's investment decision is characterised by two types of inaction zones: the first having to do with irreversibility and the second with financial constraints. For firms with high levels of retained earnings or net worth, actual investment behaviour is determined by the irreversibility constraint, uncertainty and the expectation of future financial constraints. For firms with lower levels of net worth, the cost of external finance varies inversely with the amount of net worth. We thus see the critical role of the firm's net worth, and of irreversibility in explaining investment.

To explore some additional implications for investment we make some simplifying assumptions. Suppose that τ_{t+1}, i_t and π_{t+1}^e are known with certainty and constant through time. Also, suppose that β is constant as well, and that $\Gamma_B = 0$. Let $\varkappa \equiv \beta_t[(1 - \tau_{t+1})(i_t + \Gamma_B(B_t, K_{t+1}) + (1 - \pi^e_{t+1})] \equiv \beta[(1 - \tau)(i + (1 - \pi^e)]$. Assume that $\varkappa < 1$. After recursive substitution we can solve (2.82) for λ^D_t as:

$$m + \lambda^D_t = E_t \left\{ \sum_{j=0}^{\infty} \varkappa^j \frac{\lambda^B_{t+j}}{p^I_{t+j} K_{t+1+j}} \right\}. \tag{2.111}$$

Hence, the shadow price of dividends, λ^D_t, reflects the sum of the expected future shadow prices of debt. The greater the expectation that the firm's debt constraint will bind in the future (that it will exceed its allowable debt to equity ratio) the greater the cost of the dividend constraint today and the greater the cost of investment today. Furthermore, the greater is the likelihood that investment will be constrained tomorrow. These effects will work to reduce current irreversible investment.

Financial constraints and asymmetric tax treatment
There is an inherent asymmetry in the corporate income tax structure such that firms' gains and losses do not receive the same treatment: when the firm has positive taxable income it must pay taxes immediately, whereas if it makes a loss and has negative taxable income, it does not receive an immediate tax refund at the corporate tax rate. Instead, the firm has the right to a partial carry-over (backward or forward) of losses. This carry-over provision is helpful in reducing the tax burden especially to firms making a temporary loss and expecting to make a profit in the next period. Nevertheless, the asymmetry in the tax system may discourage firms from making risky investments. Another asymmetry in the tax system concerns the treatment of different modes of financing. Thus for example, equity finance is not tax-deductible, while the interest expense incurred when issuing debt is deductible from taxable income. This differential tax treatment also affects firms' financing decisions. Furthermore, in the presence of irreversibility and of uncertainty about future demand conditions, it reduces the expected return on capital, since firms may have long periods of negative or positive profits because they are either reluctant to increase their capital stock for fear of having too much capital in the future, or unable to reduce their capital stock in view of the high costs involved.

In a model where firms face an irreversibility constraint, fixed operating costs, fixed costs of entry, output price uncertainty as well as a credit ceiling, Faig and Shum (1999) show that the asymmetry in the tax system affects both the level of investment of active firms and the entry decision of firms, and also affects their financing decisions. The asymmetry does not affect firms that are either highly profitable or highly unprofitable, but affects firms that have moderate profitability and face the probability of making a loss in the future. Such firms choose full debt financing, but unlike highly profitable firms, also face a binding constraint with respect to their debt ceiling. In this case firms have to be even more cautious in their investment decision since in the event of future losses, they may be unable to use full debt financing in the future and may have to resort to some equity financing. The desired capital stock of moderately profitable firms is lower under the asymmetric tax system than under the neutral symmetric system. The impact on the desired capital stock is larger the greater the degree of irreversibility faced by the firm.

An additional and much larger effect comes however through the entry decision of firms. In the presence of a non-deductible fixed entry cost, only the most profitable firms decide to enter, thus reducing the level of investment. Faig and Shum find that the asymmetry of the tax system has a quantitatively greater impact on investment through firms' entry decisions than through its impact on active firms.[81]

Empirical evidence
There exists a vast literature which attempts to test for the impact of financial constraints on investment within a cost-of-adjustment framework.[82] Empirical studies typically rely on firm-level panel data and find that investment is significantly correlated with changes in net worth and that the correlation is stronger for firms which are likely to face financial market imperfections. As explained by Hubbard (1998), these studies have been confronted with three challenges: identifying a proxy for investment opportunities, typically Q; finding sorting criteria which are related to the firm's information problems such as firm size or dividend policy so as to discriminate between constrained and unconstrained firms; and identifying a proxy for net worth or changes in net worth which is uncorrelated with investment opportunities. Cash flow is typically used as an imperfect proxy for the firm's net worth.[83] Studies usually classify firms in the panel according to whether they are constrained or unconstrained. However, as Hubbard argues, 'it is more plausible that firms switch between "constrained" and

---

[81] Faig and Shum (1999) caution that a thorough investigation of these issues should be conducted in a general equilibrium framework.
[82] See Chirinko (1993) and Hubbard (1998) for surveys.
[83] Cash flow reflects accounting decisions thus reducing the correlation with net worth.

"unconstrained" regimes depending upon shifts in investment opportunities and the availability of internal or external financing'.

Scaramozzino (1997) considers a model of irreversible investment with
financial constraints and quadratic costs of adjustment. He adopts Q-theory
and investigates the effects of irreversibility for firms who are likely to be
financially constrained using a British company panel. In his model there
are two departures from the costs-of-adjustment model with Q-theory:
the irreversibility constraint and financial constraint. Thus, a regression of
investment on Q would be misspecified. He divides the sample into firms
below and above median dividend payout ratios and those below and above
investment ratios.[84] For firms whose investment ratio is below the median
Q-theory performs poorly, namely the coefficient on Q has the wrong sign
and the explanatory variables are not jointly significant. For firms whose
dividend to market value ratio is below the median, the coefficient on
Q is of the right sign but is not significant. Finally, his results confirm
that for firms which have either below-median dividends or below-median
investment and are constrained on one account, the Q-model performs
well, in particular with respect to the size and significance of the coefficient
on Q in the investment regression.

Further work is needed to explore the empirical implications of financial
constraints when investment is irreversible. Finally, tests need to be devised
to discriminate between the predictions of the irreversibility of investment
and financial constraints.[85]

4.9 The long-run effects of irreversibility

So far we have considered the short-run impact of irreversibility and uncertainty. Abel and Eberly (1999) have analysed the long-run effect of output
price risk on the expected long-run capital stock. In addition to the short-
run effect of risk or uncertainty in the presence of irreversibility (termed a
'user cost effect' or 'hurdle rate effect'), they also identify a 'hangover effect'
which occurs when a firm finds itself with too much capital. This arises
because in states of low demand, a firm may wish to sell capital but under
irreversibility, the only way it can dispose of its stock of capital is by letting
it depreciate. Thus, it may turn out that the expected long-run capital stock
is higher under irreversibility compared to reversibility.

---

[84] Hubbard, Kashyap and Whited (1995) also split the sample according to the payout ratio.
[85] Hubbard suggests examining investment in industries characterised by irreversibility to see if hurdle
rates vary according to the predictions of theories of imperfect financial markets and similarly for
industries characterised by well-functioning resale markets and where investment is not irreversible.

We will compare the long-run optimal capital stocks under irreversibility and reversibility by making the following simplifying assumptions: (1) the demand shock, α_t follows a geometric Brownian motion with growth rate of ω; (2) the capital stock does not depreciate, that is, $\delta = 0$; (3) the discount factor, $\beta = (1 + r)$; (4) the price of capital and tax rates are constant over time; (5) there are no taxes; (6) the wage rate is constant; (7) the production function is $F(K_t, L_t) = L_t^{1-\eta} K_t^{\eta}$ has CRS. As a result, the Jorgensonian frictionless cost of capital, c, reduces to $c = rp^k$ and the short-run profit function, Π, reduces to: $\Pi = (1 - \mu)^{-1} v \alpha_t^{\mu} K_t^{1-\mu}$ where $\mu = [\eta(1 + \varepsilon) - \varepsilon]^{-1} > 0$ and $v > 0$.

For the irreversible investment model under uncertainty, Abel and Eberly (1999) find the user cost of capital, c^I, to be:

$$c^I = (1 - \mu/\varsigma)rp^k, \qquad (2.112)$$

where ς is the negative root of a fundamental quadratic equation. Assume $\alpha_0 = 1$ and that the growth rate of α_t is ω. The capital stock at t and the expected capital stock as of time 0 can readily be found as:

$$K_t^I = \left(\frac{c^I}{v}\right)^{-1/\mu} \max_{s \leq t} \alpha_s \qquad (2.113)$$

$$E_0 K_t^I = \left(\frac{c^I}{v}\right)^{-1/\mu} E\left\{ \max_{s \leq t} \alpha_s \,|\, \alpha_0 = 1 \right\}. \qquad (2.114)$$

Assuming that the frictionless capital stock, K_t^f, is chosen under certainty, the capital stock at time t for the firm facing reversible investment can be obtained as:

$$K_t^f = \left(\frac{c}{v}\right)^{-1/\mu} [(\alpha_t)^{\mu}]^{\frac{1}{\mu}}. \qquad (2.115)$$

The expectation as of time 0 of K_t^R can be obtained as:

$$E_0 K_t^f = \left(\frac{c}{v}\right)^{-1/\mu} E(\alpha_t \,|\, \alpha_0 = 1). \qquad (2.116)$$

Since

$$E(\alpha_t \,|\, \alpha_0 = 1) = e^{\omega t}. \qquad (2.117)$$

A comparison of the two expected capital stocks can be readily achieved. To evaluate the effect of irreversibility on the long-run expected capital stock, we can take the ratios of $E_0(K_{t+1}^I)$ and $E_0(K_{t+1}^f)$ as

$$\frac{E_0(K_t^I)}{E_0(K_t^f)} = D \times H(t), \qquad (2.118)$$

where

$$D = \left(\frac{c^I}{c}\right)^{-\frac{1}{\mu}} < 1,$$

and

$$H(t) \equiv \frac{E\{\max_{0 \leq s \leq t} \alpha_s \mid \alpha_0 = 1\}}{E[\alpha_t \mid \alpha_0 = 1]} \geq 1.$$

The first term, D, reflects the 'user cost effect' of irreversibility on the expected long-run capital stock. Since irreversibility increases the user cost relative to the frictionless case, the effect of irreversibility through the user cost is to depress the expected long-run capital stock. The second term, $H(t)$, introduces a second effect of irreversibility, which Abel and Eberly (1999) call the 'hangover effect'. Since the historical peak of the demand shock α_s is at least as large as the current value, the hangover effect tends to increase the long-run optimal capital stock. Thus, depending on which effect dominates, irreversibility may decrease or increase the long-run optimal capital stock relative to the situation in which investment is fully reversible.

Abel and Eberly show that greater uncertainty strengthens both the user cost effect and the hangover effect. They find that increased uncertainty raises the expected capital stock under irreversibility but it can raise it even more under reversibility. They show that a high growth rate of demand lowers the expected capital stock under irreversibility relative to reversibility. Finally, a low interest rate, a high capital share in output and a high elasticity of demand also lower the expected capital stock under irreversibility relative to reversibility.

4.10 Learning

The literature on investment behaviour has typically abstracted from the role of learning and subjective uncertainty and has focused on the implications of risk. Yet whenever the environment of the firm changes, due, for example, to shifts in demand, productivity or cost of investing, tax policy reform or other forms of regime shifts, the firm may not know with certainty the distributions of the random variables that affect its investment decisions. Hence, it may face additional subjective uncertainty. This distinction between objective and subjective uncertainty was stressed by Frank Knight.

There are many reasons to believe that subjective uncertainty is important. The firm's environment is continuously changing. The firm may be subject to shifts in demand owing to changes in tastes for particular products (for example, changes in fashion) or to phases of the business cycle (recessions and booms). The firm may be subject to productivity improvements or negative productivity shocks. It may also face shifts in the cost of investing due to technological discoveries in the manufacturing of new capital equipment. However, the firm may not know with certainty the new distribution of demand, productivity or costs, nor for how long they will last.

Arrow and Fisher (1974), Bernanke (1983), Cukierman (1980) and Henry (1974), analyse the investment problem of a firm facing a number of alternative irreversible investment projects in a context where the firm acquires information through time and learns about the expected returns on the projects it is considering. In these analyses all uncertainty is subjective. Given that its investment decisions are irreversible, there is an incentive for the firm to wait before investing in order to acquire more information and reduce the extent of uncertainty about the returns. There is thus an option value to waiting which, however, vanishes once learning is complete. At that point in time, the firm chooses a project and invests. Thus, investment is akin to an optimal stopping problem. There is no gradual adjustment of the capital stock to its desired level. By contrast, in the presence of objective uncertainty, the option value of waiting is always kept alive by the riskiness of the environment. M. Demers (1985, 1991) introduces both subjective and objective uncertainty, and analyses the investment decision at both the intensive and extensive margins – that is, the decision of the firm as to whether or not to invest as well as the quantity invested. The combination of objective and subjective uncertainty together with irreversibility leads to a gradual adjustment of investment, and the option value of waiting does not vanish even when learning is complete, due to the presence of objective uncertainty.

In what follows, we examine the impact of learning behaviour (without experimentation) on investment decisions when firms follow a Bayesian learning process. The learning model allows us to incorporate the effects of firms' prior beliefs and of imperfect information explicitly into the dynamics of the investment process. We then examine other learning models including those based on experimentation.

Informational structure and learning dynamics

In principle, the firm may face simultaneously subjective uncertainty with respect to the state of demand, productivity, the corporate tax rate, the ITC and the cost of investing. To describe the informational structure of the model and the implication of learning we will focus on a single source of subjective uncertainty, namely the state of demand. The firm knows the possible states of demand but does not know with certainty which one is the true state. Let $\overline{A} \equiv \{\overline{\alpha}_1, \ldots, \overline{\alpha}_n\}$ be the set of possible states. The firm has a prior probability distribution about the true state $\overline{\alpha}$ denoted by Ψ^0, where $\Psi^0 = [\psi_1^0, \ldots, \psi_n^0]$, $\psi_i^0 > 0$, $i = 1, \ldots, n$, and $\sum_{i=1}^n \psi_i^0 = 1$; ψ_i^0 is the prior probability that $\overline{\alpha} = \overline{\alpha}_i$, $i = 1, \ldots, n$.

Each period the firm observes the realisation of α_t and the realisation of a non-price signal b_t which is informative about $\overline{\alpha}$ and which may consist of various pieces of information such as the monetary growth rate, financial surveys, etc. We denote by H^α the set of all possible signals $h_t^\alpha \equiv (\alpha_t, b_t)$.

Letting $f_j(x_t | \overline{\alpha}_i)$, $j = 1, 2$, be the density of x_t, conditional on $\overline{\alpha}_i$ being the true state, $x_t = \alpha_t, b_t$, we can define $\lambda(h_t^\alpha | \overline{\alpha}_i) \equiv f_1(\alpha_t | \overline{\alpha}_i) f_2(b_t | \overline{\alpha}_i)$ as the likelihood of observing h_t^α given that the true state is $\overline{\alpha}_i$. The firm revises its prior probability distribution Ψ^0, by applying Bayes' law. That is

$$\psi_i^t = \frac{\lambda(h_t^\alpha | \overline{\alpha}_i) \psi_i^{t-1}}{\sum_{j=1}^n \lambda(h_t^\alpha | \overline{\alpha}_j) \psi_j^{t-1}} \qquad h_t^\alpha \in H^\alpha, \quad i = 1, \ldots, n, \quad t = 1, 2, \ldots$$

(2.119)

$\Psi^t(h_t^\alpha) = [\psi_1^t(h_t^\alpha), \ldots, \psi_n^t(h_t^\alpha)]$ represents the firm's state of information at time t. For all t, $\Psi^t \in D(\overline{A})$ is the set of all probability distributions on $\overline{A}$. The evolution of the information state can be expressed as

$$\Psi^t(h_t^\alpha) = g(\Psi^{t-1}, h_t^\alpha),$$

(2.120)

where g denotes the law of motion of the information state and updating according to Bayes' law. Note that g does not have a time subscript since the revision process is time-invariant. Furthermore, the evolution of the information state has the Markov property since the past information states $\Psi^1, \ldots, \Psi^{t-2}$ are irrelevant to the revision process at time t as long as Ψ^{t-1} is known. In other words, Ψ^{t-1} completely describes the state of information at time $t - 1$. Let $h_t \equiv (\alpha_t, A_t, w_t)$. The firm solves

$$
\max_{\{I_t\}_{t=1}^{\infty}} \left\{ \Pi(K_1, h_1) - p_1^k I_1 \right.
$$
$$
\left. + \sum_{t=2}^{\infty} \beta^{t-1} \int_{H^{\alpha\, t-1}} \left[\Pi(K_t, h_t) - p_t^k I_t \right] \Theta\left(h_2^{\alpha t} \mid \Psi^1\right) dh_2^{\alpha t} \right\} \quad (2.121)
$$

subject to (2.29), (2.51), (2.120), K_1 and Ψ^1 given, where $0 < \beta < 1$ is the discount factor and $\Theta(h_2^{\alpha t} | \Psi^1)$ is the predictive density of the sequence of observations $h_2^{\alpha t}$ defined as $h_2^{\alpha t} \equiv \{h_2^{\alpha}, h_3^{\alpha}, \ldots, h_t^{\alpha}\}$. Thus, the firm chooses a sequence of strategies for future investment plans $\{I_t\}_{t=1}^{\infty}$ which specify future investment as a function of the state of information Ψ^t and the capital stock K_t to maximise the expected present value of future net cash flows conditional on the state of information, subject to the irreversibility constraint and the laws of motion for the capital stock and the state of information, K_1, Ψ^1 given. Let E_t denote the expectation operator using the predictive density $\Theta(h_{t+1}^{\alpha} | \Psi^t)$. Using dynamic programming, we can express the problem recursively as

$$
V\left(K_t, \Psi^t, h_t, p_t^k\right) = \max_{I_t} \left\{ \Pi(K_t, h_t) - p_t^k I_t \right.
$$
$$
\left. + \beta E_t V\left(K_{t+1}, \Psi^{t+1}\left(h_{t+1}^{\alpha}\right), h_{t+1}, p_{t+1}^k\right) \right\} \quad (2.122)
$$

subject to (2.29), (2.51), (2.120), K_t, Ψ^t given. The first-order necessary and sufficient condition for the optimisation problem at time t are

$$
-p_t^k + \beta E_t V_K\left(K_{t+1}, \Psi^{t+1}\left(h_{t+1}^{\alpha}\right), h_{t+1}, p_{t+1}^k\right) = 0 \quad \text{if } I_t^* > 0
$$
$$
\leq 0 \quad \text{if } I_t^* = 0.
$$
$$
(2.123)
$$

Using the envelope theorem, the shadow value of capital can be expressed as

$$
V_K\left(K_{t+1}, \Psi^{t+1}\left(h_{t+1}^{\alpha}\right), h_{t+1}, p_{t+1}^k\right)
$$
$$
= \Pi_K(K_{t+1}, h_{t+1}) + (1 - \delta) \min\left[p_{t+1}^k, \beta E_{t+1} V_K \right.
$$
$$
\left. \times \left((1 - \delta) K_{t+1}, g\left(\Psi^{t+1}, h_{t+2}^{\alpha}\right), h_{t+2}, p_{t+2}^k\right)\right]. \quad (2.124)
$$

Also, let:

$$
\Phi_t^L = (1 - \delta) \left\{ E_t p_{t+1}^k - E_t \min\left[p_{t+1}^k, \beta E_{t+1} V_K \right.\right.
$$
$$
\left.\left. \times \left((1 - \delta) K_{t+1}, g\left(\Psi^{t+1}, h_{t+2}^{\alpha}\right), h_{t+2}, p_{t+2}^k\right)\right]\right\}. \quad (2.125)
$$

Assume that an interior solution obtains at t. After substituting for V_K and for $\beta = (1 + r)^{-1}$, (2.123) can be rearranged as:

$$c_t + \Phi_t^L = E_t \Pi_K(K_{t+1}, h_{t+1}). \tag{2.126}$$

The right-hand side of (2.126) is the marginal benefit of investing an additional unit. The left-hand side is the total cost of investing which is the sum of the Jorgensonian cost of capital and of a time-varying marginal risk premium when the firm invests an additional unit. In a model with learning, this opportunity cost of investing varies through time with the firm's state of information.[86]

We can alternatively present the optimality condition with the marginal call option, C_{Kt}^L. Assume that $\alpha_t \geq \alpha_t^H$ so that $I_t > 0$:[87]

$$
\begin{aligned}
p_t^k &+ \beta C_{Kt}^L\left(K_{t+1}, p_{t+1}^k\right) \\
&= \beta E_t\left\{\Pi_K(K_{t+1}, h_{t+1}) + \beta(1 - \delta)\right. \\
&\quad \left. \times E_{t+1} V_K\left((1 - \delta)K_{t+1}, g\left(\Psi^{t+1}, h_{t+2}^\alpha\right), h_{t+2}, p_{t+2}^k\right)\right\} \\
&\equiv Q_t + \Upsilon_t,
\end{aligned} \tag{2.127}
$$

where C_K is as defined earlier except that it varies with the firm's state of subjective uncertainty and learning. Similarly, Q_t and the gain in future value due to future call or growth options, Υ_t, also embody the learning process.[88]

In a model of a perfectly competitive firm where the firm has a decreasing returns to scale production function and faces uncertainty with respect to demand, M. Demers (1985, 1991) shows that irreversibility, subjective uncertainty and learning provide an alternative explanation of the gradual adjustment of the capital stock over time towards the desired level which is defined as the capital stock which is optimal given full knowledge of the distribution of demand. In Altug, Demers and Demers (1999), irreversibility in conjunction with the anticipation of receiving information and learning about the permanent level of the cost of investing also leads to a gradual adjustment of the capital stock towards the desired level, where the latter is defined as the stock that the firm would choose if it knew the true value of the state of costs, $\overline{p}^k$.[89]

[86] Φ_t^L can be interpreted as the 'cost-of-adjustment' term which arises *endogenously*. Note that c_t is not to be confused with the cost of capital which accounts for irreversibility, c_t^H.

[87] α_t^H is defined as in (2.34) except that with learning E_t denotes that expectation is taken with respect to the predictive density, $\Theta(h_{t+1}^\alpha \mid \Psi^t)$.

[88] We could equivalently express the optimality of investment in terms of a cost of capital, c_t^H which accounts for irreversibility (see below).

[89] For a proof and discussion of convergence to the steady state, see Altug, Demers and Demers (1999).

The impact of greater information

Now, suppose that the firm anticipates receiving greater non-price information which helps it form more precise estimates of the unknown state
of demand. What are the implications for irreversible investment? We use
Blackwell's (1951) notion of greater information. We say that an experiment $\widehat{b}_t$ is more informative than another experiment b_t if there exists a
positive stochastic transformation $\eta(b_t, \widehat{b}_t)$ defined on $B \times \widehat{B}$ such that

$$\lambda(b_t|\overline{\alpha}) = \int_{\widehat{B}} \eta(b_t, \widehat{b}_t)\widehat{\lambda}(\widehat{b}_t|\overline{\alpha})d\widehat{b}_t, \quad \overline{\alpha} \in \overline{A}, b_t \in B$$

and $\int_B \eta(b_t, \widehat{b}_t)db_t = 1$ for all $\widehat{b}_t \in \widehat{B}$ where $\eta(b_t, \widehat{b}_t)$ does not depend on
the unknown $\overline{\alpha}$. If greater information in the Blackwell sense is anticipated
in the future, for example, if some current uncertainty about the impact of
consumer confidence on the distribution of the state of demand is expected
to be resolved in the future, the marginal risk premium will rise and current
investment will fall as the firm adopts a wait and see attitude.

The impact of greater risk

Altug, Demers and Demers (1999) assume that the price of capital p_t^k
is log-normally distributed so that $\log(p_t^k) = \overline{p}^k + u_{kt}$ follows a normal
distribution with mean an $\overline{p}^k$ and variance σ_k^2. In this specification, the
firm does not know with certainty which value $\overline{p}^k$ takes on. However, the
firm has a uniform prior probability distribution about the true state $\overline{p}^k$.

Altug, Demers and Demers examine the impact of changes in σ_k^2. In a
learning model the latter involves a risk as well as an information effect.
Adopting a uniform prior they show that even if the transitory shocks to the
price of capital are independently and identically distributed, the impact
of doubling σ_k^2 is to induce a dramatic decline in investment expenditures,
and a much greater frequency with which firms delay current investment:
an 85.7 per cent increase in the incidence of the binding irreversibility
constraint, and a 68.6 per cent reduction in the average level of investment.
Even with an informative prior, the decline in total investment is still very
substantial. In contrast, in a model without learning the same increase in
risk elicits only a 2 per cent increase in the incidence of a binding constraint
and a 10 per cent fall in investment. Taken together, the results of Altug,
Demers and Demers (1999) suggest that policies that are aimed at reducing
subjective uncertainty will have a greater impact in increasing investment
than policies that are aimed at reducing the cyclical variation in the price
of capital or other components of the costs of investing.

The impact of changes in prior beliefs

Altug, Demers, and Demers (1999) examine the impact of optimism and pessimism by firms on their investment decisions. They model optimism and pessimism as prior distributions that place most mass on the lowest and highest values of the price of capital, respectively. They compare these scenarios with one in which the firm has an informative prior, modelled as one which puts the most mass on the average value of the price of capital. They find when the firm overestimates the costs of investing, the noisy observations that it receives on the permanent component of the price of capital tend to reinforce its prior beliefs, and it refrains from investing compared to the case in which it has an informative prior. By contrast, when the firm underestimates the costs of investing, investment actually falls compared to the case in which it overestimates them.[90] Thus, changes in the prior beliefs of firms may have significant effects on their investment behaviour.

Convergence to the desired capital stock

A learning model permits the following distinction between the actual and the desired capital stock. The desired capital stock is the capital stock that would be optimally chosen by a firm that knows the true state of the world. By contrast, the actual capital stock is the capital stock that would be optimally chosen by a firm on the basis of its posterior beliefs about the true state. In what follows, we provide a discussion of convergence to the steady state for the model with learning.

First, suppose that the only source of uncertainty is the state of demand, α_t. Assume that firms do not know the permanent component of α_t and must learn about it through a Bayesian learning process. We define $\alpha_t = \bar{\alpha} + u_{\alpha,t}$, where $u_{\alpha,t}$ is IID. Now the capital stock follows the law of motion $K_{t+1} = (1 - \delta)K_t + I(K_t, \Psi^t) \equiv \gamma(K, \Psi^t)$. First, it can be shown that the firm's state of information, Ψ^t, will converge almost surely to a vector Ψ^* which assigns probability one to the true state of demand. In this case, K_{t+1} converges to K^*, where K^* is the fixed point of $\gamma(K^*, \Psi^*) = K^*$, since γ is a contraction mapping with modulus less than $(1 - \delta)$. Next, suppose that Ψ^t is in an neighbourhood of Ψ^*, the joint convergence of K_{t+1} and Ψ^t to K^* and Ψ^* follow since γ is a continuous function of (K_t, Ψ^t). Thus, once learning is complete and the true state of demand $\bar{\alpha}$ is known with certainty, the firm's capital stock reaches the desired level.

---

[90] This occurs because the subjective distribution which underestimates the true state has a lower subjective mean than the one which overestimates the true state.

Since the state of demand does not appear as a state variable in the firm's problem when it follows an IID process, the long-run desired capital stock is a constant that does not vary with the state of demand.

If the source of subjective uncertainty in the firm's problem arises from the costs of investing, the desired capital stock is stochastic.[91] Following the analysis above, suppose that the price of capital can be expressed as the sum of an unknown permanent component and a transitory component as $p_{k,t} = \overline{p}^k + u_{k,t}$ where $u_{k,t}$ is IID. The firm's desired stock of capital is the capital stock achieved by the firm when learning is complete and the firm's state of information has converged to a vector Ψ^* which assigns probability one to the true state of costs $\overline{p}^k$. In view of cost uncertainty, the long-run capital stock is no longer a constant and the vector (K^*, Ψ^*) is an element of the ergodic set $\Gamma \equiv \{(K, \Psi) \mid K \in [K^l, K^h], \Psi = \Psi^*\}$ where $\underline{u}_k$ and $\overline{u}_k$ are, respectively, the lower and upper bounds of $u_{k,t}$.[92] Define the vector $s_{t+1} = [K_{t+1}, \Psi^t]$. The law of motion for s_{t+1} can be expressed as $s_{t+1} = \Phi(s_t, h_t)$ where Φ is continuous in s_t for all h_t and is measurable with respect to the σ-algebra of H for all s_t. As a result, one obtains a transition probability on the state space, which induces a Markov operator $\mathcal{T} : \mathcal{C}(\mathcal{S}) \to \mathcal{C}(\mathcal{S})$. By demonstrating that the adjoint operator $\mathcal{T}^*$ of $\mathcal{T}$, which maps probability measures into probability measures, satisfies the properties of irreducibility, equi-continuity and quasi-compactness, one can conclude that there exists a unique steady-state measure μ^* and that convergence to the steady state will take place.[93]

Other learning models

If the objective uncertainty in the model involves regime shifts (i.e. the underlying objective distribution of the random variables is itself subject to change), then subjective uncertainty will also persist or be renewed by the regime shift. Thus, for example, an economy may be subject to regime shifts due to political risk, structural change or changes in policy. In this context, subjective uncertainty is continuously renewed and the subjective uncertainty component of the option value of waiting is always present.

---

[91] Alternatively, if the source of uncertainty is the state of demand and the latter follows a Markov process, the desired capital stock will also be stochastic.

[92] K^l and K^h solve

$$\overline{p}^k + \overline{u}_k = \beta E V_K((1 - \delta)K + I(K, \Psi^*, \overline{p}^k + \overline{u}_k))$$
$$\overline{p}^k + \underline{u}_k = \beta E V_K((1 - \delta)K + I(K, \Psi^*, \overline{p}^k + \underline{u}_k)).$$

[93] For a proof of the convergence to the steady state for this case, see Altug, Demers and Demers (1999).

This idea is explored in Altug, Demers and Demers (2000) in an analysis of political risk. In this case, investors may not know with certainty the distributions characterising the state of demand or the costs of investing in the different regimes, but may form beliefs about various moments on the basis of socio-economic variables.[94]

Learning may also have important implications in the context of tax policy. A firm that is faced with tax reform (a regime shift) may not know with certainty whether the tax reform that is enacted is permanent. It may also be unsure with respect to the exact nature of the tax reform. It therefore forms subjective beliefs about the tax policy parameters which it subsequently revises as new information becomes available. As emphasised by Judd (1987) the 'anticipation effect' and duration (permanent versus transitory) of investment tax credits have a particularly strong impact on investment. Cummins, Hassett and Hubbard (1994, 1996) have stressed that the net return to investing typically depends on 'firms' beliefs about the likelihood and significance of tax reforms,' which firms revise on the basis of economic and political indicators. Altug, Demers and Demers (2002a) examine these issues in a model of tax policy.

Some authors have also considered learning by experimentation (also referred to as 'endogenous learning' and 'Bayesian learning-by-doing') in the context of irreversible investment. In this case, economic agents who face uncertain payoffs can by their actions (say, by investing) affect the rate at which learning takes place. Their investment decisions reveal relevant information which helps them revise their expectations about their payoffs. In this case we have 'endogenous learning.' In this framework, the agent chooses the action that achieves two simultaneous goals: maximising the payoff and yielding the maximum information.[95] In general, this leads to optimal actions that differ from the ones that apply in an analogous problem with an uncertain payoff, but where the action taken by the agent does not affect the information stream.

Zeira (1987) analyses the choice of the capital stock by a perfectly competitive firm that faces irreversibility and does not know with certainty

---

[94] In a related analysis, Brock and Durlauf (2001) argue that a 'robust' decision-theoretic approach that allows for model uncertainty can be used to relax many of the implausible assumptions that underlie the current literature on the empirics of growth. They employ a Bayesian Model Averaging approach that permits uncertainty regarding the appropriate theoretical model and heterogeneity uncertainty arising from differences in the historical experience of the countries under study.

[95] See Grossman, Khilstrom and Mirman (1977). Whenever the economic agents' actions affect the information on the basis of which beliefs are revised, learning will be complete, i.e. lead to the true distribution of the unknown variable, only under restrictive assumptions. Thus, in some instances learning may never be complete. See Aghion *et al.* (1991) for a more general analysis of this point.

its optimal desired capital stock (and hence its production function). The firm has prior beliefs about the optimal capital stock, and revises these beliefs after observing the realisation of output each period. Hence, each period, the firm chooses the optimal amount of capital to maximise its anticipated payoff as well as to generate information about the unknown optimal capital stock. Note that there is only subjective uncertainty and no objective uncertainty in this model. Once learning is complete, the firm knows its true desired capital stock. However, since increasing the capital stock also generates information, the adjustment of the capital stock to its desired level will be gradual even though adjustment costs are linear and there is only subjective uncertainty.

Rob (1991) analyses a similar problem in the context of a multi-agent framework. He considers a perfectly competitive industry with sequential entry. There is a constant returns to scale technology and firms face delays and substantial costs to disinvesting (i.e. investment is at least partially irreversible). There are linear adjustment costs to investment. There is a fixed entry cost in the form of payment for a piece of machinery that is needed to produce output. Owing to irreversibility, part of that investment is a sunk cost. There is also a proportional variable cost of operating the machinery. Potential entrants must decide whether to invest (i.e. enter) or not in the face of uncertainty about the size of the market and the future demand for their product. They revise their expectations by observing the equilibrium outcome of the actions of the current incumbents. Thus the incumbents generate an information externality by their actions. (Hence there is a divergence between the private and social optimum.) The equilibrium outcome is not always fully revealing. Since investment is partially irreversible and there are sunk costs, it is costly to enter if the market limit has been reached, and the prospective entrants will wait to have more information. Rob (1991) shows that the adjustment of productive capacity occurs *gradually* through free entry and exit of firms into the industry.[96]

---

[96] Caplin and Leahy (1993) analyse a similar problem in a general equilibrium framework. We discuss their contribution below in the context of general equilibrium models. The importance of learning for economic behaviour in general equilibrium models has been investigated in many different contexts. Miller (1984) studies a dynamic model of job matching and occupational choice in which there is Bayesian learning about the unknown job match parameter. F. Demers (1985) shows how lack of confidence, underestimation and overestimation of productivity and monetary shocks lead to cyclical effects and that Bayesian learning leads to a propagation of shocks in an equilibrium model of business cycles. Bertocchi and Wang (1996) introduce Bayesian learning into a growth model with overlapping generations and show that learning about the technological parameters may not only affect capital accumulation in the transition but also its stationary long-run value.

4.11 Testing the irreversibility model and testing for the impact of uncertainty

In this section we survey empirical studies with respect to tests of the irreversibility model and tests of the impact of uncertainty on irreversible investment.

There have been numerous tests of the irreversible investment model under uncertainty.[97] A number of empirical studies have focused on the behaviour of hurdle rates or thresholds at which investment will occur. For a cross-section of thirty countries Pindyck and Solimano (1993) calculate a measure of the marginal profitability of capital, for a Cobb–Douglas technology and use the volatility of this measure as a proxy for uncertainty together with its extreme values for the threshold at which investment will be triggered. Using panel regressions of the investment share on the mean and standard deviation of the change in the marginal profitability of capital, they find a significant negative relationship between the investment ratio and volatility for the LDCs but not for the OECD countries.

Caballero and Pindyck (1996) argue that a test of their irreversibility model of industry equilibrium should be based on the trigger point U at which firms enter or expand their productive capacity. When uncertainty increases the trigger point U rises. Thus, tests of the irreversibility model and of the impact of uncertainty should be based on U. However, U cannot be observed directly. Nevertheless, it is possible to estimate the marginal profitability of capital up to a scale factor, conditional on a production function and market structure as a proxy for U.

Caballero and Pindyck (1996) assume a Cobb–Douglas production function and calculate the marginal profitability of capital, Π_K which is the value of output for an average productive unit, B_t. For each of the industries they use data on real output, real inputs of capital, materials and labour and the corresponding price deflators. They obtain a time series for $\log B_t$ for the period 1958–86 for two-digit industries, b_{2t}, and for four-digit industries, b_{4t}. They calculate the sample standard deviation for the first series as a measure of aggregate uncertainty and for the second series as a measure of aggregate and idiosyncratic uncertainty. They then use these standard deviations to ascertain the impact of uncertainty on $\log B_t$, the proxy used for the trigger. They find a sizable effect of uncertainty.

Patillo (1998) uses a panel of manufacturing firms for Ghana from 1994–5 where questions were asked to detect entrepreneurial perceptions of uncertainty. In the data set, one half of the firms do not invest in a

---

[97] For recent reviews of the empirical investment literature, see Carruth, Dickerson and Henley (2000).

year. When firms invest the measured marginal revenue product of capital is equal to the trigger. She exploits this information to estimate the determinants of the trigger, including measures of uncertainty. She proceeds in three steps. First, she estimates a reduced form probit of the decision to invest or not; second, she runs a selection bias corrected regression for Π_K which conditional on positive investment, is equal to the trigger; third, she estimates a structural probit to test for significance. She finds that greater uncertainty raises the hurdle rate and that uncertainty has a negative effect on irreversible investment.

Harchaoui and Lasserre (2001) test the options model of investment for Canadian copper mines. They circumvent the problems due to the unobservability of trigger prices by using option theory to derive the value of capacity investment projects (the option to invest) which in turn allows them to calculate the investment threshold. Their results support the irreversibility model.

A number of studies have analysed the relationship between uncertainty and investment more generally. Leahy and Whited (1996) study the relationship between uncertainty and investment in a panel study using Compustat data. They regress the firm's investment to capital ratio on Q and a measure of uncertainty, defined as the variance of the daily stock price, and do not obtain significant results. However, they also find that the variance has a negative and statistically significant effect on Q, thus indicating an indirect effect on investment. This suggests that irreversibility constitutes the explanation for this relationship.

Guiso and Parigi (1999) find a negative relationship between firms' perceptions of future product demand and irreversible investment based on a cross-section of Italian manufacturing firms. They use different indicators such as the standard deviation of future demand scaled by the capital stock or the variance of the rate of growth of demand. They also show that uncertainty affects investment independently of financial constraints such as cash flows. Finally, they find a stronger negative effect of uncertainty for firms with high market power and high irreversibility.

Aizenman and Marion (1999) examine the relationship between private and public investment and various measures of volatility for over forty developing countries. They find that there is a negative impact of uncertainty and volatility on private investment in developing countries. Darby et al. (1999) analyse an open economy irreversible investment model that allows for disinvestment and the effects of exchange-rate misalignment. In their empirical analysis, they find that both misalignment and volatility of the exchange rate have significant negative impact on investment. Their empirical analysis is conducted using aggregate investment data for four European countries for the 1980s and 1990s. Using a 4-digit panel of foreign direct investment (FDI) flows, Campa (1993) finds a negative relationship between exchange-rate volatility and (FDI), especially for Japanese foreign direct investment.

Abel and Eberly (1994) develop a Q-model of investment when there are flow fixed costs, costly irreversibility and convex adjustment costs. As a result investment will respond to changes in Q in a non-linear way. In particular, investment may not respond to changes in Q for some range of values of Q. Barnett and Sakellaris (1998) provides an empirical test of this model using firm-level data on publicly traded corporations (Compustat) between 1960 and 1987. They find evidence that the elasticity of investment with respect to Q is highly variable thus implying a non-linear relationship between Q and investment. Abel and Eberly (1996) use Compustat data from 1974 to 1993 to estimate investment and disinvestment. The results support a non-linear (concave) cost-of-investment function so that the response of investment to Q is monotonically declining. They also show that the non-linear model tracks investment better than the quadratic costs-of-adjustment model. Finally, Abel and Eberly (1996) consider a model with fixed costs and heterogeneity with respect to the capital stock. In the latter case, the firm decides which type of capital goods to purchase (extensive margin) and how much to buy (the intensive margin). The empirical evidence further supports non-linearities. Eberly (1997) estimates an asymmetric adjustment cost model for the period 1981–94 using a company-level international comparative panel data set for eleven countries. She finds a significant role for non-linearities for all but two of the countries.

5 AGGREGATE INVESTMENT

Up to now, we have conducted our analysis in terms of the investment decision of the single firm, or at times, in terms of the representative firm. Most of the literature on investment analysed the firm's investment decision as a proxy for explaining the behaviour of aggregate investment. The heterogeneity of firms was not considered in these models. More recently, the literature has distinguished between firm-level investment and aggregate investment. It has focused on the fact that investment at the firm level is not only intermittent as also suggested by the irreversibility model, but is also characterised by large spurts where the firm undertakes a substantial adjustment in its capital stock in a single period or in a few consecutive periods. Yet, since we do not observe such very pronounced spikes interspersed with periods of inaction in the aggregate investment series, we need to explain how the firm-level decisions, *when aggregated*, lead to the relatively smooth aggregate investment series that we observe. We now turn to a type of model that can explain the spikes characterising individual firm investment decisions by introducing fixed adjustment costs. By assuming that these costs are random and idiosyncratic to the firm, this model is also capable of addressing the aggregation issue.

5.1 Models of lumpy investment

There exists substantial evidence suggesting that investment projects at the firm level are not only intermittent but also lumpy. Doms and Dunne (1993), who study the investment behaviour of 12,000 large manufacturing establishments from 1972 to 1988 from the Longitudinal Research Database (LRD), have found that more than half of establishments have capital growth of close to 50 per cent in a single year. Moreover, more than 25 per cent of an average plant's investment occurs in a single year/project. They also note that the second largest spike came right before or right after the largest spike. As Caballero and Engel (1999) conclude, '40 percent of the sample investment of the median establishment probably corresponds to a single investment episode.'

These findings are confirmed in Doms and Dunne (1998) using a sample of 13,700 manufacturing plants drawn from 300 industries at the 4-digit level (also from the LRD). More than half of the plants in their sample experience an adjustment of 37 per cent in their capital stock in a single year, indicating lumpiness in investment activity at the plant level. At the same time, 80 per cent of the plants in the sample adjust their capital stock by less than 10 per cent in a given year. They find evidence that plants adjust their capital stock only when the difference between their desired and actual capital stock is substantial. This evidence supports the notion that investment is intermittent and is consistent with irreversibility. Doms and Dunne (1998) also find evidence that lumpiness at the plant level influences aggregate investment. They indicate that the lumpy investment activity of a few firms may have a large impact on aggregate investment. They report that in 1977 and 1987 the largest 500 investment projects accounted for 35.7 per cent and 32.1 per cent of total investment, respectively, in those years leading to a very skewed distribution of investment for the population as a whole. Using a Herfindahl index for investment in each year, they find that a change in the frequency of plants undertaking large investment projects partly accounts for periods of high aggregate investment (see Doms and Dunne 1998, figures 6 and 7: 425–6).[98]

The evidence presented by Doms and Dunne is greatly supportive of models of irreversibility and of lumpy investment. Furthermore, their evidence indicates a substantial impact on aggregate investment of lumpiness at the plant level.

Bertola and Caballero (1990) and Caballero and Leahy (1996) consider (S, s) models of lumpy and intermittent adjustment of consumer durables and investment respectively. The lumpiness of investment arises from a fixed cost which the firm must pay if it undertakes an investment decision. Owing to this fixed cost which does not depend on the quantity invested it is optimal for the firm to bunch investment.

In their study of aggregate dynamics for US manufacturing establishments, Caballero and Engel (1999) go a step beyond the standard (S, s) model by assuming that the fixed cost is random, implying that the zone of inaction will not be fixed over time. Furthermore, the random fixed costs are modelled as a firm-specific shock that leads to firm heterogeneity. After characterising the individual firm's investment decision, they aggregate across firms in order to obtain the aggregate investment level. They also present empirical evidence in support of their model. We now present their model in more detail and then discuss their aggregation procedure and econometric evidence. We also discuss some related empirical literature.

5.2 A generalised (S, s) model

The firm's problem

Let θ_t be a random shock that combines demand, productivity and wage shocks. Let r and δ be the interest and depreciation rates. The short-run profit function at time t, $\Pi(K_t, \theta_t)$, net of flow payments to capital, $(r + \delta)K_t$, is given by:

$$\Pi(K_t, \theta_t) \equiv \theta_t K_t^{\mu} - (r + \delta)K_t, \tag{2.128}$$

where $0 < \mu < 1$. Thus, the profit function is increasing and concave in K_t. This profit function can be derived under the assumptions of an iso-elastic industry demand curve and a Cobb–Douglas production function.

---

[98] The Herfindahl index is given by $\Sigma(I_i/I)^2$ where I_i/I is plant i's investment share of aggregate investment.

Next, define the firm's frictionless stock of capital K_t^* as the solution to the maximisation of (2.128) with respect to K_t such that

$$\theta_t = \xi K_t^{*1-\mu}, \tag{2.129}$$

where $\xi \equiv (r + \delta)/\mu$. Defining the disequilibrium variable z_t as the log-difference of the actual and frictionless capital stock $z_t \equiv \ln(K_t/K_t^*)$ and substituting (2.129) into (2.128) yields:

$$\Pi(z_t, K_t^*) = \pi(z_t)K_t^* = \xi[\exp(\mu z_t) - \mu \exp(z_t)]K_t^*, \tag{2.130}$$

where $\pi(z_t)$ is the short-run profit function per unit of frictionless capital.

Adjustment costs are modelled by assuming that firms must shut down operations for a fixed period of time when replacing capital.[99] Thus, adjustment costs are proportional to forgone profits due to re-organization:

$$\text{Adjustment costs} = \omega_t[\Pi(K_t, \theta_t) + (r + \delta)K_t] = \omega_t\theta_t K_t^\mu, \tag{2.131}$$

where ω_t is the fraction of profits forgone due to the capital stock adjustment. Since $\mu < 1$, notice that adjustment costs display increasing returns, that is, costs fall by less than the multiple of any expansion of the capital stock. This feature of the model is intended to capture the lumpy and intermittent nature of the investment process. Using (2.129) together with the definition of the disequilibrium variable z_t yields

$$\text{Adjustment costs} = \omega_t\xi \exp(\mu z_t)K_t^*. \tag{2.132}$$

One difference between the standard (S, s) framework and Caballero and Engel's model is that ω_t is assumed to be a random variable with distribution function $G(\omega_t)$ which is independent over time and over firms. Thus, this assumption allows the consideration of heterogeneity in adjustment costs at any point in time, and time variation in these costs over time for any firm.

The firm's decision involves whether to adjust its capital stock or not. Given the nature of the adjustment cost technology, this decision will not involve smooth and gradual adjustments. Instead the optimal policy will be characterised by periods of inaction followed by sudden spurts of investments. Therefore, the firm's problem will involve two regimes: action and inaction. The solution to the firm's problem will require partitioning the (ω, z) space in terms of these two regimes.

---

[99] Another possibility is to assume that the purchase price of capital goods is greater than the resale price.

To characterise the optimal investment policy, θ_t is assumed to follow a geometric random walk with drift and normally distributed errors. Then, using (2.129) it is straightforward to show that K^* will also follow the same process. Similarly, z_t will also follow the same process when there are no adjustments to the capital stock. Given these assumptions, the state vector for the firm's problem is comprised of (ω_t, z_t, K_t^*). Thus, the value of a firm with before-adjustment disequilibrium z_t, frictionless capital stock K_t^* and current adjustment cost parameter ω_t, denoted by $V(z_t, K_t^*, \omega_t)$, is equal to the maximum of the value of the firm given that it does not adjust, $V(z_t, K_t^*)$, and the value of the firm given that it does adjust, $V(c, K_t^*) - \omega_t \xi \exp(\mu z_t) K_t^*$, where c is the optimally determined target point of adjustment. That is:

$$V^*(z_t, K_t^*, \omega_t) = \max\{V(z_t, K_t^*), V(c, K_t^*) - \omega_t \xi \exp(\mu z_t) K_t^*\}.$$

(2.133)

The evolution of the value of a firm that does not adjust in the current period is

$$V(z_t, K_t^*) = \pi(z_t) K_t^* + \beta E_t[V^*(z_{t+1}, K_{t+1}^*, \omega_{t+1})],$$

(2.134)

where $\beta = (1+r)^{-1}$. Since the profit and adjustment cost functions are homogeneous of degree one in K_t^*, given z_t, so are the value functions $V(z_t, K_t^*)$ and $V^*(z_t, K_t^*, \omega_t)$. Therefore, we can re-write the value functions in terms of the value per unit of frictionless capital as $v(z) = V(z, K^*)/K^*$ and $v^*(z, \omega) = V^*(z, K^*, \omega)/K^*$. Using the fact that

$$\frac{K_{t+1}^*}{K_t^*} = (1 - \delta) \exp(-\Delta z_{t+1})$$

and dividing both sides of (2.133) and (2.134) by K^* yields

$$v^*(z_t, \omega_t) = \max\{v(z_t), v(c) - \omega_t \xi \exp(\mu z_t)\}$$

(2.135)

$$v(z_t) = \pi(z_t) + (1 - \delta)\beta E_t[v^*(z_{t+1}, \omega_{t+1}) \exp(-\Delta z_{t+1})].$$

(2.136)

From value matching (i.e. equating the two terms on the right-hand side of (2.135)) we find the optimal policy function $\Omega(z_t)$ for a given capital imbalance z_t as:

$$\Omega(z_t) = \xi^{-1} \exp(-\mu z_t)(v(z_t) - v(c)).$$

(2.137)

$\Omega(z_t)$ is the maximum cost of adjustment such that the firm finds it advantageous to adjust its capital stock. Note that $\Omega(c) = 0$, implying that when the level of capital imbalance z is equal to c the firm would adjust only if the adjustment costs were zero. After differentiation of (2.137) with respect to z_t, evaluating at $z_t = c$ and using the first-order condition $v'(c) = 0$, we find the smooth pasting condition: $\Omega'(c) = 0$.

Let $L(\omega_t)$ and $U(\omega_t)$ be the maximum shortage and excess of capital which is tolerated by the firm when its cost of adjustment is ω_t. The interval $(L(\omega_t), U(\omega_t))$ is the inaction zone. For any given realisation of ω_t the firm acts only when ω_t lies outside the interval $(L(\omega_t), U(\omega_t))$ in which case the firm invests so as to bring z_t back to c. Thus, for a *given* value of ω the investment policy is defined by a (L, c, U) type policy which corresponds to a two-sided (S, s) model. The shape and location of $\Omega(z_t)$ and its inverse $(L(\omega_t), c, U(\omega_t))$ depend on the distribution function of the cost of adjustment, $G(\omega)$.

Adjustment hazard

An important step in the aggregation process consists of using knowledge of the distribution $G(\omega)$. Thus, we find the probability that a firm with imbalance z_t adjusts. Let $x_t \equiv z_t - c$, denote the firm's imbalance relative to its target point. The firm adjusts if ω_t is small enough, that is if $\omega_t < \Omega(x_t + c)$. Let $\Lambda(x_t) = G(\Omega(x_t + c))$ be the probability that a firm with an imbalance equal to x_t adjusts its capital stock. $\Lambda(x_t)$ is thus the *adjustment hazard*. The adjustment hazard can be found if the form of $G(\omega)$ is known. Caballero and Engel (1999) assume that $G(\omega_t)$ is a Gamma distribution. Conditional on adjusting its capital stock, a firm with imbalance x_t will invest the following amount

$$(e^c - e^{z_t})K_t^* = (e^{-x_t} - 1)e^{z_t}K_t^* = (e^{-x_t} - 1)K_t(x_t). \quad (2.138)$$

Furthermore, the probability that a firm with imbalance x_t will invest is given by $\Lambda(x)$. Thus, the expected investment of firm i with imbalance x_t before adjusting its capital stock at t is given by:

$$E\left[I_t^i(x_t)\big|x_t\right] = \Lambda(x)(e^{-x_t} - 1)K_t^i(x_t) \approx -x\Lambda(x_t)K_t^i(x_t). \quad (2.139)$$

In general, $-x\Lambda(x_t)$ is a non-linear function of x. The non-linearity of expected investment reveals that a firm's incentives to invest rise more than proportionately with its imbalance.

Aggregation

Since the firm-specific adjustment cost ω is IID across firms and it is assumed that there are a large number of firms, we can apply the Law of

Large Numbers to find the *average*[100] investment to capital ratio of firms with imbalance x from (2.139) as:

$$\left(\frac{I_t}{K_t}\right)_x = -x\Lambda(x), \qquad (2.140)$$

where the subscript x identifies the group of firms by the magnitude of their imbalance. Let $\overline{f}(x, t)$ denote the cross-sectional density of firms according to their imbalances just before adjustment. The aggregate investment to capital ratio across all firms $(I_t/K_t)^A$ is obtained as:

$$\left(\frac{I_t}{K_t}\right)^A = -\int x\Lambda(x)\overline{f}(x, t)dx. \qquad (2.141)$$

As noted above, since in general $-x\Lambda(x)$ is non-linear in x, aggregate investment in general depends on all the moments of the cross-sectional distribution of imbalances. $\Lambda(x)$ admits of a variety of specifications. Thus, when it doesn't depend on x then the first moment of the cross-sectional distribution (i.e. the average imbalance before adjustment) suffices to determine the aggregate investment rate. This is akin to a partial adjustment model with implications that are similar to a quadratic adjustment cost model for a representative firm. However, for other specifications, this function will be highly non-linear and it will be necessary to consider higher-order moments. For example, when the adjustment hazard is quadratic,

$$\Lambda(x) = \lambda_0 + \lambda_1 x + \lambda_2 x^2 \qquad (2.142)$$

we need to know the first *three* moments of the cross-sectional distribution of imbalances in order to derive aggregate investment.

As is well known, the aggregate investment series does not exhibit intermittence nor lumpiness, but is instead relatively smooth. In order to explain this smoothness of the aggregate investment series there is a need to assume that both aggregate and idiosyncratic shocks affect the firms' decisions to invest. As Bertola and Caballero (1994) point out, without idiosyncratic shocks (and with only aggregate shocks) the investment of individual units would differ only by the initial conditions and in the limit $f(x, t)$ would

---

[100] For simplicity, we follow Caballero (1999) in assuming that aggregate investment is given by the average of investment instead of the weighted average of the investment of firms with imbalance x. Caballero and Engel (1999) also make the simplifying assumption that the adjustment hazard is independent of the capital stock before adjustment for firms with imbalance x. They also carry out the analysis without making the simplifying assumption in an appendix, but indicate that the loss of accuracy due to the approximation is small. Furthermore, this simplifying assumption is also confirmed to be a close approximation in the context of US manufacturing data for the 1970s and 1980s by Caballero, Engel and Haltiwanger (1995).

converge to a spike and aggregate investment would be characterised by intermittence which is counterfactual. In fact, idiosyncratic shocks prevent the cross-sectional density from converging into a spike. In other words, they prevent a perfect synchronisation of inactivity. Hence, aggregate investment is a smoothed version of the non-linear discontinuous investment policies of individual firms. If on the other hand there were no aggregate shocks and only idiosyncratic shocks, then to the extent that these are independently distributed across a large number of firms, their impact will vanish in the aggregate. The firms' actual capital stock would be very close to the frictionless capital stock, average capital imbalances would be close to zero and would exhibit low persistence.[101]

Thus to capture the impact of the interaction of aggregate and firm-specific shocks on aggregate investment, Caballero and Engel assume that the shocks to wages, demand and productivity which affect the desired stock of capital can be decomposed into an aggregate (or sectoral) component, v_t, and an idiosyncratic component, ε_t which are exogenous to the firm and the sector. The evolution of the desired capital stock is given by

$$K_t^* = K_{t-1}^* e^{v_t + \epsilon_t} \tag{2.143}$$

so that when the firm does not adjust, x_t evolves according to:

$$\Delta x_t = -(\delta + v_t) - \epsilon_t, \tag{2.144}$$

where δ is the depreciation rate. Thus, the cross-sectional distribution of imbalances will evolve through time due to the aggregate and idiosyncratic shocks that are realised each period as well as due to depreciation. Let $f(x, t-1)$ denote the cross-sectional density at the end of $t-1$. After the realisation of the aggregate shock at time t and after depreciation, the cross-sectional density becomes $\overline{f}(x, t) = f(x + \delta + v_t, t-1)$. Then the cross-sectional density is further modified by taking into account those firms that adjust and those that do not in accordance with the adjustment hazard function. Finally the idiosyncratic shocks are realised, leading to the cross-sectional density $f(x, t)$ at the end of period t which is given by

$$f(x, t) = \left[\int \Lambda(y) f(y + \delta + v_t, t - 1) dy \right] g_\epsilon(-x) + \int [1 - \Lambda(x + \epsilon)]$$
$$\times f(x + \epsilon + \delta + v_t, t - 1) g_\epsilon(-\epsilon) d\epsilon, \tag{2.145}$$

---

[101] Doyle and Whited (2001) test the proposition that the persistence of capital imbalances should increase as the ratio of aggregate to idiosyncratic shocks increases. They find evidence supporting the presence of both kinds of shocks and that the observed smooth aggregate investment is the result of aggregation across firms that behave in a non-synchronised manner.

where $g_\epsilon(\epsilon)$ is the density of ϵ. From (2.141) and the cross-sectional density just before adjustment $\overline{f}(x, t) = f(x + \delta + v_t, t - 1)$ we find the following aggregate investment equation where the influence of aggregate shocks is explicit:

$$\frac{I_t^A}{K_t^A} = \int (e^{-x_t} - 1)\Lambda(x_t) f(x_t + \delta + v_t, t - 1)dx. \quad (2.146)$$

Given an initial cross-section distribution $f(x, 0)$ and a sequence of aggregate shocks $\{v_t\}$ we can obtain the sequence of aggregate investment from (2.145) and (2.146).

In this framework, the response of aggregate investment to shocks (that is, to changes in the cost of capital, in productivity or demand) is time-varying and depends on the history of shocks. Suppose that there has been a sequence of favourable shocks. Then most firms will find themselves with a large capital shortage or 'pent-up investment demand.' In such a case, aggregate investment becomes very sensitive to further shocks, since a positive shock may induce a large number of firms to simultaneously decide to increase their investment and eliminate their capital imbalance. There will be a synchronised increase in investment across firms which will influence aggregate investment. Alternatively, a negative shock (following this sequence of positive ones) will dissuade these firms from investing, and the take-off will not occur. Thus, as Caballero (1999: 841) points out, the elasticity of aggregate investment to these shocks 'captures the aggregate impact of changes in the degree of synchronization of large adjustments'. As shown by Caballero and Engel (1999) with aggregate data, it also helps explain the higher moments of aggregate investment such as its high skewness and kurtosis.

Empirical evidence

Caballero and Engel (1999) use aggregate (2-digit-level) macroeconomic data for equipment and structures in the US manufacturing sector for 1947–92, to undertake an empirical test. They find further supporting evidence for irreversibility and for the fixed cost effect, and demonstrates that microeconomic non-linearities matter at the aggregate level.

They limit the number of parameters to be estimated to those which characterise the distribution of adjustment costs, $G(\omega)$, or the hazard function, $\Lambda(x)$. They fix the remaining parameters, concentrate them out of the likelihood function or show that they play a limited role. In view of the large data requirements to estimate non-linearities from time series Caballero and Engel impose a common $G(\omega)$, or $\Lambda(x)$ across all sectors. Sectoral shocks are multivariate normal and independent over time.

Two models are estimated. In the semi-structural model the parameters, λ_0 and λ_2 of an ad hoc adjustment hazard are estimated:

$$\Lambda(x) = 1 - e^{-\lambda_0 - \lambda_1 x - \lambda_2 x^2}. \tag{2.147}$$

In the structural model $G(\omega)$ is assumed to have a gamma distribution:

$$G(\omega) = \frac{1}{\phi^p \Gamma(p)} \int_0^\omega \eta^{p-1} e^{\frac{-\eta}{\phi}} d\eta. \tag{2.148}$$

The parameters of $G(\omega)$, namely the mean and coefficient of variation, are estimated and the adjustment hazard is found as a solution to the dynamic programming problem.

In contrast to other work in the literature, Caballero and Engel use single-step maximum likelihood estimation which does not necessitate the separate estimation of frictionless capital and hence avoids the measurement errors, small sample bias problems and specification errors that may arise in this context. Both the results of the semi-structural model and the structural model confirm the presence of an increasing hazard for equipment and structures. Caballero and Engel then compare their model against two models: an $AR(1)$ where the correlation coefficient is the same across sectors and an $AR(2)$ where the correlation coefficients differ:[102]

$$\frac{I_{it}^A}{K_{it}^A} = a_i + \rho \frac{I_{it-1}^A}{K_{it-1}^A} + v_{it} \tag{2.149}$$

$$\frac{I_{it}^A}{K_{it}^A} = a_i + \rho_{1i} \frac{I_{it-1}^A}{K_{it-1}^A} + \rho_{2i} \frac{I_{it-2}^A}{K_{it-2}^A} + v_{it}. \tag{2.150}$$

Caballero and Engel reject the null hypothesis that these two models are equivalent to the structural non-linear model. With respect to out-of-sample performance the structural model outperforms the $AR(2)$ model even though the former imposes the same distribution of adjustment costs across sectors.

Finally, Caballero and Engel analyse the predictive accuracy of the $AR(2)$ and structural model. The study concludes that the structural model is better able to track aggregate investment when there occurs large changes in investment. The estimated hazards magnify or dampen the response of investment to aggregate shocks. Hence, these non-linearities improve

---

[102] The $AR(1)$ is equivalent to a quadratic cost-of-adjustment model.

the aggregate performance of dynamic investment equations. In particular, after the tax reform of 1986 when some tax incentives were removed, the fall in investment is found to be 20 per cent larger than with a quadratic cost-of-adjustment model.

Caballero and Engel also find strong evidence in favour of an increasing adjustment hazard rate: that is, the probability that the firm will adjust its capital stock grows more than proportionately with the capital imbalance x. In conclusion, Caballero and Engel's empirical study demonstrates that microeconomic non-linearities matter at the aggregate level.

5.3 Other empirical evidence

In the context of irreversible investment (but without fixed costs), Bertola and Caballero (1994) consider the aggregation problem when firms face both idiosyncratic and aggregate shocks. They estimate their model using aggregate US manufacturing data and find evidence generally supporting it.

Bertola and Caballero estimate the irreversible investment model in continuous time with Brownian motions for aggregate and idiosyncratic shocks. The study constructs an annual Γ_t series as the ratio of gross investment in non-residential capital equipment to the capital stock over the 1954–86 period. They construct a predicted aggregate gross investment path $\widehat{\Gamma}_t$ which is decomposed as the sum of Γ_t^* (the frictionless series) and of changes in the mean of the cross-sectional density of firms according to their capital imbalance (i.e. the gap between their actual and desired capital stock). The hypothetical frictionless series, Γ_t^*, depends only on the cross-sectional first moments. Assuming that $\Pi(K_t, Z_t) = K_t^\mu \theta_t$ where $0 < \mu < 1$, they obtain:

$$\Gamma_t^* = \left(\frac{1}{1-\mu} \Delta \ln \Pi_{it} - \Delta \ln c_t \right) - \frac{\mu}{1-\mu} \Gamma_{it} + \frac{1}{1-\mu} \delta, \quad (2.151)$$

where c_t is the cost of capital. Equation (2.151) is estimated. This equation corresponds to the hypothetical investment rate that would be observed if there did not exist an irreversibility constraint nor any other friction. Finally, some moments of the predicted aggregate investment series are matched to the moments of actual investment.

Bertola and Caballero find that the constant drift and variance assumptions of the Brownian motions are not contradicted by the data. They note that the actual Γ_t series is substantially less variable than the Γ_t^* series. The irreversibility of investment is a plausible explanation for this observation. Bertola and Caballero choose the standard deviation of the idiosyncratic shock, σ_I, to match the volatility and serial correlation of the observed series. When $\sigma_I = 0.6$ the model can explain 36 per cent of the variability in the investment series; the standard deviation of desired investment $= 0.015$ compared to 0.017 in the data, and the first order serial correlation is 0.66 compared to 0.68 in the data. Bertola and Caballero's study reveals that the volatility of desired capital would need to be very high to rationalise empirical evidence at the aggregate level without appealing to other sources of smoothness.[103] One should also note that Bertola and Caballero assume heterogeneity with respect to the structural parameters.

Caballero, Engel and Haltiwanger (hereafter, CEH, 1995) use data at a very disaggregated level, specifically, 7,000 plants from the LRD, to analyse whether the microeconomic (plant-level) data reveal non-convexities in the adjustment technology, and to investigate the issue of aggregation in the presence of lumpy investment at the microeconomic level.

CEH focus on equipment investment. They first measure the capital imbalance of plants in their sample, and obtain the period-t cross-sectional distribution of plants according to their capital imbalance, $f(x, t)$. Thus, for example, the fraction of plants at time t with capital imbalance between x and $x + \Delta x$ would be given by $f(x, t)\Delta x$. As in Caballero and Engle (1999), the cross-sectional distribution of plants varies with time, and is affected by both aggregate and idiosyncratic shocks.[104] Secondly, grouping together plants that have similar levels of x before investing in period t, CEH compute the average actual investment of each group as a fraction of their respective capital imbalances, and obtain the adjustment hazard. The investment rate of plants with imbalance x at time t is given by $-x\Lambda(x, t)$[105], and the aggregate investment level at time t is obtained as

$$I_t \equiv \int -x\Lambda(x, t) f(x, t) dx. \qquad (2.152)$$

While I_t is the average investment rate, if one assumes that investment is independent of the beginning-of-period capital stock, then I_t represents

---

[103] When σ_I is large the irreversibility constraint will bind for some units and for some time periods so that changes in the cross-section smooth out the response of Γ_t to $\Delta\Gamma_t^*$.

[104] See Caballero (1999: 840), Caballero and Engel (1999) and Caballero, Engel and Haltiwanger (1995: Appendix A) for a description of the law of motion of the cross-sectional distribution, and how this evolution is affected by the distribution of idiosyncratic shocks, aggregate shocks, as well as by the fraction of plants that adjust (either fully, ending up with $x = 0$, or partially, moving to a different x-group).

[105] Here we follow the notation and convention of Caballero and Engel (1999). CEH define the capital imbalance to be the negative of that in Caballero and Engel.

the aggregate investment-to-capital ratio. CEH indicates that the data are consistent with this assumption.

As we have mentioned above, $\Lambda(x, t)$ is in general highly non-linear, and knowing simply the first moment of the cross-sectional distribution does not suffice to compute aggregate investment. In cases such as an asymmetric adjustment cost model with different adjustment costs for investing and disinvesting, or alternatively a two-sided (S, s) model of investment characterised by a (L, c, U)-type investment policy, this function will be highly non-linear and it will be necessary to consider higher-order moments. For example, in the latter case it is necessary to know the fraction of plants below the lower threshold and their average capital imbalance the fraction of plants above the higher threshold and their average capital imbalance and the fraction in the inaction zone in order to calculate aggregate investment. Hence, it is necessary to conduct a meticulous accounting of the activities of firms in each group and to track the time-varying distribution of firms. On the basis of their data set, CEH obtain the adjustment hazard and find that it is highly non-linear and that it is indeed necessary to consider higher moments of the distribution to calculate aggregate investment. CEH also find that the adjustment hazard (i.e. the probability that a firm with imbalance x adjusts) is increasing in the magnitude of the imbalance. Thus, the higher the imbalance, the higher the probability that the firm adjusts.

The results of the CEH's study indicate that the long-run elasticity of capital with respect to the cost of capital is quite large, varying from -0.1 to -2.0, while the short-run elasticities are smaller and more variable, varying between 7 per cent and 12 per cent of the long-run elasticities. The reason why aggregate elasticities are so variable is that plants are likely to make large adjustments to their capital stock when there are large capital shortages, but may not react very much when the shortage is small or when they have excess capital. These results are quite consistent with irreversibility and with fixed costs of adjustment implying increasing returns in the adjustment technology. Another interesting finding is that tax reforms have had a substantial impact on aggregate (equipment) investment. Thus, the 1981 tax reform had a large positive impact, while the tax reform of 1986, and the removal of the ITC, had a large negative impact. These results confirm at a more disaggregated level, the findings of Caballero and Engle (1999).

In conducting their study with microeconomic data, CEH use a cointegration procedure to estimate a series of desired capital stocks for each plant and then a measure of the deviation x for each plant. Caballero and Engel (1999) by contrast, use more aggregate data (at the 2-digit level) with a postulated cross-sectional distribution of firms, but use a maximum likelihood procedure that does not require the construction of a desired capital stock series.

Cooper, Haltiwanger and Power (1999) focus on an analysis of the timing of large investment expenditures at the plant level and its relationship to aggregate fluctuations. They consider the firm's discrete decision choice of whether or not to replace an existing piece of machinery each period. Thus they focus only on the extensive margin (the decision to invest or not), and do not consider the intensive margin (the quantity of investment). In the presence of both proportional and fixed costs of adjusting the capital stock, as well as aggregate and idiosyncratic productivity shocks, they derive a hazard function (the probability that the firm will replace the machine) that is a function of the aggregate productivity level, and the age of the current capital stock.[106] Using the hazard function and the cross-sectional distribution of plants according to the age of their capital stock, they obtain an aggregate investment level that depends on the aggregate productivity shock.

Both their simulations and their empirical investigation (that makes use of the LRD) reveal that the hazard function is increasing in the time since last replacement. Since the convex cost-of-adjustment model predicts a negatively sloped hazard function, this result is viewed as evidence against the cost-of-adjustment model. The hazard function also tends to be pro-cyclical, thus supporting a variant of their model with only large fixed replacement costs rather than proportional costs, and aggregate productivity shocks with a high degree of persistence.

They find strong evidence that plant-level investment is characterised by large investment episodes, or investment spikes, and that these episodes substantially contribute to fluctuations in aggregate investment. They conclude that taking into account the evolution of the cross-sectional distribution of firms according to their capital vintage (the age of their capital) is very important in predicting investment changes and that ignoring it could lead to substantial prediction errors.

Doyle and Whited (2001) focus on quarterly 2-digit industry-level investment data in order to avoid the time-aggregation problem that could blur the lack of synchronisation across firms. They construct an uncertainty measure by using stock market returns in order to capture the relative importance of aggregate and idiosyncratic shocks that affect firms' investment decisions. They find evidence in favour of lumpy plant-level investment and

---

[106] Note that the hazard function here is different from the one in Caballero and Engel (1999) where it depends on the deviation of the beginning-of-period capital stock from the desired capital stock.

intermittent capital adjustment that is also asynchronous. They also find evidence in favour of the importance of idiosyncratic shocks, indicating the heterogeneity of agents, and providing evidence against the representative agent paradigm. They conclude that it is the aggregation across heterogeneous firms that leads to smooth aggregate fluctuations in investment.

5.4 Fixed costs and Q-theory

Caballero and Leahy (1996) emphasise that not only marginal-Q affects investment but also investment affects Q. This simultaneity problem is assumed away by a CRS production function and perfect competition, in which case marginal-Q is independent of investment. Furthermore, when costs of adjustment are convex firms smooth investment over time. However, with fixed costs, investment is intermittent and lumpy. Thus, positive demand or productivity shocks which may raise the current marginal profitability of capital may lower the value of an installed unit because they increase the probability of of investment in the future. Caballero and Leahy demonstrate that when the profit function is concave in capital and fixed costs are present investment is no longer a monotonic function of Q and thus, its inverse no longer exists. They show that under strong homogeneity conditions namely, Π is homogeneous of degree one in the shock, θ, and in K, average-Q is a sufficient statistic for investment. However, if either the homogeneity conditions fails or the shock does not follow a random walk average-Q will not in general be a sufficient statistic.

6 GENERAL EQUILIBRIUM MODELS WITH IRREVERSIBILITY AND FIXED COSTS

We now turn to general equilibrium models with irreversibility and with fixed costs. While earlier models have tended to use the framework of the one-sector growth model, more recent models have introduced heterogeneity of firms and adopted the multi-sector growth model approach in order to analyse the general equilibrium implications of irreversibility and of fixed costs.

6.1 The one-sector stochastic growth model with irreversibility

One notable seminal contribution in this context is Sargent (1980) who incorporates an irreversibility constraint in a one-sector stochastic growth model developed earlier by Brock and Mirman (1972) and Mirman and Zilcha (1975). Sargent derives the optimal investment policy function under irreversibility and shows the existence of a competitive equilibrium with irreversible investment. He puts emphasis on the interpretation of Q-theory in a general equilibrium framework. In particular, he indicates that Q, interpreted as the ratio of the value of existing capital to its replacement cost, should always be equal to one in the absence of any source of friction that prevents the adjustment of the price of existing capital from being equal to the current price of capital. Irreversibility is one possible source of such friction. In the presence of irreversibility, aggregate investment will be positively correlated with Q. Sargent emphasises that Q is endogenously determined, and that it both affects *and* is affected by firms' investment decisions. Since irreversibility makes the investment problem dynamic and forward-looking, even when individual firms are justified in regarding Q as exogenous to their own individual investment decisions, their problem cannot be represented as a myopic decision relating current investment to current Q. In other words, Q cannot be a sufficient statistic that summarises the totality of agents' expectations about the future.

In Sargent's model once installed, capital cannot be consumed. However, there exists a market where claims to the existing capital may be traded at a competitively determined price p^k measured in units of the consumption good per unit of capital, whereas the price of newly produced capital in terms of the consumption good is unity. The price p^k represents Tobin's Q. The representative consumers' preferences are defined over consumption sequences and are subject to a taste shock. Labour is inelastically supplied. A random multiplicative productivity shock affects output each period. The irreversibility constraint will be binding for some realisations of the taste and productivity shocks, and it is at these points where investment is zero that q will be less than unity. In this model where irreversibility prevents a downward adjustment of the capital stock but does not prevent a smooth upward adjustment, Q cannot exceed one. A costly upward adjustment of investment would be needed to obtain a value of Q greater than one. Sargent also points out that it is quite possible for *aggregate* investment to be positive with a value of Q less than one. This would occur, for example, if the economy is made up of several sectors, and some of these are experiencing binding irreversibility while others have positive investment.

Olson (1989) generalises Sargent's model by proving the existence of a competitive equilibrium for both continuous and discrete distributions of the productivity shocks, which in his framework, are not necessarily multiplicative and hence do not imply an ordering of output levels according to the random productivity levels. He also uses a Kuhn–Tucker approach to the solution as opposed to the contraction mapping arguments used by Sargent.

6.2 The multi-sector stochastic growth model with irreversibility

Dow and Olson (1992) analyse a two-sector stochastic growth model where aggregate investment is subject to a non-negativity constraint. Setting the moments of the aggregate productivity shock in accordance with the Solow residual, they find that the irreversibility constraint is never binding because the variance of the aggregate productivity shock emanating from the data is too small. They thus conclude that irreversibility has no impact on aggregate investment.

Coleman (1997) emphasises the importance of sectoral shocks in analysing the aggregate impact of irreversibility. He attributes the lack of aggregate impact observed by Dow and Olson to their imposition of an aggregate irreversibility constraint. Coleman examines the impact of investment irreversibility in a multi-sector, stochastic growth model where there is no exogenous aggregate uncertainty, but where each sector j ($j = 1, \ldots, n$) is subject to an idiosyncratic productivity shock and to an irreversibility constraint such that $x' \geq (1 - \delta) x$ where x' denotes next period's capital stock and δ is the rate of depreciation. The representative household has logarithmic preferences over consumption and inelastically supplies one unit of labour to each sector. In this framework, irreversibility has important aggregate effects, especially on equilibrium interest rates. In particular, Coleman shows that the irreversibility of investment prevents an equalisation of the marginal productivity of capital across sectors. Sectors that face a binding irreversibility constraint and cannot disinvest will have a below-average marginal productivity of capital while sectors that have positive investment will have above-average marginal productivity of capital. Since an important determinant of real interest rates is the marginal productivity of investment, real interest rates will reflect the marginal productivity of capital in the high productivity sectors where investment is positive. All of the variations in investment in the sectors where investment is positive will be reflected in consumption and hence will affect the real interest rate. In the absence of irreversibility, there would be disinvestment in the low-productivity sector and capital would flow from that sector to the high productivity sector, thus leaving aggregate variables such as investment, consumption and the interest rate unchanged.

Coleman simulates his model and finds that for most parameter values, the real interest rate is negatively correlated with output and consumption, positively correlated with the investment–output ratio and positively autocorrelated. All of these variations are a consequence of the irreversibility of investment and the inability of capital to flow from the low- to the high-productivity sector. In the absence of irreversibility such adjustments would take place and the aggregate variables would be constant. In the presence of irreversibility, an increase in uncertainty concerning sectoral shocks[107] and hence the future return to capital, has an overall ambiguous and weak impact on current aggregate investment (leading to an increase or decrease of investment depending on parameter values) but always leads to a lower real interest rate.[108] These effects are due to the desire to smooth consumption. Greater uncertainty as to which sector to invest in reduces investment while consumption-smoothing motives tend to increase investment. These two opposing effects are responsible for the weak response of aggregate investment to greater uncertainty.

Coleman (1997) concludes that the impact of irreversibility should be studied in a disaggregated multi-sector setting rather than a one-sector setting because the variance of aggregate shocks is not large enough for the representative firm to be constrained by irreversibility. In a multi-sector model with irreversible investment, sectoral shocks may have an important impact on aggregate variables such as interest rates, output and consumption, and do not tend to average out as in a one-sector growth model. Coleman also notes that the presence of irreversibility in his model 'weakens the relationship between interest rates and aggregate variables such as aggregate output or investment.' This is consistent with empirical observations which conclude that the risk-free rate is less pro-cyclical than predicted by flexible investment models.

Ramey and Shapiro (1998) analyse the impact of an increase in government expenditures in a two-sector stochastic optimal growth model where it is costly to relocate capital across the two sectors, but where labour is perfectly mobile across sectors. The increase in demand for goods by the government affects only one of the two sectors and thus represents a sectoral shock in demand. Taking their cue from the characteristics of the aerospace industry,[109] the study makes three assumptions about the relocation costs for capital. First, it assumes that the relocation of capital from one sector to the other may entail a substantial (25 per cent in one case and 50 per cent in another) loss of capital. Second, it also assumes that capital purchased from sector 1 can become productive only with a one-period lag in sector 2.

---

[107] The increase in uncertainty is modelled as a regime shift (occurring with a fixed exogenous transition probability) between two distributions, the first with a low level of uncertainty (a degenerate distribution), and the second with a high level of uncertainty.

[108] This is true both when sectoral shocks are negatively correlated (so that when some sectors receive a positive shock the others receive a negative shock) and when the sectoral shocks are IID so that all sectors could receive a negative shock.

[109] The characteristics of the aerospace industry were analysed by the authors in Ramey and Shapiro (1998).

Finally, it also assumes that sector-specific capital can be produced only in the sector itself. This assumption captures the fact that there is specialisation and vertical integration in the production of capital goods and that most capital goods producers cater only to a few downstream industries. If both sectors could produce both types of capital, then the effect of the sectoral demand shock would be offset.

An aggregate productivity shock affects output in both sectors. Two different production technologies are considered. A CRS Cobb–Douglas specification is compared with a Leontief specification where there are only limited substitution possibilities between capital and labour. In this latter specification, capital and labour must be used in fixed proportions, but the utilisation rate (the work-week) of capital and labour may vary. The households' preferences are specified as being logarithmic over consumption of two goods and leisure, as they are in the Cobb–Douglas technology case, but in addition, also display an increasing marginal disutility for overtime work in the Leontief technology with variable utilisation of capital and labour. This increasing marginal disutility for overtime work implies that firms desiring to increase the work-week will face increasing marginal costs.

Calibrating their model to match some key aspects of the economy, Ramey and Shapiro analyse their model's predictions about the impact of an increase in government demand such as the one that occurred before the Korean War. Relative to the frictionless economy without relocation costs for capital[110] they find that a costly relocation of capital has a significant impact on several macroeconomic variables. In the Cobb–Douglas case while the impact on output is small, the impact of frictions in capital mobility leads to an increase in hours worked that is 15 per cent higher than in the frictionless case. Although the results are qualitatively similar across the two types of technologies, they find that the costly reallocation of capital has a larger impact, for most variables, but especially on output, when technology is of the Leontief type than when it is of the Cobb–Douglas form. That is, when comparing a frictionless economy to the costly capital reallocation economy, the impact of costly reallocation is larger when the technology is of the Leontief type. The real interest rate falls, remains lower than its initial level for several periods, then increases well above the initial level before reaching a somewhat higher than initial steady-state value.

Faig (2001) also considers a multi-sector stochastic optimal growth model with irreversibility, and with N types of capital. For the sake of

---

[110] This frictionless model essentially amounts to the one-sector model since capital will easily flow instantaneously and costlessly to the sector experiencing an increase in demand.

tractability, labour is omitted as a factor of production.[111] The production function is given by

$$x = G(k, z), \tag{2.153}$$

where x denotes output, $k \in R^N$ denotes the vector of the N types of capital and $z \in R^M$ represents the realisation of the productivity shocks (that will be in one of M states). Output x includes both production and the inherited capital stock valued at cost. The function G is concave, linearly homogeneous and continuously differentiable in k and measurable in z. Thus, a CRS technology is assumed.

As opposed to Coleman's framework, the degree of irreversibility may vary across sectors in Faig's model. Firms in sector i that have higher capital stocks than desired can at most divest a portion $(1 - \mu_i)$ of the excess capital. That is, with $0 \leq \mu_i \leq 1$,

$$k_i' \geq \mu_i (1 - \delta) k_i, \tag{2.154}$$

where $\mu_i = 0$ represents full flexibility and $\mu_i = 1$ represents full irreversibility.

Preferences are specified to be of the Kreps–Porteus–Epstein–Zin type (see Epstein and Zin 1989). That is, the representative household's preferences are given by

$$u = \left\{ (1 - \beta)c^{1-\sigma} + \beta \left[E\left(u'^{(1-\gamma)} \right) \right]^{(1-\sigma)/(1-\gamma)} \right\}^{1/(1-\gamma)}, \tag{2.155}$$

where u is current utility, u' is next period utility, σ is the inverse of the intertemporal elasticity of substitution along a deterministic path, and γ is the constant relative risk aversion parameter for atemporal lotteries.[112] These preferences are recursive, homothetic and independent across states but not time-additive. Households maximise the above preference functional subject to the set of irreversibility constraints and subject to the overall resource constraint given by

$$c + \sum_{i=1}^{N} k_i' \leq x. \tag{2.156}$$

---

[111] Faig points out that some types of capital may be interpreted as human capital.
[112] For $\sigma = \gamma$ the above functional reduces to the time-separable expected utility function with constant relative risk aversion and where the measure of risk aversion is equal to the inverse of the elasticity of intertemporal substitution. For $\sigma \neq \gamma$ these preferences imply that the individual is not indifferent to the timing of the resolution of uncertainty. Furthermore, while β represents the subjective discount factor under certainty, the subjective discount factor under uncertainty is in general both time and state-dependent.

As shown in Epstein and Zin (1989), there exists a value function V over (k, z) sequences which is continuously differentiable, concave and linearly homogeneous. The first-order conditions are

$$(1 - \beta)V^\sigma c^{-\sigma} = \lambda \qquad (2.157a)$$

$$\lambda - V^\sigma \beta \Big[E\left(V^{(1-\gamma)}\right)^{(\gamma - \sigma)/(1-\gamma)}\Big] \times E[V'^{-\gamma}(\partial V'/\partial k_i')] = v_i \geq 0 \qquad (2.157b)$$

for $i = 1, \ldots N$, where λ is the Lagrange multiplier for the overall resource constraint, while v_i is the Lagrange multiplier for the irreversibility constraint in the ith sector. v_i is positive whenever the irreversibility constraint is binding, and zero otherwise. Irreversibility in sector i thus drives a wedge between the marginal value of wealth λ and the marginal value of sector i's capital. Using the envelope theorem, $\partial V/\partial k_i = \lambda(\partial G/\partial k_i) - v_i \mu_i(1 - \delta_i)$. Making use of the linear homogeneity of both the production function and of the value function and the homotheticity of preferences, one can show that the value function as well as consumption are proportional to wealth. Thus,

$$V = \lambda \left[\sum_{i=1}^{N} \partial V/\partial k_i\right] = \lambda \widetilde{x} \qquad (2.158)$$

$$c = (1 - \beta)^{1/\sigma} \lambda^{1-1/\sigma} \widetilde{x} \qquad (2.159)$$

$$where \ \widetilde{x} = x - \sum_{i=1}^{N} \frac{v_i}{\lambda} \mu_i (1 - \delta_i) k_i, \qquad (2.160)$$

where v_i/λ denotes the shadow capital losses incurred due to the binding irreversibility constraint, and where (2.159) is obtained by using (2.157a) and (2.158). $\widetilde{x}$ is the market value of all goods produced this period and of the inherited capital stock, and constitutes the market value of total wealth in the economy. Note that $\widetilde{x}$ is less than x in the presence of binding irreversibility, but is equal to x in its absence. It can be shown that the resource constraint can now be expressed as $qk' = \widetilde{x} - c$ where $q = 1 - v_i/\lambda \leq 1$ is Tobin's Q. Since $q = 1$ and $\widetilde{x} = x$ under flexibility, the resource constraint is simply $k' = x - c$ in that case.

Comparing a fully flexible economy with an irreversible one, investment in the flexible economy is lower than in the irreversible economy. Irreversibility has three effects in this model. First, it prevents capital destruction in periods when one may wish to consume part of the existing capital stock. Second, there is a substitution effect that arises from the option value lost when investment does occur by constraining the future value of the capital stock. Third, there is a wealth effect in general equilibrium in that the irreversibility constraint reduces the set of feasible paths for the economy. The substitution effect discourages capital creation while the wealth effect encourages capital creation. This occurs because the existence of the irreversibility constraint makes the representative consumer poorer and leads to less consumption and more saving in equilibrium. If the intertemporal elasticity of substitution is less than or equal to one, then the wealth effect dominates the substitution effect, implying that investment will be higher under irreversibility than reversibility.

Despite the higher investment levels under irreversibility, in the long run the economy without irreversibility constraints may grow faster and have a larger capital stock. The reason is that in a model with multiple capital goods, irreversibility changes not only the amount of investment but also its composition. Resources are diverted from irreversible to flexible types of capital, sacrificing productivity and lowering the aggregate return on capital. Thus, even if smaller amounts are invested in a flexible economy, they may on average yield higher output and higher capital accumulation over the long run. If the assumption of linear homogeneity of the production function is relaxed, then with a strictly concave production function, which implies the existence of a fixed factor of production, it may be shown that investment in such an economy will be lower than in the irreversible economy.

Faig also distinguishes between an economy with multiple sectors where each sector faces an individual irreversibility constraint (as the one just described) and one where all sectors share the same degree of irreversibility μ and face an *aggregate* irreversibility constraint such that $\Sigma_{i=1}^{N} k_{t+1,i} = \mu \Sigma_{i=1}^{N} (1 - \delta) k_{ti}$. This latter economy is characterised by the possibility of *relocating* capital across sectors even though the economy as a whole faces irreversibility. He then compares the latter economy with a special case of the former economy where the degree of irreversibility in each individual sector is assumed to be equal to the degree of aggregate irreversibility, i.e. where $\mu_i = \mu$ for $\forall i$. He finds that investment is lower in the economy with relocation than in the irreversible economy, provided that the intertemporal elasticity of substitution is less than or equal to one.

Irreversibility also affects asset returns by two channels. The first is a direct effect since irreversibility may lead to capital gains or losses. The second is an indirect effect: irreversibility affects the variability of consumption and of the market return, and hence, the price of risk. In particular, considering an analytically tractable special case where there is only one sector and where the productivity shocks are multiplicative and IID, Faig finds that the price of risk and the risk premium are higher in the irreversible economy relative to the flexible one. Furthermore, the irreversible economy exhibits a risk-free rate and a risk premium that are counter-cyclical, while these tend to be pro-cyclical in equilibrium models excluding irreversibility. This result accords with observations of a countercyclical risk premium in the USA, as well as with empirical evidence that the risk-free-rate is less pro-cyclical than predicted by flexible investment equilibrium models. This finding is in line with Coleman's finding mentioned above that irreversibility in a multi-sector setting weakens the relationship between the interest rate and output.

We now review two contributions to the general equilibrium literature on irreversible investment which are also based on multi-sector RBC models and which, contrary to the other multi-sector optimal growth models reviewed so far, arrive at results that indicate little or no significant impact of irreversibility or lumpiness on aggregate investment. Veracierto (2002) and Thomas (2002) undertake a calibration exercise, and compare a model economy with irreversible investment (in the case of Veracierto) or lumpy investment (in the case of Thomas) with the actual economy and with a baseline model of flexible investment. We review each model in turn.

Veracierto argues that the reason why irreversibility has an impact on aggregate investment in multi-sector growth models such as Coleman (1997), Faig (2001), and Ramey and Shapiro (1998, 2001) is due to their assumption of unrealistically large sectoral shocks. Similarly, according to Veracierto, the reason why aggregate investment displays lower variability in the presence of irreversibility when firms are subject to idiosyncratic shocks in Bertola and Caballero (1994) is due to their assumption of a very large variance for these idiosyncratic shocks. Veracierto argues that when the size of sectoral shocks is consistent with that observed in the data, the aggregate impact of irreversible investment disappears in a general equilibrium framework.

Veracierto considers an optimal multi-sector growth model with a continuum of *ex ante* identical households who have preferences given by

$$\sum_{t=0}^{\infty} \beta^t [\log(c_t) + v(l_t)] \tag{2.161}$$

defined over consumption and leisure. Leisure is assumed to be indivisible as in Hansen (1985) and Rogerson (1988), so that leisure can take only two values, ω and $\omega - 1$, where ω denotes the time endowment of households.

Thus, the period utility function takes the form $u_t = [\log(c_t) + v(l_t)] = \log(c_t) - \alpha \eta_t$ where $\alpha = v(\omega) - v(\omega - 1)$ and where η_t is the fraction of the population that works at time t. Households own plants[113] that produce output y_t using capital (k_t) and labour (n_t) and that are subject to both aggregate (z_t) and idiosyncratic (s_t) productivity shocks:

$$y_t = e^{z_t} s_t k_t^\theta n_t^\gamma, \tag{2.162}$$

where $\theta + \gamma < 1$. Output can be either consumed or invested. Labour is perfectly mobile across plants.

Each period, households receive a constant endowment ν of new plants with a zero initial capital stock, and that have a random initial idiosyncratic productivity level taking on the low and high values ($s^L = 1, s^H = \lambda$), $\lambda \geq 1$, with probability ($\psi(1), \psi(\lambda)$). The plants already existing at time t face an idiosyncratic shock that takes on one of three possible values (s^E, s^L, s^H) where $s^E = 0$ and represents a state where the plant exits. The three states follow a Markov process with transition matrix Π, where

$$\Pi = \begin{bmatrix} 1 & 0 & 0 \\ \zeta & \phi(1-\zeta) & (1-\phi)(1-\zeta) \\ \zeta & (1-\phi)(1-\zeta) & \phi(1-\zeta) \end{bmatrix} \tag{2.163}$$

and where ζ represents the probability of exit, while ϕ is the probability of remaining in the same productivity state (conditional on not exiting). The exit state is an absorbing state so that once a plant exits, it is no longer in operation, and its owner recuperates a share q of its undepreciated capital stock $(1 - \delta)k_t$ where q may take values between $(0, 1)$ representing the different possible degrees of irreversibility of the economy ranging from the fully irreversible ($q = 0$) to the fully flexible ($q = 1$). The idiosyncratic shocks are independently distributed across plants. Thus, there is an exogenously given birth rate ν and death rate ζ of plants such that in the long run, the number of plants is constant.

All plants also face a common aggregate productivity shock z_t that follows a first-order autoregressive process, such that $z_t = \rho z_{t-1} + \varepsilon_t$ where ε_t is a normally distributed IID shock with zero mean and variance σ_ε^2.

Plants' investment decisions each period are subject to an irreversibility constraint such that the investment decision is given by $\{k_{t+1} - (1 - \delta)k_t\}$

---

[113] Doms and Dunne (1998) distinguish between plant-level, line-of-business-level and firm-level investment. Their findings indicate that plant-level investment tends to be more lumpy than line-of-business-level investment, which in turn is more lumpy than the more aggregated firm-level investment. They point out that this greater smoothness of investment at the firm level may be an indication of the existence of finance constraints.

when the latter magnitude is positive and by $q\{k_{t+1} - (1 - \delta)k_t\}$ when the latter is negative, q denoting the degree of irreversibility faced by all plants in the economy. Thus total irreversibility is represented by $q = 0$, in which case the plant allows its capital stock to depreciate when $\{k_{t+1} - (1 - \delta) k_t\}$ is negative. When $0 < q \leq 1$, there exist resale markets such that a portion q of the capital stock's value may be recuperated. There are proportional costs to disinvesting (as long as $q < 1$), but no adjustment costs to investing. Investment is *intermittent* in Veracierto's model, but it is not *lumpy* due to the absence of fixed investment costs. The decision rules have the (S, s) form, and lead to upper and lower boundaries to the inaction zone that are state-contingent and depend on the realisation of the idiosyncratic shock.

Each period t, a measure x_t defined over capital stocks and current realisations of the idiosyncratic shocks describes the distribution of plants of each type. In addition, the author defines an x-measurable function n_t that describes the distribution of workers across plant types such that

$$\int n_t(k, s)dx_t \leq \eta \qquad (2.164)$$

and an x-measurable function g_{t+1} that describes next period's stock of capital across plant types. The resource constraint faced by households is given by

$$c_t \leq \int \{e^{z_t}s k^\theta n_t(k, s)^\gamma - [g_{t+1}(k, s) - (1 - \delta)k] D[k, g_{t+1}(k, s)]\}dx_t$$

$$(2.165)$$

$$+ \int (1 - \delta)g_t(k, s)q\pi(s, 0)dx_{t-1}. \qquad (2.166)$$

Here, D is an indicator function that takes the value 1 when $k' \geq (1 - \delta) k$ and positive (or zero) investment takes place, and the value q when $k' \leq (1 - \delta) k$ and disinvestment takes place (so that only the fraction q of $\{k' - (1 - \delta)k\}$ becomes available for consumption due to irreversibility). The first integral is output minus investment across all plant types, while the second integral captures all plants that exit at time t, so that the households recuperate a fraction q of their capital stocks net of depreciation. The law of motion of the distribution of plants is given by:

$$x_{t+1}(B, s') = \int_{(k,s):g_{t+1}(k,s)\in B} \pi(s, s')dx_t + \nu\psi(s')\chi(0 \in B), \quad (2.167)$$

where B is the set capital stocks, χ is an indicator function that takes a value of one when $0 \in B$, and of zero otherwise, while $\pi(s, s')$ denotes the transition probability. Thus, $x_{t+1}(B, s')$ represents the number of plants that have capital stocks that are elements of B and that draw an idiosyncratic shock s'. If the set B includes the value zero, then the second term on the right-hand side of (2.167) also captures the newly born plants. Since the state variables of the problem include the period t decision rule g_t and the measures x_t and x_{t-1}, the dynamic programming problem has a high dimensionality. In order to solve this problem, Veracierto reduces its dimensionality by making use of the (S, s) form of the decision rule. The history of investment decision rules $\{g_{t+1-j}(k, s)\}_{j=1}^{J}$ can be described in terms of the upper and lower boundaries of the inaction zone[114]

$$g_{t+1-j}(k, s) \left\{ \begin{array}{ll} = a_{t-j}(s) & if \ (1 - \delta)k_t < a_{t-j}(s) \\ = A_{t-j}(s) & if \ (1 - \delta)k_t > A_{t-j}(s) \\ = (1 - \delta)k_t & otherwise \end{array} \right\} \qquad (2.168)$$

such that $\{g_{t+1-j}(k, s)\}_{j=1}^{J} = \{a_{t-j}(1), a_{t-j}(\lambda), A_{t-j}(1), A_{t-j}(\lambda)\}_{j=1}^{J}$ which can be expressed as $\{(\mathbf{a}_j, \mathbf{A}_j)\}_{j=1}^{J} \equiv (\mathbf{a}, \mathbf{A})$. Thus, the pair of vectors $(\mathbf{a}, \mathbf{A})$ describe the entire history of the thresholds that characterise the decision rule. The measure x_t is obtained by first initialising x_{t-J} to be x^*, the deterministic steady state value, and then by using the history of upper and lower thresholds for each period and by iterating J times with the law of motion given by (2.167). The measure x_{t-1} is similarly obtained by iterating $J - 1$ times. Then, maximizing 'wealth' given by the right-hand side of (2.165) subject to (2.164), a consumption function $c(\mathbf{a}, \underline{\mathbf{A}}, z, \mathbf{a}^c, \mathbf{A}^c, \eta)$ is obtained where $(\mathbf{a}^c, \mathbf{A}^c)$ denote the current thresholds that define the decision rule g_{t+1}. Using this consumption function the Social Planner's problem is defined as

$$V(\mathbf{a}, \underline{\mathbf{A}}, z) = \max\{\ln c(\mathbf{a}, \underline{\mathbf{A}}, z, \mathbf{a}^c, \mathbf{A}^c, \eta) - \alpha\eta + \beta E V(\mathbf{a}', \underline{\mathbf{A}}', z')\}$$

$$subject \ to \qquad\qquad\qquad\qquad (2.169)$$

$$\mathbf{a}'_{j+1} = \mathbf{a}_j \ and \ \mathbf{A}'_{j+1} = \mathbf{A}_j \ for \ j = 1, 2, \ldots, J - 1 \quad (2.170)$$

$$\mathbf{a}'_1 = \mathbf{a}^c \ and \ \mathbf{A}'_1 = \mathbf{A}^c \qquad\qquad\qquad (2.171)$$

$$z' = \rho z + \varepsilon'. \qquad\qquad\qquad\qquad (2.172)$$

---

[114] The upper bound J on the history of thresholds is taken to be a large enough number, such that due to the depreciation of the capital stock, the solution of the model with history $\widehat{J} > J$ will be the same as the solution for J. See our discussion of Thomas (2002) below for a similar argument for truncating the history of capital vintages.

Since the constraints are linear and the variables that are subject to non-negativity constraints are all positive in the steady state, the problem is solved by taking a quadratic approximation around the deterministic steady state.

First, looking at the plants' problem in a partial equilibrium framework for the purposes of illustration, Veracierto heuristically argues that in the absence of idiosyncratic shocks and when all plants face an aggregate productivity shock with a small variance, the growth rate of the capital stock k_{t+1}/k_t in a totally flexible economy would exceed $(1 - \delta)$ with probability one, so that desired investment would be positive with probability one. Since empirical evidence indicates that aggregate productivity shocks have a low variance, Veracierto suggests that it is unlikely that aggregate shocks alone could increase the incidence of binding constraints in an irreversible economy.

The question remains as to whether persistent idiosyncratic shocks could substantially increase the number of plants facing a binding irreversibility constraint so that we may observe the impact of irreversibility in the aggregate. This would require an 'intermediate' degree of persistence since in the case of a permanent idiosyncratic shock (the certainty case) and in the case of an IID shock, plants have a constant expectation of future idiosyncratic productivity so that the choice of investment will be the same in the two cases and will be determined only by the aggregate productivity shock. As the persistence of the idiosyncratic shocks decreases plants will make more frequent but smaller adjustments and the desired capital stocks will be more similar across plants. An increase in the size of the idiosyncratic shock will increase the number of plants making large adjustments. Furthermore, larger differences across idiosyncratic productivity levels (i.e. a larger value of λ) will lead to larger differences in the desired capital stock across plants.

Even if a large number of plants are bound by the irreversibility constraint due to idiosyncratic shocks, it may not be clear that irreversibility could have an impact on aggregate variables as long as aggregate productivity shocks have a small variance and are persistent. To illustrate this point Veracierto compares two irreversible economies (with $q = 0$) whose plants face slightly different levels of aggregate productivity under certainty (one productivity level being zero, and the other being slightly negative). He shows that first the number of plants with a binding irreversibility constraint would be the same in both economies, while the investment level of the investing plants would be slightly lower in the low-productivity economy. Since investment at the extensive margin is not affected and the only difference is at the intensive margin, the aggregate investment levels of the fully irreversible and fully reversible economies will be the same. As Veracierto argues, if aggregate productivity shocks have *lower* persistence, then irreversibility constraints could have an important impact on aggregate investment. A plant that faces a high probability of a low idiosyncratic productivity shock and hence of facing a binding irreversibility constraint is likely to be less responsive to a positive aggregate shock when the latter is known to have a short duration since, given the high probability of a low realisation of the idiosyncratic shock, it is likely to end up with too much capital once the aggregate productivity level has returned to normal. Veracierto maintains that aggregate productivity shocks are characterised by high persistence and low variability and that therefore this scenario is unlikely.

Turning to the general equilibrium implications of his model, Veracierto compares a benchmark model where $q = 1$ (no irreversibility) to the actual US economy for the period 1960–93, as well as to alternative model economies obtained by varying the value of q from 1 to 0. The model parameters are calibrated using data from the actual economy. The parameters ζ, ϕ and λ of the model are calibrated to fit the data on job-creation and job-destruction as given in Davis and Haltiwanger (1990). First comparing the benchmark model (BM) with data from the actual economy, the standard deviation of investment is higher in the BM (5 times the standard deviation of output as opposed to 3.75 times in the data) while the standard deviation of output is slightly higher (by 6 per cent) and that of consumption is considerably lower than in the data (35 per cent of the standard deviation of output as opposed to 65 per cent in the data). Productivity measured as output divided by hours is less variable in the BM than in the data (35 per cent of the standard deviation of output as opposed to 57 per cent in the data). Productivity is also highly correlated with output in the BM (with a correlation coefficient of 0.91, whereas the coefficient is −0.16 for the data). Nevertheless, the benchmark model without irreversibility is deemed to be broadly consistent with the actual US economy.

The results indicate that as the degree of irreversibility increases, the variability of output, investment and hours worked decreases, but the variability of consumption increases. The standard deviation of investment falls as the degree of irreversibility varies from $q = 1$ to $q = 0$ (from 5 times to 4.4 times the standard deviation of output). However, in view of the fact that the comparison is between two extreme cases of complete reversibility and complete irreversibility, the difference is not very large, according to the author.

A sensitivity analysis conducted by varying the degree of persistence ϕ of the idiosyncratic shocks as well as their magnitude λ,[115] leads essentially to the same conclusion, but also reveals that the variability of investment falls somewhat as q goes from 1 to 0 *irrespective* of the presence or absence of idiosyncratic uncertainty. In order to understand this result, consider the case where there are no idiosyncratic shocks and plants are homogeneous. The variability of investment could fall as irreversibility increases either because the variability of the desired capital stock itself falls or because the level of the desired capital stock falls significantly due to the impact of the aggregate productivity shock which leads to a binding irreversibility constraint. Looking at the impulse response of a negative productivity shock equal to one standard deviation, it can be observed that the variability of the aggregate shock is not large enough to significantly reduce the desired capital stock. In order for the irreversibility constraint to become binding, the aggregate productivity shock would need to be eighteen times more variable, which is counterfactual. Hence, the lower variability of investment as q goes from 1 to 0 must be due to the fact that the desired capital stock itself must become less variable. Furthermore, this must be a general equilibrium effect since irreversibility has no effect in the partial equilibrium framework with homogeneous plants (due to the low variability of aggregate shocks). Veracierto indicates that the main channel through which irreversibility affects aggregate investment is, in fact, related to the exit rate. The latter affects the 'effective' depreciation rate $\widetilde{\delta}(q)$ that plants face, namely:

$$1 - \widetilde{\delta}(q) = (1 - \zeta)(1 - \delta) + \zeta(1 - \delta)q. \qquad (2.173)$$

That is, given that there is a positive probability of exiting, the plant's optimal investment decision takes into account the fact that a fraction q of its capital stock may be lost if it exits. Its rate of effective depreciation is consequently increased, and its rate of return on investment is lowered. Due to a lower rate of return, investment becomes less responsive to aggregate productivity shocks, and hence less variable. This is clearly a general equilibrium effect. Equilibrium prices adjust and the variability of investment falls.

Even though the aggregate impact of irreversibility is not large, its impact at the plant level is quite important. Looking at the distribution of capital

---

[115] A value of $\lambda = 1.4$ leads to a more significant reduction in the variability of investment as q goes to zero. However, Veracierto points out that such a value of λ would imply implausibly high rates of job creation and job destruction. Varying the degree of persistence from $\phi = 0.5$ (the IID case) to $\phi = 1$ also leads to the conclusion that idiosyncratic shocks do not play an important role in explaining the fall in the variability of aggregate investment as q goes from 0 to 1.

growth rates reveals that when $q = 1$ a large number of plants make small adjustments to their capital stock while a small number make very large positive or negative adjustments. When $q = 0$ on the other hand, the number of plants making small adjustments diminishes substantially, the number of plants in the inaction zone increases substantially and the changes in the capital stock are smaller than in the flexible-economy case. Thus capital adjusts more gradually with irreversibility. Another observation is that even a small degree of irreversibility may have an important impact at the plant level, an observation that is also made in Abel and Eberly (1996). Thus the behaviour of capital growth rates is almost identical when $q = 0.9$ as when $q = 0$. Veracierto concludes that irreversibility at the plant level, though very important to the individual plant, does not have a large impact on aggregate investment.

Thomas (2002) introduces fixed costs in a general equilibrium framework. Taking a stochastic neoclassical growth model (an RBC model) as a starting point, she introduces a generalised (S, s) model of investment in the Caballero and Engel (1999) sense. In Thomas' model, plants do not face any irreversibility constraint, but face fixed costs that are randomly drawn from a known distribution. This setup leads to lumpy investment at the plant level. As mentioned in section 5, the generalised (S, s) model allows for inactivity zones that are state-dependent and hence probabilistic. The likelihood that the firm will undertake a discrete adjustment in its capital stock increases as the deviation of its current capital stock from its desired level increases, thus yielding an increasing adjustment hazard as has been observed in the data (see Caballero and Engel 1999; Caballero, Engel and Haltiwanger 1995). The likelihood that the firm will undertake a discrete adjustment in its capital stock also increases as the time-since-last-adjustment increases (as was found by Cooper, Haltiwanger and Power 1999). The stochastic nature of the adjustment costs leads to investment that is lumpy at the plant level, but smoother at the aggregate level.

Consider a continuum of plants in the unit measure, differentiated by their capital stock. A plant that last adjusted its capital stock j periods ago has an output level given by

$$y_{jt} = A_t k_{jt}^\gamma n_{jt}^\nu \qquad (2.174)$$

with decreasing returns to scale technology where k_{jt} is the capital stock that is predetermined at time t, n_{jt} denotes employment and A_t denotes the aggregate productivity shock which has a deterministic component X_t with growth rate θ_A, and a stochastic component z_t. That is, $A_t = X_t z_t$ where z_t

follows a first-order autoregressive process in logs with zero-mean normally distributed errors. In other words, $z_t = z_{t-1}^\rho e^{\varepsilon_t}$ with $\varepsilon_t \sim N(0, \sigma_\varepsilon^2)$. While labour can be adjusted costlessly, adjustments of the capital stock are subject to fixed (non-convex) costs. Each plant is affected by a random idiosyncratic adjustment cost given by ξw_t where w_t is the real wage measured in units of output. Thus, the random adjustment cost is proportional to the wage. The shock ξ is independently and identically distributed through time and across plants. After observing the realisation of the aggregate and plant-specific shocks, the plant determines whether to invest or not. All plants share the same production technology, the same realisation of the aggregate shock and the same distribution $G(\xi)$ of adjustment costs. Hence, all firms that decide to invest at time t have the same expected present value of future marginal revenues, and hence adjust to the same desired capital stock, irrespective of their beginning-of-period capital stock. They are thus identical right after investing, in the sense that they all own the same amount of capital stock. The law of motion of the capital stock is thus:

$$k_{0,t+1} = (1 - \delta) k_{jt} + i_{jt} \quad \text{if the firm adjusts} \qquad (2.175)$$
$$k_{j+1,t+1} = (1 - \delta) k_{jt} \qquad \text{if the firm does not adjust.} \quad (2.176)$$

Determining the cross-sectional distribution of plants according to their capital levels and its evolution through time requires tracking the behaviour of plants that have the same vintage of capital stock, that is, that have last invested j periods ago. The fraction of plants of each vintage j that decide to adjust, α_{jt}, can be obtained as that fraction of plants that draws an adjustment cost value less than or equal to the critical cost level that will just make investing profitable for that vintage of plants. Thus, α_{jt} (which also represents the probability that a plant with vintage j capital stock adjusts) can be obtained from the distribution of the adjustment costs, $G(\xi)$. Let θ_{jt} denote the fraction of plants with vintage j capital stock at t, so that θ_{0t} indicates the fraction of firms that adjusted their capital stock at $t - 1$ *after* production took place. Thus the fraction of plants with each vintage of capital is given by the vector $\Theta_t = \{\theta_{jt}\}$. Clearly, as plants decide to invest or not, the fraction of plants in each vintage will vary through time. Thus, the law of motion of the θ_{jt} is given by

$$\theta_{0,t+1} = \sum_{j=0}^{\infty} \alpha_{jt}\theta_{jt} \qquad (2.177)$$
$$\theta_{j+1,t+1} = \theta_{j,t}(1 - \alpha_{jt}). \qquad (2.178)$$

Households are assumed to have logarithmic preferences defined over consumption and leisure and, as in Veracierto, labour is assumed to be indivisible in the sense of Hansen (1985) and Rogerson (1988). Specifically the period utility function is given by $u(c, L) = \log c + \zeta L$. The resource constraints for the economy are given, respectively, by the budget constraint for the consumers and the time constraint for employment and adjustment activities, where N_t denotes total available time for market activities at t:

$$c_t \leq \sum_{j=0}^{\infty} \theta_{jt} y_{jt} - \theta_{jt} \alpha_{jt} i_{jt} \tag{2.179}$$

$$\sum_{j=0}^{\infty} \theta_{jt} n_{jt} + \sum_{j=0}^{\infty} \theta_{jt} \Xi(\alpha_{jt}) \leq N_t. \tag{2.180}$$

$\Xi(\alpha_{jt})$ is the average adjustment costs paid by that fraction of plants with vintage j capital that adjusts its capital stock, and is defined by

$$\Xi(\alpha_{jt}) \equiv \int_0^{G^{-1}(\alpha_{jt})} x \, dG(x). \tag{2.181}$$

Thomas (2002) finds that there is an endogenously determined upper bound vintage level J such that plants fully adjust their capital stock. This is due to the fact that the distribution of adjustment costs has a bounded support and that the capital stock depreciates. Thus, given that there is an upper bound to costs on the one hand and that capital depreciates through time on the other, there comes a point where the gain of adjusting the capital stock exceeds the cost. Thus plants do not allow their capital stock to depreciate for more than J periods without adjusting. This truncation in the history of vintages reduces the dimensionality of the problem. The planner's problem can be stated as

$$V(\mathbf{k}_t, \boldsymbol{\Theta}_t, A_t) = \max_{\{c_t, \mathbf{n}_t, N_t, \mathbf{i}_t, \alpha_t, \boldsymbol{\Theta}_{t+1}, k_{0,t+1}\}} u(c_t, 1 - N_t)$$
$$+ \beta E_t V(\mathbf{k}_{t+1}, \boldsymbol{\Theta}_{t+1}, A_{t+1}) \tag{2.182}$$

subject to the budget constraint, time constraints as well as the laws of motion of the capital stock and of Θ as given in (2.179), (2.180), (2.175), (2.176), (2.177) and (2.178) and where output is given by (2.174). The optimality conditions for consumption and leisure are given by

$$\lambda_t = u_1 (c_t, 1 - N_t) \tag{2.183}$$

$$w_t = \frac{u_2 (c_t, 1 - N_t)}{u_1 (c_t, 1 - N_t)}, \tag{2.184}$$

where λ_t is the Lagrange multiplier on the budget constraint, or equivalently the shadow value of output. Employment satisfies

$$n_{jt} = \left(\frac{v A_t k_{jt}^\gamma}{w_t} \right)^{1/(1-v)}$$

and the optimality condition for investment can be found to be

$$\lambda_t = E_t \left\{ \beta \lambda_{t+1} \left[\frac{\partial y_{0,t+1}}{\partial k_{0,t+1}} + (1 - \delta) \alpha_{0,t+1} \right] \right.$$

$$+ \beta^2 \lambda_{t+1} (1 - \delta) \varphi_{0,t+1} \left[\frac{\partial y_{1,t+2}}{\partial k_{1,t+2}} + (1 - \delta) \alpha_{1,t+2} \right] + \cdots$$

$$+ \beta^J \lambda_{t+J} (1 - \delta)^{J-1} \varphi_{J-2,t+J-1} \left[\frac{\partial y_{J-1,t+J}}{\partial k_{J-1,t+J}} + (1 - \delta) \alpha_{J-1,t+J} \right]$$

$$\left. + \beta^{J+1} \lambda_{t+J+1} (1 - \delta)^J \varphi_{J-1,t+J} \left[\frac{\partial y_{J,t+J+1}}{\partial k_{J,t+J+1}} + (1 - \delta) \right] \right\},$$

$$\tag{2.185}$$

where $\varphi_{j,t+1+j} \equiv \Pi_{i=0}^{j} (1 - \alpha_{i,t+1+i})$ is the probability as of time t that the capital stock (which is adjusted at t) will not be adjusted again through period $t + j + 1$. The marginal utility of current consumption is equated to the discounted sum of the expected future marginal utility weighted stream of expected future marginal revenues accruing to the plant from the additional unit of investment at time t (conditional on not adjusting its capital stock again in $1, 2, .., J$ periods from now). Equation (2.185) indicates that the expectation as of time t of random variables for $J + 1$ periods into the future will affect the current decision with respect to investment.

Thomas parameterises the above model by assuming a logarithmic utility function for households and a uniform distribution $G(\xi)$ for adjustment costs. The model is calibrated to fit the US economy for the 1953–97 period, and also so as to be consistent with the findings of Doms and Dunne

(1993, 1998) on investment spikes. The 'state-dependent' model (SD) described above with non-convex adjustment costs (where plant investment depends on the realisation of the random fixed cost) is compared to three other models which are essentially similar to the one described above but which differ in terms of the specification of the adjustment costs. The first is a benchmark model (BM) in which there are no adjustment costs of investment, so that plants are no longer heterogeneous and their optimal choice of capital is the frictionless capital stock. The second model is one where there are non-convex but constant adjustment costs (CA), that is, where the fraction of plants indexed by their vintage of capital stock is constant rather than time varying, and where the constant fraction of plants adjusting every period is fixed at 29 per cent (which is the stationary value of the fraction of plants that adjust in the state dependent model). Thus, in this model the cross-sectional distribution of plants and the adjustment hazard are taken to be equal to their long-run counterparts that emanate from the state-dependent model. In this model, the capital stock can be adjusted at the intensive margin (how much to invest) but not at the extensive margin, that is, the decision as to whether to invest or not is predetermined since the fraction of plants that decide to invest each period is fixed *a priori*. The third model (PA), a partial adjustment model, is characterised by traditional convex adjustment costs where plants adjust their capital stock only gradually in response to shocks.

The benchmark model is a standard RBC model, and consequently suffers from the same difficulties in terms of matching the moments of various series in the data. Thus, for example, relative to the actual economy, it generates too low a standard deviation for output, consumption and employment, but too high a standard deviation for investment. However, the model is still useful as a benchmark for comparing the behaviour of the other models featuring alternative cost of adjustment mechanisms. In fact, the standard deviation for output, investment, employment and consumption are found to be identical for the benchmark economy and for the state-dependent adjustment economy.[116] The first- and second-order autocorrelations of output, investment, employment and consumption and the contemporaneous correlation of the latter three with output are also very similar across the BM, SD and CA models, except for slightly higher autocorrelations of investment, output and employment, and a slightly higher contemporaneous correlation of investment with output in the case

---

[116] The indivisible labour assumption implies that the wage rate is proportional to consumption. Hence, the moments of these two series are identical across all models considered.

of the CA model. The partial adjustment model exhibits a markedly lower standard deviation for investment, higher first- and second-order autocorrelation for investment and higher contemporaneous correlation of investment with output than the other three models. The PA model also exhibits a higher standard deviation of consumption, a lower standard deviation of employment, a higher contemporaneous correlation of consumption and employment with output and lower first- and second-order autocorrelations of consumption that the other three models.

Thus the BM, SD and CA models are strikingly similar in terms of the time series they generate in spite of the lumpiness in investment activity at the plant level that characterises the SD and CA models. This lumpiness does not seem to have any impact on investment at the aggregate level. While the BM, SD and CA models are almost identical in terms of the behaviour of output, investment, consumption and employment, the standard deviation of the interest rate is somewhat higher in the SD model than in the BM model and even higher in the CA model relative to the BM. This observation seems to indicate that interest rate and wage adjustments, that is, general equilibrium effects due to the desire for consumption smoothing, are responsible for the similarity of aggregate investment across models. To verify this conjecture Thomas (2002) simulates the models again by fixing the wage and the interest rate. In this case, the models exhibit a marked difference in terms of the path of investment. The SD model exhibits a smoother and more gradual response to a shock than the BM model, while investment responds even less to a shock and is much smoother in the CA than in the SD model. When price changes are suppressed, a 1 per cent increase in productivity leads to a doubling of the number of investing firms. With equilibrium price adjustments however there occur only small changes in the cross-sectional distribution of plants. First, an increase in the equilibrium interest rate reduces the incentive to invest. Secondly, a rise in the real wage increases the opportunity cost of adjusting and thereby reduces again the incentive to invest. These effects dampen the variability of investment at the aggregate level. Pointing to these results, Thomas concludes that price adjustments that occur due to general equilibrium effects are responsible for the failure of plant-level lumpiness to affect aggregate investment.

6.3 Conclusions

We have looked at a number of multi-sector growth models incorporating different specifications of irreversibility or of fixed costs of adjustment.

While most of these models have found a significant impact of plant-level irreversibility on aggregate investment, the last two models that we have surveyed both find little or no significant impact of these rigidities at the aggregate level.

The interesting and remarkable conclusion of both Veracierto and Thomas is that irreversibility or lumpiness at the plant level does not affect aggregate investment significantly once general equilibrium effects such as consumption-smoothing motives leading to endogenous price adjustments are taken into account. Yet, Doms and Dunne (1998) as well as Caballero and Engel (1999), working with aggregate data, found a highly significant impact of non-linear adjustment costs on aggregate investment. Even though Caballero and Engel's analysis is not conducted in a general equilibrium framework, as Caballero (1999) emphasises, 'An important point to note is that since only aggregate data were used, these microeconomic nonlinearities must matter at the aggregate level, for otherwise they would not be identified.' These conclusions lead to an empirical puzzle.

A number of avenues may be worth exploring. In particular, Veracierto assumes a high degree of persistence for aggregate shocks, and notes that, while being empirically implausible, if aggregate shocks had *lower* persistence, then irreversibility might have an aggregate impact in the presence of idiosyncratic shocks. Now, while irreversibility has been modelled at the plant level, the aggregate productivity shocks are considered to be the economy-wide aggregates. It may be worth investigating whether individual plants are susceptible to productivity shocks at lower levels of aggregation, that is to *sectoral* or *industry-level* productivity shocks which exhibit lower persistence, thus potentially giving a greater role to irreversibility at the aggregate level.

Alternatively, one may consider introducing some additional rigidities that may prevent prices from adjusting the way they do in these models and annulling the impact of plant-level rigidities at the aggregate level. For example, changing the way in which the labour market is modelled may lead to somewhat different results. Both Veracierto and Thomas assume that labour is perfectly mobile across plants. This latter feature may be a factor that compensates for the rigidity faced by plants given that capital and labour are substitutable according to the Cobb–Douglas specification of technology and may be responsible for softening the impact of the inflexibility faced by plants in terms of their capital adjustments. Thus, for example, in the presence of heterogeneity of labour due to industry-specific skills, labour would be less mobile across sectors. Other factors such as efficiency wage considerations may also limit the wage adjustments in the economy.

Experimenting with different production technology specifications and different preferences that alter the intertemporal substitution effects and hence alter the behaviour of market-clearing interest rates and wages may be useful. Departing from the Hansen–Rogerson type of indivisible labour and from logarithmic preference specifications may lead to different general equilibrium effects. As Faig has found in a model with Epstein–Zin-type preferences, the negative substitution effect along with the income and positive wealth effects that are induced by irreversibility have an important impact on asset returns. In addition, such a model generates a countercyclical risk-free rate that also is in accordance with the data (see Thomas 2002, table 5) whereas all the models considered by Thomas (as in most RBC-type models) imply a strongly pro-cyclical interest rate. The increase in interest rates coinciding with a positive productivity shock are responsible for reducing the incentive to invest and thus smoothing out the lumpiness observed at the aggregate level.

There is also some evidence that models with fixed adjustment costs are sensitive to the specification of the distribution of adjustment costs. Thus, Dotsey, King and Wolman (1999), in an (S, s) model with fixed costs of price adjustments, indicate that the distribution of fixed costs are an important determinant of the response to money shocks, and that a uniform distribution of fixed costs leads to larger price adjustments and smaller output adjustments.

Alternatively, the introduction into the model of some incentives aimed directly at stimulating investment, such as ITCs and depreciation allowances, may also permit plant-level lumpiness in investment to have a larger aggregate effect, as is pointed out by Thomas (2002).

Another element that may introduce some additional rigidity may be financial constraints at the plant and at the household level. At the same time, one may consider the impact of another type of aggregate shock, namely, monetary shocks. Thus, for example, financial accelerator models of investment find that financially constrained firms' investment responds three times as strongly to a monetary expansion than that of firms which are not constrained (see Bernanke, Gertler and Gilchrist 1999).

Incomplete information may yet be another channel to explore. Caplin and Leahy (1993) show that the interaction of irreversibility with incomplete information may have important aggregate implications in a multi-sector general equilibrium framework. In particular, this interaction leads to allocational inefficiencies, causes even purely sectoral shocks to have important aggregate effects and leads to a propagation of temporary shocks that persist in their impact on macroeconomic variables such as capital and consumption. Thus, a temporary sectoral demand shock leads to a loss of informational capital which can be replaced only gradually, and therefore has persistent effects on aggregate investment.

In conclusion, the models developed by Veracierto and Thomas lead to an interesting empirical puzzle that is bound to spawn a new direction of research.

7 CONCLUSIONS

In this chapter, we have provided an overview of the alternative approaches underlying modern investment theory. Starting with the neoclassical theory of investment and the cost-of-adjustment model as well as the Q-theory of investment, we then turned to models of irreversible investment. We first presented a general framework of partial irreversibility and expandability. Then, we specialised this framework by focusing on the complete irreversibility model of investment under uncertainty. We discussed the impact of demand uncertainty, cost uncertainty, tax policy and liquidity constraints and imperfect capital markets on the level of irreversible investment. We have shown that features of the firm's economic environment such as time-to-build, regime shifts and subjective uncertainty and learning lead to a rich set of dynamic relationships. We then discussed the behaviour of the capital stock in the long run as well as empirical evidence on irreversibility models. Turning to an analysis of aggregate investment, we first examined Caballero and Engel's (1999) generalised (S, s) model of lumpy investment, and then surveyed empirical evidence on the aggregation of lumpy and irreversible investment. There exists strong empirical evidence indicating that models of intermittent and lumpy investment at the firm level can explain the behaviour of aggregate investment. We then turned to general equilibrium models of irreversible investment. The central question that is addressed is whether the intermittence and lumpiness observed at the firm level also affects investment at the aggregate level once general equilibrium effects are taken into account. While some of the models we have reviewed find that firm-level irreversibility has important aggregate effects, two recent studies (Thomas 2002; Veracierto 2002) find no impact of firm-level irreversibility and lumpiness at the aggregate level. The mixed results emanating from the general equilibrium studies contrast with the strong empirical evidence pointing to the important aggregate effects of firm-level irreversibility and lumpiness, leading to an interesting 'aggregate investment puzzle.'

BIBLIOGRAPHY

Abel, A. B. (1979). *Investment and the Value of Capital*, New York: Garland
   (1982). 'Dynamic Effects of Permanent and Temporary Tax Policies in a *q* Model of Investment', *Journal of Monetary Economics*, 9, 353–73
   (1983). 'Optimal Investment under Uncertainty', *American Economic Review*, 73, 228–33
   (1990). 'Consumption and Investment', in B. M. Friedman and F. H. Halm (eds.), *Handbook of Monetary Economics*, 2, Amsterdam: North-Holland, 725–78
Abel, A. B. and Blanchard, O. J. (1986). 'The Present Value of Profits and Cyclical Movements in Investments', *Econometrica*, 54, 249–74
Abel, A. B. and Eberly, J. (1994). 'A Unified Model of Investment Under Uncertainty', *American Economic Review*, 84, 1369–84
   (1996a). 'Investment and q with Fixed Costs: An Empirical Analysis', mimeo
   (1996b). 'Optimal Investment with Costly Reversibility', *Review of Economic Studies*, 63, 581–93
   (1999). 'The Effects of Irreversibility and Uncertainty on Capital Accumulation', *Journal of Monetary Economics*, 44(3), 339–77
Abel, Andrew B., Dixit, A. K., Eberly, J. and Pindyck, R. S. (1996). 'Options, the Value of Capital, and Investment', *Quarterly Journal of Economics*, 111(3), 753–77
Aghion, P., Bolton, P., Harris, C. and Julien B. (1991). 'Optimal Learning by Experimentation', *Review of Economic Studies*, 58, 621–54
Aizenman, J. and Marion, N. (1993). 'Policy Uncertainty, Persistence and Growth', *Economica*, 1(2), 145–63
   (1999). 'Volatility and Investment: Interpreting Evidence from Developing Countries', *Economica*, 66, 157–79
Altug, S. (1989). 'Time-to-Build and Aggregate Fluctuations: Some New Evidence', *International Economic Review*, 30, 889–920
   (1993). 'Time-to-Build, Delivery Lags, and the Equilibrium Pricing of Capital Goods', *Journal of Money, Credit, and Banking*, 25, 301–19
Altug, S. and Labadie, P. (1994). *Dynamic Choice and Asset Markets*, San Diego: Academic Press
Altug, S., Demers, F. S. and Demers, D. (1999). 'Cost Uncertainty, Taxation, and Irreversible Investment', In A. Alkan, C. Aliprantis and N. Yannelis (eds.), *Current Trends in Economics: Theory and Applications*, Boston: *Springer-Verlag Studies in Economic Theory*, 8, 41–72
   (2000). 'Political Risk and Irreversible Investment', CEPR Discussion Paper, 2405
   (2001). 'The Impact of Tax Risk and Persistence on Investment Decisions', *Economics Bulletin*, Spring

(2002a). 'Tax Policy and Irreversible Investment', Unpublished manuscript

(2002b). 'The Corporate Tax Rate and Irreversible Investment', Unpublished manuscript

(2002c). 'Learning about Tax Policy', Unpublished manuscript

Alvarez, Luis H. R., Kanniainen, V. and Sodersten, J. (1998). 'Tax Policy Uncertainty and Corporate Investment: A Theory of Tax-Induced Investment Spurts', *Journal of Public Economics*, 69, 17–48

Arrow, K. J. (1968). 'Optimal Capital Policy with Irreversible Investment', in J. N. Wolfe (ed.), *Value, Capital, and Growth: Papers in Honour of Sir John Hicks*, Edinburgh: Edinburgh University Press

Arrow, K. J. and Fisher, A. (1974). 'Environmental Preservation, Uncertainty and Irreversibility', *Quarterly Journal of Economics*, 88, 312–20

Auerbach, Alan J. (1989). 'Tax Reform and Adjustment Costs: The Impact on Investment and Market Value', *International Economic Review*, 30, 939–62

Auerbach, A. J. and Hassett, N. (1991). 'Recent US Investment Behavior and the Tax Reform Act of 1986: A Disaggregate View', *Carnegie–Rochester Conference Series on Public Policy*, 35, 185–215

(1992). 'Tax Policy and Business Fixed Investment', *Journal of Public Economics*, 47, 141–70

Auerbach, A. J. and Hines, J. R. (1988). 'Investment Tax Incentives and Frequent Tax Reforms', *American Economic Review*, 78, 211–16

Baldwin, C. Y. (1982). 'Optimal Sequential Investment when Capital is not Readily Reversible', *Journal of Finance*, 37, 763–82

Bar-Ilan, A. and Strange, W. C. (1996). 'Investment Lags', *American Economic Review*, 86, 610–22

Bar-Ilan, A., Sulem, A. and Zanello, A. (2002). 'Time-to-Build and Capacity Choice', *Journal of Economic Dynamics and Control*, 26, 69–98

Barnett, S. A. and Sakellaris, P. (1998). 'Nonlinear Response of Firm Investment to Q: Testing a Model of Convex and Non-Convex Adjustment Costs', *Journal of Monetary Economics*, 42(2), 261–88

Bernanke, B. S. (1983). 'Irreversibility, Uncertainty and Cyclical Investment', *Quarterly Journal of Economics*, 98, 85–106

Bernanke, B., Gertler, M. and Gilchrist, S. (1996). 'The Financial Accelerator and the Flight to Quality', *Review of Economics and Statistics*, 78, 1–15

(1999). 'The Financial Accelerator in a Quantitative Business Cycle Framework', in J. Taylor and M. Woodford (eds.), *Handbook of Macroeconomics*, I, North Holland: Elsevier Science, chapter 21

Bertocchi, G. and Yong Wang (1996). 'Imperfect Information, Bayesian Learning, and Capital Accumulation', *Journal of Economic Growth*, 1, 487–503

Bertola, G. (1988). 'Dynamic Programming, Option Pricing and Irreversible Investment', MIT, mimeo

Bertola, G. and Caballero, R. (1990). 'Kinked Adjustment Costs and Aggregate Dynamics', in O. J. Blanchard and S. Fischer (eds.), *NBER Macroeconomics Annual*, Cambridge, MA: MIT Press, 237–88

(1994). 'Irreversibility and Aggregate Investment', *Review of Economic Studies*, 61, 223–46

Bizer, D. and Judd, K. (1989). 'Taxation and Uncertainty', *American Economic Review*, 79(2), 331–6

Blackwell, D. (1951). 'Comparison of Experiments', *Proceedings of the 2nd Berkeley Symposium on Mathematical Statistics and Probability*, Berkeley: University of California Press

Blanchard, O. J. and Fischer, S. (1989). *Lectures on Macroeconomics*, Cambridge, MA: MIT Press

Bond, S. and Meghir, C. (1994). 'Dynamic Investment Models and the Firm's Financial Policy', *Review of Economic Studies*, 61, 197–222

Brennan, M. J. and Schwartz, E. (1985). 'Evaluating Natural Resource Investments', *Journal of Business*, 58, 135–57

Brennan, M. J. and Trigeorgis, L. (2000). *Project Flexibility, Agency and Competition*, Oxford: Oxford University Press

Brock, W. A. and Durlauf, S. N. (2001). 'Growth Economics and Reality', *World Bank Economic Review*, 15, 235–60

Brock, W. A. and Mirman, L. J. (1972). 'Optimal Economic Growth and Uncertainty: The Discounted Case', *Journal of Economic Theory*, 4, 479–513

Caballero, R. (1991). 'On the Sign of the Investment–Uncertainty Relationship', *American Economic Review*, 81, 279–88

(1994). 'Small Sample Bias and Adjustment Costs', *Review of Economics and Statistics*, 76, 52–8

(1999). 'Aggregate Investment', in J. Taylor and M. Woodford (eds.), *Handbook of Macroeconomics*, I, North Holland: Elsevier Science, chapter 12

Caballero, R. J. and Engel, E. M. R. A. (1999). 'Explaining Investment Dynamics in US Manufacturing: A Generalised (*S, s*) Approach', *Econometrica*, 67, 783–826

Caballero, R. J. and Leahy, J. V. (1996). 'Fixed Costs: The Demise of Marginal q', National Bureau of Economic Research Working Paper, 5508

Caballero, R. J. and Pindyck, R. S. (1996). 'Uncertainty, Investment and Industry Evolution', *International Economic Review*, 37, 641–62

Caballero, R. J., Engel, E. M. R. A. and Haltiwanger, J. (1995). 'Plant Level Adjustment and Aggregate Investment Dynamics', *Brookings Papers on Economic Activity*, 2, 1–39

Campa, J. M. (1993). 'Entry by Foreign Firms in the United States under Exchange Rate Uncertainty', *Review of Economics and Statistics*, 75(4), 614–22

Caplin, A. and Leahy, J. (1993). 'Sectoral Shocks, Learning and Aggregate Fluctuations', *Review of Economic Studies*, 60, 777–94

Carruth, A., Dickerson, A. and Henley, A. (2000). 'What Do We Know About Investment Under Uncertainty?', *Journal of Economic Surveys*, 14, 119–53

Chang, L. J. (1995). 'Business Cycles with Distorting Taxes and Disaggregated Capital Markets', *Journal of Economic Dynamics and Control*, 19, 985–1009

Chirinko, R. S. (1988). 'Business Tax Policy, The Lucas Critique and Lessons from the 1980s', *American Economic Review*, 78, 206–10

(1993). 'Business Fixed Investment Spending: Modelling Strategies, Empirical Results, and Policy Implications', *Journal of Economic Literature*, 31, 1875–1911

Chirinko, R. S. and Schaller, H. (1996). 'Bubbles, Fundamentals, and Investment: A Multiple Equation Testing Strategy', *Journal of Monetary Economics*, 38, 47–76

(2001). 'Business Fixed Investment and "Bubbles": The Japanese Case', *American Economic Review*, 91, 663–80

Cochrane, J. (2001). *Asset Pricing*, Princeton: Princeton University Press

Coleman, W. J. (1997). 'The Behavior of Interest Rates in a General Equilibrium Multi-Sector Model with Irreversible Investment', *Macroeconomic Dynamics*, 1, 206–27

Cooper, R., Haltiwanger, J. and Power, L. (1999). 'Machine Relacement and the Business Cycle: Lumps and Bumps', *American Economic Review*, 89, 921–46

Cukierman, A. (1980). 'The Effects of Uncertainty on Investment under Risk Neutrality with Endogenous Information', *Journal of Political Economy*, 88, 462–75

Cummins, J. G., Hasset, K. A. and Hubbard, R. G. (1994). 'A Reconsideration of Investment Behavior Using Tax Reforms as Natural Experiments', *Brookings Papers on Economic Activity*, 2, 1–74

(1996). 'Tax Reforms and Investment: A Cross-Country Comparison', *Journal of Public Economics*, 62(1–2), 237–73

Damodaran, A. (1999). *Applied Corporate Finance*, New York: John Wiley

Darby, J., Hughes-Hallet, A., Ireland, J. and Pescitelli, L. (1999). 'The Impact of Exchange Rate Uncertainty on the Level of Investment', *Economic Journal*, 109(454), C55–67

Davis, S. J. and Haltiwanger, J. (1990). 'Gross Job Creation and Destruction: Microeconomic Evidence and Macroeconomic Implications', in O. J. Blanchard and S. Fischer (eds.), *NBER Macroeconomics Annual*, Cambridge, MA: MIT Press, 123–68

DeLong, B. and Summers, L. H. (1991). 'Equipment Investment and Economic Growth', *Quarterly Journal of Economics*, 106, 445–502

Demers, F. (1985). 'Bayesian Learning as a Propagating Mechanism in a Dynamic General Equilibrium Model of Business Cycles', PhD dissertation, Johns Hopkins University

Demers, M. (1985). 'Investment under Uncertainty, Irreversibility and the Arrival of Information over Time', Essay 1, PhD dissertation, Johns Hopkins University

(1991). 'Investment under Uncertainty, Irreversibility and the Arrival of Information Over Time', *Review of Economic Studies*, 58, 333–50

Demers, F. S., Demers, M. and Schaller, H. (1994). 'Irreversible Investment and Costs of Adjustment', *CEPREMAP* Working Paper, 9416

Dixit, A. K. (1989). 'Entry and Exit Decisions under Uncertainty', *Journal of Political Economy*, 97, 620–38

Dixit, A. K. and Pindyck, R. S. (1994). *Investment Under Uncertainty*, Princeton: Princeton University Press

Doms, M. and Dunne, T. (1998). 'Capital Adjustment Patterns in Manufacturing Plants', *Review of Economic Dynamics*, 1, 409–29

Dotsey, M., King, R. and Wolman, A. (1999). 'State-Dependent Pricing and the General Equilibrium Dynamics of Money and Output', *Quarterly Journal of Economics*, 114, 655–90

Doyle, J. M. and Whited, T. (2001). 'Fixed Costs of Adjustment Coordination, and Industry Investment', *Review of Economics and Statistics*, 83(4), 628–37

Dow, J. and Olson, L. J. (1992). 'Irreversibility and the Behavior of Aggregate Stochastic Growth Models', *Journal of Economic Dynamics and Control*, 16, 207–23

Eberly, J. (1997). 'International Evidence on Investment and Fundamentals', *European Economic Review*, 41, 1055–78

Eisner, R. and Strotz, R. H. (1963). 'Determinants of Business Investment', Commission on Money and Credit, *Impacts of Monetary Policy*, Englewood Cliffs: Prentice-Hall, 60–138

Epstein, L. and Zin, S. (1989). 'Substitution, Risk Aversion, and the Temporal Behavior of Consumption and Asset Returns: A Theoretical Framework', *Econometrica*, 57, 937–69

Faig, M. (2001). 'Understanding Investment Irreversibility in General Equilibrium', *Economic Inquiry*, 39, 499–510

Faig, M. and Shum, P. (1999). 'Irreversible Investment and Endogenous Financing: An Evaluation of the Corporate Tax Effects', *Journal of Monetary Economics*, 43, 143–71

Fazzari, S. M., Hubbard G. R. and Petersen, B. C. (1988). 'Financing Constraints and Corporate Investment', *Brookings Papers on Economic Activity*, 1, 141–95

Federer, J. P. (1993). 'The Impact of Uncertainty on Aggregate Investment Spending: An Empirical Analysis', *Journal of Money, Credit and Banking*, 25, 30–48

Gould, J. P. (1967). 'Adjustment Costs in the Theory of Investment of the Firm', *Review of Economic Studies*, 35, 47–55

Grossman, S., Khilstrom, R. and Mirman, L. (1977). 'A Bayesian Approach to the Production of Information and Learning by Doing', *Review of Economic Studies*, 44, 533–47

Guiso, L. and Parigi, G. (1999). 'Investment and Demand Uncertainty', *Quarterly Journal of Economics*, 114, 185–228

Hadar, J. and Russell, W. E. (1971). 'Stochastic Dominance and Diversification', *Journal of Economic Theory*, 3, 288–305

Hall, R. E. and Jorgenson, D. W. (1967). 'Tax Policy and Investment Behavior', *American Economic Review*, 57, 391–414

Hansen, G. D. (1985). 'Indivisible Labor and the Business Cycle', *Journal of Monetary Economics*, 16, 309–27

Harchaoui, T. M. and Lasserre, P. (2001). 'Testing the Option Value Theory of Irreversible Investment', *International Economic Review*, 42, 141–66

Hartman, R. (1972). 'The Effects of Price and Cost Uncertainty on Investment', *Journal of Economic Theory*, 5, 258–66

(1973). 'Adjustment Costs, Price and Wage Uncertainty and Investment', *Review of Economic Studies*, 40, 259–67

Hassett, K. and Hubbard, G. (2002). 'Tax Policy and Business Investment', in A. J. Auerbach and M. Feidstein (eds.), *Handbook of Public Economics*, 3, Amsterdam: Elsevier Science

Hassett, K. and Metcalf, G. E. (1999). 'Investment with Uncertain Tax Policy: Does Random Tax Policy Discourage Investment?', *Economic Journal*, 109, 372–93

Hayashi, F. (1982). 'Tobin's Marginal q and Average q: A Neoclassical Interpretation', *Econometrica*, 50, 213–24

Henry, C. (1974). 'Option Values in the Economics of Irreplaceable Assets', *Review of Economic Studies*, 41, 89–104

Hopenhayn, H. (1992). 'Entry, Exit and Firm Dynamics in Long Run Equilibrium', *Econometrica*, 60, 1127–50

Hubbard, R. (1994). 'Investment under Uncertainty: Keeping One's Options Open', *Journal of Economic Literature*, 32, 1816–31

(1998). 'Capital-Market Imperfections and Investment', *Journal of Economic Literature*, 36, 193–225

Hubbard R. G., Kashyap, A. and Whited, T. M. (1995). 'Internal Finance and Firm Investment', *Journal of Money, Credit, and Banking*, 683–701

Jones, C. (1994). 'Economic Growth and the Relative Price of Capital', *Journal of Monetary Economics*, 34, 359–82

Jorgenson, D. W. (1963). 'Capital Theory and Investment Behavior', *American Economic Review*, 53, 47–56

(1972). 'Investment Behavior and the Production Function', *Bell Journal of Economics and Management Science*, 3, 220–51

Jorgenson, D. W. and Auerbach, A. J. (1980). 'Inflation-Proof Depreciation of Assets', *Harvard Business Review*, 58(5), 113–18

Jorgenson, D. W. and Yun, K.-Y. (1990). 'Tax Reform and US Economic Growth', *Journal of Political Economy*, 98(5), S151–S193

Judd, K. L. (1987). 'The Welfare Cost of Factor Taxation in a Perfect-Foresight Model', *Journal of Political Economy*, 95, 675–709

Kydland, F. and Prescott, E. C. (1982). 'Time-to-Build and Aggregate Fluctuations', *Econometrica*, 50, 1345–70

Lambson, V. E. (1991). 'Industry Evolution with Sunk Costs and Uncertain Market Conditions', *International Journal of Industrial Organization*, 9, 171–96

Leahy, J. (1993). 'Investment in Competitive Equilibrium', *Quarterly Journal of Economics*, 108, 1103–33

Leahy, J. and Whited, T. (1996). 'The Effect of Uncertainty on Investment: some stylized facts', *Journal of Money, Credit, and Banking*, 28, 64–83

Levine, R. and Renelt, D. (1992). 'A Sensitivity Analysis of Cross-Country Growth Regressions', *American Economic Review*, 82, 42–63

Lucas, R. E. (1967). 'Adjustment Costs and the Theory of Supply', *Journal of Political Economy*, 75, 321–34

(1976). 'Econometric Policy Evaluation: A Critique', *Journal of Monetary Economics*, 1(2) (Supplementary Series), 19–46

Lucas, R. E. and Prescott, E. (1971). 'Investment under Uncertainty', *Econometrica*, 39, 659–81

McDonald, R. and Siegel, D. (1985). 'Investment and the Valuation of Firms when there is an Option to Shut Down', *International Economic Review*, 26, 331–49

(1986). 'The Value of Waiting to Invest', *Quarterly Journal of Economics*, 101, 331–49

MacKie-Mason, J. (1990). 'Some Nonlinear Tax Effects on Asset Values and Investment Decisions under Uncertainty', *Journal of Public Economics*, 42, 301–28

Majd, S. and Pindyck, R. S. (1987). 'Time to Build, Option Value and Investment Decisions', *Journal of Financial Economics*, 18, 7–27

Marschak, J. (1949). 'Role of Liquidity under Complete and Incomplete Information', *American Economic Review*, 39, 183–95

Meyer, J. R. and Kuh, E. (1957). *The Investment Decision: An Empirical Study*, Cambridge, MA: Harvard University Press

Miller, R. (1984). 'Job Matching and Occupational Choice', *Journal of Political Economy*, 92, 1086–1120

Milne, A. and Whalley, A. E. (2000). 'Time to Build, Option Value and Investment Decisions: A Comment', *Journal of Financial Economics*, 56, 325–32

Mirman, L. J. and Zilcha, I. (1975). 'One Optimal Growth Under Uncertainty', *Journal of Economic Theory*, 11, 329–39

Myers, S. and Majluf, N. S. (1984). 'Corporate Financing and Investment Decisions When Firms Have Information That Investors Do Not Have', *Journal of Financial Economics*, 13, 187–221

Nickell, S. J. (1977). 'Uncertainty and Lags in the Investment Decisions of Firms', *Review of Economic Studies*, 44, 249–63

(1978). *The Investment Decisions of Firms*, Cambridge: Cambridge University Press

Oliner S. D., Rudebusch, G. D. and Sichel, D. (1995). 'New and Old Models of Business Investment: A Comparison of Forecasting Performance', *Journal of Money Credit, and Banking*, 27, 806–26

Olson, L. J. (1989). 'Stochastic Growth with Irreversible Investment', *Journal of Economic Theory*, 47(1), 101–29

Patillo, C. (1998). 'Investment, Uncertainty and Irreversibility in Ghana', *IMF Staff Papers*, 45, 522–53

Pindyck, R. S. (1988). 'Irreversible Investment, Capacity Choice and the Value of the Firm', *American Economic Review*, 78, 969–85

(1991). 'Irreversibility, Uncertainty and Investment', *Journal of Economic Literature*, 29, 1110–52

(1993a). 'A Note on Competitive Investment Under Uncertainty', *American Economic Review*, 83, 273–7

(1993b). 'Investments of Uncertain Cost', *Journal of Financial Economics*, 34, 53–76

Pindyck, R. S. and Solimano, A. (1993). 'Economic Instability and Aggregate Investment', in O. J. Blanchard and S. Fischer (eds.), *NBER Macroeconomics Annual*, Cambridge, MA: MIT Press, 259–303

Ramey, V. and Shapiro, M. D. (1998). 'Costly Capital Reallocation and the Effects of Government Spending', *Carnegie-Rochester Conference Series on Public Policy*, 48, 145–94

(2001). 'Displaced Capital: A Study of Aerospace Plant Closings', *Journal of Political Economy*, 109, 958–92

Rob, R. (1991). 'Learning and Capacity Expansion under Demand Uncertainty', *Review of Economic Studies*, 58, 655–76

Rodrik, D. (1991). 'Policy Uncertainty and Private Investment in Developing Countries', *Journal of Development Economics*, 36, 229–42

Rogerson, R. (1988). 'Indivisible Labor, Lotteries and Equilibrium', *Journal of Monetary Economics*, 21, 3–16

Rothschild, M. (1971). 'On the Cost of Adjustment', *Quarterly Journal of Economics*, 85, 605–22.

Sargent, T. (1980). ' "Tobin's q" and the Rate of Investment in General Equilibrium', *Carnegie-Rochester Conference Series on Public Policy*, 12, 107–54

Scaramozzino, P. (1997). 'Investment Irreversibility and Finance Constraints', *Oxford Bulletin of Economics and Statistics*, 59(1), 89–108

Serven, L. and Solimano, A. (1993). 'Private Investment and Macroeconomic Adjustment: A Survey', in L. Serven and A. Solimano (eds.), *Striving for Growth after Adjustment: The Role of Capital Formation*, Washington, DC: World Bank

Stiglitz, J. and Weiss, A. (1981). 'Credit Rationing in Markets with Imperfect Information', *American Economic Review*, 71, 393–410

Summers, L. H. (1981). 'Taxation and Corporate Investment: A 'q' Theory Approach', *Brookings Papers on Economic Activity*, 1, 67–127

Tobin, J. (1969). 'A General Equilibrium Approach to Monetary Policy', *Journal of Money, Credit, and Banking*, 1, 15–29

Thomas, J. (2002). 'Is Lumpy Investment Relevant for the Business Cycle?', *Journal of Political Economy*, 110, 508–34

Treadway, A. B. (1968). 'On Rational Entrepreneurial Behavior and the Demand for Investment', *Review of Economic Studies*, 36, 227–39

Veracierto, M. L. (2002). 'Plant-Level Irreversible Investment and Equilibrium Business Cycles', *American Economic Review*, 92, 181–97

Whited, T. M. (1992). 'Debt, Liquidity Constraints and Corporate Investment: Evidence from Panel Data', *Journal of Finance*, 47, 1425–60

Zeira, J. (1987). 'Investment as a Process of Search', *Journal of Political Economy*, 95, 204–10

Zhou, C. (2000). 'Time-to-Build and Investment', *Review of Economics and Statistics*, 82, 273–82

3

Taxes and welfare in a stochastically growing economy

Stephen J. Turnovsky

1 INTRODUCTION

During recent years economists have again been devoting attention to the issue of economic growth. In contrast to the neoclassical growth models derived in the Solow (1956)–Swan (1956) tradition, in which the steady-state rate of growth is given exogenously by technological and demographic factors, in the more recent literature the long-run growth rate is *endogenously* determined as the equilibrium outcome of the system; see, e.g., Barro (1990), Ireland (1994), Jones and Manuelli (1990), Lucas (1988), Rebelo (1991), Romer (1986) and Turnovsky (1996, 2000b). This is important, since it assigns a potentially significant role to fiscal policy as a determinant of long-run growth performance, something that is infeasible in the Solow–Swan framework. While the endogenous growth framework is not without its limitations, it provides an attractive and tractable approach to addressing issues pertaining to fiscal policy in an intertemporal context.[1]

Most of the endogenous growth literature is based on perfect certainty. However, the endogenous growth framework can be easily extended to a stochastic context and thereby analyse issues relating to risk-taking and economic growth. The objective of this chapter is to construct such a stochastic growth model and to use it to analyse aspects of fiscal policy in the context of a stochastically growing economy. The formulation and solution of the problem employs continuous-time intertemporal optimising methods, rather than adopting the more familiar discrete-time approach. The main reason for this choice is that although continuous-time problems are tractable only under restrictive conditions, when these conditions are met, the solutions they yield are highly transparent, providing substantial

---

[1] The endogenous growth model has been criticised on the basis of its 'knife-edge' characteristics (Solow 1994) and the fact that it is often associated with 'scale effects' (Jones 1995; Stokey and Rebelo 1995).

insights into the characteristics of the equilibrium and the role of risk in its determination.

We should emphasise that our focus is on characterising the macroeconomic equilibrium, and to deriving its implications for macroeconomic policy-making – particularly fiscal policy – rather than on dwelling on the technical details of the solution procedures. At the same time, we should stress that the solutions themselves do involve substantial technical details and that the solutions to these stochastic growth models can be quite challenging.

A key assumption necessary to sustain a steady stochastic growth equilibrium is that all random disturbances are proportional to the current state of the economy, as represented by the capital stock or wealth. This is not an unreasonable assumption; in fact the idea of the magnitude of stochastic shocks being linked to the size of the economy is much more plausible than the more prevalent alternative where they are taken to be additive and thus independent of the scale of the economy. Assuming a constant relative risk averse utility function, this specification leads to an equilibrium having ongoing stochastic growth, in which the means and variances of relevant endogenous variables are jointly and consistently determined. Such an equilibrium, which can be termed a *mean–variance equilibrium*, is analogous to that familiar from finance theory, the elements of which may thereby be incorporated into a complete macroeconomic framework in a straightforward way.

One characteristic of the equilibrium we shall consider is that portfolio shares remain constant over time. Given the stationarity of the structure of the model and that it yields a recurring ongoing equilibrium, this is not an unreasonable property for it to have. But while the derivation of such a consistent equilibrium is tractable, it involves a certain amount of technical detail.[2] Again, the analogy here with the rational expectations methodology is useful. The general strategy to be adopted for determining the macroeconomic equilibrium is to posit specific forms for the stochastic processes facing the agents in the economy and then to determine restrictions on these processes that make them consistent with optimising behaviour and market clearance.[3]

---

[2] A detailed discussion of the basic solution procedures is provided by Chow (1979) and Malliaris and Brock (1982). Turnovsky (2000a) provides a brief summary of the basic results, as well as some of the details for the simplest model being presented here.

[3] This procedure will be recognised as being an application of the method of undetermined coefficients, which is one of the standard solution procedures for solving linear rational expectations equilibria.

The structure of the chapter is as follows. We begin in section 2 by briefly reviewing some of the previous applications of continuous-time stochastic methods to economics. While the applications have been quite far-ranging, they are also quite sparse. Section 3 sets out a basic canonical stochastic growth model, which in structure will be seen to be a direct extension of a standard AK growth model. Sections 4 and 5 then investigate the effects of fiscal policy on the equilibrium growth rate, and characterise optimal fiscal policy. The remainder of the chapter considers alternative extensions to the model, in varying amounts of detail.

Section 6 introduces money and notes its impact on the equilibrium and its role in optimal policy-making. The basic model assumes that investment is costless, so section 7 introduces adjustment costs in investment, along the lines proposed by Hayashi (1982). Here we again focus on the modification to the macroeconomic equilibrium and the effect on optimal tax policy. Most growth models, both deterministic and stochastic, make the restrictive assumption that labour supply is inelastic. Section 8 relaxes the assumption and discusses its consequences for fiscal policy. Despite the technical difficulties of endogenising labour supply, the equilibrium can be summarised by a pair of equilibrium relationships relating employment to the growth rate. This has the advantage of rendering the formal analysis of tax policy to be quite tractable. Thus far, the analysis assumes that government expenditure has no benefits and is simply a drain on resources. This is unrealistic and section 9 extends the model to the case where the government has a positive impact on the productivity of private capital. The optimal size of government and the optimal tax structure are characterised and compared to the corresponding results due to Barro (1990) and others in a deterministic framework.

The implications of risk for international taxation are discussed in section 10, using a simple extension of the basic model. One important aspect is that key 'knife-edge' conditions, restricting tax policy in the absence of risk, no longer hold in a stochastic model. In other words, the introduction of risk introduces important (and plausible) flexibility in international tax policy. The second-best and first-best tax policies are also characterised in a special case.

The constant elasticity utility function (of which the logarithmic utility function is a special case) is the most widely used representation of preferences. As is well known, this imposes a severe restriction on two key preference parameters, the coefficient of relative risk aversion and the intertemporal elasticity of substitution. Section 11 briefly considers the case of recursive preferences, which permits these two parameters to be introduced separately. The issue we focus on here concerns the potential errors in analysing the effects of fiscal policy that one may make by employing the constant elasticity utility function rather than the more general preferences. In fact we show by example that the biases can be quite significant even for plausible estimates of the key parameters. Finally, section 12 briefly discusses the issue concerning the composition of debt and the extent to which this matters insofar as the impact of fiscal policy is concerned. Section 13 is a final comment.

2 SOME PREVIOUS APPLICATIONS OF CONTINUOUS-TIME STOCHASTIC METHODS TO ECONOMICS

Before commencing the analysis it is useful to review briefly some of the previous applications of the continuous-time stochastic optimisation approach to economics. It would be fair to say that these have been sporadic. This is in part a reflection of the fact that they involve a certain amount of technical apparatus, not that familiar to economists, and in part a consequence of the fact that they are often intractable. But one can argue that when they are tractable, continuous-time methods yield transparent solutions that significantly facilitate one's understanding of the particular issue.

As a historical matter, continuous-time stochastic optimisation methods have been more readily adopted by finance theorists than by economists. Most practitioners would agree that the application of such methods, particularly to finance but also to economics, was pioneered by Robert Merton. A collection of his seminal contributions has been brought together in his book Merton (1990), which also contains an extensive bibliography. A review of many of the examples in both finance and economics is provided by Malliaris and Brock (1982). Among the earliest applications to finance, the contributions by Black and Scholes (1973) to the option pricing model and Merton (1973) to the capital asset pricing model (CAPM) should be mentioned; see also Cox, Ingersoll and Ross (1985a). Important applications to the term structure of interest rates were first presented by Vasicek (1977) and subsequently by Cox, Ingersoll and Ross (1985b) and more recently by Duffie, Schroder and Skiadias (1997). In the portfolio area, the seminal contributions are due to Merton (1969, 1971, 1973) and a more recent application is by Jin (1998). Important extensions to international portfolio theory are due to Adler and Dumas (1983) and Stulz (1981, 1983, 1987). Applications to target zone models include Krugman (1991) and Krugman and Miller (1992).

Among the first applications of continuous-time stochastic methods to investment theory are the contributions by Abel (1983), Abel and Eberly (1994) and Pindyck (1982) and a comprehensive treatment of investment theory using these methods is provided by Dixit and Pindyck (1994). The early applications to neoclassical economic growth theory include Bismut (1975), Bourguignon (1974) and Merton (1975). The applications to macroeconomics are relatively sparse, although they are increasing. Tax policy was first analysed in a stochastic endogenous growth model such as the canonical model of section 3, by Eaton (1981). Monetary policy was first studied by Gertler and Grinols (1982), who were interested in studying the effects of monetary uncertainty on investment, and later by Stulz (1986), who analysed the effects on the interest rate. More complete macroeconomic general equilibrium models, directed at analysing integrated debt, tax and monetary policies have been developed more recently by Gong and Zou (2002), Grinols and Turnovsky (1993, 1998a, 1998b) and Smith (1996). General equilibrium applications to international economics include Devereux and Saito (1997), Grinols and Turnovsky (1994), Obstfeld (1994a) and Turnovsky (1995), among others.

3 A CANONICAL STOCHASTIC GROWTH MODEL WITH PROPORTIONAL DISTURBANCES

We consider a real economy in which the household and production sectors are consolidated. To describe the economy, the behaviour of the representative private agent and the government must be considered.

3.1 Structure of the economy

The representative private agent consumes output over the period $(t, t + dt)$ at the non-stochastic rate $dC = C(t)dt$. Output is produced by the simple linear technology in which the stochastic disturbances in output are assumed to be proportional to the mean level of output in accordance with

$$dY = \alpha K(dt + dy) \qquad (3.1)$$

where dY denotes the flow of output over the period $(t, t + dt)$, K is the stock of capital, and dy is a productivity shock assumed to be a temporally independent, normally distributed, stochastic process having zero mean and variance, $\sigma_y^2 dt$. We abstract from labour, in which case capital should be interpreted broadly to include human as well as physical capital (see Rebelo 1991).

With output determined by (3.1), and in the absence of adjustment costs, the stochastic real rate of return on capital is

$$dR_K = \frac{dY}{K} = \alpha dt + \alpha dy \equiv r_K dt + du_K. \tag{3.2a}$$

The economy is assumed to include a second asset in addition to physical capital, namely government bonds. To enhance tractability, these are assumed to be perpetuities paying a fixed coupon of one unit of output over the period dt. The price of these bonds, expressed in terms of output, is P so that $B = Pb$ (where b denotes the quantity of bonds outstanding). However, the price of these bonds now becomes stochastic, reflecting the random influences in the economy.

The stochastic real rate of return on bonds, dR_B, is postulated to be of the form

$$dR_B = r_B dt + du_B, \tag{3.2b}$$

where r_B and du_B will be determined endogenously in the macroeconomic equilibrium to be derived. As will become apparent, the equilibrium will determine only the *value* of the outstanding bonds, rather than their specific price. Accordingly, the nature of the process generating their price is unimportant and will reflect the characteristics of the bonds.

Government expenditure in this economy is determined according to the rule

$$dG = g\alpha K dt + \alpha K dz, \tag{3.3}$$

where dz is an intertemporally independent, normally distributed random variable with zero mean and variance $\sigma_z^2 dt$. According to this specification, the mean level of public expenditure is assumed to be a fraction g of the mean level of output, with a proportional stochastic disturbance, which for simplicity we assume to be uncorrelated with the output shock, dy. Equations (3.1) and (3.3) are stochastic analogues to the specification of production and government expenditure in typical linear endogenous growth models and with an appropriate utility function will lead to a stochastic endogenous growth equilibrium. Such a model was first discussed by Eaton (1981) and serves as a convenient vehicle for analysing the impact of distortionary taxes under stochastic conditions.[4]

---

[4] One constraint we should note is we require all quantities to be non-negative. If the stochastic shock in output is sufficiently negative, it is possible for $dG < 0$, implying a negative government expenditure flow. In this case, for the government to absorb risk it would need to add resources to the private sector. In general, we shall assume that the probability distribution on output shocks

Since the after-tax rate of return on government bonds will adjust to whatever market level is necessary for bonds to be held in equilibrium, only the tax on capital has any real impact on the equilibrium. Thus one may assume, without any loss of generality, that taxes are levied on only the income from physical capital, namely:

$$dT = \tau r_K K \, dt + \tau' K \, du_K = \tau \alpha K \, dt + \tau' \alpha K \, dy. \qquad (3.4)$$

Allowing the tax rate τ on the deterministic component of income to differ from τ', the tax rate on the stochastic component reflects the possibility that the tax code might include offset provisions, having the effect of taxing the two components of income differently. The extent to which the potential existence of these differential tax rates is significant from a welfare point of view will be seen below.

In order to generate an equilibrium of ongoing growth, equilibrium consumption must grow with wealth. One convenient utility function generating this property is the constant elasticity utility function, with the logarithmic utility function corresponding to $\gamma = 0.$[5] Thus, the stochastic optimisation problem of the representative consumer is expressed as being to choose the consumption–wealth ratio, C/W, and the portfolio shares, n_B, n_K to

$$\max E_0 \int_0^\infty (1/\gamma) C(t)^\gamma e^{-\beta t} dt \quad -\infty < \gamma \leq 1 \qquad (3.5a)$$

subject to

$$\frac{dW}{W} = \left(n_B r_B + n_K (1 - \tau) r_K - \frac{C}{W} \right) dt + dw \qquad (3.5b)$$

$$n_B + n_K = 1, \qquad (3.5c)$$

where we denote the stochastic component of dW/W by

$$dw \equiv n_B du_B + n_K (1 - \tau') du_K. \qquad (3.5d)$$

In performing the optimisation, the representative agent takes the rates of returns of the assets, and the relevant variances and covariances as

---

is sufficiently small so that this tail of the distribution can be effectively ignored, an assumption that empirical evidence strongly supports. In the improbable event that $dG < 0$, we shall assume that the government can provide this flow from an available contingency stock of public capital.

[5] Strictly speaking, the logarithmic utility function emerges as $\lim_{\gamma \to 0}[(C^\gamma - 1)/\gamma]$. This function differs from (3.5a) by the subtraction of the term -1 in the numerator; the two forms of utility function have identical implications.

given, though these will all ultimately be determined in the macroeconomic equilibrium.

The first-order optimality conditions can be written in the form:[6]

$$\frac{C}{W} = \frac{\beta - \rho\gamma - \frac{1}{2}\gamma(\gamma - 1)\sigma_w^2}{1 - \gamma} \tag{3.6a}$$

$$\left(r_B - \frac{v}{\varphi\gamma\,W^\gamma}\right)dt = (1 - \gamma)\text{cov}(dw, du_B) \tag{3.6b}$$

$$\left(r_K(1 - \tau) - \frac{v}{\varphi\gamma\,W^\gamma}\right)dt = (1 - \gamma)\text{cov}(dw, (1 - \tau')du_K), \tag{3.6c}$$

where v is the Lagrange multiplier associated with the normalised wealth constraint (5c), φ is a constant determined from the stochastic Bellman equation (and its value reported in (3.17)), and

$$\rho \equiv n_B r_B + n_K(1 - \tau)r_K;$$

$$\sigma_w^2 \equiv \frac{E(dw)^2}{dt} = n_B^2\sigma_B^2 + n_K(1 - \tau')^2\sigma_K^2 + 2n_B n_K(1 - \tau')\sigma_{BK}.$$

$$\tag{3.6d}$$

The form of the consumption–wealth ratio in (6a) is standard. If $\gamma \neq 0$, an increase in the expected net of tax return ρ, will raise the consumption–wealth ratio if $\gamma < 0$, and raise it otherwise. This is because an increase in expected income can be broken down into a positive income effect $d\rho$, inducing more consumption, and a negative substitution effect, $-d\rho/(1 - \gamma)$, encouraging a switch away from consumption, with the net effect on the consumption–wealth ratio being $-\gamma d\rho/(1 - \gamma)$. An increase in the variance of wealth σ_w^2 can be decomposed in an analogous (but opposite) way. As long as the agent is risk averse ($1 > \gamma$), a higher variance is equivalent to a reduction in income and therefore leads to a reduction in the consumption–wealth ratio. At the same time, the higher variance raises the risk associated with savings, thereby inducing more consumption. These two effects are exactly offsetting in the case of the logarithmic function, and also for the risk neutral agent, when they are both separately equal to zero.

Equations (3.6b) and (3.6c) are asset pricing relationships, familiar from finance theory, with the term $v/\varphi\gamma\,W^\gamma$ representing the real rate of return

---

[6] The formal solution to this stochastic optimisation problem is provided by Turnovsky (2000a).

on the asset whose return is uncorrelated with dw. In the absence of risk, (3.6b) and (3.6c) imply equality of after-tax real rates of return. Otherwise, the covariance expressions on the right-hand side of these equations determine the risk premium associated with the two assets. Solving (3.6b), and (3.6c), in conjunction with the normalised wealth constraint (3.5c), one can determine the agent's portfolio demands n_B, n_K (together with the Lagrange multiplier, v).

Equations (3.2) and (3.4) describe government expenditure policy and tax policy, both of which are proportional to current output. In the absence of any lump-sum taxation, these are linked by the government budget constraint:

$$d(Pb) = (Pb)dR_B + dG - dT \qquad (3.7)$$

which, dividing both sides by W, and combining with (3.3) and (3.4), can be written in the form

$$\frac{d(Pb)}{Pb} = \left[r_B + \alpha \frac{n_K}{n_B}(g - \tau) \right] dt + du_B + \alpha \frac{n_K}{n_B}(dz - \tau' dy). \quad (3.7')$$

The model is completed by assuming product market equilibrium, namely $dK = dY - Cdt - dG$, which using (3.1), (3.2) and dividing by K, can be expressed as

$$\frac{dK}{K} = \left[\alpha(1 - g) - \frac{C}{n_K W} \right] dt + \alpha(dy - dz) \equiv \psi dt + \alpha(dy - dz).$$

$$(3.8)$$

This equation will ultimately determine the equilibrium stochastic growth rate of the economy.

3.2 Macroeconomic equilibrium

In equilibrium, the economy determines the rates of consumption and savings; the value and rates of return on all assets; the economy's investment and growth rate; and the risk characteristics of each asset. The exogenous variables include the government policy parameters: government expenditure (g); tax rates (τ, τ'); preference and technology parameters, γ, β and α. The exogenous stochastic processes consist of government expenditure (dz) and productivity shocks (dy), both of which for convenience only are taken to be mutually uncorrelated. The remaining stochastic disturbances: real rate of return on bonds du_B, and real wealth, dw, are endogenous and will be determined. Remaining key endogenous variables include the following: the consumption–wealth ratio; the mean growth rate in the economy, the expected real returns on the two assets (r_B, r_k) and the corresponding portfolio shares (n_B, n_K). At each moment of time, b and K are predetermined.

The objective is to reduce the components of subsection 3.1 to a simple set of core relationships that jointly determine the deterministic and stochastic components of the macroeconomic equilibrium. From the relationships in (3.6) it is reasonable to posit that if assets have the same stochastic characteristics through time, then they will generate the same allocation of portfolio holdings, as well as the same consumption–wealth ratio. The strategy, therefore, is to look for an equilibrium in which portfolio shares, n_i and the C/W ratio are non-stochastic functions of the underlying parameters of the model and show that the restrictions thus implied are in fact consistent with this assumption.[7]

3.3 Determination of stochastic components

The intertemporal constancy of portfolio shares implies

$$\frac{dW}{W} = \frac{dK}{K} = \frac{d(Pb)}{Pb} \tag{3.9}$$

so that all real assets grow at a common stochastic rate. To solve for the equilibrium, one must first consider the stochastic components of the wealth-accumulation equation (3.5b), the government budget constraint (3.7′), and the product market-clearing condition (3.8). These equations, together with the definitions (3.2b) and (3.5c), and the proportionality relationship (3.9) imply

$$dw = n_B du_B + n_K(1 - \tau')\alpha dy = du_B + \alpha \frac{n_K}{n_B}(dz - \tau' dy)$$

$$= \alpha(dy - dz) \tag{3.10}$$

only two of which are independent. The following solutions for dw and du_B are obtained:

$$dw = \alpha(dy - dz) \tag{3.11a}$$

$$du_B = \frac{\alpha}{n_B}[(n_B + n_K\tau')dy - dz]. \tag{3.11b}$$

<hr />

[7] As in all rational expectations equilibria, this procedure need not rule out other equilibria, in which these constancy properties do not prevail. But if such an equilibrium can be found, it is certainly a legitimate one, and one that by the virtue of its simplicity is of real economic significance.

These two expressions enable one to compute all the necessary variances and covariances. In particular, the following expressions, which appear in the consumer optimality conditions (3.6) may be noted:

$$\sigma_w^2 = \alpha^2 \left(\sigma_y^2 + \sigma_z^2 \right) \tag{3.12a}$$

$$\text{cov}(dw, du_B) = \frac{\alpha^2}{n_B} \left[(n_B + n_K \tau') \sigma_y^2 + \sigma_z^2 \right] \tag{3.12b}$$

$$\text{cov}(dw, (1 - \tau') du_K) = \alpha^2 (1 - \tau') \sigma_y^2. \tag{3.12c}$$

Observe that (3.12b) is not a complete solution as it involves the equilibrium portfolio shares n_i which are yet to be determined.

3.4 The complete system

The equations of the complete model may now be collected. First, combining (3.12a), (3.12b) with the consumer optimality condition (3.6b), (3.6c), implies the following expression for r_B

$$r_B = \alpha(1 - \tau) + \frac{1 - \gamma}{n_B} \alpha^2 \left[\tau' \sigma_y^2 + \sigma_z^2 \right], \tag{3.13a}$$

where the second term on the right-hand side of this equation represents the differential risk premium on bonds over capital.[8] Next, equating the deterministic components of the rate of growth of government bonds from the government budget constraint (3.7′) and the rate of growth of capital from the product market equilibrium condition (3.8) (in accordance with (3.9)), leads to:

$$\psi = \alpha \frac{n_K}{n_B} (g - \tau) + r_B. \tag{3.13b}$$

Equations (3.13a) and (3.13b), together with the consumption–wealth ratio (3.6a) (after substituting for ρ and σ_w^2), the deterministic component of the market-clearing condition (3.8), and the portfolio adding-up condition (3.5c) form a complete system determining the equilibrium values of: (i) the consumption–wealth ratio, C/W; (ii) the portfolio shares n_B, n_K; (iii) the real rate of return on government bonds r_B; (iv) the equilibrium growth rate ψ. Substituting further for the portfolio shares n_B, n_K into (3.11b), the reduced form solution for the stochastic component of the

---

[8] In this model, bonds, being perpetuities, are risky, and indeed with the return on capital being denominated in units of final output, may in fact be riskier than capital.

price of bonds can be derived. In addition, the definitions of n_B, n_K add two further relationships

$$W(0) = \frac{K_0}{n_K} \quad P(0)b_0 = \frac{n_B}{n_K}K_0 \tag{3.13c}$$

which solve for initial wealth $W(0)$, and market value of bonds, $P(0)b_0$ in terms of the endogenously determined portfolio shares and the pre-determined stock of capital. This is an appropriate point to observe that the equilibrium described is indeed one in which portfolio shares and the consumption–wealth ratio are constant, thereby validating the assumption made at the outset.[9]

3.5 Equilibrium solutions

To obtain closed form solutions for the key variables, it is useful to observe that (3.5b), (3.6d) and (3.8), together imply the equilibrium relationship:

$$\psi = \rho - \frac{C}{W}. \tag{3.14}$$

This equation is just the equality between the real rate of growth of assets, given by the left-hand side of (3.14) and the growth of savings. Using this equation, the following solutions for the consumption–wealth ratio, C/W, the real growth rate, ψ; and the portfolio share of capital, n_K, obtain:

$$\frac{C}{W} = \frac{1}{1-\gamma}\left(\beta - \gamma\alpha(1-\tau) + \frac{1}{2}\gamma(\gamma-1)\alpha^2\left((2\tau'-1)\sigma_y^2 + \sigma_z^2\right)\right); \tag{3.15a}$$

$$\psi = \alpha(1-\tau) - \frac{C}{W} + \alpha^2(1-\gamma)\left(\tau'\sigma_y^2 + \sigma_z^2\right); \tag{3.15b}$$

$$n_K = \frac{(C/W)}{\alpha(\tau-g) + (C/W) - \alpha^2(1-\gamma)\left(\tau'\sigma_y^2 + \sigma_z^2\right)}. \tag{3.15c}$$

Equation (3.15a) is derived by substituting (3.6d), together with (3.13a) into (3.6a) and thus describes a closed form solution for the consumption–

---

[9] The fact that the equilibrium determines only the market value of bonds implies that it is invariant with respect to the particular type of bond offered. The specific characteristics of the bond, such as the nature of its coupon, its maturity, are therefore unimportant. This is because what is relevant to consumers is the real rate of return the bond offers, and this is ultimately determined by the after-tax rate of return on the productive asset, capital, in accordance with the relationship (3.13a). Given the type and quantity of the bond, its price adjusts as required to support this equilibrium.

wealth ratio. Equation (3.15b) is obtained by substituting (3.6d) and (3.13a) into (3.14) and describes goods market equilibrium, while (3.15c) combines (3.15b) with (3.8). The portfolio share of the other asset, government bonds, is determined residually from the stock constraint (3.5c), which then determines the equilibrium rate of return on government bonds from (3.13a). This last characteristic implies that the equilibrium would be independent of any tax on government bonds. If a tax were imposed on interest income all that would happen would be that the before-tax real return on government bonds would adjust so as to produce the necessary after-tax return required to ensure that the equilibrium relationship (3.13a) is met.

The equilibrium as determined by (3.15) must also satisfy certain feasibility conditions. The first of these is the transversality condition, which for the constant elasticity utility function is

$$\lim_{t \to \infty} E[W^\gamma e^{-\beta t}] = 0. \tag{3.16}$$

Using (3.8) and (3.9), this condition can be shown to reduce to the condition $C/W > 0$, as originally shown by Merton (1969).[10] With the equilibrium being one of balanced real growth, in which all real assets grow at the same stochastic rate, (3.16) also implies that the intertemporal government budget constraint is met. Using (3.15a), the condition (3.16) implies the following constraint on the tax rates on capital τ, τ', and other parameters:

$$\beta - \gamma \alpha (1 - \tau) + \frac{1}{2} \gamma (\gamma - 1) \alpha^2 \big[(2\tau' - 1)\sigma_y^2 + \sigma_z^2 \big] > 0.$$

This condition is automatically met for the logarithmic utility function ($\gamma = 0$). In other cases, this condition may impose restrictions in order for the tax rate to remain feasible.

Second, with non-negative stocks of capital, the equilibrium portfolio share of capital is $n_K \geq 0$. Thus in addition to (3.16), the denominator of (3.15c) must be positive. If private agents are permitted to borrow from the government, then no restriction on n_B is imposed. However, if such borrowing is ruled out, the additional restriction $n_K \leq 1$ must be met.

4 FISCAL POLICY AND GROWTH

The equilibrium is one of stochastic endogenous growth and our particular interest here is to determine its response to fiscal policy.

---

[10] See Turnovsky (2000a).

4.1 Growth and taxes

An examination of the equilibrium relationships (3.15) reveals that taxes on capital income impinge on the equilibrium through the linear combination

$$T \equiv \tau - \alpha(1 - \gamma)\sigma_y^2 \tau'$$

from which it is seen that raising the tax rate τ' on the *stochastic* component of capital income has the opposite effect to raising the tax rate τ on the *deterministic* component of income. On the one hand, an increase in τ reduces the after-tax return to capital, thereby inducing a reduction in the holdings of capital, and reducing the equilibrium growth rate. By contrast, an increase in τ' reduces the variances and associated risk on the return to capital, inducing investors to hold a higher fraction of their portfolios in capital, thereby increasing the growth rate. The qualitative effect of a uniform increase in the tax on capital $d\tau = d\tau'$ thus depends upon $1 - \alpha(1 - \gamma)\sigma_y^2$. It follows that the qualitative effects of a uniform tax increase applied under certainty continue to hold under uncertainty if and only if $1 > \alpha(1 - \gamma)\sigma_y^2$. However, if this inequality is reversed, the stochastic effect prevails, and a tax increase in this circumstance will reverse those that would obtain under certainty.[11]

The proposition that under uncertainty a tax on corporate capital income may increase economic performance has also been discussed by Gordon (1985). He argues that by taxing capital income, the government absorbs a certain fraction of both the expected return and its associated risk, and in his analysis these two effects are largely offsetting. Further implications of changing tax rates will be presented in section 6, in connection with the discussion of optimal tax policy.

4.2 Growth and government expenditure

The equilibrium growth rate ψ is independent of the mean proportion of government expenditure g, just as it is in the deterministic economy under the present assumption that government expenditure does not impact on private utility or on private production. While an increase in g reduces the growth rate directly (see (3.8)), this is exactly offset by the fact

---

[11] As a practical matter the condition $1 > \alpha(1 - \gamma)\sigma_y^2$ will hold for any plausible parameterisation of risk and risk aversion (see, e.g., Turnovsky (2000c) for an example of calibrating a stochastic growth model of the present type).

that it also increases the portfolio share of capital n_K, thereby increasing the consumption–capital ratio and maintaining the overall rate of growth unchanged; see also Eaton (1981).

By contrast, the growth rate increases with the *variance* of government expenditure. This is because an increase in σ_z^2 increases the relative risk on government bonds, inducing agents to switch to holding more capital, thereby increasing the growth rate.[12]

5 WELFARE AND OPTIMAL CAPITAL TAX

An important topic that has attracted much attention is the effect of a capital tax on economic welfare, and in particular the optimal tax on capital from a welfare point of view. Almost all of the existing discussion has been carried out in the absence of risk. It is straightforward to analyse these issues in the present framework, although to do so requires the introduction of a welfare criterion. For this purpose, the welfare of the representative agent, as specified by the intertemporal utility function (3.5a)) evaluated along the optimal path is taken to be the measure of welfare. By definition, this equals the value function used to solve the intertemporal optimisation problem.

For the constant elasticity utility function, the optimised level of utility starting from an initial stock of wealth $W(0)$ is given by:[13]

$$X(W(0)) = \varphi W(0)^\gamma, \text{ where}$$

$$\varphi \equiv \frac{1}{\gamma}\left(\frac{\hat{C}}{W}\right)^{\gamma-1} \tag{3.17}$$

and $\hat{C}/W$ is the equilibrium value given in (3.15a). However, $W(0)$ is itself endogenously determined and using the relationship (3.13c) the welfare criterion (3.17) can be expressed in terms of the initially given capital stock, as

$$X(K_0) = \frac{1}{\gamma}n_K^{-\gamma}\left(\frac{C}{W}\right)^{\gamma-1}K_0^\gamma, \tag{3.18}$$

where C/W, n_K are obtained from (3.15a) and (3.15c). Assuming that these solutions are positive implies $\gamma X(K_0) > 0$, as well.

---

[12] One issue that has gained a lot of attention is the relationship between volatility and growth. This model provides a very convenient framework for analysing this issue.

[13] See Turnovsky (2000a).

Taking the differential of (3.18) yields

$$\frac{dX}{X} = -\gamma \frac{dn_K}{n_K} + (\gamma - 1)\frac{d(C/W)}{C/W}. \tag{3.19}$$

It is seen that the effect of any policy change on welfare can be assessed in terms of its impact on: (i) the equilibrium consumption–wealth ratio, C/W, and (ii) the equilibrium portfolio share of capital, n_K. The expression for $X(K_0)$ becomes more intuitive in the case of the logarithmic utility function ($\gamma \to 0$) when (3.18) can be shown to reduce to

$$X(K_0) = \frac{1}{\beta} \ln \beta + \frac{\psi}{\beta^2} - \frac{1}{2\beta^2} \alpha^2 (\sigma_y^2 + \sigma_z^2) - \frac{1}{\beta} \ln n_K + \frac{1}{\beta} \ln K_0. \tag{3.18$'$}$$

This expression indicates the channels whereby policy impacts on welfare. First, to the extent that the policy stimulates growth, ψ, it increases future consumption possibilities and is welfare-improving. Second, to the extent that it increases the variance along the growth, σ_w^2, it is welfare-deteriorating. Third, to the extent that it leads to an instantaneous increase in the portfolio share n_K it generates an initial drop in the price of bonds, $P(0)$, causing a welfare-deteriorating decline in wealth. Optimal welfare policy involves trading off these effects. If one were to abstract from this last effect, then the fact that a tax on the mean income reduces growth, while having no effect on the variance, would imply that the optimal tax, $\hat{\tau} = 0$. Likewise, the fact that τ' is growth-enhancing would imply that it would be optimal to tax the stochastic component of capital income fully, i.e. $\hat{\tau}' = 1$. However, the initial jump in $P(0)$ induced by such a policy cannot be ignored, and in fact once it is taken into account, the optimal tax policy is an interior one.

We have already seen that the effects of a change in the tax on capital impact on the equilibrium through the linear combination $T \equiv \tau - \alpha(1 - \gamma)\sigma_y^2 \tau'$. Differentiating the expressions in (3.15), with respect to T yields:

$$\frac{d(C/W)}{dT} = \frac{\alpha\gamma}{1 - \gamma}; \quad \text{sgn}\left(\frac{d(C/W)}{dT}\right) = \text{sgn}(\gamma) \tag{3.20a}$$

$$\frac{d\psi}{dT} = -\frac{\alpha}{1 - \gamma} < 0 \tag{3.20b}$$

$$\frac{1}{n_K}\frac{dn_K}{dT} = \frac{\alpha}{(1 - \gamma)(C/W)}(\gamma - n_K) \tag{3.20c}$$

and using (3.20a) and (3.20c) in (3.19), the net effect on welfare is:

$$\frac{dX}{dT} = \frac{\alpha(\gamma X)}{(1-\gamma)(C/W)}(n_K - 1). \qquad (3.20d)$$

We have already commented that an increase in T will lower the growth rate, while the effect on the consumption–wealth ratio depends upon γ, which reflects the net impact of the income and substitution effects of the higher tax rate. As a benchmark case, it is useful to focus on the logarithmic utility function, $\gamma = 0$, when C/W is independent of the tax rate. An increase in T, by lowering the return to capital, will cause agents to switch away from capital towards bonds. The net effect on welfare in this case depends upon $n_K - 1 \equiv -n_B$. On the one hand, the decrease in growth caused by the higher tax rate reduces the expected future income flow, thereby reducing welfare by the amount $-\alpha^2/\beta$. At the same time, the reduction in n_K reduces the negative wealth effect resulting from the price rise (measured by $-(1/\beta)d\ln n_K/dT = \alpha n_K/\beta^2$) and this is welfare-improving. The same argument applies when $\gamma \neq 0$.

As long as the private sector cannot borrow from the government, that is as long as $n_B \geq 0$, it is clear that the optimal tax policy is to eliminate government bonds, setting $n_B = 0$. This result is identical to the result under certainty and is achieved by driving the equilibrium price of government bonds to zero (see Turnovsky 1996). There it was shown that if government expenditure does not impact on the utility of the private agent – the assumption being made here – then the optimal fraction of government debt in the agent's portfolio is zero, just as is found here. The deterministic result, thus extends to the present stochastic context.

To determine the optimal tax itself, set $n_K = 1$ in (3.15c). This leads to the relationship

$$T \equiv \tau - \alpha(1-\gamma)\sigma_y^2\tau' = g + \alpha(1-\gamma)\sigma_z^2. \qquad (3.21)$$

In the absence of risk, (3.21) reduces to $\tau = g$, so that the tax on capital should just equal the share of output claimed by the government. In the presence of risk, this relationship is modified by terms involving the amount of stochastic income taxed by the government and the stochastic component of its own expenditure.

Further understanding of this relationship is obtained by considering the government budget constraint, when the government ceases to issue additional debt. Focusing on the deterministic component of (3.7′), this leads to

$$\alpha n_K g + r_B n_B = \alpha n_K \tau. \qquad (3.22)$$

This equation asserts that the tax revenues on capital must suffice to finance total government expenditures plus the interest owing on its outstanding debt. Now let $n_K \to 1$, $n_B \to 0$, as the optimal tax policy requires. In the absence of risk, (3.22) reduces to $\tau = g$.

As long as the economy starts with a strictly positive stock of government bonds, the share n_B is reduced to zero, by driving their corresponding price to zero. Thus, in the present stochastic environment, as this occurs, the risk premium on these bonds implied by (3.13a) tends to infinity. So that in the presence of risk, these bonds, though negligible as a fraction of wealth, in the limit actually generate non-zero interest income:

$$\lim_{n_B \to 0} r_B n_B = (1 - \gamma)\alpha^2 [\tau' \sigma_y^2 + \sigma_z^2]. \qquad (3.23)$$

Substituting (3.23) into (3.22) thus yields (3.21). A further observation is that any combination of τ and τ' satisfying the linear constraint (3.23) will succeed in reaching the optimum. Thus the flexibility of being able to tax the deterministic and stochastic components of capital income at differential rates has no welfare benefits. The same can be achieved by taxing both components uniformly.

But this optimal equilibrium can hold only as a limit. If, instead, the economy sets the actual quantity of bonds to zero, thereby attaining the equilibrium $n_B = 0$ exactly, then the government's budget would need to balance at all times, that is $dG = dT$ in (3.7). Equating the deterministic and stochastic components in this case, implies $\tau = g$, $dz = \tau' dy$. In order for this to be sustainable, the government can no longer set its stochastic expenditures independently, but instead must adjust them in response to the stochastic component of tax receipts. Another possibility may be to introduce a state-dependent tax rate.

Interest in the question of the optimal tax on capital was stimulated by Chamley (1986), who showed that asymptotically the optimal tax on capital should converge to zero. That result was obtained in a standard neoclassical growth model in which the government sets the *level* of its expenditures exogenously. The framework employed in the present chapter differs from this in one key respect, that accounts for the difference in the nature of the optimal taxation of capital. By specifying government expenditure to be a fraction of output, its level is no longer exogenous, but instead, is proportional to the size of the growing capital stock. The decision to accumulate capital by the private sector enlarges the economy and leads to an increase in the supply of public goods in the future. Since the private sector treats government expenditure as being independent of its own investment decision, (when in fact it is not), a tax on capital is necessary to correct this distortion.

6 INTRODUCTION OF MONEY

It is straightforward to add money to the model, and this has been carried out by Grinols and Turnovsky (1998a, 1998b). In their analysis money yields direct utility, along with consumption, and is represented in the utility function

$$\int_0^\infty \frac{1}{\gamma} \left(C^\theta \left(\frac{M}{P} \right)^{1-\theta} \right)^\gamma e^{-\beta t} dt \quad 0 \le \theta \le 1, \qquad (3.24)$$

where M/P represents real money balances, and θ reflects the relative weight on money in utility.

The nominal stock of money is assumed to grow in accordance with the stochastic monetary growth rule

$$\frac{dM}{M} = \phi dt + dx,$$

where ϕ is the mean monetary growth rate and dx is its stochastic component, having the usual properties and a variance $\sigma_x^2 dt$.

This modification to the model can be solved along the lines outlined in section 3 and leads to several results that are worth noting:

(i) The equilibrium consumption–wealth ratio, the rate of growth and the equilibrium share of capital, are all independent of both the mean rate of nominal monetary growth ϕ and its variance σ_x^2. Thus the superneutrality of money associated with the Sidrauski (1967) model extends to this stochastic economy. Also as in the Sidrauski model, monetary growth does affect welfare through the equilibrium real money balances. There is an optimal rate of monetary growth, which is to reduce the stock of bonds to its lowest feasible level, presumably $n_B = 0$, thereby maximising the utility gained from real money balances. However, for the present constant elasticity utility function the optimal rate of monetary growth is obtained as a corner solution, rather than as an interior optimum which corresponds to the satiation level of real money balances.

(ii) The optimal tax policy is no longer to drive bonds to zero, but rather is now characterised by $n_K = \theta(1 + \gamma n_M)$, where n_M is the portfolio share of money. This relationship reduces to the optimum derived in section 5, when money is absent or yields no utility.

(iii) There is a jointly optimal tax–monetary policy obtained by combining (i) and (ii), and characterised by

$$n_M = \frac{1 - \theta}{1 + \theta\gamma} \geq 0; \quad n_B = 0; \quad n_K = \frac{\theta(1 + \gamma)}{1 + \theta\gamma} \geq 0$$

in which both money, which yields direct utility, and capital are held in strictly positive quantities in equilibrium.

These results are sensitive to the nature of the government bonds and to the specification of government debt policy. Under other assumptions, for example if the government deficit is residually financed by a neutral wealth tax, the non-neutrality of money breaks down.

7 ADJUSTMENT COSTS IN INVESTMENT

The model considered thus far has treated investment as being costless. It is possible to impose adjustment costs on investment along the lines of Hayashi (1982). In order to retain tractability, this must be done in a specific way, so as to retain the proportionality of the equilibrium. Benavie, Grinols and Turnovsky (1996) adopt a formulation in which installation costs are proportional to the planned rate of investment. Assuming a quadratic function, where the marginal installation costs are represented by hI/K, the equilibrium growth rate and the Tobin-q are related by

$$\psi = \frac{q - 1}{h} \tag{3.25}$$

and the macroeconomic equilibrium is described by

$$(1 - \gamma)\left(\frac{q - 1}{h}\right) = \frac{(1 - \tau)}{q}\left(\alpha + \frac{(q - 1)^2}{2h}\right) - \beta$$

$$+ (1 - \gamma)\left(\frac{\alpha}{q}\right)^2 \left[\left(\tau' - \frac{\gamma}{2}\right)\sigma_y^2 + \left(1 - \frac{\gamma}{2}\right)\sigma_z^2\right] \tag{3.26a}$$

$$\frac{C}{W} = \beta - \gamma\left(\frac{q - 1}{h}\right) - \frac{1}{2}\gamma(\gamma - 1)\left(\frac{\alpha}{q}\right)^2 (\sigma_y^2 + \sigma_z^2) \tag{3.26b}$$

$$n_K = \frac{q(C/W)}{\alpha(1 - g) - (q^2 - 1)/2h}. \tag{3.26c}$$

This equilibrium has the following recursive structure. First, (3.26a), which is essentially product market equilibrium, determines the equilibrium price q in terms of the exogenous parameters. Given q, (3.25) determines the equilibrium growth rate, while (3.26b) determines the equilibrium consumption–wealth ratio, with (3.26c) then yielding the equilibrium portfolio share. Indeed, (3.26) is directly analogous to (3.15) presented in section 3, to which it reduces in the limiting case $h \to 0, q \to 1$. The key point to observe about (3.26) is that the equilibrium q is a function of the variances in the economy it remains deterministic and changes only when there is a change in the stochastic structure. Abel and Eberly (1994) develop a continuous-time stochastic model in which q itself evolves stochastically.

7.1 Optimal capital tax

The qualitative effects of a capital tax remain essentially as in the basic model. However the introduction of adjustment costs does impinge on the optimal tax. Indeed, one can show that in the presence of adjustment costs, it is no longer optimal to eliminate bonds from the equilibrium, as was the case in section 5.

To see this, we return to the equilibrium solution (3.26) from which it is seen that the only channel through which the two tax rates τ, τ' impact on n_K, C/W, and hence on welfare, $X(K_0)$ is through the relative price of installed capital, q. Thus the optimal tax policy is tantamount to choosing the optimal q. Having determined q, this can then be attained by the appropriate choice of either tax independently, or a by a linear combination of the two.

Taking the differentials of (C/W), and n_K from (3.26b) and (3.26c), and substituting into (3.19), we can obtain the following expression for the resulting change in welfare:

$$
\frac{dX}{X} = \frac{\gamma}{h(C/W)} \left\{ (1 - n_K)q - \beta h + \gamma(q - 1) \right.
$$

$$
\left. + \frac{(\gamma - 1)(\gamma - 2)}{2} \left(\frac{\alpha}{q} \right)^2 h\left(\sigma_y^2 + \sigma_z^2\right) \right\} \frac{dq}{q}. \tag{3.27}
$$

The optimal tax policy is attained when the term in parentheses in (3.27) is set to zero, i.e when

$$
\hat{n}_K = 1 - \frac{\beta h}{\hat{q}} + \gamma \frac{(\hat{q} - 1)}{\hat{q}} + \frac{(\gamma - 1)(\gamma - 2)}{2\hat{q}^3} \alpha^2 h\left(\sigma_y^2 + \sigma_z^2\right), \tag{3.28}
$$

where $\hat{\ }$ denotes the optimum. Equation (3.28), in conjunction with (3.26b) and (3.26c), jointly determine the welfare-maximising values of the portfolio share of capital, $\hat{n}_K$; consumption–wealth ratio, $\hat{C}/W$, and the relative price of installed capital, $\hat{q}$. And having determined the latter, (3.26a), then determines the corresponding optimal tax rate, $\hat{\tau}$ or $\hat{\tau}'$.

To understand the nature of the optimal policy further, it is useful to begin with the benchmark case of freely adjustable capital, $h = 0$, when $q = 1$. In this case (3.28) reduces to $\hat{n}_K = 1$, and the corresponding optimal tax rate can be shown to reduce back to (3.21). When the accumulation of capital involves adjustment cost, optimal policy no longer calls for the elimination of government bonds and a balanced government budget. The fact that capital is costly to adjust permits bonds to play an independent welfare-enhancing role. Using the definitions of C/W, and σ_w^2, (3.28) can be expressed as

$$\hat{n}_B = h \left[\frac{1}{q} \left(\frac{\hat{C}}{W} \right) + (\gamma - 1)\hat{\sigma}_w^2 \right]. \tag{3.28'}$$

In the presence of adjustment costs a positive equilibrium consumption–wealth ratio generates a positive welfare role for government bonds. However, this is offset by the presence of equilibrium real risk and if this latter effect dominates, the optimal tax policy will call for the government to be a net creditor to the private sector.

8 ENDOGENOUS LABOUR SUPPLY

8.1 Some general issues

The introduction of endogenous labour supply into the stochastic growth model has proved problematical and like most deterministic endogenous growth models, these models almost all assume that labour is supplied inelastically.[14] But this assumption has strong implications for fiscal policy, and it is important that it be relaxed.

---

[14] Two exceptions to this in the deterministic literature include Benhabib and Perli (1994) and Ladrón-de-Guevara, Ortigueira and Santos (1997), who focus on issues relating to non-uniqueness of equilibrium generated by endogenous labour. Brief discussions of the effects of taxation in models of endogenous growth with endogenous labour are provided by Rebelo (1991) and Stokey and Rebelo (1995). Corsetti (1997), Tenc (2002), Turnovsky (2000c) are among the papers to analyse fiscal policy in a stochastic growth model with endogenous labour supply, although each introduces labour in a somewhat different way. Bodie, Merton and Samuelson (1992) examine labour supply flexibility and portfolio choice in a related stochastic life cycle model.

Although endogenising labour supply leaves some of the characteristics of the fixed-employment equilibrium unchanged, other aspects of the equilibrium turn out to be affected in significant ways. Whereas with inelastic labour supply the consumption and wage tax both operate as lump-sum taxes, when the supply of labour is endogenised, both these forms of tax have real effects. In addition, debt-financed government consumption expenditure, which with inelastic labour supply also has no effect on the equilibrium growth rate, now does influence that variable. While these effects of endogenising labour supply on fiscal policy also apply in a deterministic economy, in a stochastic economy one further important dimension is introduced.[15] By influencing the productivity of capital, the (endogenous) fraction of time allocated to labour influences the magnitude of the technology shocks as they impinge on the economy. This provides an important channel whereby tax policy is able to influence the variance of the equilibrium growth rate. In particular, the tax on labour income with its direct impact on the labour–leisure decision, has a particularly strong impact on the equilibrium risk in the economy.

With endogenous labour supply the individual production function is assumed to be constant returns to scale in private capital and labour. In order for the equilibrium to be one of steady endogenous growth, the aggregate production must be of the AK form. For this to occur, given constant returns to scale in private capital and labour, the individual production function must be subject to an externality, such as that introduced by Romer (1986).[16] This introduces an interesting methodological issue in solving for the equilibrium. Specifically, the individual agent in solving his stochastic optimisation faces two state variables: his own private stock of wealth, and the economy-wide aggregate stock of wealth. In general, two state variable continuous time stochastic models require the solution of non-linear partial differential equations and are therefore highly intractable. But under the assumption of identical representative agents, in equilibrium the individual and aggregate stocks of assets are directly proportional. The stochastic macrodynamic equilibrium is therefore generated by a single state variable, so that an analytical solution in fact turns out to be feasible. Details of these calculations are provided by Turnovsky (2000c).

Despite the rather complex equilibrium, the real part can be conveniently depicted in terms of two tradeoff loci relating the equilibrium balanced growth rate to the fraction of time devoted to leisure. The first

---

[15] These issues are analysed in some detail in a deterministic growth model by Turnovsky (2000b).

[16] Alternative sources of externalities that serve a similar purpose include a productive government input and congestion.

locus describes the combinations of these two quantities that maintain consistency among rates of return; the second describes the combinations of these two quantities consistent with product market equilibrium. These relationships are non-linear, and an equilibrium may or may not exist in which both conditions are met simultaneously.

This representation offers simple pedagogic advantages. The two equilibrium relationships enable us to see how the degree of production risk, together with the government's response to risk through the stochastic component of its taxation and expenditure policies, can influence the balance between these rates of return, and thus in part determine the existence of an equilibrium. Simple manipulation of these two equilibrium tradeoff loci permits us to conduct a number of comparative static exercises with respect to the equilibrium growth–leisure (employment) tradeoff, as well as the associated equilibrium risk. For example, it is straightforward to show that all tax rates reduce the labour supply, the equilibrium growth rate, and its risk.[17]

8.2 Production structure

In introducing endogenous labour supply it is critical to ensure that the production structure is consistent with an equilibrium of ongoing stochastic growth. To do this, we assume that the representative agent is endowed with a unit of time that can be allocated either to leisure, l, or to work, $1 - l$, $[0 < l < 1]$. The representative agent produces output in accordance with the stochastic Cobb–Douglas production function:

$$dY = \alpha\big((1 - l)\overline{K}\big)^{\eta} K^{1-\eta}(dt + dy) \equiv Z(dt + dy) \quad 0 < \eta < 1, \tag{3.29a}$$

where K denotes the individual firm's stock of capital, $\overline{K}$ is the average economy-wide stock of capital, so that $(1 - l)\overline{K}$ measures individual labour in efficiency units (see Corsetti 1997; Turnovsky 2000c). This stochastic production function exhibits constant returns to scale in the private decisions, the fraction of time to devote to work and the private capital stock. In addition, the average stock of capital yields an externality such that in equilibrium, when $K = \overline{K}$, the production function is linear in the accumulating stock of capital, as in Romer (1986). Aggregate (average) output is thus represented by:

$$d\overline{Y} = \alpha(1 - \bar{l})^{\eta}\overline{K}(dt + dy) \equiv \overline{Z}(dt + dy). \tag{3.29b}$$

---

[17] These and related issues are discussed by the current author in a companion chapter (chapter 10) in this volume, as well as in Section 8.4 below. Extensive numerical simulations are carried out by Turnovsky (2000c).

We assume that the wage rate, a, over the period $(t, t + dt)$ is determined at the start of the period and is set equal to the expected marginal physical product of labour over that period. The total rate of return to labour, dA, over the period is thus specified non-stochastically by:

$$dA = adt = E\left(\frac{\partial Z}{\partial (1 - l)}\right)_{K=\overline{K}, l=\overline{l}} dt = \eta\alpha(1 - \overline{l})^{\beta - 1}dt. \quad (3.30a)$$

The private rate of return to capital, dR_K over the period $(t, t + dt)$, is thus determined residually by

$$dR_K = \frac{d\overline{Y} - \delta\overline{K} - LdA}{\overline{K}} \equiv r_K dt + du_K, \quad (3.30b)$$

where

$$r_K \equiv \left(\frac{\partial Z}{\partial K}\right)_{K=\overline{K}, l=\overline{l}} = (1 - \eta)\alpha(1 - \overline{l})^{\eta}; \quad du_K \equiv \frac{\overline{Z}}{\overline{K}}dy$$

$$= \alpha(1 - \overline{l})^{\eta}dy.$$

According to this specification, the wage rate, a, is fixed over the period $(t, t + dt)$, with all short-run fluctuations in output being reflected in the stochastic return to capital. While this allocation of risk may seem extreme, casual empirical evidence suggests that the returns to capital are far more volatile than are wages.[18] Equations (3.30a) and (3.30b) imply, further, that the mean rate of return to capital is constant through time, while the wage rate grows with the equilibrium capital stock. These features are important for the equilibrium.

8.3 Equilibrium growth–employment–risk tradeoff

The other modification is to consumer preferences, which we assume is of the form

$$U \equiv \int_0^{\infty} \frac{1}{\gamma}(Cl^{\delta})^{\gamma}e^{-\beta t}dt. \quad (3.5a')$$

This form of utility function ensures that the equilibrium ensures that the consumption–wealth ratio remains constant, while at the same time the agent's allocation of time between leisure and labour is constant,

---

[18] In the USA, for example, the relative variability of real stock returns over the period 1955–95 have been around 32 per cent per annum, while the relative variability of wages has been comparable to that of output, 2 per cent.

consistent with having a fixed endowment of time. The rest of the model is a straightforward generalisation of Grinols and Turnovsky (1998a) and leads to a stochastic macroeconomic equilibrium having the same general structure. In particular, the dichotomy of the equilibrium in the fixed employment continues to hold, with money being super-neutral in both the mean and variance of the growth rate. Also, the real growth equilibrium is independent of the tax rates on interest income, while taxes on capital income operate through a linear combination analogous to T defined on p. 168.

With substitution, the real part of the balanced growth equilibrium can be summarised by the following pair of core equations (where for convenience the bars denoting aggregates are deleted):

$$\textbf{RR: } \psi = \frac{1}{1-\gamma}\{(1-\tau_K)(1-\eta)\alpha(1-l)^\eta - \beta$$
$$+ (1-\gamma)\alpha^2(1-l)^{2\eta}\Omega\} \tag{3.31a}$$

$$\textbf{PP: } \psi = \alpha(1-l)^\eta\left[(1-g) - \left(\frac{1-\tau_W}{1+\tau_C}\right)\frac{\eta}{\delta}\left(\frac{l}{1-l}\right)\right], \tag{3.31b}$$

where

$$\Omega \equiv (1-g')[(\tau_K' - g') - (\gamma/2)(1-g')]\sigma_y^2$$

and τ_K, τ_K' denote the tax rates on the deterministic and stochastic components of capital income, τ_W denotes the tax rate on the (deterministic) wage income, τ_C denotes the consumption tax, and g, g' denote government expenditure out of the deterministic and stochastic income components, (i.e. $dG = Z(g\,dt + g'dy)$).

These two equations jointly determine the steady-state equilibrium growth rate, ψ, and fraction of time devoted to leisure (labour), $\bar{l}$. Equation (3.31a) describes the relationship between the equilibrium growth rate and the long-run level of leisure that ensures the equality between the after-tax rate of return on capital and the return on consumption. The rates of return on both consumption and investment are risky, and the quantity Ω reflects the risk premium on consumption over investment. An increase in τ_K' reduces the stochastic component of the after-tax return to capital and thus increases the relative riskiness of consumption. An increase in the stochastic component of output claimed by the government, g', will probably (but not necessarily) reduce the relative variability of consumption.

For expository purposes we shall assume $\Omega > 0$; sufficient conditions to ensure that this is so include: $\tau_K' > g'; \gamma < 0$.

The formal properties of the RR locus are derived by Turnovsky (2000c), where we show that its slope is uniformly negative. Intuitively, a higher fraction of time devoted to leisure reduces the productivity of, and returns to, capital. For the rates of return to remain in equilibrium, the rate of return on consumption must fall correspondingly and this requires the growth of the marginal utility of consumption to rise, that is, the balanced growth rate of the economy must decline. Of course, a higher fraction of time devoted to leisure also impacts on the relative risk of the two returns, though if $\Omega > 0$, this reinforces the effect just described.

The relationship (3.31b), denoted by PP, describes the tradeoff between the equilibrium growth rate and the fraction of time devoted to leisure that ensures product market equilibrium is maintained. This, too, is unambiguously negatively sloped. In this case a higher fraction of time devoted to leisure reduces the productivity of capital. It also increases the consumption–output ratio, thus having an adverse effect on the growth rate of capital in the economy.

Under plausible conditions, both tradeoff relationships PP and RR are concave with respect to the origin, raising the question of whether or not an equilibrium balanced growth path consistent with $0 < l < 1$ exists. We can show that a sufficient condition for a unique steady-state balanced growth path to exist is

$$\frac{(1 - \tau_K)(1 - \eta)}{1 - \gamma} - (1 - g)$$

$$< \min\left[\left(\frac{1 - \tau_W}{1 + \tau_C}\right)\frac{1}{\delta} - \frac{2\alpha\Omega}{1 - \gamma}, \frac{(\beta/\alpha) - \alpha\Omega}{1 - \gamma}\right]. \quad (3.32)$$

We may observe that this condition is met in a benchmark logarithmic economy $(\gamma = 0)$ in which all tax and expenditure rates are set equal $[\tau_K = \tau_W = g]$. Note that the likelihood of (3.32) being satisfied increases if $\Omega < 0$, i.e. if the relative risk premium on the return to capital is larger.

From the properties of the RR and PP loci, we can show that in the neighbourhood of the equilibrium the PP curve is steeper. Also, having determined equilibrium employment from RR and PP, the relationship:

$$\textbf{SS:} \quad \sigma_w = \alpha(1 - l)^\eta(1 - g')\sigma_y \quad (3.31c)$$

determines the associated degree of risk (volatility) along the equilibrium growth path.

8.4 Fiscal shocks

The qualitative effects of changes in alternative fiscal instruments on the core growth–employment–risk tradeoffs are readily obtained by considering shifts in the *RR*, *PP* and *SS* curves. In all cases, we assume that the fiscal changes are financed by accommodating changes in debt. For convenience we restrict ourselves to positive equilibrium growth rates so that the *PP* and *RR* loci can be confined to the positive quadrant.

Increase in deterministic tax rates
An increase in any of the tax rates, τ_K, τ_W, τ_C has the same qualitative effects, decreasing the fraction of time devoted to work, thereby reducing the equilibrium growth rate and its risk:

$$\frac{\partial \bar{l}}{\partial \tau_i} > 0; \quad \frac{\partial \bar{\psi}}{\partial \tau_i} < 0; \quad \frac{\partial \bar{\sigma}_\psi}{\partial \tau_i} < 0; \quad i = K, W, C. \quad (3.33a)$$

These responses are illustrated in figure 3.1, where an increase in the tax on capital, τ_K, with subsequent accommodation by debt financing, is reflected by a downward shift in the *RR* locus.[19] Suppose the initial equilibrium is at A, then given the fraction of time devoted to leisure, this leads to an immediate reduction in the growth rate, as measured by the move from A to E. This reduces the return on consumption, causing a substitution of leisure for labour, and reducing the rate of return on capital to that of consumption.[20] This decrease in employment reduces output, leading to a further reduction in the growth rate. The ultimate shift in equilibrium is thus represented by a move from A to B along the *PP* locus. The increase in l (decrease in labour) leads to a reduction in σ_w which is represented by a move LH along SS, illustrating clearly how the reduction in the growth rate is accompanied by an increase in stability.

An increase in the tax on wage income or on consumption leads to an upward rotation in the *PP* locus, illustrated in figure 3.2. Given leisure, this leads to an immediate reduction in the consumption–output ratio, and a corresponding rise in the growth rate of output, from A to E. This raises the

---

[19] It is actually a rotation through the point $l = 1$, $\psi = -\beta/(1 - \gamma)$.
[20] The rate of return on consumption equals $\beta - E(dX_w)/X_w$, which varies positively with the growth rate, ψ.

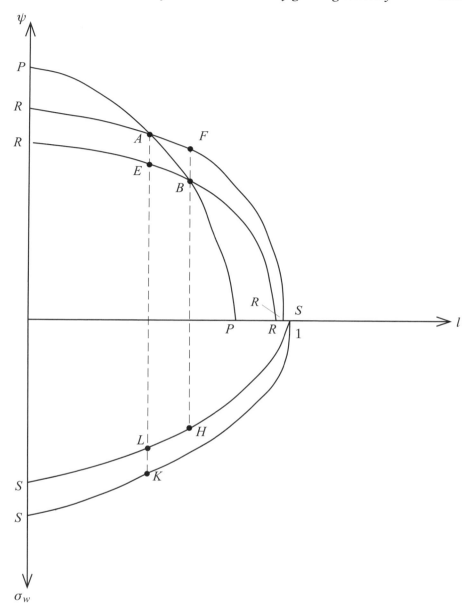

Figure 3.1 Effects due to shifts in *PR* and *SS* curves

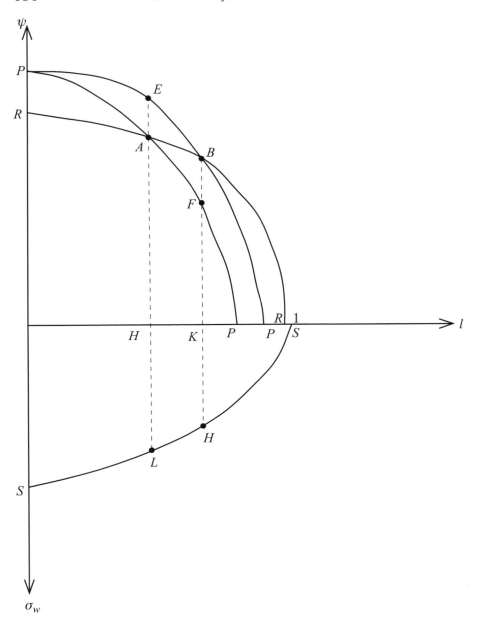

Figure 3.2 Effects due to shift in *PP* curve

return on consumption, causing agents to increase consumption and leisure over work. This causes a reduction in output and the growth rate, leading to a reduction in the return to capital and in consumption. The eventual shift in equilibrium is thus represented by a move from A to B along the RR locus. This reduction in the mean growth rate is accompanied by a reduction in its standard deviation as represented by the move LH along the SS locus.

Increase in rates of government expenditure
An increase in the mean government consumption expenditure financed by debt, can be shown to raise employment, the growth rate, and its standard deviation:

$$\frac{\partial \bar{l}}{\partial g} < 0; \quad \frac{\partial \bar{\psi}}{\partial g} > 0; \quad \frac{\partial \bar{\sigma}_\psi}{\partial g} > 0. \tag{3.33b}$$

An increase in government consumption expenditure is qualitatively directly opposite to an increase in either τ_C or τ_W and is represented by a downward shift in the PP curve in figure 3.2. Starting from an initial equilibrium at B, this leads to an immediate reduction in the growth rate of capital, measured by BF. This reduces the rate of return on consumption and induces the agent to substitute away from consumption toward labour, leading to less leisure and more growth. The new equilibrium is represented by a move along BA along PP. Given that the PP locus is steeper than the RR locus, the ultimate increase in the growth rate exceeds the immediate reduction represented by the downward shift in the PP curve. The corresponding increase in the variability of the growth rate is represented by the movement HL along SS.

The expansionary effect of the increase in the fraction of output devoted to government consumption expenditure contrasts with the well-known result discussed on p. 168 that a debt-financed (or lump-sum-financed) increase in government consumption expenditure simply crowds out private consumption leaving the growth rate unaffected. In the present case, the higher taxes and the associated reduction in wealth, raises the marginal utility of wealth, inducing workers to devote a larger fraction of their time to work, thereby increasing the long-run growth rate.

Risk, stochastic expenditures and taxes
Risk and the stochastic components of fiscal policy all operate through the term Ω, and its impact on the relative risk premium to consumption. These are illustrated in figure 3.2 by shifts in RR and in some cases the SS curve.

Consider first the case of an increase in the variance of the productivity shock, σ_y^2, in the more likely case that $\Omega > 0$, when consumption yields a more risky utility return. This is represented by an upward rotation of the RR locus, and in this respect operates like a decrease in τ_κ. Suppose the initial equilibrium is at B, then given the fraction of time devoted to leisure, this leads to an immediate increase in the growth rate as measured by the shift up along BF. This increases the rate of return on consumption, causing a substitution of labour for leisure and increasing the rate of return on capital to that of consumption. This increase in employment increases output leading to a further increase in the growth rate. The ultimate shift is from B to A on the PP curve. But in addition, the higher variance σ_y^2 also causes the SS curve to rotate down, so that the equilibrium variability, associated with the equilibrium growth–employment configuration is increased from H to K.

As noted, an increase in the tax rate on the stochastic component of income, τ_κ', is qualitatively similar to a decrease in τ_κ. It increases Ω and is thus reflected by an upward rotation in RR so that the change in equilibrium is represented by a shift from B to A. Since this tax shock has no effect on the SS curve, the increase in σ_ψ is along H to L. In contrast, an increase in the stochastic component of government expenditure, g', is equivalent to a decrease in σ_y^2, causing both a downward rotation of the RR curve and upward rotation of the SS curve. Suppose that the initial leisure-growth equilibrium is at A, with the corresponding variability at K. Then a higher absorption of stochastic output by the government will reduce both the mean growth rate and the time devoted to labour, as well as the associated risk; the new leisure–growth equilibrium will be at B, with the corresponding variability being at H.

9 PRODUCTIVE GOVERNMENT EXPENDITURE

Thus far we have assumed that government expenditure is 'useless' and represents a pure drain on the economy. In contrast, much of the recent literature on endogenous growth models has emphasised the role of public expenditure as an important determinant of long-run national growth rates and growth rate differentials. Beginning with Barro (1990), a number of authors have introduced government expenditure as an argument in the production function, to reflect its impact on the productive capacity of the economy.[21] This has led to a number of important propositions relating

---

[21] See, e.g., Cazzavillan (1996), Glomm and Ravikumar (1994, 1997) and Turnovsky (1996, 1997).

the growth rate to the size of government, and to the characterisation of optimal expenditure policy. However, these models are purely deterministic and therefore abstract from all considerations of risk.

Turnovsky (1999) extends the Barro model of productive government expenditure by analysing its role in a growing economy subject to stochastic productivity shocks. One crucial issue in introducing a government-provided input concerns its public-good characteristics. A natural starting point is to treat it as a non-rival pure public good, but this treatment fails to take account of the congestion that several authors have argued is typically associated with public goods. Accordingly, there is a growing literature associating various forms of congestion with public goods in endogenous growth models (see, e.g., Barro and Sala-i-Martin 1992; Glomm and Ravikumar 1994, 1997; Turnovsky 1996, 1997). The degree of congestion is important in that it introduces an externality that plays a key role in determining the appropriate optimal tax structure under which the decentralised economy is able to replicate the first-best outcome of the central planner. We will parameterise the degree of congestion, thereby enabling us to incorporate a range of public goods, extending from pure non-rival to pure rival but non-excludable, public goods, the latter sharing many of the characteristics of private goods.

9.1 Productive government expenditure, congestion and output

The key issue involves the introduction of congestible public expenditure in the production function, and for simplicity we return to the previous assumption of inelastic labour supply. In order to capture congestion, we consider an economy populated by N identical representative agents who consume and produce a single good. The flow of output, dY, produced by the typical individual over the period $(t, t + dt)$ is determined by his privately owned capital stock, K, and the rate of flow of services, H_s, derived from his use of a public good, in accordance with the stochastic production function:[22]

$$dY = Z(dt + dy) \equiv \alpha H_s^{\eta} K^{1-\eta} [dt + dy] \quad 0 < \eta < 1, \qquad (3.34)$$

where dy is a proportional productivity shock common to all agents, that is independently and normally distributed over time, having zero mean and variance $\sigma_y^2 dt$. Equation (3.34) asserts that the individual's mean rate of

---

[22] Corsetti (1997) obtains a similar technology by considering an externality that assumes that labour efficiency is proportional to the flow of a productive government expenditure.

output flow, z, is subject to positive, but diminishing, marginal physical product, in both the level of services of public expenditure, H_s, and his individual capital stock, k, and constant returns to scale in these two factors of production, together. The assumption that the productivity shock is proportional to the current mean level of output, Z, implies that an increase in the *deterministic* flow of government services, H_s, amplifies the magnitude of the stochastic productivity shock, du.

The productive services derived by the agent from the deterministic expenditure on the public good are represented by

$$H_s = H(K/\overline{K})^{1-\pi} \quad 0 \le \pi \le 1, \tag{3.35}$$

where H denotes the aggregate deterministic rate of flow of public expenditure and $\overline{K} \equiv NK$ denotes the aggregate stock of private capital.[23]

Equation (3.35) characterises what one may call *relative congestion*, in that the productive services derived by an agent from a given rate of public expenditure depend upon the usage of his individual capital stock relative to aggregate usage. This is a plausible assumption, a good example of which is the use of highway services. Unless an individual drives his car he derives no benefits from a publicly provided highway, and in general the level of services he does enjoy is adversely affected by the total usage of cars by others insofar as this causes congested roads. The fact that the benefits from the public good are tied to the individual's use of his capital encourages private investment and is important in the determination of the optimal tax rate.[24]

The exponent π parameterises the relative congestion associated with the public good. The case $\pi = 1$ corresponds to a non-rival, non-excludable public good that is available equally to each agent, independent of the size of the economy; there is no congestion. There are few, if any, examples of such pure public goods, so that this case should be treated largely as a benchmark. Alternatively, if $\pi = 0$, then only if H increases in direct proportion to the aggregate capital stock, $\overline{K}$, does the level of the public service available to

---

[23] In introducing productive government expenditure one must choose between formulating it as flow or as a stock, a choice that involves a tradeoff between tractability and realism. Most specifications introduce it as a flow, leading to an equilibrium in which the economy is always on its balanced growth path. But to the extent that such expenditures are intended to represent public infrastructure, it is arguably the accumulated stock that is the relevant measure. This formulation generates an equilibrium characterised by transitional dynamics. Analytical tractability of the stochastic model leads us to adopt the flow specification, so that the model is therefore a direct stochastic analogue to Barro (1990).

[24] A natural alternative specification of congestion is to assume that it is of the *absolute* form $H_s = H\overline{K}^{\pi-1}$. However, this formulation is consistent with an equilibrium of ongoing endogenous growth only under restrictive conditions.

the individual firm remain fixed, given his individual stock. We shall refer to this case as being one of *proportional* relative congestion, meaning that the congestion grows in direct proportion to the size of the economy. In this case the public good is rival, but not excludable. It is like a private good in that in equilibrium the typical agent receives his proportionate share of the good. In between, $0 < \pi < 1$, describes less congestion, where H can increase at a slower rate than does $\overline{K}$ and still maintain a fixed level of public services to the firm.[25]

Substituting (3.2) into (3.1), the individual firm's production function can be expressed as

$$dY = \alpha H^{\eta}(K/\overline{K})^{\eta(1-\pi)} K^{1-\eta}[dt + dy]$$
$$= \alpha(H/\overline{K})^{\eta}(\overline{K}/K)^{\eta\pi} K[dt + dy]. \qquad (3.34')$$

As long as $\pi < 1$, so that the public good is associated with some congestion, aggregate capital is introduced into the production function of the individual firm in an analogous way to Romer (1986).[26]

The flow of resources claimed by the government over the period $(t, t + dt)$ is specified by:

$$dG = Hdt + H'dy, \qquad (3.36)$$

where H denotes the deterministic (expected) rate of expenditure over the period dt and H' denotes the current stochastic expenditure flow, as a proportion of the stochastic output shock.[27] We shall let $\overline{Z} = NZ$ denote the aggregate mean rate of output flow and assume that the government sets H, and H' as fractions of the current deterministic and stochastic rates of flow of aggregate output:

$$H = hZ; \quad 0 < h < 1; \qquad (3.37a)$$
$$H' = h'Z; \quad 0 < h' < 1. \qquad (3.37b)$$

Thus the fraction, h, represents the policy-maker's choice of the (deterministic) size of government, while $h'(0 \le h' \le 1)$ represents the fraction of the aggregate output shock, Zdy, absorbed by the government. If h is

---

[25] The case $\pi < 0$ describes an extreme situation in which the congestion is such that the public good must grow faster than the economy in order to maintain the level of services. Although we do not discuss it, substantial empirical evidence exists to support this case.

[26] If $\pi = 0$, so that we have proportional relative congestion, then the production function (3.34') implies constant returns to scale in K.

[27] The assumption of proportional disturbances implies that the standard deviation of output shocks is more or less stationary, an assumption consistent with the data.

constant, the government is claiming a fixed share of the growing (mean) output, so that an increase in h parameterises a deterministic expansion in expenditure in a growing economy.

The production function (3.34) assumes that only the deterministic component of government expenditure is productive. This is a plausible benchmark case, since one may argue that the productive application of resources by the government takes time. Information on the stochastic component of output, dy, during the period $(t, t + dt)$ arrives at the end of the instant, and the government's share of that output is known too late to be used productively during that same instant of time. Instead, it may be assumed to be devoted to some consumption good that does not interact directly with private consumption in yielding utility to the representative agent.

Combining (3.37a), (3.35) and (3.34′) the rate of output of the individual firm can be expressed as:

$$dY = Z(dt + dy) = (\alpha h^\eta N^\eta)^{1/(1-\eta)}(K/\overline{K})^{(\eta[1-\pi]/[1-\eta])} K(dt + dy).$$
(3.38)

With all agents being identical and the stochastic shock dy being identical for all N agents, in equilibrium, individual output and aggregate output, $d\overline{Y} = NdY$, may be expressed as

$$dY = Z(dt + dy) = (\alpha h^\eta N^{\pi\eta})^{1/(1-\eta)} K(dt + dy)$$
(3.39)

$$d\overline{Y} = \overline{Z}(dt + dy) = (\alpha h^\eta N^{\eta\pi})^{1/(1-\eta)} \overline{K}(dt + dy).$$
(3.39′)

Henceforth, for notational convenience we shall let

$$\Gamma(h, \pi) \equiv (\alpha h^\eta N^{\eta\pi})^{1/(1-\eta)} \equiv \overline{Z}/\overline{K} = Z/K \quad \Gamma_h > 0, \Gamma_\pi > 0$$

denote the equilibrium average productivity of capital, both at the aggregate and at the individual level. Observe that the equilibrium individual and aggregate production functions are both of the 'AK form', where the productivity of capital increases with the deterministic share of output devoted to productive government, and decreases with the degree of congestion. Observe also, that as long as $\pi \neq 0$, the productivity of capital depends upon the population; the economy is characterized by 'scale effects'.[28] The

---

[28] The dependence of the growth rate upon the population size is emphasised by Glomm and Ravikumar (1994). The empirical relevance of this has been called into question and represents one of the motivations for the development of 'non-scale' models proposed by Jones (1995) and others.

intuition for this result is simply that the individual productivity depends upon aggregate government spending, $H = hN$, so that more agents in the economy implies a bigger externality, unless completely offset by congestion. The critical difference between the perception of the world as seen by the representative agent and as seen by the central planner in their respective decision making is as follows. The individual treats the aggregate capital stock, $\overline{K}$, as given and views the production function as specified in (3.38). The central planner, on the other hand, internalises the relationship $\overline{K} = NK$ when determining his decisions; he therefore operates in accordance with (3.39′) or (3.39).

Using this notation, the flow of resources claimed by the government over the period $(t, t + dt)$, (3.36) may be written as:

$$dG = \overline{Z}[hdt + h'dy] = \Gamma(h, \pi)\overline{K}[hdt + h'dy]. \tag{3.40}$$

But there need be no presumption that the government will have the flexibility to spend in the short run. In the absence of any flexibility, $h' = 0$, and government expenditure is non-stochastic at each instant of time, as we shall assume for private consumption to be; see Corsetti (1997). To implement the expenditure rule (3.40) the government must be able to distinguish between the deterministic and stochastic movement of output. If, on the other hand, the government observes only aggregate movements in output, $d\overline{Y}dy$, then $h' \equiv h$ and the expenditure rule is constrained to be:

$$dG = hd\overline{Y} = h\overline{Z}[dt + dy]. \tag{3.40′}$$

The individual agent consumes this good at the (non-stochastic) rate $dC = C(t)dt$, so that aggregate consumption evolves according to $d\overline{C} = \overline{C}(t)dt$. All activities are subject to the aggregate resource constraint:

$$d\overline{K} = d\overline{Y} - d\overline{C} - dG \tag{3.41}$$

which upon substitution, becomes

$$d\overline{K} = [(1 - h)\Gamma(h, \pi)\overline{K} - \overline{C}]dt + \Gamma(h, \pi)\overline{K}(1 - h')dy. \tag{3.42}$$

9.2 Optimal size of government

One of the striking results associated with the deterministic Barro model is that setting $h = \eta$ will maximise both the equilibrium growth rate and consumer welfare. In contrast, one of the main results of the present model is that the coincidence of these two objectives no longer applies in the presence of risk. The details of the analysis are provided by Turnovsky (1999) and here we summarise the relevant relationships and some of the underlying intuition.

Specifically, we can show that the (expected) growth-maximising deterministic and stochastic government expenditure shares, $\bar{h}, \bar{h}'$ can be characterised as follows:

$$
\begin{aligned}
&\textit{if } \gamma > 0, \text{ set: } \bar{h}' = 1; \; \bar{h} = \eta \\
&\textit{if } \gamma < 0, \text{ set: } \bar{h}' = 0; \; \bar{h} = \eta \left(1 - \gamma(1 - \gamma)\Gamma(\bar{h}, \eta)\sigma_y^2\right).
\end{aligned}
\tag{3.43}
$$

The extent to which maximising the expected growth rate requires the elimination of risk depends upon the degree of risk aversion. What is required is to choose the degree of stochastic intervention, h', to minimise the consumption–capital ratio given the existing risk, thereby maximising the amount of output available for investment. With a low degree of risk aversion ($\gamma > 0$) this is accomplished by setting $h' = 1$ and completely eliminating risk. This allows the government to set a larger deterministic scale than otherwise, and indeed to set the same scale as in the absence of risk. With a high degree of risk aversion ($\gamma < 0$) the consumption–capital ratio is minimised by setting $h' = 0$ and letting the private sector absorb all the risk. In this case consumption is reduced drastically, thus permitting the government to set its deterministic scale larger than it would in the absence of risk.

By contrast, optimising with respect to h, we can show that the welfare-maximising deterministic fraction of output devoted to productive government expenditure is defined implicitly by:[29]

$$
\hat{h} = \eta\left(1 - (1 - \gamma)\Gamma(\hat{h}, \pi)(1 - h')^2\sigma_y^2\right) \le \eta.
\tag{3.44}
$$

In the absence of risk, $\hat{h} = \eta$, as shown by Barro (1990). The introduction of risk thus reduces the welfare-maximising (deterministic) share of government expenditure. This is because an increase in exogenous risk raises the variance of the return to capital. In order to maximise welfare, the government must offset that risk by reducing the scale of its activity. As a consequence, there is a negative tradeoff between the optimal deterministic

---

[29] It is easy to show that (3.44) always has an interior optimum: $0 < \hat{h} < \eta < 1$. For certain values of η, there may be multiple solutions for $\hat{h}$, though for relevant numerical ranges always yield unique interior optima.

fraction of the government, $\hat{h}$, and an arbitrarily set response to the stochastic shocks, h'.

We can also show that the welfare-maximising stochastic intervention is to set $h' = 1$, and thereby fully insulate the private sector from the production risk. Combining this condition with (3.44) the corresponding deterministic optimality condition reduces to $\hat{h} = \eta$. Thus the overall optimal expenditure policy is for the government to absorb all the risk and to set its deterministic scale as it would in a riskless economy.

In the absence of risk, (3.43) and (3.44) imply $\hat{h} = \bar{h} = \eta$, so that the welfare-maximising and growth-maximising shares of government expenditure coincide; Barro (1990). Except if the agent is risk neutral ($\gamma = 1$), risk leads to a divergence between the objectives of growth maximisation and welfare maximisation; $\hat{h} < \bar{h}$. The intuition is that the maximisation of the growth rate entails more risk than the risk averse agent, concerned with his time profile of consumption, finds to be optimal. If the planner responds optimally to risk, by setting $h' = 1$, and if $\gamma > 0$, then for low degrees of risk aversion both growth maximisation and welfare maximisation reduce to $\hat{h} = \bar{h} = \eta$. But in the empirically more relevant case of high risk aversion, $\gamma < 0$, the stochastic elements introduce a conflict between these two objectives.

9.3 First-best optimal tax structure

We now describe the nature of the optimal tax structure that will enable the decentralised economy to attain the first-best optimum equilibrium. In doing so, we assume that the deterministic size of government, h, in the two economies are set equal. To replicate the centrally planned economy the deterministic and stochastic tax rates (τ, τ', respectively) in the decentralised economy must be set so as to mimic the deterministic and stochastic components of the growth rates. Setting $\tau' = h'$ ensures that the stochastic shocks to the growth rate in the decentralised economy replicate those in the centrally planned economy. Setting the deterministic income tax, $\hat{\tau}$, in accordance with:

$$\hat{\tau} = \frac{1}{1 - \eta\pi} \left\{ h - \eta\pi \left(1 - (1 - \gamma)(1 - h')^2 \Gamma(h, \pi)\sigma_y^2 \right) \right\} \quad (3.45)$$

ensures that the deterministic component is mimicked. Recalling the expression for the optimal deterministic share of government expenditure, given in (3.44), enables the optimal tax on capital income to be expressed in the following convenient form:

$$\hat{\tau} = \frac{1}{1 - \eta\pi}\{(h - \hat{h}) + \eta\pi(1 - \gamma)(1 - h')^2\sigma_y^2(\Gamma(h, \pi)$$
$$- \Gamma(\hat{h}, \pi)) + \hat{h}(1 - \pi)\}. \tag{3.46}$$

From (3.46) we see that for arbitrarily set h and h', the optimal income tax $\hat{\tau}$, [which may be a subsidy] depends upon: (i) the deviation in h from its socially optimal share, $\hat{h}$, and (ii) the degree of congestion as measured by $1 - \pi$. In general, if h is not at its optimum and is subject to congestion, government expenditure generates an externality in the capital market that requires a tax on capital income to correct. Furthermore, provided the degree of congestion is not proportional $\pi \neq 0$, this externality is compounded by risk.

In general, there is a tradeoff between the tax rate on capital, given in (3.46) and the tax rate on consumption (not reported), and that this depends crucially upon the degree of congestion. In the case of a pure public good ($\pi = 1$), income should be taxed only to the extent that the deterministic share of government expenditure deviates from its social optimum. In the case of proportional congestion, ($\pi = 0$), expenditure should be fully financed by an income tax. Finally, if both the deterministic and stochastic components of government expenditure are set optimally ($\hat{h} = \eta$, $\hat{h}' = 1$), the overall first-best tax rate on capital is given by:

$$\hat{\tau} = \frac{\eta(1 - \pi)}{(1 - \eta\pi)} \tag{3.47}$$

which is identical to the corresponding optimal rate in the risk-free economy (see Turnovsky 1996).

10 STOCHASTIC SMALL OPEN ECONOMY

International taxation is an important issue for which the present model is most applicable. It is an area that is beginning to attract a lot of attention among public finance economists (see, e.g., Frenkel, Razin and Sadka 1991 and Ihori 1991). Most of the literature is based on complete certainty and the arbitrage conditions that characterise efficient capital markets severely constrain the choice of taxation. The introduction of risk adds flexibility, as well as realism, to the analysis. In particular the corner solutions characterising the viability of alternative taxation regimes under certainty are seen to be an artifact of excluding risk. Once risk is included, each agent will choose his individual portfolio in response to the risks, his own degree of risk aversion and the tax rates he faces. Equilibrium in the world capital markets will be brought about through adjustments in the before-tax yields on the traded world assets to ensure that all capital is willingly held.

10.1 A simple international model

We shall illustrate the international application using the simplest model of a small open economy, which comprises an infinitely lived representative agent who produces a single traded good. The agent has the option of consuming that good or accumulating it as capital, K, which is tradable. Domestic output continues to be produced by the simple production function (3.1), so that in the absence of adjustment costs to investment, the (before-tax) return to capital over the period $(t, t + dt)$ continues to be given by (3.2a). In addition, the agent may accumulate a traded bond, F, which over the same period yields the stochastic rate of return

$$dR_F = s\,dt + de, \tag{3.48}$$

where s denotes the mean return and de is a Brownian motion process having zero mean and variance $\sigma_e^2 dt$. For simplicity, dy and de are assumed to be uncorrelated.

The agent accumulates wealth stochastically in accordance with the accumulation equation

$$\frac{dW}{W} = \left\{ n_K(1 - \tau_K)\alpha + n_F(1 - \tau_F)s - \frac{C}{W} \right\}$$
$$+ n_K(1 - \tau_K)\alpha\,dy + n_F(1 - \tau_F)de, \tag{3.49}$$

where for simplicity we assume that both the deterministic and stochastic components of domestic income are taxed at the uniform rate τ_K, and both components of foreign income are taxed correspondingly at the rate τ_F. The agent's objective is to choose his (deterministic) rate of consumption $dC = C(t)dt$ to maximise the logarithmic utility function

$$\int_0^\infty [\ln C + \eta \ln G] e^{-\beta t} dt, \tag{3.50}$$

where G denotes some utility-enhancing government expenditure, which the government accumulates at the non-stochastic rate $dG = G(t)dt$. In making his consumption and savings decisions, the agent takes G as given.

The government finances its deterministic rate of expenditure in accordance with the budget constraint:

$$\frac{G}{W} = \tau_K \alpha n_K + \tau_{FS} n_F. \tag{3.51a}$$

Taxes, however, are levied uniformly on all income and all tax revenues collected on the stochastic component of capital income, are rebated in accordance with:

$$dv = \tau_K \alpha n_K dy + \tau_{FS} n_F de. \tag{3.51b}$$

The macroeconomic equilibrium in this simplified small open economy comprises the following relationships:

$$n_K = \frac{\alpha(1 - \tau_K) - s(1 - \tau_F)}{\left[\alpha^2(1 - \tau_K)\sigma_y^2 + (1 - \tau_F)\sigma_e^2\right]} + \frac{(1 - \tau_F)\sigma_e^2}{\alpha^2(1 - \tau_K)\sigma_y^2 + (1 - \tau_F)\sigma_e^2};$$

$$n_F = 1 - n_K \tag{3.52a}$$

$$\frac{C}{W} = \beta, \tag{3.52b}$$

$$\frac{G}{W} = \tau_K \alpha n_K + \tau_{FS} n_F; \tag{3.52c}$$

$$\psi = \alpha n_K + s n_F - \frac{C}{W} - \frac{G}{W}; \tag{3.52d}$$

$$\sigma_w^2 = \alpha^2 n_K^2 \sigma_y^2 + n_F^2 \sigma_e^2. \tag{3.52e}$$

Despite its simplicity, this system brings out some of the main issues raised by considering international taxation in a stochastic environment.

First, choosing n_K, n_F in accordance with (3.52a) ensures the equality of the risk-adjusted after-tax rates of return on the two traded assets. The optimal portfolio share n_K is determined by two sets of factors. The first is the speculative component, which is proportional to the expected differential after-tax real rate of return on the two assets, and inversely related to its variance. The second reflects the hedging behaviour on the part of the investor. This depends upon the covariance of the after-tax asset return with wealth.

Equation (3.52a) also brings out the importance of risk in the analysis of taxation in a small open economy. In the absence of risk, $\sigma_e^2 = \sigma_y^2 = 0$, and this relationship reduces to the arbitrage condition

$$\alpha(1 - \tau_K) = s(1 - \tau_F). \tag{3.52a'}$$

With the before-tax rates of return α, s being parametrically given to the small open economy, the constraint on the tax rates imposed by the arbitrage condition (3.52a') becomes clear; a change in τ_K requires a compensating change in τ_F in order for (3.52a') to hold. In the presence of risk, the representative agent is able to adjust his portfolio share in accordance with his risk tolerance, thus permitting the two tax rates to be set independently. In this respect the presence of risk introduces important flexibility that enables an interior solution for portfolio shares, rather than a corner solution, to obtain.

From the equilibrium set out in (3.52) we see that the effect of taxes on the growth rate and its volatility depend critically upon the adjustment in portfolio shares. To determine these it is necessary to begin by considering (3.52a). Differentiating this expression with respect to the two tax rates implies the following

$$\frac{\partial n_K}{\partial \tau_K} = -\frac{\alpha}{\left[\alpha^2(1-\tau_K)\sigma_y^2 + (1-\tau_F)\sigma_e^2\right]}\left[1 - \alpha n_K \sigma_y^2\right] < 0 \quad (3.53a)$$

$$\frac{\partial n_K}{\partial \tau_F} = \frac{s - n_F \sigma_e^2}{\left[\alpha^2(1-\tau_K)\sigma_y^2 + (1-\tau_F)\sigma_e^2\right]} > 0. \quad (3.53b)$$

Consider first the tax on domestic capital. The sign in (3.53a), is predicated on the assumption that $1 > \alpha n_K \sigma_y^2$, which will be met as long as the variance of the productivity shocks is not too large. Indeed, this condition will be met under any plausible conditions. The interpretation of this condition is as follows. On the one hand, an increase in τ_K reduces the after-tax mean return to capital, thereby inducing investors to shift away from capital in their portfolios. At the same time, it reduces the associated risk, and this encourages the holding of capital. The restriction we have imposed assumes that the former effect dominates and in this case an increase in the tax rate on capital will reduce the share of capital in the traded portion of the agent's portfolio. An increase in the tax on foreign bonds, τ_F has precisely the opposite effect.

The effect of increases in the tax rate on the mean equilibrium growth rate can be written as

$$\frac{\partial \psi}{\partial \tau_K} = -\alpha n_K + [\alpha(1-\tau_K) - s(1-\tau_F)]\frac{\partial n_K}{\partial \tau_K} \quad (3.54a)$$

$$\frac{\partial \psi}{\partial \tau_K} = -s\,n_F + [\alpha(1-\tau_K) - s(1-\tau_F)]\frac{\partial n_K}{\partial \tau_F}. \quad (3.54b)$$

An increase in either tax has two effects on the growth rate. Consider τ_K. First, given the existing portfolio share n_K, it reduces the risk-adjusted after-tax return to capital, thereby reducing the growth rate. Second, it causes a portfolio shift from domestic capital to traded bonds, thus reducing n_K. Whether such a shift in the portfolio raises or lowers the mean growth rate depends upon whether the mean after-tax return to domestic capital is greater than or less than the mean after-tax return on foreign bonds. And this in turn depends upon the relative riskiness of the two assets.

For example, if the only source of risk is domestic, domestic assets will tend to have higher rates of return than do foreign assets to compensate. In that case an increase in the portfolio share of foreign assets will tend to reduce the growth rate [i.e. $\partial\psi/\partial n_K > 0$], thereby accentuating the reduction in the growth rate due to the first effect. On the other hand, if the primary sources of risk are foreign, foreign assets will tend to have higher rates of return, so that a portfolio shift toward foreign assets will raise the growth rate [i.e. $\partial\psi/\partial n_K < 0$]. This will tend to offset the reduction in the growth rate due to the first effect. Indeed it is possible for the portfolio shift to be of sufficient magnitude for this second effect to dominate, so that a higher tax on domestic capital income is actually growth-enhancing, in contrast to its known adverse effect on growth under certainty.

The effects of a higher tax rate on the variance of the growth rate are given by

$$\frac{\partial\sigma_w^2}{\partial\tau_i} = 2\left(\left[\alpha^2\sigma_y^2 + \sigma_e^2\right]n_K - \sigma_e^2\right)\frac{\partial n_K}{\partial\tau_i} \quad i = K, F. \tag{3.55}$$

Thus assuming the sign of (3.53a), an increase in the tax on domestic capital income, τ_K, will stabilise the growth rate (i.e. reduce σ_w^2) if $\omega > \overline{\omega} \equiv (\sigma_e^2/[\alpha^2(\sigma_y^2 + \sigma_z^2) + \sigma_e^2])$ and destabilise it otherwise. An increase in τ_F will have precisely the opposite effect. This is because $\overline{\omega}$ is the variance-minimising portfolio and any tax changes that shifts the portfolio toward $\overline{\omega}$ is stabilising.

10.2 Optimal policy

The optimal fiscal policy problem confronting the policy-maker is to choose the two tax rates, τ_K, τ_F, together with government expenditure, G, to maximise the agent's utility (3.50) subject to the equilibrium conditions (3.52) and its balanced budget condition (3.51). Omitting details, the following optimality conditions obtain:

$$\frac{G}{W} = \eta\beta \qquad (3.56a)$$

$$\tau_K = \left(\frac{\eta\beta}{\alpha}\right) \frac{\left[1 - s\, n_F \sigma_e^2\right]}{\left[1 - n_K n_F\left(\alpha\sigma_y^2 + s\sigma_e^2\right)\right]} \qquad (3.56b)$$

$$\tau_F = \left(\frac{\eta\beta}{s}\right) \frac{\left[1 - \alpha n_K \sigma_y^2\right]}{\left[1 - n_K n_F\left(\alpha\sigma_y^2 + s\sigma_e^2\right)\right]}, \qquad (3.56c)$$

where n_K and n_F are given by (3.52a) and (3.52b). Substituting for these expressions into (3.56a)–(3.56c) one can obtain explicit solutions determining the optimal income tax rates, τ_K, τ_F.

The following inferences can be drawn. The optimal ratio of public to private consumption equals η, the (percentage) marginal rate of substitution between the two goods in the utility function. But in contrast to a riskless world, the tax rates on the two sources of residents' income, τ_K, τ_F are *not* in general equal. Instead, they reflect differences in the risk characteristics of the underlying assets.

The optimum set in (3.56) is only second best. Because of the externality generated by government expenditure, capital income taxes alone are incapable of achieving the first-best outcome of the central planner. Some additional tax is necessary to correct for the externality generated by the growing level of government consumption expenditure. To see the issue, we begin by solving the command optimum.

The central planner's problem is to choose C, G, n_K, and n_F directly to maximise the discounted utility function (3.50), subject to the economy-wide stochastic wealth accumulation equation:

$$\frac{dW}{W} = \left(\alpha n_K + s\, n_F - \frac{C}{W} - \frac{G}{W}\right) dt + \alpha n_K dy + n_F de. \quad (3.57)$$

Performing the optimisation leads to the following first-best equilibrium outcome for the domestic economy:

$$n_K = \frac{\alpha - s}{\alpha^2 \sigma_y^2 + \sigma_e^2} + \frac{\sigma_e^2}{\alpha^2 \sigma_y^2 + \sigma_e^2}; \quad n_F = 1 - n_K \qquad (3.58a)$$

$$\frac{C}{W} = \frac{\beta}{1 + \eta} \qquad (3.58b)$$

$$\frac{G}{W} = \eta \frac{C}{W} \tag{3.58c}$$

$$\psi = \alpha n_K + s n_F - (1 + \eta)\frac{C}{W} \tag{3.58d}$$

$$\sigma_w^2 = \alpha^2 n_K^2 \sigma_y^2 + n_F^2 \sigma_e^2. \tag{3.58e}$$

The main difference between this optimal centralised equilibrium and the corresponding decentralised equilibrium summarised in (3.52a)–(3.52e), is that the central planner internalises the externality generated by G in his choice of the optimal private consumption ratio C/W. Comparing the two equilibria, it is clearly impossible to replicate the command optimum by setting only the two tax rates, τ_K, τ_F in the decentralised system. By failing to recognise the positive externality generated by government expenditure on private consumption, and the fact that the government is choosing G (along with taxes on capital) optimally, private agents choose to overconsume, relative to the command optimum, resulting in too slow a growth rate. An additional tax is necessary to correct for the distortion and it turns out that this can be most easily accomplished by introducing a general consumption tax.

It is a straightforward exercise to re-solve the decentralised equilibrium in the case where in addition to the two tax rates on capital, the representative agent is subject to a tax on consumption, τ_C say. The macroeconomic equilibrium now consists of (3.52a), (3.52d), together with

$$\frac{C}{W} = \frac{\beta}{(1 + \tau_C)} \tag{3.52b'}$$

$$\psi = \alpha n_K + s n_F - (1 + \eta)\frac{C}{W} \tag{3.52c'}$$

and the government budget constraint

$$\tau_K \alpha n_K + \tau_F s n_F = (\eta - \tau_C)\frac{C}{W}. \tag{3.51a'}$$

Comparing this equilibrium with the command optimum (3.58a)–(3.58e), it is evident that the addition of the third tax rate now enables the latter to be replicated. Specifically, if the tax rates on capital are both set to zero, $(\tau_K = \tau_F = 0)$, so that government expenditure is fully financed by the consumption tax, $(\tau_C = \eta)$, the decentralised economy will replicate the first-best optimum of the centrally planned economy. This optimal fiscal structure is thus seen to be identical to the overall optimal fiscal structure, when government expenditure is set optimally along with tax rates. When government expenditure is set arbitrarily, however, capital will need to be taxed to correct for the distortion created by government not being at its socially optimal level. Unlike the deterministic case, the size of this distortion, and therefore the appropriate tax, will depend upon the risk in the economy.

11 MORE GENERAL PREFERENCES

We have pointed out that in order to sustain an equilibrium of ongoing growth, the utility function must yield a consumption level that is proportional to the state of the economy, parameterised by its growing stock of capital or wealth. The constant elasticity utility function that we have employed throughout this analysis has this important property. But while this specification of preferences is convenient, it is also restrictive in that two key parameters critical to the determination of the equilibrium growth path – the intertemporal elasticity of substitution and the coefficient of relative risk aversion – become directly linked to one another and cannot vary independently. This is a significant limitation, and one that can lead to seriously misleading impressions of the effects that each parameter plays in determining the impact of risk and return on the macroeconomic equilibrium and its welfare.

The coefficient of relative risk aversion, R say, introduced by Arrow (1965) and Pratt (1964) is a static concept, one that is well defined in the absence of any intertemporal dimension. By contrast, the intertemporal elasticity of substitution, ε say, emphasised by Hall (1988), Mankiw, Rotemberg and Summers (1985) and others, emphasises intertemporal preferences and is well defined in the absence of risk. The standard constant elasticity utility function has the property that both these parameters are constant, though it imposes the restriction $R = 1/\varepsilon$, with logarithmic utility function corresponding to $R = \varepsilon = 1$.

The empirical evidence for both these parameters is far-ranging. Estimates for ε vary from near zero by Campbell and Mankiw (1989) and Hall (1988) to near unity by Beaudry and van Wincoop (1995). Epstein and Zin (1991) estimate a range for ε between 0.05 and 1, and estimates by Ogaki and Reinhart (1998) suggest values of around 0.4. The empirical evidence for estimates of R show even wider dispersion. Epstein and Zin (1991) find values of R around unity, consistent with the logarithmic utility function, while the 'equity premium puzzle' literature proposes values of R as high as 18 (Obstfeld, 1994a), or even 30 (Kandel and Stambaugh

1991). Constantinides, Donaldson and Mehra (2002) suggest that a plausible range for R is between 2 and 5.

Given this wide range of estimates, one certainly cannot rule out the constraint $R = 1/\varepsilon$ and hence the constant elasticity utility function. For example, $R = 2.5$ and $\varepsilon = 0.4$ is a plausible combination for which the constant elasticity utility function is appropriate. However, the empirical evidence suggests that a plausible range for $R\varepsilon$ may lie anywhere between 0.1 to 5, certainly well away from 1, so that the constant elasticity utility function is inappropriate.

Several authors, including Epstein and Zin (1989) and Weil (1990) have represented preferences by a more general recursive function, which enables one to distinguish explicitly between R and ε.[30] This is important for two reasons. First, R and ε impinge on the economy in independent, and often conflicting ways. They therefore need to be disentangled if the correct effect of each is to be determined. Second, the biases introduced by imposing the compatibility condition $R = 1/\varepsilon$ can be quite large (in terms of both growth and welfare), in both magnitude and direction, even for relatively weak violations of this relationship.

Chatterjee, Giuliano and Turnovsky (2002) analyse the effects of capital income taxes on the equilibrium stochastic growth path in an economy in which preferences are represented by Epstein–Zin recursive preferences. Their characterisation of the equilibrium clarifies how the separation of R and ε is potentially important. Risk aversion impinges on the equilibrium through the portfolio allocation process and thus through the equilibrium risk that the economy is willing to sustain. It also determines the discounting for risk in determining the certainty equivalent level of income implied by the mean return on the assets. The intertemporal elasticity of substitution then determines the allocation of this certainty equivalent income between current consumption and capital accumulation (growth).

They focus on the following question: how do the qualitative and quantitative effects of a particular government policy vary as we move away from a constant elasticity utility function? In other words, what kind of biases can a particular policy induce if the policy-maker uses the wrong specification of preferences? They show that erroneous preferences may be drawn about the evaluation of a particular policy measure if the policy-maker say, assumes an isoelastic utility function, but if the true preference structure is more recursive in nature. Supplementing the analytical results with extensive numerical simulations, they characterise the nature of bias – both its

---

[30] Giuliano and Turnovsky (2002), Obstfeld (1994) and Smith (1996) are among the few who have employed recursive preference structures in the context of stochastic growth models.

magnitude and direction – of the effects of a policy shock for both an open and closed economy on the equilibrium growth rate, welfare and portfolio choice if the preference structure of individuals is misspecified.

For our purposes it suffices to consider only the closed economy for which intuition is sharpest. We consider a simplified version of the model outlined in section 3, in which the preferences are represented by the Epstein–Zin preferences, and the government taxes capital and spends in accordance with

$$dT = \alpha \tau K \, dt + \tau' K \, dy \qquad (3.59a)$$

$$dG = \alpha g K \, dt + g' K \, dy, \qquad (3.59b)$$

respectively. For such an economy the equilibrium mean growth rate is

$$\psi = \varepsilon[(1 - \tau)\alpha - \beta] + \varepsilon R(1 - g')(\tau' - g')\sigma_y^2 + \frac{(1 - \varepsilon)R}{2}\sigma_y^2 \quad (3.60)$$

from which we immediately infer

$$\frac{\partial \psi}{\partial \tau} = -\varepsilon \alpha < 0; \qquad \frac{\partial \psi}{\partial \tau'} = \varepsilon R(1 - g')\sigma_y^2 > 0. \qquad (3.61)$$

An increase in the tax rate on the deterministic component of income reduces the mean growth rate, while increasing the tax on the stochastic component, reduces the risk and raises the growth rate. The deterministic tax effect depends only upon the intertemporal elasticity of substitution, whereas the stochastic tax effect depends upon the product of the intertemporal elasticity of substitution with the coefficient of relative risk aversion. This is because R converts the stochastic component to a 'certainty equivalent' quantity to which ε applies.

The issue concerns the comparison of the tax effects in (3.61) obtained using the above more general representation of preferences with that obtained from the conventional constant elasticity utility function, $C^{1-\kappa}/(1-\kappa)$, which implies a coefficient of relative risk aversion and an intertemporal elasticity of substitution equal to $R_C = \kappa$, $\varepsilon_C = 1/\kappa$, respectively. In interpreting the constant elasticity function, we shall assume[31]

$$\kappa = \lambda R + (1 - \lambda)\frac{1}{\varepsilon} \quad 0 \leq \lambda \leq 1 \qquad (3.62)$$

[31] Kocherlakota (1990) disentangles the coefficient of risk aversion and the intertemporal elasticity of substitution in a pure consumption model. He shows that in that context the optimality conditions stemming from the constant elasticity utility function are observationally equivalent to those corresponding to recursive preferences, a result that does not extend to the present production-growth environment. He also argues that empirically, at least for the USA, the elasticity in the constant elasticity function is a more accurate measure of the coefficient of relative risk aversion than of the intertemporal elasticity of substitution; in terms of (3.16), $\lambda \approx 1$.

where λ reflects the relative weight assigned to R and $1/\varepsilon$ in the constant elasticity κ. Thus the biases of κ as measures of R and $1/\varepsilon$ are, respectively,

$$\kappa - R = \frac{1-\lambda}{\varepsilon}(1 - R\varepsilon) \qquad (3.63a)$$

$$\kappa - \frac{1}{\varepsilon} = \frac{\lambda}{\varepsilon}(R\varepsilon - 1). \qquad (3.63b)$$

The elasticity κ will be an unbiased measure of both parameters simultaneously if and only if $R\varepsilon = 1$. Otherwise it will understate (overstate) R and overstate (understate) $1/\varepsilon$ if $R\varepsilon > (<)1$, and in general $R\varepsilon - 1$ measures the degree of incompatibility of the constant elasticity utility assumption. The corresponding equilibrium growth rate for the constant elasticity utility function is

$$\psi = \frac{1}{\kappa}[(1 - \tau)\alpha - \beta] + (1 - g')(\tau' - g')\sigma_y^2 + \frac{(\kappa - 1)}{2}\sigma_y^2 \qquad (3.60')$$

which implies the following effects of the tax rates on the mean growth rate:

$$\left(\frac{\partial\psi}{\partial\tau}\right)_C = -\frac{\alpha}{\kappa} < 0; \qquad \left(\frac{\partial\psi}{\partial\tau'}\right)_C = (1 - g')\sigma_y^2 > 0. \qquad (3.61')$$

Subtracting the corresponding expressions in (3.61') from (3.61) and using (3.62) we obtain the biases obtained from using the constant elasticity function:

$$\left(\frac{\partial\psi}{\partial\tau}\right)_C - \frac{\partial\psi}{\partial\tau} = \frac{\alpha\lambda\varepsilon}{\kappa}\left(R - \frac{1}{\varepsilon}\right) \qquad (3.64a)$$

$$\left(\frac{\partial\psi}{\partial\tau'}\right)_C - \frac{\partial\psi}{\partial\tau'} = (1 - g')\sigma_y^2\varepsilon\left(\frac{1}{\varepsilon} - R\right). \qquad (3.64b)$$

In the event that the compatibility condition $R\varepsilon = 1$ is met, the constant elasticity responses give correct estimates of the true responses, but otherwise they are generally biased. Thus, for example, if $R\varepsilon > 1$, the constant elasticity utility function understates both the adverse effects of an increase in τ and the positive effects of an increase in τ'. If $R\varepsilon < 1$ these responses are overstated. Note, however, if $\lambda = 0$ so that the elasticity in the constant elasticity utility function reflects only the intertemporal elasticity of substitution, then the constant elasticity utility function will also yield a correct estimate of the effect of τ on the growth rate irrespective of the compatibility condition.

Moreover, the biases can be large, even for plausible magnitudes of the parameters. Equations (3.64a) and (3.64b) imply

$$\frac{(\partial\psi/\partial\tau)_C - (\partial\psi/\partial\tau)}{(\partial\psi/\partial\tau)} = -\frac{\lambda}{\lambda R + (1-\lambda)(1/\varepsilon)}\left(R - \frac{1}{\varepsilon}\right) \quad (3.65a)$$

$$\frac{(\partial\psi/\partial\tau')_C - (\partial\psi/\partial\tau')}{(\partial\psi/\partial\tau')} = \frac{1}{R}\left(\frac{1}{\varepsilon} - R\right). \quad (3.65b)$$

Taking $\lambda = 1$, $R = 2.5$, $\varepsilon = 0.2$ as plausible parameters we see that (3.65a) implies that the constant elasticity utility function overestimates the deterministic tax effect by 100 per cent and underestimates the stochastic tax effect by 100 per cent. These are big errors, obtained from very realistic parameters, well within the standard bounds of estimation. The message to be drawn is that the constant elasticity utility function needs to be used with caution.

12 COMPOSITION OF DEBT

In the models we have discussed, government debt has always been long-term debt, and in particular perpetuities. This has been done basically to preserve flexibility with respect to fiscal and debt policy, while maintaining tractability. The bonds we have introduced have had the property that their relative price has been endogenously determined in such a way as to enable the economy to always be on its balanced growth path. We have not had to consider transitional dynamics, which although clearly realistic, are intractable.

Nevertheless, Grinols and Turnovsky (1993, 1998b) have introduced short-term debt into a stochastic growth model of the generic type discussed in this chapter. In their 1993 paper, they assumed that government debt was all short term. In order to permit the economy always to be on its balanced growth path, with constant portfolio shares, this necessitated a debt policy in which the ratio of (short-term) government debt to nominal money was assumed to be constant. With the money supply assumed to evolve in an exogenous stochastic way, and debt policy tied to the nominal supply of money, the deterministic and stochastic components of the tax rate on wealth were then assumed to adjust endogenously to meet the government budget constraint. With government debt and money closely linked in this way, the neutrality of money noted in section 6 did not apply. But in order to derive a closed form solution, debt policy had to be specified in an overly restrictive and unappealing way.

In Grinols and Turnovsky (1998b) they introduce both short-term and long-term bonds simultaneously and thus are able to address issues pertaining to the term structure of interest rates in the context of a stochastically growing economy. The main proposition they establish is the neutrality of debt policy with respect to growth and welfare. A change in the composition of government debt has no effect on either the current level of consumption, the growth rate, or future consumption levels, and therefore welfare. The general conclusion is that the composition of government debt does not matter, suggesting an invariance property analogous to Ricardian Equivalence in government finance, and the Modigliani and Miller proposition, in corporate finance.

13 FINAL COMMENT

In this chapter we have developed a series of stochastic endogenous growth models and have used them to analyse the effects of tax policy on economic growth and welfare. The examples we have introduced are quite diverse and illustrated the flexibility of the framework to deal with a wide range of circumstances. But in concluding, two important limitations of our analysis should be noted.

First, in all of the models the economy has always been on its equilibrium stochastic balanced growth path. This has been possible, in part, because of the nature of the government (outside) bonds, the price of which could jump as necessary to bring about the instantaneous adjustment to the balanced growth path. But the absence of transitional dynamics is a severe limitation, since in reality economies are never on a balanced growth path, stochastic or otherwise. Furthermore, empirical evidence suggesting that convergence speeds are slow (perhaps of the order of 2–3 per cent per annum) highlights the importance of studying transitional paths relative to the steady state. But the extension of the continuous-time stochastic growth models we have been discussing to deal with transitional dynamics is not easy, but it is important if we are to understand the short-term effects of fiscal policy in a stochastic environment.

A second feature of these models is that although the introduction of risk is very important from a theoretical standpoint, the quantitative magnitudes involved for developed countries such as the OECD economies are small. This is because what we have considered are aggregate (economy-wide) risks, which typically are measured by the standard deviation of the relative volatility of output. For countries like the USA or the UK these are of the order of 2 per cent per annum, and given that they appear in the analysis as variances, their impact may be negligible. Indeed, this suggestion is not new. Lucas (1987) using a stationary model argued that the gains from stabilising for aggregate shocks was of the order of 0.1 per cent of consumption per annum, and Turnovsky (2000b) reached a similar conclusion by calibrating the model of section 8. This does not mean that the models are irrelevant, since they are important in identifying the channels through which risk impinges on the economy. But rather it signifies that more work needs to be done to increase the quantitative significance of risk. In this respect the extension of the model to allow for transitional dynamics may prove to be important, since even small risks will with slow adjustment, compound through time to yield much larger long-run effects. Second, the decomposition of risk into aggregate and idiosyncratic components suggests that, whereas aggregate risks may be small, individual risk that influences individual behaviour and welfare is indeed much more substantial. The careful introduction of these aspects into the type of stochastic model we have been discussing would seem to be important if our understanding of the effects of macroeconomic policy in a stochastic world is to be enhanced.

BIBLIOGRAPHY

Abel, A. B. (1983). 'Optimal Investment under Uncertainty,' *American Economic Review*, 73, 228–33
Abel, A. B. and Eberly, J. (1994). 'A Unified Model of Investment Under Uncertainty', *American Economic Review*, 84, 1369–84
Adler, M. and Dumas, B. (1983). 'International Portfolio Choice and Corporation Finance: A Synthesis', *Journal of Finance*, 38, 925–84
Arrow, K. J. (1965). *Aspects of the Theory of Risk-Bearing*, Yrjö Jahnsson Foundation, Helsinki
Barro, R. J. (1990). 'Government Spending in a Simple Model of Endogenous Growth', *Journal of Political Economy*, 98, S103–S125
Barro, R. J. and Sala-i-Martin, X. (1992). 'Public Finance in Models of Economic Growth', *Review of Economic Studies*, 59, 645–61
Beaudry, P. and van Wincoop, E. (1995). 'The Intertemporal Elasticity of Substitution: An Exploration using US Panel of State Data', *Economica*, 63, 495–512
Benavie, A., Grinols, E., and Turnovsky, S. J. (1996). 'Adjustment Costs and Investment in a Stochastic Equilibrium Macro Model', *Journal of Monetary Economics*, 38, 77–100
Benhabib, J. and Perli, R. (1994). 'Uniqueness and Indeterminacy: On the Dynamics of Endogenous Growth', *Journal of Economic Theory*, 63, 113–42

Bismut, J. M. (1975). 'Growth and Intertemporal Allocation of Risks', *Journal of Economic Theory*, 10, 239–57

Black, F. and Scholes, M. (1973). 'The Pricing of Options and Corporate Liabilities', *Journal of Political Economy*, 81, 637–54

Bodie, Z., Merton, R. C. and Samuelson, W. F. (1992). 'Labor Supply Flexibility and Portfolio Choice in a Life Cycle Model', *Journal of Economic Dynamics and Control*, 16, 427–49

Bourguignon, F. (1974). 'A Particular Class of Continuous-Time Stochastic Growth Models', *Journal of Economic Theory*, 9, 141–58

Campbell, J. and Mankiw, N. G. (1989). 'Consumption, Income, and Interest Rates: Reinterpreting the Time Series Evidence', in O. Blanchard and S. Fischer (eds.), *NBER Macroeconomic Annual*, Cambridge, MA: MIT, 185–216

Cazzavillan, G. (1996). 'Public Spending, Endogenous Growth, and Endogenous Fluctuations', *Journal of Economic Theory*, 71, 394–415

Chamley, C. (1986). 'Optimal Taxation of Capital Income in General Equilibrium with Infinite Lives', *Econometrica*, 54, 607–22

Chatterjee, S., Giuliano, P. and Turnovsky, S. J. (2002). 'Capital Income Taxes and Growth in a Stochastic Economy: A Numerical Analysis of the Role of Risk Aversion and Intertemporal Substitution', *Journal of Public Economic Theory*, forthcoming

Chow, G. C. (1979). 'Optimum Control of Stochastic Differential Equation Systems', *Journal of Economic Dynamics and Control*, 1, 143–75

Constantinides, G. M., Donaldson, J. B. and Mehra, R. (2002). 'Junior Can't Borrow: A New Perspective on the Equity Premium Puzzle', *Quarterly Journal of Economics*, 117, 269–96

Corsetti, G. (1997). 'A Portfolio Approach to Endogenous Growth: Equilibrium and Optimal Policy', *Journal of Economic Dynamics and Control*, 21, 1627–44

Cox, J. C., Ingersoll, J. E. and Ross, S. A. (1985a). 'An Intertemporal General Equilibrium Model of Asset Prices', *Econometrica*, 53, 363–84

(1985b). 'A Theory of the Term Structure of Interest Rates', *Econometrica*, 53, 385–408

Devereux, M. B. and Saito, M. (1997). 'Growth, Convergence, and Risk-Sharing with Incomplete International Asset Markets', *Journal of International Economics*, 42, 453–81

Dixit, A. K. and Pindyck, R. S. (1994). *Investment Under Uncertainty*, Princeton: Princeton University Press

Duffie, D., Schroder, M. and Skidias, C. (1997). 'A Term Structure with Preferences for the Timing of Resolution of Uncertainty', *Economic Theory*, 9, 3–22

Eaton, J. (1981). 'Fiscal Policy, Inflation, and the Accumulation of Risky Capital', *Review of Economic Studies*, 48, 435–45

Epstein, L. and Zin, S. (1989). 'Substitution, Risk Aversion, and the Temporal Behavior of Consumption and Asset Returns: An Empirical Analysis', *Journal of Political Economy*, 99, 263–86

(1991). 'Substitution, Risk Aversion, and the Temporal Behavior of Consumption and Asset Returns: A Theoretical Framework', *Econometrica*, 57, 937–69

Frenkel, J. A., Razin, A. and Sadka, E. (1991). *International Taxation in an Integrated World Economy*, Cambridge, MA: MIT Press

Gertler, M. and Grinols, E. (1982). 'Monetary Randomness and Investment', *Journal of Monetary Economics*, 10, 239–58

Giuliano, P. and Turnovsky, S. J. (2003). 'Intertemporal Substitution, Risk Aversion, and Economic Performance in a Stochastically Growing Open Economy', *Journal of International Money and Finance*, 22, 529–56

Glomm, G. and Ravikumar, B. (1994). 'Productive Government Expenditures and Long-Run Growth', *Journal of Economic Dynamics and Control*, 21, 183–204

(1997). 'Public Investment in Infrastructure in a Simple Growth Model', *Journal of Economic Dynamics and Control*, 18, 1173–88

Gong, L. and Zou, H. F. (2002). 'Direct Preferences for Wealth, the Risk Premium Puzzle, Growth and Policy Effectiveness', *Journal of Economic Dynamics and Control*, 26, 247–70

Gordon, R. H. (1985). 'Taxation of Corporate Capital Income: Tax Revenues Versus Tax Distortions', *Quarterly Journal of Economics*, 100, 1–27

Grinols, E. and Turnovsky, S. J. (1993). 'Risk, the Financial Market, and Macroeconomic Equilibrium', *Journal of Economic Dynamics and Control*, 17, 1–36

(1994). 'Exchange Rate Determination and Asset Prices in a Stochastic Small Open Economy', *Journal of International Economics*, 36, 75–97

(1998a). 'Risk, Optimal Government Finance, and Monetary Policies in a Growing Economy', *Economica*, 65, 401–27

(1998b). 'The Consequences of Debt Policy in a Stochastically Growing Monetary Economy', *International Economic Review*, 39, 495–521

Hall, R. E. (1988). 'Intertemporal Substitution in Consumption', *Journal of Political Economy*, 96, 339–57

Hayashi, F. (1982). 'Tobin's Marginal q, Average q: A Neoclassical Interpretation', *Econometrica*, 50, 213–24

Ihori, T. (1991). 'Capital Income Taxation in a World Economy: A Territorial versus a Residence System', *Economic Journal*, 101, 958–65

Ireland, P. N. (1994). 'Supply Side-Economics and Endogenous Growth', *Journal of Monetary Economics*, 33, 559–71

Jin, X. (1998). 'Consumption and Turnpike Theorems in a Continuous-Time Finance Model', *Journal of Economic Dynamics and Control*, 22, 1001–26

Jones, C. (1995). 'Time Series Tests of Endogenous Growth Models', *Quarterly Journal of Economics*, 110, 495–527

Jones, L. E. and Manuelli, R. (1990). 'A Convex Model of Equilibrium Growth: Theory and Policy Implications', *Journal of Political Economy*, 98, 1008–38

Kandel, S. and Stambaugh, R. F. (1991). 'Asset Returns and Intertemporal Preferences', *Journal of Monetary Economics*, 27, 39–71

Kocherlakota, N. (1990). 'Disentangling the Coefficient of Relative Risk Aversion from the Elasticity of Substitution: An Irrelevance Result', *Journal of Finance*, 45, 285–304

Krugman, P. (1991). 'Target Zones and Exchange Rate Dynamics', *Quarterly Journal of Economics*, 106, 669–82

Krugman, P. and Miller, M. H. (eds.) (1992). *Exchange Rate Targets and Currency Bands*, Cambridge: Cambridge University Press

Ladrón-de-Guevara, A., Ortigueira, S. and Santos, M. (1997). 'Equilibrium Dynamics in Two-Sector Models of Economic Growth', *Journal of Economic Dynamics and Control*, 21, 115–43

Lucas, R. E. (1987). *Models of Business Cycles*, Oxford: Basil Blackwell
  (1988). 'On the Mechanics of Economic Development', *Journal of Monetary Economics*, 22, 3–42

Malliaris, A. G. and Brock, W. A. (1982). *Stochastic Methods in Economics and Finance*, Amsterdam: North-Holland

Mankiw, N. G., Rotemberg, J. J. and Summers, L. H. (1985). 'Intertemporal Substitution in Macroeconomics', *Quarterly Journal of Economics*, 100, 225–51

Merton, R. C. (1969). 'Lifetime Portfolio Selection Under Uncertainty: The Continuous-Time Case', *Review of Economics and Statistics*, 51, 247–57
  (1971). 'Optimum Consumption Rules in a Continuous-Time Model', *Journal of Economic Theory*, 3, 373–413
  (1973). 'An Intertemporal Capital Asset Pricing Model', *Econometrica*, 41, 867–87
  (1975). 'An Asymptotic Theory of Growth Under Uncertainty', *Review of Economic Studies*, 42, 375–93
  (1990). *Continuous-Time Finance*, Oxford: Blackwell

Obstfeld, M. (1994). 'Risk-Taking, Global Diversification, and Growth', *American Economic Review*, 84, 1310–29

Ogaki, M. and Reinhart, C. M. (1998). 'Measuring Intertemporal Substitution: The Role of Durable Goods', *Journal of Political Economy*, 106, 1078–98

Pindyck, R. S. (1982). 'Adjustment Costs, Demand Uncertainty, and the Behaviour of Firms', *American Economic Review*, 72, 415–27

Pratt, J. W. (1964). 'Risk Aversion in the Small and in the Large', *Econometrica*, 32, 122–36

Rebelo, S. (1991). 'Long-run Policy Analysis and Long-Run Growth', *Journal of Political Economy*, 99, 500–21

Romer, P. M. (1986). 'Increasing Returns and Long-Run Growth', *Journal of Political Economy*, 94, 1002–37

Sidrauski, M. (1967). 'Rational Choice and Patterns of Growth in a Monetary Economy', *American Economic Review*, 57, 534–44

Smith, W. T. (1996). 'Taxes, Uncertainty, and Long-Term Growth', *European Economic Review*, 40, 1647–64

Solow, R. M. (1956). 'A Contribution to the Theory of Economic Growth', *Quarterly Journal of Economics*, 70, 65–94

(1994). 'Perspectives on Economic Growth', *Journal of Economic Perspectives*, 8, 45–54

Stokey, N. L. and Rebelo, S. (1995). 'Growth Effects of Flat Taxes', *Journal of Political Economy*, 103, 519–50

Stulz, R. (1981). 'A Model of International Asset Pricing', *Journal of Financial Economics*, 9, 383–406

(1983). 'The Demand for Foreign Bonds', *Journal of International Economics*, 15, 225–38

(1986). 'Interest Rates, and Monetary Policy Uncertainty', *Journal of Monetary Economics*, 17, 331–47

(1987). 'An Equilibrium Model of Exchange Rate Determination and Asset Pricing with Nontraded Goods and Imperfect Information', *Journal of Political Economy*, 95, 1024–40

Swan, T. W. (1956). 'Economic Growth and Capital Accumulation', *Economic Record*, 32, 334–61

Tenc, T. (2002). 'Taxation, Risk-Taking and Growth: A Continuous-Time Stochastic General Equilibrium Analysis with Labor–Leisure Choice', unpublished manuscript

Turnovsky, S. J. (1995). 'Optimal Tax Policies in a Stochastically Growing Economy', *Japanese Economic Review*, 46, 125–47

(1996). 'Optimal Tax, Debt, and Expenditure Policies in a Growing Economy', *Journal of Public Economics*, 60, 21–44

(1997). 'Public and Private Capital in an Endogenously Growing Economy', *Macroeconomic Dynamics*, 1, 615–39

(1999). 'Productive Government Expenditure in a Stochastically Growing Economy', *Macroeconomic Dynamics*, 3, 544–70

(2000a). *Methods of Macroeconomic Dynamics*, 2nd edn., Cambridge MA: MIT Press

(2000b). 'Fiscal Policy, Elastic Labor Supply, and Endogenous Growth', *Journal of Monetary Economics*, 45, 185–210

(2000c). 'Government Policy in a Stochastic Growth Model with Elastic Labor Supply', *Journal of Public Economic Theory*, 2, 389–433

Vasicek, O. (1977). 'An Equilibrium Characterization of the Term Structure', *Journal of Financial Economics*, 5, 177–88

Weil, P. (1990). 'Non-Expected Utility in Macroeconomics', *Quarterly Journal of Economics*, 105, 29–42

4

Recent developments in the macroeconomic stabilisation literature: is price stability a good stabilisation strategy?

Matthew B. Canzoneri, Robert E. Cumby and Behzad T. Diba

1 INTRODUCTION

A New Neo-classical Synthesis (NNS) is merging three traditions that have dominated macroeconomic modelling for the last thirty years.[1] In the 1970s, Sargent and Wallace (1975) and others added rational expectations to the IS-LM models that were then being used to evaluate monetary policy;[2] somewhat later, Calvo (1983) and Taylor (1980) introduced richer dynamic specifications for the nominal rigidities that were assumed in some of those models. In the 1980s, Kydland and Prescott (1982) and others introduced the Real Business Cycle (RBC) model, which sought to explain business cycle regularities in a framework with maximising agents, perfect competition, and complete wage/price flexibility.[3]

The NNS reintroduces nominal rigidities and the demand determination of employment and output. Monopolistically competitive wage- and price-setters replace the RBC model's perfectly competitive wage- and price-takers; monopoly markups provide the rationale for suppliers to expand in response to an increase in demand; and the Dixit and Stiglitz (1977) framework – when combined with complete sharing of consumption risks – allows the high degree of aggregation that has been a hallmark of macroeconomic modelling.

In this chapter, we present a simple model that can be used to illustrate elements of the NNS and recent developments in the macroeconomic stabilisation literature. We do not attempt to survey this rapidly growing

We would like to thank, without implicating, Dale Henderson for useful discussions of the material presented here. We would also like to thank two anonymous referees for their careful reading and helpful suggestions.

[1] Goodfriend and King (1997) described this synthesis, gave it its name, and cited a number of early references. Ongoing work includes draft chapters of Michael Woodford's *Interest and Prices* (Woodford forthcoming).

[2] McCallum (1980) surveys this literature.

[3] Cooley (1995) provides a representative sampling of this literature.

literature. Instead, we focus on a set of papers that are key to a question that is currently being hotly debated: is price stability a good strategy for macroeconomic stabilisation?[4] If so, some of the generally accepted tradeoffs in modern central banking would seem to evaporate. For example, inflation (or price-level) targeting need not be seen as a choice that excludes Keynesian stabilisation, and it would be unnecessary to give price stability such primacy in the statutes of the new central bank in Europe.

In section 2, we present our model and discuss some fundamental characteristics of the NNS. Our model is simpler than that which appears in much of the literature because we have replaced the dynamic Calvo and Taylor specifications of nominal rigidity with the assumption that some wages and/or prices are set one period in advance. This allows us to derive closed form equilibrium solutions for a class of utility functions and assumptions about the distribution of macroeconomic shocks.[5] On the other hand, our model is somewhat more complicated than that which appears elsewhere because we allow for an arbitrary number of sectors within the economy. Much of the current debate over stabilisation policy revolves around asymmetries – asymmetries in wage and/or price setting, and asymmetries in the stochastic processes driving productivity. Our multi-sector model is designed to capture these asymmetries in a very tractable way.

NNS models have much in common with the IS-LM models that preceded them, but a provocative new element has been added. Wage- and price-setters' prediction errors – errors in predicting macroeconomic shocks and monetary policy – continue to make employment and output deviate from their expected levels. However, in the NNS models, second moments also affect the average (or expected) level of employment and output. In our NNS model, for example, we will see that an increase in monetary uncertainty can lower the level of economic activity, and that a monetary policy that attenuates the negative covariance between employment and productivity can increase the level of economic activity. Put another way, stabilisation policy in NNS models does more than just reduce variances; it also raises the expected level of economic activity by manipulating the second moments.

In section 3, we use our model to discuss normative aspects of the NNS, and in particular monetary policy. Household utility provides the makings

---

[4] Contributions to the debate include Aoki (2001), Benigno (2001), Erceg and Levin (2002), Erceg, Henderson and Levin (2000), Goodfriend and King (1997, 2001), King and Wolman (1999), Rotemberg and Woodford (1997, 1999).

[5] The cost of course is that we cannot discuss dynamic issues (such as persistence in the effects of macroeconomic shocks) that the Calvo and Taylor specifications were designed to capture, and are currently a hot topic in the literature. See for example Chari, Kehoe and McGrattan (2000).

for a natural measure of national welfare, and it turns out that the fully flexible wage/price benchmark is a 'constrained' optimum. The recent literature has produced what at first blush appears to be a bewildering array of statements on the merits of price stability as a guide for macroeconomic stabilisation: Goodfriend and King (1997, 2001) and King and Wolman (1999) said that monetary policy should stabilise the aggregate price level, or equivalently the average markup of price over marginal cost; Aoki (2001) said that 'core' prices should be stabilised; Benigno (2001) said that a weighted average of regional prices should be stabilised; Blanchard (1997) said that wage rigidity changes the arguments for price stability; and Erceg, Henderson and Levin (2000) said there was a tradeoff between price and wage stability. We will review each of their arguments. Basically, the dispute is over which kinds of nominal inertia are important, whether there are asymmetries in nominal inertia and shocks across sectors and whether wage rigidities constrain the efficient allocation of labour.

In section 4, we summarise the present state of the policy debate, and identify some of the empirical issues that are at its core.

2 A MULTI-SECTOR ECONOMY WITH MONOPOLISTIC COMPETITION AND NOMINAL INERTIA

Our economy consists of S sectors. Sectors are defined by supply-side characteristics: their nominal rigidities and their productivity shocks. Sectors are indexed by $s = 1, 2, \ldots S$. Each sector has a continuum of price-setting firms. Firms are indexed by $f \in [1, S + 1]$, with firms in $[1, 2)$ belonging to sector 1, firms in $[2, 3)$ belonging to sector 2, and so on. Each firm has a continuum of wage-setting households working for it. Households are indexed by $(h, f) \in [0, 1] \otimes [1, S + 1]$.[6] Our notation keeps track of time period, sector and individual entity; so for example, $W_{s,t}(h, f)$ is the wage of household h at firm f in sector s in period t, and $Y_{s,t}(f)$ is output of firm f in sector s in period t.[7]

Our multi-sector framework allows us to analyse a wide variety of economic structures. There is a mass of one household working at each firm, a mass of one firm in each sector, and S sectors in all; so, the total mass

---

[6] In our model, each household works at just one firm. In other models, each household supplies labour to all of the firms; see for example Erceg and Levin (2002) or Erceg, Henderson and Levin (2000). We will return to this issue in section 4.3.

[7] At this point, the sectoral subscript, s, may be viewed as notational overkill, since the sector can be inferred from the firm's index, f. However, in equilibrium, all of the firms and households in a given sector will be identical, and we will be able to drop the indices in parentheses; only the subscripts will matter.

of firms and households is S. In a multi-country version of our model, S would measure the size of the economy. We can also use the number of sectors to represent the relative importance of different kinds of nominal rigidity in the economy, or the relative importance of different productivity shocks. For example, if wage rigidity is thought to affect twice as many firms as price rigidity, then we can specify two sectors with wage rigidity and one with price rigidity.

2.1 Households and bundlers

Household (h, f)'s utility in period t is given by

$$
U_t(h, f) = E_t \sum_{\tau=t}^{\infty} \beta^{\tau-t} [u(C_\tau(h, f)) - g(N_{s,\tau}(h, f))
$$
$$
+ v(M_\tau(h, f)/P_\tau)] \tag{4.1}
$$

where $C_\tau(h, f))$ is the household's consumption of a composite consumption good (to be defined later) and P_τ is its price; $N_{s,\tau}(h, f)$ is the household's work effort, and $M_\tau(h, f)$ are the household's money balances. In what follows, we will generally restrict our attention to the constant elasticity functions: $u(C_\tau) \equiv (1 - \gamma)^{-1} C_\tau^{1-\gamma}$ and $g(N_\tau) \equiv A_\tau(1 + \chi)^{-1} N_\tau^{1+\chi}$. A_τ may be viewed as a stochastic preference shock, essentially a 'laziness' shock. In section 3, we shall further restrict $u(\cdot)$ to the case of log utility.

The household's optimisation problem can be divided into an *intratemporal* problem – which determines the demand for the components of composite goods – and an *intertemporal* problem – which determines savings and overall consumption.[8] Chari, Kehoe and McGrattan (2000) use the artifice of a competitive 'bundler' to derive the results of the intratemporal problem. Here, we use the notion of a 'bundler' to aggregate labour (at the firm level) and output (both at the sectoral level and economywide). A bundler buys the sectoral goods $Y_{s,t}$ at prices $P_{s,t}$ and bundles them into a composite consumption good

$$
Y_t = \Pi_{s=1}^{S} Y_{s,t}^{1/S}. \tag{4.2a}
$$

The bundler's cost-minimisation problem gives the demands for the S sectoral goods

$$
Y_{s,t}^d = (1/S)(P_t/P_{s,t})Y_t, \quad s = 1, 2, \ldots, S \tag{4.2b}
$$

[8] See for example Blanchard and Fischer (1989, chapter 8), Frenkel and Razin (1987, chapter 6). The artifice of bundlers, described next, arrives at the same result with less algebra; see Canzoneri, Cumby and Diba (2002b) Note 4: Unbundling the bundler.

and the price

$$P_t = S\Pi_{s=1}^{S} P_{s,t}{}^{1/S} \tag{4.2c}$$

at which the bundler sells the composite consumption good to households.

Each sectoral good is itself a composite of the outputs of firms in the sector. A sectoral bundler buys the firms' outputs $Y_{s,t}(f)$ at the price $P_{s,t}(f)$ and bundles them into the sectoral good

$$Y_{s,t} \equiv \left[\int_s^{s+1} Y_{s,t}(f)^{(\theta-1)/\theta} df \right]^{\theta/(\theta-1)}, \tag{4.3a}$$

where $\theta > 1$ is the elasticity of substitution across differentiated products within a sector. (Note that (4.2a) implies that the elasticity of substitution across sectoral goods is one; this restriction – first introduced by Corsetti and Pesenti (2001) – simplifies the algebra that follows; as we shall see, it is not entirely innocent.) This bundler's cost-minimisation problem gives the demand for each firm's product

$$Y_{s,t}^d(f) = (P_{s,t}/P_{s,t}(f))^\theta Y_{s,t}, \tag{4.3b}$$

and the price

$$P_{s,t} = \left[\int_s^{s+1} P_{s,\tau}(f)^{1-\theta} df \right]^{1/(1-\theta)}, \tag{4.3c}$$

at which the bundler sells the sectoral good to the bundler of the composite consumption good.

We can also use the artifice of a bundler to describe the production technology. Recall that each firm f has a continuum of households (h, f) working for it. A bundler for firm f pays the wage $W_{s,t}(h, f)$ for the labour services $N_{s,t}(h, f)$ and assembles them into a composite labour input

$$N_{s,t}(f) \equiv \left[\int_0^1 N_{s,t}(h, f)^{(\phi-1)/\phi} dh \right]^{\phi/(\phi-1)}, \tag{4.4a}$$

where $\phi > 1$. The bundler's cost-minimisation problem gives the demand for household (h, f)'s labour

$$N_{s,t}^d(h, f) = (W_{s,t}(f)/W_{s,t}(h, f))^\phi N_{s,\tau}(f) \tag{4.4b}$$

and the price at which the bundler sells the composite labour input to the firm

$$W_{s,t}(f) = \left[\int_0^1 W_{s,t}(h, f)^{1-\phi} dh \right]^{1/(1-\phi)}. \qquad (4.4c)$$

Production is linear and stochastic; $Y_{s,t}(f) = Z_{s,t} N_{s,t}(f)$, where $Z_{s,t}$ is the sectoral productivity shock.

Household (h, f)'s budget constraint for period τ is given by

$$M_\tau(h, f) + E_\tau[\delta_{\tau,\tau+1} B_{\tau+1}(h, f)] + P_\tau C_\tau(h, f) + P_\tau T_\tau$$
$$= W_{s,\tau}(h, f) N_{s,\tau}^d(h, f) + M_{\tau-1}(h, f) + B_\tau(h, f) + D_\tau(h, f) \quad (4.5)$$

where $B_{\tau+1}(h, f)$ is a state-contingent claim on other households, and $\delta_{\tau,\tau+1}$ is the stochastic discount factor.[9] $D_t(h, f)$ are household (h, f)'s dividends, and T_t is a lump-sum tax (which the government uses to balance its budget each period).[10]

Household (h, f)'s intertemporal optimisation problem is to choose $B_{t+1}(h, f)$, $C_t(h, f)$, $M_t(h, f)$, and $W_{s,t}(h, f)$ to maximise (4.1) subject to (4.4b) and (4.5). Differentiation with respect to the first three variables produces standard first-order conditions that do not depend upon where the household works (or assumptions about nominal rigidities):

$$\delta_{t,t+1} = \beta \lambda_{t+1}(h, f)/\lambda_t(h, f) \qquad (4.6)$$

$$\lambda_t(h, f) = u'(\cdot)/P_t \qquad (4.7)$$

$$v'(\cdot) = u'(\cdot)[1 - E_t(\delta_{t,t+1})], \qquad (4.8)$$

where $\lambda_t(h, f)$ is household (h, f)'s marginal utility of nominal wealth.

Why have we modelled contingent claims markets? Without them, households working in different sectors would generally have different incomes, different levels of consumption and different marginal utilities of

---

[9] The parsimonious notation for contingent claims in (4.5) comes from Woodford (1997). Cochrane (2001, chapter 3) introduces contingent claims in the following way: let $p(B) = \sum_\sigma pc(\sigma) B(\sigma)$ be the price of a portfolio B of contingent claims; the σs denote states of nature, $pc(\sigma)$ is the price of a claim on one dollar received in $\tau + 1$ contingent on the state σ occurring, and $B(\sigma)$ is the number of such claims in portfolio B. Letting $\pi(\sigma)$ be the probability of state σ, $p(B) = \sum_\sigma \pi(\sigma)[pc(\sigma)/\pi(\sigma)] B(\sigma) = E[\delta(\sigma) B(\sigma)]$, where $\delta(\sigma) \equiv pc(\sigma)/\pi(\sigma)$ is called the 'stochastic discount factor'. $B_{\tau+1}(h, f)$ and $\delta_{\tau,\tau+1}$ in (5) correspond to $B(\sigma)$ and $\delta(\sigma)$. All households face the same asset prices and have the same subjective probabilities; so, all households face the same discount factor, $\delta_{\tau,\tau+1}$, in (5).

[10] We may assume that each household owns a representative share in all of the firms. We have suppressed the buying and selling of shares since, as explained below, state-contingent claims make the distribution of dividends irrelevant in this model.

wealth. It is very difficult to derive an equilibrium in such a model (even with simulation). So, NNS models generally postulate complete sharing of consumption risk, and all households face the same stochastic discount factors. Then, in an equilibrium in which all households have the same initial wealth, the Euler equation (4.6) implies that the marginal utility of wealth equalises across households, and (4.7) implies that consumption equalises across households, even though labour incomes, work efforts or dividends may not.[11] Equation (4.8) gives the household's demand for real money balances. Consider a 'risk-free' bond that costs 1 dollar in period t and pays I_t dollars in period $t + 1$ for all states of nature; then, $1 = E_t[\delta_{t,t+1} I_t]$ or $I_t^{-1} = E_t[\delta_{t,t+1}]$. Equation (4.8) relates the demand for real money balances to the level of consumption and the gross nominal interest rate, I_t.

If household (h, f) works in a sector with flexible wages, then optimal wage-setting requires

$$g'(\cdot) = (1/\mu_w)(W_{s,t}(h, f)/P_t)u'(\cdot) \qquad (4.9)_{flex}$$

where $\mu_w \equiv \phi/(\phi - 1) > 1$ is a 'markup factor'. The left-hand side of $(4.9)_{flex}$ is the disutility of working one more hour; the right-hand side is the utility of spending the proceeds, $(1/\mu_w)(W_{s,t}(h,f)/P_t)$. The proceeds are less than the original real wage, $W_{s,t}(h, f)/P_t$, because the household faces a downward-sloping demand curve, (4.4b); it has to lower its wage to induce the extra hour of work. This is a source of inefficiency. Monopolistic wage setting implies the MRS ($= g'(\cdot)/u'(\cdot)$) is less than the real wage; so, the work effort will be too small. As $\phi \to \infty$, the labour demand curve becomes infinitely elastic, $\mu_w \to 1$, and the distortion is eliminated.

If household (h, f) works in a sector with fixed wages, then $W_{s,t}(h, f)$ is set at the end of period $t - 1$, with the information available at that time; optimal wage-setting requires

$$E_{t-1}[g'(\cdot)N_{s,t}(h, f)] = E_{t-1}[(1/\mu_w)(W_{s,t}(h, f)/P_t)u'(\cdot)N_{s,t}(h, f)].$$
$$(4.9)_{fixed}$$

When wages are fixed, labour is demand-determined. The household will want to work more in response to an increase in demand as long as the marginal disutility of work is less than the marginal utility of spending the proceeds: $g'(\cdot) < (W_{s,t}(h, f)/P_t)u'(\cdot)$. Since $g'(\cdot)$ is increasing while

---

[11] Alternatively, we could assume that all of the households supply labour to all of the firms in all of the sectors, and share equally in the profits of all the firms. Then, we could dispense with the contingent claims markets.

$u'(\cdot)$ is decreasing, there is a limit as to how much the household will want to increase its work effort; this limit is known as the 'participation constraint'.[12] The participation constraint, if taken seriously, poses some technical difficulties. We can limit the support of random variables (and monetary policy) so that the constraint is never binding, or we can deal with the discontinuities that the constraint entails. In practice, the constraint is generally given short shrift.[13]

2.2 Firms

The market value of firm f is

$$MV_t(f) = E_t \sum_{\tau=t}^{\infty} \delta_{t,\tau} R_\tau(f), \qquad (4.10)$$

where $\delta_{t,\tau}$ is the stochastic discount factor (representing the current price of a dollar claim in a particular state in period τ) and $R_\tau(f) \equiv P_{s,\tau}(f) Y_{s,\tau}(f) - W_{s,\tau}(f) N_{s,\tau}(f)$ is the firm's net revenue. Firm f sets $P_{s,\tau}(f)$ to maximise (4.10) subject to (4.3b) (and $N_{s,t}(f) = Y_{s,t}(f)/Z_{s,t}$). If firm f is in a flexible price sector, then

$$P_{s,t}(f) = \mu_p[W_{s,t}(f)/Z_{s,t}], \qquad (4.11)_{flex}$$

where $\mu_p \equiv \theta/(\theta-1) > 1$; price is set at a constant markup, μ_p, over marginal cost.

Monopolistic price-setting, like monopolistic wage-setting, is a source of inefficiency. The inefficiency is most easily explained in a one-sector model. Efficiency requires that the MRS be equal to the MPL. Here, monopolistic price-setting drives a wedge between the MPL and the real wage; that is, MPL $= Z = \mu_p(W/P)$. As noted above, monopolistic wage setting drives a wedge between the real wage and the MRS. Combining $(4.9)_{flex}$ and $(4.11)_{flex}$, we have MRS $= (1/\mu_w\mu_p)$MPL; $\mu \equiv \mu_w\mu_p$ measures the combined distortion (or markup). Both distortions make the work effort too small.[14] Similar reasoning applies in our multi-sector model.

---

[12] With perfect competition, the household would never have wanted to supply more labour; monopolistic competition rationalises the demand determination within a limited range.

[13] Some macroeconomists think that macroeconomic shocks are more important than microeconomic distortions (like monopolistic competition). Tobin (1977), for example, asserts that: 'It takes a heap of Harberger Triangles to fill an Okun Gap.' This suggests that limiting the size of macroeconomic shocks may not be the right choice; we may ultimately be forced to deal with the participation constraint in a more direct way.

[14] See Erceg, Henderson and Levin (2000) and Galí, Gertler and Lopez-Salido (2001) for a fuller discussion of the welfare loss arising from the distortion of this margin in models with sticky wages and prices.

If firm f is in a fixed-price sector, then $P_{s,t}(f)$ is set in period $t-1$, and

$$P_{s,t}(f) = \mu_p E_{t-1}[(u'(\cdot)/P_t)Y_{s,t}(f)(W_{s,t}(f)/Z_{s,t})]/E_{t-1} \\ \times [(u'(\cdot)/P_t)Y_{s,t}(f)], \qquad (4.11)_{fixed}$$

where the Euler equation (4.6) was used to eliminate $\delta_{t-1,t}$ and then (4.7) was used to eliminate λ_t. When prices are fixed, output is demand-determined. Once again, there is a participation constraint; the firm will want to expand to meet an increase in demand as long as $P_{s,t}(f) > W_{s,t}(f)/Z_{s,t}$.

Since the first-order conditions for households and firms in a given sector are identical, we look for an equilibrium in which: $N_{s,t}(h, f) = N_{s,t}(f) \equiv N_{s,t}$, $W_{s,t}(h, f) = W_{s,t}(f) \equiv W_{s,t}$, $P_{s,t}(f) = P_{s,t}$. The market for sector s output will clear when consumption by households (regardless of the sector in which they are employed) is equal to the output of sector s: $\int_1^{S+1}[\int_0^1 C_{s,t}(h, f)dh]df = SC_{s,t}(h, f) \equiv SC_{s,t} = Y_{s,t} \equiv Y_{s,t}(f) = [\int_s^{s+1} Y_{s,t}(f)^{(\theta-1)/\theta}df]^{\theta/(\theta-1)}$. In equilibrium, aggregate consumption is equal to aggregate output: $\int_1^{S+1}[\int_0^1 C_t(h, f)dh]df = SC_t(h, f) \equiv SC_t = Y_t \equiv \Pi_{s=1}^S Y_{s,t}^{1/S}$. Note that we have defined $C_{s,t}$ to be consumption per household of sectoral good s; $Y_{s,t}$ is defined to be output per worker in sector s. Since the measure of households is S, while the measure of workers in any given sector is one, $SC_{s,t} = Y_{s,t}$ in equilibrium. Consumption and output of the composite good, C_t and Y_t, are similarly defined. Before describing the equilibria in detail, we discuss a fundamental relationship optimising households impose between the expected utility of leisure and the expected utility of consumption.

2.3 A fundamental relationship between leisure and consumption

The decentralisation of the economy into households and firms is somewhat artificial in the present model. We can combine the wage-setting behaviour in $(4.9)_{fixed}$ with the price-setting behaviour in $(4.11)_{fixed}$ to arrive at a relationship between leisure and consumption that would also hold in a Yeoman–Farmer framework.[15] With constant elasticity utility functions, and a Cobb–Douglas aggregator for the final consumption good, this relationship implies that the expected utility of consumption is proportional to the expected disutility of work.

---

[15] Canzoneri, Cumby and Diba (2002b) show that the relationships in lemma 1, below, hold in a Yeoman–Farmer framework.

Lemma 1: Consumption–leisure tradeoff

(A) $(4.9)_{fixed}$, $(4.11)_{fixed}$ and $(4.2b)$ $\Rightarrow E_{t-1}[(u'(\cdot)C_t]$
$$= \mu E_{t-1}[g'(\cdot)N_{s,t}]$$

(B) $u(C) = (1-\gamma)^{-1}C^{1-\gamma}$ and $g(N) = A(1+\chi)^{-1}N^{(1+\chi)}$
$$\Rightarrow E_{t-1}[u(\cdot)] = [(1+\chi)/(1-\gamma)]\mu E_{t-1}[g(\cdot)]$$

(C) $u(C) = (\log C)$ and $g(N) = A(1+\chi)^{-1}N^{(1+\chi)} \Rightarrow E_{t-1}[g(\cdot)]$
$$= [\mu(1+\chi)]^{-1}$$

Proof   The proof is straightforward using $(4.9)_{fixed}$, $(4.11)_{fixed}$ and $(4.2b)$.

Lemma 1 will have important implications for the normative analysis in section 3.

In equilibrium, the sectoral wage and price equations become (for $s = 1, 2, \ldots, S$):

$$W_{s,t}/P_t = \mu_w[g'(N_{s,t})/u'(C_t)] \quad \text{for flex-wage sectors} \qquad (4.12)_{flex}$$
$$W_{s,t} = \mu_w E_{t-1}[g'(N_{s,t})N_{s,t}]/E_{t-1}[(u'(C_t)/P_t)N_{s,t}]$$
$$\text{for fixed-wage sectors} \qquad (4.12)_{fixed}$$
$$P_{s,t} = \mu_p[W_{s,t}/Z_{s,t}] \quad \text{for flexible-price sectors} \qquad (4.13)_{flex}$$
$$P_{s,t} = \mu_p E_{t-1}[(u'(C_t)/P_t)Y_{s,t}(W_{s,t}/Z_{s,t})]/E_{t-1}[(u'(C_t)/P_t)Y_{s,t}]$$
$$\text{for fixed-price sectors.} \qquad (4.13)_{fixed}$$

The other equilibrium conditions are:

$$P_t C_t = S P_{s,t} C_{s,t} \qquad (4.14)$$
$$P_t = S\Pi_{s=1}^{S} P_{s,t}^{1/S} \qquad (4.15)$$
$$I_t^{-1} = \beta E_t[u'(C_{t+1})/u'(C_t))(P_t/P_{t+1})] \qquad (4.16)$$
$$v'(M_t/P_t) = u'(C_t)\left[1 - I_t^{-1}\right]. \qquad (4.17)$$

Expenditure on each sectoral good is proportional to total expenditure because of the Cobb–Douglas aggregator.[16] It is natural to take nominal income as the instrument of monetary policy: in sectors with sticky prices, output and employment rise and fall with nominal income; in sectors with sticky wages and flexible prices, $(4.13)_{flex}$ and (4.14) imply that output and employment move with both nominal income and sectoral productivity

---

[16] The constant expenditure shares embodied in (4.14) effectively separate the sectors from each other. For this reason, the Cobb–Douglas aggregator is often used in models that assume multiple goods or sectors; see for example Corsetti and Pesenti (2001) and Obstfeld and Rogoff (2001).

shocks. In what follows, we let $\Omega_t \equiv P_t C_t = P_t Y_t / S = P_{s,t} Y_{s,t}$ be the instrument of monetary policy; Ω may be a function of the macroeconomic shocks if the Central Bank has information on them.

In practice, of course, the Central Bank's instrument is either the money supply or the interest rate, and the Central Bank would have to offset demand shocks (which we have not modelled here) to control nominal expenditure; it would do this via (4.16) and (4.17), which can be thought of as IS and LM curves. The new literature tends not to dwell on these issues, and our discussion in section 3 will focus on the optimal response of nominal income to supply-side shocks.[17]

2.4 The flexible wage/price solution

The flexible wage/price solution will be a useful benchmark in what follows. It is instructive to solve $(4.12)_{flex}$, $(4.13)_{flex}$, $(4.14), \ldots, (4.17)$ for a specific set of utility functions.

Lemma 2: the flexible wage/price solution
If $u(C_t) = \log(C_t)$ and $g(N_t) = A_t (1 + \chi)^{-1} N_t^{1+\chi}$, then

(A)
$$P_{s,t}{}^* = \mu_p (W_{s,t}{}^* / Z_{s,t})$$

(B)
$$N_{s,t}{}^* = \mu^{-1/(1+\chi)} A_t^{-1/(1+\chi)} \quad \text{and}$$

(C)
$$Y_{s,t}{}^* = Z_{s,t} N_{s,t}{}^* = \mu^{-1/(1+\chi)} A_t^{-1/(1+\chi)} Z_{s,t} = S C_{s,t}{}^*$$

(D)
$$C_{s,t}{}^* / C_{s',t}{}^* = P_{s',t}{}^* / P_{s,t}{}^* = Z_{s,t} / Z_{s',t} \quad \text{and}$$
$$P_{s',t}{}^* / P_t{}^* = (\Pi_{s=1}^S Z_{s,t}^{1/S}) / S Z_{s',t}$$

(E)
$$C_t{}^* = (1/S) \mu^{-1/(1+\chi)} A_t^{-1/(1+\chi)} \Pi_{s=1}^S Z_{s,t}^{1/S}$$

(F)
$$P_t{}^* = \Omega_t S \mu^{1/(1+\chi)} A_t^{1/(1+\chi)} \Pi_{s=1}^S Z_{s,t}^{-1/S} \quad \text{and}$$
$$W_{s,t}{}^* = \mu_w \mu^{-\chi/(1+\chi)} A_t^{1/(1+\chi)} \Omega_t$$

where *'s denote flexible wage/price values and $\mu \equiv \mu_p \mu_w$ is the combined markup.

---

[17] King and Wolman (1999), and Ireland (1996) adopt cash-in-advance frameworks, and nominal expenditure is equal to the money supply. We have followed most of the recent literature in using a money-in-the-utility function (MIUF) framework. In Canzoneri, Cumby and Diba (2002b), we consider explicit interest rate rules, in the spirit of Henderson and Kim (1999). See Giannoni and Woodford (2001) for a discussion of interest rate rules.

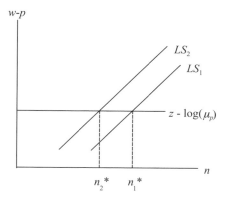

Figure 4.1a A positive leisure shock

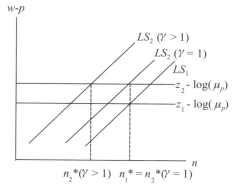

Figure 4.1b A positive productivity shock

Monopolistic wage- and price-setting does not, by itself, break up the Classical Dichotomy. Everything real – output levels, employment levels, real wages, relative prices – is determined by productivity factors (the productivity shocks, $Z_{s,t}$) and the disutility of work (the laziness shock, A_t). Monetary policy, Ω, does not appear in lemma 2 until (F), where it determines the nominal levels of wages and prices. As Goodfriend and King (1997) have noted, the flexible wage/price solution is essentially an RBC model with monopolistic competition added on.

According to lemma 2, employment in each sector reacts to the preference shock, A_t, but not to the productivity shocks, $Z_{s,t}$. The response of employment to supply shocks can be interpreted by looking at the labour market. Labour demand is given by $W_{s,t}{}^*/P_{s,t}{}^* = (1/\mu_p)Z_{s,t}$. Labour supply is given by $W_{s,t}/P_t = \mu_w[g'(\cdot)/u'(\cdot)]$. Starting with a more general specification of the utility of consumption – $u(C_t) = (1 - \gamma)^{-1}C_t^{1-\gamma}$ – and letting small letters represent the logs of capital letters, the labour supply and demand curves become:

$$w_{s,t}{}^* - p_{s,t}{}^* = \text{constant} + (\gamma + \chi)n_{s,t}{}^* + a_t + [1 + (\gamma - 1)(1/S)]z_{s,t}$$

$$+ (\gamma - 1)(1/S) \sum_{s' \neq s} z_{s',t} \qquad (4.18a)$$

$$w_{s,t}{}^* - p_{s,t}{}^* = \text{constant} + z_{s,t}. \qquad (4.18b)$$

The leisure shock is easy enough to understand. As shown in figure 4.1a, an increase in a_t shifts labour supply up and lowers employment. The productivity shock is a little more complicated. As shown in figure 4.1b, an increase in $z_{s,t}$ shifts labour supply and labour demand up by the same amount if $\gamma = 1$ and $n^*_{s,t}$ does not respond; labour supply shifts up more than labour demand if $\gamma > 1$, and $n^*_{s,t}$ falls.[18] The assumption of log utility (or $\gamma = 1$) in lemma 2 greatly simplifies the model, but at some cost.

2.5 Sticky wage and/or price solutions

Per capita nominal income is determined by monetary policy – $\Omega_t \equiv P_t C_t = P_{s,t} Y_{s,t}$. In sectors with fixed prices, the price is determined by $(4.13)_{fixed}$, and then consumption and output are determined by (4.14), and employment is determined by $N_{s,t} = Y_{s,t}/Z_{s,t}$. As Henderson and Kim (1999) have noted, when the price is fixed, it does not matter whether the wage is fixed or flexible; the solutions for output and employment are the same either way. The real wage determines the distribution of revenue between workers and the firm's owners, but with complete sharing of consumption risks, this does not affect consumption. In sectors with fixed wages and flexible prices, the wage is determined by $(4.12)_{fixed}$, and then the price is determined by $(4.13)_{flex}$, consumption and output are determined by (4.14) and employment is determined by $N_{s,t} = Y_{s,t}/Z_{s,t}$.

With constant elasticity utility functions, the model is nicely log linear. So, it is natural to assume that the supply shocks – A_t and $Z_{s,t}$ – have a log-normal distribution.[19] Under this assumption, we can find exact closed form solutions. Letting small letters represent the logs of capital letters, letting $\psi \equiv 1 + \chi$, and denoting flexible wage/price solution values by a^*, we have:

Lemma 3: sticky wage/price solutions
Let $u(C_t) = \log(C_t)$ and $g(N_t) = A_t(1+\chi)^{-1} N_t^{1+\chi}$, and let $\{A_t, Z_{s,t}\} \sim$ log normal; then:

In sectors where wages are fixed and prices are flexible:

(A) $$w_{s,t} = \psi^{-1} \log(\mu) - \log(\mu_p) + E_{t-1}[\omega_t + (a_t/\psi)]$$
$$+ (\psi/2)\text{VAR}_{t-1}[\omega_t + a_t/\psi]$$

---

[18] In addition, labour supply responds to productivity shocks in other sectors if $\gamma \neq 1$.

[19] A quick review of log-normality: let small letters represent the logs of capital letters. Let Q have a log-normal distribution; so, $q \equiv \ln Q \sim N(\bar{q}, \sigma_q^2)$ and $\ln Q^k = kq$ imply $Q^k = exp\{kq\}$ *or* $E(Q^k) = E(exp\{kq\}) = exp\{k\bar{q} + {}^1/_2 k^2 \sigma_q^2\}$; and finally, $\ln E(Q^k) = k\bar{q} + {}^1/_2 k^2 \sigma_q^2$.

The log-normal distribution has an unbounded support; so, the participation constraints will be violated for 'large' realisations of the shocks. Similarly, monetary policies that have Ω respond automatically to the values of shocks may violate the zero bound for nominal interest rates. Following standard practice, we set these issues aside.

(B) $\quad y_{s,t} = y_{s,t}{}^{*} + \{\omega_t - E_{t-1}[\omega_t]\} + \{(a_t/\psi) - E_{t-1}[a_t/\psi]\}$
$\qquad - (\psi/2)\text{VAR}_{t-1}[\omega_t + a_t/\psi]$

(C) $\quad w_{s,t} = w_{s,t}{}^{*} - \{\omega_t - E_{t-1}[\omega_t]\} - \{(a_t/\psi) - E_{t-1}[a_t/\psi]\}$
$\qquad + (\psi/2)\text{VAR}_{t-1}[\omega_t + a_t/\psi].$

In sectors where prices are fixed and wages are either fixed or flexible:

(D) $\quad p_{s,t} = \psi^{-1}\log(\mu) + E_{t-1}[\omega_t - z_{s,t} + (a_t/\psi)]$
$\qquad + (\psi/2)\text{VAR}_{t-1}[\omega_t - z_{s,t} + a_t/\psi]$

(E) $\quad y_{s,t} = y_{s,t}{}^{*} + \{\omega_t - E_{t-1}[\omega_t]\} - \{z_{s,t} - E_{t-1}[z_{s,t}]\} + \{(a_t/\psi)$
$\qquad - E_{t-1}[a_t/\psi]\} - (\psi/2)\text{VAR}_{t-1}[\omega_t - z_{s,t} + a_t/\psi]\}$

(F) $\quad p_{s,t} = p_{s,t}{}^{*} - \{\omega_t - E_{t-1}[\omega_t]\} + \{z_{s,t} - E_{t-1}[z_{s,t}]\} - \{(a_t/\psi)$
$\qquad - E_{t-1}[a_t/\psi]\} + (\psi/2)\text{VAR}_{t-1}[\omega_t - z_{s,t} + a_t/\psi]\}.$

Proof To get (A), note that part (C) of Lemma 1 and (4.14) imply $W_{s,t} = (\mu^{1/\psi}/\mu_p)\{E_{t-1}[A_t\Omega_t{}^{\psi}]\}^{1/\psi}$, and use log-normality. To get (D), note that part (C) of Lemma 1 and (4.14) imply $P_{s,t} = \mu^{1/\psi}\{E_{t-1}[A_t(\Omega_t/Z_{s,t})^{\psi}]\}^{1/\psi}$, and use log-normality. The other results are straightforward to derive using (A), (D), the expressions in lemma 2 and the definition of ω_t.

In the sticky wage/price solutions, policy prediction errors and shock prediction errors cause output (and employment) to deviate from their flexible wage/price values. This is familiar from the earlier IS-LM cum rational expectations models of Gray (1976) and Fischer (1977). The second-moment terms are what is new here. In fixed-wage/flexible-price sectors, wage-setters set wage rates so that $E_{t-1}[y_{s,t}] = E_{t-1}[y_{s,t}{}^{*}] - (\psi/2)\text{VAR}_{t-1}[\omega_t + a_t/\psi]$, and in fixed-price sectors, firms set prices so that $E_{t-1}[y_{s,t}] = E_{t-1}[y_{s,t}{}^{*}] - (\psi/2)\text{VAR}_{t-1}[\omega_t - z_{s,t} + a_t/\psi]$; if monetary policy does nothing ($\omega = 0$), economic activity is on average lower than it would be with flexible wages and prices. As in the Fischer–Gray models, the Central Bank can (if it has sufficient information) make the money prediction error offset the shock prediction errors, and this would achieve the flexible-wage/price solution in this sector.[20] Here, however, the

---

[20] For example, the policy $\omega_t = z_{s,t} - a_t/\psi$ eliminates the prediction errors and the variance term in the fixed-price solution in this sector. In section 4.3, we will see that if there are other sectors with different kinds of nominal rigidity and/or productivity shocks, monetary policy cannot achieve the flexible-wage/price solution economy-wide; optimal policy will involve tradeoffs in eliminating the output gaps in various sectors.

Central Bank does so by raising the expected level of economic activity in addition to stabilising output and employment around their flexible-wage/price levels.

Part of the intuition for how stabilisation policy works is again familiar from the earlier Fischer–Gray literature. From parts (C) and (F) of lemma 3, the policy that achieves the flexible-wage/price solution also has the property that it brings notional (starred) wages and prices to their actual (pre-set) values. If aggregate demand policy can change quantities so that the notional values are equal to the actual values, then there is no need for wage or price flexibility. In the language of Canzoneri, Henderson and Rogoff (1983), monetary policy can eliminate the costs of frequent re-contracting by making re-contracting redundant. Or, looking ahead to the next section (where the flexible-wage/price solution will be seen to be a constrained optimum), the monetary policy problem has two representations: a 'primal' and a 'dual'. In the primal representation, the optimal policy brings quantities to their optimal values; in the dual representation, the optimal policy brings notional prices (which can be regarded as shadow prices) to their actual values.

The variance terms in lemma 3 are both new and provocative. Where do they come from? And how does monetary policy affect them? Consider, for example, sectors with fixed wages and flexible prices, and note that with log-normality, the expected disutility of work can be written as:

$$\log E_{t-1}\left[A_t N_{s,t}{}^{\psi}\right] = E_{t-1}[a_t] + \psi E_{t-1}[n_{s,t}] + \frac{1}{2}\mathrm{VAR}_{t-1}[a_t]$$

$$+ \frac{1}{2}\psi^2 \mathrm{VAR}_{t-1}[n_{s,t}] + \mathrm{cov}_{t-1}[a_t, \psi n_{s,t}].$$

Consider first pure nominal instability. If a_t and $z_{s,t}$ are non-stochastic, lemma 3 implies $E_{t-1}[y_{s,t}] = E_{t-1}[y_{s,t}{}^*] - (\psi/2)\mathrm{VAR}_{t-1}[\omega_t]$. Monetary instability in and of itself can lower the average level of economic activity.[21] Why is this? Fluctuations in ω_t lead to fluctuations in $n_{s,t}$, and given the curvature of the disutility of work, this increases the expected disutility. Households raise their wage rates to lower the average work effort.[22] Consider next instability in the disutility of work (or stochastic a_t shocks). If $\mathrm{cov}_{t-1}[a_t, \psi n_{s,t}] > 0$, then work effort is high when the disutility of work is high, and this covariance increases the expected disutility of work. Once again, households raise their wage rates to lower the average work

[21] For other utility functions, monetary instability can actually increase the average level of employment. See the Yeoman–Farmer example in Canzoneri, Cumby and Diba (2002b).
[22] Note that the variance term remains even if the disutility of work is linear ($\psi \equiv 1 + \chi = 1$). This is because we are working in logs instead of levels of employment.

effort. Monetary policy can eliminate this covariance (if a_t is observable) and increase the average level of employment.

The notion that monetary policy can work through second moments to affect the first moments of equilibrium variables is not exactly new,[23] but it certainly is provocative. The literature has not focused much on this aspect of monetary policy, and we know of no empirical evidence suggesting that these variance terms are large. At this point, it is hard to know what to make of them.

3 OPTIMAL STRATEGIES FOR MONETARY POLICY

Goodfriend and King (1997, 2001) and King and Wolman (1999) have argued that the optimal strategy for monetary policy is to stabilise the aggregate price level. Aoki (2001) argued that the 'core' price level should be stabilised. Blanchard (1997) argued that it may be wages that should be stabilised instead of prices, and Erceg, Henderson and Levin (2000) argued that there may be a tradeoff between price and wage stabilisation. Basically, we will see that the dispute is over which kinds of nominal inertia are most important in the economy. We will also see that the stochastic structure of sectoral productivity shocks matters.

In this section, we ask when a full information policy (in which the Central Bank can identify all of the shocks) can achieve a 'constrained' optimum. Since the information requirements of a full information policy are considerable, we also ask when a simpler strategy – such as stabilising an appropriate price level – can achieve the same goal. First, we describe the goals of monetary policy.

3.1 The goals of monetary policy

There is a natural measure of national welfare embodied in the household utility functions, though we will have to find a way of aggregating the utility of heterogeneous households.[24] The distortions inherent in monopolistic wage- and price-setting imply that the level of economic activity is too low, and the Central Bank will have an incentive to expand more than expected once wages and/or prices have been set. This makes NNS models a natural framework for revisiting the issue of 'time inconsistency'. We will,

---

[23] For example, Canzoneri and Dellas (1998) noted that monetary policy can affect the risk premium on nominal assets by changing the covariance between the price level and consumption.

[24] Recall that the work effort will not, in general, be the same across households employed in different sectors.

however, follow a branch of the literature that assumes the Central Bank is committed to a monetary policy rule that maximises the expected value of national welfare.

It is also common in this branch of the literature to ignore the utility of money (because it is presumed to be small). Thus, we assume the goal of monetary policy is to choose a rule that maximises the expected value of average household utility, minus the real balance term:[25]

$$J_t \equiv E_{t-1} \sum_{\tau=t}^{\infty} \beta^{\tau-t} \left[u(C_\tau) - (1/S) \sum_{s=1}^{S} g(N_{s,\tau}) \right].$$
(4.19)

Lemmas 1 and 3 give us three useful characterisations of this problem.

Proposition 1: Let $u(C_t) \equiv \log(C_t)$ and $g(N_t) \equiv \psi^{-1} A_t N_t^{\psi}$; let A_t and the $Z_{s,t}$ have a log-normal distribution; let W be the set of sectors that have fixed wages and flexible prices, and let P be the set of sectors that have fixed prices; and let $g_{s,t} \equiv y_{s,t} - y_{s,t}^*$ be the 'output gap' in sector s. Then, the goal of monetary policy is to choose a rule, $\omega(\cdot)$, that maximises $\sum_{s=1}^{S} E_{t-1} c_{s,t}$, and $\sum_{s=1}^{S} E_{t-1} c_{s,t}$ can be expressed in three ways:

(A) $\displaystyle\sum_{s=1}^{S} E_{t-1} c_{s,t} = -S \log(S) + \sum_{s=1}^{S} E_{t-1} y_{s,t}^* - \frac{1}{2} \sum_{s \in W} \mathrm{VAR}_{t-1}$

$$\times [\omega_t + a_t/\psi] - \frac{1}{2} \sum_{s \in P} \mathrm{VAR}_{t-1}[\omega_t - z_{s,t} + a_t/\psi]$$

(B) $\displaystyle\sum_{s=1}^{S} E_{t-1} c_{s,t} = -S \log(S) + \sum_{s=1}^{S} E_{t-1} y_{s,t}^*$

$$- \frac{1}{2} \sum_{s \in W} \mathrm{VAR}_{t-1}[g_{s,t}] - \frac{1}{2} \sum_{s \in P} \mathrm{VAR}_{t-1}[g_{s,t}]$$

(C) $\displaystyle\sum_{s=1}^{S} E_{t-1} c_{s,t} = -S \log(S) + \sum_{s=1}^{S} E_{t-1} y_{s,t}^*$

$$- \frac{1}{2} \sum_{s \in W} \mathrm{VAR}_{t-1}[w_{s,t}^*] - \frac{1}{2} \sum_{s \in P} \mathrm{VAR}_{t-1}[p_{s,t}^*].$$

Proof Lemma 1 implies $J_t = E_{t-1} \sum_{\tau=t}^{\infty} \beta^{\tau-t}[\log(C_t) - (\mu\psi)^{-1}]$, and since there are no state variables, the maximisation problem is essentially static. Monetary policy cannot affect the expected disutility of work;

---

[25] Alternatively, (4.19) could be viewed as the expected utility of the representative household before households are randomly assigned to sectors.

the goal reduces to maximising $E_{t-1} \log(C_t)$, which is proportional to $\sum_{s=1}^{S} E_{t-1} c_{s,t}$. Expressions for $\sum_{s=1}^{S} E_{t-1} c_{s,t}$ follow from lemma 3.

We can use part (A) of proposition 1 to derive the optimal policy rule. If, for example, the Central Bank has full information on all of the shocks, it would choose $\omega(a_t, z_{1,t}, \ldots, z_{S,t})$ to minimise the sum of variances; the optimal policy may not be able to reduce all these variances to zero. Part (B) of proposition 1 is the 'primal' representation of the problem. We will see that monetary policy cannot always eliminate all of the output gaps in a multi-sector economy. Part (B) will be useful in characterising the tradeoffs confronting policy-makers. Part (C) is the 'dual' representation of the problem, stated in terms of shadow or 'notional' wages and prices. It provides an alternative way of characterising the tradeoffs. Part (C) also illustrates an observation we made in the last section: if wages or prices are fixed, monetary policy should move employment and output in such a way that wage and price changes are redundant.

One interesting result (noted by Obstfeld and Rogoff 2001) follows immediately from proposition 1. The best monetary policy can do is to achieve the flexible-wage/price solution.[26]

Corollary 1 (Obstfeld and Rogoff): When monetary policy is characterised by pre-set rules, the constrained optimum is the flexible-wage/price solution. The monopolistic distortions that make employment and output too low do not interact with the stabilisation problem.

3.2 Is price stability a good new-Keynesian policy in economies with fixed prices?

The answer to this question generally depends on the symmetry or asymmetry of nominal rigidities and productivity shocks across sectors. We can illustrate the various possibilities by examining a series of economies with different sectoral constellations. We begin with the simplest, and we assume that $u(C_t) \equiv \log(C_t)$, $g(N_t) \equiv \psi^{-1} A_t N_t^{\psi}$ and A_t and the $Z_{s,t}$ have a log-normal distribution for the remainder of the chapter.

Economy 1: One sector with fixed prices
In this framework, Ireland (1996) showed that monetary policy could achieve the optimal flexible-wage/price solution while at the same time implementing Friedman's zero interest rate rule.

---

[26] This result also holds for $u(C) \equiv (1-\gamma)^{-1} C^{1-\gamma}$.

Proposition 2 (Ireland):   Suppose the economy consists of one sector with fixed prices; wages can be either fixed or flexible. For any pre-set target path for the price level, $\{p_\tau^T\}$, there is a monetary policy that makes:

(A) $\qquad\qquad\qquad\qquad p_{p,t} = p_t^T$, and

(B) $\qquad\qquad\qquad\qquad y_{p,t} = y_{p,t}^*$.

Furthermore, there is a target path, $\{p_\tau^T\}$, that makes:

(C) $\qquad\qquad\qquad\qquad i_t = 0$.

Proof   The Central Bank can announce the target path $\{p_\tau^T\}$ one period in advance, and commit to the following state-contingent path for *per capita* nominal income: $\omega_\tau = p_\tau^T - \psi^{-1}\log(\mu) - a_\tau/\psi + z_{p,\tau}$. With this rule, $\mathrm{VAR}_{t-1}[\omega_t - z_{p,t} + a_t/\psi] = \mathrm{VAR}_{t-1}[p_t^T - \psi^{-1}\log(\mu)] = 0$. Then, from part (D) of lemma 3, $p_{p,t} = \psi^{-1}\log(\mu) + E_{t-1}[\omega_t - z_{p,t} + (a_t/\psi)] = \psi^{-1}\log(\mu) + E_{t-1}[p_t^T - \psi^{-1}\log(\mu)] = p_t^T$, establishing part (A). To get part (B), note that $\mathrm{VAR}_{t-1}[\omega_t - z_{p,t} + a_t/\psi] = 0 \Rightarrow \omega_t - z_{p,t} + a_t/\psi = E_{t-1}[\omega_t - z_{p,t} + a_t/\psi] \Rightarrow \{\omega_t - E_{t-1}[\omega_t]\} - \{z_{s,t} - E_{t-1}[z_{s,t}]\} + \{(a_t/\psi) - E_{t-1}[a_t/\psi]\} = 0$, and use part (E) of lemma 3. To get part (C), the target path $\{p_\tau^T\}$ must satisfy $p_\tau^T \equiv p_{\tau-1}^T + y_{\tau-1}^* + \log(\beta) - E_{\tau-1}[y_\tau^*] - \frac{1}{2}\mathrm{VAR}_{\tau-1}[y_\tau^*]$. This makes $\log(I_t) = 0$, as can be confirmed by taking the log of the Euler equation (4.16).

Friedman's rule eliminates seigniorage distortions.[27] So in this economy, there is no conflict between Keynesian stabilisation and Lucas' (1986) admonition that monetary policy should be viewed in terms of the principles set out in the public-finance literature.

While the nominal interest rate is being held constant, monetary policy is actually following an active rule – $\omega_\tau = p_\tau^T - \psi^{-1}\log(\mu) - a_\tau/\psi + z_{p,\tau}$ – to stabilise the economy. It decreases nominal income in response to a laziness shock (a positive a_t), and it increases nominal income in response to a positive productivity shock. Why are these responses necessary? Optimal monetary policy has to get the labour–leisure margin right, as specified by the flexible-wage/price benchmark described in the last section. Work should fall in response to a laziness shock. However, absent a change in nominal income, the combination of fixed prices and fixed expenditure

---

[27] Carlstrom and Fuerst (1998) point out that there is an indeterminacy in Ireland's (1996) model when the nominal interest rate is set equal to zero; we sidestep the problem by never referring to real money balances.

shares, (4.14), implies that output remains constant, and so does the work effort. Work should not respond at all to a productivity shock (with log utility of consumption). However, absent a change in nominal income, fixed prices and fixed expenditure shares mean that output remains constant, and that the work effort would have to fall. The activist policy postulated in proposition 2 gets the work effort right for both shocks.

The fundamental reason why the Friedman Rule can also be achieved is that there is no tradeoff between price-level targeting and optimal macroeconomic stabilisation. Since we are free to select any path for the price level, we can choose a path that is consistent with zero nominal interest rates.

The information requirements of this policy are, however, rather daunting. Employment and output are demand-determined, and (absent an accommodating monetary policy) they will not respond to the preference shock, a_t.[28] So, the Central Bank has to somehow intuit that households are having a fit of laziness (a positive a_t shock), and lower nominal income accordingly. The next economy we consider admits an optimal monetary policy that is much less demanding.

Economy 2: Two sectors with asymmetric price setting, but a common productivity shock

King and Wolman (1999) showed that strict price-level targeting would achieve the optimal flexible-wage/price solution in this economy. Their result is both provocative and practical: it says that there is no conflict between those who advocate price stability and those who advocate an activist stabilisation policy, and it shows that the optimal stabilisation policy can be characterised in an implementable way, without the strong information requirements of Ireland's example. The result is also rather intuitive; in King and Wolman's words, 'it is perhaps not surprising that sticky prices make it optimal for the price level not to vary. After all, if the price level never changes, then in a sense it doesn't matter whether prices are sticky.'

Following Taylor (1980), King and Wolman (1999) postulated a 'staggered' price-setting scheme: prices are set for two periods, and half of the firms are resetting their prices each period. We can capture some – but not all – aspects of their analysis in our simpler framework of one-period price stickiness.[29] A flexible-wage/price sector can represent the firms that

---

[28] Employment would fall in response to a positive productivity shock. Productivity shocks are, in this sense, more identifiable. And, absent a_t shocks, optimal policy in this economy might be describes as stabilising employment.

[29] One aspect of their analysis that we can not capture is that with Taylor's (1980) pricing scheme, there is actually an optimal rate of inflation. In our setup, price-level targeting is optimal, but any rate of inflation will do. See Wolman (2001) for a recent discussion of these issues.

are resetting their prices, and a fixed-price sector can represent firms who set their prices last period.

Proposition 3 (King and Wolman): Suppose the economy consists of a fixed-price sector (denoted by 'p') and a flexible-wage/price sector (denoted by 'f') with a common productivity shock ($z_{f,t} = z_{p,t}$). Then, the optimal monetary policy eliminates price uncertainty, in the sense that $\text{VAR}_{t-1}[p_t] = 0$, and attains $y_{s,t} = y_{s,t}{}^*$ for s $= f, p$.

Proof   By part (C) of proposition 1, the optimal policy minimises VAR_{t-1} $[p_{p,t}{}^*]$. As in proposition 2, this variance term can be set to zero using the rule: $\omega_\tau = p_{p,\tau}{}^T - \psi^{-1}\log(\mu) - a_\tau/\psi + z_{p,\tau}$. Lemma 3 implies $y_{p,t} = y_{p,t}{}^*$ and $p_{p,t} = p_{p,t}{}^*$; price and output in the flexible-wage/price sector take care of themselves: $y_{f,t} = y_{f,t}^*$ and $p_{f,t} = p_{f,t}^*$. Since the two sectors have the same productivity shock, $p_{p,t}{}^* = p_{f,t}{}^*$. So, $p_t = \log(2) + {}^1\!/_2 p_{p,t} + {}^1\!/_2 p_{f,t} = \log(2) + p_{p,t}{}^*$. And since the optimal policy makes $\text{VAR}_{t-1}[p_{p,t}{}^*] = 0$, $\text{VAR}_{t-1}[p_t] = 0$.

How does this policy work? There is a common productivity shock, so marginal cost equalises across sectors. The two sectoral goods should sell for the same price. If they do not, consumption of the composite good will not be maximised for a given amount of household expenditure. When there is, say, a positive productivity shock (or a negative preference shock), firms in the flexible-price sector will lower their prices, and (absent monetary policy) there will be an output gap in the fixed-price sector. Part (C) of proposition 1 says that monetary policy has to increase nominal income, bringing flexible prices back up to the level that was set in the fixed-price sector, and eliminating the output gap in the fixed-price sector.

Following Lucas' (1986) admonition, Goodfriend and King (1997, 2001) interpret price-level targeting as optimal tax smoothing. When wages are flexible, lemma 2 implies

$$P_{p,t}/MC_{p,t} = P_{p,t}/(W_{p,t}{}^*/Z_{p,t}) = (P_{p,t}/P_{p,t}{}^*)\mu_p \quad (4.20a)$$

$$(W_{p,t}{}^*/P_{p,t})/MP_{p,t} = (P_{p,t}{}^*/P_{p,t})(W_{p,t}{}^*/P_{p,t}{}^*)/Z_{p,t}$$

$$= (P_{p,t}{}^*/P_{p,t})(1/\mu_p) \quad (4.20b)$$

where $MP_{p,t}(= Z_t)$ is the marginal product of labour in the fixed-price sector and $MC_{p,t}(= W_{p,t}/Z_t)$ is marginal cost. When prices are flexible ($P_{p,t} = P_{p,t}{}^*$), firms set their prices at a constant markup ($\mu_p > 1$) over marginal cost, or equivalently, they offer a real wage at a constant markdown

$(1/\mu_p < 1)$ from the marginal product of labour. The markdown of the real wage is like a tax on labour; it makes employment and output too small. With fixed prices, the size of the markup (or markdown) fluctuates with $P_{p,t}/P_{p,t}^*$. Monetary policy cannot affect the average 'tax' rate, μ_p, but price-level targeting makes $P_{p,t}/P_{p,t}^* = 1$, and this smooths the 'tax' distortion around its flexible price level.

Blanchard (1997) notes that this analogy with the public-finance literature is not very robust: 'The focus on the markup and on stabilizing the markup is appealing. But it is misleading. It is appropriate only in a model in which firms face the right marginal cost, thus in a world where, in particular, there is no nominal wage rigidity. If there is nominal wage rigidity, the marginal cost faced by the firm does not vary enough, and it is then optimal to destabilize the markup.'[30]

King and Wolman's (1999) basic result is that there is no conflict between those who advocate price stability and those who advocate an activist stabilisation policy. When monetary policy stabilises prices in the flexible-price sector, it eliminates the output gap in the fixed-price sector. This result is important from an operational point of view. It changes the Central Bank's mandate from stabilising unobservable output gaps to stabilising observable prices. Much of the rest of this section will be devoted to a discussion of the robustness of this provocative result.

Economy 3: Two sectors with asymmetric price setting and asymmetric productivity shocks

It is traditional in macroeconomic modelling to assume that there is a single, economy-wide productivity shock, but there is no empirical reason for doing so. In fact, the Balassa–Samuelson literature suggests that the stochastic processes driving productivity in the service and manufacturing sectors are quite different. Our first qualification to King and Wolman's (1999) result is that it requires a common productivity shock. If sectoral productivity shocks are asymmetric, then strict price level targeting can not be optimal.

Proposition 4: Suppose the economy consists of a fixed-price sector (denoted by 'p') and flexible-wage/price sector (denoted by 'f'). Suppose productivity shocks are not perfectly correlated, then optimal monetary policy attains $y_{s,t} = y_{s,t}^*$ for $s = f, p$, but implies $\mathrm{VAR}_{t-1}[p_t] > 0$.

---

[30] To see this explicitly, note that when wages are also fixed in the fixed price sector, $P_{p,t}/MC_{p,t} = P_{p,t}/(W_{p,t}/Z_{p,t}) = (P_{p,t}/P_{p,t}^*)(W_{p,t}^*/W_{p,t})/(W_{p,t}^*/P_{p,t}^* Z_{p,t}) = (P_{p,t}/P_{p,t}^*)(W_{p,t}^*/W_{p,t}) \mu_p$. The optimal policy makes $P_{p,t}/P_{p,t}^* = 1$, and the optimal markup is $(W_{p,t}^*/W_{p,t})\mu_p$, not μ_p.

Proof   As in proposition 2, optimal policy reduces $\text{VAR}_{t-1}[p_{p,t}{}^*]$ to zero. But, if the two sectors experience different productivity shocks, we now have $p_{p,t}{}^* \neq p_{f,t}{}^* = p_{.f,t}$. So, $\text{VAR}_{t-1}[p_{f,t}] > 0$ and $\text{VAR}_{t-1}[p_t] > 0$.

The intuition for proposition 4 is straightforward: relative sectoral prices must reflect relative marginal costs; if they do not, the composite consumption good will not be maximised for a given amount of household expenditure. When relative marginal costs $(z_{f,t} - z_{p,t})$ fluctuate, optimal monetary policy has to make relative prices fluctuate. Since one price is fixed, monetary policy must make the flexible-price, and the aggregate price level, fluctuate to achieve the optimal flexible-wage/price solution.

Aoki (2001) develops an interesting result that we can now explain by combining several of the lessons we have already learned. Consider an economy with the two sectors of proposition 3: a fixed-price sector, a flexible-price sector, and a common productivity shock. Think of the price index of these sectors as the 'core' price level. Now add a third sector with flexible prices and a different productivity shock, as in proposition 4. Optimal policy in this economy will be to stabilise the 'core' price index; the non-core sector has flexible prices and takes care of itself.

Proposition 5 (Aoki):   Suppose the economy consists of a 'core' sector consisting of flexible and fixed price subsectors having a common productivity shock. Suppose the remaining sector has flexible prices and a possibly different productivity shock. The optimal policy in this economy is to stabilise the core price index.

Proof   The proof follows from propositions 3 and 4.

Aoki's observation is quite clever. Central Banks often pay more attention to core inflation than to overall inflation, and Aoki's result seems to rationalise that view. The prices that are typically excluded from core inflation – energy prices and food prices – are excluded on the basis of volatility; it would be interesting to verify that energy prices and food prices are actually 'flexible'.

Another observation follows fairly quickly from the previous discussion. If an economy has two fixed-price sectors, with different productivity shocks, then even a fully informed monetary policy cannot achieve the optimal flexible-wage/price solution. Canzoneri, Cumby and Diba (2002a) provide an example with traded and non-traded goods, and Erceg and Levin (2002) provide an example with durable and non-durable goods.

Proposition 6 (Canzoneri, Cumby and Diba 2002a; Erceg and Levin 2002): Suppose the economy consists of two fixed-price sectors (denoted by p and p'), and suppose productivity shocks are not perfectly correlated across sectors. Then, there is no full information policy rule, $\omega_t(a_t, z_{p,t}, z_{p',t})$, that can make $y_{s,t} = y_{s,t}^*$ and $y_{s',t} = y_{s',t}^*$.

Proof This can be seen from part (E) of lemma 3: we can't simultaneously make $\omega_t = z_{p,t} - a_t/\psi$ and $\omega_t = z_{p',t} - a_t/\psi$.

If both sectoral prices are fixed, there is no way to make their ratio (the relative price) reflect fluctuations in marginal cost. The consumption index will not be maximised for a given level of household expenditure.

Of course, this does not mean that monetary policy is impotent. When there are multiple fixed-price sectors, proposition 1 says $\omega(a_t, z_{p,t}, z_{p',t})$ should be chosen to minimise an average of variances $-\sum_{s \in P} \text{VAR}_{t-1}[\omega_t - z_{s,t} + a_t/\psi]$ – or equivalently an average of variances of output gaps – $\sum_{s \in P} \text{VAR}_{t-1}[g_{s,t}]$ – or equivalently an average of variances of notional prices $-\sum_{s \in P} \text{VAR}_{t-1}[p_{s,t}^*]$. Our multi-sector framework can be used to analyse monetary policy in a variety of interesting settings. One such example is Benigno's (2001) currency union.

Economy 4: A currency union with fixed prices and asymmetric national productivity shocks

Benigno (2001) showed that the optimal union policy could be characterised as stabilising a weighted average of the two national price levels. Benigno assumed a Calvo-style staggered pricing scheme, but once again, we can capture much of his analysis in our simpler framework. Suppose the union consists of two countries: Country A has a fixed-price sector (denoted by 'ap'), a flexible-price sector (denoted by 'af'), and a national productivity shock, $z_{a,t}$. Country B is bigger than Country A. It has two fixed-price sectors (each denoted by 'bp'),[31] one flexible-price sector (denoted by 'bf'), and a national productivity shock, $z_{b,t}$. Benigno (2001) shows that the optimal policy can be characterised as stabilising a weighted average of the national price levels.

Proposition 7 (Benigno 2001): Suppose a currency union consists of the two countries, A and B, described above. Then,

---

[31] We can let the two fixed price sectors in country B be denoted by the same subscript since they will be identical in equilibrium.

(A) there is no full information policy rule that can achieve the optimal flexible wage/price solution union-wide
(B) the optimal policy rule sets $\text{VAR}_{t-1}[\omega_t - (1/3)z_{a,t} - (2/3)z_{b,t} + a_t/\psi] = 0$
(C) the optimal policy can also be characterised as $\text{VAR}_{t-1}[(1/3)p_{ap,t}{}^* + (2/3)p_{bp,t}{}^*] = \text{VAR}_{t-1}[(1/3)p_{af,t} + (2/3)p_{bf,t}] = 0$.

Proof
(A) This result, like proposition 6, follows directly from lemma 3.
(B) Part (A) of proposition 1 implies that the optimal monetary policy minimises $\text{VAR}_{t-1}[\omega_t - z_{a,t} + a_t/\psi] + 2\text{VAR}_{t-1}[\omega_t - z_{b,t} + a_t/\psi]$. After some algebra, this expression reduces to $3\text{VAR}_{t-1}[\omega_t - (1/3)z_{a,t} - (2/3)z_{b,t} + a_t/\psi] + (2/3)\text{Var}_{t-1}[z_{a,t} - z_{b,t}]$, establishing part (B).
(C) This follows from part (B) above. Using lemma 2, we have $\omega_t - (1/3)z_{a,t} - (2/3)z_{b,t} + a_t/\psi = (1/3)p_{ap,t}{}^* + (2/3)p_{bp,t}{}^* - \psi^{-1}\log(\mu)$, and since the notional prices in the fixed-price sectors are equal to the actual prices in the flexible-price sector, $(1/3)p_{ap,t}{}^* + (2/3)p_{bp,t}{}^* = (1/3)p_{af,t} + (2/3)p_{bf,t}$.

Both countries have fixed prices, and monetary policy cannot make consumption of the two national goods (or the terms of trade) reflect fluctuations in marginal costs. As in the previous example, the consumption index will not be maximised for a given level of household expenditure. The optimal policy gives more weight to stabilising prices in the country with more fixed-price sectors; in our model, a country could have more fixed-price sectors because it is larger, or because it has more nominal rigidity.

3.3 Is price stability a good policy in economies with fixed wages and flexible prices?

As Blanchard (1997) noted in his comments on Goodfriend and King (1997), things change when the nominal rigidity shifts to wages. When wages are fixed, instead of prices, then it may be optimal to stabilise the aggregate wage level, rather than the aggregate price level.

Economy 5: Two sectors with asymmetric wage setting, but a common productivity shock

Here, the structure is analogous to the one we used to discuss King and Wolman (1999), but it is wages, not prices, that are sticky. We have a proposition that is analogous to proposition 3.

Proposition 8:   Suppose the economy consists of a fixed-wage sector (denoted by 'w') and a flexible-wage/price sector (denoted by 'f') with a common shock ($z_{f,t} = z_{w,t} \equiv z_t$). Then, optimal monetary policy eliminates wage uncertainty, in the sense that $\text{VAR}_{t-1}[w_t] = 0$, and attains $y_{s,t} = y_{s,t}{}^*$ for $s = f, w$.

Proof   The proof is analogous to that of proposition 3. By part (C) of proposition 1, optimal policy minimises $\text{VAR}_{t-1}[w_{w,t}{}^*]$. This variance term can be set to zero to attain $y_{s,t} = y_{s,t}{}^*$, for $s = f$. Since the two sectors experience the same shocks, we have $w_{w,t}{}^* = w_{f,t}$, and $\text{VAR}_{t-1}[w_t] = \text{VAR}_{t-1}[w_{f,t}] = \text{VAR}_{t-1}[w_{w,t}{}^*] = 0$.

Here, prices are flexible and relative sectoral prices move automatically with relative marginal costs. Monetary policy would not have to be concerned with maximising the consumption index even if the productivity shocks did differ across sectors; this can be seen from parts (B) and (C) of lemma 3, where the productivity shocks are absent. Here, the labour–leisure margin is the concern of monetary policy. The economy has to contract in response to a 'laziness' shock (a positive shock to a_t). Productivity shocks do not matter with log utility of consumption, for reasons that were discussed in the last section. Moreover, if monetary policy were to stabilise the price level, instead of the wage rate, it would have to respond to the productivity shock. And this would distort the labour–leisure margin. The basic insight of Canzoneri, Henderson and Rogoff (1983) and King and Wolman (1999) still holds. Monetary policy can make frequent wage contracting redundant by making movements in the notional wage unnecessary. Here, too, wage targeting would seem to be operationally feasible, though few (if any) Central Banks would describe their current operating procedures in this way.

Some of the propositions that follow proposition 3 would have obvious counterparts here. Aggregate wage targeting would no longer be optimal if the sectors had asymmetric preference shocks, though the motivation for this observation is perhaps not as appealing: would one sector's households wake up lazy, while another sector's woke up energetic? If we generalised the utility of consumption to a constant elasticity specification, then asymmetric productivity shocks would once again be an issue. Finally, if wages were fixed in both sectors, and if the relevant sectoral shocks were asymmetric, then there would be no full information policy that could achieve the optimal flexible wage/price solution.

Economy 6: Three sectors with asymmetric nominal rigidities, but a common productivity shock

Erceg, Henderson and Levin (2000) showed that price-level targeting is not optimal if there are asymmetries in both wage- and price-setting; moreover, there is no full information policy that can achieve the optimal flexible-wage/price solution. Erceg, Henderson and Levin (2000) assumed Calvo-style staggering for both wage- and price-setting, and this makes their analysis more difficult. Once again, we can capture some – but not all – of their results in our simpler framework.

Proposition 9 (Erceg, Henderson and Levin 2000): Suppose the economy consists of a fixed-wage sector (denoted by 'w'), a sticky-price sector (denoted by 'p'), and a flexible-wage/price sector (denoted by 'f'). Suppose productivity shocks are perfectly correlated across sectors ($z_{p,t} = z_{w,t} = z_{f,t} \equiv z_t$). Then:

(A) There is no rule, $\omega(a_t, z_t)$, that makes $y_{p,t} = y_{p,t}^*$ and $y_{w,t} = y_{w,t}^*$ for all z_t.

(B) A policy that targets the aggregate price level (makes $p_t = p_t^T$) implies $y_{p,t} = y_{p,t}^*$.

(C) A policy that targets the aggregate wage rate (makes $w_t = w_t^T$) implies $y_{w,t} = y_{w,t}^*$.

(D) The optimal policy rule sets $\text{VAR}_{t-1}[\omega_t - (1/2)z_t + a_t/\psi] = 0$.

(E) The optimal policy can also be characterised as $\text{VAR}_{t-1}[(1/2)p_{p,t}^* + (1/2)w_{w,t}^*] = \text{VAR}_{t-1}[(1/2)p_{f,t} + (1/2)w_{f,t}] = 0$.

Proof

(A) Lemma 3 implies that: (1) to get the fixed-price sector right, ω_t must respond to both a_t and z_t and (2) to get the fixed-wage sector right, ω_t must respond to a_t alone.

(B) The proof is similar to the proof of proposition 3.

(C) The proof is similar to the proof of proposition 8.

(D) From part (A) of proposition 1, the optimal monetary policy minimises $\text{VAR}_{t-1}[\omega_t - z_t + a_t/\psi] + \text{VAR}_{t-1}[\omega_t + a_t/\psi]$. After some algebra, this expression reduces to $2\text{VAR}_{t-1}[\omega_t - (1/2)z_t + a_t/\psi] + (1/2)\text{VAR}_{t-1}[z_t]$. Since the second variance does not depend on monetary policy, optimal policy sets the first variance equal to zero.

(E) This follows from (D) above. Using lemma 2, we have $\omega_t - (1/2)z_t + a_t/\psi = (1/2)p_{p,t}{}^* + (1/2)w_{w,t}{}^* - \psi^{-1}\log(\mu) + (1/2)\log(\mu_p)$. Since the notional wages and prices in the fixed sectors are equal to the actual wages and prices in the flexible sector, $(1/2)p_{p,t}{}^* + (1/2)w_{w,t}{}^* = (1/2)p_{f,t} + (1/2)w_{f,t}$.

The intuition for this result combines the intuition from previous examples. To get the consumption mix right in the fixed-price sector, monetary policy has to respond to the productivity shock, but this would distort the labour–leisure margin in the fixed-wage sector. The fundamental problem is one of instrument insufficiency: one monetary instrument can not simultaneously stabilise the aggregate price level and the aggregate wage rate.[32] From proposition 1, the optimal policy can be characterised as trading off the variances of notional wages and prices, or trading off the sectoral output gaps. As in proposition 7, the optimal policy can be characterized as stabilising an index of nominal variables, but this time comprised of prices and wages.

4 THE CURRENT STATE OF THE DEBATE ON THE OPTIMALITY OF PRICE STABILITY

Goodfriend and King (1997, 2001) and King and Wolman (1999) outlined the case for price-level targeting. Blanchard (1997) and Erceg, Henderson and Levin (2000) showed that there are major qualifications to their arguments when nominal inertia resides in wages as well as prices. Goodfriend and King (2001) admit that: 'There is a large body of evidence showing about the same degree of temporary rigidity in nominal wages as in nominal prices.'[33] However, they question its relevance, reasoning that 'there is a fundamental asymmetry between product and labor markets. The labor market is characterized by long term relationships where there is opportunity for firms and workers to neutralize the allocative effects of temporarily sticky nominal wages. On the other hand, spot transactions predominate in product markets where there is much less opportunity for the effects of

---

[32] Actually, our framework differs rather substantially from Erceg, Henderson and Levin (2000), and while we come to much the same conclusion, the intuition in their setup is somewhat different. Erceg, Henderson and Levin postulate a composite labour input that is used by all firms. Wage dispersion (due to their Calvo-style staggered wage setting) leads to an inefficient work effort. But in our framework and in theirs, the fundamental problem is the same: monetary policy can not simultaneously stabilise wages and prices.

[33] See, for example, Taylor's (1999) survey. Taylor concludes that there is no empirical reason to build a model in which wages are flexible while prices are sticky (or vice versa).

sticky nominal prices to be privately neutralized.' To our knowledge, this hypothesis has yet to be formalised and subjected to empirical testing.[34]

We also showed that asymmetries in productivity can lead to policy trade-offs that question the optimality of price stabilisation, or at least question which price aggregate should be stabilised. There has been little discussion in the recent literature of asymmetric shocks, perhaps because it is traditional in macroeconomic modelling to assume a common, economy-wide process for productivity. However, there is also a well-established empirical literature on the Balassa–Samuelson hypothesis that would question the wisdom of that tradition.

Currently there are few 'stylised facts' guiding the macroeconomic modelling of these new policy evaluation models. Which sectors show the most price inertia? Which show the least? Which sectors show the most wage inertia? Does wage inertia matter as much as price inertia? Where do the greatest asymmetries in productivity lie? Analyses of the European Monetary Union (EMU) often postulate asymmetries across countries, rather than sectors.[35] Should the Euro area be modelled differently than the USA? One might speculate that asymmetries in price-setting are determined by economic factors, while asymmetries in wage-setting are determined by national legislation, but is this true? Developing appropriate stylised facts would greatly help this new and promising modelling effort.

BIBLIOGRAPHY

Aoki, K. (2001). 'Optimal Monetary Policy Responses to Relative Price Changes', *Journal of Monetary Economics*, 48, 55–80

Benigno, P. (2001). 'Optimal Monetary Policy in a Currency Area', January, mimeo

Blanchard, O. (1997). ' "Comment" on Goodfriend and King, "The New Neoclassical Synthesis and the Role of Monetary Policy" ', *NBER Macroeconomics Annual*, Cambridge, MA: MIT Press, 289–93

Blanchard, O. and Fischer, S. (1989). *Lectures on Macroeconomics*, Cambridge, MA: MIT Press

Benigno, P. and Lopez-Salido, D. (2001). 'Inflation Persistence and Optimal Monetary Policy in the Euro Area', October, mimeo

Calvo, G. (1983). 'Staggered Prices in a Utility Maximizing Framework', *Journal of Monetary Economics*, 12, 383–98

Canzoneri, M., Cumby, R. and Diba, B. (2002a). 'On the Need for International Policy Coordination: What's Old, What's New and What's Yet to Come', *NBER Working Paper*, 8765

---

[34] An alternative hypothesis is that wages are flexible, but that equilibrium wages are highly persistent.
[35] See for example, Benigno (2001) and Benigno and Lopez-Salido (2001).

(2002b). 'Notes on Models with Monopolistic Competition and Sticky Prices (and/or Wages)', available on Matthew Canzoneri's web page

Canzoneri, M. and Dellas, H. (1998). 'Real Interest Rates and Central Bank Operating Procedures', *Journal of Monetary Economics*, 42(3), 471–94

Canzoneri, M., Henderson, D. and Rogoff, K. (1983). 'The Information Content of the Interest Rate and the Optimal Monetary Policy', *Quarterly Journal of Economics*, November, 545–66

Carlstrom, C. and Fuerst, T. (1998). 'A Note on the Role of Countercyclical Monetary Policy', *Journal of Political Economy*, 106(4), 860–6

Chari, V. V., Kehoe, P. J. and McGrattan, E. R. (2000). 'Sticky Price Models of the Business Cycle: Can the Contract Multiplier Solve the Persistence Problem?', *Econometrica*, 68(5), 1151–79

Cochrane, J. (2001). *Asset Pricing*, Princeton and Oxford: Princeton University Press

Cooley, T. (ed.) (1995). *Frontiers of Business Cycle Research*, Princeton: Princeton University Press

Corsetti, G. and Pesenti, P., (2001). 'Welfare and Macroeconomic Interdependence', *Quarterly Journal of Economics*, 116(2), 421–46

Dixit, A. and Stiglitz, J. (1977). 'Monopolistic Competition and Optimum Product Diversity', *American Economic Review*, 6, 297–308

Erceg, C. and Levin, A. (2002). 'Optimal Monetary Policy and Durable/Non-Durable Goods Prices', June

Erceg, C., Henderson, D. and Levin, A. (2000). 'Optimal Monetary Policy with Staggered Wage and Price Contracts', *Journal of Monetary Economics*, 46(2), 281–313

Fischer, S. (1977). 'Long-term Contracts, Rational Expectations, and the Optimal Money Supply Rule', *Journal of Political Economy*, February

Frenkel, J. and Razin, A. (1987). *Fiscal Policies and the World Economy*, Cambridge, MA: MIT Press

Galí, J., Gertler, M. and Lopez-Salido, D. (2001). 'Markups, Gaps, and the Welfare Costs of Business Fluctuations', mimeo

Giannoni, M. and Woodford, M. (2001). 'Optimal Interest-Rate Rules', December, mimeo

Goodfriend, M. and King, R. (1997). 'The New Neoclassical Synthesis and the Role of Monetary Policy', *NBER Macroeconomics Annual*, Cambridge, MA: MIT Press, 231–83

(2001). 'The Case for Price Stability', *NBER Working Paper*, 8423

Gray, J. A. (1976). 'Wage Indexation: A Macroeconomic Approach', *Journal of Monetary Economics*, 2

Henderson, D. and Kim, J. (1999). 'Exact Utilities under Alternative Rules in a Simple Macro Model with Optimizing Agents', *International Tax and Public Finance*, 6(4), 507–35

Ireland, P. (1996). 'The Role of Countercyclical Monetary Policy', *Journal of Political Economy*, 4, 704–23

King, R. and Wolman, A. (1999). 'What Should the Monetary Authority Do When Prices are Sticky?', in J. Taylor (ed.), *Monetary Policy Rules*, Chicago: University of Chicago Press

Kydland, F. and Prescott, E. (1982). 'Time to Build and Aggregate Fluctuations', *Econometrica*, 50, 1345–70

Lucas, R. (1986). 'Principles of Fiscal and Monetary Policy', *Journal of Monetary Economics*, 17

McCallum, B. (1980). 'Rational Expectations and Macroeconomic Stabilization Policy', *Journal of Money Credit, and Banking*, November

Obstfeld, M. and Rogoff, K., (2001). 'Global Implications of Self-Oriented National Monetary Rules', June, mimeo

Rotemberg, J. and Woodford, M. (1997). 'An Optimization Based Framework for the Evaluation of Monetary Policy', in B. Bernanke and J. Rotemberg (eds.), *NBER Macroeconomics Annual*, Cambridge, MA: MIT Press, 297–346

    (1999). 'Interest Rate Rules in an Estimated Sticky Price Model', in J. Taylor (ed.), *Monetary Policy Rules*, Chicago: University of Chicago Press

Sargent T. and Wallace, N. (1975). 'Rational Expectations, and the Optimal Monetary Instrument, and the Optimal Money Supply Rule', *Journal of Political Economy*, April 1975

Taylor, J. (1980). 'Aggregate Dynamics and Staggered Contracts', *Journal of Political Economy*, 88, 1–24

    (1999). 'Staggered Price and Wage Setting in Macroeconomics', in J. Taylor and M. Woodford (eds.), *Handbook of Macroeconomics*, 1B, Amsterdam: Elsevier Science, 1009–50

Tobin, J. (1977). 'How Dead is Keynes?', *Economic Inquiry*, 15(4), 459–68

Woodford, M. (1997). 'Control of Public Debt: A Requirement for Price Stability?', in G. Calvo and M. King (eds.), *The Debt Burden and Monetary Policy*, London: Macmillan

    forthcoming. *Interest and Prices*, book in progress, chapters available on Michael Woodford's webpage

Wolman, A. (2001). 'A Primer on Optimal Monetary Policy with Staggered Price-Setting', *Federal Reserve Bank of Richmond Economic Quarterly*, 87(4), 27–52

5

On the interaction of monetary and fiscal policy

Jagjit S. Chadha and Charles Nolan

1 INTRODUCTION

In this chapter we consider the interaction of monetary policy with aggregative fiscal policy. By 'aggregative' we mean that our focus is primarily on the effects of debts and deficits in the presence of lump-sum taxation.[1] We shall, in particular, be concerned with the ways monetary and fiscal policies may need to be coordinated to ensure 'good' macroeconomic outcomes. To that end, we shall be largely occupied with two issues: (a) the fundamental linkages between the government's budget constraint and the setting of interest rates and (b) on the stabilisation issues thrown up by systematic fiscal and monetary policy over the economic cycle.

More specifically, we study how monetary policy may be influenced by doubts over the wider fiscal solvency of the public sector. In an important contribution Sargent and Wallace (1981) argued that the money stock and taxes were substitutes in the backing of government debt. This discussion brings to the fore the fact that monetary and fiscal policies are linked via a budget constraint. However, many countries have recently delegated control of monetary policy to an independent monetary authority, partly in response to the kind of concerns raised by Sargent and Wallace. There now seems to be some concern that monetary and fiscal policy may actually not be well coordinated under such an institutional structure. The issue seems less to do with solvency, and more to do with aggregate demand

We should like to thank for useful comments on this research, Willem Buiter, Matthew Canzoneri, Sugata Gosh, Dale Henderson, Andrew Hughes Hallett, Campbell Leith, Bennett McCallum, Patrick Minford, Anna Schwartz, Frank Smets, Gabriel Talmain, Mike Wickens, Simon Wren-Lewis and conference participants at Birkbeck College, Cardiff University, Dundee University, Manchester University, York University and the European Central Bank. Anne Mason provided excellent assistance in the preparation of this chapter. All remaining errors are due to the authors.

[1] Chapter 3 in this volume by Turnovsky discusses a number of central issues raised by the existence of distortionary taxes in the stochastic growth model. Chari and Kehoe (1999) is a recent comprehensive review of (Ramsey) optimal monetary and fiscal policies in the presence of distortionary taxation.

management over the economic cycle: if monetary policy is too 'rigid', then fiscal policy may need to compensate by being more 'flexible'. So the second issue we discuss is how monetary and fiscal policies might be set jointly in order to smooth the economic cycle.

In the next section we set out the contents of the chapter in some more detail.

1.1 Key themes

Following Sargent and Wallace (1975, 1981) macroeconomists generally argued that there were two key requirements for monetary policy to retain control over nominal magnitudes. First, monetary policy ought to be characterised by control over the money stock as opposed to an interest rate peg. However, since fiscal policy may hamper the effective control of the money supply by requiring excessive seigniorage revenue – the tax revenue generated from money creation – this is not, in general, a sufficient condition. As we show in sections 2 and 3, the consolidated public-sector budget constraint is the key equation linking the joint feasible sequences of monetary and fiscal variables through time. A government which runs a persistent deficit may require monetary policy to plug the hole in the public-sector finances. Consequently, for monetary policy to retain control over nominal magnitudes in the economy, fiscal policy must take seigniorage as given and provide a temporal, (state-dependent) sequence of net deficits in order that debt satisfies a no-Ponzi condition.

Through the 1980s the USA started to run large and what were expected to be long-lasting fiscal deficits, and the concerns of Sargent and Wallace (1981) moved centre stage. However, McCallum (1984) argued that it was not at all apparent that persistent deficits would compromise the ability of monetary policy to control the price level. He showed that a key issue was how one defined the deficit. If one included interest payments in the definition of the deficit, as is common, then permanent deficits were perfectly feasible without recourse to seigniorage revenue.

In a related analysis, Aiyagari and Gertler (1985) demonstrated that if bonds were not fully backed by taxes then the price level would show a proportionate relationship to the value of outstanding bonds.

Although focusing on different fiscal rules, these two contributions are essentially refinements of the Sargent and Wallace (1981) intuition. However, one may question whether the issues considered in these analyses are of first-order importance. In many models, the real side of the economy, consumption, real interest rates, and so on, is largely immune to fiscal policy developments by virtue of Ricardian Equivalence.[2] However, a more recent approach to analysing the interaction of monetary and fiscal policy, the fiscal theory of the price level, argues that the requirements for a rational expectations equilibrium to obtain in standard models of a monetary economy, are stricter than is often acknowledged. And in so arguing it demonstrates that prices *and output* may indeed be influenced strongly by fiscal policy, even without distortionary taxes, liquidity constraints, and so on.

The fiscal theory of the price level (FTPL), developed by, among others, Cochrane (2001a), Leeper (1991), Sims (1994, 1999) and Woodford (1995, 1997, 1998a), argues that the public-sector budget constraint imposes few restrictions on the joint choices for monetary and fiscal variables. In the FTPL the government's present-value budget constraint (PVBC) determines the equilibrium price level. That is, if the expected discounted sequence of net surpluses or deficits is not identically equal to outstanding debt, then the price level must change in order to bring these magnitudes into equality. For holders of nominal government debt such changes in the price level alter the value of real consumption units to which the nominal debt lays claim. The resulting wealth effect changes equilibrium consumption, output, interest rates and the price level. However, this approach has proved controversial, encouraging a sometimes vigorous debate amongst its supporters and detractors.[3]

One advantage that the FTPL may have is that it resolves the problem of price level indeterminacy under an interest rate rule. This problem was highlighted by the earlier contribution of Sargent and Wallace (1975). If the present-value budget constraint ties down the price level, we might consider the monetary authority to be setting the interest rate in a way that may be consistent with how Central Banks act in practice.[4] However, this comes at a price as monetary policy no longer controls inflation (although it may still influence expected inflation), and macroeconomic stability may have more to do with fiscal policy than monetary policy. That said it may be very hard in practice to disentangle the effects of monetary and fiscal

---

[2] We are being a little cavalier here. While the statement is basically right in representative agent models with lump-sum taxes (given a path of government expenditure), real variables will in general respond to shocks to government expenditure. See for example, Baxter and King (1993) and Aiyagari, Christiano and Eichenbaum (1992). Ricardian Equivalence can, of course, break down for a number of other reasons, such as incomplete markets (e.g. liquidity constraints), distortionary taxation, non-rational expectations, and so on.

[3] See for example, Buiter (1998, 1999) who is highly critical of the FTPL and Cochrane (1998, 2001a, 2001b), who is strongly supportive.

[4] Whether or not the FTPL does indeed resolve this indeterminacy issue is a matter, like much else related to the FTPL, of some controversy; see McCallum (2001).

rules. However the overriding criticism of the FTPL appears to be that it permits the fiscal sector to operate without respecting a budget constraint, even though the PVBC will be satisfied in equilibrium.

It is increasingly common for theoretical macroeconomics to assume that the short-term nominal interest rate (as opposed to the money supply) is the instrument of monetary policy. In section 4–6, therefore, as a prelude to our discussion of the joint conduct of monetary and fiscal policy over the business cycle, we investigate further the implications of the PVBC for monetary policy. In sections 7–10 we develop a highly stylised dynamic stochastic general equilibrium model in which both monetary and fiscal policy have leverage over aggregate demand. We necessarily incorporate the consolidated public-sector budget constraint, but assume that fiscal policy is set over time to ensure that the PVBC is met. We then investigate the jointly optimal policies for monetary policy and fiscal policy given a key objective of stabilising aggregate demand and find that our interest rate rule ends up being parameterised remarkably closely to the original recommendations of Taylor (1993). Our rule for fiscal policy also ends up being parameterised such that the implied deficit to GDP ratio tracks reasonably closely recently observed values in both the USA and UK. We also analyse what might happen if one or the other policy rule 'misbehaves'.

We offer some conclusions and suggestions for further research in section 11.

2 SARGENT AND WALLACE (1981) AND WHAT CAME NEXT

For expositional ease, and for consistency with what we present in sections 7–10, we shall present the key results in this section using a representative agent framework. We do not model the factor markets and we assume that there is no population growth. This setup means we cannot analyse all the issues raised in some of the original contributions that we draw on. However, we do find it easier to relate the analyses to one another and more recent contributions. Finally, until section 7 we shall in general consider only perfect foresight economies under price flexibility, although there are some important exceptions in between. We shall make clear when we drop these assumptions.

Consider a closed economy inhabited by a large number of identical agents. Each agent's utility is defined over the real consumption stream, $\{C_t\}_{t=0}^{\infty}$, and the stream of real money balances, $\{\frac{M_t}{P_t}\}_{t=0}^{\infty}$. We motivate the incorporation of base money in the utility function, in the manner of Brock (1975) and Sidrauski (1965), by appealing to the notion that money eases transactions costs. The discounted present value of utility is therefore given by

$$V_t = \sum_{t=0}^{\infty} \beta^t U\left(C_t, \frac{M_t}{P_t}\right), \tag{5.1}$$

where $U(\cdot)$ denotes a utility function increasing in both arguments, strictly concave and obeying familiar Inada-type conditions (see Obstfeld and Rogoff 1983). In addition, we shall also find it convenient to assume that $U(\cdot)$ is separable in its arguments. This keeps the analysis somewhat simpler than it otherwise would be in one or two places. Specifically, we shall assume that $U(\cdot) = u(C_t) + v(M_t/P_t)$. $\beta \in (0, 1)$ is the discount factor which equals $(1 + \delta)^{-1}$, where $\delta > 0$ is the subjective rate of time preference. The representative agent maximises (5.1) each period subject to the following sequence of flow budget constraints

$$P_t C_t + M_t + \frac{B_t}{1 + i_t} \le M_{t-1} + B_{t-1} + P_t Y_t - P_t T_t \quad \forall t \ge 0, \tag{5.2}$$

M_{-1} and B_{-1} given. P_t is the price-level in period t, M_t and B_t are, respectively, nominal money balances and one period (discount) nominal debt held at the end of period t. Y_t is the endowment in period t and T_t denotes lump-sum taxes. The first-order conditions for an interior optimum include (5.2) with equality at each date t, a relationship equating the marginal utility of money holdings to the marginal cost

$$\frac{v'(M_t/P_t)}{u'(C_t)} = \frac{i_t}{1 + i_t} \quad \forall t \ge 0, \tag{5.3}$$

and a relationship characterising optimal consumption and savings through time:

$$\beta \frac{u'(C_{t+1})}{u'(C_t)} \frac{P_t}{P_{t+1}} = \frac{1}{1 + i_t} \quad \forall t \ge 0. \tag{5.4}$$

It follows that the price level will be governed by the following non-linear difference equation

$$P_{t+1} = i_t \beta P_t \left[\frac{u'(C_{t+1})}{v'(M_t/P_t)}\right]. \tag{5.5}$$

It is well known that this equation will admit multiple equilibria, some of which may be ruled out via appeal to familiar conditions on the budget set, as in Obstfeld and Rogoff (1983), but others which cannot. These conditions essentially constrain the optimal consumption programme such that borrowing is limited by lifetime resources. This condition is implied by the intertemporal sequence of equations in (5.2), along with the requirement that

$$\lim_{T \to \infty} \left\{ \prod_{j=0}^{T-1} (1 + i_{t+j}) \right\}^{-1} W_{t+T} \to 0. \tag{5.6}$$

Here we denote $W_t \equiv M_{t-1} + B_{t-1}$. This is often labelled the 'no-Ponzi' finance condition and permits us to rule out equilibria in which, for a given money stock, the price level tends to zero. (5.6) is therefore also considered a requirement for an optimum.

The question now is: in what way does the fiscal–monetary framework affect the workings of this simple economy? As a first pass at this issue, we shall consider the economy outlined above in steady state. Specifically, consider a steady state in which $M_t/M_{t-1} = P_{t+1}/P_t = \mu = \pi_{t+1} + 1$. Since, as we just indicated, the evolution of prices need not necessarily be consistent with this steady state we ought to establish that such a steady state is worthy of our interest. In practice many economists have been persuaded of the importance of this steady state since otherwise self-fulfilling hyperinflations or hyperdeflations result.[5] When we analyse below the fiscal theory of the price level we shall return to this equilibrium selection issue. Then, with lower case letters generally denoting real steady-state values, the representative consumer's optimality conditions become

$$\delta = r, \tag{5.7}$$

$$\frac{v'(m)}{u'(c)} = \frac{r}{1+r}, \tag{5.8}$$

and

$$c - (\mu - 1)m - b\left(\frac{r}{1+r}\right) = y - t. \tag{5.9}$$

Now note that the government per-period budget constraint is given by

$$\frac{B_t}{(1+i_t)} = B_{t-1} + P_t(G_t - T_t) - (M_t - M_{t-1}) \quad \forall t \geq 0. \tag{5.10}$$

---

[5] Or, to put the matter more succinctly, many economists have been persuaded by Milton Friedman that inflation is a monetary phenomenon.

The variables in (5.10) are as defined previously, with G_t now denoting real government expenditure. This expression is analogous to the agent's flow constraint and together (5.2) and (5.10) implies the economy-wide resource constraint

$$C_t + G_t = Y_t \quad \forall t \geq 0. \tag{5.11}$$

And since the representative agent's optimal consumption programme is constrained by lifetime resources it follows that the sequence of equations (5.10) will be consistent with the representative agent's consumption programme iff a requirement analogous to (5.6) is imposed on the government's net issue of debt

$$\lim_{T \to \infty} \left\{ \prod_{j=0}^{T-1} (1 + i_{t+j}) \right\}^{-1} W_{t+T} \to 0. \tag{5.12}$$

In turn, then, it follows that (5.10) and (5.12) together imply that

$$B_{t-1} + M_{t-1} = \sum_{j=0}^{\infty} \left\{ \prod_{s=j}^{j-1} \left(\frac{1}{1 + i_{t+s}} \right) \left[P_{t+j}(T_{t+j} - G_{t+j}) \right. \right.$$
$$\left. \left. + \frac{i_{t+j}}{1 + i_{t+j}} M_{t+j} \right] \right\}. \tag{5.13}$$

The traditional interpretation of (5.13) is that it determines the necessary discounted value of taxation (including seigniorage) given the outstanding real value of government liabilities, $(B_{t-1} + M_{t-1})/P_t$. This interpretation is, therefore, entirely analogous to the interpretation of the representative agent's PVBC, and implies that (5.13) is a constraint that holds identically for all feasible price-level sequences. In turn, such a restriction implies that the fiscal–monetary programme will operate to ensure that whatever the real outstanding level of government liabilities, sufficient net taxation will be forthcoming to ensure that (5.13) holds identically. A key implication of this perspective is that monetary and fiscal policy, in setting the left-hand side of (5.13), are potential substitutes in the backing of outstanding liabilities. Most obviously, a rise in outstanding interest-bearing liabilities that does not elicit an equal present-valued increase in tax revenue requires necessarily an increase in seigniorage. Equally, there exists an additional requirement upon the joint design of fiscal–monetary policy such that monetary policy is capable of determining the evolution of nominal magnitudes in the economy.

There are a number of useful ways to view the restrictions typically associated with the government's financing constraint. First let us consider the budget constraint in the constant inflation steady state set out above. In addition, consider what happens in that steady state when it is also characterised by a constant level of interest-bearing debt. We emphasise that there is nothing special about such a steady state, particularly with respect to our assumption of steady-state debt. In particular, as we shall see, debt need not in fact be constant in the steady state, even with a constant inflation rate. However, for now, it will help fix ideas to consider such a situation. In that case the government's budget constraint implies

$$b = \left[\frac{1+r}{r} \right] (G - T) + \left[\frac{1+r}{r} \right] (\mu - 1)m. \qquad (5.14)$$

Following Calvo (1985) assume further a situation in which in this steady state the government raises sufficient funds via taxation to cover government expenditure. In that case, we find that

$$\pi = \frac{b}{m} \left(\frac{r}{1+r} \right). \qquad (5.15)$$

Equation (5.7) pins down the steady-state interest rate (making it equal to the subjective rate of discount), while (5.8) determines the steady-state demand for money, given the steady-state level of consumption and the discount rate. Hence (5.15) in turn implies a positive relationship between inflation and bonds. This is the essence of the Sargent and Wallace (1981) contention that control of monetary policy, and hence control of inflation, may be compromised when the fiscal authority is 'dominant', which may imply a stronger commitment technology. Equation (5.15) indicates that a rise in outstanding bonds, absent any change in the steady-state net primary surplus, implies that steady-state inflation must be higher. The mechanism is clear: the budget constraint needs to be met and if taxes do not adjust then it falls to seigniorage to meet the shortfall. In each of the subsequent analyses, except for the fiscal theory of the price level, it is this simple logic that requires monetary and fiscal policy to be linked.

Let us now consider another implication of the joint sequence of (5.10) and (5.12). First, note that $P_{t+1}/P_t \equiv (1 + \pi_{t+1})$, and also that, for any variable X_t, deflated by the previous-period price level it will be convenient to write $X_{t+1}/P_t = (X_{t+1}/P_{t+1})(1 + \pi_{t+1})$. In real terms, the flow period t constraint may be written as

$$\frac{b_t}{1 + r_t} = b_{t-1} + G_t - T_t - [m_t(1 + \pi_{t+1}) - m_{t-1}] \qquad (5.16)$$

where $m \equiv M/P$. Let us assume that the real interest rate is constant. Iterating forward on this equation in the usual way, we find that

$$b_{t-1} + m_{t-1} = \frac{b_{t+T} + m_{t+T}}{(1+r)^{T+1}}$$

$$+ \sum_{j=0}^{T} \left[\frac{[(r + (1+r)\pi_{t+j+1})/(1+r)]m_{t+j}}{(1+r)^j} \right]$$

$$+ \sum_{j=0}^{T} \left[\frac{\tau_{t+j} - g_{t+j}}{(1+r)^j} \right]. \tag{5.17}$$

However, as we noted above, the other side of the representative agent's transversality condition is an analogous condition on fiscal–monetary sequences, such that as $T \to \infty$ we have that

$$b_{t-1} + m_{t-1} = \sum_{j=0}^{\infty} \left(\frac{1}{1+r} \right)^j \left[\frac{r + (1+r)\pi_{t+j+1}}{1+r} \right] m_{t+j}$$

$$+ \sum_{j=0}^{\infty} \left(\frac{1}{1+r} \right)^j [\tau_{t+j} - g_{t+j}], \tag{5.18}$$

since in that case

$$\lim_{T \to \infty} \frac{b_{t+T} + m_{t+T}}{(1+r)^{T+1}} = 0. \tag{5.19}$$

Some of the issues raised by Sargent and Wallace may now be observed from the standpoint of the PVBC. Let K denote the present value of outstanding liabilities and net of interest deficits. That is,

$$\sum_{j=0}^{\infty} \left(\frac{1}{1+r} \right)^j \left[\frac{r + (1+r)\pi_{t+j+1}}{1+r} \right] m_{t+j} = K. \tag{5.20}$$

Crucially, we assume that the arm of government responsible for seigniorage revenue takes the right-hand side of (5.20) as given. Consider, now, the consequences of a temporary change in seigniorage revenue raised in period t, but compensated for with a one-off rise in period $t + T$. It follows that,

$$\frac{dm_{t+T}}{dm_t} = -\frac{[r + (1+r)\pi_{t+1}](1+r)^T}{[r + (1+r)\pi_{t+T+1}]}. \tag{5.21}$$

In other words, any change in the real money stock requires a larger change (in the opposite direction) in T-periods time, with a factor of proportionality that is rising through time.[6] It appears that postponing the raising of seigniorage runs the risk of a proportionately larger inflation in the future than may be required 'today'.[7]

The overriding concern raised by Sargent and Wallace boils down to the institutional framework surrounding monetary and fiscal policy. For example, might policy-makers find it optimal *and feasible* to extricate themselves from a highly indebted position via an inflation of the price-level? Sargent (1987: 176) attributes to Wallace the view that monetary and fiscal authorities may be engaged in a 'game of chicken' with either side trying to force the other's hand to meet the obligations of the PVBC. If such a game were to take place then there must be a presumption that the fiscal authority has an in-built advantage in the real world. Consequently, in the presence of some limit to the demand for bonds, a sequence of deficits may simply end up forcing the monetary authority to step in and provide the requisite seigniorage revenue.[8]

2.1 How constrained is monetary policy?

Through the second half of the 1970s fiscal deficits became more persistent in the USA and ballooned in the 1980s and first half of the 1990s. The concerns raised by Sargent and Wallace (1981) seemed very relevant. Indeed these persistent deficits caused some economists even to question whether or not the public sector was meeting the PVBC.[9] However, arguably a more fruitful line of enquiry was to enquire just how tolerant monetary policy could be of persistent deficits without surrendering *de facto* control of inflation. How extensive would the effects be on inflation of a run of deficits, or even a *permanent* sequence of deficits? This was the subject of

---

[6] Our example of the Sargent and Wallace concerns is clearly somewhat simplified. Sargent (1987), proposition 5.5, p. 173, extends the above example of a one-off shift in the money stock to the case of changes in the temporal sequence of the money supply. The intuition is, however, the same.

[7] Actually, the authorities may not be able to put off the fiscal day of reckoning. If the price level is a forward-looking variable rational agents may anticipate the higher future price level.

[8] Would fiscal authorities find such shifts in the price level optimal? The Ramsey-inspired approach to policy tradeoffs identifies some important factors. On the one hand a bout of inflation acts like a lump-sum tax. If the only other sources of revenue are via distortionary taxation, then inflation may have an obvious attraction. On the other hand, if there are rigidities in private-sector price-setting unanticipated inflation is far from costless. Results presented in Schmitt-Grohé and Uribe (2000) suggest that optimal policy will ensure substantial stability in the aggregate price level.

[9] The key contribution to this literature is Hamilton and Flavin (1986). However, see Bohn (1995) for a critical assessment of the literature following Hamilton and Flavin (1986).

McCallum (1984). McCallum enquired whether or not monetary policy might retain control of the price level in the face of just such a sequence of permanent deficits. Following McCallum let us define a 'monetarist equilibrium' in which inflation is zero. Let us set $\mu = 1$. In that case we have, $\pi = 0$, since $\pi = \mu - 1$. Alternatively, $m_t(1 + \pi_{t+1}) - m_{t-1} = 0$, $\forall t$. We shall investigate the extent to which fiscal policy might exclude such a situation from being a feasible outcome. First of all note that this implies that (5.16) may be rewritten as

$$\frac{b_t}{1 + r_t} = b_{t-1} + (g_t - \tau_t). \tag{5.22}$$

We adopt the following notation: $(g_t - \tau_t) = d$, $\forall t$. It follows then, assuming a constant interest rate, that

$$b_{t+T} = (1 + r)^{T+1} b_{t-1} + (1 + r)d \sum_{j=0}^{T} (1 + r)^j. \tag{5.23}$$

In turn this implies that

$$\frac{b_{t+T}}{(1 + r)^{T+1}} = b_{t-1} + d \sum_{j=0}^{T} \left(\frac{1}{1 + r}\right)^j. \tag{5.24}$$

The final term on the right-hand side may be written as

$$d \left[\frac{1 - \left(\frac{1}{1+r}\right)^T}{1 - \left(\frac{1}{1+r}\right)} \right].$$

This expression does not converge to zero through time, since as $T \to \infty$ we see that

$$\frac{b_{t+T}}{(1 + r)^{T+1}} = b_{t-1} + \frac{1 + r}{r} d. \tag{5.25}$$

However, since the PVBC must hold, a zero inflation equilibrium is not feasible under rule (5.22); permanent deficits in this sense are indeed inconsistent with the monetarist equilibrium. In contrast to (5.22), now consider a process for debt of the following sort:

$$b_t = b_{t-1} + d_t^*(1 + r) \tag{5.26}$$

where d^* denotes the deficit inclusive of interest payments, $d_t^* \equiv (g_t + \frac{r b_{t-1}}{1+r} - \tau_t)$. Furthermore, let us assume that the fiscal authority attempts to fix the deficit to its value at time t for all $t + j$, for $j \geq 0$. This rule implies that at time T the outstanding level of debt will be given by

$$\frac{b_{t+T}}{(1+r)^{T+1}} = \frac{b_{t-1}}{(1+r)^{T+1}} + \frac{(T+1)d^*}{(1+r)^T}. \qquad (5.27)$$

We note that the first term on the right-hand side of this expression clearly converges to zero for $T \rightarrow \infty$. The second term on the right-hand side follows a somewhat circuitous route, rising initially before falling. Intuitively, while the numerator is rising linearly through time, the denominator is rising exponentially through time. As $T \rightarrow \infty$, it follows then that $\frac{b_{t+T}}{(1+r)^{T+1}} \rightarrow 0$, as required. The intuition is that by including interest payments in the definition of the deficit, the government repays a sufficient amount of debt each period and hence meets the PVBC.[10] In *this* sense permanent deficits are a feasible policy for the fiscal authority in the presence of a zero inflation monetary policy.

However, even on this definition of the deficit, there are some unappealing implications for the evolution of taxes. In particular, the sequence of taxes required to support such a permanent deficit is itself unbounded. It can be shown that the sequence of taxes necessary for $d_t^* = d^*$ for all t is given by

$$\{\tau_{t+j}\}_{j=0}^{\infty} = \left\{ g_{t+j} + \frac{r b_{t-1}}{1+r} + (1 - jr) d \right\}_{j=0}^{\infty},$$

which in turn can be used in (5.27) to yield a formula for the deficit inclusive of interest:

$$\frac{r}{1+r} \left[\sum_{j=0}^{\infty} \left\{ \left(\sum_{s=0}^{j-1} b_{t+s} - b_{t+s-1} \right) + (1 - jr) d \right\} \right],$$

where the first term within the summation is a sequence of terms in the growth of outstanding debt.[11] We see, therefore, that taxes are rising linearly through time. Although the level of debt is rising through time the constant valued deficit implies a growth in interest payments that is declining through time. Consequently, the growth in taxes is also falling through time but necessarily at a rate initially less than that of the debt service. The primary deficit is therefore constrained in this setup to fall without bound

[10] The ever-rising interest payments on the outstanding debt enable agents to pay the ever-rising taxes.
[11] We adopt the convention, $\sum_s \equiv 0$, for $j = 0$.

such that taxes raised are sufficient to meet the ever-rising interest bill on the rising stock of debt.[12]

Aiyagari and Gertler (1985) widen the notion of 'monetarism' relative to McCallum's. In addition to the notion that the price level is determined by the money supply, they also investigate whether or not money is unique in its effects on other economic variables, whether it matters if fiscal policy or monetary policy causes variation in the money stock, and whether a strict Fisher relation obtains between nominal interest rates and expected money growth. It is not possible to review all the results in this contribution. However, a notable result, that the price level may be closely tied to the level of government debt, has been of more recent interest since it has become something of a forerunner of the fiscal theory of the price level. Consider a rule for raising tax revenues of the following sort.

$$T_t = \left[G_t + \psi B_{t-1} - \frac{\psi B_t}{1 + i_t} \right]. \tag{5.28}$$

For $0 < \psi < 1$, this says that outstanding government bonds are not completely backed by taxes. Using this in (5.10) and simplifying we get that

$$\frac{(1 - \psi)}{1 + i_t} B_t = (1 - \psi) B_{t-1} - M_t + M_{t-1}. \tag{5.29}$$

As before we may write this in real terms, such that

$$\frac{1 + \pi_{t+1}}{1 + i_t} \left[(1 + i_t) \frac{M_t}{P_{t+1}} + (1 - \psi) \frac{B_t}{P_{t+1}} \right] = (1 - \psi) \frac{B_{t-1}}{P_t} + \frac{M_{t-1}}{P_t}. \tag{5.30}$$

Using (5.2) under the assumption of log separability (that is $U = \log C + \chi \log(M/P)$, $\chi > 0$) we get that

$$\frac{1}{1 + r_t} \left[\frac{M_t}{P_{t+1}} + (1 - \psi) \frac{B_t}{P_{t+1}} \right] + \chi C_t = (1 - \psi) \frac{B_{t-1}}{P_t} + \frac{M_{t-1}}{P_t}, \tag{5.31}$$

where we have used that

$$\frac{1 + \pi_{t+1}}{1 + i_t} i_t \frac{M_t}{P_{t+1}} = \chi \left(\frac{1 + \pi_{t+1}}{1 + i_t} \right) (1 + i_t) C_t = \chi \frac{1 + i_t}{1 + r_t} C_t. \tag{5.32}$$

---

[12] In addition McCallum also demonstrates that the deficit growth need not, even in this no-growth economy, literally go to zero to ensure fiscal solvency, although there is a bound on the possible growth rate which is determined by the steady-state rate of interest in the economy. We postpone until section 5.4 discussion of the interaction between fiscal solvency and the interest rate.

It is straightforward to rearrange (5.32) and recover an expression governing the evolution of the equilibrium price level of the form (5.5) (or (5.37) below, using our assumed functional forms). However, following Walsh (1998), it may be more useful to solve for the steady-state price level in this setup. In the steady state we have that $C = Y$, $i = r = \delta$. Therefore from (5.32) we see that

$$P = \frac{\delta}{1 + \delta} \frac{M + (1 - \psi)B}{\chi Y}. \tag{5.33}$$

In the event that taxes fully back debt issue, then a steady-state equilibrium of our model exists in which the price level will be directly proportional to the money supply in the way the simple quantity theory might suggest. However, to the extent that taxes do not fully support debt issue then we see that the price level will bear a proportionate relationship to the stock of outstanding debt. Indeed there exists a continuum of solutions for the price level indexed on ψ. The intuition is essentially that of Sargent and Wallace, if 'real' taxes are not backing public sector liabilities then seigniorage will be required.

2.2 The fiscal theory of the price level

In all of the above contributions, the tension between monetary and fiscal policy was as a result of the PVBC. This needed to be met identically for all feasible values of the model's variables (and in all feasible states, in a stochastic environment). But need monetary policy so constrain fiscal policy? Indeed, need fiscal policy so constrain monetary policy? If we relax the assumption that the PVBC is an identity, how does the equilibrium of our simple model change? A recent literature due to Cochrane (2001a), Leeper (1991), Sims (1994, 1999) and Woodford (1995, 1997, 1998a) relaxes the requirement that the PVBC is an identity, although it is retained as an equilibrium relationship (as it must in fact be for the representative agents' budget set to be well defined, in the usual sense). A defining characteristic of this fiscal theory of the price level (FTPL) is a presumption that in the real world, monetary and fiscal authorities do not typically coordinate their 'actions' – specifically their temporal (contingency) sequences for the money stock (or interest rates), tax rates and government expenditure. In the absence of such coordination does this simply lead, in Buiter's (2002) terminology, to default or supersolvency? The fiscalist writers argue in the negative. They point out that with the nominal value of debt predetermined, and the future (expected) discounted stream of net deficits in some sense exogenous, the price level today (and in the future, see Cochrane 2001) can 'jump' to ensure that *in equilibrium*, the PVBC does nevertheless hold. Specifically, let us continue to use the simple framework outlined above, which assumes two types of government liabilities, one-period discount nominal debt, and base money that returns no interest to its holder. As before, we may write the PVBC facing the public sector (loosely, the consolidated government and Central Bank balance sheet) as follows:

$$\frac{B_{t-1} + M_{t-1}}{P_t} = \sum_{j=0}^{\infty} \left(\frac{1}{1+r}\right)^j \left[\frac{r + (1+r)\pi_{t+j+1}}{1+r}\right] m_{t+j}$$

$$+ \sum_{j=0}^{\infty} \left(\frac{1}{1+r}\right)^j [\tau_{t+j} - g_{t+j}]. \tag{5.34}$$

As we noted, since $B_{t-1} + M_{t-1}$ are predetermined *nominal* variables and the sum on the right-hand side is the result of 'disjoint' public policy decisions, there is little hope that for any given price level the requirement that (5.34) nonetheless hold in equilibrium is satisfied. Is there a contradiction here? If instead we view (5.34) as an equation itself defining the equilibrium price level, then the FTPL argues there is no contradiction. Indeed, some fiscal theory writers argue that this approach to price level determination resolves an issue of some importance in monetary theory – the indeterminacy of the price level under an interest rate rule (see Woodford 1997).

2.3 A specific example

Using the model developed above, we exposit a simple example of the FTPL based on McCallum (2001). Let us continue with our simple endowment economy, in which the agent receives y units of non-storable output each period. The government confiscates a given amount each period, $\tau_t - g > 0$ where τ is also assumed constant through time. We assume a period utility function as in the previous section. In this case, the Euler equation for consumption yields,

$$(1 + i_t) = (1 + \delta)\frac{P_{t+1}}{P_t}. \tag{5.35}$$

The demand for money is, in turn, given by

$$\frac{M}{P_t} = \chi C\left(\frac{1+i_t}{i_t}\right), \tag{5.36}$$

where we have assumed a constant money stock for all t. Combining these two equations as we did in deriving (5.5), we find that the price level evolves in the following way

$$P_{t+1} = (1 + \delta)^{-1} P_t \left(1 + \frac{P_t \chi C}{M - P_t \chi C} \right). \qquad (5.37)$$

As we noted above, this equation, familiar in this class of models (see for example Brock 1975 or Obstfeld and Rogoff 1983), has a number of interesting properties. First it is an unstable difference equation with fixed points at zero and at some positive level, P^*. For $P > P^*$, the price level rises without bound, while for $P < P^*$, the price level falls without bound. Some of these paths are usually ruled out as equilibria as they are taken to imply a breach of (5.19) above.[13]

Our assumptions mean that debt evolves in the following manner

$$\frac{b_t}{1 + r_t} = b_{t-1} + (g - \tau_t). \qquad (5.38)$$

However, as we saw above, this policy for the deficit implies a debt level that is inconsistent with the requirement that government meets a no-Ponzi requirement, itself driven by a similar consideration on the representative agent's optimal consumption programme. However, if real debt in this period were somehow to equal

$$b_{t-1} = \frac{1 + \delta}{\delta} (\tau_t - g), \qquad (5.39)$$

then it follows that debt would forever remain at this level. We return to this point shortly.

2.4 A monetarist equilibrium

That the above model supports a monetarist equilibrium is straightforward to see. First, note that in this case $P = P^*$. Then we have that $(1 + i_t) = (1 + \delta)$, and $M/P^* = \chi C (1 + \delta)/\delta$. Notice, we have not used (5.39) in our construction of this equilibrium. Indeed, we have assumed that unstable debt processes are inadmissible: (5.39) would be no part of a fiscal authority's plan for the evolution of debt. McCallum (2001) also argues that such an equilibrium does not contradict our assumption that $\tau_t - g > 0$.

---

[13] Although, McCallum (2001) argues that (5.19) above may not be the appropriate version of the no-Ponzi condition. We leave that issue to one side for present purposes.

He argues that in such a situation it means that the fiscal authority must in effect be providing transfer payments to households so that the apparent surplus is being offset by transfer payments to the public. He concludes that the fiscal authority's primary surplus is constrained necessarily to equal zero.

2.5 A FTPL equilibrium

The fiscal theorists would identify an alternative equilibrium of the model. First note that we may rewrite (5.39) as,

$$\frac{B_{t-1}}{P_t} = \frac{1+\delta}{\delta}(\tau_t - g). \tag{5.40}$$

The FTPL locates the equilibrium expression for the price level in (5.40).[14] Let this expression determine the initial price level. Consequently, then, the evolution of the price level is again given by (5.37), and the path of prices is unrelated to the value of the money stock. Buiter (2002) refers to this example as a fiscal theory of the initial price level.

Critics of the FTPL have generally adopted one of three approaches. First, some have argued that it is difficult to interpret real-world data from the perspective of the fiscal theory. For example, Canzoneri, Cumby and Diba (1999) analyse the response, over the post-war period, of US debt to an innovation in the federal government's budget balance. They find that debt responds negatively to the primary surplus and conclude that the post-war US data are most plausibly interpreted as consistent with a Ricardian regime. Looking at the 'reverse' response, Bohn (1998a) finds that US fiscal surpluses respond positively to debt. He interprets this as evidence that US fiscal policy has been sustainable and although he does not comment directly on the fiscal theory of the price level, his results are again consistent with 'traditional' views.

Using a long run of UK data covering the period 1705–1996, Janssen, Nolan and Thomas (2002) adopt a structural VAR approach modelling the long-run relationships between money, debt and prices. They find, as in the shorter-run studies using US data, that debt leads surpluses, while the reverse does not hold. In addition they find that money leads prices but that the reverse does not hold. They argue that the Sargent and Wallace concerns appear unfounded in practice and that the FTPL may be hard to reconcile with the data.

---

[14] Recall that $\tau_t - g > 0$. Note the criticism of Buiter (2002) mentioned below.

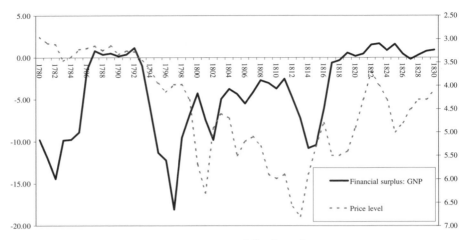

Figure 5.1 Price and fiscal surpluses

Nevertheless many find these empirical exercises unpersuasive. Indeed some argue that the FTPL is an untestable theory. They point out that all data are equilibrium observations and since both Ricardian and non-Ricardian fiscal policies retain the PVBC as an equilibrium relationship there is no way of using time-series data to distinguish between regimes.[15] Indeed episodic evidence shows how difficult it is to test theories on long-run data, particularly when such theories require the development of expectations of infinite sums. We illustrate with a simple example of the fiscal–monetary programme adopted by the British government during the Napoleonic Wars.[16] Figure 5.1 shows the relationship between fiscal

---

[15] The issue of the testability of the FTPL is taken up in Christiano and Fitzgerald (2001) and in Janssen, Nolan and Thomas (1999).

[16] We concentrate on the period 1780–1830, during which time a number of interesting experiments on the fiscal–monetary programme were run. Government expenditure on the Napoleonic Wars, 1793–1815, set the national debt to income ratio on a path which led to it rising from 1.6 in both 1780 and 1793 to as high as 2.7 in 1821; in fact this ratio has subsequently only been equalled in 1946. Great Britain fixed the price of Sterling in terms of gold in 1717 but adopted a rolling programme of temporary suspensions of the standard during the wars and the immediate post-war reconstruction period. This suspension of the gold standard was associated with monetary accommodation of public and private demand during which time annual commodity price inflation, which had averaged 0.5 per cent from 1717 to 1792, averaged over 3.5 per cent from 1797 to an inflationary peak in 1813. Subsequently, the price level fell to approximately its pre-war level by 1822. Sargent and Velde (1995) consider the myriad problems of French finance during this complicated period in detail. Gayer, Rostow and Schwartz (1953), mainly from *British Parliamentary Papers*, provide the data we used in compiling the graphs. Fetter (1965) provides a clear picture of the policy choices made in this period.

Money supply and price level (rhs) (1780–1830)

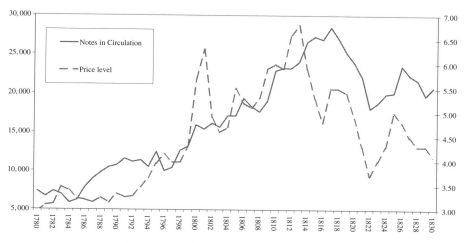

Figure 5.2 Money and prices, 1780–1830

surpluses and price-level adjustment to be complicated. During gold standard maintenance, persistent deficits had little or no relationship with the price level but following 1797, the fiscal deficits clearly lead the increase in the price level. But we note a sharp fall in the price level in 1814 some three years before the sequence fiscal deficits head to near zero in 1817. Figure 5.2 shows that there is some evidence to suggest that money led prices in the period leading up to gold standard suspension in 1797 but that towards the end of the Napoleonic Wars there was a clear adjustment of the price level prior to the reduction of Bank of England notes issued. We leave further analysis of this period to future work.

A second line of attack, forcefully pursued by Buiter (1998, 2002), is that the FTPL involves an unwarranted weakening of the government's PVBC. In requiring this to hold only in equilibrium, the FTPL enables the government to breach a fundamental requirement of a market economy: all agents must respect their budget constraints. He argues that the FTPL gives rise to certain anomalies which mean that the FTPL has to be 'switched off' arbitrarily if the price level is to be determinate. Here we give two examples from Buiter (2002). Consider what happens if there is no nominal debt, and all government liabilities are real (i.e. index linked). In that case there can be no fiscal theory of price determination.[17] Buiter also argues that there is no reason for us to expect under the FTPL that both sides of (5.34)

---

[17] The same is true if all debt is foreign-currency-denominated.

have the same sign. However, the price level cannot be negative, and so he argues that once again the FTPL needs to be arbitrarily 'switched off'.

A final line of criticism of the FTPL has been pursued by McCallum (2001). He argues that the FTPL involves an implausible/unattractive equilibrium selection in that bubble solutions are favoured over the minimum state variable (MSV), or fundamentals, solution. He argues that since in the model under consideration the money stock is constant (there is no relevant state variable), and since the price level is a jump variable ($P_t = \phi(E_t P_{t+1})$), the MSV solution is of the following form, $P_t = c$, where c denotes some constant value. In that case one can show that $P_t = P^*$. He goes on to argue that while the fiscalist equilibrium is logically coherent it depends on the introduction of an extraneous state variable, that is a solution essentially of the form, $P_t = \phi(P_{t-1})$.[18]

3 FISCAL POLICY AND INTEREST RATE BOUNDS

Much of the literature that we have touched on has characterised monetary policy as the evolution through time (and across states) of the money stock. In addition, it has tended to assume that prices are flexible. These assumptions have been useful in developing many of the key points outlined above. However, a plausible case can be made that neither assumption is particularly realistic, so it is an interesting exercise to investigate what may happen if we adopt alternative assumptions. In the next section we characterise monetary policy as a sequence of interest rates and we assume that prices are to some extent inflexible. It turns out that adopting this perspective does offer new insights. In sections 7–10, we shall characterise monetary policy in just these terms. We identify the sorts of bounds required on interest rates to ensure fiscal solvency. We shall find this information of some use in sections 7 and beyond when we formulate fiscal rules for the purpose of simulation.

There has been considerable recent interest in characterising monetary policy in terms of the choice of the (optimal) interest rate sequence. As Taylor (1999) demonstrates, it seems that monetary policy can be usefully characterised as a feedback rule for the short-term nominal interest rate.[19] In addition, Woodford (1997) demonstrates that modelling the monetary authority as controlling the short-term nominal interest rate is

---

[18] This debate is on going. While Woodford (2001) rejects this line of criticism, McCallum (2003) has recently enlarged on his concerns to argue that the fiscalist equilibrium is not learnable, in the sense of Evans and Honkapohja (2001).

[19] As well as outlining this principle, Taylor (1999) also outlines the general scope of the finding through time and across several countries.

consistent with a determinate (at least, locally) unique rational expectations equilibrium.

In the next section, we analyse the relation between interest rates and fiscal variables, within the confines of the public sector's PVBC. We analyse a number of simple scenarios for the evolution of fiscal policy and derive the corresponding implications for the interest rate. The PVBC makes clear that monetary and fiscal policy are closely linked, and perhaps more so than one might conclude from viewing monetary policy as simply control over the money supply. Whether this implies any practical constraint for monetary policy is, however, an open issue – the restrictions we derive on the interest rate imply bounds on the interest rate sequence possibly far out in the future.

4 BUDGET CONSTRAINTS AND INTEREST RATES

We continue to work within a deterministic framework. Financial wealth takes one of two forms: money, which earns no interest, and one-period nominal bonds which do earn interest.[20] We may think of a fiscal authority setting fiscal variables (taxes and debt, given expenditure), and a monetary authority determining the path for the interest rate. The seigniorage sequence determined as a result of the interest rate sequence is assumed to be determined endogenously (via a money demand equation which we do not explicitly model). As before, the one-period public sector flow budget constraint is given by:

$$\frac{B_t}{(1 + i_t)} = B_{t-1} + P_t(G_t - T_t) - (M_t - M_{t-1}). \quad (5.41)$$

B_{t-1} is the nominal quantity of debt issued last period, and maturing this period, i_t is the nominal interest rate between period t and $t + 1$, P_t is the aggregate price level, $(G_t - T_t)$ is the real primary deficit in period t and $(M_t - M_{t-1})$ is seigniorage raised in period t. A central assumption is that the monetary–fiscal sequences avoid Ponzi schemes,[21] such that,

$$\lim_{T \to \infty} B_{t+T} \left(\prod_{j=0}^{T} (1 + i_{t+j}) \right)^{-1} = 0. \quad (5.42)$$

[20] The following analysis, based on Chadha and Nolan (2001), does not incorporate the behaviour of the private sector, as the main points can be made without doing so.

[21] As we noted before, the no-Ponzi game restriction is consistent with optimal private sector behaviour. O'Connell and Zeldes (1988) demonstrate that no rational individual will hold the liabilities of a government that attempts to run a Ponzi game. That is because the welfare of any individual holding such government debt for any period will be strictly lower than under an alternate feasible consumption programme.

What we found in section 2 was that a condition similar to (5.42) is sufficient to ensure that the PVBC is satisfied. This condition ensures that for a given level of outstanding liabilities at the start of any time period the ensuing intertemporal sequence of net surpluses plus seigniorage is sufficient to meet those liabilities.

We shall analyse fiscal rules (or regimes) of the following form:

$$T_t = \lambda_t G_t - \frac{(M_t - M_{t-1})}{P_t} + \gamma \frac{B_{t-1}}{P_t}, \qquad (5.43)$$

where T_t denotes tax revenue generated in period t. Fiscal policy is characterised by the sequence $\{(\lambda_{t+s}, \gamma_{t+s})\}_{s=0}^{T}$. In other words, we may think of fiscal policy as determining the amount of debt retired, and the size of the primary deficit (i.e. γ and $(1 - \lambda_{t+s})G_{t+s}$). We assume that $\gamma \in (0, 1)$, is fixed for all time. This is a useful assumption that makes it more easy to characterise the kind of restrictions on the interest rate and γ that we are seeking. Finally, again for simplicity, we assume that seigniorage revenue is rebated lump sum to the private sector. The particular fiscal rules that we analyse will then be indexed simply by restrictions on the sequence $\{\lambda_{t+s}\}_{s=0}^{T}$.

Equation (5.42) is a very general statement of the kind of restrictions we require on monetary and fiscal policy. However, we can rewrite it in a manner more applicable to the class of fiscal rules under consideration. First, since $\gamma > 0$, the fiscal authority, looking forward from any time t, will always do enough to repay the outstanding debt in existence at the start of time t, that is

$$\lim_{T \to \infty} (1 - \gamma)^{T+1} B_{t-1} = 0.$$

Consequently, for monetary and fiscal policy to be consistent with fiscal solvency there must be a sufficient amount of (discounted) net surpluses looking forward from date t. Therefore $\lim_{T \to \infty} B_{t+T}(\prod_{j=0}^{T}(1 + i_{t+j}))^{-1} = 0$ iff

$$\sum_{s=0}^{T} \left[\left\{ \prod_{j=0}^{s-1}(1 + i_{t+j}) \right\}^{-1} (1 - \gamma)^{T-s}(1 - \lambda_{t+s})P_{t+s} G_{t+s} \right] \to 0. \qquad (5.44)$$

4.1 A balanced budget regime

The first regime we analyse is one in which the government is not permitted (or does not desire) to deviate from a zero balance on the primary deficit.

Some debt was issued in the past, and the government is committed to repaying that at a constant rate, γ. Fiscal policy is simply the sequence $\{(\lambda, \gamma)\}_{s=0}^{T}$ with $\lambda = 1$ and $0 < \gamma < 1$, $\forall s$. Monetary policy is the sequence of one-period decisions denoted by $\{i_{t+s}\}_{s=0}^{T}$. In period t the tax yield is given by (5.45):

$$T_t = G_t - \frac{(M_t - M_{t-1})}{P_t} + \gamma \frac{B_{t-1}}{P_t}. \qquad (5.45)$$

Using (5.45) in (5.41) reveals that

$$\frac{B_t}{(1 + i_t)} = (1 - \gamma) B_{t-1}. \qquad (5.46)$$

Iterating on this expression demonstrates that such a fiscal rule satisfies the no-Ponzi game condition *independently* of monetary policy, that is the sequence of interest rates, since

$$\lim_{T \to \infty} B_{t+T} \left(\prod_{j=0}^{T} (1 + i_{t+j}) \right)^{-1} = \lim_{T \to \infty} (1 - \gamma)^{T+1} B_{t-1} = 0. \qquad (5.47)$$

To confirm this result, set $\lambda = 1$, $\forall s$ in (5.44). In this case, there is no linkage between fiscal variables and the interest rate. Outstanding debt will become vanishingly small in finite time, and there is no constraint on monetary policy.

4.2 Permanent deficits

We now go to the opposite extreme and enquire as to the feasibility of permanent deficits. The existence of a permanent deficit may be taken to imply that $\lambda \in (0, 1)$, $\forall t$. We continue to assume that there is a lower bound on taxes determined by the debt repayment parameter γ. The fiscal rule is now:

$$T_t = \lambda G_t - \frac{(M_t - M_{t-1})}{P_t} + \gamma \frac{B_{t-1}}{P_t}. \qquad (5.48)$$

Substituting (5.48) into (5.41) yields

$$\frac{B_t}{(1 + i_t)} = (1 - \gamma) B_{t-1} + (1 - \lambda) P_t G_t. \qquad (5.49)$$

The public sector is now running a deficit in every period. This policy is sustainable if the following expression goes to zero in the limit:

$$B_{t+T} \left(\prod_{j=0}^{T} (1 + i_{t+j}) \right)^{-1}$$

$$= (1 - \gamma)^{T+1} B_{t-1} + (1 - \lambda) \sum_{s=0}^{T} \left[\left\{ \prod_{j=0}^{s-1} (1 + i_{t+j}) \right\}^{-1} \right.$$

$$\left. \times (1 - \gamma)^{T-s} P_{t+s} G_{t+s} \right]. \tag{5.50}$$

The analysis in subsection 4.1 demonstrates that we require the second term on the right-hand side of this expression to converge to zero. As (5.50) is a special case of (5.44) it will be convenient to make some simplifying assumptions. A useful special case is where the sequence of nominal government expenditures is fixed:

$$(1 - \lambda) P_{t+s} G_{t+s} = (1 - \lambda) \overline{PG} \quad \forall s. \tag{5.51}$$

Now substitute (5.51) into (5.50) to see that the second expression on the right-hand side of (5.50) may be written as

$$(1 - \lambda) \overline{PG} \sum_{s=0}^{T} \left[\left\{ \prod_{j=0}^{s-1} (1 + i_{t+j}) \right\}^{-1} (1 - \gamma)^{T-s} \right]. \tag{5.52}$$

This expression brings out clearly the potential tension between monetary and fiscal policy. Given the rate of retirement of outstanding debt (γ), it is left to monetary policy to ensure convergence of this expression to zero. On the other hand, if the monetary authority had a stronger commitment technology we would regard (5.52) as determining a bound on γ. An interesting example of the implications for monetary policy is where interest rates are set at the level given in (5.53)

$$i_{t+s} = \{(1 - \gamma)^{-2} - 1\} \quad \forall s \geq 0. \tag{5.53}$$

If monetary policy follows this path then (5.52) can be written as

$$(1 - \gamma)^{T} \sum_{s=t}^{T} [(1 - \gamma)^{s-t} (1 - \lambda) \overline{PG}], \tag{5.54}$$

where the expression in square braces converges to

$$\frac{1-\lambda}{\gamma}\overline{PG}. \tag{5.55}$$

Consequently, as $T \to \infty$ (5.54) tends to zero. Although it is clear that (5.53) is not unique,[22] in the spirit of McCallum (1984) we find that (5.53) is a sufficient condition for permanent deficits to be a feasible fiscal policy. But, and more importantly, we find that permanent fiscal deficits effectively place an upper bound on the sequence of feasible interest rates and so do not imply complete 'separability' in the feasible set of monetary and fiscal choices. The result here is intuitive insofar as the bound increasingly constrains the interest rate sequence as the fiscal authority's chosen rate of debt retirement becomes smaller.

5 TAX SMOOTHING AND INFLEXIBLE PRICES

We have shown that the separability of monetary from fiscal policy is not complete under a regime of permanent fiscal deficits. In this section we illustrate the generality of this conclusion.

The assumption of completely fixed prices is not crucial to our arguments. What is critical, as we now make explicit, is that, for a given value of γ, the monetary authority needs *sufficient* control over the real short-term interest rate. We continue to assume that government expenditure is constant. Rewriting solvency condition (5.54) in real terms yields

$$(1-\lambda)\overline{G}\sum_{s=0}^{T}\left[\left\{\prod_{j=0}^{s-1}\frac{(1+\pi_{t+1+j})}{(1+i_{t+j})}\right\}(1-\gamma)^{T-s}\right]. \tag{5.56}$$

As in the previous example, the expression in square braces must tend to zero in the limit if the requirements of fiscal solvency are to be met. Expression (5.56) can usefully be rewritten as

$$(1-\lambda)(1-\gamma)^{T}\overline{G}\sum_{s=0}^{T}\left[\left\{\prod_{j=0}^{s-1}\frac{(1+\pi_{t+1+j})}{(1+i_{t+j})}\right\}\left(\frac{1}{1-\gamma}\right)^{s}\right]. \tag{5.57}$$

A sufficient condition for this expression to reach zero in the limit is simply that the term in square braces is convergent, as opposed to having a zero

---

[22] There are a number of ways to see this non-uniqueness. Perhaps the most obvious is to note that if $i_{t+s} = \{(1-\gamma)^{-2} - 1\} \; \forall s \geq 0$ is a feasible equilibrium sequence then so too must be $i_{t+s} = \{[2(1-\gamma)]^{-2} - 1\} \; \forall s \geq 0$.

limiting value.[23] It can then be shown that this will be the case when the following requirement is (eventually) met infinitely often:[24]

$$i_s - \pi_{s+1} < \gamma \quad \forall s \geq T. \tag{5.58}$$

This expression has a very obvious interpretation in that it requires that the fiscal authority must eventually repay a sufficient portion of the debt each period.[25] An alternative interpretation is that the debt retirement schedule places an upper bound on the feasible real interest rate sequence.

5.1 Tax smoothing

Permanent zero balances or permanent deficits are clearly extreme cases and obvious, more realistic, intermediate cases present themselves. For example, consider a deficit in period zero that is declining steadily through time. Such a policy may be viewed as a simple form of tax smoothing. That is consider a deficit $D_t = \rho D_{t-1}$, where $\rho > 1$ and where $D_t \equiv (1 - \lambda) P_t G_t$. Then one can show that a condition analogous to (5.58) occurs:

$$(1 - \rho) + i_s - \pi_{s+1} < \gamma \quad \forall s \geq T. \tag{5.59}$$

Expression (5.59) tells us that under a regime in which the deficit is temporary but persistent the constraint on monetary policy is clearly eased, as compared to one where it is permanent, but that it is not entirely absent either.

6 SOME CONCLUSIONS CONCERNING BUDGETARY ARITHMETIC

The results in this section compliment those of Sargent and Wallace (1981) and especially McCallum (1984). The latter showed that incorporating the interest burden into the arithmetic of fiscal solvency is important for the independence of monetary policy. However, if instead we view monetary policy as control of the short-term real interest rate, the constraint imposed on monetary policy by a permanent deficit takes the form of an upper bound on the interest rate sequence. And even under less extreme fiscal policies, such as a temporary but persistent deficit, monetary conduct

---

[23] See Rudin (1976), theorem 3.3(c), p. 49.

[24] We are essentially drawing on d'Alembert's ratio test. This says that for a convergent series: $\lim_{n \to \infty} \sup |a_{n+1}/a_n| < 1$. In the text, however, we are unwinding the unstable roots forward to ensure convergence.

[25] Actually this expression is an approximation, since we ignore the cross term: $[(p_{t+1}/p_t) - 1] \times \gamma$.

may be hampered. This latter result may also shed some light on why some monetary policy-makers, such as at the European Central Bank (ECB), may support strict controls on the fiscal policies of member states. That said, it is also the case that these constraints on monetary policy may not be quantitatively that large. To the extent that the solvency requirements analysed above require interest rates to be sufficiently accommodative *eventually*, the pressures may be more apparent than real. Nevertheless, our analysis must be regarded as somewhat preliminary as we have not nested our budgetary arithmetic in a complete dynamic general equilibrium model. In the next section, we shall do just that, and some of the implications of the foregoing section will be useful.

7 A MODEL FOR BUSINESS CYCLE ANALYSIS UNDER RICARDIAN FISCAL–MONETARY REGIMES

So far, our main concern has been with the constraints which monetary and fiscal policy can impose upon one another by virtue of the PVBC. That reflects the dominant concern in the literature which followed Sargent and Wallace (1981). And indeed those concerns have been influential in policy design. The Pact for Stability and Growth which governs those countries which are part of the Euro-zone is in large part, it seems, motivated by concerns that fiscal policy could otherwise distort monetary policy decisions. However, these constraints could also impose costs on these economies. Having lost the ability to set monetary policy with regard to domestic considerations, it may appear desirable to retain some flexibility in setting fiscal policy. Indeed, the desirability of a flexible fiscal response goes beyond the countries of the Euro-area.

In this and the following sections we present a prototype model in which both monetary and fiscal policy are feasible instruments with which to stabilise the economy. As regards fiscal policy, the model in some sense lies between the traditional Ricardian-type fiscal analyses (as in Sargent and Wallace 1981), and the new fiscal theory of the price level. It shares with the literature growing out of the Sargent and Wallace tradition an insistence that the government budget constraint be met for all feasible price and interest rate sequences. In our setup that will mean that the price level or inflation rate will be determined without reference to the issue of fiscal solvency. Nevertheless, it shares with the fiscal theory a recognition that there may well be wealth effects associated with government deficits, although the catalyst for these wealth effects will be somewhat different to the fiscal theory.

The model is constructed around a finite horizon model, following Blanchard (1985) and Yaari (1965). We extend this framework in a number of important directions. First following Buiter (1990), Cardia (1991), Chadha and Nolan (2002b) and Chadha, Janssen and Nolan (2001) we translate the model into discrete time. We incorporate an imperfectly competitive production technology to motivate the existence of sticky prices. A similar model in continuous time is developed by Leith and Wren-Lewis (2000) to analyse the joint requirements on monetary and fiscal policy that might be required for control of inflation to be possible. Like the latter authors, we model price stickiness in the manner of Calvo (1983), in what has become something of a benchmark for sticky-price models (see Woodford 1997). The utility function for the representative agent, j, is given by

$$V_0 = E_0 \sum_{t=0}^{\infty} \left\{ \left(\frac{1}{1+\delta} \right)^t \left(\frac{1}{1+\lambda} \right)^t U \left(C_t^j, \frac{M_t^j}{P_t}, L_t^J \right) \right\}. \quad (5.60)$$

Here δ is the subjective discount rate and λ is the probability of death. We assume that both these parameters are constant. As we demonstrate in an appendix (p. 297), this setup is consistent with the expected remaining lifetime of the agent being equal to λ^{-1}. Because of this the model is sometimes dubbed the 'perpetual youth' model. We make the usual assumptions on the shape of the utility function. Expected utility is maximised subject to a sequence of per period budget constraints

$$P_t C_t^j + M_t^j + \frac{B_t^j}{(1+i_t)} \leq (1+\lambda) M_{t-1}^j + (1+\lambda) B_{t-1}^j + P_t Y_t^j - T_t^j, \quad (5.61)$$

where, $P_t C_t^j = \int_0^1 \int_0^1 p_t(k, z) c_t^j(k, z) \, dz \, dk$, and $P_t Y_t^j = \int_0^1 \int_0^1 p_t(j, z) y_t(j, z) \, dz$, and where (5.61) holds for all $t \geq 0$, and in each state of nature. Here $c_t^j(k, z)$ denotes the representative agent's consumption of good (k, z) where z indexes agents in the economy. Similarly, $y_t(j, z)$ indicates the amount of output produced by the agent. This formulation follows Woodford (1997) and assumes that each agent is a monopoly supplier of all goods that it supplies, while each agent also consumes a basket of all goods. In this way, we partial out any wealth effects that might otherwise have occurred due to price rigidity.[26] B_t^j denotes the bond portfolio, M_t^j

---

[26] By not modelling factor markets and the corporate sector explicitly, we can develop the key aggregate equations with a minimum of fuss. However, in adopting this approach we gloss over some important aggregation issues present in the overlapping-generations framework. For example different cohorts are at different stages of their life cycle and hence consumption and saving are not constant across

denotes money balances, P_t is the aggregate price level, Y_t denotes non-financial income and T_t^j denotes lump-sum taxes. The evolution of wealth is given by

$$W_t^j = (1 + \lambda) M_{t-1}^j + (1 + \lambda) B_{t-1}^j, \qquad (5.62)$$

where we assume, following Blanchard (1985), that perfect capital markets return all financial wealth to the population as windfall dividends in the event of death. Combining (5.61) and (5.62), we get that

$$W_t^j = \left(\frac{1}{1 + i_t} \right) \left(\frac{1}{1 + \lambda} \right) E_t W_{t+1}^j + P_t C_t^j - P_t Y_t^j + \frac{i_t}{1 + i_t} M_t^j, \qquad (5.63)$$

which implies if $\lim_{T \to \infty} (\frac{1}{1+\lambda})^T E_0 \prod_{j=0}^{T-1} (1 + i_{t+j})^{-1} W_{t+T}^j \to 0$, that

$$W_t^j = -E_t \sum_{s=t}^{\infty} \prod_{j=t}^{s-1} \left\{ \left(\frac{1}{1 + i_{t+j}} \right) \left(\frac{1}{1 + \lambda} \right)^{s-t} \right.$$
$$\left. \times \left[P_s \left(C_s^j - Y_s^j \right) + T_s^j + \frac{i_s}{1 + i_s} M_s^j \right] \right\}. \qquad (5.64)$$

We note that both (5.63) and (5.64) now reflect the probability faced by the agent of not being alive in any subsequent period. The simple way we have incorporated this effect means that the probability of death serves merely to act to increase the effective rate of discount. Consumption is defined over the Dixit–Stiglitz aggregator function,

$$C_t^j \equiv \left[\int_0^1 \int_0^1 c_t^j (k, z)^{\frac{\theta-1}{\theta}} \, dz dk \right]^{\frac{\theta}{\theta-1}}, \qquad (5.65)$$

with the aggregate price level defined accordingly as:

$$P_t \equiv \left[\int_0^1 \int_0^1 p_t (j, z)^{1-\theta} \, dz dj \right]^{\frac{1}{1-\theta}}. \qquad (5.66)$$

cohorts. Consequently different cohorts have different stocks of wealth, and hence different marginal utility of consumption. And because of this, optimal labour supply will also differ. If we now consider the effects of shocks that affect currently alive cohorts but perhaps not those yet to be born, the situation seems very complex.

However, in practice the key problem centres around the labour supply function – most other elements are straightforward. And with respect to the labour supply function if we assume that our utility function is a log-specification that complication also disappears. For a more detailed discussion, see Chadha and Nolan (2002e) and an appendix to that paper, available on request.

If we let $\{\mu_s\}_{s=t}^{\infty}$ denote the sequence of positive undetermined multipliers, we may form the Lagrangian function:

$$
\mathcal{L} = E_0 \sum_{t=0}^{\infty} \left\{ \left(\frac{1}{1+\delta} \right)^t \left(\frac{1}{1+\lambda} \right)^t U\left(C_t^j, \frac{M_t^j}{P_t}, L_t^j \right) \right\}
$$
$$
+ E_0 \sum_{t=0}^{\infty} \left\{ \left(\frac{1}{1+\delta} \right)^t \mu_t^j \left[(1+\lambda)M_{t-1}^j + (1+\lambda)B_{t-1}^j \right. \right.
$$
$$
\left. \left. + P_t Y_t^j - T_t^j - \frac{B_t^j}{(1+i_t)} - M_t^j - P_t C_t^j \right] \right\}. \qquad (5.67)
$$

7.1 The demand side

The first-order conditions of the representative agent from any cohort are familiar, except that we now see the effect of the probability of death. At each date and in each state we have that an interior optimum will be characterised by, among other conditions, (5.68), (5.69) and (5.70):

$$
\left(\frac{1}{1+\lambda} \right)^t U_c'(C_t^j, M_t^j/P_t, L_t^j) = \mu_t^j P_t, \qquad (5.68)
$$

$$
\left(\frac{1}{1+\lambda} \right)^t U_M'(C_t^j, M_t^j/P_t, L_t^j)/P_t + \left(\frac{1}{1+\delta} \right)(1+\lambda)E_t\mu_{t+1}^j = \mu_t^j, \qquad (5.69)
$$

$$
\left(\frac{1}{1+\delta} \right) E_t\mu_{t+1}^j(1+\lambda)(1+i_t) = \mu_t^j. \qquad (5.70)
$$

These three expressions can be combined and yield immediately the following two expressions:

$$
\frac{1}{1+\delta} \frac{E_t U'(C_{t+1}^j)}{P_{t+1}}(1+i_t) = \frac{U'(C_t^j)}{P_t}, \qquad (5.71)
$$

$$
\frac{U_M'(C_t^j, M_t^j/P_t, L_t^j)}{U_c'(C_t^j, M_t^j/P_t, L_t^j)} = \frac{i_t}{1+i_t}. \qquad (5.72)
$$

Despite the probability of death we see no tilting of consumption towards the present, and no reduction in the demand for money, as one might have supposed. In fact, given our assumptions on the operation of the capital/equity markets and the money market this makes perfect sense. Any windfall gain from agents dying and leaving unconsumed real resources (either in the form of 'unspent' bonds or money) are simply passed on to those agents left alive. However, those agents, in turn, face an excess interest premium (in order to ensure a zero profit equilibrium). These two effects cancel.

Finally, optimality requires that the flow budget constraint holds with equality in each period and in each state, and the following no-Ponzi finance condition be satisfied:

$$\lim_{T \to \infty} \left(\frac{1}{1+\lambda} \right)^T E_0 \left\{ \prod_{j=0}^{T-1} (1 + i_{t+j}) \right\}^{-1} W_{t+T} \to 0. \quad (5.73)$$

Again this is a familiar expression, save for the inclusion of the probability of death factor.

7.2 The supply side

Agents are assumed to meet demand at the posted price, whether or not prices have been changed in the current period. We follow Calvo (1983), then, and many subsequent analysts and assume that when a price is set in period t it will remain at that nominal level with probability, α ($0 \le \alpha < 1$). More generally, an agent that reprices some part of her output this period faces the probability α^k of having to charge the same price in k-periods' time. We consider the repricing by agent j of one good, z. We demonstrate that the optimal price is a function of aggregate economy-wide variables only. As a consequence we can easily aggregate across all goods in our economy, given (5.66). It will be convenient now to introduce a specific functional form for our utility functional and we shall assume the following $U(C_t^j, \frac{M_t^j}{P_t}, L_t^j) \equiv \log C + \log(M/P) - \int_0^1 \varpi [y_t(j, z)] dz$. This will also be the functional form assumed in our simulation results reported in section 10. $\int_0^1 \varpi [y_t(j, z)] dz$ denotes the disutility of supplying labour across all z goods. For any individual good, then, it follows that the optimal level of $p(z)$, say, p_t^* will be that which maximises the following function

$$\Phi = E_0 \sum_{k=0}^{\infty} (\alpha \beta')^k \left\{ \mu_{t+k} p(z) \left(\frac{p(z)}{P_{t+k}} \right)^{-\theta} Y_{t+k} - \varpi \left[\left(\frac{p(z)}{P_{t+k}} \right)^{-\theta} Y_{t+k} \right] \right\}.$$

$$(5.74)$$

So calculating $\frac{\partial \Phi}{\partial p(z)}$ it is easy to show that

$$E_0 \sum_{k=0}^{\infty} \left\{ (\alpha \beta')^k \mu_{t+k} \left(\frac{p(z)}{P_{t+k}} \right)^{-\theta} Y_{t+k} p(z) \frac{1-\theta}{\theta} \right\}$$

$$= -E_0 \sum_{k=0}^{\infty} \left\{ (\alpha \beta')^k \mu_{t+k} \left(\frac{p(z)}{P_{t+k}} \right)^{-\theta} Y_{t+k} \varpi' \left[\frac{\left(\frac{p(z)}{P_{t+k}} \right)^{-\theta} Y_{t+k}}{\mu_{t+k}} \right] \right\},$$

and hence finally that

$$p_t^* = \frac{\theta}{\theta - 1} \frac{E_0 \sum_{k=0}^{\infty} \left\{ (\alpha \beta')^k \mu_{t+k} \left(\frac{p(z)}{P_{t+k}} \right)^{-\theta} Y_{t+k} \varpi' [\cdot] \right\}}{E_0 \sum_{k=0}^{\infty} \left\{ (\alpha \beta')^k \mu_{t+k} \left(\frac{p(z)}{P_{t+k}} \right)^{-\theta} Y_{t+k} \right\}}. \tag{5.75}$$

Here μ_{t+k} is a measure of aggregate marginal utility, and $\beta = \beta'(1+\lambda)^{-1}$. Expression (5.75) indicates that the optimal price is a function of expected future demand and cost conditions. It follows that the evolution of the aggregate price level is given by

$$P_t = \left[(1-\alpha) p_t^{*1-\theta} + \alpha P_{t-1}^{1-\theta} \right]^{1/(1-\theta)}. \;^{27} \tag{5.76}$$

7.3 Aggregation

Our aggregator function is a discrete time analogue of Blanchard (1985). See Chadha and Nolan (2002b) and Chadha, Janssen and Nolan (2001) for a detailed description of our discretisation of the Blanchard (1985) model.

First we note that the size of the cohort born each period is given by

$$\left(\frac{\lambda}{1+\lambda} \right) \left(\frac{1}{1+\lambda} \right)^t.$$

Naturally death means that the size of the cohort decreases monotonically with time, and the sum of all currently alive cohorts is equal to unity,

---

[27] A strict interpretation of our setup implies, then, that a proportion of each cohort will never get to price some of its output. This is an artifact of combining a yeoman-farmer with a probability of death setup. If we modelled the corporate sector separately, as in Chadha and Nolan (2002e), this anomaly disappears. Consequently, we ignore it in what follows. Alternatively, one may think of the newly born agents inheriting the price tags of the currently expiring agents.

that is[28]

$$\frac{\lambda}{1+\lambda} \sum_{j=-\infty}^{t} \left(\frac{1}{1+\lambda}\right)^{(t-j)} = 1.$$

This makes aggregating the model, for the most part, straightforward. In Chadha and Nolan (2002e) we provide more detail on these calculations. In particular, for any variable x_t^a it follows that

$$x_t^a = \frac{\lambda}{1+\lambda} \sum_{s=-\infty}^{t} \left(\frac{1}{1+\lambda}\right)^{t-s} x_{s,t}. \tag{5.77}$$

The derivation of aggregate consumption dynamics is slightly more involved and we go through that derivation in detail in an appendix (p. 297). We show that aggregate consumption dynamics are given by the following expression,

$$E_t P_{t+1} C_{t+1} = (1+i_t)\beta P_t C_t - \lambda\phi E_t W_{t+1}. \tag{5.78}$$

In the infinite horizon case (where $\lambda = 0$) this expression is simply $E_t P_{t+1} C_{t+1} = (1+i_t)\beta P_t C_t$, the familiar consumption Euler equation. This equation describes how aggregate consumption evolves through time – and importantly we see that temporal variations in financial wealth play no part in determining contemporaneous consumption. In other words, in the absence of distortionary taxation, liquidity constraints (or other financial frictions), deviations from rational expectations and in the presence, as we make clear below, of a Ricardian fiscal policy (and other ingredients which cook up Ricardian Equivalence, see Barro 1974), we see that it makes no odds to the economy whether taxes are raised now or in the future. Agents will consume out of their present value of net wealth, and since lower taxes now resulting in higher taxes in the future does not alter the present value of net wealth, there will be no leverage for fiscal policy to operate in this model via the level of outstanding government debt. However, in the case of finite horizons $\lambda \neq 0$, variations in the temporal allocation of taxes are not 'neutral'. Net wealth is affected by the time profile of taxes. In our simple setup, that is essentially because the probability of a currently alive cohort facing a given tax bill has fallen and hence the consumption set has expanded.

---

[28] We outline in more detail in an appendix (p. 297) the construction of our discrete approximation to the continuous exponential density.

8 MONETARY AND FISCAL POLICY

We shall in general consider policy-makers as setting the per-period interest rate and taxes in order to stabilise both output and inflation. That is we are envisaging policy rules of the following sort:

$$i_t = \phi(i)[Y_t, \pi_t, E_t\pi_{t+1}, i_{t-1}], \qquad (5.79)$$

and

$$T_t = \phi(T)[G_t, \gamma B_{t-1}], \qquad (5.80)$$

where i_t is the short nominal interest rate set in period t, Y_t is real aggregate output, π_t is the inflation rate in period t, and T_t is the per-period lump-sum taxes. While the monetary rule is fairly standard the rule for tax needs some explanation. We shall assume that the process for government expenditure is essentially exogenous. We shall further assume that the fiscal authority sets taxes in response to the level of contemporaneous government expenditure and crucially the level of outstanding debt at the start of the period. The parameter γ indicates the proportion of debt that is retired each period. We shall assume that seigniorage is remitted lump-sum to the private sector.

9 THE GOVERNMENT BUDGET

As we saw above in sections 4–6, γ is a key parameter in ensuring that fiscal policy is Ricardian. Here we give another example in this vein for the case of a fiscal rule that we actually use in our simulations below. Recall that the period public-sector budget constraint, reproduced here for convenience, may be written as,

$$\frac{B_t}{(1+i_t)} = B_{t-1} + P_t(G_t - T_t) - (M_t - M_{t-1}). \qquad (5.81)$$

The rule for taxes mentioned above is given by

$$T_t = \chi_t G_t - \frac{(M_t - M_{t-1})}{P_t} + \gamma \frac{B_{t-1}}{P_t}. \qquad (5.82)$$

Together these two equations imply that real debt will evolve in the following manner,

$$\frac{b_t}{1+r_t} = (1-\gamma)b_{t-1} + (1-\chi_t)G_t. \qquad (5.83)$$

So we call $(1 - \chi_t)G_t$ the per-period deficit, which we denote, D_t. Following the same steps as in section 4, we see that (5.83) at $t = T$ implies

$$E_t \frac{b_{t+T}}{\prod_{j=0}^{T}(1 + r_{t+j})} = (1 - \gamma)^{T+1} b_{t-1}$$

$$+ E_t \sum_{s=0}^{T} \prod_{j=0}^{s-1} \left(\frac{1}{1 + r_{t+j}} \right) (1 - \gamma)^{T-s} D_{t+s}. \quad (5.84)$$

To ensure that fiscal solvency is obtained via the fiscal authority's choice over the sequence $\{T\}_{t=0}^{\infty}$, we shall assume that the coefficient γ is sufficiently large. In particular that will ensure that policy is Ricardian and that the PVBC is satisfied for any feasible path for the relevant variables.

9.1 Why does fiscal policy matter in this model?

In our discussion of consumption dynamics we indicated one way in which fiscal policy has leverage over the economy. In this section we demonstrate this point explicitly. Recall that fiscal policy matters for the level of aggregate demand in this model because it affects the discounted present value of human wealth. Define human wealth, H_t, as equal to the difference between present-value income (let Y_t denote income in period t) and present-value lump-sum taxes (where T_t denotes such taxes in period t). That is,

$$H_t = \sum_{j=0}^{\infty} \left\{ \left(\frac{1}{1+r} \right)^j \left(\frac{1}{1+\lambda} \right)^j Y_{t+j} \right\}$$

$$- \sum_{j=0}^{\infty} \left\{ \left(\frac{1}{1+r} \right)^j \left(\frac{1}{1+\lambda} \right)^j T_{t+j} \right\}. \quad (5.85)$$

For simplicity we assume here that the real interest rate is constant, although it will be apparent that nothing crucial hinges on this assumption. Now consider a change in the temporal profile of taxes such that the present discounted value of government surpluses remain unchanged. That is, consider a variation in taxes at time t offset by a one-time change at $t + j$,

$$T_t(1 + \Delta) + \left(\frac{1}{1+r} \right)^j (1 + \Delta) T_{t+j} = 0.$$

That is,

$$\Delta T_{t+j} = -(1 + r)^j \Delta T_t, \quad (5.86)$$

such that

$$B_{t-1} = \sum_{j=0}^{\infty} \left\{ \left(\frac{1}{1+r}\right)^{t+j} T_{t+j} \right\} - \sum_{j=0}^{\infty} \left\{ \left(\frac{1}{1+r}\right)^{t+j} G_{t+j} \right\}. \quad (5.87)$$

In the simple representative agent model such an amendment to fiscal policy would leave all real variables unaltered since it would leave the present value of human wealth unchanged, $\triangle H = 0$. Here, however, it is straightforward to show that this will not be the case. First note that the change in human wealth will be given by

$$\triangle H_t = T_t(1 + \triangle) + \left\{ \left(\frac{1}{1+r}\right)^j \left(\frac{1}{1+\lambda}\right)^j \right\} (1 + \triangle) T_{t+j}. \quad (5.88)$$

It follows that for $\lambda \neq 0$

$$\triangle H_t = \triangle T_t \left\{ 1 - \left(\frac{1}{1+\lambda}\right)^j \right\} \neq 0. \quad (5.89)$$

Clearly, if the representative agent here faces a zero (anticipated) probability of death, then the change in present-value of human wealth is identically zero, $\triangle H_t = 0$, and the time profile of consumption remains the same despite the temporal reallocation of taxes. So a government that cuts taxes today but leaves fiscal solvency intact can nevertheless influence the level of private-sector demand. And the longer the fiscal authority waits to tighten fiscal policy to offset today's relaxation, the larger will be the impact on aggregate demand.

However there are additional effects from fiscal policy. To see this note that in our model aggregate demand is simply given by

$$Y_t^d = C_t + G_t. \quad (5.90)$$

The *aggregate* consumption function at time t is given by

$$C_t = \frac{1 + \lambda - \beta}{1 + \lambda}$$
$$\times \left[b_{t-1} + E_t \sum_{s=t}^{\infty} \prod_{j=t}^{s-1} \left\{ \left(\frac{1}{1+r_{t+j}}\right) \left(\frac{1}{1+\lambda}\right)^{s-t} (Y_s - T_s) \right\} \right],$$
$$(5.91)$$

where we are ignoring the effect of money balances. We see that the path of taxes impacts negatively on consumption as it reduces net wealth. Following Blanchard (1985) we construct an index of fiscal stance, IFS_t, which characterises the net effect of fiscal variables on aggregate demand:

$$IFS_t = G_t - \frac{1+\lambda-\beta}{1+\lambda}\left[E_t\sum_{s=t}^{\infty}\prod_{j=t}^{s-1}\left\{\left(\frac{1}{1+r_{t+j}}\right)\left(\frac{1}{1+\lambda}\right)^{s-t}G_s\right\}\right]$$
$$+\frac{1+\lambda-\beta}{1+\lambda}\left[b_{t-1}+E_t\sum_{s=t}^{\infty}\prod_{j=t}^{s-1}\right.$$
$$\left.\times\left\{\left(\frac{1}{1+r_{t+j}}\right)\left(\frac{1}{1+\lambda}\right)^{s-t}(G_s-T_s)\right\}\right]. \tag{5.92}$$

The first line is the effect of government expenditure on aggregate demand when it is financed out of contemporaneous taxation, while the second line is the effect of financing via debt issue. To see this more clearly, recall that the government's present-value budget is

$$b_{t-1} = -E_t\sum_{s=t}^{\infty}\prod_{j=t}^{s-1}\left\{\left(\frac{1}{1+r_{t+j}}\right)(G_s-T_s)\right\}, \tag{5.93}$$

where we have again partialled out the seigniorage term. Hence the index may now be written as

$$IFS_t = G_t - \frac{1+\lambda-\beta}{1+\lambda}\left[E_t\sum_{s=t}^{\infty}\prod_{j=t}^{s-1}\left\{\left(\frac{1}{1+r_{t+j}}\right)\left(\frac{1}{1+\lambda}\right)^{s-t}G_s\right\}\right]$$
$$+\frac{1+\lambda-\beta}{1+\lambda}\left[E_t\sum_{s=t}^{\infty}\prod_{j=t}^{s-1}\left\{\left(\frac{1}{1+r_{t+j}}\right)\right.\right.$$
$$\left.\left.\times\left[1-\left(\frac{1}{1+\lambda}\right)^{s-t}\right](G_s-T_s)\right\}\right]. \tag{5.94}$$

Here, if $\lambda = 0$ we see that the second line is identically zero, and there is no net wealth effect from bonds. If, however, $\lambda \neq 0$ and $b_{t-1} > 0$, then outstanding bonds will tend to boost aggregate demand. The correspondence between the second line in this expression and (5.89) is clear.

9.2 Why does monetary policy matter in this model?

Monetary policy matters in this framework because of the monetary policy authority's ability to alter the short-term real interest rate. In other words a change in the level of the nominal interest rate in the presence of sticky prices means that the real interest rate must have changed, and hence that the marginal utility of consumption this period compared with next period must have altered.[29]

10 OPTIMAL SIMPLE RULES FOR FISCAL AND MONETARY POLICY

There has been much recent interest in the performance of quantitative models, such as the one developed here, under the assumption that monetary policy follows a simple rule for the interest rate. This interest can be traced largely to the insightful analysis of US monetary policy by John Taylor (1993). Taylor found that to a large extent US monetary policy appeared to be characterised by a systematic response of the Fed Funds rate to inflation and output deviations from target or trend levels. Taylor (1999), Chadha and Nolan (2002a) and Christiano and Gust (1999) are recent evaluations of the Taylor rule in a variety of quantitative theoretical environments. We cannot review in detail the results from that literature but basically interest rate rules which entail a more than one-for-one change in the nominal interest rate in response to a rise in inflation (referred to as the 'Taylor principle') while responding very little to output appear to have desirable operating characteristics.[30] In our setup policy-makers need to decide on monetary policy *and* fiscal policy. Rather than simply impose a monetary rule that conforms to the Taylor principle we therefore optimise over the parameter space that spans both the monetary and fiscal policy rules, for a given functional form for both rules. In this way we shall see in what ways the addition of fiscal policy affects the optimal simple monetary rule – which in principle need not now conform to the Taylor principle.[31]

---

[29] There are other effects of variations in the real rate of interest, such as via the government budget constraint, but these appear to be of second-order importance.

[30] In fact, Christiano and Gust (1999) argue that the feedback coefficient should be zero on output. As we show below, our results offer qualified support for this as far as monetary policy goes but argue strongly to the negative as far as fiscal policy is concerned. See also the discussion in Woodford (2000).

[31] We extend the King and Watson (1997) code to perform what is, in effect, a grid search over the policy parameters such that the policy-maker's loss function is minimised. Alternative code has been written by Richard Dennis (2001) to solve for optimal simple rules under rational expectations. This latter algorithm, however, requires something close to what we call the B matrix in (5.95) to be non-singular. For larger models that is often inconvenient since then some manual system reduction is required. Our code requires neither A nor B to be singular. The King and Watson (1997) reduction

Table 5.1a *US business cycle dynamics*

	σ_i	$\frac{\sigma_i}{\sigma_y}$	y_{t-4}	y_{t-3}	y_{t-2}	y_{t-1}	y_t	y_{t+1}	y_{t+2}	y_{t+3}	y_{t+4}
y_t	1.563	1.0	0.140	0.415	0.696	0.912	–	–	–	–	–
i_t	1.500	0.960	0.435	0.554	0.631	0.627	0.513	0.308	0.039	−0.235	−0.464
s_t	0.772	0.494	0.367	0.563	0.713	0.776	0.724	0.541	0.285	0.018	−0.205
$\hat{i}_t$	2.141	1.370	0.669	0.610	0.436	0.306	0.100	−0.116	−0.293	−0.420	−0.493
$\hat{s}_t$	3.794	2.427	0.625	0.828	0.946	0.946	0.824	0.603	0.344	0.094	−0.109

Table 5.1b *UK business cycle dynamics* [a,b,c,f]

	σ_i	$\frac{\sigma_i}{\sigma_y}$[d]	y_{t-4}[e]	y_{t-3}	y_{t-2}	y_{t-1}	y_t	y_{t+1}	y_{t+2}	y_{t+3}	y_{t+4}
y_t[g]	1.458	1.0	0.255	0.508	0.751	0.932	–	–	–	–	–
i_t	1.496	1.026	0.605	0.624	0.591	0.487	0.310	0.085	−0.155	−0.372	−0.536
s_t	1.503	1.031	0.033	0.122	0.181	0.204	0.201	0.190	0.187	0.195	0.207
$\hat{i}_t^h$	3.973	2.275	0.424	0.314	0.156	−0.039	−0.240	−0.413	−0.526	−0.566	−0.536
$\hat{s}_t^h$	5.423	3.719	0.466	0.550	0.608	0.626	0.599	0.522	0.419	0.306	0.199

Notes: [a] All data are from 1955:1 to 2001:4; [b] We show the results for band-pass filtered series with a 12-quarter moving average window; [c] Hodrick–Prescott filtered series are available on request; [d] Column (2) is the standard deviation of the filtered series, i; [e] Column (3) is the standard deviation scaled by output; [f] We examine the correlation with output at leads and lags; [g] The first row gives the autocorrelation function of output; [h] The final two rows are the simulated policy instruments of interest rates and the fiscal surplus.

To be more specific, we shall assume that monetary and fiscal policy are set jointly optimal, under the assumption of perfect credibility and assuming that the policy-maker has a quadratic criterion function in annualised output, inflation and interest rates. In effect, then, there is here a single policy-maker which determines monetary and fiscal policy jointly, subject to a requirement that fiscal policy must at all times ensure that policy is Ricardian, in the sense of section 5.2.[32]

Table 5.1 presents some business cycle moments on monetary and fiscal policy over the post-war business cycle in the UK and USA. The band-pass

---

algorithm deals with singular A matrices while our method of calculating the model's asymptotic variance–covariance matrix does not require the inversion of B at any step along the way. Dennis' (2001) code, however, can also be used to solve for the case when pre-commitment is not feasible.

[32] There have been a few recent studies which have solved for optimal (simple) rules. These are Erceg, Henderson and Levin (2000) and Williams (1999). These studies both focused on Taylor-type rules. Batini, Harrison and Millard (2001) subject an open economy DSGE model to a battery of optimised rules, including Taylor rules, nominal income targeting rules, exchange rate rules and inflation targeting rules. None of the above papers has focused on fiscal policy issues.

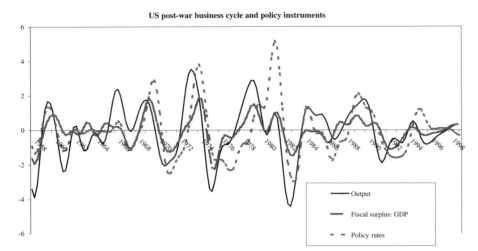

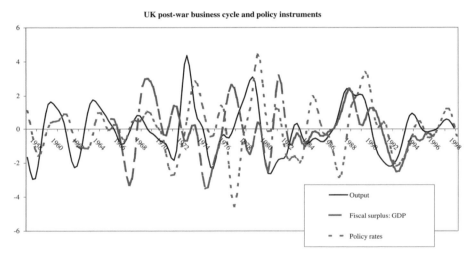

Figure 5.3 Business cycle in the USA and UK

filtered series for output, the policy rate and the fiscal surplus as a percentage of GDP are presented in figure 5.3. The policy instruments' business cycle association data is thus reasonably clear: (policy) interest rates and the fiscal surplus are pro-cyclical, although policy rates have negative leads for output.[33] The systematic and positive association of the instruments of stabilisation policy, nominal rates and the fiscal surplus, with the business

---

[33] The main difference between the two economies is that the volatility of the price level, inflation and, in particular, the fiscal surplus seems substantially higher in the UK compared to the USA.

cycle motivate our use of simple rules for understanding monetary and fiscal policy.

10.1 Solving the model and optimal simple rules

In this section we describe how we solve and simulate the model and how we solve for the optimal simple rules. We use our model developed in the previous section to solve for equilibrium processes for the evolution of aggregate wealth, consumption, money holdings, inflation, the short term nominal interest rate, the level of taxation, the level of government interest-bearing debt and aggregate output. To do this we used the following equations (converted into aggregate form as required): (5.62), (5.71), (5.72), (5.75) and (5.76), (5.79) and (5.80) and (5.81), together with an equation describing the aggregate economy-wide resource constraint. The feedback coefficients in the policy rules, (5.79) and (5.80), are left unspecified and we solve for these adopting a quadratic criterion for the policy-maker. In practice that means we need to calculate, for a given stochastic structure for the economy's driving processes, the asymptotic variance–covariance matrix for the economy's endogenous variables. We first linearise the model around its non-stochastic steady state. Then we make an initial guess about the optimal policy parameters (given the other parametric assumptions we have made) and verify that the model admits a unique stable rational expectations equilibrium under this parameter constellation.[34] In the event that such an equilibrium exists we are able to calculate the loss function of the policy-maker. We then redo this calculation for an alternative selection of policy rule parameter values, and compare losses, and continue in this way until a minimum for the loss function is located. The linearised model can be represented in the following way with all variables in percentage deviation from the steady state:

$$AE_t y_{t+1} = By_t + Cx_t \quad \forall t \geq 0, \tag{5.95}$$

where y_t is a vector of endogenous variables comprising both predetermined and non-predetermined variables including policy rules for the nominal interest rate and taxes, x_t is a vector of exogenous variables, and A, B and C are matrices of fixed, time-invariant, coefficients. E_t is the expectations operator conditional on information available at time t. King and Watson

---

[34] We verify that our model, under the policy rules in place, meets the Blanchard–Kahn criteria by applying the state reduction algorithm described in King and Watson (1997). This is convenient since we encountered, as is generally the case in DSGE models of the sort developed in this chapter, singularities in what we label the A matrix. See the discussion below for more details.

(1997) demonstrate that if a solution to (5.95) exists and is unique then we may write that solution in state-space form as follows,

$$y_t = \Pi s_t$$
$$s_t = M s_{t-1} + G e_t, \qquad (5.96)$$

where the s_t matrix includes the state variables of the model (predetermined variables along with exogenous state variables), and e_t is a vector of shocks to the state variables. The y_t matrix has also been augmented to include the model's exogenous state variables. Let npd denote the number of predetermined variables, nx the number of exogenous state variables and let $nnpd$ denote the number of non-predetermined variables. The dimensions of our system are as follows: y_t is $[(nnpd + npd + nx) \times 1]$, s_t is $[(npd + nx) \times 1]$, Π is $[(nnpd + npd + nx) \times (npd + nx)]$, M is $[(npd + nx) \times (npd + nx)]$, and G is $[(npd + nx) \times (npd + nx)]$. We can use (5.96) to calculate the asymptotic variance–covariance matrix for the model's endogenous variables. (We outline this calculation in a somewhat informal manner. The interested reader should consult Hansen and Sargent 1998.) To proceed, iterate on the second set of equations. Since there are a sufficient number of stable roots, we have that

$$s_t = G \sum_{j=0}^{\infty} M^j e_{t-j}. \qquad (5.97)$$

Using this in the first set of equations in (5.96) we get that

$$y_t = \sum_{j=0}^{\infty} \Phi M^j e_{t-j}, \qquad (5.98)$$

where $\Phi \equiv \Pi G$ is $[(nnpd + npd + nx) \times (npd + nx)]$. Since the stochastic shocks to the economy are assumed to be covariance stationary, it then follows that we may write,

$$y_t y_t' \equiv \Sigma = \sum_{j=0}^{\infty} \Phi M^j \Omega M^{j'} \Phi', \qquad (5.99)$$

where a prime denotes a transpose and $\Omega \equiv e_t e_t'$.[35] Let Σ_x denote the asymptotic variance of the annualised value of x. Then, using the relevant

---

[35] To derive (5.99) we have used the result that for any two conformable matrices A and B, $(AB)' = B'A'$. Note also that since our shocks are stationary, we have that $e_t e_{t-j}' = 0 \ \forall j > 0$.

Table 5.2A *The simple Taylor Rule*

Interest rate rule		Fiscal rule	
$\pi_t - \pi^*$	1.1513	$\pi_t - \pi^*$	0
$y_t - y_t^*$	0.0631	$y_t - y_t^*$	1.7522
R_{t-1}	0.2511	D_{t-1}	0.5712

entries from the Σ matrix for given policy rules we can evaluate the policy-maker's loss function which we assume is given by

$$L = \alpha_1 \Sigma_\pi + \alpha_2 \Sigma_y + \alpha_3 \Sigma_i. \qquad (5.100)$$

In what follows we generate sequences of systems (5.96) under alternative guesses on the optimal parameters in our policy rules which we then evaluate using (5.100). Our aim, of course, is to find parameter values which minimise (5.100), given the functional form of the rules under consideration.

10.2 Results of simulations

There are a number of interesting thought experiments that one could conduct in this setup. We limit ourselves here to a small number of experiments (more are contained in Chadha and Nolan 2002e). First we looked to see how a simple Taylor-type rule for monetary policy might be affected in the presence of a stabilising fiscal policy. Second, how do our results change if we extend the monetary rule to incorporate feedback from expected inflation? Finally, how does one arm of policy react when the other is constrained to act in a suboptimal manner?

Recall from the literature on Taylor rules (see for example, Woodford 2000) that it is often argued that a weight of greater than unity on inflation and a weight close to zero on contemporaneous output has desirable stabilising properties (see also Christiano and Gust 1999). In fact, in most studies these parameters are simply imposed and the behaviour of the model analysed under these imposed rules. Our results are given in table 5.2A.

The numbers in this table correspond to the values of the optimised coefficients associated with the arguments (indicated to the left) in the reaction functions. So, for example, the interest rate rule reported in table 5.2A is given by

$$R_t = 1.15 \times (\pi_t - \pi^*) + 0.0631 \times (y_t - y_t^*) + 0.2511 \times R_{t-1}.$$

In all of the simulation results reported we have constrained fiscal policy not to react to inflation. We see, then, that the Taylor principle is respected in our optimised rule, with a feedback on inflation of just over 1.5. Taylor (1993) himself argued that a value of 1.5 fits the US data. There is also, at the optimum, a weak contemporaneous feedback from output (0.06). Interest rates are autocorrelated, although to a degree that appears somewhat less than one might expect. Turning to the deficit rule, we see that the deficit reacts robustly to the output gap. The surplus to GDP ratio responds contemporaneously to the output gap with a coefficient of 0.75 (somewhat higher than Taylor's recommendation), and is more highly autocorrelated than the nominal interest rate. In Chadha and Nolan (2002e) we calibrated these simple optimised rules to the US and UK data. This exercise is intended to see if these rules – particularly for the deficit – look plausible. Figures 5.4 and 5.5 are taken from that earlier paper. Returning to table 5.1 we note that the final two rows give the band-pass filtered policy instrument series for both the US and UK, where we find that the model delivers instruments with appropriate dynamics with respect to the business cycle.

We see that the rules can to some extent track actual data, although the fit is somewhat closer in the case of the UK. Towards the start of the sample, however, the optimised fiscal rules in both countries appear to imply large swings in the deficit. This reflects relatively large swings in the output gaps in both countries and the effects of the strong feedback from the output gap in our optimised rule. Our assumption that all government expenditure is on final goods and that it is financed ultimately only out of lump-sum tax means that it is relatively costless for the fiscal authority to design a systematic component for fiscal policy that implies such wide swings in net expenditure. Nevertheless, given that our model has such a simple structure, its ability to capture some of the movement in actual data provides us with some comfort that our results provide insight.

There has been much recent interest in the welfare and stabilisation properties of inflation (forecast) targeting regimes. This interest has, of course, been the result of a number of countries adopting such a nominal regime, and with a degree of success that has often appeared elusive under alternative nominal frameworks.[36] Some analysts have argued that feedback from expected inflation may have desirable stabilisation properties. We therefore augmented our simple Taylor rule to include the

---

[36] See Canzoneri, Nolan and Yates (1997) for a discussion of why this may be the case when credibility is an issue.

Optimal Taylor Rule and Federal Funds Rate: US 1990–2000

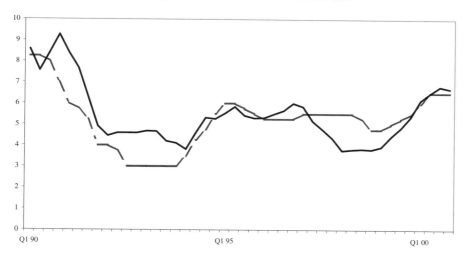

Optimal Fiscal Rule and fiscal surplus: US 1990–2000

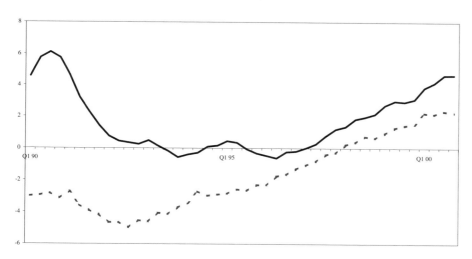

Figure 5.4 US policy, 1990–2000

possibility of some feedback from expected inflation. The results are given in table 5.2B.

Here we see that the inclusion of expected inflation in the monetary rule results in little change to the feedback parameter on output (in either rule). However, the feedback on contemporaneous inflation rises somewhat, and the feedback on expected inflation also appears large, however the feedback

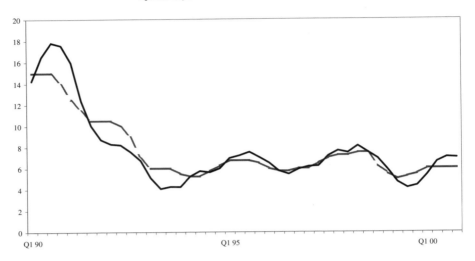

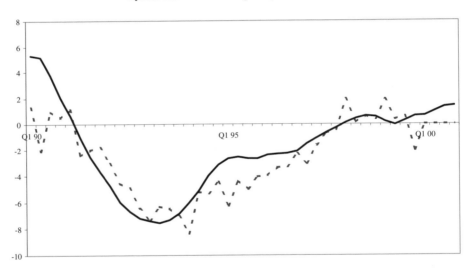

Figure 5.5 UK policy, 1990–2000

from the lagged interest rate goes almost to zero. That indicates that the smoothing of interest rates and the (credible) targeting of inflation may be substitutes in the inflation targeting framework. In practice, the impulse responses suggest that there is little difference in the behaviour of this model economy under the two simple monetary-fiscal regimes outlined in tables

Table 5.2B *Inflation expectations augmented
Taylor Rule*

Interest rate rule		Fiscal rule	
$\pi_t - \pi^*$	1.0981	$\pi_t - \pi^*$	0
$E_t\pi_{t+1} - \pi^*$	0.2927	$E_t\pi_{t+1} - \pi^*$	0
$y_t - y_t^*$	0.0548	$y_t - y_t^*$	1.8151
R_{t-1}	0.0958	D_{t-1}	0.5271

5.2A and 5.2B.[37] Perhaps unsurprisingly, under credible pre-commitment and coordination of monetary and fiscal policy the precise form of the monetary policy rule may not matter much.

10.3 Impulse responses

Before assessing a number of different policy scenarios, we discuss the impulse responses, given in figure 5.6, 5.7 and 5.8 of output, interest rates, the fiscal balance and inflation to 1 per cent shocks from each of the forcing variables given the optimised coefficients reported in table 5.2A. From the plots of these responses, a picture emerges of monetary and fiscal policy working as a complementary sequence of choices and of little real difference between the two rules (i.e. whether inflation or expected inflation is targeted). Consequently our comments in this section apply to the behaviour of our model economy under either rule.

In response to a symmetric persistent productivity shock, output responds positively and with a high degree of persistence. Inflation mirrors the response, as falling marginal costs put downward pressure on firms' prices. The optimal policy response sees the nominal interest rate fall below base, while the fiscal surplus rises. Nominal interest rates are cut in order to stabilise falling inflation and lump-sum taxation tempers aggregate demand.

Following an unanticipated monetary tightening, output remains below its steady-state level for some ten quarters, although it is within 0.1 per cent of base after only three quarters. Output falls because a monetary policy shock increases real rates. Fiscal policy responds to this monetary tightening by running a (persistent) deficit. The maximal response is in the first period. Inflation responds quickly to the monetary shock, falling by

---

[37] We present impulse responses for table 5.2A and those for table 5.2B, which are very similar, are available on request.

Output in response to productivity shock

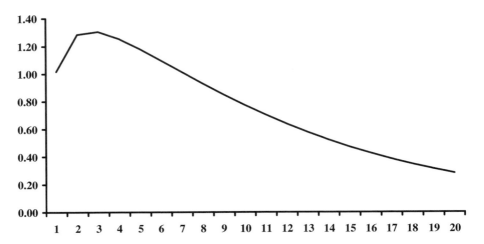

Nominal interest in response to productivity shock

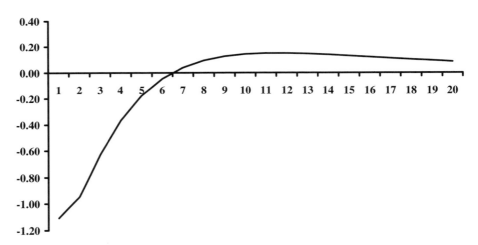

Figure 5.6 Key responses to a productivity shock

just under 0.5 per cent in period 1 and returns more than halfway to base by period 2.

A fiscal shock impacts on output via government expenditure and bonds. The increase in output and inflation caused by the impact on aggregate demand leads to a persistent but small rise in nominal interest rates. The

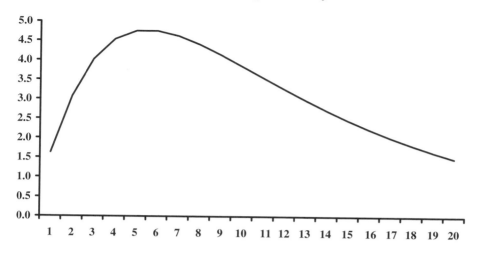

Surplus in response to productivity shock

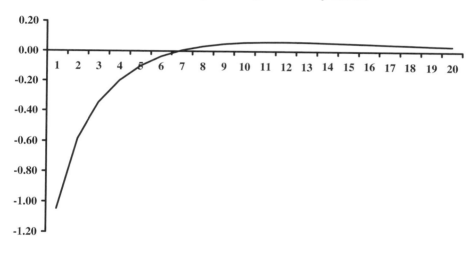

Inflation in response to productivity shock

Figure 5.6 (*cont.*)

effects of government expenditure are analysed in Baxter and King (1993). Briefly, a rise in government expenditure on final goods results in a rise in labour supply which boosts aggregate output (despite pushing down on aggregate consumption). It turns out that the transmission channel of fiscal policy identified by Baxter and King (1993) is also dominant in the current setup. In other words the wealth effect of outstanding government bonds is

Output in response to monetary shock

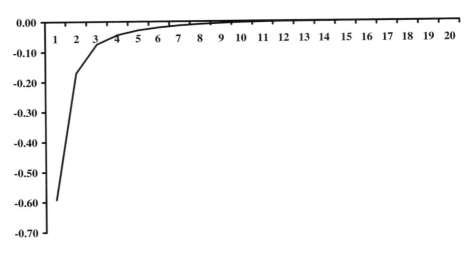

Nominal interest in response to monetary shock

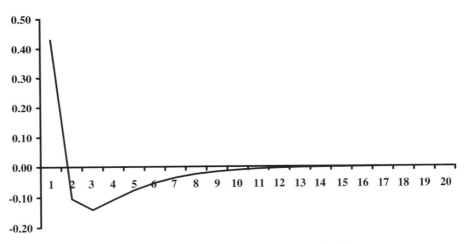

Figure 5.7 Key responses to a monetary shock

of second-order importance. Chadha and Nolan (2002e) demonstrate this point in more detail.

Monetary–fiscal interactions
We now turn briefly to two further experiments. First we assess a suggestion of Robert Mundell (1971) that monetary policy should focus on

Surplus in response to monetary shock

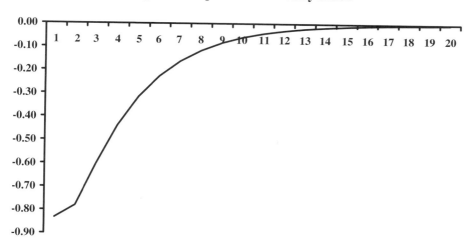

Inflation in response to monetary shock

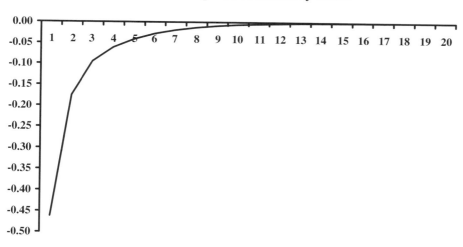

Figure 5.7 *(cont.)*

inflation control, and fiscal policy on real objectives. Table 5.2C shows that the weights in the optimal rules derived in tables 5.2A and 5.2B are not particularly far from that which would be implied by the implementation of Mundell's (1971) suggestion.

Our final illustration in table 5.2D shows the implications for fiscal policy from a monetary policy-maker who places a high weight on inflation

Output in response to fiscal shock

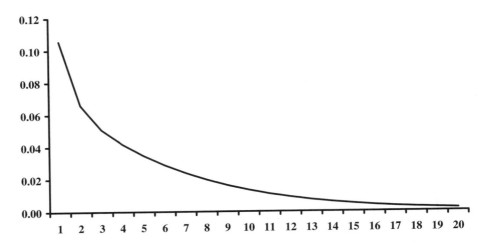

Nominal interest in response to fiscal shock

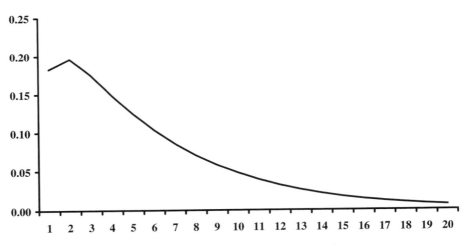

Figure 5.8 Key responses to a fiscal shock

stabilisation. Table 5.2D shows that active monetary policy in this case engenders similarly active fiscal policy in order to reach the optimum. This means that overly aggressive monetary policy will be complemented by a similar fiscal policy in order to stabilise the economy optimally: aggression breeds aggression. In Chadha and Nolan (2002e) a number of further experiments are conducted. However the same basic intuition is present, in that when one rule is constrained to deviate from its optimised form,

Surplus in response to fiscal shock

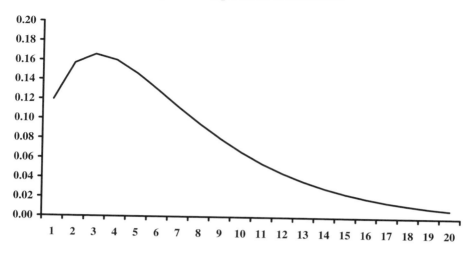

Inflation in response to fiscal shock

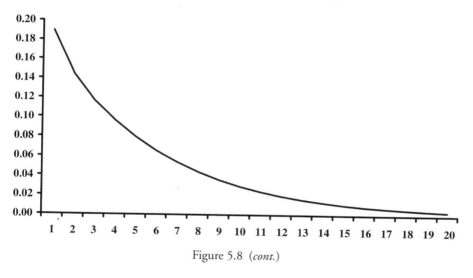

Figure 5.8 (*cont.*)

the other rule ends up acting to try to compensate for such suboptimal behaviour.

The four simulations in this section indicate a number of issues worth pursuing further. The Mundellian assignment strategy is near the optimum of our constrained optimal rules. Inflation targeting, or at least our version of it, does not appear to make much difference to the behaviour of our model economy as the feedback from anticipated inflation substitutes for

Table 5.2C *Mundell Assignment Rule*

Interest rate rule		Fiscal rule	
$\pi_t - \pi^*$	1.07	$\pi_t - \pi^*$	–
$y_t - y_t^*$	–	$y_t - y_t^*$	1.11
R_{t-1}	0.19	D_{t-1}	0.65

Table 5.2D *Fiscal policy implications of the high inflation aversion*

	IRR[a]	FDR[a]	IRR	FDR	IRR	FDR	
π_t	4.5	–	3.5	–	2.0	–	π_t
y_t	0.1	3.06	0.1	3.03	0.1	2.57	y_t
R_{t-1}	0.2	0.44	0.2	0.47	0.2	0.52	D_{t-1}

Note: [a] The columns headed IRR refer to Interest Rate Rule and those headed FDR refer to the Fiscal Deficit Rule. For IRR go to the LHS column for a key and for FDR go to the RHS column for a key.

the lack of a feedback from the lagged interest rate. Finally, suboptimal behaviour in one rule generates a response from the other: in our final example an aggressive monetary policy optimally engendered an aggressive fiscal policy.

11 CONCLUSIONS

This chapter has focused on two main issues in the study of the interaction of monetary and fiscal policy. First, because monetary and fiscal policy are linked via the public sector's PVBC, the seigniorage and real tax sequences need to be coordinated over the 'long run'. In practice a number of countries have adopted independent Central Banks with a primary objective being price stability. Implicitly, and sometimes explicitly, this institutional setup implies that fiscal solvency should be a primary goal of fiscal policy. However, this has led to a concern that monetary and fiscal policy may not be coordinated at the business cycle frequencies, with the implication that output and employment may be more volatile than necessary. We develop a model in which the optimal design of monetary and fiscal policy can be considered.

APPENDIX

A.1 EXPONENTIAL AND DISCRETE DENSITY FUNCTIONS

Here we informally show how the exponential density can be approximated by the discrete density we use in the chapter. The exponential density is given by (A.1)

$$f(\lambda) = \int_0^\infty \lambda e^{-\lambda t} dt \tag{A.1}$$

where λ is the constant probability of death, as in Blanchard (1985), and $1/\lambda$ is the expected value of remaining life. That is, the expected value of a random variable is given by

$$E(x) = \int x f(x) \, dx \tag{A.2}$$

which in the case of the exponential density just becomes

$$E(.) = \int_0^\infty t \lambda e^{-\lambda t} dt. \tag{A.3}$$

Integrating (A.3) by parts yields

$$E(.) = -te^{-\lambda t}]_0^\infty + \int_0^\infty e^{-\lambda t} dt = \frac{1}{\lambda}. \tag{A.4}$$

Now, to translate this continuous density to its discrete time analogue note that:

$$e^{-\lambda t} \simeq \left(\frac{1}{1+\lambda}\right)^t. \tag{A.5}$$

The exponential density is pre-multiplied by λ, however in discrete time the above factor is not pre-multiplied by $1/{1+\lambda}$ as one might initially suppose. Note that λ is the (negative) of the instantaneous growth rate of the function $e^{-\lambda t}$, so that the discrete time analogue is simply

$$\frac{\left(\frac{1}{1+\lambda}\right)^t - \left(\frac{1}{1+\lambda}\right)^{t-1}}{\left(\frac{1}{1+\lambda}\right)^{t-1}} = \left(\frac{\lambda}{1+\lambda}\right). \tag{A.6}$$

Intuitively this ensures that at each point the probability of death is constant:

$$\sum_{t=0}^{\infty} \left(\frac{\lambda}{1+\lambda}\right) \left(\frac{1}{1+\lambda}\right)^t. \qquad (A.7)$$

The expected value of this distribution is then derived as follows

$$E(.) = \left(\frac{\lambda}{1+\lambda}\right) \sum_{t=0}^{\infty} t \left(\frac{1}{1+\lambda}\right)^t. \qquad (A.8)$$

Focusing on the terms to be integrated, we see that the sum, S, is given by

$$S = 0 + \left(\frac{1}{1+\lambda}\right) + 2 \left(\frac{1}{1+\lambda}\right)^2 + 3 \left(\frac{1}{1+\lambda}\right)^3$$
$$+ \cdots + n \left(\frac{1}{1+\lambda}\right)^n. \qquad (A.9)$$

Similarly,

$$\left(\frac{1}{1+\lambda}\right) S = \left(\frac{1}{1+\lambda}\right)^2 + 2 \left(\frac{1}{1+\lambda}\right)^3 + \cdots + n \left(\frac{1}{1+\lambda}\right)^{n+1}. \qquad (A.10)$$

It then follows that

$$\left(\frac{\lambda}{1+\lambda}\right) S = \left(\left(\frac{1}{1+\lambda}\right) + \left(\frac{1}{1+\lambda}\right)^2 + \left(\frac{1}{1+\lambda}\right)^3 \right.$$
$$\left. + \cdots + \left(\frac{1}{1+\lambda}\right)^n\right) - n \left(\frac{1}{1+\lambda}\right)^{n+1}.$$

Simplifying this expression and evaluating the sum as $n \to \infty$, gives that

$$S = \frac{\left(\frac{1}{1+\lambda}\right)}{\left(\frac{\lambda}{1+\lambda}\right)^2}. \qquad (A.11)$$

Using this in expression (A.8) confirms that expected remaining life is constant and equal to λ^{-1}.

A.2 CALCULATING AGGREGATE CONSUMPTION

As we indicated in the text, the strong symmetry assumptions adopted mean that aggregation is generally easy. For example, whenever a given variable is constant across cohorts, we employ (5.18) in the main text in a straightforward way. Similarly, the aggregate evolution of wealth is the same as the representative cohort's except that $\lambda = 0$. In this part of the appendix we show how we calculated (5.19) in the main text which is the expression governing aggregate consumption dynamics. We ignore the j-superscripts in what follows (since all cohorts are identical). In the usual way we can calculate the expected present value of consumption. Thus, iterating on the consumption Euler equation and using the PVBC we find that,

$$
E_t \sum_{s=t}^{\infty} \prod_{j=t}^{s-1} \left(\frac{1}{1+i_{t+j}} \right) \left(\frac{1}{1+\lambda} \right)^{s-t} P_s C_s
$$

$$
= W_t + E_t \sum_{s=t}^{\infty} \prod_{j=t}^{s-1} \left\{ \left(\frac{1}{1+i_{t+j}} \right) \left(\frac{1}{1+\lambda} \right)^{s-t} \right.
$$

$$
\left. \times \left[P_s Y_s - T_s - \frac{i_s}{1+i_s} M_s \right] \right\}.
$$

Assuming log separability as in our characterising of the key supply-side equations, we get that the left-hand side of the above expression can be written as $^{1+\lambda}/_{1+\lambda-\beta} P_t C_t$, so that we have

$$
P_t C_t = \frac{1+\lambda-\beta}{1+\lambda} \left[W_t + E_t \sum_{s=t}^{\infty} \prod_{j=t}^{s-1} \left\{ \left(\frac{1}{1+i_{t+j}} \right) \left(\frac{1}{1+\lambda} \right)^{s-t} \right. \right.
$$

$$
\left. \left. \times \left[P_s Y_s - T_s - \frac{i_s}{1+i_s} M_s \right] \right\} \right], \tag{A.12}
$$

which is the solved out consumption function for a given cohort. We now want to calculate *aggregate* $P_{t+1} C_{t+1} - P_t C_t$. First we economise on some notation, rewriting (A.12) as

$$
P_t C_t = \Psi \left[W_t + E_t \sum_{s=t}^{\infty} \prod_{j=t}^{s-1} \left\{ \left(\frac{1}{1+i_{t+j}} \right) \left(\frac{1}{1+\lambda} \right)^{s-t} \Theta_s \right\} \right] \tag{A.13}
$$

where $\Psi \equiv {}^{1+\lambda-\beta}/_{1+\lambda}$, and $\Theta_s \equiv P_s Y_s - T_s - {}^{i_s}/_{1+i_s} M_s$. We shall also avoid carrying around expectations operators. We construct $P_{t+1} C_{t+1} - P_t C_t$ in two steps. First we derive an expression for the evolution of aggregate 'human' wealth, Θ_s, and then we calculate an analogous expression for aggregate financial wealth. The sum of these two expressions delivers aggregate consumption dynamics. First, then, we look to the change in aggregate 'human' wealth. Since human wealth is, by assumption, equal across cohorts (productivity is equal, the first-order conditions of money holdings are the same and there is no difference across cohorts *vis-à-vis* taxes levied) we get that,

$$\Psi \left[W_{t+1} + \Theta_{t+1} + \left(\frac{1}{1+i_{t+1}}\right)\left(\frac{1}{1+\lambda}\right)\Theta_{t+2} + \right.$$
$$\left. \left(\frac{1}{1+i_{t+1}}\right)\left(\frac{1}{1+i_{t+2}}\right)\left(\frac{1}{1+\lambda}\right)^2 \Theta_{t+3} + \cdots \right]$$

$$-\Psi \left[W_t + \Theta_t + \left(\frac{1}{1+i_t}\right)\left(\frac{1}{1+\lambda}\right)\Theta_{t+1} \right.$$
$$\left. + \left(\frac{1}{1+i_t}\right)\left(\frac{1}{1+i_{t+1}}\right)\left(\frac{1}{1+\lambda}\right)^2 \Theta_{t+2} + \cdots \right].$$

Collecting terms we see that

$$\Psi \left[-\Theta_t + \left(1 - \left(\frac{1}{1+i_t}\right)\left(\frac{1}{1+\lambda}\right)\right)\Theta_{t+1} \right.$$
$$\left. + \left(1 - \left(\frac{1}{1+i_t}\right)\left(\frac{1}{1+\lambda}\right)\right)\left(\frac{1}{1+i_{t+1}}\right)\left(\frac{1}{1+\lambda}\right)\Theta_{t+2} \right]$$
$$+ \left(1 - \left(\frac{1}{1+i_t}\right)\left(\frac{1}{1+\lambda}\right)\right)\left(\frac{1}{1+i_{t+1}}\right)\left(\frac{1}{1+i_{t+2}}\right)$$
$$\times \left(\frac{1}{1+\lambda}\right)^2 \Theta_{t+3} + \cdots$$

This expression can, with a little rearrangement, be rewritten as

$$\Psi \left[\Theta_t + \frac{(1+\lambda)(1+i_t) - 1}{(1+\lambda)(1+i_t)} \right.$$
$$\left. \times \left[\sum_{s=t+1}^{\infty} \prod_{j=t}^{s-1} \left\{ \left(\frac{1}{1+i_{t+j}}\right)\left(\frac{1}{1+\lambda}\right)^{s-(t+1)} \Theta_s \right\} \right] \right]. \quad \text{(A.14)}$$

We now calculate an expression for $\Psi[W_{t+1} - W_t]$. First we recall that we now need to work with aggregate financial wealth. That is

$$W_t = M_{t-1} + B_{t-1}.$$

Using this in the flow budget constraint we find after some manipulation that

$$W_t + P_t C_t + \frac{W_{t+1}}{1 + i_t} - \Theta_t.$$

Therefore the change in wealth may be written as,

$$\Psi \left[\frac{i_t}{1 + i_t} W_{t+1} + \Theta_t - P_t C_t \right]$$

and combining this with expression (A.14) we get that

$$P_{t+1} C_{t+1} - P_t C_t$$
$$= \Psi \left[\begin{array}{l} -\Theta_t + \dfrac{(1 + \lambda)(1 + i_t) - 1}{(1 + \lambda)(1 + i_t)} \left[\displaystyle\sum_{s=t+1}^{\infty} \prod_{j=t}^{s-1} \left\{ \left(\dfrac{1}{1 + i_{t+j}} \right) \right. \right. \\ \left. \left. \times \left(\dfrac{1}{1 + \lambda} \right)^{s-(t+1)} \Theta_s \right\} \right] + \dfrac{i_t}{1 + i_t} W_{t+1} + \Theta_t - P_t C_t \end{array} \right].$$
$$\text{(A.15)}$$

However, we already know that

$$P_{t+1} C_{t+1} = \Psi \left[W_{t+1} + \sum_{s=t+1}^{\infty} \prod_{j=t}^{s-1} \left\{ \left(\frac{1}{1 + i_{t+j}} \right) \left(\frac{1}{1 + \lambda} \right)^{s-(t+1)} \Theta_s \right\} \right]$$

so we can re-write (A.15) as

$$P_{t+1} C_{t+1} - P_t C_t$$
$$= \Psi \left[-\Theta_t + \frac{(1 + \lambda)(1 + i_t) - 1}{(1 + \lambda)(1 + i_t)} \left[\frac{P_{t+1} C_{t+1}}{\Psi} - W_{t+1} \right] \right]$$
$$+ \Psi \left[\frac{i_t}{1 + i_t} W_{t+1} + \Theta_t - P_t C_t \right]$$

And straightforward simplification results in:

$$E_t P_{t+1} C_{t+1} = (1 + i_t) \beta P_t C_t - \lambda \phi E_t W_{t+1}, \qquad \text{(A.16)}$$

which is (5.78) in the main text.

Table 5A.1 *Calibration parameters for quarterly model*

Symbol	Value	Description
λ	0.00357	Expected life remaining: 70 years
r	0.0125	Real interest rate
β	0.95	Subjective discount factor
δ	0.053	Subjective discount rate
γ	0.06	Rate of debt retirement
$\frac{c}{y}$	0.6	Steady-state consumption–output ratio
$\frac{m}{w}$	0.1	Steady-state money–wealth ratio
κ	0.5	Phillips curve slope
$\frac{w}{c}$	0.7	Steady-state wealth–consumption ratio

A.3 PARAMETERISATION OF THE MODEL

Table 5A.1 outlines the baseline parameter values that we adopt for the calibration of the model. More discussion of these and the driving processes that we adopt can be found in Chadha and Nolan (2002e). The post-Second World War UK and US data set is standard. The US data set runs from 1955:1 to 2000:4: we use the Federal Funds rate as the policy instrument in the Taylor Rule; annual inflation is measured as the four-quarter percentage change in the All-Items CPI; GDP in 1995 constant prices is detrended by a quadratic time trend and the Federal Government surplus or deficit is given as as a proportion of GDP. For the UK, we use the base rate as the policy instrument; annual inflation is measured as the four-quarter percentage change in the RPI; GDP in 1995 constant prices is detrended by a quadratic time trend and the Public Sector Cash Requirement is given as a proportion of GDP, after being seasonally adjusted by X12.

The model is calibrated at a quarterly frequency using more or less standard parameter values. We assume that λ is determined as a result of the representative agent expecting to live to 70. The discount factor, β, is set at 0.95. Numerical investigations led us to set the debt retirement rate, γ, to 0.06. The consumption–income ratio, c/y, is equal to 0.6, while the steady-state money–wealth ratio, m/w, was chosen to be 0.1. Roughly speaking the average size of the UK debt to GDP ratio over the post-war period has been some 40 per cent. Together with our assumption for c/y, this implies that the steady-state wealth–income ratio for this simple model economy is 0.7.

Let a_t, f_t, and h_t denote the log-detrended processes for productivity, fiscal and monetary innovations, respectively. We then assume they can be described adequately for our purposes as follows,

$$
\begin{bmatrix} a_t \\ f_t \\ h_t \end{bmatrix} = \begin{bmatrix} \rho_a & 0 & 0 \\ 0 & \rho_f & 0 \\ 0 & 0 & \rho_q \end{bmatrix} \begin{bmatrix} a_{t-1} \\ f_{t-1} \\ h_{t-1} \end{bmatrix} + \begin{bmatrix} x_t \\ g_t \\ q_t \end{bmatrix}
$$

where x_t, g_t and q_t are the shocks, respectively, to productivity, fiscal and monetary innovations. We adopted an agnostic strategy for setting the covariance structure of the forcing variables. First we estimated Solow residuals, Taylor rules and Fiscal rule equations on US and UK data and found little difference in the standard errors of the respective equations. Similarly Cardia (1991) found that the standard deviation of shocks to the monetary and fiscal processes were of similar magnitude in the US data, while in the German data the standard deviations of fiscal and productivity shocks were of a similar size. In practice, then, we decided simply to set $\sigma_a = \sigma_f = \sigma_q = 0.01$. In terms of the persistence parameters we chose the following: $\rho_a = 0.9$, $\rho_f = 0.9$ and $\rho_q = 0$. In Chadha and Nolan (2002e) we discuss these stochastic settings further. We found that our results were fairly insensitive to alternative plausible assumptions *vis-à-vis* persistence and volatility of underlying shocks.

BIBLIOGRAPHY

Aiyagari, S. R., Christiano, L. J. and Eichenbaum, M. (1992). 'The Output, Employment, and Interest Rate Effects of Government Consumption', *Journal of Monetary Economics* (30)1, 73–86

Aiyagari, S. R. and Gertler, M. (1985). 'The Backing of Government Bonds and Monetarism', *Journal of Monetary Economics*, 16(1), 19–40

Barro, R. J. (1974). 'Are Government Bonds Net Wealth?', *Journal of Political Economy*, 82(6), 1095–1117

(1979). 'On the Determination of the Public Debt', *Journal of Political Economy*, 87(5), part 1, 940–71

(1981). 'Output Effects of Government Purchases', *Journal of Political Economy*, 89(6), 1086–1121

Batini, N., Harrison, R. and Millard, S. P. (2001). 'Monetary Policy Rules for an Open Economy', Bank of England Working Paper, 149

Bauxter, M. and King, R. G. (1993). 'Fiscal Policy in General Equilibrium', *American Economic Review*, 83(3), 315–34

Blanchard, O. J. (1985). 'Debts, Deficits and Finite Horizons', *Journal of Political Economy*, 93, 223–47

Bohn, H. (1995). 'The Sustainablility of Government Deficits in a Stochastic Economy', *Journal of Money Credit, and Banking*, 27(1), 257–71

(1998a). 'The Behaviour of US Public Debt and Deficits', *Quarterly Journal of Economics*, 113(3), 949–63

(1998b). 'Comment on John Cochrane, "A Frictionless View of US Inflation"', in B. S. Bernanke and J. J. Rotemberg (eds.), *NBER Macroeconomics Annual*, Cambridge, MA: MIT Press, 323–84

Brock, W. A. (1975). 'A Simple Perfect Foresight Monetary Model', *Journal of Monetary Economics*, 1, 133–50

Buiter, W. H. (1990). *Principles of Budgetary and Financial Policy*, Cambridge, MA: MIT Press

(1998). 'The Young Person's Guide to Neutrality, Price Level Indeterminacy, Interest Rate Pegs and Fiscal Theories of the Price Level', *NBER Working Paper*, 6396, Cambridge, MA

(2002). 'The Fallacy of the Fiscal Theory of the Price-Level': A Critique, *Economic Journal*, 112, 459–80

Calvo, G. A. (1983). 'Staggered Prices in a Utility Maximising Framework', *Journal of Monetary Economics*, 12(3) 983–98

(1985). 'Macroeconomic Implications of the Government Budget Constraint: Some Basic Considerations', *Journal of Monetary Economics*, 15, 95–112

Canzoneri, M. B., Cumby, R. E. and Diba, B. T. (2001). 'Is The Price Level Determined by the Needs of Fiscal Solvency?', *American Economic Review*, 91(5), 1221–38

Canzoneri, M. B., Nolan, C. and Yates, A. (1997). 'Mechanisms for Achieving Monetary Stability: Inflation Targeting versus the ERM', *Journal of Money Credit, and Banking*, 29(1), 46–60

Cardia, E. (1991). 'The Dynamics of a Small Open Economy in Response to Monetary, Fiscal and Productivity Shocks', *Journal of Monetary Economics*, 28(3), 411–34

Chadha, J. S. and Nolan, C. (2002a). 'Inflation versus Price-Level Targeting in a New Keynesian Macro-Model', *The Manchester School*, 70(4), 570–95

(2002b). 'Supply Shocks and the Natural Rate of Interest: An Exploration', in P. J. Sinclair *et al.* (eds.), *The Theory and Practice of Monetary Transmission in Diverse Economies*, Cambridge: Cambridge University Press.

(2002c). 'Output, Inflation and the New Keynesian Phillips Curve', *DAE Working Paper*, 0204

(2002d). 'The Interaction of Monetary and Fiscal Policy: When Does Aggregative Fiscal Policy Matter?', in preparation

(2002e). 'Operating Characteristics of Simple Rules for the Conduct of Monetary Policy and Fiscal Policy', in preparation.

Chadha, J. S., Janssen, N. and Nolan, C. (2001). 'Productivity and Preferences in a Small Open Economy', *The Manchester School*, 69(1), 57–80

Chari, V. V. and Kehoe, P. (1999). 'Optimal Fiscal and Monetary Policy', in J. Taylor and M. Woodford (eds.), *Handbook of Macroeconomics*, Amsterdam: North-Holland

Christiano, L. J. and Fitzgerald, T. J. (2000). 'Understanding the Fiscal Theory of the Price Level', *Federal Reserve Bank of Cleveland Economic Review*, 36(2), 1–37

Christiano, L. J. and Gust, C. J. (1999). 'Taylor Rules in a Limited Participation Model', *De Economist*, 147(4), 437–60

Cochrane, J. (1998). 'A Frictionless View of US Inflation', in B. S. Bernanke and J. J. Rotemberg (eds.), *NBER Macroeconomics Annual*, Cambridge, MA: MIT Press, 323–84

(2001a). 'Long Term Debt and Optimal Policy in the Fiscal Theory of the Price Level', *Econometrica*, 69(1), 69–116

(2001b). 'Money as Stock', revised June 2001 (original August 1999), Chicago, mimeo

Dennis, R. (2001). 'Solving for Simple Rules in Rational Expectations Models', *Federal Reserve Bank of San Francisco Working Paper*, 00–14

Erceg, C., Henderson, D. and Levin A. (2000). 'Optimal Monetary Policy with Staggered Wage and Price Contracts', *Journal of Monetary Economics*, 46, 281–313

Evans, G. W. and Honkapohja, S. (2001). *Learning and Expectations in Macroeconomics*, Oxford: Oxford University Press and Princeton: Princeton University Press

Fatas, A. and Mihov, I. (1999). 'Government Size and Automatic Stabilisers: International and International Evidence', *CEPR Working Paper*, 2259

Fetter, F. W. (1965). *Development of British Monetary Orthodoxy, 1797–1875*, Cambridge: MA: Harvard University Press

Friedman, M. and Schwartz, A. J. (1963). *A Monetary History of the United States, 1867–1960*, Princeton: Princeton University Press

Gayer, A., Rostow, W. and Schwartz, A. (1953). *The Growth and Fluctuations of the British Economy*, Oxford: Clarendon Press

Hamilton, J. D. and Flavin, M. A. (1986). 'On the Limitations of Government Borrowing: A Framework for Empirical Testing', *American Economic Review*, 76(4), 808–19

Hansen, L. P. and Sargent, T. J. (1998). *Recursive Linear Models of Dynamic Economies*, Chicago: Chicago University Press

Janssen, N., Nolan, C. and Thomas, R. S. (2002). 'Money, Debt and Prices in the UK 1705–1996', *Economica*, 69(275), 461–79

Kocherlakota, N. and Phelan, C. (1999). 'Explaining the Fiscal Theory of the Price Level', *Federal Reserve Bank of Minneapolis Quarterly Review*, 23(4), 14–23

Leeper, E. (1991). 'Equilibria Under "Active" and "Passive" Monetary Policies', *Journal of Monetary Economics*, 27(1), 129–47

Leith, C. and Wren-Lewis, S. (2000). 'Interactions Between Monetary and Fiscal Policy Rules', *Economic Journal*, 110(462), C93–C108

Lucas, R. E., Jr. (1996). 'Nobel Lecture: Monetary Neutrality', *Journal of Political Economy*, 104(4), 661–82

McCallum, B. T. (1984). 'Are Bond-Financed Deficits Inflationary? A Ricardian Analysis', *Journal of Political Economy*, 91(1), 123–35

(2001). 'Indeterminacy, Bubbles and the Fiscal Theory of Price-Level Determination', *Journal of Monetary Economics*, 47(1), 19–30

(2003). 'The Fiscal Theory of the Price-Level is not Learnable', Carnegie–Mellon University, mimeo; forthcoming in the *Scottish Journal of Political Economy*

Mundell, R. A. (1971). 'The Dollar and the Policy Mix: 1971', *Essays in International Finance*, 85, International Finance Section, Princeton University

Obstfeld, M. and Rogoff, K. (1983). 'Speculative Hyperinflations in Maximizing Models: Can We Rule Them Out?', *Journal of Monetary Economics*, 91(4), 675–87

O'Connell, S. A. and Zeldes, S. P. (1988). 'Rational Ponzi Games', *International Economic Review*, 29, 431–50

Rudin, W. (1976). *Principles of Mathematical Analysis*, 3rd edn., New York: McGraw-Hill

Sargent, T. J. (1987). *Dynamic Macroeconomic Theory*, Cambridge, MA: Harvard University Press

Sargent, T. J. and Velde, F. R. (1995). 'Macroeconomic Features of the French Revolution', *Journal of Political Economy*, 103(3), 474–518

Sargent, T. J. and Wallace, N. (1975). ' "Rational Expectations", the Optimal Monetary Instrument, and the Optimal Money Supply Rule', *Journal of Political Economy*, 83(2), 241–54

(1981). 'Some Unpleasant Monetarist Arithmetic', *Federal Reserve Bank of Minneapolis Quarterly Review*, 5(3), 1–17

Schmitt-Grolé, S. and Urike, M. (2000). 'Price Level Determinary and Monetary Policy under a Balanced-Budget Requirement', *Journal of Monetary Economics*, 45(1), 211–46

Sidrauski, M. (1965). 'Rational Choice and Patterns of Growth in a Monetary Economy', *American Economic Review*, 57(2), 534–44

Sims, C. (1994). 'A Simple Model for the Study of the Price Level and the Interaction of Monetary and Fiscal Policy', *Economic Theory*, 4(3), 381–99

(1999). 'The Precarious Fiscal Foundations of EMU', *De Economist*, 147(4), 415–36

Taylor, J. B. (1993). 'Discretion versus Rules in Practice', *Carnegie–Rochester Conference Series on Public Policy*, 39, 195–214

(1999). *Monetary Policy Rules*, Chicago: University of Chicago Press for NBER

Walsh, C. (1998). *Monetary Theory and Policy*, Cambridge, MA: MIT Press

Williams, J. C. (1999). 'Simple Rules for Monetary Policy', Board of Governors of the Federal Reserve System, *Finance and Economics Discussion Paper*, 1999–12, Washington, DC

Woodford, M. (1995). 'Price Level Determinacy without Control of a Monetary Aggregate', *Carnegie–Rochester Conference Series on Public Policy*, 43, 1–46

(1997). 'Control of the Public Debt: A Requirement for Price Stability?', in G. A. Calvo, and M. A. King (eds.), *The Debt Burden and Monetary Policy*, London: Macmillan

(1998a). 'Public Debt and the Price Level', Princeton University, mimeo

(1998b). 'Comment on John Cochrane, "A Frictionless View of US Inflation"', in B. S. Bernanke and J. J. Rotemberg (eds.), *NBER Macroeconomics Annual*, Cambridge, MA: MIT Press, 400–28

(2000). 'A Neo-Wicksellian Framework for the Analysis of Monetary Policy', Princeton University, mimeo

(2001). 'Fiscal Requirements for Price Stability', *Journal of Money, Credit, and Banking*, 33(3), 669–728

Yaari, M. E. (1965). 'Uncertain Lifetime, Life Insurance, and the Theory of the Consumer', *Review of Economic Studies*, 32, 137–50

6

Dynamic general equilibrium analysis: the open economy dimension

Philip R. Lane and Giovanni Ganelli

1 INTRODUCTION

This chapter highlights some key topics in understanding the dynamic general equilibrium (DGE) behaviour of open economies. In line with the evolution of best practice in closed economy macroeconomic theory, DGE models are now the standard workhorse in the international macroeconomics literature. In addition, the incorporation of nominal rigidities and imperfect competition means that the current generation of open economy DGE models is also able to address the concerns of policy-makers regarding potential inefficiencies in adjusting to fundamental shocks. In this way, the 'new open economy macroeconomics' (NOEM) is a direct descendant of the traditional Mundell–Fleming–Dornbusch model (Rogoff 2001). While respecting this lineage, the microfounded nature of the new generation of models means that much more can be done in terms of providing a rigorous welfare evaluation of alternative policy regimes.

An open economy DGE model must contain a number of essential elements. Household preferences must be specified: this is more complex than in a closed economy model since the elasticity of substitution between home- and foreign-produced goods must be specified. This also applies to the specification of production functions since imported intermediate goods represent a potentially important linkage across economies. The international dimension of asset trade must also be specified, detailing whether home and foreign households share risks via state-contingent assets or just engage in bond trade or face even more restricted opportunities for international financial transactions.[1] Of course, the form of nominal rigidities must also be determined (sluggishness in goods prices versus wages; the duration of rigidities): in an open economy, the researcher

---

[1] See chapter 7 in this volume by Arellano and Mendoza for examples of these more restricted international financial transactions.

faces the problem of deciding the currency denomination of these sticky goods or factor prices. Finally, the nature of monetary and fiscal policies must be incorporated. Again, policy formation in an open economy involves extra dimensions in fixing the domestic policy response to foreign disturbances and evaluating whether there are gains to international policy coordination.

Lane (2001a) and Sarno (2001) provide broad surveys of this recent literature on 'sticky' DGE (NOEM) models that was initiated by the seminal 'Redux' model of Obstfeld and Rogoff (1995). Our strategy in this chapter is to focus on some key issues that are at the core of current research on open economy DGE modelling. In particular, we consider: the currency denomination of sticky prices; the role of the current account and net foreign assets in adjustment dynamics; and the analysis of fiscal policy in an open economy. As already noted, the first two topics raise issues that are by definition absent from closed economy analysis; we also highlight the third topic, since it has received comparatively less attention than monetary analysis in the recent literature but represents a critical channel by which policy-makers influence the behaviour of the international economy.

The structure of the rest of the chapter is as follows. Section 2 considers the currency denomination of sticky prices. The role of the current account and net foreign assets in the adjustment process is considered in section 3. We turn to the analysis of fiscal policy in NOEM models in section 4. Conclusions are offered in section 5.

2 THE CURRENCY DENOMINATION OF STICKY PRICES

2.1 Optimal exchange rate and monetary policies

Obstfeld and Rogoff (1995, 1996) assumed that prices were sticky in the currency denomination of the producer: US firms set prices in dollars, Japanese firms in yen and so on. Such producer currency pricing (PCP) implies an active expenditure-switching role for the nominal exchange rate: if the dollar depreciates, this implies a reduction in the Euro-currency price of US exports which in turn should raise demand for these goods from Eurozone purchasers.

Betts and Devereux (1996, 2000) and others have rather preferred an alternative specification under which firms set prices in the currency of the purchaser: such local currency pricing (LCP) of course requires that the firm is able to segment markets since prices to purchasers in different locations are potentially different under this scheme.[2] Under LCP, the exchange-rate does not have a direct allocative role: a surprise nominal depreciation does not alter the prices facing purchasers and so does not induce substitution between domestic and imported goods. Rather, exchange-rate movements just have income effects by altering the rate at which given foreign currency revenues convert into domestic currency and vice versa.

In general, this 'pass-through' debate concerns the elasticity

$$\frac{\partial p}{\partial e} = \lambda, \tag{6.1}$$

where p is the (log) domestic-currency purchase price, e is the (log) nominal exchange rate and λ is the elasticity. Full PCP and LCP correspond to $\lambda = 1$ and $\lambda = 0$ respectively, with intermediate values representing partial degrees of pass-through. As emphasised by Obstfeld (2001), p need not refer to a consumer price: intermediates comprise much of international trade. Moreover, it should be recognised that LCP is not the only source of a weak contemporaneous relation between exchange rates and consumer prices – as is surveyed by Engel (2002), shipping costs, non-traded distribution services and optimal price discrimination may also inhibit exchange rate pass-through.

The recent literature has paid much attention to the comparison of PCP and LCP (i.e. differences in degree of pass-through from exchange rates to the prices facing purchasers) in terms of its implications for optimal monetary and exchange-rate policies. Although the initial contributions in the NOEM field focused on certainty equivalence settings, the work that has followed Obstfeld and Rogoff (1998) has adopted an explicitly stochastic framework in evaluating policy regimes. This is important, since it highlights the role of uncertainty in determining the average levels of macroeconomic variables: risk averse agents will typically build in risk premia into wages and prices in response to an uncertain environment. In turn, this implies that uncertainty has first-order effects on welfare.[3]

Under PCP, the standard finding is that a floating exchange rate system is optimal in allowing economies to adjust to asymmetric real shocks for

---

[2] It is empirically well documented that deviations from the Law of One Price are widespread even for goods that are commonly traded in international markets (see, for example, Engel 1993; Froot and Rogoff 1995). Smets and Wouters (2002) find a significant amount of sticky import price behaviour in their empirical model of the Eurozone economy.

[3] Another literature – as laid out in Woodford (2002) – also emphasises the role of uncertainty in affecting welfare. In the Woodford approach, staggered pricing means that shocks lead to a dispersion in prices in the economy and variable production effort across firms, which is welfare-decreasing. Sutherland (2001a) shows that there are basic equivalences between the two approaches.

standard Friedmanite reasons (see Obstfeld and Rogoff 2001, 2002). Under LCP, the gains to floating in adjusting to shocks are reduced, since the exchange rate does not facilitate stabilisation in that case (Devereux and Engel 2001a).

Corsetti and Pesenti (2002a) make the point that LCP limits the desirability of exchange-rate flexibility, even if output could be perfectly stabilised under a float. The reason is that exchange-rate movements under LCP imply deviations from the law of one price. In turn, this increases the risk facing foreign exporters, who respond by incorporating a risk premium into prices that reduces the average real incomes of domestic households – in general, the optimal policy must trade off a larger output gap against lower import prices. However, Sutherland (2001a) shows that a flexible exchange rate may be desirable with even a low degree of pass-through if the elasticity of labour supply is low.[4] The reason is that exchange-rate volatility induces exporters to set high prices, which has the effect of improving the terms of trade.

Devereux and Lane (2001) provide a quantitative exploration for a small open economy. Their setup involves a competitive export sector that faces exogenously determined world prices and a monopolistic non-traded sector that displays Calvo-style nominal price stickiness. The consumption good is imported. Two scenarios for the degree of pass-through for import prices are considered: complete pass-through; and partial pass-through, set at the same degree of rigidity as shown by prices in the non-tradable sector. Shocks to world interest rates and the terms of trade are considered. The results of the numerical simulations are shown in table 6.1 for three monetary rules: the targeting of non-tradables inflation; CPI targeting; and an exchange rate peg.[5]

The findings in the upper panel of table 6.1 show that the first regime is easily dominant in the case of full pass-through. By allowing the nominal and real exchange rate to vary in response to shocks, targeting non-tradables' inflation achieves much lower volatility in output and investment, even if CPI inflation is less stable. For an open economy with full pass-through, targeting CPI inflation is much closer to a pegged regime, since exchange-rate movements must be suppressed in order to maintain a stable CPI. In contrast, the lower panel of table 6.1 shows that partial/delayed pass-through

---

[4] The other papers in this literature typically assume an infinitely elastic labour supply.

[5] See Devereux and Lane (2001) for details concerning the calibration of the model. This paper also considers the impact of financial frictions and liability dollarisation, as discussed on p. 313 below. Galí and Monacelli (2002) provide a related analysis but only for the case of complete pass-through and their model does not have a non-tradables sector. See also Smets and Wouters (2002).

Table 6.1 *Macroeconomic volatility and pass-through*[d]

	Output	Investment	RER	NER	Inflation
PT[a]					
NT	0.14	3.9	1.22	2.43	1.76
Pstab	0.99	6.29	0.45	0.51	0
Peg	1.11	6.65	0.34	0	0.3
DPT[b]					
NT[c]	0.1	1.74	2.66	2.88	0.25
Pstab[c]	0.4	3.42	1.69	0.71	0
Peg[c]	1.1	6.62	0.35	0	0.3

Notes: [a]PT is full pass-through case; [b]DPT is the partial/delayed pass-through case, [c]NT, Pstab and Peg refer to the policy rules of targeting non-tradables inflation, CPI inflation and fixing the exchange, respectively. [d]Standard deviations reported where shocks to terms of trade and world interest rate are jointly estimated from a VAR using Asian data.
Source: For more details, see Devereux and Lane (2001).

sharply improves the relative performance of the CPI targeting regime. With partial pass-through, a tight link between the nominal exchange rate and the CPI is broken, permitting exchange-rate adjustment without sacrificing overall price stability. In this case, the CPI rule is actually preferable to targeting non-tradables' inflation: although aggregate output and investment volatility are higher, CPI inflation is stabilised and the lower amount of exchange-rate volatility limits excessive reallocations between traded and non-traded sectors. Overall, the results in table 6.1 indicate that a low degree of pass-through may be a prerequisite for CPI inflation targeting to be a desirable monetary regime for a small open economy.

Another recent strand of the literature has focused on the currency denomination of asset contracts, instead of product prices. In particular, the effects of foreign-currency debt are considered. The typical finding is that such liability dollarisation reduces the net gain to exchange-rate flexibility: depreciation raises the real domestic value of foreign-currency debt and this tends to depress investment and production in models exhibiting financial constraints. Some authors have emphasised that this mechanism can give rise to multiple equilibria and crisis episodes: depreciation depresses investment, which in turn justifies depreciation (Aghion, Bacchetta and Banerjee 2001). Others have incorporated this channel into otherwise standard DGE models and found that it does not alter the usual ranking of alternative exchange-rate regimes: with pass-through, flexible exchange rates are still preferable despite the negative net worth effect (Cespedes, Chang and Velasco 2001; Devereux and Lane 2001; Gertler, Gilchrist and Natalucci 2001). However, Devereux and Lane (2002) show that a fixed exchange rate may be preferable if a trade financing constraint means that a fall in net worth raises the cost of imported intermediates – in this case, the combination of foreign-currency debt and depreciation directly depresses output by raising production costs.

Finally, Devereux and Engel (2002) show that LCP is helpful in reconciling high exchange-rate volatility with exchange-rate 'disconnect': the fact that volatile nominal exchange rates appear to have little impact on overall macroeconomic behaviour. In particular, Devereux and Engel (2002) achieve this result by combining LCP with other market imperfections: incomplete international financial markets; a particular structure of international distribution systems; and stochastic deviations from uncovered interest rate parity (UIP) that are driven by noise trader activity in financial markets. In related fashion, by eliminating offsetting expenditure responses, LCP raises the sensitivity of the exchange rate to disturbances. A further implication is that international consumption correlations are lowered (since real exchange-rate movements are larger), while international output correlations are raised (since the expanding country raises demand for imports from overseas).

2.2 Endogeneity of PCP versus LCP

The preceding discussion begs the question of the endogenous determination of the currency denomination of sticky prices. A DGE approach highlights that firms should take into account the covariance between exchange rates and the marginal utility of consumption of its household shareholders in setting prices. In contrast, the partial equilibrium literature typically assumes a risk neutral firm, which rules out consideration of such general equilibrium effects.

Devereux and Engel (2001b) study this problem in a general equilibrium setting in which money supplies are subject to random variability and households are risk averse.[6] These authors find that only relative monetary volatility matters under full risk-sharing: all firms will set prices in the most stable currency, in order to minimise uncertainty. If the home country has the more stable monetary regime, this means that home firms practice PCP but foreign firms follow LCP *vis-à-vis* home consumers, with foreign

---

[6] See also the numerical simulations in Bacchetta and van Wincoop (2001a).

consumers facing uncertain prices. If financial markets are incomplete, in contrast, a symmetric LCP equilibrium is feasible so long as absolute monetary variability is not too large in either country and the degree of risk aversion is not too low. However, a symmetric PCP equilibrium is feasible only in the knife-edge case when monetary variability is identical in the two countries.

Bacchetta and van Wincoop (2001b) provide an alternative approach and highlight that two key factors are the market share of home firms in the foreign market and the greater market power of individual firms.[7] If home firms have a high market share and the elasticity of intra-sectoral substitutability is low, then a PCP equilibrium is likely. This is reinforced by a strategic complementarity in price-setting: PCP is more attractive, the more other home firms also pursue this strategy.[8]

Corsetti and Pesenti (2002b) make a useful contribution to this debate. Rather than focusing on monetary uncertainty, they allow monetary policies to be optimally determined. In addition, firms are free to choose any degree of pass-through. They show that there are two equilibria. In one equilibrium, exchange rates float and firms select PCP strategies; in the other, the exchange rate is fixed and an LCP equilibrium is feasible. In this way, a currency union can be self-validating, since fixed exchange rates are an optimal monetary policy response to LCP strategies, given that exchange-rate shifts have no allocative role in that case. However, it is important to note that these equilibria are Pareto-rankable: the float/PCP equilibrium offers higher expected welfare compared to the fix/LCP alternative. The reason, of course, is that the former configuration allows the exchange rate to be a helpful adjustment mechanism in the face of asymmetric macroeconomic shocks.

Country size and, relatedly, the nature of the distribution process are also surely important. For instance, Devereux, Engel and Tille (1999) conjecture that the introduction of the Euro will make it more likely that imports into the Eurozone will be priced in Euro rather than in foreign currency. Since such a switch insulates the Eurozone price level from exchange rate volatility, the welfare of European consumers is enhanced. Moreover, under international risk-sharing, foreign agents also benefit through an associated increase in European asset prices.

---

[7] Devereux and Engel (2001a, 2001b) consider a unit elasticity of substitution between home and foreign goods.

[8] Bacchetta and van Wincoop (2001b) also have an interesting discussion on the implications of allowing for wage rigidity in addition to price rigidity.

Undoubtedly, much remains to be done in terms of understanding the currency denomination of prices. The highest priority is surely the acquisition of improved empirical evidence on the price-setting behaviour: in this regard, the formation of EMU provides a natural experiment. In related fashion, a better understanding of the determination of the currency denomination of debt contracts is also an important desideratum.[9]

3 THE CURRENT ACCOUNT AND NET FOREIGN ASSETS IN THE ADJUSTMENT PROCESS

A fundamental difference between a closed and open economy is that earned income and expenditure can diverge in the latter via access to international capital markets. With purchasing power parity (PPP), a full international risk-sharing equilibrium implies that domestic consumption depends only on global output, with full insulation from idiosyncratic domestic shocks. Of course, by the same token, this exposes domestic consumption to external disturbances that shift global output, even if domestic production is unchanged. As a modelling strategy, the assumption of complete international financial markets is attractive, since asymmetric shocks do not alter the international wealth distribution.[10]

Even if PPP does not hold (as under LCP, for instance), this assumption also provides an extremely simple relation between relative consumption and the real exchange rate

$$\left(\frac{C}{C^*}\right)^{-\rho} = \frac{P}{E\,P^*},\tag{6.2}$$

where ρ is the coefficient of relative risk aversion, P and P^* are the home and foreign consumer price levels, respectively, and E is the level of the nominal exchange rate. Here, we have assumed that complete insurance extends to nominal incomes: at an optimum, transferring a dollar between home and foreign agents cannot be a Pareto-improvement. Of course, however elegant, the tight link between the real exchange rate and relative consumption in (6.2) is profoundly rejected in the data (Ravn 2001).

---

[9] See Chamon (2001) for one recent contribution on this problem.

[10] Tille (2000) points out that moving from autarky to complete financial integration is not necessarily welfare-improving for all countries. Consider two countries with differing levels of domestic monetary volatility. Financial integration raises the volatility of the exchange rate and induces the high-volatility country to restrict production – on net, the low-volatility country may lose out via a decline in its terms of trade.

As is emphasised by Corsetti and Pesenti (2001, 2002a), another way to eliminate international wealth redistributions is to restrict consumption preferences in a particular way.[11] Suppose initial non-monetary wealth is zero and utility from consumption is given by

$$U = \sum_{s=t}^{s=\infty} \beta^{s-t} \left[\ln C_s\right] \qquad 0 < \beta < 1, \tag{6.3}$$

where C_s is an unitary-elasticity aggregate over home and foreign goods

$$C_s = C_{Hs}^{\gamma} C_{Fs}^{1-\gamma} \tag{6.4}$$

and the corresponding consumer price index is

$$P_s = \frac{1}{\gamma^{\gamma}(1-\gamma)^{1-\gamma}} P_{Hs}^{\gamma} P_{Fs}^{1-\gamma} \tag{6.5}$$

with the same preferences applying also to foreign households. Then, it can be shown that households just spend their income each period

$$P_s C_s = R_s, \tag{6.6}$$

where R_s is the revenue from sales to domestic and export markets. Under PCP, this result applies even for a non-unitary intertemporal elasticity of substitution: it is sufficient that the elasticity of intra-temporal substitution is one. The intuition is straightforward: current account imbalances will tend not to arise if there is limited substitutability between home and foreign products in consumption.

Although it promotes model tractability, ruling out current account and net foreign asset dynamics by either approach is quite limiting. The original 'Redux' model emphasised that a monetary shock could be non-neutral even in the long run, since it generates a short-run current account surplus and a corresponding long-run improvement in the net foreign asset position. In turn, this generates permanent wealth effects that alter the long-run patterns of consumption, work effort and the terms of trade.

The 'Redux' model adopted a certainty-equivalence framework and just considered a one-time unanticipated monetary shock. In a more general stochastic DGE setting, permanent changes in the net foreign asset position provide technical problems since solution techniques typically rely on the existence of a stationary steady state: a unit root in the net foreign asset

---

[11] See also Cole and Obstsfeld (1991), Obstfeld and Rogoff (1998), Svensson and van Wijnbergen (1989) and Tille (2001).

position is obviously inconsistent with model stationarity. However, it is not difficult to ensure stationarity and the speed of convergence can be set at any desired rate. For instance, Schmitt-Grohé and Uribe (2001) consider several alternatives: an endogenous discount factor; a debt-elastic interest rate premium; convex portfolio adjustment costs; and, of course, completeness of international asset markets.[12] Alternatively, Cavallo and Ghironi (2002) and Ghironi (2002) achieve stationarity by imposing an overlapping-generations (OLG) structure, although this imposes a lot of additional structure on the standard NOEM model.[13]

At an empirical level, net foreign asset positions tend to be quite persistent (Lane and Milesi-Ferretti 2000, 2002a), suggesting that current account innovations can be an important source of dynamics in open economy DGE models. Moreover, the net foreign asset position has an important influence on the long-run values of real exchange rates and potentially also real interest rate differentials and country risk premia (Lane and Milesi-Ferretti 2000, 2002a, 2002b).[14]

At an empirical level, there is evidence that the current account does respond to monetary shocks. Lane (2001b) studies a variety of identified VAR models for the US economy and finds that a monetary shock, after an initial lag, moves the current account into surplus. That said, as is also emphasised by earlier work in the RBC tradition, productivity and terms of trade shocks may represent more important sources of cyclical fluctuations in the current account (Cardia 1991; Mendoza 1991).

It is important to recognise that the long-run wealth effects induced by such cyclical current account shocks are likely to be quantitatively minor. For instance, for an infinitely lived household, a real interest rate of

---

[12] Benigno (2001) and Kollmann (2002) provide examples of employing a debt-elastic interest rate premium to ensure stationarity. Lane and Milesi-Ferretti (2002a) document some suggestive evidence in support of such a 'portfolio balance' effect: there is a positive correlation between the ratio of net external liabilities to exports and real interest rate differentials.

[13] These authors find very slow convergence back to the steady state. In part, this is because they follow Weil (1989) and assume households are infinitely lived but population growth means that new cohorts are born each period, rather than adopting the finite horizon formulation as in Blanchard (1985). Ghironi (2002) argues that slow convergence is attractive since univariate tests indicate that it is hard to reject non-stationarity of the net foreign asset position. However, a unit root in the net foreign asset position could be consistent with rapid adjustment to business cycle shocks if the stochastic trend is driven by other persistent factors (e.g. demographic variables). See also the discussion in the next paragraph.

[14] Lane and Milesi-Ferretti (2000, 2002b) emphasise the relative price of non-tradables as an important component of the real exchange rate that endogenously responds to the net foreign asset position. The real exchange rate effect obviously varies with country size. Lane and Milesi-Ferretti (2002a) document a strong inverse correlation between net foreign asset positions and real interest rate differentials.

4 per cent means that a 1 per cent of GDP improvement in the net foreign asset position implies only a relatively trivial 0.04 per cent increase in the long-run level of consumption.[15]

In contrast, significant net foreign asset positions may also be accumulated as the result of long-term trend differences in savings and investment behaviour rather than business cycle shocks. Lane and Milesi-Ferretti (2002a) show that relative income levels, public debt and demographic patterns are important for the evolution of net foreign asset positions. For business cycle analysis, these accumulated imbalances – regardless of their origin – may be important, since exchange-rate and asset price fluctuations then also operate via a revaluation channel on the value of foreign assets and liabilities. For instance, Benigno (2001) shows that the business cycle response to shocks is quantitatively quite different if the initial net foreign asset position is, say, 30–50 per cent of GDP rather than zero, as is assumed in most of the literature.

Moreover, the asymmetry created by non-zero net foreign asset positions (if the home country is a net debtor, the rest of the world by definition is a net creditor) also implies potentially large gains to international policy coordination. In this model, for zero initial net foreign asset positions, the first best can be well approximated by a policy of targeting domestic producer price inflation.[16] However, such a policy induces excessive volatility in interest rates and hence inefficient cross-country wealth redistributions if initial net foreign asset positions are non-zero and policy coordination in this case can substantially improve welfare. As Benigno (2001) puts it: 'A producer-price stability policy is a symmetric policy in an asymmetric world.'

Cavallo and Ghironi (2002) consider the impact of current account dynamics in a setting in which Central Banks follow Taylor-style interest rate rules of the form

$$i_{t+1} = \alpha_1 y_t + \alpha_2 \pi_t^{CPI} + \xi_t, \qquad (6.7)$$

where y_t and π_t^{CPI} are the deviation of output and CPI inflation from their steady-state (trend) values.[17] This particular monetary policy rule leads to some interesting dynamics. For instance, consider the impact of an accumulation of net foreign assets. Since this generates a positive wealth

---

[15] The increase in consumption will be somewhat higher if there is mean-reversion in the net foreign asset position, for instance if the model is set up to generate stationarity of the steady state.
[16] This is the optimal policy under complete financial integration. If initial net foreign asset positions are zero, it is also not far from the optimum with bond-only international asset trade.
[17] See also Lane (2002).

effect that leads to a reduction in work effort, domestic output falls even though domestic consumption is raised.

The Taylor rule in (6.7) instructs the Central Bank to reduce interest rates whenever it observes a fall in output below its steady-state value (regardless of its source): the positive accumulated net foreign asset position is thereby associated with a depreciation of the nominal exchange rate. Another implication of this rule is that there is a forecastable component to the nominal exchange rate: the accumulated net foreign asset position predictably influences the interest rate under (6.7), through the wealth effect on labour supply and thereby on the level of output.[18]

This example highlights the importance of carefully specifying the loss function for the Central Bank in an open economy. Obstfeld and Rogoff (1995) strongly emphasised that the behaviour of output is not a good welfare indicator in an open economy, since real income and output can diverge due to investment income flows and terms of trade movements and the value of leisure time needs also to be incorporated into an overall welfare evaluation. Since a monetary policy rule like (6.7) appears suboptimal from a normative perspective in an open economy, it would be interesting to also study optimising monetary policy strategies.[19] At an empirical level, it would be interesting to compare the fit of a welfare-maximising rule relative to the 'positive' rule embodied in (6.7).

It should be recognised that a significant net external liability position also leaves a country vulnerable to a financing crisis, which can in itself be a source of business cycle volatility. In turn, a sharp turnaround in the trade balance may require a large real depreciation, especially in the presence of nominal rigidities. Such 'sudden stops' in capital inflows have been a recurrent problem for emerging market economies in recent years but are also potentially relevant for major debtor nations such as the USA (Obstfeld and Rogoff 2000).

Integrating the macroeconomic impact of dramatic shifts in international financial market sentiment into the NOEM framework appears to be a useful direction for future research.[20] Of course, understanding the sources of these market swings is a primary concern in assessing the net gains to international financial integration. A related issue is that allowing non-fundamental financial market shocks (in conjunction with incomplete

---

[18] The strength of this mechanism is the larger, the higher the degree of substitutability between domestic and foreign goods in consumption. This model maintains the PCP assumption.

[19] Examining the behaviour of such rules for the flexible-price case also seems to be a digression, since such monetary policy rules only make sense if there is some degree of nominal rigidity.

[20] Cook and Devereux (2001) provide an interesting application of such a model to the Asian crisis.

risk-sharing) can help improve the empirical performance of NOEM models. For instance, Devereux and Engel (2002) and Kollmann (2002) both allow for stochastic deviations from UIP in their calibration models and find that it is helpful in improving the fit to the data.[21]

Finally, a complete treatment of the net foreign asset position requires the introduction of capital accumulation into the model: investment dynamics are central to understanding current account behaviour. In this regard, Betts and Devereux (1999), Chari, Kehoe and McGrattan (1998) and Kollmann (2001) provide interesting numerical analyses of the impact of introducing capital into NOEM models. It would be desirable to also allow for international trade in equities in addition to trade in bonds, especially if the objective is to capture the unusual behaviour of the US net foreign asset position since the mid-1990s (Ventura 2001). In related fashion, reintroducing portfolio balance considerations in modelling current account dynamics may add an interesting dimension to the role played by the net foreign asset position as a key state variable in NOEM models.

4 FISCAL POLICY IN NOEM MODELS

In this section we survey how NOEM models have been used to analyse fiscal issues. Despite the fact that this framework is equipped to study the effects of fiscal shocks, relatively few authors focus on them. We start by illustrating how government spending can be introduced into the 'Redux' model, and we subsequently look at the effects of fiscal shocks in variants of the basic model that incorporate various features such as LCP strategies; financial frictions; perfect risk-sharing; home bias; non-separability between private and public consumption; fixed exchange rates; and deviations from Ricardian Equivalence.

4.1 Government spending in the 'Redux' model

Government spending is introduced in the basic 'Redux' model by Obstfeld and Rogoff (1995) in the form of a composite of public consumption that aggregates across the differentiated goods produced by the individual agents in the same way as for private consumption, with the same elasticity of

---

[21] Kollmann (2002) studies a small open economy. He argues that shocks to UIP actually improve welfare, since the country will hold higher net foreign assets in response and hence enjoy a greater mean level of consumption.

substitution. Accordingly, domestic government spending is given by

$$G = \left[\int_0^1 g(z)^{\frac{\theta-1}{\theta}} \, dz \right]^{\frac{\theta}{\theta-1}}, \tag{6.8}$$

where $[0, 1]$ is the continuum of goods produced in the domestic and foreign countries and θ is the elasticity of substitution between varieties. Formula (6.8) also illustrates the absence of home bias in government spending in the 'Redux' model. In this framework world government spending G_t^w enters as an exogenous shock to the demand schedule faced by every agent for its product

$$y_t^d(z) = \left[\frac{p_t(z)}{P_t} \right]^{-\theta} \left(C_t^w + G_t^w \right), \tag{6.9}$$

where $[p_t(z)/P_t]$ is its relative price and C_t^w and G_t^w are global private and government consumption spending, respectively. In the 'Redux' model, a permanent balanced-budget increase in home government spending reduces short-run relative consumption and depreciates the exchange rate. The intuition for this result is that, with no home bias in government spending, such a policy increases the demand for both domestic and foreign goods, while the tax bill falls only on domestic residents. This implies a negative wealth effect for home agents, who react by reducing their consumption relative to foreigners. Because money demand is a positive function of consumption, the fall in relative consumption brings about a depreciation of the domestic currency.

A domestic balanced-budget increase in government spending also raises output in the home country and lowers it abroad. The positive effect on domestic output is consistent with results previously derived in the RBC tradition.[22] Under flexible prices, this can be explained by the fact that an increase in taxes reduces wealth, inducing agents to reduce their consumption of leisure and increase labour supply. In contrast, under sticky prices, output is demand-determined and so its positive response cannot be explained by supply-side factors. An intuition for the increase in domestic output can rather be found in the expenditure-switching effect that follows the depreciation of the domestic currency which raises demand for domestic goods.[23] Since both leisure and consumption provide utility in

---

[22] For example, Baxter and King (1993).

[23] By the same token, we can explain the decrease in foreign output following a domestic expansion. Since the domestic effect is stronger in absolute value, world output increases.

this framework, the above analysis suggests that a domestic fiscal expansion has *beggar-thyself* and *prosper-thy-neighbour* welfare implications.

The effects of permanent fiscal expansions on the current account and on the real interest rate are in stark contrast with the implications of flexible-price, representative agent models. If $\theta + 1$ is bigger than the elasticity of intertemporal substitution of real balances ϵ, the home country runs a current account surplus following a domestic expansion.[24] This is due to the fact that, unlike in flexible-price models, the presence of sticky prices means that an unanticipated permanent increase in government spending can tilt the time profile of output, thereby inducing current account effects.

A permanent fiscal policy shock reduces the short-run real interest rate.[25] The intuition is that the effect on output is larger in the short run than in the long run on account of the temporary nominal rigidity. This implies a declining path of output available for private consumption. It follows that a decrease in the short-run real interest rate is required, in order to make the individual optimal consumption smoothing consistent with this dynamics.

While all the effects discussed above refer to an increase in government spending that is financed with lump-sum taxes, Obstfeld and Rogoff (1995) also consider the case of an income tax. When distortionary taxation is introduced, initial steady-state output is lower than in the case in which the only distortion is imperfect competition. It follows that both countries potentially gain more from an unanticipated increase in world demand than in the case of lump-sum taxes. In the case of a monetary shock, the overall benefit is redistributed towards the depreciating country, that can reduce the distortion due to income taxes at foreign expense.

A feature of the 'Redux' model, as it is clear from (6.9), is a constant elasticity of demand, that implies a fixed markup of prices on marginal costs. While enhancing tractability, this rules out some interesting possibilities. Rotemberg and Woodford (1992), for example, show that allowing for intra-industry strategic collusion can generate a counter-cyclical markup following an unexpected fiscal shock. Dixon and Rankin (1994) and Galí (1994) make the point that changing the public–private spending mix also

---

[24] Note that this condition is always satisfied in the particular case of logarithmic preferences, in which $\epsilon = 1$. This follows from the fact that the elasticity of substitution between goods θ must be bigger than unity in order to have well-defined demand functions. Note that the consumption elasticity of money demand in the model is given by $1/\varepsilon$.

[25] This is a novelty compared to the flexible-price textbook result of no effect on the interest rate (Barro 1993).

alters the elasticity of total demand if the elasticity of public spending is different from that of private spending.[26] In this way, endogenising the degree of imperfect competition could improve our understanding of the effects of fiscal policy. The subsequent literature that has built on the 'Redux' model has also highlighted some other limitations of the basic framework, as well as its flexibility in terms of introducing more realistic assumptions. In what follows, we illustrate how researchers have attempted to deal with some of these issues in relation to fiscal policy.

4.2 Fiscal policy: PCP versus LCP

As was discussed in section 6.2, a feature of the 'Redux' model that has been deemed as unrealistic is the PCP assumption that requires the Law of One Price (LOOP) and PPP to always hold. Most of the contributions that deal with fiscal policy, however, use the PCP approach. This modelling choice can probably be considered less problematic when dealing with fiscal shocks than when dealing with monetary ones, in light of the results illustrated in Betts and Devereux (1999). Using calibration experiments, these authors show that deviations from the LOOP, although crucial in affecting the transmission mechanism of monetary shocks, are relatively unimportant for the case of fiscal shocks.[27] The interdependence pattern following a tax-financed increase in government spending is essentially the same as in the 'Redux' model regardless of the denomination of sticky prices.

A noteworthy exception is that with LCP the nominal exchange rate slightly overshoots in the short run. This difference with the 'Redux' result of no overshooting is due to the fact that with LCP the foreign price level does not move immediately and the rise in the price level is smaller than in the PCP case. This in turn implies that the reduction in relative consumption is slightly reduced and hence an overshooting of the exchange rate is required to clear the money market.

Senay (1998) analyses the impact of fiscal policy in a LCP framework that also incorporates financial frictions. Senay confirms, in a LCP framework, that financial integration reduces the volatility of consumption, output and the nominal exchange rate following an asymmetric fiscal shock.[28]

---

[26] In empirical work, Lombardo (2001) finds a negative relationship between the government share and the markup.

[27] On the other hand, the asset market structure is very important in the fiscal case (see p. 324 below), and irrelevant in the monetary one.

[28] The same result is found by Sutherland (1996).

However, she finds that the way in which financial integration operates does not significantly depend on the degree of LCP in the economy.

4.3 Fiscal policy and perfect risk-sharing

Betts and Devereux (1999) also show that the asset market structure is crucial in affecting the results following a fiscal shock. When asset markets are complete, the wealth effects of financing the increased government spending are shared equally by the two countries. Domestic and foreign variables therefore react in the same way. Both home and foreign output increase, while consumption falls, and there are no exchange rate and current account effects.

In the 'Redux' model, the degree of monopolistic competition and the elasticity of substitution between home and foreign goods is equal. As was discussed in section 6.2, Corsetti and Pesenti (2001) develop a model that sets a unitary elasticity of substitution between home and foreign goods. Under PCP, this formulation provides the same kind of risk-sharing implied by complete markets for the case of fiscal shocks. The fiscal results of these authors, however, differ from those of Betts and Devereux (1999), since they introduce complete home bias in government spending. When a domestic fiscal shock stimulates the demand for home goods only, foreign output, the nominal exchange rate, home and foreign consumption are unaffected in the short run, while home output increases on a one-to-one basis.[29]

It follows that the welfare spillover of a fiscal expansion is determined solely by the long-run effects. A foreign increase in government spending affects the home economy through two channels. The first channel is a depreciation of the domestic real exchange rate, that reduces the domestic PPP and consumption. The welfare spillover of this channel is unambiguously negative. Since a fiscal expansion in the foreign country reduces the amount of foreign goods available to world consumers, the world demand for domestic goods increases if domestic and foreign goods are substitutes, and decreases if they are complements. The sign of the welfare spillover is negative when the two national goods are substitutes, because domestic production increases and domestic leisure falls. Corsetti and Pesenti (2001)

---

[29] This property, which can be labelled 'quasi-neutrality', is common in models with home bias in government spending (an early example is Rankin 1990). Ganelli (2000) argues that introducing home bias in government spending in the 'Redux' model generates 'quasi-neutrality' of fiscal shocks. Warnock (1998) introduces home bias in the 'Redux' model in the form of idiosyncratic preferences, rather than in the composition of spending, finding that a higher degree of home bias increases the depreciation of the domestic currency and therefore increases the probability that the home country runs a surplus following a domestic fiscal expansion.

conclude that the negative channel prevails for a wide range of parameters. In their model therefore, unlike in the 'Redux' one, fiscal spillovers are likely to be *beggar-thy-neighbour*.

A feature of the way Corsetti and Pesenti (2001) specify preferences is that solutions can be derived in closed form, without resorting to linearisation. Their model is therefore well equipped to carry out a choice-theoretic analysis of policy coordination. In particular, they analyse the interplay between monetary and fiscal policy links, by deriving the optimal monetary policy as a function of the parameters of the model and of the other (domestic and foreign) policy variables. Since a home fiscal expansion increases domestic output in the short run, bringing the domestic economy closer to potential output at unchanged terms of trade, the optimal monetary response is a contraction of domestic money supply. As noted above, domestic fiscal shocks have no impact on the foreign economy in the short run. The foreign authorities therefore do not need to react directly to such a policy, but they will implement the optimal response to any monetary contraction of the home country caused by a domestic fiscal shock.

4.4 Useful government spending

Ganelli (2000) introduces utility-enhancing government spending in the 'Redux' model, by modelling private and public consumption as substitutes in private utility. The representative agent therefore maximises the following utility function:

$$U_t^j = \sum_{s=t}^{\infty} \beta^{s-t} \left[\log(C_s^j + \gamma G_s) + \chi \log \frac{M_s^j}{P_s} - \frac{\kappa}{2} Y_s(j)^2 \right], \quad (6.10)$$

where γ is the marginal rate of substitution between private and public consumption, M_s^j / P_s is the level of real balances and $Y_s(j)$ is the level of work effort. This formulation implies a direct crowding-out effect of government spending on private consumption, that tends to have a negative effect on the domestic and international consumption multipliers, in both the short and the long run.

Ganelli (2000) also shows that introducing utility-enhancing government spending increases home welfare, following a domestic expansion, compared to the 'Redux' benchmark. This follows from the fact that the direct increase in utility caused by such an expansion more than offsets the negative welfare effect arising from the reduction in consumption due to direct crowding-out. The differential effect of introducing $\gamma > 0$ therefore moderates the *beggar-thyself* nature of fiscal policy highlighted by Obstfeld and Rogoff (1995).

4.5 Fiscal policy under fixed exchange rates

Caselli (2001) develops a fixed-exchange-rate version of the 'Redux' model. Her main interest is to evaluate the welfare effects of fiscal contractions under two alternative global monetary arrangements. In the first regime, the foreign country pursues its own monetary policy aimed at long-run price stability, and the home country is unilaterally responsible for pegging the exchange rate. In the second regime, the home and foreign countries cooperate to maintain fixed exchange rates at unchanged world money supply. Caselli (2001) interprets the first regime as a proxy of the situation faced by several EU countries that carried out fiscal contractions in the 1980s and 1990s, while pegging their currencies to the Deutsche Mark.

Symmetrically to what happens in the 'Redux' model following a fiscal expansion, a home contraction in public spending in this framework increases private relative consumption, therefore increasing home money demand. Unlike in the 'Redux' model, with fixed exchange rates the equilibrium cannot be restored by a nominal appreciation. An implication is that, contrary to the conventional wisdom dictated by the Mundell–Fleming approach, monetary policy under unilateral pegging has to become more expansionary in order to stabilise the exchange rate in the face of a fiscal contraction.

Caselli (2001) also tests empirically some implications of the model using EU data. A panel regression shows that, in line with the theoretical analysis, the differential (home minus foreign) in private consumption growth rates is negatively affected by a domestic expansionary fiscal policy and positively affected by a foreign expansion.

4.6 Macroeconomic effects of government debt

A common feature of all the policy experiments considered so far is that they are balanced budget expansions or contractions. This follows from the fact that, with infinitely lived agents, Ricardian Equivalence holds and there is no role for government debt. Ganelli (2002) departs from Ricardian Equivalence by introducing overlapping generations of the Blanchard type (1985) in a NOEM framework. This enables a non-trivial analysis of the real effects of government debt.

In this framework, each agent faces in every period a constant probability of death $1 - q$. Unlike in the infinitely lived models previously described, it is here necessary to differentiate agents by age. The representative domestic agent of age a at time t therefore maximises the expected utility function:

$$E(U_t) = \sum_{s=t}^{\infty} (\beta q)^{s-t} \left[\log(C_{a+s-t,s}) + \chi \log \frac{M_{a+s-t,s}}{P_s} \right.$$
$$\left. + \psi \log(1 - L_{a+s-t,s}) \right], \tag{6.11}$$

where q is the probability of surviving to next period. $C_{a+s-t,s}$ denotes consumption of an agent of age $a + s - t$ at time s, and an analogous notation holds for the other variables. L denotes the amount of labour supplied in a perfectly competitive labour market.[30] Since the endowment of time in each period is normalised to 1, $1 - L$ denotes leisure. It is possible to derive *per capita* macroeconomic variables, by solving the optimisation problem of the representative agent, aggregating across ages and dividing by the size of the population. Ganelli (2002) evaluates the short-run and long-run effects on *per capita* macroeconomic variables of a debt-financed temporary reduction in taxes, with long-run taxes increasing endogenously to meet the increased interest payment.

If such a policy is carried out by the domestic country, short-run relative (domestic minus foreign) consumption increases. This is achieved by means of an increase in the domestic level of consumption, while the effect on foreign consumption is ambiguous but likely to be positive as well. The fact that relative and absolute home consumption increase following a domestic fiscal shock illustrates the existence of a wealth effect that is not at work in the Ricardian models previously considered. Because of the deviation from Ricardian Equivalence, home agents are aware of the fact that there is a positive probability that they will not be alive next period, and therefore they will not have to pay the future tax bill implied by the increase in debt. This explains why short-run domestic consumption increases. The latter result is consistent with some recent empirical evidence regarding the effects of fiscal policy.[31]

---

[30] The departure from the yeoman-farmer model used in the 'Redux,' where agents are both consumers and producers, is necessary to make aggregation across ages possible.

[31] Fatás and Mihov (2001), using a VAR approach to study the effects of fiscal policy shocks in the USA, stress the contrast between the positive effect on consumption that is in the data and the negative impact in their standard RBC theoretical model. They conclude that one important item in the agenda of research on fiscal policy is to develop theoretical models that bring theory closer to reality.

The fact that short-run relative consumption increases implies an appreciation of the exchange rate and a decrease in relative output. The short-run international output spillover is unambiguously positive. In contrast to the 'Redux' model, introducing deviations from Ricardian Equivalence can thereby make the NOEM paradigm more consistent with the predictions of the traditional Mundell–Fleming–Dornbusch framework.

The long-run movements of output and consumption depend on the effect on net foreign assets. Ganelli (2002) shows that net foreign assets are a positive function of the short-run nominal exchange rate and a negative function of short-run relative consumption.[32] It follows that net foreign assets unambiguously decrease following a temporary debt-financed tax cut. Since there is an inverse steady-state relation between net foreign assets and the trade balance, long-run relative consumption and leisure must fall to offset the reduction in net foreign assets.

This discussion illustrates that it is clearly possible to attribute real macroeconomic effects to government debt policies once the NOEM framework is suitably adapted to allow for deviations from Ricardian Equivalence. The analysis of Evans (1991) does suggest that the impact of simply moving from the representative-agent infinite horizon case is quantitatively limited. However, Faruqee and Laxton (2000) show that the public debt can have larger effects if combined with non-flat age–earnings profiles and a low intertemporal elasticity of substitution. At an empirical level, Lane and Milesi-Ferretti (2002a) document that the level of government debt is an important driver of the net foreign asset position for both industrial and developing countries. The magnitude of the elasticity is larger for the latter group, which is in line with the view that departures from Ricardian Equivalence are likely to be larger for developing countries that are characterised by more severe financial constraints on household and corporate borrowing.

4.7 Fiscal policy: other dimensions

One direction for future research is to incorporate the stylised fact that a substantial proportion of government spending is used not for public consumption of privately produced goods but rather to pay for employment in the public sector. None of the models that we have surveyed incorporates this feature. Finn (1998), using a flexible-price RBC model, shows

---

[32] The net foreign asset position is also a negative function of relative government spending, that is kept constant in the policy under consideration.

how failing to distinguish between these two different subaggregates of government expenditure can lead to overestimation of the government's impact on the economic cycle. Lane and Perotti (2001) in a reduced form sticky-wage sticky-price model show how the composition of government spending interacts with the exchange-rate regime and empirically matters for macroeconomic outcomes. Incorporating this distinction into a micro-founded NOEM model could provide a better understanding of the role of fiscal policy. In addition, embedding the concerns of the 'fiscal theory of the price level'[33] literature into a NOEM setting may also be a useful direction for new theoretical work.

Since the econometric analysis of fiscal policy is still in its infancy, it is also obvious that more empirical work aimed at testing the fiscal implications of these models would be welcome. Here, extending the recent techniques of Blanchard and Perotti (2001) and Fatás and Mihov (2001) to an open economy setting would be a welcome innovation: it would be extremely helpful to have evidence concerning the impact of fiscal policy on the exchange rate, the current account and interest rate differentials. As is illustrated by Favero (2002), it is also important to study the joint impact of monetary and fiscal policies by allowing for interdependencies between the two instruments of macroeconomic policy management.

5 CONCLUSIONS

This chapter has discussed some key elements in DGE analysis of open economies and, along the way, has also signalled key issues to be addressed by future researchers.[34] One contribution of the NOEM literature has been to highlight the wide range of possible choices that exist in the specification of microfounded international DGE models: the fixed assumptions in the Mundell–Fleming–Dornbusch model concerning the relation between exchange rates and prices and the role played by the current account have been challenged, with myriad alternatives being offered. In terms of modelling strategy, we have emphasised that the choices required to obtain closed form solutions may be potentially misleading in terms of identifying quantitatively relevant specifications.

Regarding the current state of the literature, there are encouraging signs that new technical progress is being made. In particular, developing

---

[33] See chapter 5 in this volume by Chadha and Nolan which discusses the fiscal theory of the price level and the interaction of monetary and fiscal policy, in a closed economy setting.

[34] For reasons of space, this chapter has comparatively neglected the use of NOEM models for the analysis of international policy coordination issues. This is an exciting current branch of the literature: Bergin (2002) provides an accessible introduction.

second-order solutions to DGE models promises to be very helpful in improving welfare evaluation and the analysis of international policy coordination issues in open economy DGE models (Kollmann 2002; Sutherland 2001b). In addition, more research on fiscal policy would counterbalance the predominance allocated to the analysis of monetary shocks in the literature to date.

Empirical implementation of the NOEM paradigm is also getting started. Bergin (2003) and Ghironi (1999) provide interesting systems-based estimation and tests. From another angle, Smets and Wouters (2002) represents an innovative attempt to calibrate a NOEM model for the Eurozone, in part deriving parameter values from an estimated VAR for the Eurozone economy. In addition to such macroeconometric studies, more microeconomic evidence on international price-setting and international financial trade is highly desirable.

BIBLIOGRAPHY

Aghion, P., Bacchetta, P. and Banerjee, A. (2001). 'Currency Crises and Monetary Policy in an Economy with Credit Constraints', *European Economic Review*, 47, 1121–50

Bacchetta, P. and van Wincoop, E. (2001a). 'A Theory of the Currency Denomination of International Trade', University of Virginia, mimeo

(2001b). 'Trade Flows, Prices and the Exchange Rate Regime', University of Virginia, mimeo

Barro, R. J. (1993). *Macroeconomics*, 4th edn., New York: Wiley

Baxter M. and King, R. (1993). 'Fiscal Policy in General Equilibrium', *American Economic Review*, 83, 315–34

Benigno, P. (2001). 'Price Stability and Imperfect Financial Integration', New York University, mimeo

Bergin, P. (2002). 'Is There a Role for International Policy Coordination?', *Federal Reserve Bank of San Francisco Economic Letter*, 2002–03

(2003). 'Putting the New Open Economy Macroeconomics to a Test', *Journal of International Economics*, 60(1), 3–34

Betts, C. and Devereux, M. (1996). 'The Exchange Rate in a Model of Pricing to Market', *European Economic Review*, 40, 1007–21

(1999). 'The International Effects of Monetary and Fiscal Policy in a Two-Country Model', University of British Columbia, mimeo

(2000). 'Exchange Rate Dynamics in a Model of Pricing-to-Market', *Journal of International Economics*, 50, 215–44

Blanchard, O. J. (1985). 'Debt, Deficits and Finite Horizons', *Journal of Political Economy*, 93, 223–47

Blanchard, O. J. and Perotti, R. (2001). 'An Empirical Characterization of the Dynamic Effects of Changes in Government Spending and Taxes on Output', MIT, mimeo

Cardia, E. (1991). 'The Dynamics of a Small Open Economy in Response to Monetary, Fiscal, and Productivity Shocks', *Journal of Monetary Economics*, 28, 411–34

Caselli, P. (2001). 'Fiscal Consolidation under Fixed Exchange Rates', *European Economic Review*, 45, 425–50

Cavallo, M. and Ghironi, F. (2002). 'Net Foreign Assets and the Exchange Rate: Redux Revived', *Journal of Monetary Economics*, 49(5), 1057–97

Cespedes, L., Chang, R. and Velasco, A. (2001). 'Balance Sheets and Exchange Rate Policy', Harvard University, mimeo

Chamon, M. (2001). 'Why Don't we Observe Foreign Lending to Developing Countries in their Currency, Even When Indexation to Inflation is Available?', Harvard University, mimeo

Chari, V. V., Kehoe, P. and McGrattan, E. (1998). 'Can Sticky Price Models Generate Volatile and Persistent Real Exchange Rates?', *Federal Reserve Bank of Minneapolis Staff Report*, 223

Cole, H. and Obstfeld, M. (1991). 'Commodity Trade and International Risk Sharing: How Much do Financial Markets Matter?', *Journal of Monetary Economics*, 28, 3–24

Cook, D. and Devereux, M. (2001). 'The Macroeconomic Effects of International Financial Panics', University of British Columbia, mimeo

Corsetti, G. and Pesenti, P. (2001). 'Welfare and Macroeconomic Interdependence', *Quarterly Journal of Economics*, 116(2), 421–45

(2002a). 'International Dimensions of Optimal Monetary Policy', University of Rome, III, mimeo

(2002b). 'Self-Validating Optimum Currency Areas', *NBER Working Paper*, 8783

Devereux, M. and Engel, C. (2001a). 'Monetary Policy in the Open Economy Revisited: Exchange Rate Flexibility and Price Setting Behavior', University of British Columbia, mimeo

(2001b). 'Endogenous Currency of Price Setting in a Dynamic Open Economy Model', *NBER Working Paper*, 8559

(2002). 'Exchange Rate Pass Through, Exchange Rate Volatility and Exchange Rate Disconnect', *Journal of Monetary Economics*, forthcoming

Devereux, M. and P. R. Lane (2001). 'Exchange Rates and Monetary Policy in Emerging Market Economies', *CEPR Discussion Paper*, 2874

(2002). 'Understanding Bilateral Exchange Rate Volatility', *CEPR Discussion Paper*, 3518

Devereux, M., Engel, C. and Tille, C. (1999). 'Exchange Rate Pass-Through and the Welfare Effects of the Euro', *NBER Working Paper*, 7382

Dixon, H. and Rankin, N. (1994). 'Imperfect Competition and Macroeconomics: A Survey', *Oxford Economics Papers*, 46, 171–99

Engel, C. (1993). 'Real Exchange Rates and Relative Prices: An Empirical Investigation', *Journal of Monetary Economics*, 32, 35–50

(2002). 'The Responsiveness of Consumer Prices to Exchange Rates and the Implications for Exchange-Rate Policy: A Survey of a Few Recent New Open-Economy Macro Models', *NBER Working Paper*, 8725

Evans, P. (1991). 'Is Ricardian Equivalence a Good Approximation?', *Economic Inquiry*, 29, 626–44

Faruqee, H. and Laxton, D. (2000). 'Life Cycles, Dynasties, and Saving: Implications for Closed and Small Open Economies', *IMF Working Paper*, WP/00/126

Fatás, A. and Mihov, I. (2001). 'The Effects of Fiscal Policy on Consumption and Employment: Theory and Evidence', INSEAD, mimeo

Favero, C. (2002). 'How Do European Monetary and Fiscal Authorities Behave?', Bocconi University, mimeo

Finn, M. G. (1998). 'Cyclical Effects of Government's Employment and Goods Purchases', *International Economic Review*, 39, 635–57

Froot, K. A. and Rogoff, K. (1995). 'Perspectives on PPP and Long-Run Real Exchange Rates', in G. M. Grossman and K. Rogoff (eds.), *Handbook of International Economics*, 3, Amsterdam: North-Holland, 1647–88

Galí, J. (1994). 'Monopolistic Competition, Business Cycles and the Composition of Aggregate Demand', *Journal of Economic Theory*, 63, 73–96

Galí, J. and Monacelli, T. (2002). 'Monetary Policy and Exchange Rate Volatility in a Small Open Economy', Universitat Pompeu Fabra, mimeo

Ganelli, G. (2000). 'Useful Government Spending, Direct Crowding-Out and Fiscal Policy Interdependence', *Warwick Working Paper* in Economics, 547, forthcoming in *Journal of International Money and Finance*

(2002). 'The New Open Economy Macroeconomics of Government Debt', Trinity College Dublin, mimeo

Gertler, M., Gilchrist, S., and Natalucci, F. (2001). 'External Constraints on Monetary Policy and the Financial Accelerator', New York University, mimeo

Ghironi, F. (1999). 'Towards New Open Economy Macroeconometrics', Boston College, mimeo

(2002). 'Macroeconomic Interdependence Under Incomplete Markets', Boston College, mimeo

Kollmann, R. (2001). 'The Exchange Rate in a Dynamic-Optimizing Business Cycle Model with Nominal Rigidities', *Journal of International Economics*, 55, 243–62

(2002). 'Monetary Policy Rules in the Open Economy: Effects on Welfare and Business Cycles', *CEPR Discussion Paper*, 3279

Lane, P. R. (2001a). 'The New Open Economy Macroeconomics: A Survey', *Journal of International Economics*, 54, 235–66

(2001b). 'Money Shocks and the Current Account', in G. Calvo, R. Dornbusch and M. Obstfeld (eds.), *Money, Factor Mobility and Trade: Essays in Honour of Robert Mundell*, Cambridge, MA: MIT Press, 385–412

(2002). 'Comment on *Net Foreign Assets and the Exchange Rate: Redux Revived*', *Journal of Monetary Economics*, 49(5), 877–1102

Lane, P. R. and Milesi-Ferretti, G. M. (2000). 'The Transfer Problem Revisited: Real Exchange Rates and Net Foreign Assets', *CEPR Discussion Paper*, 2511

(2002a). 'Long-Term Capital Movements', *NBER Macroeconomics Annual*, 16

(2002b). 'External Wealth, the Trade Balance and the Real Exchange Rate', *European Economic Review*, forthcoming

Lane, P. R. and Perotti, R. (2001). 'The Importance of Composition of Fiscal Policy: Evidence from Different Exchange Rate Regimes', *Journal of Public Economics*, forthcoming

Lombardo, G. (2001). 'Sticky Prices, Markups and the Business Cycle: Some Evidence', Deutsche Bundesbank, mimeo

Mendoza, E. (1991). 'Real Business Cycles in a Small Open Economy', *American Economic Review*, 81, 797–818

Obstfeld, M. (2001). 'International Macroeconomics: Beyond the Mundell–Fleming Model', *International Monetary Fund Staff Papers*, 47S, 1–39

Obstfeld, M. and Rogoff, K. (1995). 'Exchange Rate Dynamics Redux', *Journal of Political Economy*, 103, 624–60

(1996). *Foundations of International Macroeconomics*, Cambridge, MA: MIT Press

(1998). 'Risk and Exchange Rates', *NBER Working Paper*, 6694

(2000). 'Perspectives on OECD Economic Integration: Implications for US Current Account Adjustment', in *Global Economic Integration: Opportunities and Challenges*, Federal Reserve Bank of Kansas City

(2001). 'New Directions for Stochastic Open Economy Models', *Journal of International Economics*, 50, 117–53

(2002). 'Global Implications of Self-Oriented National Monetary Rules', *Quarterly Journal of Economics*, 117(2), 503–35

Rankin, N. (1990). 'Macroeconomic Interdependence, Floating Exchange Rates, and Product Substitutability', in A. S. Courakis and M. P. Taylor (eds.), *Private Behaviour and Government Policy in Interdependent Economies*, Oxford: Oxford University Press

Ravn, M. (2001). 'Consumption Dynamics and Real Exchange Rates', *CEPR Discussion Paper*, 2940

Rogoff, K. (2002). 'Dornbusch's Overshooting Model After Twenty-Five Years', *International Monetary Fund Working Paper*, 02/39

Rotemberg, J. and Woodford, M. (1992). 'Oligopolistic Pricing and the Effects of Aggregate Demand on Economic Activity', *Journal of Political Economy*, 100, 1153–1207

Sarno, L. (2001). 'Toward a New Paradigm in Open Economy Modeling: Where Do We Stand?', *Federal Reserve Bank of St Louis Review*, 83(3), 21–36

Schmitt-Grohé, S. and Uribe, M. (2001). 'Closing Small Open Economy Models', University of Pennsylvania, mimeo

Senay, O. (1998). 'The Effects of Goods and Financial Market Integration on Macroeconomic Volatility', *The Manchester School Supplement*, 66, 39–61

Smets, F. and Wouters, R. (2002). 'Openness, Imperfect Exchange Rate Pass-Through and Monetary Policy', *Journal of Monetary Economics*, 49(5), 947–81

Sutherland, A. (1996). 'Financial Market Integration and Macroeconomic Volatility', *Scandinavian Journal of Economics*, 98, 521–39

(2001a). 'Incomplete Pass Through and the Welfare Effects of Exchange Rate Volatility', University of St Andrews, mimeo

(2001b). 'A Simple Second-Order Solution Method for Dynamic General Equilibrium Models', University of St Andrews, mimeo

Svensson, L. and van Wijnbergen, S. (1989). 'Excess Capacity, Monopolistic Competition and International Transmission of Monetary Disturbances', *Economic Journal*, 99, 785–805

Tille, C. (2000). 'Is the Integration of World Asset Markets Necessarily Beneficial In the Presence of Monetary Shocks?', Federal Reserve Bank of New York, mimeo

(2001). 'The Role of Consumption Substitutability in the International Transmission of Shocks', *Journal of International Economics*, 53(2), 421–44

Ventura, J. (2001). 'A Portfolio View of the US Current Account Deficit', *Brookings Papers on Economic Activity*, 1, 241–53

Warnock, F. E. (1998). 'Idiosyncratic Tastes in a Two-Country Optimizing Model: Implications of a Standard Presumption', *International Finance Discussion Paper*, 631, Board of Governors of the Federal Reserve System

Weil, P. (1989). 'The Equity Premium Puzzle and the Risk-Free Rate Puzzle', *Journal of Monetary Economics*, 24(3), 401–22

Woodford, M. (2002). *Interest and Prices: Foundations of a Theory of Monetary Policy*, Princeton: Princeton University Press, forthcoming

7

Credit frictions and 'Sudden Stops' in small open economies: an equilibrium business cycle framework for emerging markets crises

Cristina Arellano and Enrique G. Mendoza

1 INTRODUCTION

The severe financial and economic crisis that hit Mexico after the devaluation of the peso in December 1994, and the unprecedented 'Tequila effect' by which Mexico's financial woes 'infected' emerging markets world-wide were a harbinger of a period of intense turbulence in international capital markets. Seven years later, in December 2001, a major crisis broke out in Argentina with an explosive combination of sovereign default, massive currency devaluation and collapse of economic activity. In the seven years separating the Mexican and Argentine crises, similar crises engulfed nearly all of the so-called 'emerging markets,' including Hong Kong, Korea, Indonesia, Malaysia, Thailand, Russia, Chile, Colombia, Ecuador, Brazil and Turkey. Interestingly, devaluation itself proved not to be a prerequisite for these crises, as the experiences of Argentina in 1995 and Hong Kong in 1997 showed. 'Contagion effects' similar to the 'Tequila effect' were also typical, as crises spread quickly to countries with no apparent economic linkages to countries in crisis. A favourite example is the correction in US equity prices in the autumn of 1998 triggered by the Russian default. The systemic nature of this correction forced the US Federal Reserve to lower interest rates and coordinate the orderly collapse of hedge fund Long Term Capital Management.

Emerging markets crises are characterised by a set of striking empirical regularities that Calvo (1998) labelled the 'Sudden Stop' phenomenon. These empirical regularities include: (a) a sudden loss of access to international capital markets reflected in a collapse of capital inflows, (b) a large

The authors gratefully acknowledge comments and suggestions from Fernando Alvarez, Franz Hamann, Jonathan Heatcote, Alejandro Izquierdo, Urban Jermann, Pedro Oviedo, Fabrizio Perri, Katherine Smith, Diego Valderrama and Stan Zin. Mendoza also thanks the Research Department of the Inter-American Development Bank, where part of this chapter was written.

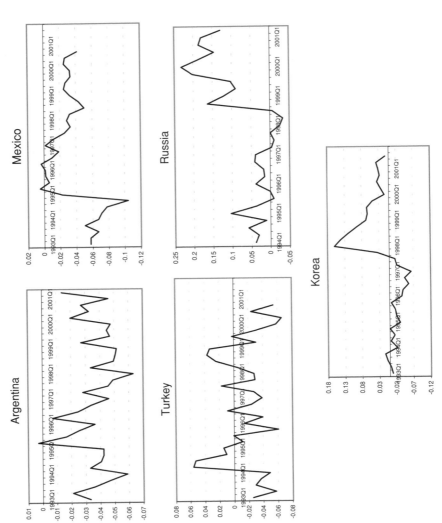

Figure 7.1 Current account balances in per cent of GDP, 1993Q1–2001Q1

Source: IMF, *International Financial Statistics*.

reversal of the current account deficit, (c) collapses of domestic production and aggregate demand, and (d) sharp corrections in asset prices and in the prices of non-traded goods relative to traded goods. Figures 7.1–7.3 illustrate some of these stylised facts for Argentina, Korea, Mexico, Russia and Turkey.[1] Figure 7.1 shows recent time series data for each country's current account as a share of GDP. Sudden Stops are displayed in these plots as sudden, large swings of the current account that in most cases exceeded five percentage points of GDP. Figure 7.2 shows data on consumption growth as an indicator of real economic activity. These plots show that Sudden Stops are associated with a collapse in the real sector of the economy. Figure 7.3 provides information on two key financial indicators for each country, the price of domestic equity (valued in US dollars) and the spread of the yield in JP Morgan's Emerging Markets Bond Index Plus (EMBI+) for each country relative to US Treasury bills. Large declines in equity prices and sudden, sharp increases in EMBI+ spreads are features of Sudden Stops, with equity prices often leading the surge of the EMBI+ spread at the monthly frequency.

The Sudden Stop phenomenon is seriously at odds with the predictions of standard models of the business cycle of the small open economy, both frictionless RBC models and models with nominal rigidities. In these models, international capital markets provide the means for small open economies to borrow in order to smooth consumption when 'bad' states of nature materialise, and to share the risk of their idiosyncratic income fluctuations with the rest of the world. A country's *sudden* loss of access to international capital markets is ruled out by assumption. Moreover, while RBC models have been successful in accounting for several features of regular business cycles in small open economies (see Correia, Neves and Rebelo 1995 and Mendoza 1991a, 1995), they cannot account for the large magnitude of the contractions in output, consumption and investment, and the large price collapses, observed during a Sudden Stop. Similarly, general equilibrium asset pricing models have difficulties in accounting for the observed large asset price declines and for the contagion of asset price volatility across countries.

The pressing need to gain a better understanding of the Sudden Stop phenomenon has led to the development of an active research programme

---

[1] Calvo and Reinhart (1999) and Milesi-Ferretti and Razin (2000) document in detail the reversals of capital inflows and the sharp contractions in economic activity associated with Sudden Stops. The document by the International Monetary Fund (1999) reviews the collapses in equity prices and the increase in their volatility. Mendoza (2002c) and Parsley (2000) show evidence of sharp changes in the relative price of non-tradables for Hong Kong, Korea and Mexico.

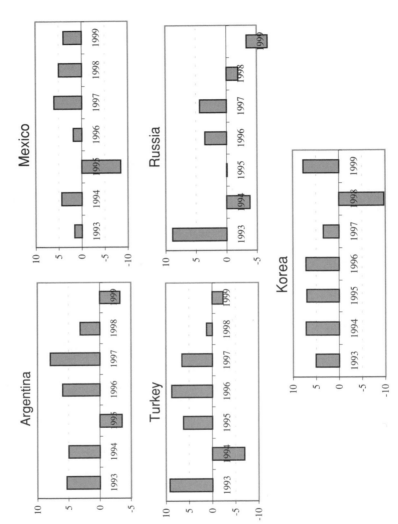

Figure 7.2 Annual growth rates in real private consumption expenditures, 1993–1999
Source: World Bank, *World Development Indicators.*

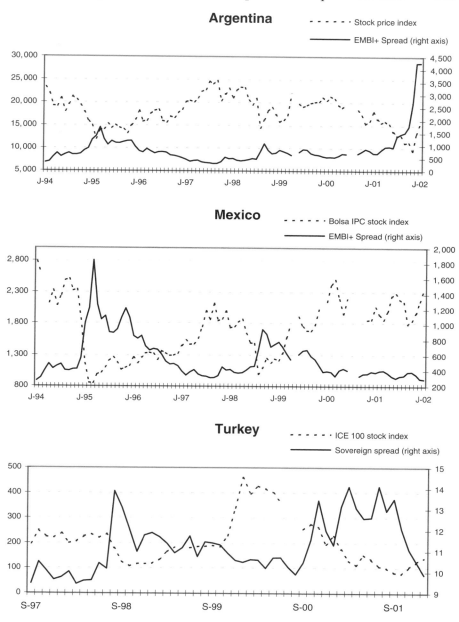

Figure 7.3 Equity prices and country risk, 1994–2002
Source: JP Morgan.

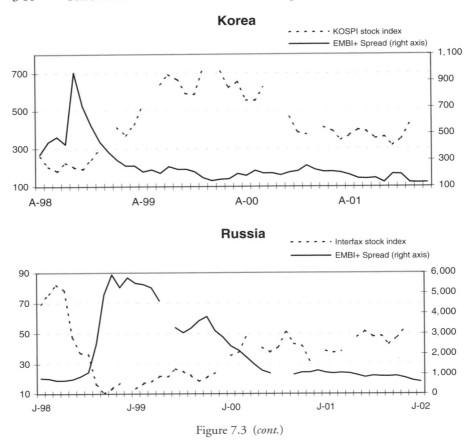

Figure 7.3 (*cont.*)

(see, for example, the November 1996 and June 2000 symposia issues of the *Journal of International Economics* or the NBER volumes edited by Edwards 2000, Frankel and Edwards 2002 and Krugman 2000). The initial step of this research programme was to recognise that an analytical framework aiming to explain the empirical regularities of emerging markets crises requires a reconsideration of the conventional approach to model international capital markets as a perfect mechanism for consumption smoothing, risk-sharing and credit allocation (see Calvo and Mendoza 1996). Moreover, since international capital markets across industrial countries are much less volatile than emerging markets, it was also important to identify at the outset factors that could explain why emerging capital markets are significantly more prone to fail than the capital markets of industrial countries (see Calvo and Mendoza 2000a, 2000b and Krugman 2000). Thus, the common starting point of much of the literature on emerging markets crises was to model international capital markets as subject to a variety of financial market imperfections, and to attribute these imperfections to various forms of informational frictions that are more pervasive in emerging markets than in industrial-country capital markets. Most of the literature focuses on theoretical partial equilibrium models that yield qualitative results consistent with some of the features that define a Sudden Stop. Very little is known yet about whether these models provide a reasonable quantitative account of a typical emerging markets crisis.

The main objective of this chapter is to analyse a framework that aims to integrate some of the financial frictions channels proposed in the recent literature on emerging markets crises with an equilibrium business cycle model for small open economies. The emphasis is on developing methods for deriving the quantitative implications of the proposed framework and on using these quantitative methods to learn about the strengths and weaknesses of financial frictions theories of the Sudden Stop phenomenon. The chapter also provides a short survey of the recent literature with the aim of highlighting the differences between the alternative financial transmission mechanisms that have been proposed.

The chapter is organised as follows. Section 2 surveys the recent literature on credit frictions models of Sudden Stops. Section 3 proposes a basic macroeconomic framework for integrating financial frictions into RBC models of the small open economy. Section 4 reviews four applications of this framework. Section 5 concludes and discusses several avenues for further research.

2 VARIETIES OF CREDIT FRICTIONS

A large portion of the recent literature on emerging markets crises proposes financial transmission mechanisms that can be roughly divided into two categories. First, a group of studies explore financial transmission mechanisms driven by a debtor's *ability to pay*. In these models, debtors may be willing to repay their debts but their ability to do so is threatened by the realisation of 'bad' states of nature. Creditors aim to cover their exposure to this default risk by imposing lending conditions on borrowers (usually in the form of collateral or liquidity requirements) or by choosing to incur monitoring costs to assess a borrower's claim not to be able to repay. The second category emphasises a debtor's *willingness to pay*. In these models, debtors decide optimally to renege on their debts when the expected lifetime payoff of defaulting, net of any default penalty, exceeds the expected lifetime payoff of repaying.

Most of the work published to date in both of the above categories is theoretical in nature and is based in part on the related literature on financial frictions and contract theory in macroeconomics, international macroeconomics and finance. Note also that the two-category classification is a natural way of organising the literature but it hides the fact that several of the existing models combine elements of ability and willingness to pay (costly monitoring models, for example, have elements of both ability to pay and willingness to pay since they deal with the inability of a lender to tell if a defaulting borrower is unable to pay or unwilling to pay without incurring the monitoring cost).

2.1 Ability-to-pay models

Models driven by ability to pay generally specify explicit constraints linking a country's ability to acquire debt to the dynamics of income and prices or to various forms of collateral. The motivation for these constraints comes from the lenders' interest in managing default risk and from informational asymmetries between borrowers and lenders.

Calvo (1998) presents a clear characterisation of an ability-to-pay framework as a mechanism for explaining Sudden Stops. He considers a perfect-foresight, three-period small open economy with traded and non-traded goods that are separable in utility. An endowment of traded goods is received only in the last period. Production of non-traded goods is planned at date 0, using a linear technology in which tradables enter as an input and output is obtained one period later. Thus, at date 0 firms borrow to import tradables to use as input in non-tradables production acting on a perceived relative price for non-tradables sold at date 1. At date 1, tradables and non-tradables are consumed, producers' debt is due and new debt is contracted to import tradables for consumption. At date 2, tradables are consumed and debt is paid. In this economy, the Pareto-optimal competitive equilibrium free of credit market imperfections obtains when the date-0 perceived non-tradables relative price equals the actual date-1 equilibrium price. Firms are always able to repay their debt.

The outcome differs sharply if there is an unexpected (as of date 0) shock to the country's ability to access capital markets in period 1, once production plans are implemented, *and* there are fixed bankruptcy costs that increase the real cost of servicing debt at date 2. In this case, the competitive equilibrium yields two mutually consistent outcomes. On the one hand, the equilibrium relative price of non-tradables is lower than the perceived date-0 price. On the other hand, firms go bankrupt because at this lower price they are unable to repay their debts. The non-tradables price falls because bankruptcy costs lower permanent income and hence consumption of tradables at dates 1 and 2. Given the predetermined supply of non-tradables, the fall in tradables' consumption at date 1 causes a fall in the equilibrium relative price of non-tradables. This price decline renders firms bankrupt because firms made zero-profits production plans at the higher Pareto-optimal price perceived at date 0.

The shock to credit market access at date 1 and the bankruptcy costs are both central to Calvo's story. If bankruptcy does not entail costs, household owners of the firms would borrow to cover the firms' obligations and the Pareto-optimal equilibrium would prevail. This model is highly stylised but its main prediction (i.e. that large relative price changes induced by credit frictions can trigger Sudden Stops) is robust to several modifications in terms of the life horizon of economic agents, the form of the utility function and the tradables endowment process. Moreover, bankruptcy *per se* is less relevant for the macroeconomic implications of Calvo's model than the shock to the ability to borrow. In particular, the equilibrium allocations of his model can be shown to be analogous to those produced by models in which there is no bankruptcy but there is an explicit borrowing constraint that depends on the relative price of non-tradables. Mendoza (2002a), for example, considers an RBC-like, two-sector model that delivers findings similar to Calvo's model by introducing a constraint that limits debt not to exceed a fraction of GDP in units of tradables (this model is discussed from p. 356).

A group of models of Sudden Stops more elaborate than Calvo's model typically emphasise collateral constraints analogous to the well-known collateral constraint studied by Kiyotaki and Moore (1997). In these models, foreign debt is constrained not to exceed the discounted liquidation value of the capital stock one period into the future. Models of this class include those of Edison, Luangaram and Miller (2000), Izquierdo (2000) and Paasche (2001).

Izquierdo (2000) and Edison, Luangaram and Miller (2000) use Kiyotaki–Moore (K–M) constraints to study how this credit market friction could explain the large real effects observed during the Tequila and East Asian crises. They find that the response of credit-constrained economies to financial shocks, such as a fall of the exchange rate, can greatly amplify the real effects of these shocks and lead to systemic financial collapse. Izquierdo argues that these magnification effects lead to an asymmetric response relative to what is observed when positive shocks hit the economy, and shows evidence of asymmetric responses in a panel for Latin America. Paasche (2001) examines the extent to which a crisis in a country can spread to another seemingly unrelated country, when two small open economies that face K–M constraints export differentiated goods to a large country. An adverse, temporary terms of trade shock triggered by a productivity shock to one of the small economies causes large capital outflows and a rapid deterioration in the current account of the other small economy.

Several other studies make use of collateral constraints different from the K–M constraints. These include Auernheimer and Garcia-Saltos (2000), Caballero and Krishnamurthy (2001), Christiano, Guts and Roldos (2002), Mendoza and Smith (2002) and Schneider and Tornell (1999). A common feature of these studies is that they produce collateral-based financial transmission mechanisms that magnify the real effects of macroeconomic shocks. Caballero and Krishnamurthy focus on differences across domestic industries in their ability to offer 'useful' collateral to international lenders. Auernheimer and Garcia-Saltos (2000) link the cost of borrowing explicitly to the market value of the capital stock, as a form of implicit collateral. Schneider and Tornell (1999) study the interaction of collateral constraints that comprise land, a fraction of risky capital and a fraction of bonds, with government bailout guarantees. Christiano, Guts and Roldos (2002) and Mendoza and Smith (2002) study collateral constraints that depend on the current liquidation value of assets, which is analogous to a margin requirement (see Aiyagari and Gertler 1999).

Quantitative applications of ability-to-pay models in an RBC setting are rare (some examples are presented in section 7.4), but there are numerical results for some of the models cited above under perfect foresight. Paasche (2001) and Auernheimer and Garcia Saltos (2000) study simulations of their models to explore the magnitude of the real effects they can produce in response to unanticipated shocks. Cespedes, Chang and Velasco (2002) and Christiano, Gust and Roldos (2002) develop quantitative models aimed at answering policy questions. Christiano, Gust and Roldos study how a change in the domestic interest rate affects output when a small open economy runs into an unanticipated, binding collateral constraint. Firms require two types of working capital: domestic currency to hire domestic inputs and foreign currency to finance imports of an intermediate input. Borrowers and lenders never anticipate the possibility of the borrowing constraint hitting the economy, so the constraint emerges as an unanticipated shock to a perfect-foresight equilibrium as in the experiments of Paasche (2001) and Auernheimer and Garcia-Saltos (2000). In this setting, an interest rate cut can produce a fall in the value of domestic assets via a nominal exchange-rate depreciation, which in turn reduces imports of the foreign input. If the foreign input is not very substitutable for domestically produced inputs, a contraction in output follows. Depending on how labour enters into production and how it responds to the interest rate cut, however, the model can also predict that an expansion could follow from the interest rate cut.

Cespedes, Chang and Velasco (2002) consider a setup of monitoring costs analogous to the Bernanke–Gertler (1995) financial accelerator model to study the relation among exchange-rate regimes, balance sheet effects, nominal rigidities and macroeconomic outcomes. In their model, balance sheet effects magnify the adverse real effects of a foreign shock that triggers a real devaluation of the currency. However, these real effects are always larger with a fixed exchange rate than with a flexible one because the former does not help the economy cope with nominal rigidities and makes no difference for the nature of the Bernanke–Gertler external financing premium.

From the perspective of developing an equilibrium business cycle approach to explain Sudden Stops, the above literature on ability-to-pay models faces two challenges. One is that in the majority of the existing models borrowing constraints are always binding along an equilibrium path. This rules out equilibrium dynamics featuring large reversals of the current account triggered by a switch from a state of nature in which the constraint did not bind to one in which it does (this is the notion implicit in Calvo's 1998 setup). The second shortcoming is that most models deal with perfect-foresight experiments in which the credit constraint arrives as an unexpected shock. Hence, economic agents are not given the opportunity to adapt their optimal plans to the possibility of being suddenly unable to access international capital markets. As shown later, optimal plans can differ sharply even if the probability of this event is negligible.

2.2 Willingness-to-pay models

The literature on international debt that emphasises willingness to pay was very active in the aftermath of the developing country debt crisis of the 1980s, and is now going through a renaissance motivated both by the emerging markets crises and the recent developments in closed economy finance theory. The premise in this literature is that credit markets are intrinsically fragile because, in the absence of efficient mechanisms for committing debtors to fulfil their obligations, debtors optimally choose to default whenever the lifetime payoff of doing so exceeds the payoff of continuing in a credit relationship. However, the implications of this incentive compatibility or participation constraint vary depending on the structure of the economic environment on which it is imposed.

Eaton and Gersovitz (1981) wrote one of the classic articles on sovereign default. In their model, a sovereign debtor in default faces permanent exclusion from international capital markets (i.e. consumption must be set at the same level of the economy's income endowment each period). Eaton and Gersovitz set this debtor in a global credit market with fully informed, risk neutral lenders that are willing to lend at a default-risk premium that equates the expected return on risky sovereign debt with that of a riskless asset (up to an endogenous maximum lending ceiling). The default risk premium is an endogenous outcome that reflects the probability that borrowers find themselves in states of nature at which it is optimal to default because the participation constraint fails. Default is observed at equilibrium when these states occur.

Atkeson (1991) considers a model in which the participation constraint interacts with a moral hazard problem in a contracting environment in which repayment schedules are contingent on output realisations. In particular, lenders cannot observe whether borrowed funds are used for investment or consumption. The optimal contract features capital outflows from the borrowing country as a solution to the moral hazard problem.

The above studies assume that countries cannot enter into other financial agreements after they renege on their debts, and thus that financial autarky is a credible threat. However, a key lingering question facing this literature is whether creditors really possess the ability to penalise debtors in this way. Bulow and Rogoff (1989a) show that a sufficient condition for the reputational mechanism implicit in satisfying the participation constraint to fail to enforce debt repayments is that countries in default may have access to a rich set of deposit contracts with foreign creditors. Thus, a country that has large expected repayments due can default and then save the resources at stake in deposit contracts, thereby enjoying a higher level of consumption (and utility) thereafter. Rational lenders foresee this outcome and so international borrowing cannot be sustained in equilibrium.

The Bulow–Rogoff paradox has been addressed in different ways. Bulow and Rogoff (1989b) provided an answer based on the notion that lenders may be able to impose direct trade sanctions on defaulting borrowers. More recently, Kletzer and Wright (2000) proposed an environment in which both lenders and borrowers lack the capacity of commitment. This limits the set of deposit contracts that defaulting economies have access to if they default. The authors show how the two-sided commitment problem they study can restore sustainable intertemporal exchange through reputation by constructing a renegotiation-proof equilibrium where payments are state contingent and contracts are incentive-compatible for both parties. Finally, Wright (2001) looks at how a country's concern for reputation can work to enforce repayment when there are also reputational incentives on the side of lenders that lead them to tacitly collude in punishing a country in default. If syndicated lending is allowed, banks collude to punish countries in default so as to preserve their own reputation for cooperation.

Quantitative applications of willingness-to-pay models applied to the study of Sudden Stops as a business cycle feature are as rare as those of the ability-to-pay models. Most of the literature focuses on examining theoretically the strategic interaction of borrowers and lenders and the properties of the resulting incentive-compatible contract, although some quantitative applications of models in this class do exist. Perri and Kehoe (2002) study business cycle comovements across industrial countries in a two-country model in which each country is required to satisfy its participation constraint in each state of nature, following the closed economy analysis of Kehoe and Levine (1993) and Kocherlakota (1996). From the perspective of emerging markets crises, however, this modelling approach has difficulties in accounting for defaults because the need to satisfy the participation constraints at all times rules them out at equilibrium.[2] Also, depending on preference and technology parameters and on the stochastic structure of the shocks hitting the economy, these models can predict that the incentives for default tend to be stronger for countries that are in *good* states of nature or that experience *less* macroeconomic volatility (one example is provided in section 4). The intuition is that a country facing a smooth income path makes small gains from accessing world credit markets to smooth consumption, and hence assigns less value to a credit relationship.

Hamann (2002) studies the quantitative implications of the Eaton–Gersovitz framework and explores its ability to account for some features of emerging markets crises, albeit in the context of a pure exchange economy. He shows how increased persistence or variance in the endowment income process can reproduce some features of a Sudden Stop in which borrowing constraints are tightened and the default risk premium is increased. To do so, he exploits the feedback between these changes in the income process, the equilibrium probability of default and the optimising behaviour of the risk neutral lenders assumed in the Eaton–Gersovitz model.

---

[2] In these models there can be states of nature in which borrowers and lenders agree to a zero payment but always as part of the contract that enforces the incentive compatibility constraint.

In summary, the growing literature studying emerging markets crises from the ability- and willingness-to-pay approaches has made important contributions to our understanding of the process that drives Sudden Stops. Related studies that have examined Sudden Stops as the outcome of self-fulfilling expectations, informational cascades, or working capital distortions (see, for example, Aghion, Bacchetta, and Banerjee 2000; Calvo 2000; Chari and Kehoe 2003; Cole and Kehoe 1998; Neumeyer and Perri 2001; Oviedo 2002; and Reif 2001) have also made valuable contributions. Yet, little is still known about the quantitative implications of these models in an equilibrium business cycle setting, and about whether the financial transmission channels they propose offer a quantitatively plausible account of the Sudden Stop phenomenon. In the next two sections we describe an equilibrium business cycle framework with financial frictions that tries to make some progress in this regard.

3 REAL BUSINESS CYCLES IN SMALL OPEN ECONOMIES WITH FINANCIAL FRICTIONS

This section proposes a modification of the standard RBC framework for the small open economy that introduces financial frictions. The standard small open economy RBC model (as in Mendoza 1991a) features a representative infinitely lived household, a representative firm operating a neoclassical production technology subject to random productivity disturbances and facing capital-adjustment costs and an international credit market of one-period, non-contingent bonds. In this model, markets of contingent claims are incomplete but the credit market is perfect (i.e. the small open economy can borrow or lend at the world-determined real interest rate any amount that is consistent with the household's no-Ponzi game condition).

In addition to the above assumptions, small open economy RBC models require extra assumptions regarding the nature of intertemporal preferences or international bond markets in order to support a well-defined long-run equilibrium. It is well known that deterministic small open economy models, with standard time-separable preferences featuring an exogenous rate of time preference and the standard global credit market with an exogenous interest rate, yield either explosive dynamics of foreign asset holdings (if the rate of time preference and the interest rate differ) or stationary equilibria that depend on initial conditions (if the rate of time preference and the interest rate are identical).

Stochastic models fail to support stationary equilibria even if the rate of interest and the rate of time preference are equal. The reason is that households striving to smooth consumption perfectly in a world of random income and incomplete markets can do so only if they end up holding an infinite amount of foreign assets. In mathematical terms, the problem is that the discounted marginal benefit of saving follows a convergent Supermartingale sequence. If the rate of time preference equals the interest rate, Supermartingale convergence requires consumption to converge to a perfectly-smooth (i.e. non-random) level, but since income is random this can be consistent with the budget constraint only if agents end up holding an infinite amount of foreign assets.

One of the first methods used to address the above problems and obtain well-defined dynamics for small open economies was to model intertemporal preferences with an endogenous rate of time preference. Obstfeld (1981) introduced preferences with this feature into a perfect-foresight small open economy model and showed how they produced a unique steady state independent of initial conditions. Similarly, the stochastic RBC model in Mendoza (1991a) used preferences with endogenous discounting in order to obtain a well-defined limiting distribution of foreign assets.

In stochastic environments, intertemporal preferences with an endogenous rate of time preference take the form of Epstein's (1983) Stationary Cardinal Utility (SCU) function:

$$E_0 \left[\sum_{t=0}^{\infty} \exp\left\{ -\sum_{\tau=0}^{t-1} v(c_\tau) \right\} u(c_t) \right]. \qquad (7.1)$$

In this expression, $u(.)$ is a standard twice-continuously differentiable and concave utility function and $v(.)$ is the time-preference function, which is assumed to be increasing, concave and twice-continuously differentiable. The SCU also imposes restrictions linking the two functions that can be interpreted as setting an upper bound on the elasticity of the rate of time preference with respect to the argument of utility. These restrictions imply that the *impatience effect*, by which changes in date-t consumption alter the rate at which all future utility flows are discounted, must be 'small' (in the sense that the rate of time preference, $\exp(v(.))$, is increasing in the argument of utility but maintaining the condition that $u_1(\cdot) \exp(-v(\cdot))$ is non-increasing). This is necessary in order to ensure that consumption at every date is a normal good and that the model supports a well-defined unique, invariant limiting distribution (see Epstein 1983).

A well-defined stochastic steady state for the small open economy RBC model can also be obtained with two other alternatives: (1) modelling households with stochastically finite lives using Blanchard–Yaari preferences (as in Cardia 1991), or (2) using standard preferences with a constant rate of time preference but one that is set higher than the rate of interest. This second alternative is based on findings from the closed economy literature on incomplete markets and precautionary savings (as in Aiyagari 1993). Agents in the small open economy RBC model face non-insurable, idiosyncratic income risk with only one non-state-contingent asset, which is a very similar environment to that modelled in closed economy, precautionary savings studies. These studies show that standard preferences with an exogenous discount factor and a real interest rate *lower* than the rate of time preference support a well-defined stochastic steady state because of the precautionary savings effect induced by the existence of non-insurable income shocks (see chapter 14 in Ljungqvist and Sargent 2000). A drawback of this approach in its small open economy application is that the long-run mean net foreign asset position is determined by the arbitrary difference between the exogenous discount factor and the exogenous world interest rate. In the closed economy literature, by contrast, the goal is to solve for the risk-free interest rate. Moreover, relative to the Blanchard–Yaari setup or the precautionary savings setup, the method that uses Epstein's SCU function has the advantage that it is consistent with two standard features of RBC models: economic agents are infinitely lived and the rate of time preference and the rate of interest are equalised in the long run.

The recent quantitative literature on stochastic equilibrium models of the small open economy has also used other methods to obtain unique, invariant limiting distributions of foreign asset holdings. These include incorporating transactions costs in foreign assets and introducing ad hoc functions that link the rate of interest to the stock of foreign debt or the rate of time preference to average consumption. In some applications, these alternative methods can yield similar results as the methods mentioned above (see Schmitt-Grohé and Uribe 2001), but this equivalence has to be established case by case and it is unlikely to hold in models of Sudden Stops that display large, non-linear adjustments in macroeconomic aggregates. Moreover, the theoretical foundations of these other methods are questionable. Ad hoc functions relating the interest rate to foreign debt are a serious deviation from microfoundations. Models like that of Eaton and Gersovitz (1981) do predict that the interest rate is *at equilibrium* a convex, increasing function of debt, but this is an equilibrium pricing function that prices the endogenously determined risk of default. It is not an ad hoc function imposed exogenously on the optimisation problem of borrowers. Similarly, Epstein's (1983) analysis of the microfoundations of SCU derives strict conditions on the specification of time-preference functions. He showed that SCU as a representation of a preference order requires *weaker* axioms of consumer theory than the ones required by time-separable utility with exogenous discounting, but a utility function that represents a preference order consistent with these axioms *exists iff* it takes the form of the SCU function. Thus, an ad hoc endogenous rate of time preference that depends on mean consumption is not consistent with the microfoundations of consumer choice for models with endogenous impatience.

In the context of models with financial frictions, preferences with endogenous discounting have the extra advantage that they allow for the possibility of modelling credit constraints that can remain binding at a steady state. This is because a binding credit constraint drives a wedge between the intertemporal marginal rate of substitution in consumption and the rate of interest. In a stationary state with a binding credit constraint the rate of time preference adjusts endogenously to accommodate this wedge. In contrast, in models with an exogenous discount factor credit constraints never bind in the long run (if the exogenous rate of time preference is set greater or equal than the world interest rate) or must always bind at a steady state (if the rate of time preference is fixed below the interest rate).

The recursive representation of the competitive equilibrium of the small open economy RBC model is characterised by optimal decision rules for the vector $y = [c, n, i]$ of control variables (where c is consumption, n is labour supply, and $i = k' - k(1 - \delta)$ is gross investment) and the vector $x' = [k', b']$ of endogenous states (where k' is capital accumulation and b' is foreign asset accumulation) that solve the following dynamic-programming form of a planner's problem:

$$V(k, b, e) = \max_{k', b', c, n} \{u(c, n) + \exp(-v(c, n)) E[V(k', b', e')]\}$$

$$\text{s.t.} \quad c = ef(k, n) - k' + k(1 - \delta) - \varphi(k, k') - b' + bR,$$

(7.2)

where $f(.)$ is a neoclassical production function, δ is the rate of depreciation of the capital stock, φ is a convex capital-adjustment-cost function, R is the world's gross real interest rate and e is a productivity disturbance that follows a Markov process with a known transition probability matrix. The initial state of the system is given by the observed realisation of e and by the vector $x = [k, b]$, where k is the initial capital stock and b the initial net foreign asset position.

The above social planner's problem can be decentralised in standard fashion to establish the equivalence between the planner's problem and the competitive equilibrium of an economy in which households own the factors of production and rent them out to profit-maximising firms. The prices and factor rental rates that support equilibrium allocations include the wage rate, w, the rental rate of capital, r, and the relative price of investment goods in terms of consumption goods, q – which is not equal to 1 because of the capital-adjustment costs. The price vector that households and firms take as given is thus defined by $p = [w, r, q]$.

Consider now a modification of the above economic environment in which financial markets are imperfect. The first change to notice is that, since financial frictions distort the competitive equilibrium, it may be necessary to study the equilibria of these economies directly in decentralised form. In some cases, it may be possible to construct a variant of a planning problem that captures the distortions induced by specific forms of financial market imperfections on the competitive equilibrium (as in some of the applications studied in section 7.4).

This chapter focuses on financial frictions that can be reduced to functional constraints on the small open economy's ability to contract foreign debt of the following form:

$$b' \geq h(k', x, y, e, p). \tag{7.3}$$

In most of the applications of this framework reviewed in the next section, this state-contingent borrowing constraint is not formally derived as a feature of an optimal credit contract between the small open economy and its international creditors (the exception is the application in which a constraint like (7.3) is derived so as to enforce participation constraints on the small open economy). However, the review of the applications relates explicit forms of the borrowing constraint to existing results for optimal credit contracts or to observed practice in actual credit markets. The above specification is general enough to include a broad range of applications, including liquidity requirements, margin constraints, borrowing ceilings set to support debt repayment incentives and collateral constraints set to the current liquidation value of assets. One exception is the K–M collateral constraint, which depends on *future* realisations of an element of p (the next period's equity price).[3]

The strategy is to begin by proposing explicit functional forms for financial frictions affecting domestic households, firms or foreign agents in a decentralised competitive equilibrium, and then explore whether this competitive equilibrium can be represented in recursive form using the aggregate borrowing constraint defined in (7.3). For example, the aggregate

---

[3] Despite this limitation, other collateral constraints included in h, like margin requirements, have similar asset pricing implications as K–M constraints (see Mendoza and Smith 2002 for details).

borrowing constraint may represent a constraint limiting households' foreign debt not to exceed a fraction of factor income or firms' ability to leverage their debt on the value of their capital. Under particular assumptions, the competitive equilibria of economies with these constraints can be shown to be equivalent to that of a planning problem in which debt is limited not to exceed a fraction of output or a fraction of the market value of the capital stock. In general, however, whether such equivalence between competitive equilibria and a planner's problem exists needs to be examined case by case.

At this level of generality it is possible to extract some important properties of small open economy RBC models that incorporate the above borrowing constraint:

(1) *The borrowing constraint is 'occasionally binding'.* Whether the constraint binds or not depends ultimately on the initial state (x, e). Since the equilibrium is represented in recursive form, the optimal decision rules for k' and y and the equilibrium pricing vector p in the right-hand side of (7.2) are also functions of x and e.

(2) *The dynamics of the borrowing constraint and equilibrium allocations and prices feature endogenous feedback effects.* Knowledge that the constraint is a feature of the financial markets in which the small open economy participates influences the optimal forward-looking plans that economic agents formulate. As a result, this knowledge also influences the equilibrium dynamics of prices and allocations, which in turn determines whether the constraint binds or not. In particular, the agents' expectations that they may face future states in which the borrowing constraint can bind influences their decisions to accumulate assets today and thus the probability that the constraint can actually bind in the future.

(3) *Suddenly binding borrowing constraints can produce non-linear dynamics and country-specific risk premia.* When the economy switches from a state in which the constraint does not bind to a state in which it binds, there are discrete jumps upward in the effective intertemporal relative price of current consumption and downward (upward) in the level of current (future) consumption. This follows from the household's consumption Euler equation, which takes the form:

$$\lambda = E[\lambda' R' + \mu], \tag{7.4}$$

where λ is the lifetime marginal utility of consumption (i.e. the non-negative Lagrange multiplier on the resource constraint facing the planner) and μ is the non-negative Lagrange multiplier on the borrowing constraint. The increased effective real interest rate in the states in which the borrowing constraint binds represents an endogenous, country-specific risk premium on external financing.

(4) *The borrowing constraint can depress asset prices and trigger Fisherian debt–deflation dynamics.* As shown in the next section, the higher effective interest rates implied by either a currently binding or expected future binding borrowing constraint depresses current equity prices by increasing the discount rates relevant for discounting dividend streams in the valuation of assets. If the specification of $h(.)$ links the borrowing constraint to asset prices, the adverse asset pricing implications of the constraint add a feedback effect in the spirit of Fisher's debt–deflation mechanism: an initial shock triggers the borrowing constraint, this leads to a decline in asset prices, which then leads to an even tighter borrowing constraint and thus a downward spiral on asset prices and access to foreign financing.

An important implication of these four properties is that the small open economy RBC framework with borrowing constraints is endowed with a self-adjustment mechanism that actually works to *weaken* the significance of the effects of financial frictions. That mechanism is the precautionary savings motive: risk averse agents respond to their non-insurable exposure to the risk of a binding borrowing limit, which adversely affects their consumption plans, by accumulating a buffer stock of assets. Precautionary savings can also distort portfolio choice in models in which foreign assets coexist with other vehicles of saving such as physical capital or equity. As mentioned earlier, this precautionary-savings effect is already present in the frictionless small open economy RBC model because the non-contingent international bond cannot fully insure agents against country-specific idiosyncratic income shocks. The effect is stronger in the presence of borrowing constraints, however, because agents in the frictionless model can rely on a perfect international credit market to support optimal consumption plans and they have the option of using domestic investment as an alternative savings vehicle.[4]

Dealing with the precautionary-savings motive is an important unfinished task for the literature on financial frictions in small open economies. The majority of models of the Sudden Stop phenomenon abstract from it by assuming perfect foresight or by focusing on experiments in which

---

[4] Mendoza (1991b) shows that, in the standard small open economy RBC model, agents adjust investment and suffer negligible welfare losses even when forced out of the world credit market.

the financial frictions are a negative unanticipated shock to the economic environment. Thus, in these experiments economic agents are not allowed to condition their behaviour on the possibility of the occurrence of states of nature in which they are forced out of international capital markets. While this assumption has proven useful for obtaining insightful analytical results, it is important to relax it in order to integrate financial frictions into equilibrium business cycle models for small open economies.

In principle, precautionary savings may seem reason to cast doubt on the potential of models with financial frictions to offer a quantitatively significant account of the empirical regularities of emerging markets crises. Yet, precautionary savings are in fact a key property of these models that enables them to mimic a central feature of the data: Sudden Stops are dramatic but relatively rare. The cyclical downturns experienced in countries that have suffered Sudden Stops were large, but they were also *abnormally* large relative to those countries' regular business cycles (see Mendoza 2002a). Thus, it seems natural to think of designing equilibrium business cycle models that aim to explain Sudden Stops by nesting these dramatic, rare events within a regular business cycle pattern.[5] It is undesirable to follow an approach with two disconnected theories of economic fluctuations for emerging economies, one for Sudden Stops and one for tranquil times, in which key assumptions regarding the ability of agents to condition their behaviour on the possibility of the economy suddenly losing access to world capital markets in the future are emphasised in the former but dismissed in the latter.

4 APPLICATIONS

This section of the chapter reviews four applications of the general framework proposed in section 3 that aim to capture financial frictions similar to those emphasised in the literature on emerging markets crises. The first application considers a liquidity requirement that *at equilibrium* reduces to a constraint on the debt to output ratio of a two-sector economy (this model is borrowed from Mendoza 2002a). The liquidity requirement incorporates the phenomenon known as 'liability dollarisation': foreign debt

---

[5] If Sudden Stops are nested as rare events within regular business cycles, the RBC approach to compare first and second statistical moments of detrended data with moments of the ergodic distribution of business cycle models will not be useful for studying Sudden Stops. Valderrama (2002) follows a more promising approach. He uses non-linear statistical techniques to extract and test the significance of statistical non-linearities in the data such as skewness, kurtosis and conditional volatility, and to assess the ability of equilibrium models to explain them.

is denominated in units of tradable goods but serviced in part with income generated in the non-tradables sector, and hence large swings in the relative price of non-tradables, or in the real exchange rate, can trigger binding borrowing constraints and sudden current account reversals. The second application reviews the asset pricing model of Mendoza and Smith (2002). This model incorporates two financial frictions. First, a friction in the international credit market analogous to a margin requirement by which a fraction of the value of equity holdings must be offered as collateral for foreign debt. Second, informational frictions in the equity market that result in transactions costs in trading the small open economy's equity with foreign securities firms. The third application looks at Arellano's (2002) analysis of borrowing constraints that enforce credit market participation constraints in an environment with incomplete insurance markets. The fourth application sketches a model with capital-adjustment costs that features a collateral constraint similar to the margin requirement used in the asset pricing model but in a setup with endogenous capital accumulation. Foreign creditors retain as collateral a fraction of the value of the economy's capital stock where this value is determined by Tobin's q.

4.1 Liquidity requirements and liability dollarisation in a two-sector economy

Consider a small open economy with two sectors, a tradable goods sector and a non-tradable goods sector. The output of tradables is a stochastic endowment $\exp(\varepsilon)y^T$, where ε is a random variable that follows a Markov process. Non-tradable goods are produced using a Cobb–Douglas production function $F(k, n) = \exp(\varepsilon)Ak^{1-\alpha}n^{\alpha}$, where A is a productivity scaling factor, n is variable labour input, k is the time-invariant capital stock and $0 < \alpha < 1$ is the output share of labour income. The production of non-tradables is subject to productivity shocks, which are assumed to be perfectly correlated with the shocks to the tradables endowment for simplicity.

Private consumption of tradables (c^T) and non-tradables (c^N) is aggregated into a composite good using a standard constant elasticity of substitution (CES) aggregator $c = [\omega(c^T)^{-\eta} + (1 - \omega)(c^N)^{-\eta}]^{-\frac{1}{\eta}}$, where $0 < \omega < 1$ and $\eta > -1$ are the standard CES parameters ($1/(1 + \eta)$) is the elasticity of substitution between c^T and c^N). The argument of utility adopts the Greenwood–Hercowitz–Huffman (1988) specification, $c - \frac{n^{\delta}}{\delta}$ (with $\delta > 1$), so the wage elasticity of labour supply is equal to $1/(\delta - 1)$.

The economy has access to a global credit market of one-period bonds (b) in which it acts as a small price-taker. The world gross real interest rate $\exp(\varepsilon^R)R$ is subject to random shocks ε^R which also follow a Markov process.

The government of the small open economy levies a consumption tax τ that is uniform across goods. This tax is intended to capture some of the distortions that can result from fiscal, monetary and exchange-rate policies in models in which money enters as an argument of the utility function or as a means to economise transactions costs (see Mendoza 2001, Mendoza and Uribe 2001 for details). Private agents perceive tax policy as uncertain and thus attach positive probability to scenarios in which the economy can switch from low- to high-tax regimes and vice versa. Hence, the consumption tax is modelled as a standard regime-switching, asymmetric Markov process.

The government also maintains a constant level of unproductive purchases of non-tradables financed by a time-invariant lump-sum tax T^N. This ensures that the dynamics of the relative price of non-tradables (p^N) are driven only by changes in private-sector supply and demand choices and not by endogenous changes in government purchases due to fluctuations in tax revenue. Fluctuations in tax revenue result in fluctuations of unproductive government purchases of tradable goods around a 'trend' level financed also by a time-invariant lump-sum tax T^T. This assumption introduces the Calvo–Drazen (1998) fiscal-induced wealth effects that Calvo and Drazen (1998) and Mendoza and Uribe (2001) found critical for explaining key features of economic fluctuations in developing countries exposed to the risk of uncertain duration of government policy.

The global credit market is imperfect. In particular, the small open economy must satisfy a liquidity requirement by which a fraction ϕ of current expenditures, tax and debt service obligations must be paid out of current income valued in the same units in which debt contracts are written (i.e. in units of tradable goods):

$$w_t n_t + \pi_t \geq \phi \left[(1 + \tau_t) \left(c_t^T + p_t^N c_t^N \right) - \exp\left(\varepsilon_t^R \right) R b_t + T_t^T + p_t^N T_t^N \right].$$

$$(7.5)$$

Here, w is the wage rate and π are rents on the time-invariant capital stock paid by firms producing non-tradables. This liquidity requirement and the household's budget constraint imply that the economy faces a borrowing constraint that limits debt not to exceed a fraction $(1 - \phi)/\phi$ of household income in units of tradables:

$$b_{t+1} \geq -\frac{1-\phi}{\phi}[w_t n_t + \pi_t]. \tag{7.6}$$

An intuitive motivation for this liquidity requirement is that it helps creditors to manage default risk because it is an ability-to-pay criterion that reduces the likelihood of observing situations in which the current income of borrowers falls short of what is needed to pay for existing debts. This is accomplished by limiting the margin by which the borrowers' current obligations can exceed their current income (i.e. by forcing borrowers to maintain a certain level of 'liquidity'). Borrowing constraints of this form are widely used by lenders in determining maximum loan amounts and setting borrowers' qualification criteria, particularly in mortgage loans and consumer debt contracts.

Despite its empirical appeal, the liquidity requirement is not modelled here as the outcome of an optimal contract between lenders and borrowers. It is not optimal from the ability-to-pay standpoint because it does not ensure that debtors will have enough current income to repay their debts (if the credit market suddenly closed) *in every state of nature*. To do so, ϕ would have to be contingent on b_t and on the stochastic processes governing the exogenous shocks. It is not optimal from the willingness-to-pay perspective because it does not ensure that borrowers will satisfy their participation constraint. These caveats imply that the use of the liquidity requirement is supported by two implicit participation assumptions. First, contract-enforcing institutions are such that borrowers are committed to honour debt contracts that feature the liquidity requirement even if they find themselves in states of nature in which it is not incentive compatible for them to do so. Second, debt contracts with the liquidity requirement also commit lenders to lend even if the borrowers' ability to repay out of current income in all future states is not guaranteed (i.e. debtors can always borrow at date t if they satisfy the liquidity requirement, even if at $t + 1$ there are some states of nature in which their income net of current expenditures and taxes is lower than their debt service obligations).

The borrowing constraint in (7.6) can be incorporated into a planner's problem that yields a solution equivalent to the model's competitive equilibrium. Since factors earn their marginal products and factor payments exhaust output, the borrowing constraint in the planner's problem adopts the form of a constraint that limits debt not to exceed the fraction $(1 - \phi)/\phi$ of GDP valued at tradables' goods prices. Defining $\psi \equiv (\varepsilon, \varepsilon^R, \tau)$ as the triple of observed realisations of the exogenous shocks and adopting explicit functional forms for the period utility and time preference functions, the planner's problem in dynamic programming form is the following:

$$V(b, \psi) \max_{b'} \left\{ \frac{\left[c - \frac{n^\delta}{\delta} \right]^{1-\sigma} - 1}{1 - \sigma} \right.$$

$$\left. + \exp\left(-\beta \left[Ln\left(1 + c - \frac{n^\delta}{\delta} \right) \right] \right) E[V(b', \psi')] \right\} \quad (7.7)$$

subject to:

$$(1 + \tau)\hat{c}^T + \tau \hat{p}^N \hat{c}^N = \exp(\varepsilon^T)y^T - b' + b \exp(\varepsilon^R)R - T^T \quad (7.8)$$

$$\hat{c}^N = \exp(\varepsilon^N)F(k, \hat{n}) - g^N \quad (7.9)$$

$$b' \geq -\left(\frac{1 - \phi}{\phi} \right) \left(\exp(\varepsilon^T)y^T + \hat{p}^N \exp(\varepsilon^N)F(k, \hat{n}) \right) \quad (7.10)$$

Period utility is a standard constant-relative-risk aversion utility function, with σ as the coefficient of relative risk aversion. The time preference function is logarithmic and β represents the elasticity of the rate of time preference with respect to $1 + c - \frac{n_t^\delta}{\delta}$. The variables in 'hats' represent solutions of a system of five non-linear simultaneous equations in the five unknowns $[\hat{c}, \hat{c}^T, \hat{c}^N, \hat{n}, \hat{p}^N]$ that satisfy a subset of the competitive equilibrium conditions for each coordinate (b, b', ψ) in the state space. If the liquidity constraint (7.10) is not binding, the five equations are: (i) the equilibrium condition equating the marginal rate of substitution between c^T and c^N with p^N, (ii) the equilibrium condition equating the marginal rate of substitution between n and c with the effective real wage (i.e. the post-tax marginal product of labour in units of tradables, $w/(1 + \tau)p^c$, where p^c is the CES relative price index of c in units of tradables, which is itself a monotonic, increasing function of p^N), (iii) the market-clearing condition in the tradable goods market (7.8), (iv) the market-clearing condition in the non-tradable goods market (7.9) and (v) the definition of the CES composite good c. If the liquidity constraint is binding, (7.10) holds with equality and replaces the labour-consumption optimality condition.

The Bellman equation in (7.7) can be solved using a variety of well-known value or policy function iteration methods. One important caveat, however, is that solution methods that iterate on policy functions using linear interpolations or methods based on Taylor-series approximations to continuously differentiable decision rules may perform poorly because of the non-linearities or kinks in the decision rule for b_{t+1} implied by the occasionally binding borrowing constraint. These kinks do not extend to the value function, which remains continuously differentiable and concave.

The transmission mechanism that drives economic fluctuations in this model combines features of RBC and policy uncertainty models with the credit-channel mechanism induced by the liquidity requirement. If the liquidity requirement never binds, the shocks to productivity and the world interest rate drive business cycles through the channels examined in the RBC literature for small open economies (see Mendoza 1991a, 1995). Tax shocks add to these channels through the wealth and substitution effects highlighted in the studies on uncertain duration of economic policies by Calvo and Drazen (1998) and Mendoza and Uribe (2001). Given a low tax at date t, the conditional expected tax for $t + 1$ is higher than the tax observed at t. This triggers an intertemporal substitution effect: prices are relatively low at t and hence agents substitute consumption intertemporally in favour of current consumption. Under uncertainty and in the presence of non-insurable income effects, due to the incompleteness of financial markets, there is also a state-contingent wealth effect. Each period that low taxes prevail, households benefit from the implicit lower level of government absorption, and this gain is added to their permanent income. This effect favours an increasing consumption path for the duration of the low-tax regime, followed by a collapse in consumption when a reversal of the tax cut takes place.

The above intuition for the effects of policy uncertainty applies fully in partial equilibrium. In general equilibrium, a shift from a low to a high tax can also induce a decline in the output of non-tradables, labour allocation and relative price of non-tradables. For the price of non-tradables to fall, the reduction in demand for non-tradables induced by the above-mentioned wealth and intertemporal substitution effects, must exceed the reduction in supply. In turn, for the supply of non-tradables to fall in equilibrium, the combined effect of the reduction in the demand for labour (resulting from the reduced value of the marginal product of labour in the non-tradables sector as p^N falls) and the fall in labour supply (induced by the tax hike) must dominate the positive effect on labour supply resulting from the decline in p^C (which is caused by the fall in the relative price of non-tradables).

The credit channel of the liquidity requirement modifies the model's business cycle transmission mechanism by introducing the following effects in states of nature in which the credit constraint binds:

(a) The effective real interest rate faced by the small open economy increases because the binding borrowing constraint forces households to reduce consumption relative to the case with perfect credit markets. Hence, the collapse in aggregate consumption and in the demand for tradables and non-tradables associated with adverse real and/or policy shocks is magnified when the economy's response to these shocks triggers the borrowing limit.

(b) The effective marginal reward to labour supply increases because the extra unit of labour enhances the household's ability to borrow. This moderates the negative effects of adverse tax and productivity shocks on labour supply.

(c) Consumption, saving, and net foreign asset accumulation (and hence the current account) exhibit intertemporal distortions that depend on the combined dynamic effects of (a) and (b) in general equilibrium. This is because the effective intertemporal relative price of aggregate consumption is the consumption-based real interest rate, $\exp(\varepsilon_t^R) R[p_t^C(1+\tau_t)/p_{t+1}^C(1+\tau_{t+1})]$, which depends on the inverse of the rate of change of the relative price of consumption (which is determined by the change in the relative price of non-tradables).

As a result of the above effects, households face an implicit risk premium in the use of foreign debt *vis-à-vis* their own saving in their efforts to smooth consumption that is analogous to the external financing premium faced by firms in models of Sudden Stops based on the Bernanke–Gertler financial accelerator. The differences are in the model proposed here, the equilibrium risk premium is determined endogenously and is influenced by the risk averse nature of the households' preferences and the economy's non-insurable aggregate risk. In contrast, in open economy extensions of the Bernanke–Gertler framework the functional form representing the external financing premium in general equilibrium is identical to the partial equilibrium solution of a costly monitoring contracting problem under risk neutrality and without aggregate risk.

Mendoza (2002a) calibrates the liquidity requirements model to Mexican data and produces numerical simulations to examine the effects of the borrowing constraint on macroeconomic dynamics and welfare. The calibration parameters are reproduced in table 7.1.

Figure 7.4 plots the ergodic distributions of foreign bond holdings with and without the liquidity requirement. The key business cycle statistical moments of the model's endogenous variables computed using each of the ergodic distributions are listed in table 7.2. Despite the marked differences between the two limiting distributions and the first moments, the majority

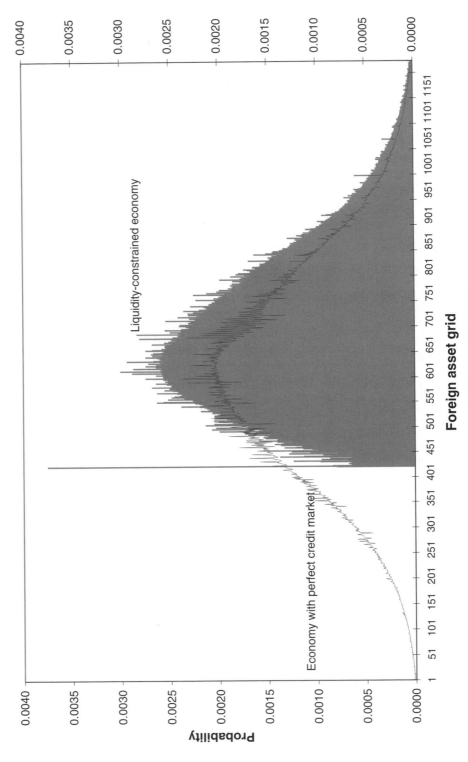

Figure 7.4 Limiting distributions of net foreign assets

Table 7.1 *Parameter values for the calibrated deterministic stationary state*

Technology		Fiscal policy		Credit market	
α	0.364	τ	0.079	R	1.016
A	1.958	*T traded*	−0.139	ϕ	0.740
YT	1.000	*T non-traded*	0.119	b/Y	−0.350
Preferences		*National accounts ratios*			
β	0.027	C/Y	0.684	CT/YT	0.665
δ	2.000	I/Y	0.217	GT/YT	0.017
η	0.316	G/Y	0.092	IT/YT	0.323
ω	0.342	NX/Y	−0.001	CN/YN	0.708
σ	2.000	YT/YN	0.648	GN/YN	0.141
				IN/YN	0.151

of the standard deviations, GDP correlations and first-order autocorrelations show negligible differences across the economies with and without the borrowing constraint (except for those pertaining to foreign assets and net exports, which figure 7.4 clearly predicts should change dramatically). Thus, in general the presence of the liquidity requirement does not alter the long-run business cycle features of the economy. As argued earlier, this is an important feature of models that aim to explain Sudden Stops as rare events nested within a setup in which 'regular' business cycles are more common. But, can the model replicate a Sudden Stop?

To answer this question, figure 7.5 plots the impact effects of a change from a state of nature with high productivity, low world interest rate and low tax rate, or the 'best' state, to the 'worst state' with the opposite features on the model's endogenous variables as functions of the foreign bond position. The plots show that in the region of negative bond positions (i.e. debt positions) in which the change from one state to the other triggers the borrowing constraint the model displays several Sudden Stop features. This Sudden Stop region is the one for which the foreign assets–output ratio rises as the bond position falls in the first plot of figure 7.5. In this region, there are large, sudden reversals in the current account, collapses in domestic production and consumption and sharp declines in the relative price of non-tradables.

Mendoza (2002a) elaborates on the economic forces that explain the markedly non-linear pattern of the impact effects shown in figure 7.5 by examining the model's optimality conditions and the distortions imposed on them by the multiplier on the borrowing constraint. Note that within

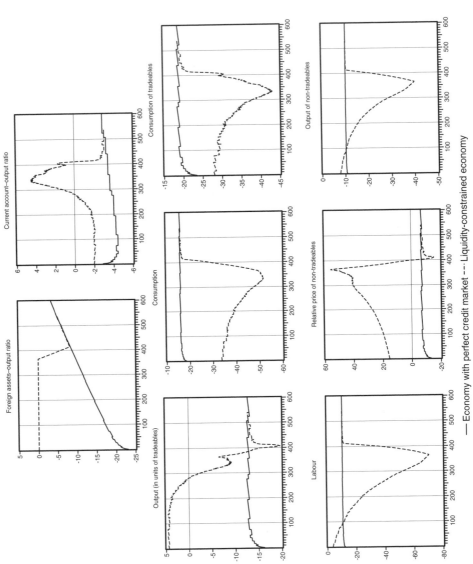

Figure 7.5 Impact effects of a shift from 'best' to 'worst' state (as a function of the foreign asset grid)

Table 7.2 *Business cycle comovements in the limiting distribution of model economies*

	Mean	Standard[a] dev.	Standard dev. relative to GDP of non-tradables	First-order autocorrelation	Correlation with GDP
Economy with perfect credit markets					
Net foreign assets	−0.097	0.883	14.274	0.999	0.321
GDP in units of tradables	2.598	7.307	1.829	0.931	1.000
Tradables GDP	1.000	3.368	0.843	0.553	0.387
Non-tradables GDP	1.548	3.995	1.000	0.633	0.387
Labour	0.524	5.003	1.252	0.928	0.976
Consumption	0.924	6.254	1.565	0.839	0.823
Consumption of tradables	0.683	10.162	2.544	0.934	0.996
Consumption of non-tradables	1.097	5.635	1.411	0.633	0.387
Net exports	0.002	25.987	6.504	0.623	−0.025
Price of non-tradables	1.033	11.925	2.985	0.815	0.874
World real interest rate	1.016	0.880	0.220	0.553	−0.071
Economy with liquidity constraint					
Net foreign assets	0.258	0.679	10.957	0.999	0.313
GDP in units of tradables	2.612	7.323	1.830	0.931	1.000
Tradables GDP	1.000	3.368	0.842	0.553	0.391
Non-tradables GDP	1.549	4.002	1.000	0.633	0.391
Labour	0.525	5.008	1.252	0.928	0.978
Consumption	0.927	6.226	1.566	0.838	0.823
Consumption of tradables	0.688	10.158	2.538	0.934	0.996
Consumption of non-tradables	1.098	5.643	1.410	0.633	0.391
Net exports	−0.004	9.150	2.287	0.599	−0.003
Price of non-tradables	1.041	11.880	2.969	0.815	0.874
World real interest rate	1.016	0.880	0.220	0.553	−0.069

Note: [a] All standard deviations are in per cent of the corresponding mean, except for the one corresponding to the net foreign asset position.

the Sudden Stops region, output, consumption and labour levels always drop and large current account reversals always occur, but the relative price of non-tradables can fall sharply or increase sharply. This feature of the model results from the elastic labour supply that is assigned fully to the

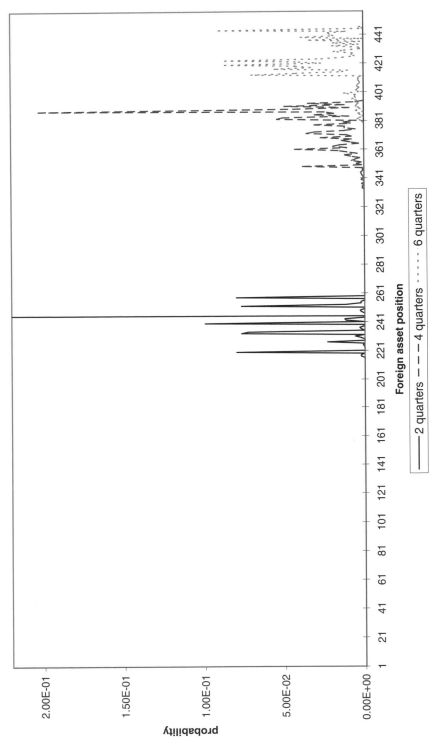

Figure 7.6 Transition distributions of net foreign assets in liquidity-constrained economy with risk aversion coefficient set at 2.0 (from largest initial debt position and random shocks in state 1)

non-tradables sector. Under these conditions, a Sudden Stop lowers the equilibrium allocations of both tradables' and non-tradables' consumption, but the relative price of non-tradables can increase or fall depending on which of the two falls by more. If instead non-tradables are modelled as being in inelastic supply when the Sudden Stop hits, as in Calvo's (1998) model, the real exchange rate would always fall. This could be done either by making labour supply inelastic or by assuming that labour is used to produce tradables. However, the fall in the relative price of non-tradables could also be obtained under less extreme assumptions (allowing for elastic labour even going into both sectors), as long as the contraction in tradables' consumption is larger than that in non-tradables.

The effect of precautionary savings is evident on the ergodic distribution of asset holdings in the economy with the liquidity requirement compared with the one with perfect credit markets (see figure 7.4). Precautionary savings rule out observing states of nature with relatively high debt positions in the long run. In fact, there is only one foreign asset position with non-zero long-run probability and a binding borrowing constraint, which shows in the plot as the leftmost spike in the limiting distribution of the model with the liquidity requirement. Interestingly, the liquidity requirement imposes directly a constraint on the debt to GDP *ratio* but this yields optimising behaviour that results in an ergodic distribution of foreign assets that is similar to the one that would be obtained with a constraint on a maximum *level* of debt. The reason is again precautionary savings: households maintain a buffer stock of saving to avoid painful large downward adjustments in the argument of utility $c - \frac{n^\delta}{\delta}$ because of the curvature of the period utility function. In particular, they do not want to be exposed to the risk that this argument could become infinitesimally small (i.e. marginal utility grows infinitely large) when the income realisation is low, initial debt is high and the borrowing constraint suddenly binds. Hence, at equilibrium, they build up precautionary savings up to the point that in the long run the *level* of bond holdings is above a minimum such that this is not possible under any triple ψ.

Precautionary savings does not imply that if the economy starts from any high debt level, including those in the Sudden Stop region, it would jump immediately out of this region and into the region of non-binding borrowing constraints. Figures 7.6 and 7.7 show the transitional dynamics of the conditional distribution of bond holdings starting from the largest debt position for $\sigma = 2$ and $\sigma = 5$. With $\sigma = 2$, the economy transitions out of the Sudden Stop range in about six quarters, but with $\sigma = 5$ it takes about fifty quarters. The economy can take a while to build up the buffer

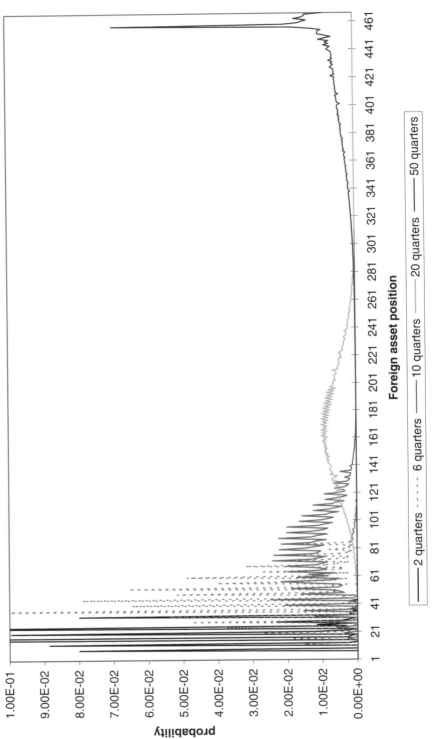

Figure 7.7 Transition distributions of net foreign assets in liquidity-constrained economy with risk aversion coefficient set at 5.0 (from largest initial debt position and random shocks in state 1)

stock of savings that permits it to part from the region of the state space in which it is exposed to Sudden Stops caused by standard productivity, interest rate and tax shocks that trigger binding borrowing constraints. These transitional dynamics reflect the fact that, even though the model behaves in the long run as if it featured a maximum debt constraint, this constraint is not binding in the short run for optimal decision rules starting from high-debt initial conditions.

4.2 Margin requirements, transactions costs and asset prices

The next application incorporates the use of a borrower's assets as collateral. As mentioned earlier, one type of collateral constraint that has been widely used in the literature on emerging markets crises is that studied by Kiyotaki and Moore (1997). In their framework, collateral is in the form of assets subject to a *credible* threat of confiscation by lenders in the event of default (with the credibility of the threat hinging on institutional arrangements that allow lenders to confiscate assets). In this setting, lenders never lend more than the expected discounted liquidation value of the collateral. An alternative type of collateral constraints commonly used in financial markets is in the form of margin requirements, which differ from K–M constraints in two key respects. First, custody of the collateral is passed onto creditors when the debt contract is entered, so there is no uncertainty regarding the lenders' ability or willingness to confiscate the assets. Second, the collateral constraint is set in terms of the *current* (or end-of-period) liquidation value of the collateral. Thus, a decline in asset prices triggers a 'margin call' by which lenders require borrowers to fill in a gap between the contracted margin requirement and the market value of the collateral under the lenders' control. If borrowers fail to meet the call, lenders liquidate the assets. Some margin requirements exist as a regulatory practice imposed by government agencies supervising financial intermediaries but many others are set as explicit or implicit clauses of credit contracts. For example, Value-at-risk collateralisation by which lenders set aside collateral to cover losses in worst-case scenarios, are also a form of margin requirements.

If margin requirements affected only the ability to contract debt of a subset of financial market participants in an environment of otherwise frictionless and efficient asset markets, margin constraints would be harmless from a macroeconomic standpoint. At least two additional asset market frictions are needed to permit margin constraints to have non-trivial effects on intertemporal plans and asset prices at the aggregate level. First, short positions on assets other than debt must be constrained. If an agent faces a binding borrowing limit in the credit market but borrowing by taking a sufficiently large short position on assets is feasible, any potentially binding credit constraint can be undone by setting debt to zero and going short on assets. Second, for asset prices to fall when margin constraints bind for some agents there must be frictions affecting asset trading with other agents. If a borrower's assets are sold to meet a margin call but aggregate asset demand is infinitely elastic at the fundamentals asset price, as it would be in a frictionless environment, the margin sale can be executed and the collateral restored without a drop in the asset price.

Consider an economy with similar preferences and technology as in the liquidity requirements model but modified to introduce margin requirements and asset trading costs. This model is a variation of a heterogeneous agents model with two agents: a small open economy and a representative foreign securities firm specialised in trading the equity of the small open economy. Since there is also a global credit market determining the world real interest rate on bonds, relative to which both the small open economy and the securities firm are very small, the large pool of lenders in world credit markets can be interpreted as representing a trivial third set of agents.

Firms producing inside the small open economy are the same as before, assuming now only a single tradable commodity for simplicity. Hence, the conditions that determine the demand for labour and dividends payments are standard marginal productivity conditions:

$$w_t = \exp(\varepsilon_t) F_n(k, n_t) \tag{7.11}$$

$$d_t = \exp(\varepsilon_t) F_k(k, n_t) \tag{7.12}$$

for $t = 0, \ldots, \infty$.

Preferences are the one-good version of those used in the liquidity requirements model, so consumption in the argument of utility $(c - \frac{n^\delta}{\delta})$ corresponds now to consumption of a single tradable good. Households maximise lifetime utility subject to this budget constraint:

$$c_t = \alpha_t k d_t + w_t n_t + q_t(\alpha_t - \alpha_{t+1})k - b_{t+1} + b_t R_t \tag{7.13}$$

where α_t and α_{t+1} are beginning- and end-of-period shares of the time-invariant domestic capital stock owned by domestic households and q_t is the price of equity. For simplicity, the world's risk-free gross real interest rate is now assumed to be deterministic and tax shocks are ignored.

The margin requirement imposes the following borrowing constraint on households:

$$b_{t+1} \geq -\kappa q_t \alpha_{t+1} k, \quad 0 \leq \kappa \leq 1. \tag{7.14}$$

This constraint limits the extent to which the small open economy can leverage its external debt position in the bond market using its equity holdings. The debt cannot exceed the fraction κ of the value of end-of-period equity holdings. Note that, given the budget constraint (7.13), the margin constraint is equivalent to a flow constraint requiring that a fraction $1 - \kappa$ of the economy's equity purchases be paid out of current saving (i.e. $\alpha_t k(d_t + q_t) + w_t n_t + b_t R_t - c_t \geq (1 - \kappa) q_t \alpha_{t+1} k$).

In addition to the budget constraint and the margin requirement, the small open economy faces a constraint that imposes a lower bound on its equity position $\alpha_{t+1} \geq \chi$ for $-\infty < \chi < 1$ for $t = 1, \ldots, \infty$. As explained earlier, this lower bound ensures that the state space of the small open economy's optimisation problem is compact and that the margin requirement is not irrelevant. A short-selling constraint is represented by $\chi \leq 0$ while $0 < \chi < 1$ can be interpreted as a portfolio requirement.

The optimality conditions of the maximisation problem faced by households and firms imply that the equilibrium of the labour market, factor payments and the level of output are determined by a set of static equilibrium conditions independent of the intertemporal elements of the model (particularly the dynamics of debt, equity and equity prices). This is because (a) the Greenwood, Hercowitz and Huffman (1988) (GHH) specification of the argument of $u(.)$ and $v(.)$ implies that the marginal rate of substitution between c and n depends on n only, so labour supply is just a function of the real wage and does not shift with c, and (b) the demand for labour is given by the standard marginal productivity condition (7.11). These static labour demand and supply conditions determine the equilibrium sequences of w_t, n_t and $\exp(\varepsilon_t) F(k, n_t)$ and given those condition (7.12) determines the equilibrium sequence of d_t. All of these sequences are stochastic because of the Markov process driving ε.

The representative foreign securities firm maximises the present discounted value of the stream of dividends that it pays to its global shareholders. These firms incur two types of costs in trading the small open economy's equity: recurrent and per-trade costs. These represent the costs that the firm incurs in gathering and processing information particular to the small open economy. Per-trade transactions costs are a common feature of the quantitative asset pricing literature (e.g. Heaton and Lucas 1996). Recurrent costs are added to capture the notion that with regard to emerging markets, foreign traders face non-trivial recurrent costs to follow economic, political and social developments in the countries they invest in.

Calvo and Mendoza (2000b) argue that an arrangement where a pool of largely uninformed global investors invests in informed securities firms, which specialise in emerging markets and pay information costs, may be an endogenous feature of globalised financial markets. The reason is that in a world with short-selling constraints, a global investor's gain of acquiring country-specific information falls as the number of markets in which to invest grows.

The problem of the foreign traders is to choose α^*_{t+1} for $t = 1, \ldots, \infty$ so as to maximise:

$$
D = E_0 \left[\sum_{t=0}^{\infty} M^*_t \left(\alpha^*_t k (d_t + q_t) - q_t \alpha^*_{t+1} k \right. \right.
$$

$$
\left. \left. - q_t \left(\frac{a}{2} \right) ((\alpha^*_{t+1} - \alpha^*_t + \theta) k)^2 \right) \right] \tag{7.15}
$$

where $M^*_0 \equiv 1$ and $M_t{}^*$ for $t = 1, \ldots, \infty$ are the exogenous stochastic discount factors representing the trader's opportunity cost of funds or (at equilibrium) the marginal rates of substitution between c_t and c_0 for the hypothetical world 'representative client' of foreign securities firms. Since these firms are very small compared to the size of the global credit market, and since the model abstracts from collateral constraints on foreign traders, setting $M_t{}^* = R^{-t}$ is a reasonable assumption. Trading costs $q_t(\frac{a}{2})((\alpha^*_{t+1} - \alpha^*_t + \theta) k)^2$ are a function of the size of the trades $(\alpha^*_{t+1} - \alpha^*_t)$ and of a recurrent entry cost θ. Even if the firm does not trade, it incurs each period a total recurrent cost equal to $q_t(\frac{a}{2})(\theta k)^2$. The parameter a is a 'speed-of-adjustment' coefficient governing marginal transactions costs.

Define the fundamentals equity price q_t^f as the conditional expected value of the stream of dividends discounted using the world's representative agent stochastic discount factors: $q_t^f \equiv E_t(\sum_{i=0}^{\infty} M^*_{t+1+i} d_{t+1+i})$. It follows from the optimality conditions of the foreign trader's problem that:

$$
(\alpha^*_{t+1} - \alpha^*_t) k = a^{-1} \left(\frac{q_t^f}{q_t} - 1 \right) - \theta. \tag{7.16}
$$

Thus, foreign securities firms follow a partial-portfolio-adjustment rule by which their demand for equity is an increasing function of the percentage deviation of the fundamentals equity price from the actual equity price. The price elasticity of this demand function is approximated by $1/a$.

Given the probabilistic processes of the exogenous shocks and the initial conditions $(b_0, \alpha_0, \alpha^*_0)$, a competitive equilibrium for this model is defined by sequences of state-contingent allocations $[c_t, n_t, b_{t+1}, \alpha_{t+1}, \alpha^*_{t+1}]$ and prices $[w_t, d_t, q_t]$ for $t = 0, \ldots, \infty$ such that: (a) domestic firms maximise dividends subject to the CRS production technology, taking factor and goods prices as given, (b) households maximise expected utility subject to the budget constraint, the margin constraint and the short-selling constraint, taking as given factor prices, goods prices, the world interest rate and the price of equity, (c) foreign securities firms maximise the expected present value of dividends net of the trading costs, taking as given equity prices and (d) the market-clearing conditions for equity, labour and goods markets hold.

How do margin constraints and trading costs affect equilibrium asset prices and macroeconomics dynamics? The lack of closed form solutions implies that this question cannot be fully answered analytically, but it is still possible to derive useful analytical results by examining the Euler equations for bonds and equities of the small open economy and the partial adjustment rule of foreign traders.

The Euler equations for b_{t+1} and α_{t+1} in the small open economy can be manipulated to yield 'partial-equilibrium' expressions for excess returns and equity prices as perceived by residents of this economy. These expressions are analogous to standard results from asset pricing models. The mean excess return on equity can be expressed as:

$$E_t\left[R_{t+1}^q\right] - R_{t+1} = \frac{\eta_t(1-\kappa) - \dfrac{v_t}{q_t} - COV_t\left(\lambda_{t+1}, R_{t+1}^q\right)}{E_t[\lambda_{t+1}]}. \qquad (7.17)$$

Here, λ_t is the Lagrange multiplier on the small open economy's budget constraint (i.e. the lifetime marginal utility of c_t), η_t is the multiplier on the margin requirement, v_t is the multiplier on the short-selling constraint, and $R_{t+1}^q \equiv (d_{t+1} + q_{t+1})/q_t$ is the return on equity.

Clearly, if the margin and short-selling constraints never bind, the expected excess return that households require to hold equity is determined by the negative of the covariance between R_{t+1}^q and λ_{t+1}, as in standard asset pricing models. If both constraints bind at date t they affect expected excess returns via the *direct* and *indirect* effects identified by Heaton and Lucas (1996). The direct effects are given by $\eta_t(1-\kappa)$ and $-v_t/q_t$. A binding margin constraint increases the excess return by the amount $\eta_t(1-\kappa)$. A binding short-selling constraint reduces the excess return by v_t/q_t. The indirect effects depend on how the reduced ability to smooth consumption implied by these two frictions alters the covariance between the marginal utility of consumption and the return on equity. The covariance is negative for risky assets like equity, and it becomes more negative in the presence of frictions hampering consumption smoothing (although the resulting effect on unconditional excess returns has been found to be small in quantitative applications like that of Heaton and Lucas 1996).

The small open economy's partial equilibrium asset pricing equation reduces to:

$$q_t = E_t \left(\sum_{i=0}^{\infty} \left[\prod_{j=0}^{i} \left(E_t[R^q_{t+1+j}] \right)^{-1} \right] d_{t+1+i} \right), \qquad (7.18)$$

where the sequence of $E_t[R^q_{t+1+j}]$ is given by (7.17). Thus, a binding margin requirement at any date $t + j$ for $j \geq 0$ increases the expected return on equity that agents in the small open economy use to discount the future stream of dividends, and hence reduces their valuation of equity at t. Interestingly, date-t equity prices fall whenever agents expect that there can be margin calls in the future, even if the margin constraint does not bind at t (a result first noted in the closed economy model of margin requirements by Aiyagari and Gertler 1999).

It follows from the above results that when a margin call takes place, agents in the small open economy rush to sell equity and adjust their debt position, and thus the equity premium they require increases. Since they meet in the equity market with foreign traders who are willing to buy more equity only if the price falls below the fundamentals level, the equilibrium equity price falls. However, this makes the margin constraint even more binding, triggering another round of margin calls in a downward spiral like the one described in Irving Fisher's classic debt-deflation mechanism.

By inverting the foreign traders' demand function in (7.16), and imposing the market-clearing condition in the equity market, $\alpha_t + \alpha^*_t = 1$ for all t, one finds that at equilibrium equity prices must satisfy $q_t = q^f_t /[1 + a(\alpha_t - \alpha_{t+1} + \theta)]$. Thus, the magnitude of the equity price decline is larger the lower the elasticity of the foreign traders' demand curve (i.e. the higher is a). This is because the higher is a the more the equity price needs to fall in order to entice foreign traders to buy the equity that the small open economy wishes to sell. As argued earlier, if their demand were infinitely elastic (i.e. $a = 0$), the small open economy could reduce its equity holdings without lowering the price. Note also that, since the short-selling constraint imposes a lower bound on equity prices, the equity price collapse in response to a margin call is larger the larger the excess of initial equity holdings relative to the level of the short-selling constraint (i.e. the larger is $\alpha_t - \chi$). This is because a binding short-selling constraint limits the magnitude of the 'fire sale' of equity that the small open economy can undertake. If the constraint binds, so $\alpha_{t+1} = \chi$, the fire sale of equity is larger the larger α_t is relative to χ. If $\alpha_t = \chi$, no equity can be sold and the equilibrium market price must remain at q_t^f.

The recurrent trading costs also play an important role in the model's dynamics. If $M_t^* = R^{-t}$ and equity is a risky asset for the small open economy at all points in the state space, a model with $\theta = 0$ ends up in the long run with foreign traders owning the maximum equity that the short-selling constraint on domestic residents permits them to own $(1 - \chi)$. This occurs because for any initial α_t, the fact that equity is a risky asset for the small open economy implies that its valuation of equity is lower than that implied by discounting dividends at the risk free rate (i.e. lower than q_t^f). However, at a price lower than q_t^f the foreign trader is always buying equity. Hence, if an equilibrium exists, it will be at a price at which the small open economy sets $\alpha_{t+1} < \alpha_t$. Thus, in the long run domestic residents always hit the short-selling constraint. On the other hand, if $\theta > 0$ the equity price at which foreign traders chose a stationary equity position is lower than the fundamentals price, making it possible to obtain states of nature in which domestic agents may set $\alpha_{t+1} \geq \alpha_t$ at the equilibrium price.

The competitive equilibrium of this model is solved by reformulating it in recursive form and by applying a recursive numerical solution method (the algorithm is described in detail in the appendix, p. 400). Define α and b as the endogenous state variables and ε as the exogenous state. The state space of equity positions spans the discrete interval $[\chi, \alpha^{\max}]$ with NA elements and the state space of debt position spans the discrete interval $[b^{\min}, b^{\max}]$ with NB elements. The endogenous state space is thus defined by the discrete set $Z = [\chi, \alpha^{\max}] \times [b^{\min}, b^{\max}]$ of NA $\times$ NB elements. Productivity shocks follow an asymptotically stationary, two-point Markov chain with realisations ε_H and ε_L, so the exogenous state space is defined by $E = \{\varepsilon_H, \varepsilon_L\}$. Since equilibrium wages, dividends and factor payments depend only on the realisation of ε, these equilibrium outcomes can be expressed by the functions $w(\varepsilon)$, $d(\varepsilon)$ and $n(\varepsilon)$.

Assume a continuous non-negative equity pricing function that is taken as given by foreign traders and the small open economy. The conjectured pricing function maps the state space into equity prices $q(\alpha, b, \varepsilon)$: $E \times Z \to R^+$. For any initial state (α, b, ε), the conjecture must satisfy $q(\alpha, b, \varepsilon) \in [q^{\min}(\alpha, \varepsilon), q^{\max}(\alpha, \varepsilon)]$, where $q^{\min}(\alpha, \varepsilon) = q^f(\varepsilon)/[1 + a(\alpha - \chi + \theta)]$ and $q^{\max}(\alpha, \varepsilon) = q^f(\varepsilon)/[1 + a(\alpha - \alpha^{\max} + \theta)]$ are the minimum and maximum equity prices along the foreign traders' demand curve for an initial state with equity holding α and productivity shock ε. These bounds of the pricing function follow from the fact that when the small open economy hits either the short-selling constraint or the upper bound α^{max}, the foreign traders are at the 'short side' of the market (assuming the equity demand curves of both players are well behaved with the one of the foreign traders always flatter than that of the small open economy).

Imposing market clearing in the equity market, the conjectured pricing function and the foreign trader's partial adjustment decision rule can be combined to formulate the following conjectured transition equation for equity holdings:

$$\hat{\alpha}'(\alpha, b, \varepsilon) = \alpha - \frac{1}{a} * \left(\frac{q^f(\varepsilon)}{q(\alpha, b, \varepsilon)} - 1 \right) + \theta. \qquad (7.19)$$

Taking as given this conjectured transition equation, the conjectured pricing function and the equilibrium functions for factor payments and labour allocations, one can formulate a dynamic programming problem that yields optimal consumption and bond holdings for the small open economy. This dynamic programming problem is:

$$V(\alpha, b, \varepsilon)$$

$$= \max_{b'} \left\{ \frac{\left[c - \frac{n(\varepsilon)^\delta}{\delta} \right]^{1-\sigma} - 1}{1 - \sigma} + \exp\left(-\beta \left[Ln\left(1 + c - \frac{n(\varepsilon)^\delta}{\delta} \right) \right] \right) \right.$$

$$\left. \times E[V(\hat{\alpha}'(\alpha, b, \varepsilon), b', \varepsilon')] \right\} \qquad (7.20)$$

subject to:

$$c = \alpha k d(\varepsilon) + w(\varepsilon)n(\varepsilon) + q(\alpha, b, \varepsilon)k[\alpha - \hat{\alpha}'(\alpha, b, \varepsilon)] - b' + bR \qquad (7.21)$$

$$b' \geq -\kappa q(\alpha, b, \varepsilon)\hat{\alpha}'(\alpha, b, \varepsilon)k. \qquad (7.22)$$

The solutions to this problem represent optimal consumption and bond accumulation choices by the small open economy for *any* given conjectured pricing function and corresponding equity transition equation. These optimal plans can then be used together with the asset pricing formulas in (7.17) and (7.18) to compute the actual equity pricing function, $\bar{q}(\alpha, b, \varepsilon)$, at which the small open economy would agree to the trades implicit in the conjectured pricing and equity transition equations in a competitive equity market. In general, for an arbitrary initial conjectured pricing function, the conjectured and the actual equity pricing functions will differ. An updated conjectured pricing function can then be created using a Gauss–Seidel algorithm until the distance between the two functions satisfies a reasonable convergence criterion.[6]

The optimal decision rules obtained after the conjectured and actual pricing functions converge constitute a recursive competitive equilibrium for the model. In a recursive equilibrium, the optimal rules determining equity holdings, bond holdings, consumption, labour, wages, dividends, foreign equity holdings and the equity pricing function are such that: (a) given equity prices, wages and dividends, the policy functions for c, b', α' and n solve the maximisation problems of households and firms in the small open economy, (b) given equity prices and dividends, the policy function for α'^* solves the maximisation problem of foreign traders and (c) the market-clearing conditions for equity, goods and labour markets hold.[7]

This model is calibrated and solved in Mendoza and Smith (2002) using similar parameters as in Mendoza (2002a). The experiments conducted here use the same calibration. Mendoza and Smith constructed a benchmark calibration in which an RBC-like calibration exercise determines the values of the parameter set $(\gamma, \sigma, \beta, \delta, R)$ and the properties of the Markov process of productivity shocks. The parameters' values are $\gamma = 0.341, \sigma = 1.1, \beta = 0.04518, \delta = 2$ and $R = 1.065^{1/4}$. The values of γ, β, and R are derived from Mexican data (see Mendoza and Smith 2002a for details). The value of σ is in line with values used in the RBC literature, although it is lower than available estimates for Mexico. The value of δ is set to yield unitary wage elasticity in labour supply. The standard deviation of productivity shocks is set to match that of Mexico's GDP of tradable goods in quarterly data (3.36 per cent), and the transition probability matrix is assumed to be symmetric with a conditional probability of switching states set to match the first-order autocorrelation of Mexico's tradables output (0.553).

The values of the financial friction parameters $(\kappa, \theta, a, \chi)$ are set first to baseline values such that the margin constraint is not binding in all

---

[6] Since this 'hog cycle' algorithm is not a contraction mapping, the Gauss–Seidel algorithm uses dampening and extrapolation corrections to improve accuracy and avoid exploding cycles.

[7] This is easy to prove noting that: (i) the Benveniste–Sheinkman equation applied to problem (7.20) yields the same Euler equation for bond holdings as the households' maximisation problem, (ii) by construction, the implied equity prices ensure that at equilibrium the households' Euler equation for equity holdings also holds (up to the error allowed by the convergence criterion), (iii) the wage, dividend and labour functions reflect optimal decisions by households and domestic firms, (iv) the conjectured transition equation for equity holdings ensures that the trades undertaken at the equilibrium equity prices solve the maximisation problem of foreign traders, and (v) the constraints (7.21) and (7.22) combined with results (i)–(iv) ensure that the market-clearing conditions, the households' budget constraint and the margin constraint are satisfied.

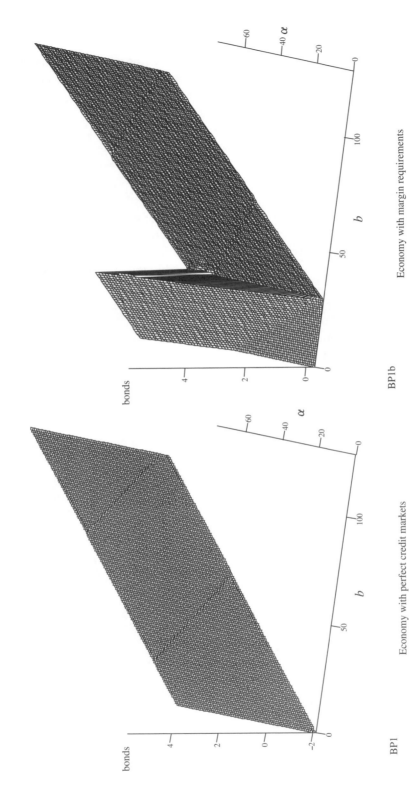

BP1

Economy with perfect credit markets

BP1b

Economy with margin requirements

Figure 7.8 Foreign bond decision rules for economies with and without margin requirements in low-productivity state (as functions of the (α, b) pairs in the discretised state space Z)

of *ExZ*, and then κ is increased to obtain a binding margin constraint. The baseline values are $\theta = 0$, $a = 0.001$ and $\chi = 0.8742$, which support unconstrained equilibrium allocation with any $\kappa \geq 0.011$ for grids with 130 evenly spaced bond positions in the interval $[-0.634, 5.691]$ and 76 evenly spaced equity positions in the interval $[0.874, 0.969]$. The simulation with binding margin requirements uses $\kappa = 0.009$.

The manifolds of the optimal decision rule for bond holdings in economies with and without margin constraints (for the low realisation of the shock) are plotted in figure 7.8. Manifolds of the corresponding equity prices are plotted in figure 7.9. Note that in the manifolds for the margin-constrained economy there is a 'low-wealth' triangular valley that should be ignored because α and b are too low for the non-negativity constraint on the argument of utility to be satisfied together with the margin constraint. In each plot, this area is set to show values of the variable being plotted equal to the value that corresponds to the lowest (α, b) pair for which a solution satisfying the non-negativity constraint exists.

Figure 7.8 shows that, even in this experiment with a very high elasticity in the equity demand of foreign traders (at $a = 0.001$ the elasticity is 100) and no recurrent trading costs, the margin constraint alters significantly foreign asset holdings. The difference in bond positions is striking, as the decision rule changes from a smooth, increasing function of α and b to a non-linear function with a sharp jump at the point in which debt is sufficiently high for the margin constraint to bind. The jump is larger the higher is α because these are also the states in which the equity price falls by more (see figure 7.9), and hence the Fisherian deflation inducing tighter margin constraints in response to falling asset prices is stronger. However, the equity price collapses were bound to be quantitatively small given that the very high elasticity of the foreign traders' demand for equity implies that their demand curve is almost horizontal at the level of the fundamentals price.

The impact effects on consumption and the current account–output ratio in response to a switch from the high productivity state to the low productivity state are plotted in figures 7.10 and 7.11, respectively. Figure 7.10, in combination with figures 7.8 and 7.9, shows a key difference between this application and the liquidity requirements model: with two assets to allocate savings into, agents have an extra degree of freedom in their efforts to mitigate the consumption effect of a binding borrowing constraint. As figure 7.10 shows, in states in which debt is high enough for the constraint to bind but initial equity holdings are large, agents manage to keep a relatively smooth consumption path (despite the large adjustments

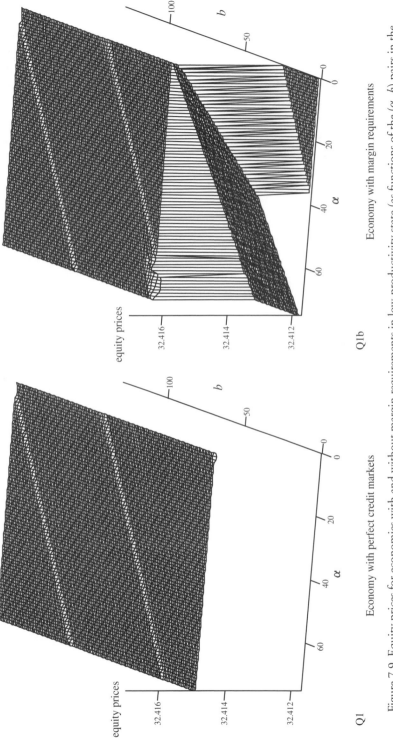

Q1

Economy with perfect credit markets

Q1b

Economy with margin requirements

Figure 7.9 Equity prices for economies with and without margin requirements in low-productivity state (as functions of the (α, b) pairs in the discretised state space Z)

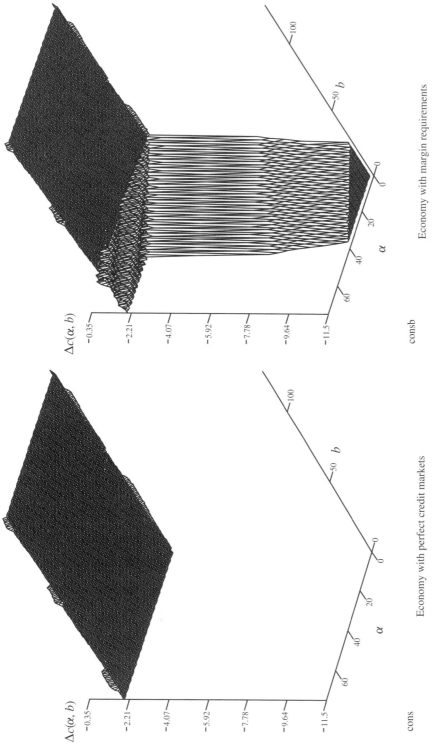

$\Delta c(\alpha, b)$

cons

Economy with perfect credit markets

$\Delta c(\alpha, b)$

consb

Economy with margin requirements

Figure 7.10 Impact effects on consumption in response to a shift from high- to low-productivity states (as functions of the (α, b) pairs in the discretised state space Z)

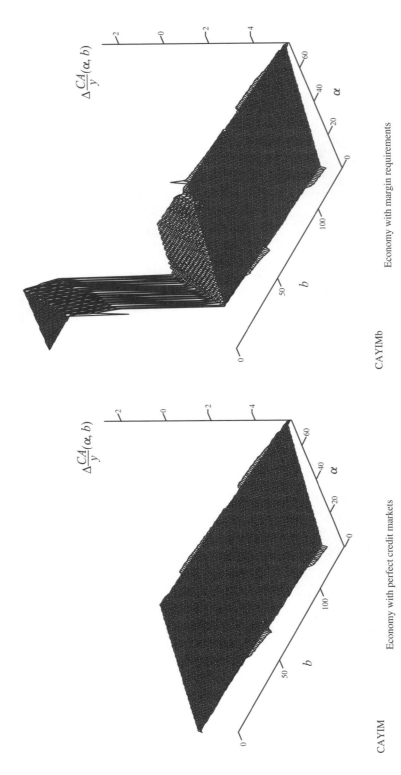

CAYIM   Economy with perfect credit markets   CAYIMb   Economy with margin requirements

Figure 7.11 Impact effects on the current account–output ratio in response to a shift from high- to low-productivity states(as functions of the (α, b) pairs in the discretised state space Z)

in both equity prices and bond holdings shown in figures 7.8 and 7.9). In states in which agents have a low equity position, consumption falls sharply. The largest consumption declines are observed when the margin constraint switches from non-binding to binding when the productivity shock hits, they can reach up to 11.5 per cent. Figure 7.11 shows a similar pattern for the response of the current account–output ratio. Small reversals of current account deficits occur in response to the productivity shock in the area of the state space in which the consumption impact effect is modest, but reversals of up to 2.5 percentage points of GDP are possible when the consumption decline is at its maximum.

4.3 The willingness-to-pay case: borrowing constraints enforcing participation constraints

Liquidity requirements and collateral constraints are features of a variety of private credit contracts but when it comes to instruments like sovereign debt there is limited scope for enforcing contracts featuring those constraints. In this context, a modelling approach based on willingness-to-pay considerations seems an appealing alternative. Hence, in this application we study a small open economy that faces a standard credit market participation constraint. In case of default, the country is punished by permanent exclusion from world financial markets, so default is optimal whenever the expected lifetime utility of staying in a credit relationship exceeds that of living permanently under financial autarky.

The analysis conducted here differs from those in Alvarez and Jermann (2000), Kehoe and Levine (1993), Kehoe and Perri (2002) and Kocherlakota (1996), in that the model retains the asset market incompleteness of the small open economy RBC setting, in contrast with the complete contingent claims markets assumed in those studies (which were not aimed at explaining Sudden Stops but at studying equilibria in which there can be as much risk-sharing as possible given that participation constraints are satisfied). As Alvarez and Jermann (2000) showed, the equilibrium with participation constraints and complete markets can be decentralised with financial markets that feature endogenous, state-contingent limits on short positions for state-contingent assets. Interestingly, the incomplete markets, small open economy RBC model with a participation constraint can also be represented as an economy that faces an endogenous borrowing constraint, but with the caveat that the constraint is not state-contingent. This brings the model closer to the analysis of participation constraints under incomplete markets by Zhang (1997) than to the models in the Kehoe–Levine–Kocherlakota line.

In the model presented here, precautionary savings interact with default incentives to give rise to the endogenous non-state-contingent borrowing constraint, which ensures that agents have incentives to repay their debts, and thus enforces the participation constraint. The borrowing constraint is determined by the highest level of foreign asset holdings for which the expected lifetime utility of staying in a credit relationship is equal to the expected lifetime utility of autarky across all productivity states of nature. This is the case because the model's only financial asset is the non-contingent bond and the decision to default is made one period in the future. In this environment, lenders seeking to enforce participation constraints in all states of nature need to set today a borrowing limit equal to the maximum b_{t+1} among those for which repayment and autarky values are equalised across all realisations of the productivity shock tomorrow. As a consequence, the borrowing constraint cannot vary with the state of nature.

Consider a one-sector small open economy similar in structure to the one examined in the previous application but without equity trading. The small open economy can be viewed as a representative agent economy facing a labour–leisure choice and non-diversifiable, idiosyncratic income risk. Labour allocations, dividends and wages are still governed by the same equilibrium functions of the productivity state $w(\varepsilon)$, $d(\varepsilon)$ and $n(\varepsilon)$. The utility function changes only in that it features now a constant discount factor. Thus, this application obtains a well-defined limiting distribution of foreign assets for the small open economy via precautionary savings. As explained in section 7.2, this requires setting $\beta R < 1$.

The households' budget constraint is:

$$c_t = d_t + w_t n_t - b_{t+1} + b_t R_t. \tag{7.23}$$

This constraint differs from the one in (7.13) only in that domestic agents are owners of the entire domestic capital stock (with $k = 1$ without loss of generality).

The small open economy also faces a standard participation constraint that ensures that it always has the incentive to repay its external debt:

$$V(b_{t+1}, \varepsilon_{t+1}) \geq V^{AUT}(\varepsilon_{t+1}) \quad \text{for all } b_{t+1}, \varepsilon_{t+1}. \tag{7.24}$$

The value of autarky in the right-hand side of (7.24) is state-dependent since it measures the expected utility of the optimal consumption–labour path obtained when consumption is set equal to domestic output at all times, and both labour and output vary with the productivity shock. Under autarky, the small open economy cannot smooth period utility because there are no international financial assets available to facilitate consumption smoothing after the economy defaults. The value of autarky solves the following straightforward functional equation:

$$V(\varepsilon) = \frac{\left(d(\varepsilon) + w(\varepsilon)n(\varepsilon) - \dfrac{n(\varepsilon)^{\delta}}{\delta}\right)^{1-\sigma} - 1}{1 - \sigma} + \beta E[V(\varepsilon')] \quad (7.25)$$

The competitive equilibrium for this economy is defined by sequences of state contingent allocations and prices $[c_t, n_t, b_{t+1}, w_t]$ for $t = 1, \dots, \infty$ such that: (a) domestic firms maximise profits given their production technology, taking factor prices as given, (b) households maximise expected lifetime utility subject to their budget constraint and participation constraint, taking as given factor prices and the world interest rate, (c) international lenders agree to loan contracts that enforce participation constraints and (d) the goods and labour markets clear.

Given that the value function in the left-hand side of (7.24) is increasing and concave in foreign bond holdings, one can translate the participation constraint into an endogenous constraint setting a maximum amount of debt (or minimum level of bond holdings), $\underline{B}$, that guarantees that condition (7.24) holds regardless of the realisation of the productivity shock:

$$b' \geq \underline{B} = \max_{\varepsilon}\{\underline{b}(\varepsilon) : V(b, \varepsilon) = V^{AUT}(\varepsilon)\}. \quad (7.26)$$

This borrowing constraint ensures that the only permissible values of b' at equilibrium are those greater or equal to the largest one, across all productivity states of nature, for which the value of debt repayment equals the value of living in financial autarky.

It is important to separate the question of how $\underline{B}$ is determined (i.e. what determines the gap between continuation and autarky values) from the question of whether this model can reproduce Sudden Stops given $\underline{B}$ (i.e. situations in which the borrowing constraint switches from non-binding to binding in response to standard productivity shocks). Once $\underline{B}$ is set, the model's solution is identical to that of a small open economy model with an exogenous, state- and time-invariant lower bound on foreign assets that just happens to have been set at $\underline{B}$. This yields similar incentives for precautionary savings and long-run distributions of assets as the Aiyagari (1993) incomplete markets model with exogenous borrowing constraints. In particular, the decision rule $b'(b, \varepsilon)$ first equals $\underline{B}$ for low values of b and all values of ε, then at some level of b (which is lower for lower values of ε) it hits a kink and slopes upward for higher values of b. This allows for the possibility that there can be a range of values of b for which $b'(b, \varepsilon) > \underline{B}$ if ε is high but $b'(b, \varepsilon) = \underline{B}$ if ε is low. In this range the model displays Sudden Stops.

The non-state-contingent nature of $\underline{B}$ does limit this model's ability to yield short-term dynamics in which the real effects of Sudden Stops can be very large and prevents it from producing outcomes in which actual Sudden Stops and the likelihood of future Sudden Stops persist for several quarters. The reason is that, in contrast with the previous two applications in which the borrowing constraint varies with the state (either with GDP in units of tradables or with the end-of-period liquidation value of equity), here the constraint is always $\underline{B}$. The economy cannot be assumed to start from higher debt positions because, by backward induction, this would imply that at some point in the past lenders agreed to debt contracts that did not support the participation constraint. Even if they did, the reversal to $\underline{B}$ would take place in one shot once the constraint was imposed.

The level of $\underline{B}$ is determined by the gap between autarky and continuation values, which in turn depends on preferences, technology, initial debt and the stochastic structure of productivity shocks. The effect of initial debt is obvious: since the value of repayment is increasing in b and the value of autarky is independent of b, the incentive for default is always higher the higher the level of debt. The effect of the productivity shocks are easiest to study in the case of a two-point, symmetric Markov chain, with high and low shocks denoted ε^l and ε^h, respectively, such that $\varepsilon^h = -\varepsilon^l = \varepsilon$ and the variance of the shocks is ε^2. In this case, the value of repayment is low the lower the realisation of the productivity shock and the higher the conditional probability of continuing in the low state of the shock. The value of autarky is high the higher the productivity shock and the higher the conditional probability of continuing in the high state of the shock. For given conditional probabilities (i.e. given the persistence of the productivity disturbances), higher variance increases debt repayment incentives, since higher variance increases the benefit of using international debt as a means to smooth consumption. Thus, *ceteris paribus*, this willingness-to-pay setup has the unappealing feature that the economies that exhibit higher income variability would be allowed to borrow more.

The households' coefficient of relative risk aversion matters for default incentives because it influences the curvature of the utility and value functions but its effect on default incentives is ambiguous. For low values of this curvature parameter, the borrowing constraint that supports the participation constraint tends to correspond to the level of debt at which repayment and autarky values are equal when the productivity shock is *high*. In this case, incentives to default are higher in good productivity states. However, for sufficiently high relative risk aversion, *ceteris paribus*, the borrowing constraint that supports the participation constraint is the level of debt at which repayment and autarky values are equal when the productivity shock is *low*. The intuition is that with greater curvature in utility, an agent hit by a negative productivity shock has a higher marginal utility of lower consumption and is thus more willing to default to get a higher consumption level under autarky, than an agent with less curvature in utility.

The controversial implication derived from these arguments is that the model can easily predict that, looking at a cross-section of small open economies identical in preferences and technology, those with more macroeconomic volatility (i.e. higher income variability) should be the ones with a higher capacity to borrow (or with lower values of $\underline{B}$). This is because the high-volatility economies enjoy more benefits from being able to smooth consumption using the global credit market and thus have weaker incentives to default. Note, however, that higher volatility by itself does not imply that the borrowing constraint of a high-volatility country will be set at a higher level than for a low-volatility country because this depends on the combination of the preference, technology and stochastic factors mentioned above.

The solution method used to solve this model is a policy function iteration algorithm that solves recursively for the endogenous borrowing constraint defined in (7.26). The method starts with a guess of $\underline{B}$. Optimal plans are then solved for via policy function iteration on the bond holding decision rules in the corresponding Euler equation. Given these solutions, the method compares the value of expected lifetime utility of continuing in the credit relationship for the given guessed value of $\underline{B}$ with the lifetime utility of autarky, and evaluates whether the pre-set borrowing constraint is the *least tight* that enforces the participation constraint in all productivity states. If it is not, the method finds the levels of bond holdings that support the participation constraints with equality for all states, and chooses the maximum among these as the new guess of $\underline{B}$. The iterations continue until the guess value of $\underline{B}$ set in the first step equals the endogenous constraint computed in the last step. This method is very similar to the one employed by Zhang (1997).

The numerical results reported below illustrate the key properties of the model, using a calibration identical to the one used in the previous application to facilitate comparisons across models. The one important difference

Experiment 1   σ = 5

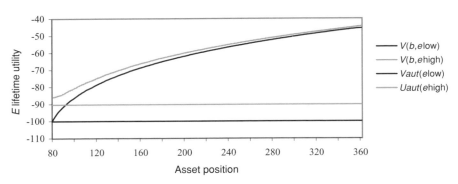

Experiment 2   σ = 2

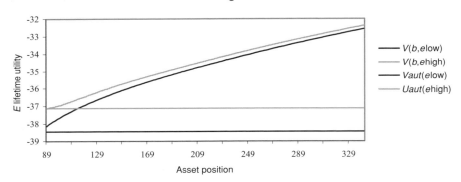

Figure 7.12 Lifetime utilities as functions of bond positions

is that this model uses preferences with a constant discount factor β set to a value such that $\beta R < 1$. That value is set at $\beta = 0.98$, which implies a gross rate of time preference of about 1.02 quarterly or 1.084 in annual terms. Results are reported for two experiments that compare repayment incentives and borrowing constraints for economies with risk aversion coefficients set at 2 and 5, respectively. In the case with $\sigma = 2$, the endogenous borrowing constraint is equivalent to 3.4 per cent of GDP, while in the case with $\sigma = 5$ the borrowing limit reaches 11.6 per cent of GDP.

Figure 7.12 plots the values of repayment and autarky under high and low productivity states as a function of the foreign bond position. These plots show how with $\sigma = 2$ the borrowing constraint is set at the level in which repayment and autarky values cross for the high productivity state, while for $\sigma = 5$ this happens at the debt position that equates the repayment and autarky values for the *low* productivity state.

Figure 7.13 shows the limiting distribution for bond holdings for the economy with $\sigma = 5$. Note that this distribution is similar to the ergodic distribution of foreign assets in the liquidity requirements economy. Recall, however, that there are non-trivial transitional dynamics in the conditional distributions of foreign assets of the liquidity requirements economy when the simulations start from high levels of debt relative to those supported by the ergodic distribution. In contrast, the model with the participation constraint can never start from bond positions below $\underline{B}$ because that would imply that at the time such high debt was acquired the participation constraint did not hold. If one assumes that such an initial high-debt state could be observed, the economy would jump to $\underline{B}$ in one shot.

Figure 7.14 shows impact effects on consumption and foreign asset holdings when the economy switches from high productivity to low productivity. As in the previous applications, the adverse productivity shock in the (high-debt) region of the space of foreign asset holdings in which the borrowing constraint becomes binding when the shock hits causes a large fall in consumption and a reduction in the current account deficit. However, these Sudden Stop effects are quantitatively smaller than those obtained with the ability-to-pay models because the model with the participation constraint can accommodate only initial debt positions that satisfy $b \geq \underline{B}$.

Summing up, the willingness-to-pay model based on a participation constraint under incomplete markets can reproduce some features of a Sudden Stop, but in some dimensions it seems to fall behind the ability-to-pay alternatives. In particular, it can yield a counterfactual prediction regarding macroeconomic volatility and the ability to acquire debt in global credit markets, and it limits the magnitude and persistence of the Sudden Stops it can produce because of the nature of the borrowing constraint it embodies. At the same time, however, this model has the advantage that it enforces *full* consistency in the incentives of borrowers and lenders, while the previous applications rely on the implicit assumption that the frictions they assumed are enough to commit debtors to repay even if debtors are in states in which they could be better off living under autarky.

4.4 Capital accumulation, collateral constraints and Tobin's q

From the perspective of business cycle analysis, the previous three applications miss one important element: capital accumulation. The interaction

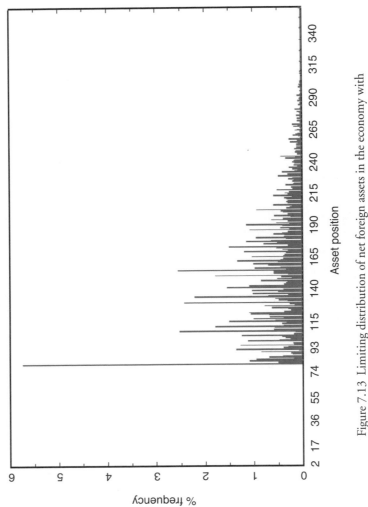

Figure 7.13 Limiting distribution of net foreign assets in the economy with participation constraints (simulation with $\sigma = 5$)

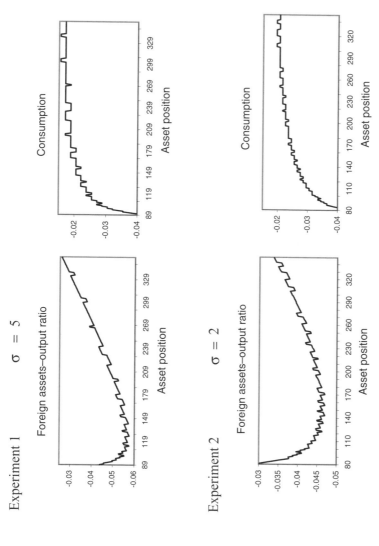

Figure 7.14 Impact effects of a shift from high productivity to low productivity

of credit frictions, the price of capital and the investment process is an important subject to explore as part of the business cycle implications of financial market imperfections. Thus, this last application sketches a full-blown RBC small open economy model with capital accumulation in which foreign debt must satisfy a collateral constraint. The collateral constraint is again in the form of a margin requirement set to a fraction of the end-of-period liquidation value of the capital stock. In this environment, the equilibrium price of equity must satisfy the households' forward-looking asset pricing condition as well as the firms' optimality condition for invest-ment decisions. Firms are assumed to face a standard linearly homogeneous, convex capital-adjustment cost function, so investment follows a Tobin-q decision rule and average q, marginal q and equity prices are the same at equilibrium.

The model shares with the asset pricing model reviewed earlier the as-sumption that a margin requirement forces households to keep their debt equal or smaller than a fraction κ of the value of the capital stock. This model differs in that all equity is held by domestic households and capital accumulation is endogenous.

Firms in this economy have a more dynamic role than in the previous models because they choose labour and investment to maximise the present value of their profits taking as given wages, the cost of funds and the price of capital. Firms operate a constant returns to scale technology and face convex adjustment costs of investment. Firms choose n_t, i_t and k_{t+1} to maximise the expected present discounted value of profits:

$$E_0 \left[\sum_{t=0}^{\infty} \left(\prod_{j=0}^{t} (\tilde{R}_j)^{-1} \right) \left(\exp(\varepsilon_t) F(k_t, n_t) - w_t n_t - i_t \left[1 + \varphi \left(\frac{i_t}{k_t} \right) \right] \right) \right]$$

(7.27)

where $\tilde{R}_0 = 1$ and $\tilde{R}_j$ for $j = 1, .., \infty$ are the stochastic discount factors (or, at equilibrium, the marginal rates of substitution in consumption) that represent the cost of funds to firms. This maximisation problem is subject to the standard capital accumulation equation:

$$i_t = k_{t+1} - k_t(1 - \delta).$$

(7.28)

Note that (7.27) implicitly assumes that firms cannot borrow directly from abroad because profits are not discounted at the world interest rate. How-ever, the assumption that at equilibrium firms discount profits with the households' stochastic discount factor implies that the model permits households, who can borrow from abroad and are the owners of the firms, to provide financing to firms at the interest rate that they find optimal to do so.

The first-order conditions of the firm's problem are:

$$\exp(\varepsilon_t) F(k_t, n_t) = w_t \tag{7.29}$$

$$\left(1 + \varphi\left(\frac{i_t}{k_t}\right) + \left[\frac{i_t}{k_t}\right]\varphi'\left(\frac{i_t}{k_t}\right)\right) = q_t \tag{7.30}$$

$$E_t\left[\left(\tilde{R}_{t+1}\right)^{-1}\left(\exp(\varepsilon_{t+1})F_K(k_{t+1}, n_{t+1})\right.\right.$$

$$\left.\left. + \left[\frac{i_{t+1}}{k_{t+1}}\right]^2\varphi'\left(\frac{i_{t+1}}{k_{t+1}}\right) + (1-\delta)q_{t+1}\right)\right] = q_t \tag{7.31}$$

where q_t is the Lagrange multiplier corresponding to the capital accumulation equation at time t, or the firms' shadow value of investing in one additional unit of capital. These optimality conditions are standard from investment theory. Equation (7.29) is the standard labour demand condition. Equation (7.30) equates the marginal cost of investment with its shadow value, and it implies that investment is an increasing function of q_t because the marginal adjustment cost is increasing in the investment–capital ratio and capital is predetermined one period in advance. Equation (7.31) is an Euler equation that equates the expected discounted marginal return of investment with its shadow value.

The Euler equation also represents an arbitrage condition in implicit form that equates (at equilibrium) the expected marginal gain of adding an extra unit to the capital stock weighed by the households' stochastic intertemporal marginal rate of substitution in consumption with the marginal cost. The expected marginal gain includes dividend payments d_{t+1}, defined as $d_{t+1} \equiv \exp(\varepsilon_{t+1})F_K(k_{t+1}, n_{t+1}) + [\frac{i_{t+1}}{k_{t+1}}]^2\varphi'(\frac{i_{t+1}}{k_{t+1}})$, plus capital gains net of depreciation. The forward solution of (7.31) yields an asset pricing expression for the firm's valuation of capital as a function of the expected present discounted value of dividends

$$(1-\delta)q_t = E_t\left[\sum_{j=0}^{\infty}\left(\prod_{i=0}^{j}\left(\frac{\tilde{R}_{t+1+i}}{(1-\delta)}\right)^{-1}\right)d_{t+1+j}\right]. \tag{7.32}$$

The households' optimisation problem is to maximise expected lifetime utility (returning now to the SCU utility function in (7.1)) subject to the following budget constraint:

$$c_t = (d_t + q_t(1 - \delta)) k_t - q_t k_{t+1} + w_t n_t - b_{t+1} + b_t R_t. \quad (7.33)$$

The collateral constraint implies that households are allowed to borrow up to a fraction κ of the end-of-period value of the capital stock:

$$b_{t+1} \geq -\kappa q_t k_{t+1}. \quad (7.34)$$

The household's problem yields an asset pricing condition similar to (7.17) with an additional depreciation component. In a decentralised competitive equilibrium, households solve their optimisation problem taking equity prices, dividends and wage rates as given. Their valuation of equity reflects the expected present discounted value of the stream of state-contingent dividends, discounted using the sequence of their stochastic discount factors (i.e. the marginal rates of substitution in consumption between date $t + 1 + j$ consumption and date t consumption, for $j = 0, \ldots, \infty$, adjusted to take into account the states in which the collateral constraint binds).

In a rational expectations equilibrium, the equity prices resulting from the households' asset pricing equation must match those obtained from the firm's investment demand decision in (7.32). In other words, at equilibrium the sequence of stochastic discount factors of households, taken as given by firms in solving their optimisation problem, must yield equity prices from the firms' side such that, taking as given those prices, the households' optimisation problem yields the same sequence of stochastic discount factors.

It is possible to use the above characterisation of the equilibrium, combined with the representative agent nature of the model, to write down a recursive formulation of the competitive equilibrium in the form of a planner's problem for the small open economy that takes as given a conjectured equity price function. The planner's problem can be solved repeatedly until convergence is attained between the conjectured pricing function and the actual prices calculated using the values of the households' stochastic discount factors obtained each time the planner's problem is solved. The conjectured pricing function can be updated at each stage using a Gauss–Siedel algorithm like the one proposed on p. 377. Moreover, the investment schedule implied by (7.30) can play the same role played by the trader's partial portfolio adjustment rule in that other application (i.e. it can be used to build a conjectured transition equation for aggregate capital given the conjectured pricing function and the initial capital stock).

Since this model's collateral constraint is a function of the capital accumulation decision, it introduces feedback effects between the constraint (or the incentives to relax it) and the production and investment decisions, wage and dividend rates and the price of capital. Suppose a realisation of the exogenous shocks makes the collateral constraint bind. If equilibrium investment declines as households try to reduce their equity stake to lessen the effect of the suddenly binding constraint on consumption, the price of capital falls by (7.30). This tightens further the constraint producing a Fisherian deflationary effect as in the equity-trading model. In contrast with that model, however, the change in capital accumulation introduces effects on the ability of the economy to generate income that persist over time, as the independence of the equilibrium paths of labour allocations, wage and dividend rates with respect to the credit friction holds longer.[8]

5 CONCLUSIONS

The seven years separating the Mexican financial crisis of December 1994 and the 2001 Argentine crisis witnessed more than a dozen similar financial débâcles across the majority of the so-called emerging markets economies. The novel feature of these crises is the 'Sudden Stop' phenomenon: a sudden loss of access to international capital markets, a marked reversal of the current account deficit, a severe contraction of domestic production and aggregate demand and a collapse in asset prices and in domestic relative prices. Emerging markets crises also displayed a high potential for contagion, as a crisis in one country infected other emerging economies with little or no direct economic linkages with the first.

Explaining Sudden Stops poses a serious challenge to international macroeconomic theory because their features are seriously at odds with the predictions of the mainstream approaches to analyse balance of payments crises and economic fluctuations in open economies. As a result, a growing literature has produced several alternative theoretical models in which financial market imperfections are put forward as a central element of the transmission mechanism that triggers Sudden Stops and contagion of crises across emerging markets. Quantitative applications of these models

---

[8] Mendoza examines the quantitative implications of this model and its ability to explain Sudden Stops in work in progress.

have lagged behind, however, and hence the potential for this approach to offer a plausible explanation of the Sudden Stop phenomenon and a solid basis for policy-evaluation models is largely undetermined.

This chapter surveyed recent developments in an area of quantitative applications of open economy equilibrium business cycle models with financial frictions that aim to fill some of the gaps in the literature on emerging markets crises. The applications featured explicit constraints on a small open economy's ability to borrow from international capital markets linked to ability-to-pay and willingness-to-pay criteria like those at the core of several theoretical and policy studies on Sudden Stops. These borrowing constraints were attached to the optimisation problems of economic agents acting independently in a decentralised competitive environment, and the resulting equilibria were then represented in recursive form. The models were solved using recursive, non-linear numerical methods that are accurate for picking up the kinks in asset accumulation decision rules and the implied non-linearities in the adjustment of macroeconomic aggregates caused by occasionally binding borrowing constraints.

The first application considers a two-sector variant of the standard RBC model for small open economies without capital accumulation in which lenders impose a liquidity requirement on borrowers, by which borrowers must pay a fraction of their current obligations out of current income. Given the households' budget constraint, the liquidity requirement is equivalent to a borrowing constraint limiting the stock of foreign debt not to exceed a fraction of income. The liquidity requirement can thus be interpreted as a tool for managing default risk, and is in line with lending criteria widely applied in credit markets (particularly mortgages and consumer credit). The two-sector nature of the model plays a key role because foreign debt is denominated in units of tradable goods but part of the income on which it is leveraged is generated in the non-tradables sector. Thus, the model captures the 'liability-dollarisation' problem faced in many emerging markets crises: sudden changes in the relative price of non-tradables in terms of tradables, or in the income generated by the non-tradables sector, compromise the ability of borrowers to service debt and magnify the effects of the loss of access to world credit markets.

The second application explores equity trading and its connection with access to international credit markets in a two-agent stochastic general equilibrium asset pricing model. The model features a one-good version of the same small open economy setup as the first application but modified to allow domestic agents to trade domestic equity abroad and to require them to offer equity as collateral for foreign debt. Collateral is modelled in the form of a margin requirement according to which debt is limited not to exceed a fraction of the end-of-period liquidation value of the domestic agents' equity position. This form of collateral is widely used in international capital markets through value-at-risk collateralisation or explicit margin clauses (such as those that featured prominently in the contagion of the Russian crisis to financial markets world-wide), and it is also often imposed on financial intermediaries by regulators. Domestic agents trade equity with specialised foreign securities firms that incur per-trade and recurrent trading costs in trading the small open economy's equity.

A margin call in this setup leads domestic agents to engage in a 'fire sale' of equity in their effort to meet the call and minimise the adverse welfare implications of the suddenly binding credit constraint. However, the trading costs incurred by foreign traders imply that their equity demand function is less than infinitely elastic. Hence, the fire sale of equity lowers equity prices below the fundamentals level and tightens further the borrowing constraint, thereby inducing a Fisherian debt-deflation with overreaction of asset prices.

The third application considers a willingness-to-pay setup. In particular, this application revisits the one-good RBC small open economy model without capital accumulation in an environment in which the economy is required to satisfy a credit market participation constraint. This constraint requires the expected lifetime utility of repaying debts not to fall below the expected lifetime utility of moving to financial autarky. A recursive representation of the equilibrium of this economy features an endogenous borrowing constraint that does not vary over time and across states of nature. This constraint is set at the highest level of debt at which the values of participation and autarky are equalised across all possible realisations of an exogenous productivity disturbance. The model can produce Sudden Stops with qualitative features that are similar to those of the ability-to-pay models but the magnitude of the current account reversals and consumption declines is significantly smaller.

The last application reconsiders collateral constraints in a full-blown RBC small open economy with endogenous investment decisions and capital-adjustment costs. In this case, households cannot borrow more than a fraction of the end-of-period liquidation value of the capital stock and investment follows decision rules consistent with Tobin's q. Endogenous capital accumulation adds a vehicle for increasing the persistence of the effects induced of a suddenly binding collateral constraint. The reason is that this model features the standard inverse relationship between the price of capital and the investment decision. Hence, the decline in the price of capital, caused by the agents' rush to liquidate capital to relax the collateral constraint, leads not only to a Fisherian deflation like the one in the equity trading application but it also lowers the future capital stock and impairs the economy's ability to generate future wage and dividend income. The decline in expected earnings feeds back into the price equity and thus interacts with the Fisherian deflation.

The framework developed in this chapter is a natural environment to study financial contagion through international capital markets. For example, an event such as the run for liquidity in global capital markets triggered by the Russian default of 1998 can be interpreted as a large shock to the world real interest rate in the ability-to-pay models. An emerging economy without any direct economic linkages with Russia but with a level of debt in the region in which it is vulnerable to a Sudden Stop could then experience a financial crisis. Contagion occurs via the financial frictions in international capital markets that trigger binding borrowing constraints for that emerging economy that become tighter as its asset prices crash because of margin calls (if debt contracts feature margin constraints) or as the relative price and/or income of its non-tradables sector crashes (if debt contracts feature liability dollarisation and liquidity requirements).

The power of the RBC-type framework augmented by financial frictions to account for key features of Sudden Stops suggests that the monetary instability and large devaluations that attract a lot of attention during emerging markets crises may be less relevant than they seem. The results reported here show that the *real* effects of *real* credit crunches are large even though monetary elements were ignored. Devaluation may be important because it triggers large domestic relative price changes, fuels expectations of large shifts in real tax-like distortions, or leads to credit crises due to liability dollarisation, and not because of the change in the nominal exchange rate itself. If this is the case, the attention given to traditional Mundellian issues regarding the role of nominal rigidities and the origin of economic shocks on the debate on exchange rate regimes may also be misplaced. Lack of policy credibility and the interaction of this lack of credibility with global financial frictions could be more important; if they are, they provide support for the view that emerging countries should abandon their domestic currencies completely and adopt hard currencies (see Mendoza 2001, 2002c).

Much remains to be done in the task of developing quantitative applications of equilibrium business cycle models that can explain Sudden Stops, yet the results summarised here suggest that models based on credit frictions can produce large current account reversals and collapses in economic activity and prices. Moreover, the precautionary savings channel inherent in all four applications enables the models to be consistent with the observation that while Sudden Stops are large and dramatic, and can entail large welfare costs (see Mendoza 2001), they are relatively rare compared with the regular business cycle of the economies in question. In addition, the four applications break away from the common assumption in the emerging markets crises literature of treating a suddenly binding borrowing constraint as an unanticipated surprise to which economic agents did not assign some probability of occurrence, however small, in forming their optimal plans. To the contrary, the agents' fear of a Sudden Stop influences critically their saving, consumption, investment, current account and portfolio decisions. It is also worth noting that all four applications yield large, non-linear real effects relying on credit market imperfections only, without recurring to nominal rigidities or multiple equilibria as in some models proposed in the theoretical literature on emerging markets crises.

The limitations of the four applications reviewed in this chapter suggest two interesting agendas for further research. One relates to exploring the policy implications of the models. Most of the proposals under consideration for reforming the facilities available to a country in crisis through international financial organisations are based on the notion that macroeconomic models can be counted on to determine 'sustainable' current account and debt positions, as well as asset prices that reflect 'normal' market conditions *vis-à-vis* prices that reflect 'imperfections' resulting from moral hazard, informational frictions, or other distortions (see, for example, Calvo 2002; Lerrick and Meltzer 2001). Clearly, developing reliable models to perform these tasks is not possible without first making progress in producing useful quantitative models of Sudden Stops.

The second agenda would address several of the weaknesses of the applications reviewed in this chapter. The ability-to-pay applications did not fully enforce ability-to-pay criteria and were not concerned with maintaining the borrowers' incentives to repay their debt even if they were able to repay. It would be interesting to develop quantitative models that incorporated both of these features. The applications also did not take into account credit frictions affecting firms directly or foreign traders in the global credit market, differences in the maturity of debt contracts, interactions of the credit frictions with government-issued debt instruments and monetary distortions and the endogenous determination of coefficients driving margin and liquidity requirements.

6 APPENDIX

6.1 Numerical solution method for the model with margin constraints and trading costs

The model of equity trading between a small open economy and specialised foreign traders described from p. 369 is solved with the following algorithm:

1. Select functional forms and parameter values for the problems of households, domestic firms and foreign securities firms, and for the Markov process of productivity shocks.

2. Specify the value of the lower bound on equity and construct discrete grids containing the interpolation nodes for the endogenous state space: $(\alpha, b) \in Z = [\chi, \alpha^{\max}] \times [b^{\min}, b^{\max}]$. The space of initial states is therefore defined by all triples (α, b, ε) in the discrete set $Z \times E$.

3. Propose an initial conjectured pricing function $q(\alpha, b, \varepsilon)$ – the fundamentals equity price is generally used as the initial conjecture.

4. Combine the conjectured pricing function with the foreign traders' demand function and the equity market-clearing condition to create the conjectured transition equation (7.19).

5. Solve the small open economy's dynamic programming problem (7.20) via value-function iteration. The initial states are given by all triples $(\alpha, b, \varepsilon) \in Z \times E$ but the maximisation step approximates the one-step-ahead value function in the right-hand side of (7.20) using bilinear interpolation so that the approximate decision rule $\hat{b}'(\alpha, b, \varepsilon)$ can be chosen off grid nodes. This decision rule is determined by solving for the optimal bond position that satisfies the first-order condition of the dynamic programming problem using the bilinear approximation to the value function within the interpolation nodes included in $Z \times E$.

6. Check the margin constraint for each $\hat{b}'(\alpha, b, \varepsilon)$ at each pass of the maximisation step. The constraint is assumed to be non-binding first. If the resulting $\hat{b}'(\alpha, b, \varepsilon)$ violates the constraint, the constraint is imposed with equality. That is, when the constraint binds the decision rule for bonds in the closed form given by the right-hand side of (7.22).

7. Value function iterations continue until convergence is attained.

8. After the value function converges, use the optimal decision rule $\hat{b}'(\alpha, b, \varepsilon)$ to compute optimal consumption plans, the multipliers on the margin constraint and the domestic equity pricing function given by (7.18). If the domestic and conjectured equity pricing functions satisfy a standard stopping rule, a recursive equilibrium for the model

has been found. If the rule fails, update the conjectured pricing function and return to step 4. Updates of the pricing function for iteration $i + 1$ follow this Gauss–Siedel algorithm: $q^{i+1}(\alpha, b, \varepsilon) = \omega^{i}(\alpha, b, \varepsilon)[\bar{q}^{i}(\alpha, b, \varepsilon) - q^{i}(\alpha, b, \varepsilon)] + q^{i}(\alpha, b, \varepsilon)$, where $\omega(\alpha, b, \varepsilon)$ is a coefficient set to dampen unstable price iterations ($\omega < 1$) or accelerate convergence of stable ones ($\omega > 1$) using an adaptive successive overrelaxation (ASOR) procedure that combines data from iterations i and $i - 1$. This is necessary because iterations on pricing functions do not follow a contraction mapping and work instead by searching for a fixed point on a 'tatônnement' process. Without ASOR, this process may not converge due to the well-known problem of unstable 'hog cycles'.

BIBLIOGRAPHY

Aghion, P., Bacchetta, P. and Banerjee, A. (2000). 'Currency Crises and Monetary Policy with Credit Constraints', Department of Economics, Harvard University, mimeo

Aiyagari, S. R. (1993). 'Explaining Financial Market Facts: The Importance of Incomplete Markets and Transactions Costs', *Federal Reserve Bank of Minneapolis Quarterly Review* 17, 17–31

Aiyagari, S. R. and Gertler, M. (1999). 'Overreaction of Asset Prices in General Equilibrium', *Review of Economic Dynamics*, 2, 3–35

Alvarez, F. and Jermann, U. J. (2000). 'Efficiency, Equilibrium, and Asset Pricing with Risk of Default', *Econometrica*, 68(4), 775–98

Arellano, C. (2002). 'Dollarisation and Borrowing Limits', Department of Economics, Duke University, mimeo

Atkeson, A. (1991). 'International Lending with Moral Hazard and Risk of Repudiation', Econometrica, 59(4), 1069–89

Auernheimer, L. and Garcia-Saltos, R. (2000). 'International Debt and the Price of Domestic Assets', *IMF Working Paper*, 00/177

Bernanke, B. and Gertler, M. (1995). 'Inside the Black Box: The Credit Channel of Monetary Policy Transmission', *Journal of Economic Perspectives*, Fall, 27–48

Bernanke, B., Gertler, M. and Gilchrist, S. (1998). 'The Financial Accelerator in a Quantitative Business Cycle Framework', *NBER Working Paper*, 6455

Bulow, J. and Rogoff, K. (1989a). 'A Constant Recontracting Model of Sovereign Debt', *Journal of Political Economy*, 97, 155–78

(1989b). 'Sovereign Debt: Is to Forgive to Forget?', *American Economic Review*, 79, 43–50

Caballero, R. J. and Krishnamurthy, A. (2001). 'International and Domestic Collateral Constraints in a Model of Emerging Market Crises', *Journal of Monetary Economics*, 48, 513–48

Calvo, G. A. (1986). 'Temporary Stabilisation: Predetermined Exchange Rates', *Journal of Political Economy*, 94, 1319–29

(1998). 'Capital Flows and Capital-Market Crises: The Simple Economics of Sudden Stops', *Journal of Applied Economics*, 1, 35–54

(2000). 'Balance of Payments Crises in Emerging Markets: Large Capital Inflows and Sovereign Governments', in P. Krugman (ed.), *Currency Crises*, Chicago: University of Chicago Press

(2002). 'Globalisation Hazard and Delayed Reform in Emerging Markets', Center for International Economics, Department of Economics, University of Maryland, mimeo

Calvo, G. A. and Drazen, A. (1998). 'Uncertain Duration of Reform: Dynamic Implications', *Macroeconomic Dynamics*, 2(4), 443–55

Calvo, G. A. and Mendoza, E. G. (1996). 'Mexico's Balance of Payments Crises: A Chronicle of a Death Foretold', *Journal of International Economics*, 41, 235–64

(2000a). 'Capital-Market Crises and Economics Collapse in Emerging Markets: An Informational-Frictions Approach', *American Economic Review: Papers and Proceedings*, May

(2000b). 'Rational Contagion and the Globalisation of Securities Markets', *Journal of International Economics*, 51(1), 79–113

Calvo, G. A. and Reinhart, C. M. (1999). 'When Capital Inflows Come to a Sudden Stop: Consequences and Policy Options', Center for International Economics, Department of Economics, University of Maryland, mimeo

Cardia, E. (1991). 'The Dynamics of a Small Open Economy in Response to Monetary, Fiscal and Productivity Shocks', *Journal of Monetary Economics*, 28, 411–34

Carroll, C. D. (2000). 'A Theory of the Consumption Function, With and Without Liquidity Constraints', Department of Economics, Johns Hopkins University, mimeo

Cespedes, L., Chang, R. and Velasco, A. (2002). 'Balance Sheets and Exchange Rate Policy', Department of Economics, New York University, mimeo

Chari, V. V. and Kehoe, P. (2003). 'Financial Crises as Herds: Overturning the Critiques', Federal Reserve Bank of Minneapolis, Staff Report, 316

Christiano, L. J., Gust, C. and Roldos, J. (2002). 'Monetary Policy in an International Financial Crisis', Research Department, International Monetary Fund, Washington, DC, mimeo

Cole, H. L. and Kehoe, T. J. (1998). 'Self-Fulfilling Debt Crises', *Review of Economic Studies*, 67(1), 91–116

Correira, I., Neves, J. and Rebelo, S. (1995). 'Business Cycles in a Small Open Economy', *European Economic Review*, 39, 1089–1113

Eaton, J. and Fernandez, R. (1995). 'Sovereign Debt', in G. M. Grossman and K. Rogoff (eds.), *Handbook of International Economics*, 3, Amsterdam: Elsevier, 2031–76

Eaton, J. and Gersovitz, M. (1981). 'Debt with Potential Repudiation: Theoretical and Empirical Analysis', *Review of Economic Studies*, 47, 289–309

Edison, H., Luangaram, P. and Miller, M. (2000). 'Asset Bubbles, Domino Effects and "Lifeboats": Elements of the East Asian Crisis', *Economic Journal*, 110(460), 309–34

Edwards, S. (ed.) (2000). *Capital Flows and the Emerging Markets Economies*, A National Bureau of Economic Research Conference Report, Chicago: University of Chicago Press

Epstein L. G. (1983). 'Stationary Cardinal Utility and Optimal Growth under Uncertainty', *Journal of Economic Theory*, 31, 133–52

Fisher, I. (1993). 'The Debt-Deflation Theory of Great Depressions', *Econometrica*, 1, 337–57

Frankel, J. and Edwards, S. (2002). *Preventing Currency Crises in Emerging Markets*, A National Bureau of Economic Research Conference Report, Chicago: University of Chicago Press

Greenwood, J., Hercowitz, Z. and Huffman, G.W. (1988). 'Investment, Capacity Utilisation and the Real Business Cycle', *American Economic Review*, June

Hamann, F. (2002). 'Sovereign Risk and Macroeconomic Volatility', Department of Economics, North Carolina State University, mimeo

Heaton, J. and Lucas, D. (1996). 'Evaluating the Effects of Incomplete Markets on Risk Sharing and Asset Pricing', *Journal of Political Economy*, 104(3), 443–87

International Monetary Fund (1999). *International Capital Markets*, International Monetary Fund, Washington, DC, September

Izquierdo, A. (2000). 'Credit Constraints, and the Asymmetric Behavior of Asset Prices and Output under External Shocks', Washington, DC: World Bank, June, mimeo

Judd, K. L., Kubler, F. and Schmedders, K. (2000). 'Computational Methods for Dynamic Equilibria with Heterogeneous Agents', Hoover Institution, mimeo

Kaminsky, G. L. and Reinhart, C. M. (2000). 'On Crises, Contagion, and Confusion', *Journal of International Economics*, 51, 145–68

Kehoe, T. J. and Levine, D. K. (1993). 'Debt-Constrained Asset Markets', *Review of Economic Studies*, 60, 868–88

Kehoe, P. and Perri, F. (2002). 'International Business Cycles with Endogenous Incomplete Markets', *Econometrica*, 70(3), 907–28

Kiyotaki, N. and Moore, J. (1997). 'Credit Cycles', *Journal of Political Economy*, 105, 211–48

Kletzer, K. M. and Wright, B. D. (2000). 'Sovereign Debt as Intertemporal Barter', *American Economic Review*, 90(3), 621–39

Kocherlakota, N. (1996). 'Implications of Efficient Risk Sharing without Commitment', *Review of Economic Studies*, 63(4), 595–609

Krugman, P. (ed.) (2000). *Currency Crises*, A National Bureau of Economic Research Conference Report, Chicago: University of Chicago Press

Krusell, P. and Smith, A. A., Jr. (1997). 'Income and Wealth Heterogeneity, Portfolio Choice, and Equilibrium Asset Returns', *Macroeconomic Dynamics*, 1, 387–422

Lerrick, A. and Meltzer, A. H. (2001). 'Blueprint for and International Lender of Last Resort', Carnegie-Mellon University, mimeo

Lucas, D. J. (1994). 'Asset Pricing with Undiversifiable Income Risk and Short Sales Constraints', *Journal of Monetary Economics*, 34, 325–41

Lucas, R. E., Jr. (1987). *Models of Business Cycles*, New York: Basil Blackwell

Ljungqvist, L. and Sargent, T. J. (2000). *Recursive Macroeconomic Theory*, Boston, MA: MIT Press

Mendoza, E. G. (1991a). 'Real Business Cycles in a Small Open Economy', *American Economic Review*, 81, 797–818

  (1991b). 'Capital Controls and the Gains from Trade in a Business Cycle Model of a Small Open Economy', *IMF Staff Papers*, 38, 480–505

  (1995). 'The Terms of Trade, The Real Exchange Rate and Economic Fluctuations', *International Economic Review*, 36, 101–37

  (2001). 'The Benefits of Dollarisation when Stabilisation Policy Lacks Credibility and Financial Markets are Imperfect', *Journal of Money, Credit, and Banking*, part 2, 33(2), 440–74

  (2002a). 'Credit, Prices, and Crashes: Business Cycles with a Sudden Stop', in J. Frankel and S. Edwards (eds.), *Preventing Currency Crises in Emerging Markets*, Chicago: University of Chicago Press

  (2002b). 'Why Should Emerging Economies Give up National Currencies: A Case for "Institutions Substitution"', *NBER Working Paper*, 8950

Mendoza, E. G. and Smith, K. A. (2002). 'Margin Calls, Trading Costs and Asset Prices in Emerging Markets: The Financial Mechanics of the "Sudden Stop" Phenomenon', *NBER Working Paper*, 9286

Mendoza, E. G. and Uribe, M. (2001). 'Devaluation Risk and the Business Cycle Implications of Exchange Rate Management', *Carnegie–Rochester Conference Series on Public Policy*, 53

Milesi-Ferreti, G. M. and Razin, A. (2000). 'Current Account Reversals and Currency Crises: Empirical Regularities', in P. Krugman (ed.), *Currency Crises*, Chicago: University of Chicago Press

Neumeyer, P. and Perri, F. (2001). 'Business Cycles in Emerging Economies: The Role of Interest Rates', Department of Economics, New York University, mimeo

Obstfeld, M. (1981). 'Macroeconomic Policy, Exchange Rate Dynamics, and Optimal Asset Accumulation', *Journal of Political Economy*, 89, 1142–61

Oviedo, P. (2002). 'Business Cycles in Small Economies with a Banking Sector', North Carolina State University, mimeo

Paasche, B. (2001). 'Credit Constraints and International Financial Crises', *Journal of Monetary Economics*, 28, 623–50

Parsley, D. (2001). 'Accounting for Real Exchange Rate Changes in East Asia', Hong Kong Institute of Monetary Research, *Working Paper*, 6/2001

Reif, T. (2001). 'The "Real" Side of Currency Crises', Columbia University, mimeo

Schmitt-Grohé, S. and Uribe, M. (2001). 'Closing Small Open Economy Models', Department of Economics, University of Pennsylvania, mimeo

Schneider, M. and Tornell, A. (1999). 'Lending Booms, Asset Price Inflation and Soft Landings', Department of Economics, University of Rochester, mimeo

Wright, M. (2001). 'Reputations and Sovereign Debt', Department of Economics, MIT, mimeo

Valderrama, D. (2002). 'The Impact of Financial Frictions on a Small Open Economy: When Current Account Borrowing Hits a Limit', Research Department, Federal Reserve Bank of San Francisco, mimeo

Zhang, H. (1997). 'Endogenous Borrowing Constraints with Incomplete Markets', *The Journal of Finance*, December

8

Asset pricing in macroeconomic models

Paul Söderlind

1 INTRODUCTION

This chapter studies the two main financial building blocks of simulation models: the consumption-based asset pricing model and the definition of asset classes. The aim is to discuss what different modelling choices imply for asset prices. For instance, what is the effect of different utility functions, investment technologies, monetary policies and leverage on risk premia and yield curves?

The emphasis is on surveying existing models and discussing the main mechanisms behind the results. I therefore choose to work with stylised facts and simple analytical pricing expressions. There are no simulations or advanced econometrics in this chapter.[1] The following two examples should give the flavour. First, I use simple pricing expressions and scatter plots to show that the consumption-based asset pricing model cannot explain the cross-sectional variation of Sharpe ratios. Second, I discuss how the slope of the real yield curve is driven by the autocorrelation of consumption by studying explicit log-linear pricing formulas of just two assets: a one-period bond and a one-period forward contract.

The plan of the chapter is as follows. Section 2 deals with the consumption-based asset pricing model. It studies if the model is compatible with historical consumption and asset data. From a modelling perspective, the implicit question is: if my model could create a realistic consumption process and has defined realistic assets (for instance, levered equity), would it then predict reasonable asset returns? Section 3 deals with how assets are defined in simulation models and what that implies for pricing. I discuss yield curves (real and nominal), claims on consumption (one-period and multi-period), options and levered equity. Section 4 summarises

---

[1] See Rouwenhorst (1995) for a survey of simulation evidence; Ferson (1995) and Reffett and Schorfheide (2000) for surveys of careful econometric modelling.

the main findings. Technical details are found in a number of appendices (p. 444).

2 PROBLEMS WITH THE CONSUMPTION-BASED ASSET PRICING MODEL

This part of the chapter takes a hard look at the consumption-based asset pricing model since it is one of the building blocks in general equilibrium models. The approach is to derive simple analytical pricing expressions and to study stylised facts – with the aim of conveying the intuition for the results.

The first sections below look at earlier findings on the equity premium puzzle and the risk-free rate puzzle and study if they are stable across different samples (see the surveys of Bossaert 2002; Campbell 2001; Cochrane 2001; and Smith and Wickens 2002). The following sections present new evidence on the ability of the consumption-based model to account for the predictability of returns and the cross-sectional variation (across portfolios formed on industries, firm size, dividend–price ratio, book to market ratio and country). The last section discusses if alternative models of the stochastic discount factor (including Epstein–Zin utility, habit persistence and idiosyncratic risk) can help in solving the problems of the consumption-based model.

2.1 The asset pricing equation

This section sets the stage for studying whether the consumption-based asset pricing model can fit the data. The basic pricing equation is specified and some stylised facts are presented.

The basic asset pricing equation says

$$\mathrm{E}_{t-1}(R_t M_t) = 1, \tag{8.1}$$

where R_t is the gross return of holding an asset from period $t-1$ to t and M_t is a stochastic discount factor (SDF). E_{t-1} denotes the expectations conditional on the information in period $t-1$, that is, when the investment decision is made. This equation holds for any assets that are freely traded without transaction costs (or taxes), even if markets are incomplete.[2]

---

[2] The existence of such an SDF is guaranteed if the Law of One Price holds (portfolios with the same payoffs have the same prices). The SDF is unique if, in addition, markets are complete (all risk can be insured). See Hansen and Richard (1987), Harrison and Kreps (1979) and Ross (1978), for textbook treatments see Cochrane (2001) and LeRoy and Werner (2001).

It is convenient to rewrite (8.1) as[3]

$$E_{t-1}(R_t) = 1/E_{t-1}(M_t) - \text{Cov}_{t-1}(R_t, M_t)/E_{t-1}(M_t), \qquad (8.2)$$

which expresses the conditional expectations of the return in terms of the conditional expectation of the SDF and the conditional covariance of the return and the SDF.[4]

Two applications of this equation will be particularly useful in the subsequent analysis. First, a (gross) risk-free rate, R_{ft}, has no conditional covariance with the stochastic discount factor (but it may still be a random variable), so (8.2) implies that the expected risk-free rate is the inverse of the expected SDF

$$E_{t-1}(R_{ft}) = 1/E_{t-1}(M_t). \qquad (8.3)$$

Second, consider the gross returns on two assets (one could be a risk-free asset) and let R^e be the excess return, that is, the difference between the two returns. Apply (8.2) on both returns and take the difference to get

$$E_{t-1}(R_t^e) = -\text{Cov}_{t-1}(R_t^e, M_t)/E_{t-1}(M_t), \qquad (8.4)$$

which shows that a positive risk premium requires a negative correlation with the SDF.

In a consumption-based model, (8.1) is the Euler equation for optimal saving in $t-1$ where M_t is the ratio of marginal utilities in t and $t-1$, $M_t = \beta u'(C_t)/u'(C_{t-1})$.[5] I will focus on the case where the marginal utility of consumption is a function of consumption only, which is by far the most common formulation. This allows for other terms in the utility function, for instance, leisure and real money balances, but they have to be additively separable from the consumption term. With constant relative risk aversion (CRRA) γ, the stochastic discount factor is

$$M_t = \beta(C_t/C_{t-1})^{-\gamma}, \text{ so} \qquad (8.5)$$

$$\ln(M_t) = \ln(\beta) - \gamma \Delta c_t, \text{ where } \Delta c_t = \ln(C_t/C_{t-1}). \qquad (8.6)$$

The second line is there only to introduce the convenient notation Δc_t for the consumption growth rate.

The next few sections study if the pricing model consisting of (8.1) and (8.5) can fit historical data. To be clear about what this entails, note the

---

[3] Recall that $\text{Cov}(x, y) = E(xy) - E(x)E(y)$.
[4] A conditional variance, $\text{Var}_{t-1}(x_t)$, is the variance of the forecast error $x_t - E_{t-1}(x_t)$; a conditional covariance, $\text{Cov}_{t-1}(x_t, y_t)$, is the covariance of the forecast errors $x_t - E_{t-1}(x_t)$ and $y_t - E_{t-1}(y_t)$.
[5] See Breeden (1979) and Lucas (1978) for early analyses of the consumption-based model.

following. First, general equilibrium considerations will not play any role in the analysis: the production side will not even be mentioned. Instead, the focus is on one of the building blocks of an otherwise unspecified model. Second, complete markets are not assumed. The key assumption is rather that the basic asset pricing equation (8.1) holds for the assets I analyse (broad US/international stock/bond portfolios). This means that the representative US investor can trade in these assets without transaction costs and taxes (clearly an approximation). Third, the properties of historical (*ex post*) data are assumed to be good approximations of what investors expected. In practice, this assumes both rational expectations and that the sample is large enough for the estimators (of various moments) to be precise.

My approach is to derive simple expressions which highlight the basic mechanisms and make the analysis more easily adaptable to other data sets (sample periods/countries/assets). These simple expressions are obtained by making assumptions about the distribution of consumption and returns.

As an example of the pros and cons of this approach, suppose we want to analyse how different values of the risk aversion coefficient γ affect the unconditional mean of the SDF, $E(M_t)$. If we make no assumptions about the distribution of consumption, then we must essentially take a data set on consumption growth, construct the variable on the right-hand side of (8.5) for a value of γ and estimate its mean. We then repeat this for other values of γ and then describe (for instance, by plotting) how the mean varies with γ. This approach is cumbersome and the findings are hard to generalise. In contrast, by assuming that consumption growth is normally distributed, then we can express $E(M_t)$ as a simple function of γ and the mean and standard deviation of consumption growth.[6] This second approach makes it much easier to interpret and extend the findings, although it comes at the price of getting only approximate answers (since data is probably not exactly normally distributed).

Table 8.1 shows the key statistics for quarterly US real returns and consumption growth for the sample periods 1947–2001 and 1970–2001. The means and standard deviations are expressed in percentages, and have been annualised by multiplying the mean by four and the standard deviation by two (as would be appropriate for an annual sum of a quarterly IID variable). Two sample periods are used since it is of interest to see how stable the results are, but also because some of the international data used later in the section is available only from 1970.

---

[6] The result is $E(M_t) = \beta \exp[-\gamma E(\Delta c_t) + \gamma^2 \sigma(\Delta c_t)^2/2]$.

Table 8.1 *US quarterly real returns and consumption growth (annualised, per cent)*[a,g]

	Mean	Std dev.	Sharpe ratio	Auto-corr.	Correlation with Δc_t	Correlation with Δc_{t+1}
1947–2001						
Consumption[c] growth, Δc_t[d]	1.94*[b]	1.10*		0.20*		0.20*
Stock Market excess return[e,f]	7.93*	15.98*	0.50*	0.05	0.14*	0.22*
Long gov. bond excess return[e,f]	1.15	9.38*	0.12	−0.04	−0.10	0.08
1-month T-bill	1.00*	1.57*		0.58*	0.13	0.27*
1970–2001						
Consumption growth, Δc_t	1.89*	0.91*		0.41*		0.41*
Stock Market excess return	6.23*	17.87*	0.35*	0.01	0.16*	0.32*
Long gov. bond excess return	3.06	11.43*	0.27	−0.08	−0.10	0.21*
1-month T-bill	1.56*	1.44*		0.69*	0.10	0.23*

Notes: [a] This table shows summary statistics of US real returns and consumption growth rates for 1947Q2–2001Q4 and 1970Q1–2001Q4.

[b] A star (*) denotes significance at the 5 per cent level, based on GMM/delta method inference, using a Newey–West (1987) estimator with one lag (see the econometrics appendix).

[c] Consumption is real *per capita* consumption of services and non-durable goods.

[d] The consumption growth rate in quarter t is $\Delta c_t = \ln(C_t/C_{t-1})$, where C_t is the consumption level in quarter t.

[e] Returns are real returns.

[f] Excess returns are real returns in excess of the real return on a one-month Treasury-Bill.

[g] To annualise, quarterly means are multiplied by four and quarterly standard deviations by two, as appropriate if the variable is a random walk.

Source: See the data appendix for details on data sources and transformations.

Table 8.1 uses a star (*) to indicate which numbers are significantly different from zero at the 5 per cent significance level. The tests are based on estimating the moments by GMM, using a Newey and West (1987) estimator for the sampling uncertainty of the moments, and then applying the delta-method (see the econometrics appendix). This means that the tests are only valid asymptotically – but are consistent even if the data is not IID (as assumed by standard tests).

We see, among other things, that consumption has a standard deviation of only 1 per cent (annualised), the stock market has had an average excess return (over a T-bill) of 6–8 per cent (annualised), and that returns are only weakly correlated with consumption growth. These figures will be important in the following sections. Two correlations with consumption growth are shown, since it is unclear if returns should be related to what is recorded as consumption this quarter or the next. The reason is that consumption is measured as a flow during the quarter, while returns are measured at the end of the quarter.

2.2 The equity premium puzzle

This section studies if the consumption-based asset pricing model can explain the historical risk premium on the US stock market.

To discuss the historical average excess returns, it is convenient to work with the unconditional pricing equation $E(R_t M_t) = 1$, which follows from applying the law of iterated expectations on (8.1). We can then derive expressions like (8.2)–(8.4) for unconditional moments instead.

To highlight the basic problem with the consumption-based model and to simplify the exposition, I assume that the excess return, R_t^e, and the log SDF, $\ln(M_t)$, have a bivariate normal distribution.[7] Stein's Lemma[8] then gives

$$\text{Cov}\big(R_t^e, M_t\big) = \text{Cov}\big[R_t^e, \ln(M_t)\big] \times E(M_t). \tag{8.7}$$

We use this in the unconditional version of (8.4) to get the excess return and Sharpe ratio as

$$E\big(R_t^e\big) = -\text{Cov}\big[R_t^e, \ln(M_t)\big], \text{ and} \tag{8.8}$$

$$E\big(R_t^e\big)/\sigma\big(R_t^e\big) = -\rho\big[R_t^e, \ln(M_t)\big] \times \sigma\big[\ln(M_t)\big] \tag{8.9}$$

where $\rho[R_t^e, \ln(M_t)]$ is the correlation of the excess return and the log SDF, and $\sigma(R_t^e)$ and $\sigma[\ln(M_t)]$ are the standard deviations of the excess return and log SDF, respectively.

---

[7] This does not imply (but is implied by) normally distributed gross returns, which would eventually violate limited liability. Even so, that would only happen once every 3,000 years or so with the means and volatilities in table 8.1. I just wonder if Psusennes I (Pharaoh 1044 B C to 994 B C) allowed limited liability. In any case, his gold mask (Egyptian Museum, Cairo) is second only to Tutanchamon's.

[8] Stein's Lemma says that if x and y have a bivariate normal distribution and $h(y)$ is a differentiable function such that $E[|h'(y)|] < \infty$, then $\text{Cov}[x, h(y)] = \text{Cov}(x, y) E[h'(y)]$. This holds also for conditional distributions. In (8.7), $x = R_t^e$, $y = \ln(M_t)$, and $h(y) = \exp(y)$ so $h'(y) = M_t$.

The log SDF in (8.6) is linear in consumption growth so the assumption of normality boils down to assuming that R_t^e and Δc_t have a bivariate normal distribution. We can then write (8.8)–(8.9) as

$$E(R_t^e) = \text{Cov}(R_t^e, \Delta c_t)\gamma, \text{ and} \tag{8.10}$$

$$E(R_t^e)/\sigma(R_t^e) = \rho(R_t^e, \Delta c_t) \times \sigma(\Delta c_t)\gamma. \tag{8.11}$$

This expression is convenient since it allows us to split the Sharpe ratio into three separate factors: the correlation of returns and consumption growth, the volatility of consumption growth and the risk aversion. In particular, the first two factors can be estimated directly from data without knowing any preference parameters, and the volatility is a constant in a cross-section (something we will use later).

Equation (8.11) shows that to get a positive expected excess return, the asset must be 'risky' in the sense that it is positively correlated with consumption growth (negatively correlated with the SDF). In that case, the asset tends to give a high return when marginal utility is low, so investors demand a risk premium. This effect is strong if consumption is very volatile and/or investors are strongly risk averse.

Table 8.1 shows that the stock market has a Sharpe ratio around 0.35–0.5 (annualised) and that the consumption growth rate has a standard deviation of around 1 per cent $= 0.01$ (annualised). The lowest value of γ which makes (8.11) hold is then $\gamma = 35$, and this would work only if the stock market were a worthless hedge against consumption fluctuations so the correlation is one.[9]

The basic problem with the consumption-based asset pricing model is that investors enjoy a fairly stable consumption series (either because income is smooth or because it is easy/inexpensive to smooth consumption by changing savings), so only an extreme risk aversion can motivate why investors require such a high equity premium. This is the *equity premium puzzle* stressed by Mehra and Prescott (1985) (although they approach the issue from another angle – more about that later).

Still higher values of γ are needed if the correlation in (8.11) is lower than one – as it certainly is. Table 8.1 shows that the correlation is around 0.1–0.3, where the higher value is for the correlation with Δc_{t+1}. If we want to be nice to the consumption-based model, then we can use the higher value. With a Sharpe ratio of 0.35 (the lowest value, once again to

[9] This is related to the approach in Hansen and Jagannathan (1991). Rewrite (8.4) as $E(R_t^e)/\sigma(R_t^e) = -\rho(R_t^e, M_t)\sigma(M_t)/E(M_t)$, which shows that the following 'volatility bound' must hold: $\sigma(M_t)/E(M_t) \geq |E(R_t^e)|/\sigma(R_t^e)$. Their approach is essentially to search in a set of returns for the portfolio with the largest Sharpe ratio and then study if a given model of the SDF satisfies the volatility bound. In the case considered here there is only one asset.

be nice) and a standard deviation of consumption of 0.01, (8.11) becomes $0.35 = 0.3 \times 0.01\gamma$, which requires $\gamma = 117$.

The low correlation therefore adds a *correlation puzzle* (see, for instance, Cochrane 2001) to the equity premium puzzle: the consumption-based model makes the aggregate US stock market look pretty safe since almost all risk is non-systematic; it would indeed take a high risk aversion coefficient to motivate the historical risk premium.

If the consumption-based model cannot (with reasonable parameter values) explain the risk premium on the aggregate US stock market, what about other 'aggregate' assets like US government bonds? Table 8.1 shows that the Sharpe ratio for bond returns is 0.12 for the long sample but as high as 0.27 for the shorter (and later) sample – but the sampling variability is so large so neither of these figures is significantly (at the 5 per cent level) different from zero. In any case, if we use the point estimates we need a risk aversion coefficient (γ) of around 10 or 25 to make (8.11) hold – which looks much more promising than for equity. However, the correlation of the bond return and consumption growth is very low, so the equity premium puzzle is also a bond premium puzzle.

The equity premium puzzle over time

The results for the two samples in table 8.1 are somewhat different, which immediately raises the question of how sensitive the conclusions are to the sample period. Figure 8.1 provides some answers by plotting the key statistics for different samples.

Figure 8.1a shows recursive estimates of the Sharpe ratio of the aggregate US stock market and the Sharpe ratio predicted by the CRRA model when the risk aversion is 100, that is, $\rho(R^e, \Delta c) \times \sigma(\Delta c) \times 100$ from (8.11). The correlations are for Δc_{t+1}. The recursive estimation means that the results for 1957Q2 use data for 1947Q2–1957Q2, the results for 1957Q3 add one data point, etc. The results for 2001Q4 are therefore the same as those in the top panel of table 8.1. Figure 8.1b shows the same statistics, but estimated on a moving-data window of ten years. For instance, the results for 1980Q2 are for the sample 1971Q3–1980Q2. Finally, figure 8.1c uses a moving-data window of five years.

Together these figures give the impression that there are fairly long swings in the data. This fundamental uncertainty should serve as a warning against focusing on the fine details of the data. It could also be used as an argument for using longer data series – provided we are willing to assume that the economy has not undergone important regime changes.

There are other interesting results in these figures. In particular, the actual Sharpe ratio and the prediction of the consumption-based model

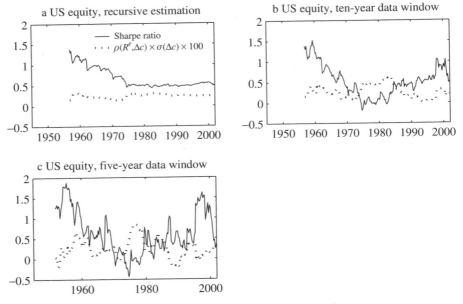

Figure 8.1 The equity premium puzzle for different samples, 1947–2001
Notes: a shows recursive estimations (longer and longer sample) of the Sharpe ratio
of the aggregate US stock market and of the correlation with Δc_{t+1} times the standard
deviation of Δc_{t+1}. b and c show the same statistics calculated on a moving data
window of ten years and five years, respectively.
Source: See the data appendix for details on data sources and transformations.

move in different directions – which is something we will return to later in
discussing time-variation of risk premia.

The Mehra–Prescott approach

The Mehra and Prescott (1985) approach to analysing the consumption-
based asset pricing model is somewhat less direct than what we did above.
However, it has had a large impact on the research community, so it is
worth summarising.

The starting point is a Lucas (1978) economy where (aggregate) consumption equals the exogenous (aggregate) endowment. To see how this
works, write the gross return as $R_t = (P_t + D_t)/P_{t-1}$, where P_t is the asset
price and D_t the dividend (per asset) in period t. We can then write (8.1)
as $P_{t-1} = \mathrm{E}_{t-1}[M_t(P_t + D_t)]$. Iterating forward, applying the law of iterated expectations, ruling out bubbles, and using the CRRA SDF in (8.5)
gives

$$P_{t-1} = \mathrm{E}_{t-1}[\beta(C_t/C_{t-1})^{-\gamma}D_t + \beta^2(C_{t+1}/C_{t-1})^{-\gamma}D_{t+1} + \cdots]. \quad (8.12)$$

The price of a real one-period bond is found by setting $D_t = 1$ and all future dividends to zero. The price of a claim to the stream of future non-storable endowments – which is interpreted as a proxy of a broad stock market index – is found by setting D_t equal to C_t. With a time series process for consumption, and values of β and γ, it is straightforward to calculate asset returns.

Mehra and Prescott (1985) construct a time series process by postulating that consumption growth follows a two-state Markov process: C_t/C_{t-1} is either low or high and the probability of which depends on whether C_{t-1}/C_{t-2} was low or high. This makes it very simple to calculate the expectations in (8.12): there is only one state variable and it can take only two values. In spite of this, the process allows both autocorrelation and time-varying volatility. The model parameters are calibrated to fit the mean, standard deviation and autocorrelation in consumption growth. With this machinery, Mehra and Prescott (1985) find that a very high value of γ is needed to explain the historical equity premium – basically because consumption is fairly smooth.

This approach is interesting, but it is a fairly indirect method for studying the equity premium, and it adds a few very strong assumptions, in particular, about the consumption process and that the stockmarket corresponds to a claim on future consumption. In any case, several extensions have been made, for instance to investigate if more extreme consumption growth processes (fat tails or 'crash states') can rescue the model – but so far with limited success (see, for instance, Bidarkota and McCulloch 2000 and Salyer 1998).

2.3 The risk-free rate puzzle

The CRRA utility function has the special feature that the intertemporal elasticity of substitution is the inverse of the risk aversion, that is, $1/\gamma$. The choice of the risk aversion parameter, for instance, to fit the equity premium, will therefore have direct effects on the risk-free rate.

A key feature of any consumption-based asset pricing model, or any consumption–saving model for that matter, is that the risk-free rate governs the time slope of the consumption profile. From the asset pricing equation for a risk-free asset (8.3) we have $E_{t-1}(R_{ft}) E_{t-1}(M_t) = 1$, which in the CRRA model becomes

$$E_{t-1}(R_{ft}) E_{t-1}[\beta(C_t/C_{t-1})^{-\gamma}] = 1. \qquad (8.13)$$

Note that we must use the conditional asset pricing equation – at least as long as we believe that the risk-free asset is a random variable. A risk-free asset is defined by having a zero conditional covariance with the SDF, which means that it is regarded as risk-free at the time of investment $(t-1)$. In practice, this means a real interest rate (perhaps approximated by the real return on a T-bill since the innovations in inflation are small), which may well have a non-zero unconditional covariance with the SDF.[10] Indeed, in table 8.1 the real return on a T-bill is as correlated with consumption growth as the aggregate US stock market.

To make progress, assume that the log SDF and the log risk-free rate $r_{ft} = \ln(R_{ft})$ have a bivariate normal distribution – which is somewhat different from our earlier assumption, but should (once again) be seen as just an approximation. We can then write (8.13) as[11]

$$E_{t-1}(r_{ft}) + \sigma_{t-1}^2(r_{ft})/2 = -\ln(\beta) + \gamma E_{t-1}(\Delta c_t) - \gamma^2 \sigma_{t-1}^2(\Delta c_t)/2.$$
(8.14)

To relate this equation to historical data, we take unconditional expectations to get

$$E(r_{ft}) + E\sigma_{t-1}^2(r_{ft})/2 = -\ln(\beta) + \gamma E(\Delta c_t) - \gamma^2 E\sigma_{t-1}^2(\Delta c_t)/2.$$
(8.15)

Before we try to compare (8.15) with data, several things should be noted. First, the log gross rate is very close to a traditional net rate ($\ln(1+z) \approx z$ for small z), so it makes sense to compare with the data in table 8.1. Second, we can safely disregard the variance terms since they are very small, at least as long as we are considering reasonable values of γ. Although the average conditional variances are not directly observable, we know that they must be smaller than the unconditional variances,[12] which are very small in table 8.1. In fact, the variances are around 0.0001 whereas the means are around 0.01–0.02.

According to (8.15) there are two ways to reconcile a positive consumption growth rate with a low real interest rate (2 per cent/year and 1 per cent–1.5 per cent, respectively in table 8.1): investors may prefer to consume later rather than sooner ($\beta > 1$) or they are willing to substitute intertemporally without too much compensation ($1/\gamma$ is high, that is, γ is low). However, fitting the equity premium requires a high value of γ, so investors must be implausibly patient if (8.15) is to hold. For instance,

---

[10] As a very simple example, let $x_t = z_{t-1} + \varepsilon_t$ and $y_t = z_{t-1} + u_t$ where ε_t are u_t uncorrelated with each other and with z_{t-1}. If z_{t-1} is observable in $t-1$, then $\text{Cov}_{t-1}(x_t, y_t) = 0$, but $\text{Cov}(x_t, y_t) = \sigma^2(z_{t-1})$.

[11] If $x \sim N(\mu, \sigma^2)$ and $y = \exp(x)$ then $E(y^k) = \exp(k\mu + k^2\sigma^2/2)$.

[12] Let $E(y|x)$ and $\text{Var}(y|x)$ be the expectation and variance of y conditional on x. The unconditional variance is then $\text{Var}(y) = \text{Var}[E(y|x)] + E[\text{Var}(y|x)]$.

with $\gamma = 25$ (which is a very conservative guess of what we need to fit the equity premium) (8.15) says $0.01 = -\ln(\beta) + 25 \times 0.02$ (ignoring the variance terms) for the long sample, which requires $\beta \approx 1.6$. The shorter sample gives a very similar number. This is the *risk-free rate puzzle* stressed by Weil (1989). The basic intuition for this result is that it is hard to reconcile a steep slope of the consumption profile and a low compensation for postponing consumption if people are insensitive to intertemporal prices – unless they are extremely patient (actually, unless they prefer to consume later rather than sooner).

Another implication of a high risk aversion is that the real interest rate should be very volatile, which it is not. According to table 8.1 the standard deviation of the real interest rate is 1.5 times the standard deviation of consumption growth. From (8.14) the volatility of the (expected) risk-free rate should be

$$\sigma[E_{t-1}(r_{ft})] = \gamma \sigma[E_{t-1}(\Delta c_t)] \tag{8.16}$$

if the variance terms are constant. The standard deviation of expected real interest rate is γ times the standard deviation of expected consumption growth. We cannot observe the conditional expectations directly, and therefore cannot estimate their volatility. However, a simple example is enough to demonstrate that high values of γ are likely to imply counterfactually high volatility of the real interest rate.

Suppose that consumption growth is an AR(1) process. In that case, $\sigma[E_{t-1}(\Delta c_t)]$ equals $\rho(\Delta c_t, \Delta c_{t+1})\sigma(\Delta c_t)$, which from table 8.1 is 0.22 per cent for the long sample and 0.37 per cent for the short sample.[13] With $\gamma = 25$, (8.16) then implies that the standard deviation of the expected real interest rate should be around 5 per cent–9 per cent. Table 8.1 shows that the unconditional standard deviation, which is an upper bound (see footnote 12), is around 1.5 per cent. This shows that an intertemporal elasticity of substitution of 1/25 is not compatible with the relatively stable real return on T-bills.

2.4 The cross-section of returns

The previous section demonstrated that the consumption-based model has a hard time explaining the risk premium on a broad equity portfolio – essentially because consumption growth is too smooth to make stocks look

---

[13] If $x_t = \alpha x_{t-1} + \varepsilon_t$, where ε_t is IID, then $E_{t-1}(x_t) = \alpha x_{t-1}$, so $\sigma(E_{t-1}x_t) = \alpha\sigma(x_{t-1})$.

particularly risky. However, the model *does* predict a positive equity premium, even if it is not large enough. This suggests that the model may
be able to explain the relative risk premia across assets, even if the scale is
wrong. In that case, the model would still be useful for some issues. This
section takes a closer look at that possibility by focusing on the relation
between the Sharpe ratio and the correlation with consumption growth in
a cross-section of asset returns.

The key equation is (8.11), which I repeat here for ease of reading

$$\mathrm{E}\big(R_t^e\big)/\sigma\big(R_t^e\big) = \rho\big(R_t^e, \Delta c_t\big) \times \sigma(\Delta c_t)\gamma. \tag{8.11}$$

The volatility of the log SDF, $\sigma(\Delta c_t)\gamma$, is the same for all assets, so the
cross-sectional variation in Sharpe ratios is due to cross-sectional variation in the correlation of the portfolio excess return and consumption
growth, $\rho(R_t^e, \Delta c_t)$. We can therefore study the cross-sectional implication of (8.11) by estimating the linear regression equation

$$\mathrm{E}\big(R_t^e\big)/\sigma\big(R_t^e\big) = a_0 + a_1\rho\big(R_t^e, \Delta c_t\big) + u, \tag{8.17}$$

where the observations are different portfolios. According to (8.11) the
slope coefficient a_1 should be positive (since $\sigma(\Delta c_t)\gamma$ is) and the coefficient of determination R^2 should be high (unity, except for sampling
variability).

In a sense, this regression is similar to the traditional cross-sectional
regressions of returns on factors with unknown factor risk premia (see, for
instance, Campbell, Lo and MacKinlay 1997, chapter 6 or Cochrane 2001,
chapter 12).

Figure 8.2 studies different cross-sections of assets by plotting the Sharpe
ratio against the correlation with consumption growth. To save some space,
only results for Δc_{t+1} are shown. To be honest, the corresponding results for
Δc_t look even less flattering. Figure 8.2a shows evidence for ten US industry
portfolios (telecom, utilities, etc.) for the sample 1970Q1–2001Q4; see
the data appendix for details on data. There seems to be a weak positive
relation between the Sharpe ratio and the correlation with consumption.
This is confirmed by the numbers at the bottom of figure 8.2: the slope
coefficient in the estimated regression equation (8.17) is 0.3, but it is not
significantly different from zero at the 5 per cent level (would have been
marked by a star * as in figure 8.2d) and the R^2 is only 0.08. The result
is no better if the odd portfolio with zero correlation (oil, gas, and coal) is
excluded.

Another way to see essentially the same result is to compare the industry portfolios with the aggregate US market (marked by a large circle in

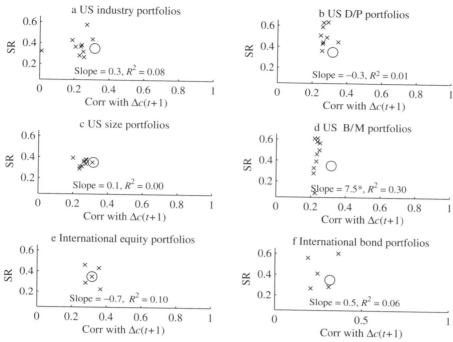

Figure 8.2 Sharpe ratios and consumption correlation, 1970–2001
Notes: a shows Sharpe ratios and correlations with Δc_{t+1} for ten US industry portfolios for 1970Q1–2001Q4. The large circle is the aggregate US stock market. The numbers at the bottom are slope coefficients and R^2 from a regression of the Sharpe ratio on a constant and the correlation. Significance at the 5 per cent level is marked by a star *. b–d are similar to a but for US dividend/price, size, and book-to-market portfolios, respectively. e–f are for international equity and bond portfolios, respectively.
Source: See data appendix for details on data sources and transformations.

figure 8.2). In figure 8.2, the market happens to have the highest correlation with consumption growth and should according to (8.11) therefore have the highest Sharpe ratio. In fact, six of the ten portfolios have higher Sharpe ratios, of which three are considerably higher.

There is also very little support for the model on US dividend/price and size portfolios (deciles of D/P and size, respectively): the R^2s are virtually zero in figures 8.2b–c. The model seems to work somewhat better on US book-to-market portfolios (figure 8.2d), but fails again on the international equity and bond portfolios (figures 8.2e–f).

It is clear that the consumption-based model has problems with explaining the cross-section of Sharpe ratios. The main problem is that there are considerable differences in Sharpe ratios, but not in correlations with consumption growth. To put it bluntly: systematic risk seems to be something other than covariance with consumption growth. However, the model is not a complete failure: four of six figures at least get a positive slope. To get a perspective on the magnitude of the problems, I will compare them with the traditional Capital Asset Pricing Model (CAPM) (Lintner 1965; Mossin 1968; Sharpe 1964).

The CAPM is most easily derived by postulating that the SDF is an affine function of the market excess return, R^e_{mt},

$$M_t = a + b\,R^e_{mt}. \tag{8.18}$$

(With a constant risk-free rate, this is the same as assuming an affine function of the market return.) Apply the unconditional version of (8.4) on the market excess return and some other excess return, R^e_t, and combine the results to get the standard CAPM expression

$$\mathrm{E}\!\left(R^e_t\right) = \frac{\mathrm{Cov}\!\left(R^e_t,\, R^e_{mt}\right)}{\sigma^2\!\left(R^e_{mt}\right)}\,\mathrm{E}\!\left(R^e_{mt}\right). \tag{8.19}$$

This says that the excess return on an asset is a regression coefficient (R^e_t regressed on R^e_{mt}) times the market excess return.

For a direct comparison with the consumption-based model in (8.11), it is more convenient to write (8.19) as

$$\mathrm{E}\!\left(R^e_t\right)\big/\sigma\!\left(R^e_t\right) = \rho\!\left(R^e_t,\, R^e_{mt}\right) \times \mathrm{E}\!\left(R^e_{mt}\right)\big/\sigma\!\left(R^e_{mt}\right), \tag{8.20}$$

which says that the Sharpe ratio is a positive linear function (with a slope equal to the Sharpe ratio of the market, that is, around 0.5) of the correlation of the asset with the market.

Figure 8.3 illustrates (8.20). The figure has the same structure as figure 8.2, except that the correlation is now with the excess return on the aggregate US market. These correlations are typically much higher than the correlations with consumption growth. However, it is hard to argue that the correlations with the stock market are much better at explaining the cross-section of Sharpe ratios: the slope coefficient is now positive in only two of six cases. In particular, the CAPM gives odd results (negative coefficients) for the dividend-price and the book-to-market portfolios (see Fama and French 1993 for a detailed analysis of these portfolios).

The conclusion is that the consumption-based model is not good at explaining the cross-section of Sharpe ratios, but it is no worse than CAPM – if it is any comfort.

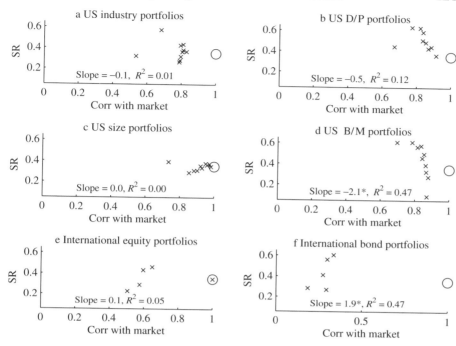

Figure 8.3 Sharpe ratios and market correlation, 1970–2001
Note: a–f show Sharpe ratios plotted against the correlation with the aggregate US market excess return; see figure 8.2 for details.

2.5 Time-variation in risk premia

In contrast to the traditional interpretation of 'efficient markets', it has been found that excess returns might be somewhat predictable – at least in the long run (a couple of years). In particular, Fama and French (1988a, 1988b) have argued that future long-run returns can be predicted by the current dividend-price ratio and/or current returns.

Table 8.2 illustrates this by showing the R^2 from the regressions

$$R^e_{t+k}(k) = a_0 + a_1 x_t + u_{t+k}, \text{ with } x_t = D_t/P_t \text{ or } R^e_t(k), \qquad (8.21)$$

where $R^e_t(k)$ is the annualised k-quarter excess return of the aggregate US stock market and D_t/P_t is the dividend-price ratio (see data appendix for details on data).

It seems as if the dividend-price ratio has some explanatory power for future returns – at least for long horizons in the long sample (first panel, 1947–2001). For instance, the R^2 is around 0.20–0.25 for the four–five

Table 8.2 *Predicting long-run excess returns on the aggregate US stock market*[a]

Horizon in quarters, (k)	1	4	8	12	16	20
1947–2001						
D_t/P_t	0.02*[b]	0.10*	0.13*	0.16*	0.20*	0.27*
$R_t^e(k)$	0.00	0.03	0.03*	0.04	0.13*	0.07*
1970–2001						
D_t/P_t	0.01	0.04	0.01	0.00	0.00	0.00
$R_t^e(k)$	0.00	0.06*	0.05	0.00	0.03	0.03

Notes: [a]This table shows results from regressing future k-quarter returns, $R_{t+k}^e(k)$, on the current dividend-price ratio (D_t/P_t) or the current k-quarter return, $R_t^e(k)$. The samples are 1947Q2–2001Q4 and 1970Q1–2001Q4.
[b]A star (*) denotes a significance at the 5 per cent level, based on GMM/delta method inference and a Newey-West (1987) estimator with $k-1$ lags.
Source: See the data appendix for details on data sources and transformations.

year horizons. However, the effect vanishes in the late sample (second panel, 1970–2001). The lagged return is a fairly weak predictor in both samples.

This evidence suggests that excess returns may perhaps have a predictable component, that is, that (*ex ante*) risk premia are changing over time. To see how that fits with the consumption-based model, assume that consumption growth is conditionally normally distributed. We then get a conditional Sharpe ratio as (compare with (8.11))

$$E_{t-1}(R_t^e)/\sigma_{t-1}(R_t^e) = \rho_{t-1}(R_t^e, \Delta c_t) \times \sigma_{t-1}(\Delta c_t)\gamma. \quad (8.22)$$

By multiplying both sides by $\sigma_{t-1}(R_t^e)$ we see that the conditional expected excess return should equal the conditional covariance times the risk aversion.

It is clear from the earlier figures 8.1a–c that the consumption-based model probably cannot generate plausible movements in risk premia. In figures 8.1a–c the conditional moments in (8.22) are approximated by estimates on different data windows (that is, different subsamples). Although this is a crude approximation, the results are revealing: the actual Sharpe ratio and the prediction of the consumption-based model move in different directions on all frequencies. In figure 8.1a (longer and longer sample) the actual Sharpe ratio is decreasing over time, whereas the prediction is mostly increasing. In Figure 8.1b the actual Sharpe ratio (on ten-year subsamples) reaches a minimum during the late 1970s and early 1980s – at the same time as the prediction is at maximum. The five-year subsamples in

Figure 8.1c seem to pick up business cycle movements, and the two series clearly move in different directions.

2.6 Refinements of the consumption-based model

There are many suggestions for how the problems with the consumption-based model can be solved. One major strand proposes changes to the utility function; another to how we measure the volatility of returns and consumption.

If we focus on the utility function, we need a high risk aversion (to get a high equity premium), a high elasticity of intertemporal elasticity of substitution (to get a low and stable real interest rate), and maybe also time-variation of the risk aversion (to fit the time-variation in expected returns). This could be produced by using a functional form that explicitly separates risk aversion from the intertemporal elasticity of substitution as in Epstein and Zin (1989a) or by certain types of habit persistence models as in Campbell and Cochrane (1999).

If we instead focus on the measurement of volatility, we need a high consumption volatility (to get a high equity premium) and time-variation in the volatility of returns and/or consumption (to get time-variation in expected returns). The first could be achieved by taking into account the effects of uninsurable idiosyncratic shocks as in Mankiw (1986); the second by a model of time-variation of second moments (typically a GARCH or regime switching model) as in, for instance, Bansal and Lundblad (2000).

There are of course many unresolved issues. First, some of the proposed 'fixes' have serious side effects. For instance, some of the habit-persistence models create implausible implications for consumption smoothing and optimal fiscal policy (see Lettau and Uhlig 2000, 2002; Ljunqvist and Uhlig 2000).

Second, it is unclear if these modifications of the SDF can improve the consumption-based model's ability to account for the cross-section of Sharpe ratios discussed on p. 418, since the cross-sectional variation often depends on the correlation with consumption growth only – just as in the CRRA model. The next few sections demonstrate this for some well-known models of time non-separable utility (Epstein and Zin 1989a), habit persistence (Campbell and Cochrane 1999) and idiosyncratic shocks (Constantinides and Duffie 1996).

Epstein–Zin utility
The basic idea of the recursive utility function in Epstein and Zin (1989b) is to form a certainty equivalent of future utility as $Z_t = [\mathrm{E}_t(U_{t+1}^{1-\gamma})]^{1/(1-\gamma)}$

where γ is the risk aversion – and then use a CES aggregator function to govern the intertemporal tradeoff between current consumption and the certainty equivalent: $U_t = [(1 - \delta)C_t^{1-1/\psi} + \delta Z_t^{1-1/\psi}]^{1/(1-1/\psi)}$, where ψ is the elasticity of intertemporal substitution.

Epstein and Zin (1989b) show that if all wealth is marketable, so the budget restriction can be written $W_{t+1} = R_{mt+1}(W_t - C_t)$ where R_{mt+1} is the market return (in a broad sense), then the Euler equation for an asset with return R_t is

$$1 = \mathrm{E}_{t-1}\big[\beta^\theta (C_t/C_{t-1})^{-\theta/\psi} R_{mt}^{\theta-1} R_t\big], \quad \text{where } \theta = (1 - \gamma)/(1 - 1/\psi). \tag{8.23}$$

This gives rise to rather complicated pricing expressions, but it is straightforward to show that the basic mechanisms are as in the CRRA model, except that the elasticity of intertemporal substitution is no longer forced to be the inverse of the risk aversion.

To illustrate that (8.23) has (approximately) the same implications for risky assets as the CRRA model, assume that consumption–wealth ratio is constant (for instance, because the market return is IID). This effectively closes down all interaction between the risk and intertemporal substitution (see Campbell 1993 and Svensson 1989). It follows from the budget constraint that consumption growth and the market return are proportional so (8.23) can be written

$$\mathrm{E}_{t-1}[(C_t/C_{t-1})^{-\gamma} R_t] = \text{constant}, \tag{8.24}$$

which is exactly the same as the CRRA model. The Epstein–Zin model therefore inherits the problem with explaining the cross-section of Sharpe ratios. This is also approximately true when the consumption–wealth ratio is not too variable. Of course, if there are large predictable movements in the market return, then it is no longer true.

To see that the intertemporal substitution is governed by the parameter ψ, close down all systematic risk by assuming that the market return is a risk-free rate (set $R_{mt} = R_t = R_{ft}$ in (8.23)) and that log consumption and the log real interest rate, r_{ft}, have a bivariate normal distribution. We then get

$$\mathrm{E}_{t-1}(r_{ft}) + \theta \sigma_{t-1}^2(r_{ft})/2 = -\ln(\beta) + \frac{1}{\psi}\mathrm{E}_{t-1}(\Delta c_t) - \frac{\theta}{\psi^2}\sigma_{t-1}^2(\Delta c_t)/2. \tag{8.25}$$

This is the same relation between the real interest rate and consumption growth as in the CRRA case (see (8.14)) – except that the elasticity of intertemporal substitution is no longer forced to be the inverse of the risk aversion.

This analysis shows that the Epstein–Zin model could help us to solve the risk-free rate puzzle (since we have a separate parameter for the elasticity of intertemporal substitution), but it can probably not do much with the equity premium (unless we are willing to accept a very high risk aversion) or the cross-sectional variation in Sharpe ratios.

Habit persistence

The utility function in the habit-persistence model of Campbell and Cochrane (1999) has the same functional form as the CRRA model, but the argument is the difference between consumption and a habit level, $C_t - X_t$, instead of just consumption. Variation in consumption and habit can both contribute to variation in marginal utility, which affects asset prices.

Campbell and Cochrane (1999) parameterise the habit in terms of the 'surplus ratio' $S_t = (C_t - X_t)/C_t$, which measures how much aggregate consumption exceeds the habit. Since this ratio is external to the investor, marginal utility becomes $(C_t - X_t)^{-\gamma} = (C_t S_t)^{-\gamma}$. We can therefore write the log SDF as

$$\ln(M_t) = \ln(\beta) - \gamma(\Delta s_t + \Delta c_t), \qquad (8.26)$$

where s_t is the log surplus ratio. The process for s_t is assumed to be a non-linear AR(1)

$$s_t = \phi s_{t-1} + \lambda(s_{t-1})\Delta c_t + \text{constant}, \qquad (8.27)$$

where $\lambda(s_{t-1})$ is a decreasing function of s_{t-1} which controls the sensitivity to (aggregate) consumption growth. The function $\lambda(s_{t-1})$ is always non-negative, so the log surplus ratio reacts positively to consumption growth (the main effect of letting λ depend on s_{t-1} is to make the risk premium move with the business cycle). Because of (8.27), a move in Δc_t will typically be accompanied by a move of Δs_t in the same direction, which increases the volatility of the SDF (8.26). In other words, a move in consumption drives the habit X_t in the opposite direction so $C_t - X_t$ varies a great deal.

Consumption growth is assumed to be conditionally normally distributed, so the conditional Sharpe ratio is (compare with (8.9))

$$\mathrm{E}_{t-1}\big(R_t^e\big)\big/\sigma_{t-1}\big(R_t^e\big) = -\rho_{t-1}\big[R_t^e, \ln(M_t)\big] \times \sigma_{t-1}[\ln(M_t)]. \qquad (8.28)$$

From (8.26) and (8.27) we note that the innovation in the log SDF is $-\gamma[\lambda(s_{t-1}) + 1]$ times the innovation in Δc_t. Since $\lambda(s_{t-1})$ is positive and known in $t-1$ this is very similar to the CRRA model, except that the conditional volatility of the log SDF (the last term in (8.28)) is scaled up. This could help explain a higher risk premium. In a way, it is very similar to just increasing the risk aversion γ (although Campbell and Cochrane 1999 show that their model does not suffer from some of the drawbacks of the CRRA model with a high γ).

However, (8.28) has the same implication for the cross-sectional variation of Sharpe ratios as the CRRA model. The reason is that the conditional correlation in (8.28) is the same as in the CRRA model since the innovation in the log SDF is proportional to the innovation in consumption growth (and the factor of proportionality cancels in the correlation).

Idiosyncratic risk

A quite different attempt to solve the problems with the consumption-based asset pricing model is to argue that aggregating individual investors into a (fictitious) representative investor is a non-trivial task. Investors who face idiosyncratic risk that they cannot insure against (incomplete markets) may be reluctant to hold risky assets. Since macro data averages out idiosyncratic components, the volatility of aggregate consumption would then underestimate the true consumption volatility of a representative investor.

However, it is surprisingly hard to make this story stick. The first problem is that only shocks that cannot be hedged qualify as 'idiosyncratic shocks': hedging means averaging out. One way of hedging consumption (if not income) is to have a savings account (see Telmer 1993). Moreover, income can sometimes be partially hedged by trading in existing assets if they are correlated with income. In practice, this means that idiosyncratic shocks are probably smaller than the income shocks estimated from micro data.

The second problem is that idiosyncratic shocks may still not matter unless their distribution is strongly tied to the state of the economy. To develop an example, note that the basic asset pricing equation (8.1) must hold for every investor (after all, it is his first-order condition), so $E_{t-1}(R_t M_{jt}) = 1$ where M_{jt} is the SDF of investor j. The conditional version of the asset pricing equation with normally distributed consumption growth (8.10) for investor j is then

$$E_{t-1}\left(R_t^e\right) = \mathrm{Cov}_{t-1}\left(R_t^e, \Delta c_{jt}\right)\gamma, \tag{8.29}$$

where Δc_{jt} is consumption growth of investor j.

We let the innovation in the consumption of investor j have two components: an aggregate innovation (common to all investors) and an idiosyncratic innovation. The idiosyncratic shock cannot be correlated with existing assets (discussed above), so it contributes nothing to the conditional covariance in (8.29): the risk premium will depend only on the covariance of the return with the aggregate innovation – as in the CRRA model. In this case the idiosyncratic shocks do not matter for the risk premium (although they will typically decrease the real interest rate as investors increase the precautionary saving).

This result is quite general. For instance, it holds for the Campbell and Cochrane (1999) model discussed above, and in any other model with a log-normal SDF where the idiosyncratic component affects the log SDF linearly (this follows directly from (8.8)).[14]

To make idiosyncratic shocks matter for risk premia, they will either have to be something less than completely idiosyncratic (for instance, affecting a group of investors who collectively have market power; see Den Haan 2001) or their distribution must depend on the aggregate shock (see Constantinides and Duffie 1996 and Mankiw 1986).

In the latter class of models, a higher risk premium requires that the volatility of the idiosyncratic shocks is stochastic and that the innovations to this volatility and of aggregate consumption are negatively correlated: bad times mean more risk. To illustrate this, consider the CRRA model where the log SDF for investor j is

$$\ln(M_{jt}) = \ln(\beta) - \gamma \Delta c_{jt}. \tag{8.30}$$

Let the innovation in consumption growth for investor j be

$$\Delta c_{jt} - \mathrm{E}_{t-1}(\Delta c_{jt}) = \varepsilon_t + u_{jt}, \tag{8.31}$$

where ε_t is the aggregate component and u_{jt} the individual component which has a variance which depends on the realisation of ε_t.

With (8.30)–(8.31) the asset pricing equation for investor j says that

$$0 = \mathrm{E}_{t-1}\left(R_t^e M_{jt}\right) \tag{8.32}$$

$$= \mathrm{E}_{R,\varepsilon,u}\left\{R_t^e \exp[\ln(\beta) - \gamma \mathrm{E}_{t-1}(\Delta c_t) - \gamma \varepsilon_t - \gamma u_{jt}]\right\}. \tag{8.33}$$

The operator $\mathrm{E}_{R,\varepsilon,u}$ is used instead of E_{t-1} to indicate that the expectations involve integrating over the random variables R_t^e, ε_t, and u_{jt}. Suppose that the distribution of u_{jt} conditional on the aggregate innovation, ε_t, is normal with zero mean and variance $v_{t-1} + \lambda(\varepsilon_t)$ where v_{t-1}

---

[14] Lettau (2002) shows that this property holds for any distribution of the consumption innovation if utility is CRRA and the distribution of the idiosyncratic component is not affected by the aggregate shock.

is known in $t - 1$ and $\lambda(\varepsilon_t)$ depends on the aggregate shock. Integrating over u_{jt} then gives

$$0 = \mathrm{E}_{R,\varepsilon}\left\{ R_t^e \exp[\ln(\beta) - \gamma \mathrm{E}_{t-1}(\Delta c_t) + \gamma^2 v_{t-1} - \gamma \varepsilon_t + \gamma^2 \lambda(\varepsilon_t)/2] \right\}$$

$$(8.34)$$

where $\mathrm{E}_{R,\varepsilon}$ indicates that we now need to integrate over R_t^e and ε_t. (This first integration works since the asset return is independent of the realisation of the idiosyncratic shock, even if not of its variance.)

I follow Lettau's (2002) approximation of assuming that ε_t and $\lambda(\varepsilon_t)$ have a bivariate normal distribution. This is only an approximation since it does not rule out negative variances, but it has the advantage of giving a very straightforward expression. The term in square brackets in (8.34) can then be interpreted as a normally distributed log SDF of the investor, which allows us to use the decomposition of the Sharpe ratio in (8.28) which I repeat here for ease of reading

$$\mathrm{E}_{t-1}\left(R_t^e\right) / \sigma_{t-1}\left(R_t^e\right) = -\rho_{t-1}\left[R_t^e, \ln(M_t)\right] \times \sigma_{t-1}[\ln(M_t)]. \quad (8.28)$$

In this model, the conditional volatility and correlation are

$$\sigma_{t-1}[\ln(M_t)] = \gamma \sigma_{t-1}[\varepsilon_t - \gamma \lambda(\varepsilon_t)/2] \quad (8.35)$$

$$-\rho_{t-1}\left[R_t^e, \ln(M_t)\right] = \rho_{t-1}\left[R_t^e, \varepsilon_t - \gamma \lambda(\varepsilon_t)/2\right]. \quad (8.36)$$

Note that setting $\lambda(\varepsilon_t) = 0$ gives the same expressions as without idiosyncratic shocks. In fact, if $\lambda(\varepsilon_t)$ is a constant, that is, if the volatility of the idiosyncratic shocks does not depend on the aggregate shock, then we also get the same expressions as without idiosyncratic shocks.

If $\lambda(\varepsilon_t)$ is decreasing in ε_t so idiosyncratic risk is larger in bad times, then the volatility in (8.35) is larger than without idiosyncratic shocks. This could help explaining the equity premium puzzle – although there are doubts about whether the idiosyncratic risk is sufficiently volatile to be quantitatively important (see Cogley 1998 and Lettau 2002).

However, this mechanism is unlikely to help the model to explain the cross-sectional variation in Sharpe ratios – which depends only on the correlation (8.36): as a first-order approximation this correlation is the same as when $\lambda(\varepsilon_t)$ is constant. For instance, if $\lambda(\varepsilon_t) = a + b\varepsilon_t$ with $b < 0$, then this is exactly so. This gives the same implications for the cross-sectional dispersion of Sharpe ratios as the model without idiosyncratic shocks – at least unless the idiosyncratic dispersion is a very non-linear function of the aggregate state.

An additional aspect of models with idiosyncratic risk is that they allow us to study the effects of transaction costs in a serious way: heterogeneous agents with idiosyncratic shocks trade, representative agents do not. The first effect of transaction costs is to transform the first-order condition of an investor to a set of inequalities $1/(1 + \tau) \leq E_{t-1}(R_t M_{jt}) \leq 1 + \tau$ where τ is the (proportional) cost of a round-trip (the upper limit is for buying the asset in $t - 1$ and selling in t; the lower limit is for the opposite). This has been used to modify the Hansen and Jagannathan (1991) bounds (see He and Modest 1995 and Luttmer 1996) with mixed results. One of the key assumptions in that analysis seems to be the length of the period: a 0.5 per cent transaction cost is quite substantive compared to a 1 per cent monthly (expected) return, but small compared to a 12 per cent annual return. We therefore need to find the equilibrium (including the endogenous trading frequency) in order to analyse the importance of transaction costs. So far, the findings indicate that the effect on prices is relatively small (unless borrowing/lending is very costly) but that the effect on turnover is large (see Heaton and Lucas 1996 and Vayanos 1998).

3 ASSETS IN SIMULATION MODELS

This part of the chapter discusses how different types of assets are incorporated into simulation models. The emphasis is on discussing the key properties of the assets when they are priced by a consumption-based model.

I first analyse a number of different asset classes: short- and long-lived claims on aggregate consumption, options and levered claims, as well as short and long real/nominal interest rates. To economise on space, I leave out some important asset classes like foreign exchange and real estate (see, for instance, Hendershott 1998, Kollman 2001, Smith and Wickens 2002 and Zimmermann 1999). At the end, I discuss some other important features of how assets are modelled: time-variation in risk premia, the effect of non-Walrasian labour contracts, and the effect of adding an asset to an existing model.

The analysis has the same basic approach as in the first part of the chapter. First, the model consists of the basic asset pricing equation (8.1) and the consumption-based stochastic discount factor (8.5). In practice, this means that we are studying equilibrium conditions on the joint behaviour of consumption growth and returns on assets that can be freely traded. This does not assume that markets are complete. However, adding an asset to a model with incomplete markets may change the consumption process, so the results we derive are valid only for assets that could be traded when the equilibrium was determined (see p. 442 for a more detailed discussion). Second, analytical pricing relations are derived by making assumptions about the distribution of returns and consumption and sometimes also by approximating complicated expressions.

Although this approach is useful for providing intuition for how different types of assets will work in a simulation model, it is clearly only a first step. In particular, this chapter never formulates and solves a full model. To do that, the other contributions to this book, the references found below and the text by Altug and Labadie (1994) should all be very useful.

3.1 Preliminaries

Many simulation models are close to log-linear and are typically fed with normally distributed shocks. This means that most variables (including returns) are approximately log-normally distributed – sometimes exactly so. I therefore derive new expressions for risk premia and Sharpe ratios (the expressions in previous sections assumed normally, not log-normally, distributed returns). These expressions will be used repeatedly in the following sections.

The asset pricing equation with the CRRA SDF is

$$1 = \mathrm{E}_{t-1}\{\beta \exp[-\gamma \Delta c_t + r_t]\},$$

where $r_t = \ln(R_t)$ is the log return. If these variables have a bivariate normal distribution, it follows (see n. 11) that the risk premium and Sharpe ratios are

$$\mathrm{E}_{t-1}\left(\tilde{r}_t^e\right) = \mathrm{Cov}_{t-1}\left(\gamma \Delta c_t, r_t^e\right), \text{ and} \qquad (8.37)$$

$$\mathrm{E}_{t-1}\left(\tilde{r}_t^e\right)/\sigma_{t-1}\left(r_t^e\right) = \rho_{t-1}\left(\Delta c_t, r_t^e\right) \times \sigma_{t-1}(\Delta c_t)\gamma. \qquad (8.38)$$

The tilde is here to indicate that the risk premium is defined as $\mathrm{E}_{t-1}(\tilde{r}_t^e) = \mathrm{E}_{t-1}(r_t^e) + \sigma_{t-1}^2(r_t)/2$, that is, the expected excess log return over the real interest rate, adjusted for Jensen's inequality. This definition of an excess return is perhaps slightly non-standard, but it captures all the aspects of interest here.

In the following sections I will make use of the fact that only innovations matter for the risk premia, since it is only innovations that are risky. For the log excess return, this means that only the innovation in the risky asset payoff matters.[15]

3.2 Claims on aggregate consumption

This section analyses the pricing of claims on aggregate consumption. Many models have considered such assets – sometimes as an approximation of equity (see, for instance, Lucas 1978 and the references on p. 44). The

---

[15] The log excess return, r_t^e is the log payoff minus the lagged log asset price (measured in real terms) minus the log real interest rate. Only the first component has an innovation.

main purpose of the discussion is to highlight that the risk premium on long-lived consumption claims depends crucially on the autocorrelation of consumption growth.

We first discuss a one-period claim and then move on to multi-period claims. The real price in $t - 1$ of a claim on aggregate consumption in t satisfies the following asset pricing equation for CRRA utility (see (8.12))

$$P_{ct-1} = \mathrm{E}_{t-1}[\beta(C_t/C_{t-1})^{-\gamma} C_t] \text{ or} \tag{8.39}$$

$$\ln(P_{ct-1}) = \ln(C_{t-1}) + \ln(\beta) + (1 - \gamma)\,\mathrm{E}_{t-1}(\Delta c_t)$$
$$+ (1 - \gamma)^2 \sigma_{t-1}^2(\Delta c_t)/2 \tag{8.40}$$

where the second line exploits log-normality. The payoff in t is obviously C_t, so the return is C_t/P_{ct-1}. Instead of evaluating this by brute force (it is not very hard, just messy), we use (8.37). Note that the innovation in the excess log return of the consumption claim, r_{ct}^e, equals the innovation in consumption growth so (8.37) gives

$$\mathrm{E}_{t-1}\big(\tilde{r}_{ct}^e\big) = \sigma_{t-1}^2(\Delta c_t)\gamma. \tag{8.41}$$

This asset has the highest possible Sharpe ratio $(\sigma_{t-1}(\Delta c_t)\gamma)$ since the return is perfectly negatively correlated with the SDF – this is yet another version of the Hansen and Jagannathan (1991) bound. This means that if the model cannot generate a high Sharpe ratio for the one-period consumption claim, then it cannot do so for any other asset either.

Most simulation models have tended to focus on long-lived claims on a consumption stream, that is, a portfolio of different claims. What is the expected return on holding such a portfolio between two periods (the holding period return)?

It is easy to get the basic intuition by considering a claim that gives aggregate consumption in t and $t + 1$. When traded in $t - 1$ this is a portfolio of two claims: a claim on C_t (discussed above) and a claim on C_{t+1}. I will call the the latter a 'C_{t+1} strip'. The time lines of these assets are shown in figure 8.4. The holding period return (between $t - 1$ and t) on this portfolio is clearly the sum of the holding period returns on its two components.

We already know the (holding period) return on the one-period claim from (8.41), so I now turn to the C_{t+1} strip. This strip becomes a one-period claim in t and its price will then be as in (8.40) but with time subscripts advanced one period

$$\ln(P_{ct}) = \ln(C_t) + \ln(\beta) + (1 - \gamma)\,\mathrm{E}_t(\Delta c_{t+1}) + (1 - \gamma)^2 \sigma_t^2(\Delta c_{t+1})/2. \tag{8.42}$$

	$t-1$	t	$t+1$
Claim on C_t:	buy claim	get C_t	
Claim on C_{t+1}:	buy claim	keep or sell claim	if kept, get C_{t+1}

Figure 8.4 Time line of $t-1$ claims on C_t and C_{t+1}

This is the only term in the excess log holding period return (between $t-1$ and t) with an innovation. Applying (8.37) therefore gives the expected holding period return (in excess of a real interest rate) of the strip

$$\mathrm{E}_{t-1}\left(\tilde{r}^e_{ht}\right) = \gamma\sigma^2_{t-1}(\Delta c_t) + \gamma(1-\gamma)\,\mathrm{Cov}_{t-1}[\Delta c_t, \mathrm{E}_t(\Delta c_{t+1})] \quad (8.43)$$

provided Jensen's inequality term is constant (or at least uncorrelated with the innovation in consumption growth).

The second term in (8.43) is zero if consumption growth is not autocorrelated[16] or if the utility function is logarithmic $\gamma=1$. In this case, the strip has the same risk premium as the one-period claim in (8.41). This should come as no surprise since lack of autocorrelation makes time irrelevant and log utility makes the discount rate effect perfectly balance the 'dividend' effect of any news.[17]

With positive autocorrelation in consumption (as table 8.1 suggests), the strip has a lower expected return than the one-period claim – provided the risk aversion is larger than unity. The intuition is as follows. The price in (8.42) is high when expected consumption growth, $\mathrm{E}_t\Delta c_{t+1}$, is low: although the expected payoff is low, it will be worth a lot since it comes at a time of scarcity (with log utility these effects cancel out). Now, if $\mathrm{E}_t\Delta c_{t+1}$ is low, then period-t consumption growth, Δc_t, is typically also low (they are positively correlated). This means that the strip generates a high-holding-period return in t (a capital gain) when consumption is scarce (high marginal utility): it is a fairly good hedge and will therefore not require a high risk premium. It is even conceivable that it could have a negative risk premium.

This extends to longer-lived claims on streams of consumption. Such assets will have a fairly low (high) risk premium if consumption is positively (negatively) autocorrelated for most leads/lags (see Campbell 1986).

[16] $\mathrm{Cov}_{t-1}[\Delta c_t, \mathrm{E}_t(\Delta c_{t+1})] = \mathrm{Cov}_{t-1}(\Delta c_t, \Delta c_{t+1})$ since $\Delta c_{t+1} - \mathrm{E}_t(\Delta c_{t+1})$ is not correlated with anything known in t.

[17] Abel (1999) assumes IID consumption growth, but reintroduces autocorrelation in the SDF through habit persistence.

3.3 Options and levered claims

This section discusses options and option-like assets. Fairly few simulation models have studied traditional options directly, but some models have dealt with option-type assets like levered equity. However, simulation models could be a useful framework for studying and solving option pricing problems. I will illustrate this by considering a very simple case: a European call option that expires next period.

On the expiry date, the owner of a European call option has the right (not the obligation) to buy a pre-specified asset for a pre-specified (strike) price, X. If the asset payoff happens to be Y_t, then the payoff of the option is zero if $Y_t < X$ (the option is not exercised) and $Y_t - X$ otherwise.

With the CRRA SDF, the price of the call option must be

$$\text{Call option price}_{t-1} = \text{E}_{t-1}[\beta(C_t/C_{t-1})^{-\gamma}\max(0, Y_t - X)]. \quad (8.44)$$

If consumption growth and the log asset payoff, $\ln(Y_t)$, have a bivariate normal distribution, then the solution to this equation is the Black and Scholes (1973)/Merton (1973) formula (see Huang and Litzenberger 1988 or Söderlind and Svensson 1997 for straightforward and not at all tedious calculations). This result is quite natural when we compare with the dynamic hedging approach typically used for deriving the Black–Scholes formula, since both approaches fundamentally rely on log-normality of the asset payoff.[18] This framework has been used by, for instance, Söderlind (2003) to study the implications of monetary policy on bond options in a simple analytical RBC model.

To get intuition for the results on option and option-like assets, it is convenient to approximate the non-linear payoff $\max(0, Y_t - X)$ with a power function

$$Z_t = Ayt^{\lambda}, \text{ with } \lambda = 1/[1 - X/\text{E}_{t-1}(Y_t)] \text{ for } X < \text{E}_{t-1}(Y_t). \quad (8.45)$$

Abel (1999) shows that this approximation gives a coefficient of variation (standard deviation divided by the mean) of the payoff which is very close to the option payoff at least for reasonably low values of X (so the probability of exercise is high). This approximate payoff is particularly convenient when Y_t is log-normally distributed since the log-normality carries over to Ayt^{λ}: if $\ln(Y_t)$ is normally distributed, so is $\ln(A) + \lambda\ln(Y_t)$.

---

[18] The result is easily derived by using the following facts: if $x \sim N(\mu, \sigma^2)$ and $y = \exp(x)$ then $\text{E}(y^k) = \exp(k\mu + k^2\sigma^2/2)$ and $\text{E}(y^k|y > a) = \text{E}(y^k)\Phi(k\sigma - a_0)/\Phi(-a_0)$, where $a_0 = [\ln(a) - \mu]/\sigma$; see Johnson, Kotz and Balakrishnan (1994).

Payoffs and distribution

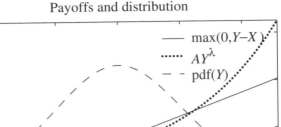

Figure 8.5 Example of option payoff and power approximation
Note: This figure shows the payoff of a call option with strike price X and a power
approximation. The value of the underlying asset is the random variable Y with
probability density function $pdf(Y)$.

Figure 8.5 illustrates how (8.45) works for a payoff with the same distribution as US annual consumption growth (mean of 2 per cent and a standard deviation of 1 per cent), where the exercise price, X, is such that there is a 93 per cent chance of exercise. The distribution of Y_t is also shown (it is log-normal, but looks almost like a normal distribution since the mean is so far from zero). The constant A in the power function payoff is chosen so that both payoffs have the same means of around 1.5 per cent. It is straightforward to calculate (using the facts in footnote 18) that both the option payoff and the approximation have standard deviations close to 1 per cent. We now use this approximation to study the implications of firm debt.

Many simulation models assume that the equity value equals the full value of a firm. However, most firms are financed by both equity and debt. Debt to assets (leverage) ratios vary a good deal, but values around 0.5 seem to be fairly typical for historical US data. Since equity is not a claim on the full value of the firm, only the residual claim, it has option-like features which is likely to make it more risky.

To illustrate the main effect of leverage, I compare the one-period claim on consumption discussed on p. 431 with a levered claim whose payoff is $max(0, C_t - X)$ where X is the debt. Leverage reduces the payoff by subtracting a fixed amount (the debt), except that limited liability means that the payoff cannot be negative. A zero payoff (a return of -100 per cent) is awfully bad for investors, so the levered claim will be considered very risky.

From (8.45) the levered claim has approximately the payoff AC_t^λ. This means that the innovation in the log payoff (which is what matters for the risk premium) is λ times the innovation in unlevered claim. It then follows directly from (8.41) that the risk premium of the levered claim, $E_{t-1}(\tilde{r}_{zt}^e)$, is λ times the risk premium on the unlevered claim

$$E_{t-1}(\tilde{r}_{zt}^e) = \lambda\sigma_{t-1}^2(\Delta c_t)\gamma. \tag{8.46}$$

The levered claim has a higher risk premium since it is more volatile ($\lambda > 1$), but the Sharpe ratio is the same.

If we interpret $X/E_{t-1}(Y_t)$ as the leverage ratio which is (on average) around 0.5, then Abel's suggestion in (8.45) gives $\lambda = 2$. With this number the risk premium on levered claims should be twice as high as the risk premium on unlevered claims.

It is more difficult to model levered long-lived claims, since the claim can only go 'bankrupt' once, so numerical methods are called for. A few simulation models have incorporated leverage and arrived at somewhat different conclusions. For instance, Rouwenhorst (1995) finds a very small effect of leverage, while Jermann (1998) finds that it adds around one percentage point to the equity premium. The main reason for the difference seems to be that the firm value is very stable in Rouwenhorst's model.

3.4 The real yield curve

This section studies the yield curve of real interest rates. The price of a k-period real bond (with a unit payoff k periods ahead) must satisfy the asset pricing equation (see (8.12))

$$B_{kt-1} = E_{t-1}[\beta^k(C_{t+k-1}/C_{t-1})^{-\gamma}]. \tag{8.47}$$

I will consider two interest rates that can be calculated from this expression. First, the one-period (log) interest rate $r_{1t-1} = \ln(1/B_{1t-1})$, is the return on holding a real bond from $t-1$ to t. Note that (according to convention) it carries the date of the investment (when the interest rate is agreed on), not the date of payoff as for most other assets. By exploiting the log-normality we get

$$r_{1t-1} = -\ln(\beta) + \gamma E_{t-1}(\Delta c_t) - \gamma^2\sigma_{t-1}^2(\Delta c_t)/2. \tag{8.48}$$

Real interest rates are time-varying only if expected consumption growth is (disregarding time-variation in Jensen's inequality term).

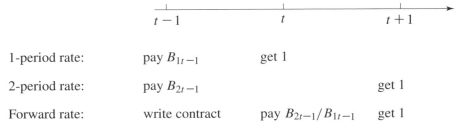

Second, we can create a portfolio of one-period and two-period real (inflation-indexed) bonds to guarantee the investor a known (as of $t - 1$) interest rate on an investment between t and $t + 1$, that is, a real forward rate.

The forward–spot parity for an asset without intermediate dividends says that the contracted forward price (to be paid next period) is

$$\text{Forward price} = \frac{\text{Spot price}}{\text{Price of bond maturing next period}}.$$

The intuition is that the forward contract is like buying the asset today, but on credit.

The 'spot way' of making sure that we get one unit (of the basket of goods) in $t + 1$ is to buy a two-period bond in $t - 1$ at the price B_{2t-1}. The price of a bond maturing next period is B_{1t-1}, so the forward price is B_{2t-1}/B_{1t-1}. This is illustrated in figure 8.6.

We then define the forward rate as the rate of return on this investment: since the bond pays off one unit in $t + 1$ and the investment was B_{2t}/B_{1t} in t, the gross forward rate is B_{1t-1}/B_{2t-1}. From (8.47) we calculate the log forward rate, $f_{t-1} = \ln(B_{1t-1}/B_{2t-1})$, as

$$\begin{aligned} f_{t-1} = &-\ln(\beta) + \gamma \, \mathrm{E}_{t-1}(\Delta c_{t+1}) \\ &- \gamma^2 \sigma^2_{t-1}(\Delta c_{t+1})/2 - \gamma^2 \mathrm{Cov}_{t-1}(\Delta c_t, \Delta c_{t+1}). \end{aligned} \quad (8.49)$$

Both the short interest rate and the forward rate can vary over time. In a one-factor model of the yield curve (see, for instance, Backus, Foresi, and Zin 1998, Cox, Ingersoll and Ross 1985 and Vasicek 1977) they move in parallel. In (8.48)–(8.49) parallel movements require that $\mathrm{E}_{t-1}(\Delta c_t)$ and $\mathrm{E}_{t-1}(\Delta c_{t+1})$ are affine functions of a single variable, *the* factor. For instance, in the special case where expected consumption is an AR (1) with positive autocorrelation, then the real interest rates would actually follow a discrete version of Vasicek's (1977) model. That holds approximately in many simple RBC models, since their dynamics are well captured by a single dynamic state variable (see Cogley and Nason 1993). This may sound awfully restrictive, but from the perspective of modelling the real yield curve, it may be acceptable. It is still a matter of debate whether the one-factor model can be rejected or not.

We now turn to studying the *average slope of the yield curve*, that is, the average over time. The risk premium is the forward rate (8.49) minus the expected (as of $t-1$) future short rate (8.48) (but with time subscripts forwarded one period)

$$f_{t-1} - \mathrm{E}_{t-1}(r_{1t}) = -\gamma^2 \mathrm{Cov}_{t-1}(\Delta c_t, \Delta c_{t+1})$$
$$+ \gamma^2 \left[\sigma_t^2(\Delta c_{t+1}) - \sigma_{t-1}^2(\Delta c_{t+1})\right]/2 \quad (8.50)$$

provided future conditional volatilities are known in advance.

The forward rate will be lower than the expected future short rate if consumption growth is positively autocorrelated (as table 8.1 suggests), disregarding the Jensen's inequality terms. The intuition is the same as on p. 432: the forward contract will generate a capital gain in t if $\mathrm{E}_t(\Delta c_{t+1})$ is low (the one-period interest rate is then low, so the price of a bond is high) and this will typically happen when consumption is scarce in t (positive autocorrelation).

This extends to longer interest rates, so the real yield curve will slope downwards (upwards) if consumption growth is positively (negatively) autocorrelated for most leads/lags. In other words, with positive autocorrelation in consumption growth, the long real (or inflation-indexed) bond is a good hedge and therefore 'safer' than the strategy of rolling over short interest rates (see Backus, Foresi and Zin 1998, Backus, Gregory and Zin 1989, Campbell 1986 and Campbell and Viceira 2002).

3.5 Money supply and nominal interest rates

This section discusses the effect of monetary policy on nominal interest rates. Simulation models with nominal variables typically introduce money through a cash-in-advance constraint, by sticking real money balances into the utility function, or by a shopping-time technology (see, for instance, Giovannini and Labadie 1991 and Labadie 1989 for asset pricing analysis with cash-in-advance constraints). In many cases, the mere introduction of money has no effect on the real equilibrium, and in most other cases the effect is only temporary and negligible (see, for instance, Cooley and Hansen 1989).

It is only when nominal rigidities are present that the real variables, including real assets, are affected – and this also gives monetary policy an important role for asset prices. For instance, a policy that aims at stabilising output is likely to achieve some short-run stabilisation of consumption, which may affect risk premia in general. On the other hand, exogenous monetary policy shifts add another source of uncertainty (as argued by Friedman and many others) which may work in the opposite direction. In any case, nominal bonds are likely to be more directly affected by monetary policy than other assets, so this section focuses on the nominal yield curve.

The real price of a nominal bond is as in (8.47) except that the real payoff is not unity but one divided by the nominal price index in $t + k - 1$, Q_{t+k-1}. Multiplying by today's price level, Q_{t-1}, converts the real price to a nominal bond price

$$B^\$_{kt-1} = \mathrm{E}_{t-1}[\beta^k (C_{t+k-1}/C_{t-1})^{-\gamma} Q_{t-1}/Q_{t+k-1}]. \qquad (8.51)$$

I assume that log consumption and the inflation rate, $\pi_t = \ln(Q_t/Q_{t-1})$, has a bivariate normal distribution. The (log) one-period nominal interest rate, $i_{1t-1} = \ln(1/B^\$_{1t-1})$, is then

$$i_{1t-1} = -\ln(\beta) + \mathrm{E}_{t-1}(\gamma \Delta c_t + \pi_t) - \sigma^2_{t-1}(-\gamma \Delta c_t - \pi_t)/2. \qquad (8.52)$$

Using the real interest rate (8.48) gives

$$i_{1t-1} - \mathrm{E}_{t-1}(\pi_t) - r_{1t-1} = -\mathrm{Cov}_{t-1}(\gamma \Delta c_t, \pi_t) - \sigma^2_{t-1}(\pi_t)/2 \qquad (8.53)$$

which is a modern version of the Fisher equation: the nominal interest rate equals the sum of expected inflation, the real interest rate and an inflation risk premium (and a Jensen's inequality term).

The Fisher equation (8.53) shows that the *movements in the nominal interest rate* come from at least two sources: expected inflation may change and the real interest rate too. Of course, in many traditional macro models the real interest rate is very stable so movements in the nominal interest rate reflect similar movements in inflation expectations (the 'Fisher effect').

The modelling of monetary policy is certainly crucial for the movements of the nominal interest rate. In models with optimal monetary policy it is often found that it is necessary to put interest rate volatility in the loss function of the policy-maker (see, for instance, Söderlind 1999, 2001b and Chadha and Nolan, chapter 5 in this volume); otherwise the interest rate becomes much too volatile compared with data.[19]

In models with exogenous (non-optimal) monetary policy it can easily happen that the implied nominal interest rate has strange dynamics. As an example, consider what could happen in the model used in Cooley

---

[19] Several articles have also analysed the effects on real aggregates and the term structure of monetary policy shocks; see, for instance, Cochrane and Piazzesi (2002b) and Rudebusch (1998).

and Hansen (1989, 1995). The utility function is logarithmic ($\gamma = 1$), so the real interest rate equals the expected consumption growth plus a constant (see (8.48)). The cash-in-advance constraint makes the nominal value of consumption equal the exogenous money supply. Together, these facts mean that $E_{t-1}(\pi_t) + r_{1t}$ on the left-hand side of (8.53) equals the expected money supply growth – and this carries over to the nominal interest rate. The money supply growth is modelled as an exogenous AR (1) process with positive autocorrelation, so this behaviour is inherited by the nominal interest rate (see n.13). It might seem innocent to change the autocorrelation coefficient to zero (so money supply becomes a random walk), but this would actually imply a constant nominal interest rate, which is slightly odd.

We now turn to discussing *the risk premium on the nominal bond* in (8.53). It is positive if the covariance of consumption growth and inflation is negative (which seems to be the case in US data). The reason is that the real return on the nominal bond (nominal return minus inflation) then tends to be low when consumption is scarce (see Cochrane and Piazzesi 2002a for a recent empirical study of bond risk premia).

This risk premium is likely to depend on many modelling choices. With predetermined inflation (which is often used in New Keynesian models), there is no risk premium at all. Monetary policy is also likely to affect the risk premium. For instance, in new Keynesian models with some kind of Phillips curve (sticky, but forward-looking, price-setting, see, for instance, Clarida, Galí and Gertler 1999) output (consumption) and inflation move in the same direction if demand shocks (random movements in the time preference rate) dominate, but in opposite directions if supply shocks (random movements in productivity or factor input prices) dominate. If the monetary policy objective is to minimise some linear combination of variances of output and inflation without any regard to interest rate volatility, then it is well known that monetary policy should neutralise all demand shocks but only some of the supply shocks. This will tend to make the risk premium positive.

3.6 Time-variation in risk premia

This section briefly discusses how a simulation model can generate time-variation in risk premia. Recall from (8.22) that the risk premium in the CRRA model is

$$E_{t-1}\left(R_t^e\right) = \text{Cov}_{t-1}\left(R_t^e, \Delta c_t\right) \tag{8.54}$$

$$= \rho_{t-1}\left(R_t^e, \Delta c_t\right) \times \sigma_{t-1}(\Delta c_t) \times \sigma_{t-1}\left(R_t^e\right)\gamma. \tag{8.55}$$

To get movements in risk premia in the consumption-based model, the conditional covariance of the excess return and consumption growth must be changing over time. Few simulation models generate this because of a combination of two features: the shocks are typically homoscedastic and the dynamics close to log-linear (so consumption growth and log returns are linear transformations of the shocks). The result is that all expected asset returns will (almost) move in parallel with the expected risk-free rate.

This can be changed by introducing heteroscedastic shocks. However, from (8.55) we see that time-variation in the volatility of returns only (with constant correlations) will make expected return move, but not Sharpe ratios. Similarly, time-variation in consumption volatility leads to proportional increases of the expected return and Sharpe ratios for all assets.

3.7 The value of a firm: labour contracts and installation costs

This section discusses how non-Walrasian labour contracts and installation costs (for new capital) affect the equity value. We put aside the issue of how the total value of a firm is split between equity holders and creditors in order to focus on the value of their combined stake. The traditional way of modelling a firm is to assume that it hires labour and finances investment through retained earnings (no debt). Any extra cash flow is distributed as dividends

$$D_t = Y_t - w_t L_t - I_t \qquad (8.56)$$

where Y_t is output, w_t the real wage rate, L_t labour input, and I_t investment costs. In reality most firms seem to smooth dividends, so D_t should probably not be directly compared with dividends, but with cash flows or earnings. Typically, the number of shares is kept constant and normalised to unity.

Most simulation models have a Cobb–Douglas production function $Y = Z_t K_t^\alpha L_t^{1-\alpha}$, where Z_t is the technology level, K_t capital stock, and L_t is labour input. The first-order condition for hiring labour is that the real wage rate equals the marginal product of labour, $w_t = (1 - \alpha) Y/L_t$. This does not require a competitive labour market, only that the firm can hire freely at the going wage rate ('right to manage'). With this assumption, we can write (8.56) as

$$D_t = \alpha Y_t - I_t. \qquad (8.57)$$

As a side remark, we note that a high capital share, α, makes dividends fairly similar to consumption (the aggregate resource constraint is $Y_t = I_t + C_t$), so the consumption claim might be a good proxy for equity in that (admittedly unrealistic) case. In other cases, the dynamics of dividends and consumption can be quite different but many models still seem to generate too stable dividends (see, for instance, Rouwenhorst 1995). The basic reason is that neither aggregate output nor aggregate investments are nearly as volatile as cash flows and earnings on listed firms.

One possibility of making the cash flow process more realistic is to allow for labour hoarding (or other types of labour contract that stabilise the wage bill) and variation in the capacity utilisation rate. Labour hoarding would make the wage bill relatively constant, rather than proportional to output as above. As a consequence, the cash flow would fluctuate more in response to movements in output. For instance, Danthine and Donaldson (2002) study the implications of different types of labour contracts in a setting where the priority status of wage claims creates an operational leverage (see also p. 433 for a discussion of leverage) – and find that this can create a sizeable risk premium.

It has also been suggested that investments should be subject to installation costs. Equations (8.56) and (8.57) are still true (I_t is the investment cost, not the gross addition of capital), but the behaviour of output, investment, and consumption will change. In particular, installation costs will make consumption more volatile since it makes consumption smoothing more costly (see, for instance, Jermann 1998 and Lettau 2000). For instance, when it is prohibitively expensive to change the investment from some steady state level, then there is no consumption smoothing. Also, cash flows in (8.57) will react stronger to output than before, since investments will no longer move in the same direction as output. Both these effects tend to increase the equity premium, although it should be admitted that increased consumption volatility is something of a cheat since that is not a free parameter. (It could also be noted that installation costs leads to movements in Tobin's q, which seems to be a salient feature of the data.)

3.8 Adding assets to a model

This section discusses if we really need fully fledged equilibrium models to analyse the pricing of assets. The asset price in (8.12) is $P_t = E_t[\sum_{s=1}^{\infty} \beta^s (C_{t+s}/C_t)^{-\gamma} D_{t+s}]$, where D_{t+s} is the 'dividend' in $t + s$. On a mechanical level, we probably need some kind of model to calculate the joint distribution of C_{t+s} and D_{t+s}. For instance, to price a one-period real bond ($D_{t+1} = 1$ and $D_{t+s} = 0$ for $s > 1$) we need the model to calculate $E_t[\beta(C_{t+1}/C_t)^{-\gamma}]$.

However, if the introduction of the asset does not change the process of consumption, then there is no need for explicitly including the asset (in the budget restriction and investment opportunity set of investors) when solving the model. This is the case when we are using a model with complete markets (the stochastic discount factor is unique in this case; see the references in n. 2). In such a model, we could always analyse the pricing of any asset, for instance, some really exotic derivative, without solving the model anew.

We are in a completely different situation when we introduce non-redundant assets, that is, when we add a non-trivial asset to a model with incomplete markets. In that case we have to solve the model with all the assets explicitly incorporated since their existence is likely to affect the equilibrium consumption process. Of course, specifying an exogenous process for non-storable endowments circumvents the problem, which may explain why that approach is so popular.

Most (simulation-based) studies of imperfect markets have concentrated on idiosyncratic income risk that cannot be insured and on borrowing constraints/transaction costs. The key findings and references are given on p. 426. Other studies have developed solution methods and analysed a different set of incomplete markets. For instance, Judd and Guu (2001) show that introducing an option on the stockmarket can lower the equity premium considerably (see also Den Haan 1996 and Marcet and Singleton 1999 for solution methods and some examples).

4 SUMMARY

The first part of this chapter studied the consumption-based asset pricing model with constant relative risk aversion (CRRA) by comparing the model predictions to the moments (means, variances and correlations) of US consumption growth and returns on broad asset classes.

It is shown that the smooth consumption growth rate observed in the US makes it hard to explain the equity premium, unless the risk aversion is very high (this is the equity premium puzzle discussed in Mehra and Prescott 1985). However, a very high risk aversion seems somewhat implausible and it creates other problems. In particular, a large risk aversion coefficient makes it hard to reconcile average consumption growth with the average return on risk-free assets (this is the risk-free rate puzzle discussed in Weil 1989) and the low volatility of real interest rates (or approximations of it).

One reaction to these problems is to say that the consumption-based model may fail to explain the magnitude of the risk premium, but that it at least can be used to understand qualitative differences in average return.

For instance, the model correctly predicts higher returns on equity than on bonds. One of the main issues in the first part of the chapter is how far that argument can be extended. Data on Sharpe ratios for different portfolios sorted on industry, dividend-price ratio, size, book-to-market and geographical location show that the consumption-based model is unable to explain the cross-sectional variation of Sharpe ratios. The basic problem seems to be that there is a lot of dispersion in Sharpe ratios, but most portfolio returns are only weakly correlated with aggregate consumption growth. It is also shown that the consumption-based model fails badly in explaining time-variation of equity premia. Although the covariance of consumption and equity returns changes over time, it does so in completely the wrong way compared with excess returns.

All these problems have spurred interest in developing the consumption-based model by changing the utility function and/or introducing heterogeneous agents. Several of these suggestions (Epstein–Zin preferences, habit formation and idiosyncratic risk) are analysed at the end of the first part of the chapter. It is found that they are quite successful in solving some of the problems, but that several remain unsolved. In particular, none of the suggestions makes much headway with the cross-sectional variation of Sharpe ratios.

The second part of the chapter is a theoretical analysis of the equilibrium relation between different asset returns and the consumption process. Simple pricing expressions (based on assumptions about log-normal returns and consumption growth) highlight the basic mechanism of (otherwise) fairly complicated pricing problems. Among the results, we find the following.

First, a positive autocorrelation of consumption growth is likely to give low risk premia on long-lived consumption claims and a negatively sloped real yield curve. Second, the properties of the Fisher equation and the risk premium on nominal bonds depend crucially on monetary policy. For instance, shocks to aggregate demand typically move consumption and inflation in the same direction, so the standard recipe for monetary policy is to cushion all such shocks. However, this policy is likely to increase the inflation risk premium since it makes inflation and consumption more negatively correlated (so the real return on the nominal bond tends to be low when consumption is scarce). Third, options and levered claims will typically have higher risk premia than the underlying asset/unlevered claim because their returns are more volatile.

Simulation models have made fine contributions to the analysis of asset pricing. In particular, they have taught us a great deal about the properties of the consumption-based asset model with constant relative risk aversion (CRRA). However, it is clear that the CRRA model has serious problems on many accounts and much of the current research is trying models with different utility functions and/or different measures of consumption. We still know too little about the properties of these new models, for instance, what side effects they have. This is likely to be the next area where simulation models can make valuable contributions to the asset pricing literature.

DATA APPENDIX

The nominal *US stock returns* are from French's (2001) website. These monthly returns are converted to quarterly returns by multiplying the monthly gross returns, for instance, the gross returns for January, February and March are multiplied to generate a quarterly gross return. The portfolios are formed from NYSE, AMEX and NASDAQ firms. The aggregate stock market return is a value weighted return of all available returns. The (equally weighted) portfolios based on industry, size, dividend/price or book-to-market are from the same data set, but with the firms sorted on the respective characteristic. The ten industry portfolios are for consumer non-durables, consumer durables, oil, chemicals, manufacturing, telecoms, utilities, wholesale and retail, financial services and other. The ten size portfolios are for deciles of firm market values; the D/P portfolios are for deciles of dividend/price; and the B/M portfolios are for deciles of book value/market values.

The dividend–price ratio for S&P500 is from Shiller (2000).

The nominal return on *long US government bonds* is from Ibbotson Associates.

The *international stock and long government bond returns* are from Ibbotson Associates, but come originally from Morgan Stanley and the IMF, respectively. The international data is for France, Germany, Japan and the UK, and has been converted into US dollar returns.

Real returns are calculated by dividing the nominal gross return by the gross inflation rate over the same period. Inflation is calculated from the seasonally adjusted CPI for all urban consumers (available at http://www.stls.frb.org/fred/).

Quarterly growth of *real consumption* per capita of non-durables and services is calculated from the seasonally adjusted number in NIPA Table 8.7 (available at http://www.bea. doc.gov/bea/dn1.htm). The growth rate is calculated as a weighted average of the growth rate of non-durables and the growth rate of services (chained 1996 dollars), where the (time-varying) weight is the relative (current dollar) size of non-durables in relation to services.

The annualised k-quarter excess returns used in the discussion of stock returns predictability are calculated as $R_t^e(k) = (R_t R_{t-1} \cdots R_{t-k+1})^{4/k} - (R_{ft} R_{ft-1} \cdots R_{ft-k+1})^{4/k}$, where R_t is the quarterly gross return of the aggregate US stock market (see above) and R_{ft} is the quarterly gross return on a short T-bill.

ECONOMETRICS APPENDIX

The tests in table 8.1 are based on t-tests from a GMM estimation and the delta method.

Testing of the mean, standard deviation, and Sharpe ratio is done in the following way. First, moment conditions for the mean (μ) and second moment (χ) of the random variable x_t are defined as

$$\sum_{t=1}^{T} m_t(\beta)/T = \mathbf{0}_{2\times 1} \quad \text{where } m_t = \begin{bmatrix} x_t - \mu \\ x_t^2 - \chi \end{bmatrix} \text{ and } \beta = \begin{bmatrix} \mu \\ \chi \end{bmatrix}.$$

GMM estimation is trivial and the estimator is asymptotically normally distributed around the true value β_0 as

$$\sqrt{T}(\hat{\beta} - \beta_0) \xrightarrow{d} N(\mathbf{0}_{2\times 1}, S_0)$$

where S_0 is the variance-covariance matrix of $\Sigma_{t=1}^{T} m_t(\beta_0)/\sqrt{T}$, which can be consistently estimated by using the point estimate of β instead of β_0 and then applying the Newey and West (1987) estimator. Second, the standard deviation and Sharpe ratio are calculated as functions of β

$$\begin{bmatrix} \sigma(x) \\ E(x)/\sigma(x) \end{bmatrix} = g(\beta) = \begin{bmatrix} (\chi - \mu^2)^{1/2} \\ \dfrac{\mu}{(\chi - \mu^2)^{1/2}} \end{bmatrix},$$

$$\text{so } \frac{\partial g(\chi, \mu)}{\partial \beta'} = \begin{bmatrix} \dfrac{-\mu}{(\chi - \mu^2)^{1/2}} & \dfrac{1}{2(\chi - \mu^2)^{1/2}} \\ \dfrac{\chi}{(\chi - \mu^2)^{3/2}} & \dfrac{-\mu}{2(\chi - \mu^2)^{3/2}} \end{bmatrix}.$$

From the delta method we then have

$$\sqrt{T}[g(\hat{\beta}) - g(\beta_0)] \xrightarrow{d} N\left(0, \frac{\partial g(\beta_0)}{\partial \beta'} S_0 \frac{\partial g(\beta_0)'}{\partial \beta}\right),$$

which is used to construct asymptotic t-tests.

A similar approach is used for *testing the correlation* of x_t and y_t, $\rho(x_t, y_t)$. For expositional simplicity, assume that both variables have zero means. The variances and the covariance can then be estimated by the moment conditions

$$\sum_{t=1}^{T} m_t(\beta)/T = \mathbf{0}_{3\times 1} \quad \text{where } m_t = \begin{bmatrix} x_t^2 - \sigma_{xx} \\ y_t^2 - \sigma_{yy} \\ x_t y_t - \sigma_{xy} \end{bmatrix} \text{ and } \beta = \begin{bmatrix} \sigma_{xx} \\ \sigma_{yy} \\ \sigma_{xy} \end{bmatrix}.$$

The covariance matrix of these estimators is estimated as before. The correlation is a simple function of these parameters

$$\rho(x, y) = g(\beta) = \frac{\sigma_{xy}}{\sigma_{xx}^{1/2}\sigma_{yy}^{1/2}},$$

$$\text{so } \frac{\partial g(\chi, \mu)}{\partial \beta'} = \begin{bmatrix} -\dfrac{1}{2}\dfrac{\sigma_{xy}}{\sigma_{xx}^{3/2}\sigma_{yy}^{1/2}} & -\dfrac{1}{2}\dfrac{\sigma_{xy}}{\sigma_{xx}^{1/2}\sigma_{yy}^{3/2}} & \dfrac{1}{\sigma_{xx}^{1/2}\sigma_{yy}^{1/2}} \end{bmatrix}.$$

The delta method formula (see above) is then applied to this case as well.

BIBLIOGRAPHY

Abel, A. B. (1999). 'Risk Premia and Term Premia in General Equilibrium', *Journal of Monetary Economics*, 43, 3–33

Altug, S. and Labadie, P. (1994). *Dynamic Choice and Asset Markets*, San Diego, London and Toronto: Academic Press

Backus, D., Foresi, S. and Zin, S. (1998). 'Arbitrage Opportunities in Arbitrage-Free Models of Bond Pricing', *Journal of Business and Economic Statistics*, 16, 13–26

Backus, D., Gregory, A. and Zin, S. (1989). 'Risk Premiums in the Term Structure: Evidence from Artificial Economies', *Journal of Monetary Economics*, 24, 371–99

Bansal, R. and Lundblad, C. (2000). 'Fundamental Values and Asset Returns in Global Equity Markets', manuscript, http://www.business.wm.edu/conference/Lundblad1.pdf

Bidarkota, P. V. and McCulloch, J. H. (2000). 'Consumption Asset Pricing with Stable Shocks – Exploring a Solution and Its Implications for the Equity Premium Puzzle', Kansas State University, mimeo

Black, F. and Scholes, M. (1973). 'The Pricing of Options and Corporate Liabilities', *Journal of Political Economy*, 81, 637–59

Bossaert, P. (2002). *The Paradox of Asset Pricing*, Princeton: Princeton University Press

Breeden, D. T. (1979). 'An Intertemporal Asset Pricing Model with Stochastic Consumption and Investment Opportunities', *Journal of Financial Economics*, 7, 265–96

Campbell, J. Y. (1986). 'Bond and Stock Returns in a Simple Exchange Model', *Quarterly Journal of Economics*, 101, 785–804

(1993). 'Intertemporal Asset Pricing without Consumption Data', *American Economic Review*, 83, 487–512

(2001). 'Consumption-Based Asset Pricing', in G. Constantinides, M. Harris and R. Stultz (eds.), *Handbook of the Economics of Finance*, Amsterdam: North-Holland

Campbell, J. Y. and Cochrane, J. H. (1999). 'By Force of Habit: A Consumption-Based Explanation of Aggregate Stock Market Behaviour', *Journal of Political Economy*, 107, 205–51

Campbell, J. Y., Lo, A. W. and MacKinlay, A. C. (1997). *The Econometrics of Financial Markets*, Princeton: Princeton University Press

Campbell, J. Y. and Viceira, L. M. (2002). *Strategic Asset Allocation: Portfolio Choice of Long-Term Investors*, Oxford: Oxford University Press

Clarida, R., Galí, J. and Gertler, M. (1999). 'The Science of Monetary Policy: A New Keynesian Perspective', *Journal of Economic Literature*, 37, 1661–1707

Cochrane, J. H. (2001). *Asset Pricing*, Princeton: Princeton University Press

Cochrane, J. H. and Piazzesi, M. (2002a). 'Bond Risk Premia', University of Chicago, mimeo

(2002b). 'The Fed and Interest Rates – a High-Frequency Identification', *AER Papers and Proceedings*, 92, 90–5

Cogley, T. (1998). 'Idiosyncratic Risk and Equity Premium: Evidence from the Consumer Expenditure Survey', Federal Reserve Bank of San Francisco, mimeo

Cogley, T. and Nason, J. M. (1993). 'Impulse Dynamics and Propagation Mechanisms in Real Busines Cycle Model', *Economics Letters*, 43, 77–81

Constantinides, G. M. and Duffie, D. (1996). 'Asset Pricing with Heterogeneous Consumers', *The Journal of Political Economy*, 104, 219–40

Cooley, T. F. and Hansen, G. D. (1989). 'The Inflation Tax in a Real Business Cycle Model', *American Economic Review*, 79, 733–48

(1995). 'Money and the Business Cycle', in T. F. Cooley (ed.), *Frontiers of Business Cycle Research*, Princeton: Princeton University Press

Cox, J. C., Ingersoll, J. E. and Ross, S. A. (1985). 'A Theory of the Term Structure of Interest Rates', *Econometrica*, 53, 385–407

Danthine, J.-P. and Donaldson, J. B. (2002). 'Labour Relations and Asset Returns', *Review of Economic Studies*, 69, 41–64

Den Haan W. J. (1996). 'Heterogeneity, Aggregate Uncertainty, and the Short-Term Interest Rate', *Journal of Business and Economic Statistics*, 14, 399–411

(2001). 'The Importance of the Number of Different Agents in a Heterogenous Asset-Pricing Model', *Journal of Economic Dynamics and Control*, 25, 721–46

Epstein, L. G. and Zin, S. E. (1989a). 'Substitution, Risk Aversion, and the Temporal Behaviour of Asset Returns: A Theoretical Framework', *Econometrica*, 57, 937–69

(1989b). 'Substitution, Risk Aversion, and the Temporal Behaviour of Asset Returns: An Empirical Analysis', *Journal of Political Economy*, 99, 263–86

Fama, E. F. and French, K. R. (1988a). 'Dividend Yields and Expected Stock Returns', *Journal of Financial Economics*, 22, 3–25

(1988b). 'Permanent and Temporary Components of Stock Prices', *Journal of Political Economy*, 96, 246–73

(1993). 'Common Risk Factors in the Returns on Stocks and Bonds', *Journal of Financial Economics*, 33, 3–56

Ferson, W. E. (1995). 'Theory and Empirical Testing of Asset Pricing Models', in R. A. Jarrow, V. Maksimovic and W. T. Ziemba (eds.), *Handbooks in Operations Research and Management Science* Amsterdam: North-Holland

French, K. R. (2001). 'US Research Returns Data', http://mba.tuck.dartmouth.edu/pages/faculty/ken.french/

Giovannini, A. and Labadie, P. (1991). 'Asset Prices and Interest Rates in Cash-in-Advance Models', *Journal of Political Economy*, 99, 1215–51

Hansen, L. P. and Jagannathan, R. (1991). 'Implications of Security Market Data for Models of Dynamic Economies', *Journal of Political Economy*, 99, 225–62

Hansen, L. P. and Richard, S. F. (1987). 'The Role of Conditioning Information in Deducing Testable Restrictions Implied by Dynamic Asset Pricing Models', *Econometrica*, 55, 587–613

Harrison, M. J. and Kreps D. M. (1979). 'Martingales and Arbitrage in Multiperiod Securities Markets', *Journal of Economic Theory*, 20, 381–408

He, H. and Modest, D. M. (1995). 'Market Frictions and Consumption-Based Asset Pricing', *Journal of Political Economy*, 103, 94–117

Heaton, J. C. and Lucas, D. J. (1996). 'Evaluating the Effects of Incomplete Markets on Risk-Sharing and Asset Pricing', *Journal of Political Economy*, 104, 443–87

Hendershott, P. H. (1998). 'Equilibrium Models in Real Estate Research: A Survey', *Journal of Real Estate Literature*, 6, 13–25

Huang, C.-F. and Litzenberger, R. H. (1988). *Foundations for Financial Economics*, New York: Elsevier Science

Jermann, U. J. (1998). 'Asset Pricing in Production Economies', *Journal of Monetary Economics*, 41, 257–75

Johnson, N. L., Kotz, S. and Balakrishnan, N. (1994). *Continuous Univariate Distributions*, 2nd edn., New York: Wiley

Judd, K. L. and Guu, S.-M. (2001). 'Asymptotic Methods for Asset Market Equilibrium Analysis', *Economic Theory*, 18, 127–57

Kollman, R. (2001). 'The Exchange Rate in a Dynamic-Optimizing Business Cycle Model with Nominal Rigidities: A Quantitative Investigation', *Journal of International Economics*, 55, 243–62

Labadie, P. (1989). 'Stochastic Inflation and the Equity Premium', *Journal of Monetary Economics*, 24, 277–98

LeRoy, S. F. and Werner, J. (2001). *Principles of Financial Economics*, Cambridge: Cambridge University Press

Lettau, M. (2000). 'Inspecting the Mechanism: Closed-Form Solutions for Asset Prices in Real Business Cycle Models', Federal Reserve Bank of New York, mimeo

(2002). 'Idiosyncratic Risk and Volatility Bounds, or Can Models with Id-iosyncratic Risk Solve the Equity Premium Puzzle', *Review of Economics and Statistics*, 84, 376–380

Lettau, M. and Uhlig, H. (2000). 'Can Habit Formation Be Reconciled with Business Cycle Facts', *Review of Economic Dynamics*, 3, 79–99

(2002). 'Sharpe Ratios and Preferences: An Analytical Approach', *Macroeconomic Dynamics*, 6(2), 242–65.

Lintner, J. (1965). 'The Valuation of Risky Assets and the Selection of Risky Investments in Stock Portfolios and Capital Budgets', *Review of Economics and Statistics*, 47, 13–37

Ljunqvist, L. and Uhlig, H. (2000). 'Tax Policy and Aggregate Demand Management Under Catching Up with the Joneses', *American Economic Review*, 90, 356–66

Lucas, R. E. (1978). 'Asset Prices in an Exchange Economy', *Econometrica*, 46, 1426–14

Luttmer, E. G. J. (1996). 'Asset pricing in Economies with Frictions', *Econometrica*, 64, 1439–67

Mankiw, G. N. (1986). 'The Equity Premium and the Concentration of Aggregate Shocks', *Journal of Financial Economics*, 17, 211–19

Marcet, A. and Singleton, K. J. (1999). 'Equilibrium Asset Prices and Savings of Heterogeneous Agents in the Presence of Incomplete Markets and Portfolio Constraints', *Macroeconomic Dynamics*, 3, 243–77

Mehra, R. and Prescott, E. (1985). 'The Equity Premium: A Puzzle', *Journal of Monetary Economics*, 15, 145–61

Merton, R. C. (1973). 'Rational Theory of Option Pricing', *Bell Journal of Economics and Management Science*, 4, 141–83

Mossin, J. (1968). 'Equilibrium in a Capital Asset Market', *Econometrica*, 35, 768–83

Newey, W. K. and West, K. D. (1987). 'A Simple Positive Semi-Definite, Heteroskedasticity and Autocorrelation Consistent Covariance Matrix', *Econometrica*, 55, 703–8

Reffett, K. and Schorfheide, F. (2000). 'Evaluating Asset Pricing Implications of DSGE Models', Arizona State University, mimeo

Ross, S. A. (1978). 'A Simple Approach to the Valuation of Risky Streams', *Journal of Business*, 51, 453–75

Rouwenhorst, K. (1995). 'Asset Pricing Implications of Equilibrium Business Cycle Models', in T. F. Cooley (ed.), *Frontiers of Business Cycle Research*, Princeton: Princeton University Press

Rudebusch, G. D. (1998). 'Do Measures of Monetary Policy in a VAR Make Sense?', *International Economic Review*, 39, 907–31

Salyer, K. D. (1998). 'Crash States and the Equity Premium: Solving One Puzzle Raises Another', *Journal of Economic Dynamics and Control*, 22, 955–65

Sharpe, W. F. (1964). 'Capital Asset Prices: A Theory of Market Equilibrium under Conditions of Risk', *Journal of Finance*, 19, 425–42

Shiller, R. J. (2000). *Irrational Exuberance*, Princeton: Princeton University Press, data available at http://www.econ.yale.edu/ shiller/data.htm

Smith, P. N. and Wickens, M. R. (2002). 'Asset Pricing with Observable Stochastic Discount Factors', *Discussion Paper*, 2002/03, University of York

Söderlind, P. (1999). 'Solution and Estimation of RE Macromodels with Optimal Policy', *European Economic Review*, 43, 813–23

   (2001). 'Monetary Policy and the Fisher Effect', *Journal of Policy Modelling*, 23, 491–5

   (2003). 'Monetary Policy and Bond Option Pricing in an Analytical RBC Model', *Journal of Business and Economics*, 55, 321–30

Söderlind, P. and Svensson, L. E. O. (1997). 'New Techniques to Extract Market Expectations from Financial Instruments', *Journal of Monetary Economics*, 40, 383–420

Svensson, L. E. O. (1989). 'Portfolio Choice with Non-Expected Utility in Continuous Time', *Economics Letters*, 40, 313–17

Telmer, C. I. (1993). 'Asset Pricing Puzzles and Incomplete Markets', *Journal of Finance*, 48, 1803–32

Vasicek, O. A. (1977). 'An Equilibrium Characterisation of the Term Structure', *Journal of Financial Economics*, 5, 177–88

Vayanos, D. (1998). 'Transaction Costs and Asset Prices: A Dynamic Equilibrium Model', *Review of Financial Studies*, 11, 1–58

Weil, P. (1989). 'The Equity Premium Puzzle and the Risk-Free Rate Puzzle', *Journal of Monetary Economics*, 24, 401–21

Zimmermann, C. (1999). 'International Business Cycles and Exchange Rates', *Review of International Economics*, 74, 682–98

9

Labour market search and monetary shocks

Carl E. Walsh

1 INTRODUCTION

In recent years, dynamic stochastic general equilibrium (DSGE) models of monetary economies have focused on the role of nominal rigidities in affecting the economy's adjustment to monetary policy and non-policy disturbances. While these rigidities appear important for understanding the impact nominal shocks have on such real variables as output and employment, models with only nominal rigidities have been unable to match the responses to monetary disturbances that have been estimated in the data. Typically, empirical studies have concluded that monetary shocks generate large and persistent real responses that display a hump shape. After a positive money shock, for example, output rises over several quarters and then declines. Christiano, Eichenbaum and Evans (1999) document this effect and provide an extensive discussion of the empirical evidence on the effects of monetary shocks. Sims (1992) finds large, hump-shaped responses of real output to monetary shocks in several OECD countries. Inflation also displays a hump-shaped response, although inflation is usually found to respond more slowly than output to monetary shocks.

The 'stylised facts' emphasised by Christiano, Eichenbaum and Evans, by Sims, and by others are illustrated in figure 9.1, which shows estimated impulse responses of output and inflation following a shock to the growth rate of money. These responses were obtained from a three-variable VAR (output, inflation, and money growth) estimated using US quarterly data for 1965–2001. Output is real GDP, inflation is measured by the Consumer Price Index, and M2 is the aggregate used to measure money. The real persistence and inflation inertia seen in figure 9.1 has been hard for

I would like to thank Ryota Kojima for research assistance, and the referees, seminar participants at UC Davis and UCSB and participants in the Brown Bag workshop at UCSC for helpful comments on this research.

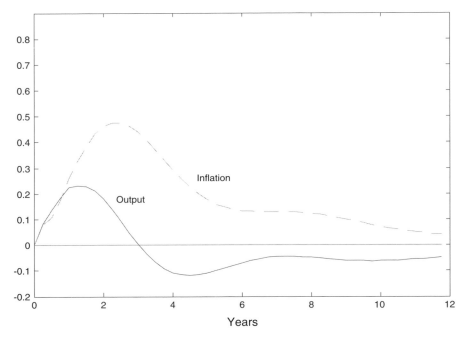

Figure 9.1 Impulse responses to a money growth rate shock (estimated VAR)

models based on nominal rigidities to match.[1] As Dotsey and King (2001) have expressed it, 'modern optimizing sticky price models have displayed a chronic inability to generate large and persistent real responses to monetary shock'.

In order to capture at least some of the real persistence seen in empirical studies, models based on nominal rigidity generally must assume a high degree of price stickiness. For example, it is common to assume that individual prices remain fixed on average for as much as nine months. Micro data on individual prices, however, suggests that prices typically change more frequently than this. Consequently, a number of researchers have recently argued that simply adding nominal rigidities to an otherwise standard DSGE model is not sufficient to match the persistence observed in the data. Instead, the real side of the economy must also be modified to capture additional factors affecting both aggregate production and aggregate spending decisions. Christiano, Eichenbaum and Evans (2001), in particular, have argued that models with nominal rigidities are capable of

[1] Chari, Kehoe and McGratten (2000) find little persistence in their model of staggered price adjustment, and Nelson (1998) demonstrates that several optimising models of price stickiness are unable to match the time series properties of inflation.

matching macro evidence but only if the real side of the model is properly specified.

Despite the recent interest on the real side of monetary models, almost all existing DSGE models of monetary economies continue to assume that labour can be costlessly and instantaneously reallocated across firms. Yet the complex process through which workers seeking jobs and firms with open vacancies are matched is likely to be important in influencing the way economic disturbances are propagated over time. The work of Mortensen and Pissarides (1994, 1999) and Pissarides (2000) has emphasised the costly and time-consuming process of matching workers seeking employment with firms seeking to fill job vacancies. How quickly unemployment returns to its steady-state level after an adverse shock, whether it is a real or nominal shock, is likely to be influenced by how efficiently the labour market is able to generate new matches between firms and unemployed workers.

In this chapter, the dynamic implications of labour market search and sticky prices are analysed. The model that is developed is the first to combine a labour market structure based on a Mortensen–Pissarides aggregate matching function with an optimising model of price rigidity. The introduction of price stickiness allows the interactions between labour market rigidities and nominal price rigidities to be investigated.

Section 2 reviews some of the related literature that has focused on the labour market and other real aspects of the economy that affect the economy's response to nominal shocks. Section 3 develops the basic model. In section 4, the dynamic adjustment of the economy to nominal money growth rate shocks is examined under flexible prices and under sticky prices. Conclusions and some suggestions for further research are discussed in section 5.

2 RELATED LITERATURE

This chapter brings together two previously unrelated strands of the literature – models such as those of Andolfatto (1996), Cooley and Quadrini (1999, 2000) and Merz (1995) that study the implications of matching models of the labour market for DSGE models of the business cycle, and models such as those of Chari, Kehoe and McGratten (2000), Goodfriend and King (1997), Rotemberg and Woodford (1997) and Yun (1996), among others, that introduce price stickiness in DSGE models of monopolistic competition. Cole and Rogerson (1999) argue that aggregate labour market matching models based on the work of Mortensen and Pissarides (1994, 1999) can replicate important aspects of business cycles, but only if the models are calibrated to imply average durations of unemployment spells that are much longer than data on actual duration suggest. Similarly, models of price stickiness are typically calibrated to imply individual prices are fixed for durations that are also much longer than suggested by evidence on individual prices (Bils and Klenow 2002). By incorporating both a labour market matching model and price stickiness within a single model, one can investigate whether the interactions of these two allow the model to match important business cycle facts with more plausible calibrations of unemployment duration and price rigidity. In fact, it has been the failure of models based solely on nominal price stickiness to account for output persistence and inertia in inflation that has led some researchers to explore the role of real factors that might interact with nominal rigidities to account for the dynamic responses seen in the data.

In an early contribution, Ball and Romer (1990) argued that real rigidities act to amplify the effects of nominal rigidities. More recently, Dotsey and King (2001) argue that 'real flexibilities' – variable capital utilisation and produced inputs – are critical for generating the persistence displayed in the data. These real flexibilities permit output to vary with relatively small effects on marginal cost, reducing the elasticity of marginal costs with respect to output. A nominal shock to aggregate demand and output has only a small impact on marginal cost, and therefore on inflation, when this elasticity is small.[2]

Similarly, Christiano, Eichenbaum and Evans (2001) (hereafter, CEE) emphasise that the interaction of real and nominal rigidities seems to be critical in matching empirical evidence. CEE allow for habit persistence in consumption, variable capital utilisation and investment adjustment costs (real rigidities) as well as both price and nominal wage stickiness. They conclude that nominal wage rigidity (as opposed to price rigidity) is critical in matching aggregate data for the USA. However, King and Goodfriend (2001: 4) take the position that nominal wage rigidity may not be important for business cycle phenomena, arguing that 'The labour market is characterised by long-term relationships where there is opportunity and reason for firms and workers to neutralise the allocative effects of temporarily sticky nominal wages'.[3]

The real rigidities introduced by long-term relationships between firms and workers has, to date, not been incorporated into models with nominal rigidities. This neglect is perhaps surprising. Jeanne (1998) combined a

---

[2] See Burnside and Eichenbaum (1996) for an earlier analysis of variable capital utilisation in a RBC model.
[3] The issue of nominal price versus nominal wage rigidity is analysed in detail in chapter 4 by Canzoneri, Cumby and Diba in this volume.

Calvo-type model of price stickiness with an ad hoc specification of the equilibrium real wage. This allowed him to exogenously vary the response of the real wage to output movements. He showed that an increase in labour market real wage rigidity reduced the degree of price stickiness that was needed to match the response of output to a monetary shock. This work suggested that the specification of the labour market might play an important role in explaining the persistent output response to nominal shocks, but his model provided no underlying theory to explain the source of the labour market rigidity.

Andolfatto (1996) and Merz (1995) have shown that a RBC model that incorporates a Mortensen–Pissarides aggregate matching function (Mortensen and Pissarides 1994, 1999; Pissarides 2000) to represent the search process in the labour market is able to provide a better match with evidence on employment and wages than do models based on a traditional Walrasian labour market. Cole and Rogerson (1999) note, however, that one must assume that workers face a small probability each period of finding a match if aggregate matching models are to capture important labour market behaviour. Den Haan, Ramey and Watson (2000) show how a search model of the labour market can serve to amplify and propagate productivity shocks. These models capture the long-term nature of employment relationships that King and Goodfriend emphasise alter the allocative implications of observed rigidity in nominal wages.

The only examples to date of monetary models with a matching model of the labour force are due to Cooley and Quadrini (1999, 2000). They introduced money into a DSGE model with a matching model of the labour market and show that monetary shocks have highly persistent impacts on inflation and the real economy. However, they assume that prices are completely flexible, and persistent real effects arise, in part, because they assume that nominal portfolios adjust slowly over time. This portfolio rigidity generates a liquidity effect (a fall in the nominal interest rate after an increase in money growth).[4] By assuming portfolio readjustments take several periods to occur, the real impact of money shocks is propagated over time in the Cooley–Quadrini model. Thus, their dynamics reflect both the specification of the labour market and the assumption of sticky portfolio adjustment.

While the work by Cooley and Quadrini has helped to highlight the role of the matching process in a monetary economy, their assumption of flexible prices meant that they were unable to study the possible interactions

---

[4] This form of limited participation model (Fuerst 1992) assumes that households cannot immediately reallocate their bond and money holdings after a monetary shock.

between the dynamic adjustment of employment through the matching process and the dynamic adjustment of inflation when prices are sticky.

3 THE MODEL ECONOMY

To study the interaction of labour search and price stickiness, I employ a model that distinguishes between wholesale and retail sectors. Goods are produced in the wholesale sector and then sold by retail firms to households. The production of wholesale goods requires that a firm and a worker be matched. Unmatched workers and firms with vacancies are matched through a process characterised by an aggregate matching function. Because some workers and firms will be matched, while others will not be, distributional issues arise. To avoid these issues, I follow Andolfatto (1996), den Haan, Ramey, and Watson (2000) and Merz (1995) in assuming that households pool consumption, both market-purchased consumption and home consumption produced by workers who do not have an employment match in period t. The output produced by worker–firm matches is sold in a competitive goods market to retail firms. These firms costlessly transform the wholesale good into retail goods that are sold to households in markets characterised by monopolistic competition. Prices at the retail level are sticky, with only a fraction of retail firms optimally adjusting their price each period. This separation between wholesale firms participating in the labour market matching process and retail firms with sticky prices follows the approach of Bernanke, Gertler and Gilchrist (1999) in their study of credit market imperfections. This separation simplifies the structure of the model.

Money is introduced through a cash-in-advance constraint.[5] Income generated in period t is not available for consumption until period $t + 1$, so the nominal interest rate affects the present discounted value of current production. This generates a channel through which nominal interest rate changes affect output and employment. An increase in the nominal interest rate reduces the present value of production and leads to an increase in job destruction, a fall in employment and a decline in output in the wholesale sector.

The role played by the labour market specification can be highlighted by considering the effects of an unanticipated increase in money growth in period t that persists for periods t and $t + 1$, after which money growth returns to its steady-state value. When prices are flexible, inflation rises immediately and remains above its steady-state value during periods t and

---

[5] For a general discussion of cash-in-advance models, see Walsh (2003, chapter 3).

$t + 1$. In period t, expected inflation also rises, causing the nominal rate of interest to rise. In period $t + 1$, the nominal rate returns to its steady-state value. In a model with an inelastic labour supply and no capital but with a standard Walrasian labour market, this money growth shock has no impact on employment or output. If labour supply is elastic, however, the rise in the nominal interest rate causes a substitution towards leisure (a 'cash' good), and employment and output fall, but only for one period.[6] In contrast, in the present model, the rise in the nominal interest rate leads to a rise in job destruction; employment and output fall. The economy enters period $t + 1$ with fewer employment matches. This propagates the output and employment decline into period $t + 1$. The matching process causes the return to the steady state to be spread over several periods. Thus, the labour market dynamics contribute to the persistence displayed by the economy in response to a money growth rate shock.

The adverse output effects of a rise in the nominal interest rate also have implications for inflation. The decline in wholesale output raises wholesale prices relative to retail prices. The fall in the retail price markup acts to raise retail price inflation. A positive impact on inflation of an increase in the nominal interest rate is variously called the 'cost channel of monetary policy' or the 'Wright Patman' effect, after the late, populist Texas Congressman. Barth and Ramey (2001) have used industry-level data to examine this cost channel. They argue that the cost channel can account for the price puzzle – the finding in empirical VARs that inflation initially rises after an interest rate increase. Christiano, Eichenbaum and Evans (2001) also incorporate a cost channel into their model, but they do not provide information on its contribution to matching the dynamic responses of output and inflation to a monetary shock.

In the remainder of this section, the details of the model are developed.

3.1 Households

The representative household consists of a worker and a shopper. Each of these actors engages in different activities during the period before reuniting at the end of each period (Lucas and Stokey 1983, 1987). There are assumed to be a continuum of such households on the interval $[0, 1]$. Shoppers carry cash balances to the goods market to purchase market consumption goods; these purchases are subject to a cash-in-advance constraint. For simplicity, households are assumed to supply their unit of labour inelasticity.

---

[6] The effect can be spread over several periods if capital is introduced into the model. See, for example, Walsh (2003, chapter 3).

Households are also the owners of all firms in the economy. Households maximise the expected present discounted value of utility:

$$E_t \sum_{i=0}^{\infty} \beta^i \left[u(C_{t+i}) + (1 - \chi_t)h - \chi_t A \right] \tag{9.1}$$

where C_t is a composite consumption good consisting of the differentiated products produced by monopolistically competitive retail firms. There are a continuum of such firms of measure 1. C_t is defined as

$$C_t = \left[\int_0^1 c_{jt}^{\frac{\theta-1}{\theta}} dj \right]^{\frac{\theta}{\theta-1}} \qquad \theta > 1. \tag{9.2}$$

The variable χ_t is an indicator variable, equal to 1 if the household's worker is employed and 0 otherwise. The disutility of work is A, and h is the utility of home production when unemployed.

Households maximise expected utility subject to two constraints. First, they face a cash-in-advance constraint that takes the form

$$P_t C_t \leq M_{t-1}^h + T_t - B_t \tag{9.3}$$

where M_t^h (B_t) is the household's nominal holdings of money (one-period nominal bonds), P_t is the retail price index and T_t is a lump-sum transfer received from the government. In the aggregate, this transfer is equal to $M_t - M_{t-1} = (G_t - 1)M_{t-1}$ where M (without the superscript h) is the aggregate nominal money stock. Note that current income is unavailable for purchasing current market consumption. This timing assumes that financial asset markets open before the goods market. Bonds purchased at the start of period t, B_t, pay a gross nominal interest rate of R_t. These interest payments are received when the asset market reopens in period $t + 1$. Thus, the budget constraint households face can be written as

$$M_t^h = P_t Y_t^l + D_t + R_t B_t + M_{t-1}^h + T_t - B_t - P_t C_t, \tag{9.4}$$

where Y_t^l is the household's real labour income and D_t is their share of aggregate profits from wholesale and retail firms.

Given prices p_{jt} for the final goods, this preference specification implies that the household's demand for good j is

$$c_{jt} = \left(\frac{p_{jt}}{P_t} \right)^{-\theta} C_t, \tag{9.5}$$

where the aggregate retail price index P_t is defined as

$$P_t = \left[\int_0^1 p_{jt}^{1-\theta} dj \right]^{\frac{1}{1-\theta}}. \tag{9.6}$$

The following two conditions, obtained from the household's first-order conditions and the cash-in-advance constraint, must hold in equilibrium:

$$\frac{u'_t}{P_t} = \beta R_t E_t \left(\frac{u'_{t+1}}{P_{t+1}} \right) \tag{9.7}$$

$$C_t = \frac{M_t}{P_t}, \tag{9.8}$$

where u' denotes the marginal utility of consumption. It will be convenient to define the one-period discount factor

$$\delta_t \equiv \beta E_t \left(\frac{P_t}{P_{t+1}} \frac{u'_{t+1}}{u'_t} \right), \tag{9.9}$$

so that (9.7) can be written as $\delta_t R_t = 1$.

3.2 The labour and goods markets

The production side of the model, and the labour market specification, is similar to that used by den Haan, Ramey and Watson (2000). Their focus is on the role of aggregate productivity shocks, and because their model does not incorporate money, they do not study the role of price stickiness. In order to simplify the non-monetary aspects of the model, I ignore the capital stock dynamics that den Haan, Ramey and Watson include. Production takes place in the wholesale sector, where firms and workers are paired through a matching process.

The wholesale sector
At the beginning of the period, there are N_t matched workers and firms; $U_t = 1 - N_t$ workers are unmatched. If a worker is part of an existing match at the start of period t, she travels to her place of employment. At that point, there is an exogenous probability $0 \leq \rho^x < 1$ that the match is terminated. For the $(1 - \rho^x)N_t$ surviving matches, the worker and firm jointly observe the current realisation of productivity and decide whether to continue the match. If the realisation of productivity is low enough, it will be unprofitable for the match to continue. If the match does continue,

production occurs. The output of a matched worker/firm pair i in period t that does produce is

$$y_{it} = a_{it} z_t \qquad (9.10)$$

where a_{it} is a serially uncorrelated, match-specific productivity disturbance and z_t is a common, aggregate productivity disturbance. The means of both productivity disturbances are equal to 1, and both are bounded below by zero. Wholesale firms sell their output in a competitive market at the price P_t^w.

Firms seeking workers must incur a cost of posting a vacancy, and workers seeking jobs must engage in a search process that takes time. As a consequence, existing matches may earn an economic surplus, and both the firm and the worker will wish to maintain a match with a positive expected surplus. The expected surplus an existing match generates depends, in part, on the value of the current output the match produces. Because of the cash-in-advance constraint, proceeds from output produced in period t are available for consumption only in period $t + 1$. Thus, the time-t value of the revenues obtained from production in period t is $\delta_t P_t^w a_{it} z_t / P_t$, where δ_t is the discount rate given by (9.9). In addition, there is a continuation value of being part of an existing match that survives into period $t + 1$. Therefore, the expected value of a match that produces in period t is

$$\delta_t \left(\frac{a_{it} z_t}{\mu_t} \right) - A + g_{it},$$

where $\mu_t = P_t / P_t^w$ is the markup of retail over wholesale prices, and g_{it} is the expected present value of a match that continues into period $t + 1$.

To simplify, assume that the share of the surplus from a match received by each participant is fixed.[7] The surplus is the difference between $(\delta_t a_{it} z_t / \mu_t) - A + g_{it}$ and the alternative opportunities available to the firm and the worker. If the firm has no alternative opportunities, the match's opportunity cost, w_t^u, is equal to the value of home consumption an unmatched worker can produce plus the present value of future worker opportunities if unmatched in period t. Define

$$q_t \equiv g_t - w_t^u$$

as the expected excess value of a match that continues into period $t + 1$. Since all matches are identical, the subscript i has been suppressed. A match continues as long as $(\delta_t a_{it} z_t / \mu_t) - A + q_t \geq 0$. Matches endogenously

---

[7] The assumption of fixed shares is common and would arise under risk neutrality in a Nash bargaining solution.

separate if the match-specific productivity shock is less than $\bar{a}_t$, where this critical value is defined using the definition of δ_t in (9.9) as

$$\bar{a}_t = \frac{\mu_t R_t (A - q_t)}{z_t}. \qquad (9.11)$$

If $A - q_t < 0$, then matches would never endogenously end since the support of a is strictly positive. When $A - q_t > 0$, matches do endogenously break up. In this case, a higher realisation of the aggregate productivity shock z_t will, *ceteris paribus*, lower $\bar{a}_t$, making it more likely that existing matches produce. A higher z_t realisation directly increases the production of all matched worker/firms (see (9.10)). It also leads more matches to produce because fewer endogenously separate (see (9.11)). Thus, the role of z_t in affecting $\bar{a}_t$ tends to amplify the impact of the aggregate productivity shock on output, an effect emphasised by den Haan, Ramey and Watson (2000). A decrease in the nominal interest rate also leads more matches to produce. Because income earned in period t is available for the household to consume only in period $t + 1$, a rise in the value of future income (as would be caused by a fall in R_t) makes current production more valuable and decreases the probability that a match will be dissolved.[8] A rise in the markup of retail over wholesale prices reduces the profitability of wholesale production and increases $\bar{a}_t$. These results are only partial equilibrium effects, since changes in aggregate productivity or the nominal interest rate also affect w_t^u, the present discounted value of unemployment, and g_t, the present discounted value of a match.

Let ρ_t^n be the aggregate fraction of matches that endogenously separate, and let F denote the cumulative distribution function of the match specific productivity shock. Then the probability match i endogenously separates is $F(\bar{a}_t)$ and, because all matches are identical, the aggregate endogenous separation rate is the probability that $a_t \leq \bar{a}_t$:

$$\rho_t^n = \Pr[a_t \leq \bar{a}_t] = F(\bar{a}_t). \qquad (9.12)$$

The aggregate total separation rate ρ_t is equal to

$$\rho_t = \rho^x + (1 - \rho^x)\rho_t^n \qquad (9.13)$$

while the survival rate, $\varphi_t \equiv (1 - \rho_t) = (1 - \rho^x)[1 - F(\bar{a}_t)]$, is decreasing in $\bar{a}$.

---

[8] The non-neutrality that this creates is similar to other cash-in-advance models that, for example, require firms to pay wages prior to the receipt of revenues from production as in Carlstrom and Fuerst (1995), Christiano, Eichenbaum, and Evans (2001), or Cooley and Quadrini (1999). For evidence on the existence of such a 'cost channel' of nominal interest rates, see Barth and Ramey (2001).

Define the joint surplus of a worker/firm pair who are matched at the start of $t + 1$ and do not separate as

$$s_{it+1} = \delta_{t+1}\left(\frac{a_{it+1}z_{t+1}}{\mu_{t+1}}\right) - A + q_{t+1}. \qquad (9.14)$$

Note that this is expressed in terms of the present value as of the beginning of period $t + 1$. Let η denote the share of this surplus received by the worker; the firm receives $1 - \eta$ of the joint surplus. If an unmatched worker in period t succeeds in making a match that produces in period $t + 1$, she receives her opportunity utility w^u_{t+1} plus the fraction η of the joint surplus, or $\eta s_{it+1} + w^u_{t+1}$. The probability of this occurring is $k^w_t(1 - \rho_{t+1})$, where k^w_t is the period t probability an unmatched worker finds a job and $1 - \rho_{t+1}$ is the probability that the match actually produces in period $t + 1$. With probability $1 - k^w_t(1 - \rho_{t+1})$ the worker either fails to make a match or makes a match that fails to survive to produce in $t + 1$. In either case, the worker is unmatched in $t + 1$ and receives w^u_{t+1}. Therefore, the expected discounted value to an unmatched worker in the labour matching market is[9]

$$w^u_t = h + \beta E_t\left(\frac{u'_{t+1}}{u'_t}\right)\left[k^w_t(1 - \rho^x)\int_{\bar{a}_{t+1}}^{\bar{a}} \eta s_{it+1} f(a_i)da_i + w^u_{t+1}\right]$$
$$(9.15)$$

since an unmatched worker is assumed to enjoy utility h while unmatched.

For a worker and firm who are already matched, the joint discounted value of an existing match is

$$g_t = \beta E_t\left(\frac{u'_{t+1}}{u'_t}\right)\left[(1 - \rho^x)\int_{\bar{a}_{t+1}}^{\bar{a}} s_{it+1} f(a_i)da_i + w^u_{t+1}\right]. \qquad (9.16)$$

Hence, subtracting (9.15) from (9.16),

$$q_t \equiv g_t - w^u_t = (1 - \rho^x)\left(1 - \eta k^w_t\right)$$
$$\times \beta E_t\left(\frac{u'_{t+1}}{u'_t}\right)\left[\int_{\bar{a}_{t+1}}^{\bar{a}} s_{t+1} f(a_i)da_i\right] - h. \qquad (9.17)$$

Unmatched firms, or firms whose matches are terminated, may choose to enter the labour matching market and post vacancies. Posting a vacancy

----

[9] The expected surplus is

$$k^w_t(1 - \rho_{t+1})\int_{\bar{a}_{t+1}}^{\bar{a}} \eta s_{t+1}\frac{f(a)}{1 - F(\bar{a}_{t+1})}da = k^w_t(1 - \rho^x)\int_{\bar{a}_{t+1}}^{\bar{a}} \eta s_{t+1} f(a)da.$$

costs γ per period. If an unmatched firm does post a vacancy and succeeds in making a match that produces in period $t + 1$, it receives $(1 - \eta)s_{t+1} - \gamma$. Otherwise (i.e. if no match is made or if the match separates before production), the firm receives nothing. If k_t^f is the probability that a vacancy is filled, free entry ensures that firms post vacancies until

$$\beta E_t \left(\frac{u'_{t+1}}{u'_t} \right) \left[k_t^f (1 - \rho^x) \int_{\tilde{a}_{t+1}}^{\bar{a}} (1 - \eta) s_{t+1} f(a) da \right] - \gamma = 0. \quad (9.18)$$

Combining (9.17) and (9.18)

$$q_t = \frac{\gamma \left(1 - \eta k_t^w \right)}{(1 - \eta) k_t^f} - h. \quad (9.19)$$

Increases in either k^w or k^f reduce the value of continuing an existing match by making it easier to find a new match.

A total of $\rho_t N_t$ matches dissolve prior to engaging in production during period t. If the worker is not part of an existing match, or if her current match ends, she travels to the labour matching market. Thus, a total of

$$u_t \equiv U_t + \rho_t N_t = 1 - (1 - \rho_t) N_t \quad (9.20)$$

workers will not produce market goods during the period and will be searching for a new match.

Based on an aggregate matching function, a fraction of workers and firms in the labour market establish new matches. These, plus the worker/firm matches that produced during the period, constitute the stock of matches that enter period $t + 1$. The number of matches is equal to $m(u_t, V_t)$ where V_t is the number of posted vacancies and $m(.)$ is the aggregate matching function. The probability an unemployed worker makes a match, k_t^w, is equal to

$$k_t^w = \frac{m(u_t, V_t)}{u_t}. \quad (9.21)$$

Similarly, the probability that a firm with a posted vacancy finds a match, k_t^f, is

$$k_t^f = \frac{m(u_t, V_t)}{V_t}. \quad (9.22)$$

The total number of matches evolves according to

$$N_{t+1} = (1 - \rho_t) N_t + m(u_t, V_t). \quad (9.23)$$

The aggregate output of the wholesale sector is obtained by aggregating over all matches that actually produce:

$$Q_t = (1 - \rho_t) N_t z_t \left[\int_{\bar{a}_t}^{\infty} a_t \left(\frac{f(a)}{1 - F(\bar{a}_t)} \right) da \right]. \qquad (9.24)$$

The retail sector

Firms in the retail sector purchase output from wholesale producers at the price P_t^w and sell directly to households. For simplicity, assume that retail firms have no other inputs. Given the structure of demand facing each retail firm (see (9.5)), all retail firms would charge the same price in a flexible price equilibrium. This price would be a constant markup over wholesale prices, with the markup equal to $\theta/(\theta - 1)$.

Rather than assume flexible prices, I assume prices at the retail level are sticky. To model this price stickiness, I adopt the approach due originally to Calvo (1983) and now widely used in macroeconomics (see, for example, Christiano, Eichenbaum and Evans 2001; Erceg, Henderson and Levin 2000; or Woodford 1999, 2000). The Calvo model is based on the assumption that each period a randomly chosen fraction of all firms are allowed to adjust their price.

Let the probability a firm adjusts its price each period be given by $1 - \omega$. If firm j sets its price at time t, it will do so to maximise expected profits, subject to the demand curve it faces. The price of retail firm j is p_{jt}. Let p_t^* be the price chosen by all firms who set prices in period t; all retail firms setting prices in period t will choose the same price. Each retail firm's nominal marginal cost is just P_t^w. Real marginal cost is $P_t^w/P_t = \mu_t^{-1}$. Using (9.5), the firm's decision problem when it adjusts its price involves picking p_t^* to maximise

$$E_t \sum_{i=0}^{\infty} \omega^i \Delta_{i,t+1} \left[\left(\frac{p_t^*}{P_{t+i}} \right)^{1-\theta} - \mu_{t+i}^{-1} \left(\frac{p_t^*}{P_{t+i}} \right)^{-\theta} \right] C_{t+i}$$

where the i-period discount factor $\Delta_{i,t+1}$ is given by $\beta^i (u'_{t+i}/u'_{t+1})$. The first-order condition implies[10]

$$\left(\frac{p_t^*}{P_t} \right) = \left(\frac{\theta}{\theta - 1} \right) \frac{E_t \sum_{i=0}^{\infty} \omega^i \Delta_{i,t+1} \left[\mu_{t+i}^{-1} \left(\frac{P_{t+i}}{P_t} \right)^{\theta} C_{t+i} \right]}{E_t \sum_{i=0}^{\infty} \omega^i \Delta_{i,t+1} \left[\left(\frac{P_{t+i}}{P_t} \right)^{\theta-1} C_{t+i} \right]}. \qquad (9.25)$$

[10] See, for example, Sbordone (2002) for a more complete derivation.

The aggregate retail price index is

$$P_t^{1-\theta} = (1 - \omega)(p_t^*)^{1-\theta} + \omega P_{t-1}^{1-\theta}. \tag{9.26}$$

Equations (9.25) and (9.26) jointly determine p_t^* and P_t.

3.3 The monetary authority

To close the model, it is necessary to specify the behaviour of the monetary authority. Most central banks implement monetary policy by controlling a short-term nominal rate of interest. Thus, one way to analyse the impact of monetary policy is to specify a rule for setting the nominal interest rate. For example, Taylor rules, in which the nominal rate responds to output and inflation, are commonly used to describe monetary policy. However, one cannot simply specify arbitrary, exogenous (stationary) rules for the nominal interest rate and compare the adjustments to policy shocks in a flexible-price version of the model with a sticky-price version. The reason is that the nominal rate must react endogenously to inflation in the sticky-price model to ensure the existence of a unique, stationary, rational expectations equilibrium (Svensson and Woodford 1999). The model may have multiple stationary equilibria if the nominal interest rate is a function solely of exogenous disturbances. It is common in recent sticky-price models to require that the policy rule satisfy the 'Taylor Principle' under which the nominal interest rate responds more than one-for-one to changes in either actual or expected inflation, yet such rules would seem less relevant when prices are perfectly flexible. Thus, to provide the most transparent comparisons between the flexible-price and sticky-price versions of the model, I assume that monetary policy can be represented by an exogenous process for the growth rate of the money supply.[11]

Specifically, let Θ_t denote the growth rate of the nominal money supply. It is assumed that

$$\Theta_t = (1 - \rho_m)\,\bar{\Theta} + \rho_m \Theta_{t-1} + \phi_t \bar{\Theta} \tag{9.27}$$

where ϕ_t is a serially uncorrelated, mean zero stochastic process. The steady-state gross inflation rate is equal to the average growth rate of money $\bar{\Theta}$. A similar stochastic process for the growth rate of the nominal money supply is employed by Cooley and Quadrini (1999) and Christiano, Eichenbaum and Evans (2001).

[11] Cooley and Quadrini (1999), Christiano, Eichenbaum, and Evans (2001) and Dostey and King (2001) are other examples of papers using money growth rate rules to evaluate the effects of monetary shocks.

3.4 Equilibrium and the steady state

The final equilibrium condition in the model requires that consumption equal aggregate household income which, in turn, is equal to production net of vacancy posting costs:

$$C_t = Y_t = Q_t - \gamma V_t = z_t(1 - \rho^x)N_t \int_{\bar{a}_t}^{\infty} a_{it} f(a)da - \gamma V_t. \quad (9.28)$$

An equilibrium in the model consists of an initial value of the nominal money stock M_t, the initial number of matchers N_t, and sequences for $\bar{a}_t$, ρ_t^n, ρ_t, q_t, u_t, V_t, k_t^w, k_t^f, N_{t+1}, Y_t, C_t, P_t, p_t^*, μ_t and R_t that satisfy equations (9.4), (9.7), (9.8), (9.11)–(9.13), (9.17), (9.19)–(9.26) and (9.28), and the Central Bank's policy rule governing the evolution of the nominal money stock M_t given by (9.27). If prices are flexible, the model consists of (9.4), (9.7), (9.8), (9.11)–(9.13), (9.17), (9.19)–(9.24), (9.27), $p_t^* = P_t$ and $\mu_t = \theta/(\theta - 1)$.

The steady state is the same for both the flexible-price and sticky-price versions of the model. In a zero-inflation steady state, (9.7) implies $R = \bar{\Theta}/\beta$. Using this in (9.11), $q = A - (\beta/\bar{\Theta}\mu)\bar{a}$. Equation (9.17) can then be written as

$$\left(\frac{\beta}{\mu}\right)\bar{a} + (1 - \rho^x)(1 - \eta k^w)\beta \left(\frac{\beta}{\mu}\right)\left[\int_{\bar{a}}^{\bar{a}} (a - \bar{a}) f(a_i)da_i\right]$$
$$= (A + h)\bar{\Theta}. \quad (9.29)$$

Rearranging this condition yields the following steady-state condition for $\bar{a}$:

$$[1 - (1 - \rho^x)(1 - \eta k^w)\beta (1 - F(\bar{a}))]\bar{a} = G(\bar{a}) \quad (9.30)$$

where $G(\bar{a}) \equiv \mu(A + h)\bar{\Theta}/\beta - (1 - \rho^x)(1 - \eta k^w)\beta[\int_{\bar{a}}^{\bar{a}} af(a_i)da_i]$. Note that this condition also depends on the endogenous k^w. Both the sides of (9.30) are continuous and increasing in $\bar{a}$. The support of a is $(0, \bar{a}]$. For a given k^w, $G(\bar{a}) = \mu(A + h)\bar{\Theta}/\beta = \mu(A + h)R$, while the left-hand side of (9.30) is equal to $\bar{a}$. Evaluated at zero, the left-hand side of (9.30) is zero and the right-hand side is equal to $G(0) = \mu(A + h)R - (1 - \rho^x)(1 - \eta k^w)\beta$ as the expected value of a is equal to 1. A unique solution $\bar{a}(k^w)$ as a function of k^w exists as long as $G(0) > 0$ and $G(\bar{a}) < \bar{a}$, or

$$(1 - \rho^x)(1 - \eta k^w)\beta < \mu(A + h)R < \bar{a}.$$

Assume A (the disutility of work) and $\bar{a}$ are such that this holds. Then $\rho = \rho^x + (1 - \rho^x)F[\bar{a}(k^w)]$ and the steady-state values of N, u, V, k^f, k^w and C are given by the solution to

$$u = 1 - (1 - \rho)N$$

$$\rho N = m(u, V)$$

$$k^f = \frac{m(u, V)}{V}$$

$$k^w = \frac{m(u, V)}{u}$$

$$\frac{\gamma(1 - \eta k^w)}{(1 - \eta)k^f} = A + h - \left(\frac{\beta}{\bar{\Theta}\mu}\right)\bar{a}(k^w)$$

$$C = (1 - \rho)N\left(\frac{1}{1 - F[\bar{a}(k^w)]}\right)\left[\int_{\bar{a}(k^w)}^{\infty} a f(a)da\right] - \gamma V.$$

The steady-state markup is equal to $\theta/(\theta - 1)$, while real money balances are equal to consumption.

4 SIMULATIONS

The recent literature in monetary economics has used simulations extensively to study the dynamic properties of stochastic general equilibrium models. To cite just a few recent examples, Dotsey and King (2001), Dotsey, King and Wolman (1999), Fuhrer (2000), Jensen (2002), McCallum and Nelson (1999) and Walsh (2002). In keeping with that literature, the model of section 3 is expressed in terms of percentage deviations and linearised around the steady state. The basic approach is described in Uhlig (1999), and the model solution and its properties are obtained using the 'toolkit' of programs written by Harald Uhlig.[12]

In solving the model, functional forms of the utility function and the aggregate matching function need to be specified. The utility function for the composite consumption good is assumed to be of isoelastic form:

$$u(C_t) = \frac{C_t^{1-\sigma}}{1 - \sigma}; \quad \sigma > 0,$$

[12] Uhlig's programs are available at http://cwis.kub.nl/~few5/center/STAFF/uhlig/toolkit.dir/toolkit.htm.

where σ is the coefficient of relative risk aversion. The matching function is taken to be

$$m(u_t, V_t) = \mu u_t^a V_t^\xi, \quad 0 < a < 1, 0 < \xi < 1. \qquad (9.31)$$

A Cobb–Douglas specification of the matching function is common, and is the form used by Cooley and Quadrini (1999). With constant returns to scale, $a + \xi = 1$.[13] Equation (9.31) does allow for the matching function to display increasing or decreasing returns to scale if $a + \xi \neq 1$.[14]

Let $\hat{z}_t$ denote the log deviation from steady state of the aggregate productivity disturbance. As is standard in the literature, $\hat{z}_t$ is assumed to follow an $AR(1)$ process with innovation ε_t:

$$\hat{z}_t = \rho_z \hat{z}_{t-1} + \varepsilon_t. \qquad (9.32)$$

4.1 The linearised model

Given the assumed functional forms, the model is linearised around the steady state.[15] Let $\hat{x}_t$ denote the percentage deviation of a variable X_t around its steady-state value. The linearised model consists of (9.32) for the aggregate productivity disturbance and the following thirteen equations:
- The policy rule for nominal money growth, (9.27):

$$\hat{\Theta}_t = \rho_m \hat{\Theta}_{t-1} + \hat{\phi}_t; \qquad (9.33)$$

---

[13] Blanchard and Diamond (1989, 1990) provide evidence that the aggregate matching function displays constant returns to scale.

[14] den Haan, Ramey and Watson (2000) assume that the matching function displays constant returns to scale and is of the form

$$m(u_t, V_t) = \frac{u_t V_t}{[u_t^s + V_t^s]^{1/s}}.$$

As den Haan, Ramey and Watson note, this functional form ensures the probabilities k^w and k^f are bounded between 0 and 1. This specification and the Cobb–Douglas form lead to similar equilibrium conditions when the model is linearised around the steady state. For example, the specification of den Haan, Ramey and Watson implies $k_t^w = V/[u_t^s + V_t^s]^{1/s}$ which is approximated by

$$\hat{k}_t^w = [1 - (k^w)^s]\hat{V}_t - (k^f)^s \hat{u}_t = [1 - (k^w)^s](\hat{V}_t - \hat{u}_t)$$

where $\hat{x}$ denotes the percentage deviation around the steady state. With constant returns to scale, (9.31) implies $k_t^w = \mu u_t^{a-1} V_t^{1-a}$ which leads to

$$\hat{k}_t^w = (1 - a)(\hat{V}_t - \hat{u}_t)$$

When $a = (k^w)^s$, the two specifications produce identical dynamic simulations. In the calibration used by Den Haan, Ramey and Watson $s = 1.27$ and $k^w = 0.45$, implying that $(k^w)^s = 0.3627$. Cooley and Quadrini set $a = 0.4$ in their base calibration, implying the two specifications are essentially identical.

[15] Details are in an appendix available at http://econ.ucsc.edu/~walshc/.

- The cash-in-advance constraint (in first-difference form), (9.8):

$$\hat{\Theta}_t = \hat{y}_t - \hat{y}_{t-1} + \hat{\pi}_t; \qquad (9.34)$$

- The evolution of the number of matches, (9.23):

$$\hat{n}_{t+1} = \varphi\hat{\varphi}_t + \varphi\hat{n}_t + \left(\frac{vk^f}{N}\right)\hat{v}_t + \left(\frac{vk^f}{N}\right)\hat{k}_t^f; \qquad (9.35)$$

- The endogenous job destruction margin, (9.11):

$$\hat{a}_t = \hat{r}_t + \hat{\mu}_t - \left(\frac{\mu Rq}{\bar{a}}\right)\hat{q}_t - \hat{z}_t; \qquad (9.36)$$

- The survival rate $\varphi_t = 1 - \rho_t$, using (9.12):

$$\hat{\varphi}_t = -\left(\frac{\rho^n}{1-\rho^n}\right)e_{F,a}\hat{a}_t; \qquad (9.37)$$

- The number of unemployed job seekers, (9.20):

$$\hat{u}_t = -\left(\frac{\varphi N}{u}\right)\hat{n}_t - \left(\frac{\varphi N}{u}\right)\hat{\varphi}_t; \qquad (9.38)$$

- The probability a vacancy is filled, (9.22):

$$\hat{k}_t^f = a\hat{u}_t - (1-\xi)\hat{v}_t; \qquad (9.39)$$

- The equality of firms filling vacancies and workers finding matches:

$$\hat{v}_t + \hat{k}_t^f = \hat{u}_t + \hat{k}_t^w; \qquad (9.40)$$

- The job-posting condition, (9.19):

$$\hat{k}_t^f = -\left(\frac{\eta k^w}{1-\eta k^w}\right)\hat{k}_t^w - \left(\frac{q}{q+h}\right)\hat{q}_t; \qquad (9.41)$$

- The output equation (9.28):

$$\hat{y}_t = \left(\frac{Q}{Y}\right)(e_{H,a}\hat{a}_t + \hat{n}_t + z_t) - \left(\frac{\gamma V}{Y}\right)\hat{v}_t; \qquad (9.42)$$

- The Euler condition from the household's optimisation problem (9.7):

$$0 = E_t\hat{y}_{t+1} - \hat{y}_t - \left(\frac{1}{\sigma}\right)\hat{r}_t + \left(\frac{1}{\sigma}\right)E_t\hat{\pi}_{t+1}; \qquad (9.43)$$

- The inflation equation from the retail firms' pricing decisions, obtained from (9.25) and (9.26):

$$0 = \beta E_t \hat{\pi}_{t+1} - \hat{\pi}_t - \kappa \hat{\mu}_t \tag{9.44}$$

- The present value condition for matches, (9.17):

$$\hat{q}_t = AB(e_{H,a} E_t \hat{a}_{t+1} - E_t \hat{\mu}_{t+1} - E_t \hat{r}_{t+1} + E_t z_{t+1})$$
$$+ \left[\frac{(1 - \eta k^w)\beta\varphi(q - A)}{q} \right] E_t \hat{\varphi}_{t+1} - \left(\frac{q + h}{q} \right) (\hat{r}_t - E_t \hat{\pi}_{t+1})$$
$$- \left(\frac{\eta k^w}{1 - \eta k^w} \right) \left(\frac{q + h}{q} \right) \hat{k}_t^w + (1 - \eta k^w)\beta\varphi E_t \hat{q}_{t+1}. \tag{9.45}$$

In these conditions, $e_{F,a}$ is the elasticity of the cumulative density function of a, $H(\bar{a}) \equiv E_t(a|a \geq \bar{a})$, $e_{H,a}$ is the elasticity of $H(\bar{a})$ with respect to $\bar{a}$, evaluated at the steady-state and

$$AB = \frac{(1 - \eta k^w)\beta H(\bar{a})}{\mu R q}.$$

Note that, while the distribution of the idiosyncratic shock a appears in the form of the function $H(\bar{a})$ and the elasticities $e_{F,a}$ and $e_{H,a}$, the actual realisations of the a_{it} shocks average out across matches, so they do not appear in the equilibrium conditions.

In the flexible-price version of the model, the markup μ is constant, equal to $\theta/(\theta - 1)$, and (9.44) is dropped.

Let $x_t = (\hat{r}_t, \hat{n}_t, \hat{\varphi}_t, \hat{y}_t, \hat{a}_t, \hat{v}_t, \hat{k}_t^f, \hat{k}_t^w, \hat{q}, \hat{u}_t, \hat{\mu}_t, \hat{\pi}_t)'$ be the vector of endogenous variables, and let $\psi_t = (\hat{\Theta}_t, z_t)'$ be the vector of exogenous aggregate disturbances. Equations (9.34)–(9.45) can be written as

$$AE_t x_{t+1} + Bx_t + CE_t \psi_{t+1} + D\psi_t = 0 \tag{9.46}$$

where

$$\psi_{t+1} = N\psi_t + \chi_{t+1},$$

and $\chi_t = (\phi_t, \varepsilon_t)'$ is the innovation vector.

If an equilibrium solution to this system of equations exists, it takes the form of stable laws of motion given by

$$x_t = Px_{t-1} + Q\psi_t.$$

Uhlig (1999) provides a complete discussion of the methods used to solve systems such as (9.46).

Table 9.1 *Calibrated parameters*

Preferences				
	β	σ	θ	h
	0.989	2	11	0

Labour market							
ρ^s	ρ^x	α	ξ	κ^f	κ^w	N	η
0.10	0.068	0.4	0.6	0.7	0.6	0.94	0.5

Price rigidity	
	ω
	0.67

Policy		
ρ_m	σ_ϕ	$\bar{\Theta}$
0.73	0.00624	1.01

Productivity		
σ_ε	ρ_z	σ_a
0.0033	0.95	0.15

4.2 Calibration

The model is characterised by five sets of parameters – those describing household preferences, those describing the aggregate matching function, those characterising the degree of price rigidity at the retail level, those specifying the behaviour of the growth rate of money and those characterising the stochastic distribution of the exogenous shocks. Parameter values are chosen to be largely consistent with those shown to match US data in non-monetary models. The baseline parameters values are shown in table 9.1 and discussed in this section.

Preferences

Household preferences are characterised by the parameters β, σ, θ, h and A. The discount rate and the coefficient of relative risk aversion appear in standard DSGE models. Choosing the time period to correspond to a calendar quarter, β is set equal to 0.989, implying a steady-state real annual return of 4.5 per cent. A value $\sigma = 2$ is chosen for the coefficient of relative risk aversion, implying greater risk aversion than log utility. The parameter θ determines the elasticity of demand for the differentiated retail goods. This elasticity in turn determines the markup μ. This markup is set equal to 1.1, corresponding to a value of $\theta = 11$. The value of home production while unemployed, h, is set equal to zero. Finally, A is determined by the steady-state condition (9.11) once q is found from the labour market calibrations.

Matching and the labour market

Den Haan, Ramey and Watson (2000) set the steady-state separation rate ρ^s equal to 0.1. This is based on Hall's conclusion that 'around 8 or 10 percent of workers separate from their employer each quarter' (Hall 1995: 235) and the Davis, Haltiwanger and Schuh (1996) finding of about an 11 per cent quarterly separation rate. This is higher than the 0.07 value adopted by Merz (1995), but lower than the 0.15 used by Andolfatto (1996). Given a value of 10 per cent for ρ^s, den Haan, Ramey and Watson use evidence on permanent job destruction to calibrate the exogenous separation probability ρ^x as 0.068. I use this value for the baseline simulations. These values for ρ^x and ρ^s imply an endogenous separation probability ρ^n of 0.0343. From this value, and the assumed distribution function for the match-specific productivity shock, the steady-state value of the cut-off productivity realization $\tilde{a}$ can be derived. I assume $\tilde{a}$ is log-normally distributed with standard deviation 0.15; this is somewhat higher than the value used by den Haan, Ramey and Watson (they set this standard deviation equal to 0.1).

For the Cobb–Douglas matching function (9.31), I follow Cooley and Quadrini and set $\alpha = 0.4$ and $\xi = 0.6$ based on the estimates of Blanchard and Diamond (1989). Both Cooley and Quadrini (1999) and den Haan, Ramey and Watson fix $k^f = 0.7$. Cooley and Quadrini (1999) cite Cole and Rogerson (1996) to set the average duration of unemployment at 1.67 quarters, which implies $k^w = 0.6$. I set $N = 0.94$, implying a steady-state unemployment rate of 0.06 and a value of 0.154 for u, the steady-state number of workers searching each period. The steady-state value of V is 0.132.[16]

I follow den Haan, Ramey and Watson and set the share of the match surplus that the worker receives, η, equal to 0.5. Finally, the steady-state value of a match q, is obtained from (9.19). Finally, (9.17) is used to calibrate γ.

Price rigidity

The degree of nominal rigidity is determined by ω, the fraction of firms each period that do not adjust their price. Empirical estimates of

---

[16] Den Haan, Ramey and Watson (2000) chose a value of 1.27 for the parameter s that appears in their matching function (see n. 9). This, together with the steady-state value of u implies a value of 0.0993 for V and 0.4515 for k^w. This last value is close to the value of 0.45 used by den Haan, Ramey and Watson and is significantly lower than the 0.6 employed by Cooley and Quadrini.

forward-looking price-setting models of the type employed here suggest prices are fixed on the order of nine months. This would imply a value of 0.67 for ω (Sbordone 2002) and this is taken as the baseline value. However, evidence based on BLS data on price changes suggests a median time between changes of six months (Bils and Klenow 2002); this would imply a value of 0.5 for ω. In the simulations, various values for ω ranging from $\omega = 0$ (price flexibility) to $\omega = 0.9$ are used to explore the impact of nominal rigidity on the dynamic response of the economy.

Policy
The process for the growth rate of M is calibrated by estimating an $AR(1)$ process for US M2 using quarterly data over the period 1965:3–2001:4. This yielded $\rho_m = 0.73$ and the standard deviation of ϕ is set to 0.00624.[17]

Shocks
In addition to the money growth rate shock, there are two other exogenous disturbances in the model: the match-specific shock and the aggregate productivity shock. The specification of the distribution of the match-specific shock has already been discussed. The log aggregate productivity shock was given in (9.32). Standard calibrations for the productivity disturbance process in the RBC literature are $\rho_z = 0.95$ and $\sigma_\varepsilon = 0.007$ (see Cooley and Prescott 1995). This calibration is, however, based on models in which the productivity disturbance is the sole source of fluctuations. In the present model there are nominal money growth shocks in addition to the aggregate productivity shocks. Thus, a smaller value of σ_ε is appropriate for matching output fluctuations. Cooley and Quadrini (1999) choose σ_ε so the model's prediction for the standard deviation of output matches the standard deviation of US real GDP. For their baseline parameter values, this implies $\sigma_\varepsilon = 0.0033$ when prices are assumed to be flexible. I employ this as the baseline value for σ_ε, together with $\rho_z = 0.95$.

4.3 Results

Flexible prices
Column (1) of table 9.2 presents standard deviations based on US data for 1959:1–1996:4; column (2) expresses these relative to the standard deviation of output. These values are taken from den Haan, Ramey and Watson (2000) and Cooley and Quadrini (1999). Columns (3) and (4) report the

---

[17] Cooley and Quadrini (1999) set the standard deviation of ϕ to 0.00623 and $\rho_m = 0.49$. Christiano, Eichenbaum and Evans (2001) set $\rho_m = 0.5$.

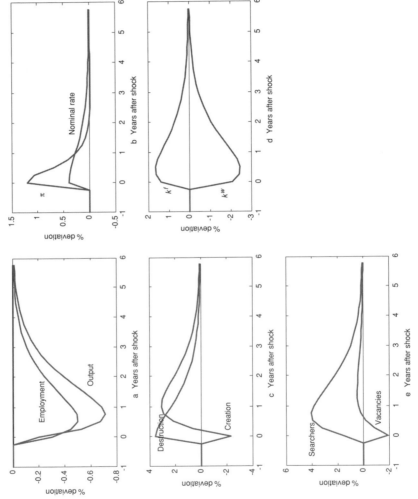

Figure 9.2 Effects of a money growth shock with flexible prices

Table 9.2 *Business cycle properties*

	US		Model outcomes				
	(1)	(2)	(3)	(4)	(5)	(6)	(7)
			$\omega = 0$	$\omega = 0$	$\omega = 0.33$	$\omega = 0.67$	$\omega = 0.9$
Variable	σ_i	σ_i/σ_y	σ_i	σ_i/σ_y	σ_i/σ_y	σ_i/σ_y	σ_i/σ_y
Output	1.60	1.00	1.18	1.00	1.00	1.00	1.00
Employment	0.99	0.62	0.66	0.56	0.53	0.57	0.78
Job creation rate	4.62	2.89	4.77	4.05	3.93	4.93	4.26
Job destruction rate	6.81	4.26	4.05	3.44	3.34	5.97	7.10
Inflation	0.56	0.35	1.05	0.89	0.96	0.84	0.14
Nominal interest rate	1.27	0.79	0.41	0.35	0.48	0.87	0.62

results from the flexible-price model. The model based on productivity and money growth rate shocks implies less output variability than is observed in the data. The model implies slightly less employment volatility relative to the standard deviation of output than found in the data (0.56 compared to 0.62), and it also reverses the relative volatility of job creation and destruction. In the data, destruction exhibits more volatility, while in the flexible price model job creation has a larger standard deviation. Greater volatility in job creation than destruction is also a property of the real model studied by den Haan, Ramey and Watson (2000). Perhaps not surprisingly, the flexible price model implies greater inflation volatility than is evident in the US data.

Figure 9.2 illustrates the impact of a money growth rate shock when prices are flexible. Nominal money growth rate fluctuations have very small real effects in a basic CIA model with a neoclassical specification of the labour market and flexible prices (for example, see Walsh 2003, chapter 3). In those models, higher inflation taxes consumption and leads households to reduce their labour supply. In the present model, labour supply is completely inelastic, so this channel is absent. Instead, fluctuations in the nominal interest rate alter the job destruction margin and have real effects even when prices are flexible. Figure 9.2 shows that a 1 percentage point money growth rate shock (which raises the nominal interest rate – see panel b) causes a fall in employment and output (panel a). For a given level of employment at the beginning of each period, fewer worker/firm matches actually remain together to produce when the nominal interest rate increases. The contraction in production at the wholesale level increases wholesale prices. With a fixed markup of retail over wholesale

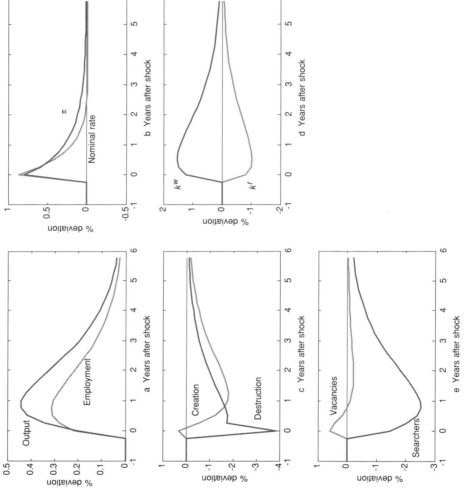

Figure 9.3 Effects of a money growth rate shock with sticky prices ($\omega = 0.67$)

prices, inflation spikes as the retail price level jumps (panel b). Job creation and job destruction initially move in opposite directions, as the number of endogenous separations rise and fewer jobs are created (panel c). However, job creation rebounds after one period. The job-finding probability falls for workers and rises for firms (panel d), reflecting the rise in the number of searching workers relative to vacancies (panel e).

The results in figure 9.2 are qualitatively similar to those reported by Cooley and Quadrini (1999) for a contractionary money shock. The key difference is the presence of a liquidity effect in the Cooley–Quadrini model and the lack of one in the present model. Thus, a *negative* money shock raises the nominal interest rate in their model while a *positive* money shock does so in the present model.

Sticky prices

When prices are sticky, monetary disturbances have traditional demand effects as well as the supply-side effects. Columns (5)–(7) of table 9.2 show the impact of increasing price rigidity on the relative variability of key variables. As expected, the relative standard deviation of inflation falls as the degree of price stickiness increases. In other sticky-price models, $\omega = 0.67$ is a common parameterisation. It implies that prices are fixed, on average, for nine months. This degree of price stickiness does provide a better match between the model's predictions for the standard deviation of inflation relative to that of output. When $\omega = 0.67$, the standard deviation of job destruction is increased relative to that of job creation, moving these statistics closer to the values found in US data.

Figure 9.3 shows how important price stickiness is in affecting the model's predictions for the response to a money supply disturbance. In contrast to figure 9.2, a positive money shock now increases real output and employment. There is a jump in job creation and a significant drop in job destruction. As a consequence, the number of workers searching for matches falls and then gradually returns to the steady state. In this CIA model, there is no liquidity effect – the nominal interest rate rises immediately in reaction to the positive shock to money growth. As expected, the inflation impact of the money growth shock is smaller when prices are sticky. Two effects operate on inflation. First, the expansion in output induced by the rise in demand increases wholesale prices and leads to a rise in retail inflation. Second, the associated rise in the nominal interest rate (reflecting the rise in expected inflation) reduces wholesale output and also contributes to an increase in wholesale prices and retail inflation. If the cost channel is eliminated,

Table 9.3 *Effects of parameter variation*

	ω	k^f	k^w	ρ_m	η	Cost Channel	Response of output					
							Multipliers			Lags		
							Impact	Peak	Total	Peak	Median	Mean
(1)	0.67	0.70	0.60	0.73	0.5	Yes	0.20	0.44	5.49	3	7	8.37
(2)	0.50	0.95	0.95	0	0.5	No	0.39	0.39	1.03	0	1	1.60
(3)	0.50	0.95	0.95	0	0.5	Yes	0.43	0.43	1.43	0	1	2.31
(4)	0.67	0.95	0.95	0	0.5	Yes	0.63	0.63	2.83	0	2	3.45
(5)	0.67	0.70	0.60	0	0.5	Yes	0.68	0.68	4.55	0	4	5.60
(6)	0.67	0.70	0.60	0.73	0.5	Yes	0.20	0.44	5.49	3	7	8.37
(7)	0.67	0.70	0.60	0.73	0.1	Yes	0.27	0.75	13.05	5	13	15.20

the standard deviation of inflation relative to output falls from 0.84 to 0.54, a 35 per cent decline.

For the baseline parameter values used for figure 9.3, the immediate impact effect on output of a 1 percentage point rise in the money growth rate is 0.20. This increases to a peak effect of 0.44, with this peak occurring three periods after the initial shock. The total multiplier is 5.49 and the mean lag is 8.37 periods. There are several elements of the model that account for the dynamic pattern displayed by this output response. First, the degree of nominal price stickiness influences the model dynamics. Second, the money growth rate process itself is serially correlated, and this accounts for some of the persistence in the output effects seen in figure 9.3. Third, the nominal interest rate affects job separation and creation, and fourth, the labour market matching process affects the evolution of employment after a shock.

Insight into how the dynamic response of output is affected by the various aspects of the model specification is provided by table 9.3. Each row of that table represents a different set of parameter values. Row (1) reports results for the baseline parameter values. Row (2) has a lower degree of price rigidity than in the baseline parameter set ($\omega = 0.50$ versus 0.67). In addition, ρ_m is set equal to 0 so that the growth rate of money is serially uncorrelated, and the direct cost channel of nominal interest rates is eliminated. Finally, both k^f and k^w are increased to 0.95 to capture a matching process in which workers and firms are able to find new matches much more quickly. As a result of these changes, the impact effect of a money growth shock on output is actually increased to 0.39, but this impact effect is also the peak effect as output starts declining in the period immediately following the shock. The response no longer displays the typical hump shape seen in estimated VARs. The total multiplier falls dramatically to 1.03 from 5.49 for the baseline parameter set (row 1), and the mean lag falls to 1.60 periods. Row (3) of table 9.3 adds back in the supply channel of the nominal interest rate. This increases the impact multiplier on output and the total impact, but it has only minor effects on the dynamic pattern of output's response. The maximum effect still occurs in the period of the shock, with output declining thereafter.

Row (4) increases the degree of price rigidity by raising ω from 0.5 to 0.67. This, like the supply channel, increases the impact of a money shock but has little impact on the shape of the response. The maximum effect occurs immediately, although the mean and median lags are both increased.

Row (5) returns k^f and k^w to their baseline values, so row (5) serves to illustrate the impact of more sluggish labour market adjustment. While the impact effect of a money shock is not significantly changed, the median lag is doubled to four periods, while the mean lag rises from 3.45 to 5.60 periods. Labour market search stretches out the response, adding to the overall persistence due to a monetary shock, but it does not induce the hump-shape response seen in VARs.

Row (5) differs from the baseline parameter set only in setting $\rho_m = 0$. If ρ_m is increased to its baseline value of 0.73, the impact is quite dramatic. To facilitate the comparison, row (6) repeats row (1), the outcomes for the baseline parameters. Comparing rows (5) and (6) shows that serially correlated money shocks reduce the impact effect of a money growth shock on output. While the impact effect is smaller, the peak effect is now both larger and delayed, occurring three periods after the shock. The total effect also rises, and the mean lag increases to over seven periods. Thus, the persistence in the money supply growth process appears to have an important effect on the response to a monetary shock, and it is serial correlation in the money shock that generates the hump-shaped response of output.

Rows (1)–(6) employed a value of 0.5 for the share parameter η. This is the value used by den Haan, Ramey and Watson (2000) and is common in other applications of the Mortensen–Pissarides framework. In contrast, Cooley and Quadrini (1999) set η equal to 0.01 and 0.1 in their alternative model economies. Row (7) of table 9.3 sets η equal to 0.1. This has a major impact on the model's response to a money growth rate shock. The impact effect rises from 0.20 in row (1) to 0.27 in row (7), the peak effect increases from 0.44 to 0.75, and the total impact rises from 5.49 to 13.05. The peak impact now occurs five periods after the shock, and the mean lag rises to over 10 periods.

The results reported in table 9.3 help to identify the key parameters affecting both the magnitude and the persistence of the response of output.

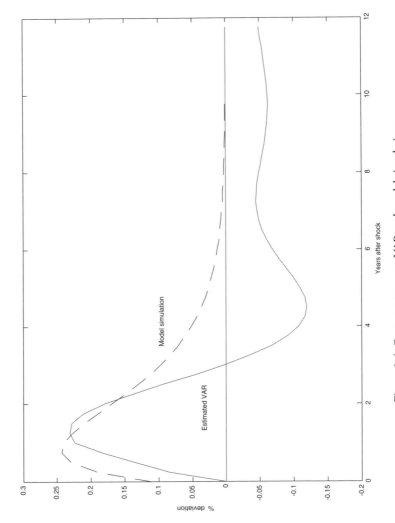

Figure 9.4 Output responses: VAR and model simulations

The magnitude of the total impact depends importantly on the values of ω, ρ_m, k_t^w, k_t^f and η. The persistence displayed by output in response to a nominal money growth shock, as measured by the median lag, is affected by the degree of price rigidity, the speed of labour market adjustment and the degree of persistence in the money growth process itself. The role of ω, the degree of price rigidity, is not surprising. Nominal rigidities have long been viewed as the key explanation for sizeable real effects of nominal disturbances. The ease with which employment matches are formed, as reflected in the values of k^f and k^w, also have a major effect on the size of the output effect of a money growth shock. The values of ω, k_t^w, and k_t^f affect mainly the total impact multiplier but not the shape of the output response. The hump-shaped response of output is determined by the degree of serial correlation in the money growth rate (ρ_m) and η (the labour share parameter).

The role of η is unexpected, in part because this share parameter plays no role in traditional dynamic general equilibrium models. Cooley and Quadrini (1999) find that the volatility of output and employment increases with η in their flexible-price model. This is no longer the case when prices are sticky, and increasing the share of the surplus going to the firm (a reduction in η) increases overall volatility.[18] As η goes to zero, (9.19) implies that the present value of a match becomes less sensitive to k^w and more sensitive to k^f. As a consequence, a contractionary monetary policy shock that reduces employment and increases the number of searching workers increases k^f and reduces the continuation value of a match. Because firms are able to find new matches more easily, the value of continuing in an existing match falls. This raises the probability of endogenous separations and, as a result, the economy takes longer to return to its steady-state level of employment. Thus, a decline in η leads to greater persistence in the real effects of a monetary policy shock.

Table 9.3 serves to separate the influence on output dynamics of various aspects of the model. To assess the 'match' between the model and the data, it is useful to compare impulse responses directly. Figure 9.4 shows the response of output to a money growth shock estimated from US data and the response obtained from the model simulations.[19] Under the baseline parameter values, the peak impact of a money shock on output is too large (0.44 – see row (1) of table 9.3 – versus 0.23 from the estimated VAR). A better match is obtained with $\omega = 0.62$, implying slightly more price

---

[18] For example, decreasing η from 0.5 to 0.1 increases the standard deviation of output from 0.73 to 1.64. Decreasing it further to 0.01 raises the standard deviation to 2.15.

[19] The estimated response for output is the same as in figure 9.1.

flexibility than with the baseline parameter values, and this value of ω is used to generate figure 9.4. The model captures the basic hump-shaped response, but there are several aspects of the estimated impulse response that are not captured by the model. The estimated output dynamics are much more complex than those exhibited by the model. The model implies output reaches a peak and then declines smoothly to the steady state; the estimate VAR shows output reaching its peak and then falling below the steady state. The impulse response function from the estimated VAR also shows output peaking five periods after the shock versus three periods in the case of the model simulation.[20]

5 CONCLUSIONS

Dynamic stochastic general equilibrium (DSGE) models are well suited for studying the interactions of real and nominal stickiness, and this chapter has examined the role of the labour market matching function and price stickiness in affecting the way the economy responds to money growth shocks. The model incorporated both an aggregate labour market matching function and price stickiness by incorporating a wholesale production sector, in which matched firms and workers produce output, and a retail sector characterised by monopolistic competition and sticky prices. Money growth shocks led to employment and output responses that were hump-shaped, just as the empirical evidence suggests. Replacing the Walrasian labour market with a simple model of labour market search appears to be a promising avenue to pursue in understanding the dynamic adjustment of the economy to monetary policy shocks.

In the sticky-price version of the model, monetary shocks had both demand and supply effects. Increases in money growth lead to increases in consumption and the nominal interest rate (via the expected inflation channel). The rise in the nominal rate reduced production among wholesale firms by altering the job destruction margin. By pushing up wholesale prices relative to retail prices, positive nominal interest rate movements also affected retail price inflation. This supply, or cost channel, effect reinforced the inflationary impact of a money growth rate increase.

As in traditional models, the response of output to monetary shocks depended on the degree of nominal price stickiness. It also depended on the degree of persistence displayed by the money process itself. Perhaps more

---

[20] However, it should be noted that the VAR impulse responses are obtain using a Choleski decomposition with money ordered last. This means that the VAR restricts money growth shocks to have no impact on output until at least one period after the shock.

interestingly, the dynamic behaviour of the model economy was sensitive to the parameter that determined how a match surplus was divided between the worker and the firm. An interesting direction for future research will be to explore further the implications of this share parameter for economic dynamics. Hosios (1990) has shown that the relationship between the share parameter and the elasticity of the vacancy matching probability with respect to labour market tightness (measured by the ratio of vacancies to searchers) is critical for determining the efficiency of the steady-state unemployment rate (Pissarides 2000, chapter 8). While Friedman argued that the optimal rate of inflation is the rate that produces a zero nominal interest rate, Cooley and Quadrini (1999) argue that the optimal level of the nominal interest rate may be positive if steady-state unemployment is inefficiently low.[21] The positive nominal rate increases job destruction and raises the average unemployment rate.

Monetary policy has been represented by a process for the growth rate of the nominal money supply. It is common in much of the recent monetary literature to represent policy by a rule for the nominal interest rate. An extension of the present model would be to replace the money growth rate rule with a nominal interest rate rule. A policy shock that raised the nominal interest rate would reduce output through a traditional demand channel and through its effect on job destruction. These channels, however, would have countervailing effects on inflation. The negative impact on wholesale output would raise wholesale prices relative to retail prices and lead to an increase in retail price inflation. The demand-side reduction in consumption would put downward pressure on inflation. These opposing effects could account for the small initial net impact on inflation of a nominal interest rate shock that is observed in the data.

BIBLIOGRAPHY

Andolfatto, D. (1996). 'Business Cycles and Labor-Market Search', *American Economic Review*, 86(1), 112–32
Ball, L. and Romer, D. (1990). 'Real Rigidities and the Nonneutrality of Money', *Review of Economic Studies*, 57, 183–203
Barth, M. J. III and Ramey, V. A. (2001). 'The Cost Channel of Monetary Transmission', *NBER Macroeconomic Annual*, Cambridge, MA: MIT Press, 199–239

---

[21] This occurs in the model of this chapter when $\eta < \alpha$, as in the calibration of Cooley and Quadrini (1999).

Bernanke, B., Gertler, M. and Gilchrist, S. (1999). 'The Financial Accelerator in a Quantitative Business Cycles Framework', chapter 21 in J. Taylor and M. Woodford (eds.), *The Handbook of Macroeconomics*, 1C, North-Holland: Elsevier Science

Bils, M. and Klenow, P. (2002). 'Some Evidence on the Importance of Sticky Prices', University of Rochester, January, mimeo

Blanchard, O. J. and Diamond, P. (1989). 'The Beveridge Curve', *Brookings Papers on Economic Activity*, 1, 1–60

(1990). 'The Aggregate Matching Functions', in P. Diamond (ed.), *Growth/Productivity/Unemployment*, Cambridge, MA: MIT Press, 159–201

Burnside, C. and Eichenbaum, M. (1996). 'Factor Hoarding and the Propagation of Business-Cycle Shocks', *American Economic Review*, 86(5), 1154–74

Calvo, G. A. (1983). 'Staggered Prices in a Utility-Maximising Framework', *Journal of Monetary Economics*, 12(3), 983–98

Carlstrom, C. T. and Fuerst, T. S. (1995). 'Interest Rate Rules vs. Money Growth Rules: A Welfare Comparison in a Cash-in-Advance Economy', *Journal of Monetary Economics*, 36(2), 247–67

Chari, V. V., Kehoe, P. J. and McGrattan, E. R. (2000). 'Sticky Price Models of the Business Cycle: Can the Contract Multiplier Solve the Persistence Problem?', *Econometrica*, 68(5), 1151–79

Christiano, L. J., Eichenbaum, M. and Evans, C. (1999). 'Monetary Policy Shocks: What Have We Learned and to What End?', chapter 2 in J. Taylor and M. Woodford (eds.), *The Handbook of Macroeconomics*, 1A, North-Holland: Elsevier Science

(2001). 'Nominal Rigidities and the Dynamic Effects of a Shock to Monetary Policy', *NBER Working Paper*, W8403, July

Cole, H. and Rogerson, R. (1999). 'Can the Mortensen–Pissarides Matching Model Match the Business Cycle Facts?', *International Economic Review*, 40(4), 933–59

Cooley, T. F. and Prescott, E. (1995). 'Economic Growth and Business Cycles', in T. F. Cooley (ed.), *Frontiers of Business Cycle Research*, Princeton: Princeton University Press, 1–38

Cooley, T. F. and Quadrini, V. (1999). 'A Neoclassical Model of the Phillips Curve Relation', *Journal of Monetary Economics*, 44(2), 165–93

Davis, S. J., Haltiwanger, J. C. and Schuh, S. (1996). *Job Creation and Job Destruction*, Cambridge, MA: MIT Press

den Haan, W. J., Ramey, G. and Watson, J. (2000). 'Job Destruction and Propagation of Shocks', *American Economic Review*, 90(3), 482–98

Dotsey, M. and King, R. G. (2001). 'Pricing, Production and Persistence', *NBER Working Paper*, 8407

Dotsey, M., King, R. G. and Wolman, A. L. (1999). 'State Contingent Pricing and the Dynamics of General Equilibrium Dynamics of Money and Output', *Quarterly Journal of Economics*, 114(2), 655–90

Erceg, C. J., Henderson, D. and Levin, A. T. (2000). 'Optimal Monetary Policy with Staggered Wage and Price Contracts', *Journal of Monetary Economics*, 46(2), 281–313

Fuerst, T. S. (1992). 'Liquidity, Loanable Funds, and Real Activity', *Journal of Monetary Economics*, 29(1), 3–24

Fuhrer, J. C. (2000). 'Habit Formation in Consumption and Its Implications for Monetary-Policy Models', *American Economic Review*, 90(3), 367–90

Goodfriend, M. and King, R. G. (1997). 'The New Neoclassical Synthesis and the Role of Monetary Policy', *NBER Macroeconomic Annual*, Cambridge, MA: MIT Press, 231–83

Hall, R. E. (1995). 'Lost Jobs', *Brookings Papers on Economic Activity*, 1, 221–56

Hosios, A. J. (1990). 'On the Efficiency of Matching and Related Models of Search and Unemployment', *Review of Economic Studies*, 57, 279–98

Jeanne, O. (1998). 'Generating Real Persistent Effects of Monetary Shocks: How Much Nominal Rigidity Do We Really Need?', *European Economic Review*, 42(6), 1009–32

Jensen, H. (2002). 'Targeting Nominal Income Growth or Inflation?', *Working Paper*, University of Copenhagen; forthcoming in *American Economic Review*, 92(4), 928–56

King, R. G. and Goodfriend, M. (2001). 'The Case for Price Stability', in *Why Price Stability?*, first ECB Central Banking Conference European Central Bank, Frankfurt am Main, November, 53–94

Lucas, R. E., Jr. and Stokey, N. (1983). 'Optimal Fiscal and Monetary Policy in an Economy without Capital', *Journal of Monetary Economics*, 12(1), 55–93

(1987). 'Money and Interest in a Cash-in-Advance Economy', *Econometrica*, 55(3), 491–514

McCallum, B. and Nelson, E. (1999). 'An Optimising IS-LM Specification for Monetary Policy and Business Cycle Analysis', *Journal of Money, Credit, and Banking*, 31(3), part 1, 296–316

Merz, M. (1995). 'Search in the Labor Market and the Real Business Cycle', *Journal of Monetary Economics*, 36(2), 269–300

Mortensen, D. T. and Pissarides, C. A. (1994). 'Job Creation and Job Destruction in the Theory of Unemployment', *Review of Economic Studies*, 61(3), 397–416

(1999). 'New Developments in Models of Search in the Labor Market', *CEPR Discussion Paper*, 2053

Nelson, E. (1998). 'Sluggish Inflation and Optimising Models of the Business Cycle', *Journal of Monetary Economics*, 42(2), 303–22

Pissarides, C. A. (2000). *Equilibrium Unemployment Theory*, Cambridge, MA: MIT Press

Rotemberg, J. and Woodford, M. (1997). 'An Optimising-Based Econometric Model for the Evaluation of Monetary Policy', *NBER Macroeconomic Annual*, Cambridge, MA: MIT Press, 297–346

Sbordone, A. M. (2002). 'Prices and Unit Labour Costs: A New Test of Price Stickiness', *Journal of Monetary Economics*, 49(2), 265–92

Sims, C. A. (1992). 'Interpretation of the Macroeconomic Time Series Facts: The Effects of Monetary Policy', *European Economic Review*, 36, 975–1000

Svensson, L. E. O. and Woodford, M. (1999). 'Implementing Optimal Policy Through Inflation-Forecast Targeting', Princeton University, mimeo

Uhlig, H. (1999). 'A Toolkit for Analyzing Non-linear Dynamic Stochastic Models Easily', in R. Marimon and A. Scott (eds.), *Computational Methods for the Study of Dynamic Economies*, Oxford: Oxford University Press, 30–61

Walsh, C. E. (2003). *Monetary Theory and Policy*, 2nd edn., Cambridge, MA: MIT Press

  (2002). 'Speed Limit Policies: The Output Gap and Optimal Monetary Policy', *American Economic Review*, 93(1), 265–78

Woodford, M. (1999). 'Optimal Monetary Policy Inertia', *NBER Working Paper*, 7261

  (2000). 'Interest and Prices', Princeton University, September

Yun, T. (1996). 'Nominal Price Rigidity, Money Supply Endogeneity, and Business Cycles', *Journal of Monetary Economics*, 37(2), 345–70

10

On the introduction of endogenous labour income in deterministic and stochastic endogenous growth models

Stephen J. Turnovsky

1 INTRODUCTION

The introduction of labour income into both deterministic, and more particularly stochastic, endogenous growth models has been somewhat problematical. The standard AK model of Barro (1990) and Rebelo (1991) assumes either explicitly or implicitly that labour income is introduced in the form of a return to human capital. Rebelo does so explicitly, by introducing human as well as physical capital in production. But Barro does so only implicitly, by assuming that capital in the AK technology is sufficiently broadly defined to be an amalgam of physical and human capital, which are assumed to be perfect substitutes in the production process. Neither of these procedures is entirely satisfactory. The assumption that the two forms of capital are perfectly interchangeable is obviously a polar one. Introducing current labour through human capital, which can be accumulated only gradually, ignores the short-run labour–leisure tradeoffs. As a consequence, taxes levied on labour income and consumption both operate as lump-sum taxes, thereby failing to capture the distortionary effects of these taxes on the growth rate of the economy; see Turnovsky (2000a).

The problem for stochastic growth models is even more acute. The solution procedure proposed by Merton's (1969, 1971) pioneering work involves explicitly solving the stochastic Bellman equation for the value function. This is a task that is tractable only under very restrictive assumptions, namely that output be generated as a linear function of current wealth (capital), thereby in effect, being represented by a stochastic AK technology. As a consequence, Merton's approach and the literature that it spawned basically restricted itself to income from assets and ignored labour income; see Eaton (1981), Gertler and Grinols (1982), Grinols and Turnovsky (1993,

The comments of Marcelo Bianconi, Santanu Chatterjee, and William Smith are gratefully acknowledged.

1998), Obstfeld (1994), and Smith (1996). Indeed, presumably for this reason the most prominent area of application of these techniques has been to portfolio allocation problems in finance; see, e.g., Adler and Dumas (1983), Stulz (1981, 1983).[1]

In this chapter we show how the equilibrium growth path can be easily obtained for both deterministic and stochastic economies in the case where the production function is of the Romer (1986) form, in which output is a linear homogeneous function of (i) private capital and (ii) labour supply expressed in efficiency units. The latter is measured as the product of labour with the average economy-wide stock of capital, which the individual agent takes as given, but which in equilibrium accumulates endogenously along with private capital. This form of production function has begun to receive increasing attention in the growth literature. Ladrón-de-Guevara, Ortigueira and Santos (1997), and Turnovsky (2000a) employ a Cobb-Douglas version of such a function in a deterministic model, while Corsetti (1997) and Turnovsky (2000b) adopt an analogous formulation in analysing tax policy in a stochastic growth context.[2]

This approach resolves key problems associated with deriving equilibrium in an endogenous growth model with labour supply. Specifically, the aggregate production function is linearly homogeneous in both the accumulating asset (capital) – thereby fulfilling the requirement for endogenous growth – as well as in the private factors of production, labour and capital, thereby fulfilling the requirements for a competitive equilibrium. It requires that the externality to private production provided by aggregate capital exactly matches the productivity of labour in private production. This of course is a knife-edge condition, albeit an extremely important one, given the prominent role played by the Romer (1986) model in the new growth theory.[3]

The main objective is to provide a tractable solution for solving for the balanced growth equilibrium in a stochastically growing economy of this type. The novel feature of the approach is that, by following the analogous procedure to that employed to solve the deterministic problem, we can solve for the stochastic equilibrium without having to solve completely for the value function. As suggested by Chow (1997), this offers an enormous

---

[1] Corsetti (1997) introduces labour income as a return on the asset, human capital.

[2] Ladrón-de-Guevara, Ortigueira and Santos (1997) consider different specifications for labour and its interaction with human capital.

[3] Note that the technological assumptions we have made ensure that the economy is always on its stochastic balanced growth path. This contrasts with Bourguignon (1974) and Merton (1975), who assume a stochastic neoclassical technology, in which case the economy evolves along a stochastic transitional growth path.

advantage, since it enables us to avoid some of the intractability associated with obtaining the complete solution. By solving for the deterministic and stochastic problems in tandem, the parallels between them become clear, and the strategy for solving the more difficult stochastic problem becomes more transparent. In addition, while the optimised value function provides the basis for conducting welfare analysis in stochastic growth models, precisely the same objective can be achieved by evaluating the agent's utility function along the equilibrium growth path, again without requiring the explicit solution for the value function.

2 EQUILIBRIUM GROWTH IN A DETERMINISTIC ECONOMY

We consider an economy populated by a number of identical representative agents, normalised to be unity. Each agent is endowed with a unit of time that may be devoted either to work, l, or to leisure, $1 - l$. We assume that output of the representative firm is described by the production function:

$$Y = F[l\overline{K}, K] \tag{10.1}$$

where K denotes the firm's private stock of capital, l denotes the agent's labour and $\overline{K}$ denotes the average stock of capital in the economy, a proxy for the economy-wide level of knowledge. The quantity $l\overline{K}$ thus represents the quantity of labour measured in terms of efficiency units. Production is assumed to have the usual neoclassical properties of positive but diminishing marginal physical products, and constant returns to scale in private capital, K, and in labour measured in efficiency units, $l\overline{K}$. This in turn means that the production function has constant returns to scale in the accumulating factors, K and $\overline{K}$, necessary for endogenous growth, and constant returns to scale in the private factors, K and l, necessary for marginal product factor pricing to be consistent with a competitive equilibrium.

Using the linear homogeneity of (1), we may write:[4]

$$Y = K F\left(\frac{l\overline{K}}{K}, 1\right) \equiv K f\left(\frac{l\overline{K}}{K}\right).$$

With all agents being identical, in equilibrium, $K = \overline{K}$, $l = \bar{l}$, $Y = \overline{Y}$, (where bars denote economy-wide averages), so that the average economy-wide output is

$$\overline{Y} = \overline{K} f(\bar{l}) \tag{10.1'}$$

[4] We shall assume $f(0) = 0$, $f'(0) \to \infty$, properties that well-behaved production functions generally exhibit.

thus illustrating the aggregate AK technology. We assume that the wage rate, $w(t)$, and the return to capital, $r(t)$, are set in accordance with the marginal conditions

$$w(t) \equiv \left(\frac{\partial Y}{\partial l}\right)_{K=\overline{K}, l=\bar{l}} = \overline{K} f'(\bar{l}) \equiv \overline{K} \psi(\bar{l}) \qquad (10.2a)$$

$$r(t) \equiv \left(\frac{\partial Y}{\partial K}\right)_{K=\overline{K}, l=\bar{l}} = f(\bar{l}) - \bar{l} f'(\bar{l}) \equiv \phi(\bar{l}). \qquad (10.2b)$$

The agent's allocation problem is to choose $C(t)$, $l(t)$, and $K(t)$ to maximise the intertemporal utility function[5]

$$\int_0^\infty \frac{1}{\gamma}(C(1-l)^\theta)^\gamma e^{-\rho t} dt \qquad -\infty < \gamma < 1, \theta > 0, 1 > \gamma(1+\theta) \qquad (10.3a)$$

subject to the accumulation equation

$$\dot{K}(t) = r(t)K(t) + w(t)l(t) - C(t), \qquad (10.3b)$$

where $w(t)$, $r(t)$ are parametrically given to the agent. The optimality conditions are given by

$$C^{\gamma-1}(1-l)^{\theta\gamma} = \lambda \qquad (10.4a)$$

$$\theta C^\gamma (1-l)^{\theta\gamma-1} = \lambda w(t) \qquad (10.4b)$$

$$\rho - \frac{\dot{\lambda}}{\lambda} = r(t), \qquad (10.4c)$$

where λ denotes the shadow value of capital.

These conditions are well known. Dividing (10.4b) by (10.4a) equates the marginal rate of substitution between leisure and consumption to the real wage (which grows with capital):

$$\frac{\theta C}{1-l} = w(t) \qquad \frac{C}{K} = \frac{(1-l)}{\theta}\psi(\bar{l}). \qquad (10.5)$$

Using (10.2a), this implies that in equilibrium ($K = \overline{K}, C = \overline{C}, l = \bar{l}$)

$$\frac{C}{K} = \frac{(1-l)}{\theta}\psi(l); \qquad \frac{\overline{C}}{\overline{K}} = \frac{(1-\bar{l})}{\theta}\psi(\bar{l}) \qquad (10.5')$$

so that the equilibrium consumption–capital ratio is a decreasing function of labour supply. From (10.5) we also see that the implied equilibrium

---

[5] The restrictions on the exponents are imposed to ensure concavity of the utility function.

consumption–output ratio is:

$$\frac{C}{Y} = \frac{(1-l)}{l\theta}\eta \qquad (10.6)$$

where $\eta \equiv f'(l)l/f(l)$ is the elasticity of output with respect to labour supply.[6]

We shall consider an economy to be characterised by a long-run balanced growth path along which consumption, capital and output all grow at the same constant (endogenously determined) rate. With the consumption–capital ratio being constant along such a path, (10.5) implies that the equilibrium allocation of the fixed time between labour and leisure must be constant as well. Such an equilibrium of ongoing growth is indeed sustained by the constant elasticity utility function, (10.3a), together with the homogeneous production function, (10.1). But in contrast to the rather general specification of the production function, the necessary constancy of the equilibrium C/K ratio survives only marginal generalisations to the utility function. Specifically, the most general felicity function for which it still obtains is $U = V(1-l)C^\alpha$, where $V(.)$ is a general concave function.[7]

2.1 Macroeconomic equilibrium

Since in macroeconomic equilibrium all agents behave identically, we can drop the distinction between individuals and averages. We shall characterise the macroeconomic equilibrium in terms of a differential equation in labour supply, l. To derive this, we begin by taking the time derivative of the optimality condition (10.4a) and combine with (10.4c), to give:

$$\frac{\dot{C}}{C} = \frac{\phi(l) - \rho - \theta\gamma\dot{l}/(1-l)}{1-\gamma}. \qquad (10.7a)$$

Next, substituting $w(t)$, $r(t)$ into the accumulation equation (10.3b), yields the product market equilibrium condition

$$\frac{\dot{K}}{K} = f(l) - c \qquad (10.7b)$$

---

[6] In the case of the Cobb–Douglas production function, the productive elasticity η is constant.

[7] The reason for this is that in order for (10.5) to generate a constant C/K ratio we require $\frac{\partial U/\partial(1-l)}{\partial U/\partial C} = h(1-l)C$, the solution to which is $U = V(1-l)C^\alpha$.

where for convenience $c \equiv C/K$. First, differentiating $c \equiv C/K$ with respect to time and utilising (10.7a) and (10.7b), and second, taking the time derivative of (10.5′), we can express the macroeconomic equilibrium by the following differential equation in the fraction of time devoted to labour:

$$\frac{dl}{dt} = \frac{G(l)}{H(l)} \tag{10.8}$$

where

$$G(l) \equiv \frac{\rho - \phi(l)}{1 - \gamma} + f(l) - \frac{1}{\theta}(1 - l)\psi(l);$$

$$H(l) \equiv \frac{1}{1 - l}\left(\frac{1 - \gamma(1 + \theta)}{1 - \gamma}\right) - \frac{\psi'}{\psi} > 0.$$

The local stability of (10.8) in the neighbourhood of the steady state, crucial to the qualitative nature of the equilibrium, depends upon

$$sgn(G'(l)) = sgn\left(f'\left(1 + \frac{1}{\theta}\right) - f''\left(\frac{1 - l}{\theta} - \frac{l}{1 - \gamma}\right)\right).$$

2.2 Balanced growth equilibrium

Steady-state equilibrium is attained when the fraction of time allocated to labour supply is constant. Setting $\dot{l} = 0$ in (10.8), the steady state is characterised by the balanced growth condition:

$$\frac{\dot{C}}{C} = \frac{\dot{K}}{K} = \frac{\dot{Y}}{Y} \equiv \tilde{\omega}.$$

Thus (10.7a) implies:

RR: $\quad \omega = \dfrac{f(l) - lf'(l) - \rho}{1 - \gamma} \equiv X(l) \tag{10.9a}$

while substituting (10.5′) into (10.7b) leads to

PP: $\quad \omega = f(l) - \dfrac{(1 - l)f'(l)}{\theta} \equiv Y(l). \tag{10.9b}$

RR and PP describe a pair of tradeoff locuses relating the equilibrium growth rate ω and labour supply l. RR describes the tradeoff locus between ω and l that ensures the equality between the rate of return on capital and the rate of return on consumption, while PP describes the corresponding tradeoff locus that ensures product market equilibrium. The intersection of these two curves, obtained by setting $X(l) = Y(l)$, determines the steady-state equilibrium labour supply, $\tilde{l}$, and the corresponding growth rate, $\tilde{\omega}$.

We can show from (10.9a) and (10.9b) that both locuses are positively sloped throughout and that[8]

$$Y'(l) - X'(l) = f'\left(1 + \frac{1}{\theta}\right) - f''\left(\frac{(1-l)}{\theta} - \frac{l}{1-\gamma}\right) = G'(l).$$
(10.10)

Imposing the condition $X(l) = Y(l)$, we see that in the neighbourhood of the equilibrium

$$Y'(l) - X'(l) = f'\left(1 + \frac{1}{\theta}\right) + \frac{f''}{f'}\left(\frac{\gamma f - \rho}{1 - \gamma}\right).$$
(10.11)

Suppose $\gamma < 0$, i.e. the intertemporal elasticity of substitution less than 1, as the empirical evidence strongly supports; see, e.g., Mankiw, Rotemberg and Summers (1985), and Ogaki and Reinhart (1998). Then, from (10.10) $Y'(l) > X'(l)$ at the point of intersection. Given the fact that $Y(0) < X(0)$, it follows that $X(l)$, $Y(l)$ intersect at a unique point, at which $G'(\tilde{l}) = Y'(\tilde{l}) - X'(\tilde{l}) > 0$.[9] It therefore follows that there is a unique stationary equilibrium and the dynamics (10.8) are associated with unstable behaviour. The only solution consistent with a balanced growth equilibrium is for $l = \tilde{l}$ at all points of time, so that the economy is always on the balanced growth path (10.9a), (10.9b).

Figure 10.1 plots the two equilibrium locuses for the Cobb–Douglas production function, $Y = A(\bar{l}K)^\beta K^\beta$ for the plausible parameter set $A = 0.6, \beta = 0.64, \gamma = -1.5, \rho = 0.04, \theta = 1.75.$[10] There is clearly a unique intersection point, at which we obtain the plausible equilibrium values $\tilde{l} = 0.285, \tilde{\omega} = 2.27$ per cent. The general shapes of the RR and

[8] That is, $X' = -lf''/(1 - \gamma) > 0$, $Y' = f'(1 + 1/\theta) - (1 - l)f''/\theta > 0$. Since a greater labour supply raises the productivity of capital, and therefore the return to capital, it must be accompanied by a higher growth rate in order for the rate of return on consumption to rise correspondingly. Likewise, since it also raises output and the consumption–capital ratio, a higher growth rate is required in order for goods market equilibrium to be maintained.

[9] Assuming that the conditions in n. 3 hold, $X(0) = -\rho/(1 - \gamma)$, $Y(0) \to -\infty$. Thus it follows that at the initial point of intersection the PP locus cuts the RR locus from below, consistent with $G'(l) > 0$. Should there be a second equilibrium point, then at that point PP would intersect RR from above, violating the condition $G'(l) > 0$, which we know holds at all equilibrium points. Therefore the two curves intersect at only one point.

[10] The exponent $\beta = 0.64$ implies that 64 per cent of output is attributable to labour; $\rho = 0.04$ is a 4 per cent rate of time discount; $\gamma = -1.5$ corresponds to an intertemporal elasticity of substitution of 0.4; $\theta = 1.75$ is the standard weight on leisure in utility assumed in the real business cycle literature; see Cooley (1995).

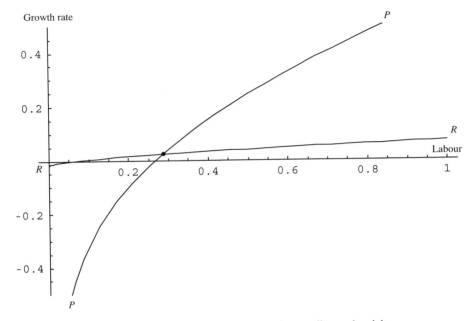

Figure 10.1 Equilibrium growth rate and time allocated to labour

PP curves are quite stable across all plausible parameter sets, and thus the qualitative nature of this equilibrium is quite robust.

Given $\bar{l}$ and $\bar{\omega}$, the product market equilibrium condition (10.7b) determines the equilibrium consumption–capital ratio, $\bar{c}$, by

$$\bar{c} = f(\bar{l}) - \bar{\omega}. \tag{10.12}$$

Substituting for $\bar{\omega}$ from (10.9a), $\bar{c}$ may be written in the more familiar form

$$\bar{c} = \frac{\rho - \gamma[f(\bar{l}) - \bar{l}f'(\bar{l})]}{1 - \gamma} + \bar{l}f'(\bar{l}) \equiv \frac{\rho - \gamma\bar{r}}{1 - \gamma} + \frac{\bar{l}\bar{w}}{K}. \tag{10.13}$$

The first term on the right-hand side of (10.13) is the standard expression for the C/K obtained in the absence of labour income. The second term adjusts this for the presence of labour income, which quantitatively dominates the first and more familiar term. For example, assuming the above parameters the first term is about 0.08, while the second term is around 0.20, implying an overall value $\bar{c}$ of about 0.28. Taking $C/Y \approx 0.6$, $K/Y \approx 3$ to be empirically plausible values, we find that empirically c is around 0.20 so that the inclusion of labour income is important for the successful calibration of this model.

The other condition to be met is the transversality condition, $\lim_{t\to\infty} \lambda K e^{-pt} = 0$. Evaluating this expression, it reduces to $\tilde{r} > \tilde{\omega}$; that is, the return on capital must exceed the equilibrium growth rate. Using (10.9a) this is equivalent to $\rho > \gamma\tilde{r}$, and from (10.13), this in turn is equivalent to $\tilde{c} > \tilde{w}\tilde{l}/\tilde{K} \equiv \tilde{l} f'(\tilde{l})$; that is, the consumption–output ratio must exceed the labour share of output, so that some consumption is financed out of asset income. In the absence of labour income, this reduces to the standard condition $\tilde{c} > 0$ (Merton 1969). Finally, combining with (10.5′), while recalling (10.2a), the transversality condition reduces to the following simple constraint on the equilibrium labour supply

$$1 > \tilde{l}(1 + \theta). \tag{10.14}$$

This condition is clearly met for the equilibrium values in figure 10.1 [$\theta = 1.75, \tilde{l} = 0.285$] and is universally met for any plausible parameterisation of the elasticity of leisure in utility, θ, and the corresponding equilibrium time devoted to labour.[11]

3 EQUILIBRIUM IN A STOCHASTICALLY GROWING ECONOMY

We turn now to the analogous stochastically growing economy and begin by presenting the stochastic generalisation of the production function formulated in section 2. Specifically, we assume that production over the period $(t, t + dt)$ takes place in accordance with

$$dY = F(\overline{lK}, K)(dt + dy) \tag{10.15}$$

where F has the properties introduced previously and dy is a Brownian motion process having mean zero and variance $\sigma_y^2 dt$ over the instant dt.[12] Given the homogeneity of F we may write

$$dY = Kf\left(\frac{\overline{lK}}{K}\right)(dt + dy)$$

---

[11] Most endogenous growth models assume an inelastic labour supply. Assuming l is fixed at $l = \hat{l}$, the optimality condition (4b) ceases to be applicable. The equilibrium growth rate and consumption to capital ratios are now jointly determined by (10.9a) and (10.12) (or (10.13)), with $l = \hat{l}$.

[12] In contrast to most stochastic growth models, which typically are restricted to the simplest production technologies, we do not impose any specific functional form on the production function F, which therefore includes more general functions such as the CES. Examples of stochastic growth models using the CES function include the two-period model of Benhabib and Rustichini (1994) and García-Peñalosa and Turnovsky (2001) who use the CES version of (10.15) to analyse the impact of volatility on income distribution.

and with all agents being identical and subject to common economy-wide shocks, the average economy-wide stochastic output is given by:

$$d\overline{Y} = \overline{K}f(\overline{l})(dt + dy).\tag{10.15'}$$

We assume that the wage rate $w(t)$ over the period $(t, t + dt)$ is determined at the start of the period and is set equal to the expected marginal physical product of labour over that period. The total rate of return to labour over the period is thus specified non-stochastically by

$$dW \equiv w(t)dt = E\left(\frac{\partial Y}{\partial l}\right)_{K=\overline{K}, l=\overline{l}} dt = \overline{K} f'(\overline{l})dt \equiv \overline{K}\psi(\overline{l})dt.\tag{10.2a'}$$

The private rate of return to capital, dR, over the period $(t, t + dt)$ is thus determined residually by

$$dR \equiv rdt + du = \frac{d\overline{Y} - \overline{l}dW}{\overline{K}} = (f(\overline{l}) - \overline{l}f'(\overline{l}))dt + f(\overline{l})dy$$

$$\equiv \phi(\overline{l})dt + f(\overline{l})dy.\tag{10.2b'}$$

According to this specification, the wage rate, w, is fixed over the period $(t, t + dt)$, with all short-run fluctuations in output being reflected in the stochastic return to capital. While this allocation of risk may seem extreme, empirical evidence suggests that the return to capital is far more volatile than are wages.[13] Equations (10.2a') thus are the stochastic analogues to (10.2b') in that assuming that the equilibrium fraction of time allocated to labour is constant, the mean rate of return to capital is constant through time, while the wage rate grows stochastically with the equilibrium capital stock.

The representative agent's stochastic optimisation problem is to choose consumption, labour supply and the rate of capital accumulation to maximise:

$$E_0 \int_0^\infty \frac{1}{\gamma}(C(t)(1 - l)^\theta)^\gamma e^{-\rho t} dt\tag{10.3a'}$$

subject to the stochastic capital (wealth) accumulation equation:

$$dK = (rK(t) + w(t)l - C)dt + K(t)du\tag{10.3b'}$$

---

[13] See chapter 3, footnote 18. The assumption that the wage rate is a non-stochastic function of the current capital stock is important to the solution procedure.

where, as before, the agent takes w, r as given, and now $du \equiv f(\bar{l})dy$. Dividing (1b) by K, we can express this equation as

$$\frac{dK}{K} = \left(r + \frac{w(t)l}{K} - \frac{C}{K} \right) dt + du \equiv \omega dt + du, \quad (10.3b'')$$

where w now denotes the mean growth rate.

Equation (10.2a′) specifies that the equilibrium wage rate is tied to aggregate capital (wealth) and thus is beyond the control of the individual agent. In equilibrium, with all agents identical, $\overline{K}$ will in fact grow at the same rate as K, in which case along the equilibrium balanced growth path, $w(t)/K$ is constant. But the individual in making his decisions does not perceive this. Instead, he perceives his wage rate as growing exogenously with time, independently of his own capital, $K(t)$, and hence we write $w(t)$.

Since the individual perceives the state variable, K, and since time appears both additively (through $w(t)$) and through the exponential time discounting, we propose a value function of the time-separable form

$$V(K, t) = e^{-\rho t}[X(K) + H(t)]. \quad (10.16)$$

Defining the differential generator of the value function $V(K, t)$ to be

$$\Psi[V(K, t)] \equiv \frac{\partial V}{\partial t} + (rK + w(t)l - C)\frac{\partial V}{\partial K} + \frac{1}{2}\sigma_u^2 K^2 \frac{\partial^2 V}{\partial K^2} \quad (10.17)$$

the individual's formal optimisation problem is to choose C, l to maximise:

$$e^{-\rho t}\frac{1}{\gamma}(C(1 - l)^\theta) + \Psi[e^{-\rho t}[X(K) + H(t)]]. \quad (10.18)$$

Taking the partial derivatives of (10.18) with respect to C, l and cancelling $e^{-\rho t}$, yields

$$C^{\gamma - 1}(1 - l)^{\theta \gamma} = X_K(K) \quad (10.19a)$$
$$\theta C^\gamma (1 - l)^{\theta \gamma - 1} = w(t)X_K(K) = \overline{K}\psi(\bar{l})\, X_K(K) \quad (10.19b)$$

where $X_K(K)$ is the marginal value of an extra unit of capital, and thus is identical to the shadow λ price introduced in the deterministic optimisation problem. Dividing (10.19b) by (10.19a) leads to (10.5) and (10.5′), which therefore continue to hold unchanged. With the consumption and labour supply implied by (10.19a), (10.19b) being deterministic functions of K and $w(t)$, the marginal rate of substitution between them is unaffected by the production risk in the economy. In principle, we may solve these equations to obtain the following expressions for the individual's consumption and labour supply[14]

$$C = C(K, w(t)) \qquad (10.20a)$$

$$l = l(K, w(t)). \qquad (10.20b)$$

In addition, the value function must satisfy the Bellman equation

$$\max_{C,l} \left\{ e^{-\rho t} \frac{1}{\gamma} (C(1 - l)^\theta)^\gamma + \Psi[e^{-\rho t}[X(K) + H(t)]] \right\} = 0 \qquad (10.21)$$

which may be expressed as (where dot denotes time derivative):

$$\frac{1}{\gamma} [C(K, w(t)) l(K, w(t))^\theta]^\gamma - \rho[X(K) + H(t)] + \dot{H}(t)$$

$$+ (rK + w(t)l(K, w(t)) - C(K, w(t)))X_K(K)$$

$$+ \frac{1}{2} K^2 X_{KK}(K) \sigma_u^2 = 0. \qquad (10.22)$$

This Bellman equation holds for all values of K, at all points of time t. Thus we can take the partial derivative of this equation with respect to K. In so doing, we note that $H(t)$ is independent of (the agent's) K, while through the optimality conditions (10.19a, 10.19b), C (and potentially l) is a function of K. Performing this calculation yields the following condition:

$$C^{\gamma-1}(1 - l)^{\theta\gamma} \partial C/\partial K - \theta C^\gamma (1 - l)^{\theta\gamma-1} \partial l/\partial K$$

$$- \rho X_K + (r - \partial C/\partial K + w \partial l/\partial K)X_K + [rK + w(t)l - C]X_{KK}$$

$$+ \sigma_u^2 K X_{KK} + \frac{1}{2} \sigma_u^2 K^2 X_{KKK} = 0$$

and using (10.19a, 10.19b) this reduces to

$$(r - \rho)X_K + [rW + w(t)l - C]X_{KK} + \sigma_u^2 K X_{KK}$$

$$+ \frac{1}{2} \sigma_u^2 K^2 X_{KKK} = 0. \qquad (10.23)$$

Consider now $X_K = X_K(K)$, the stochastic differential of which is:

$$dX_K = X_{KK} dK + \frac{1}{2} X_{KKK}(dK)^2. \qquad (10.24)$$

---

[14] It can be shown that l in (10.20b) is an increasing function of $w(t)$ but a decreasing function of K. This is because, while an increase in the real wage encourages a substitution toward more labour, an increase in K reduces the marginal utility of wealth (capital) thereby inducing the agent to supply less labour. In equilibrium w increases linearly with K so that these two effects are exactly offsetting and the labour supply is in fact constant, independent of the growing capital stock.

Taking expected values of (10.24), and dividing by dt, implies

$$\frac{E(dX_K)}{dt} = [rK + w(t)l - C]X_{KK} + \frac{1}{2}\sigma_u^2 K^2 X_{KKK} \qquad (10.25)$$

and substituting (10.25) into (10.23) leads to the relationship:

$$\frac{E(dX_K)}{X_K dt} = (\rho - r) - \sigma_u^2 \frac{K X_{KK}}{X_K}. \qquad (10.26)$$

The solution to this equation is by trial and error. Given the form of the objective function, we propose:

$$X(K) = \varepsilon K^\gamma \qquad (10.27)$$

where the parameter ε is to be determined. Evaluating the partial derivatives $X_K(K)$, $X_{KK}(K)$ and substituting into (10.26), the expected marginal utility evolves in accordance with:

$$\frac{E(dX_K)}{X_K dt} = (\rho - r) + \sigma_u^2 (1 - \gamma). \qquad (10.28)$$

The key observation is that (10.28) is the stochastic analogue to the standard deterministic intertemporal efficiency condition (10.4c). It asserts that the expected utility return to consumption, $\rho - E(dX_K)/X_K dt$, equals the risk-adjusted expected return to investment, $r - (1 - \gamma)\sigma_u^2$. From (10.24) the actual marginal utility follows the stochastic process

$$\frac{dX_K}{X_K} = \left(\rho - r + \sigma_u^2 (1 - \gamma)\right)dt - (1 - \gamma)du.$$

Any positive shock to productivity, by making capital more abundant, induces a negative shock to its marginal utility.

3.1 Macroeconomic equilibrium

As in the deterministic economy, in macroeconomic equilibrium we can drop the distinction between individuals and average. In view of the fact that the analogous deterministic economy is always on its balanced growth path, it is reasonable to focus on the stochastic balanced growth path, along which both C and K evolve at the same stochastic rate, so that C/K remains constant. The optimality condition equation (10.5′) – which we have noted continues to apply to the stochastic economy – then implies the associated equilibrium with a constant fraction of time allocated to labour.

To determine the equilibrium growth path, we follow a procedure analogous to that adopted in the deterministic case, and begin by recalling the optimality condition (10.19a). Taking the stochastic differential of this equation, with l constant, implies

$$\frac{dX_K}{X_K} = (\gamma - 1)\frac{dC}{C} + \frac{1}{2}(\gamma - 1)(\gamma - 2)\left(\frac{dC}{C}\right)^2$$

and taking expected values yields:

$$\frac{E(dX_K)}{X_K} = (\gamma - 1)\frac{E(dC)}{C} + \frac{1}{2}(\gamma - 1)(\gamma - 2)E\left(\frac{dC}{C}\right)^2. \quad (10.29)$$

Now consider (10.3b''), which along a stochastic balanced growth path when C/K is constant becomes

$$\frac{dC}{C} = \frac{dK}{K} = \left(r + \frac{w(t)l}{K} - \frac{C}{K}\right)dt + du \equiv \omega dt + du.$$

From this equation we obtain

$$\frac{E(dC)}{C} = \omega dt; \quad E\left(\frac{dC}{C}\right)^2 = \sigma_u^2 dt$$

and substituting these quantities into (29) we may write:

$$\frac{E(dX_K)}{X_K dt} = (\gamma - 1)\omega + \frac{1}{2}(\gamma - 1)(\gamma - 2)\sigma_u^2. \quad (10.30)$$

Equating (10.28) and (10.30) we may express the equilibrium growth rate in the form

$$\omega = \frac{r - \rho + (1/2)\gamma(\gamma - 1)\sigma_u^2}{1 - \gamma}. \quad (10.31)$$

Recalling the definitions of r and $du = f(l)dy$, we obtain $\sigma_u^2 = f(l)^2\sigma_y^2$, enabling (10.31) to be written:

$$\textbf{RR:} \quad \omega = \frac{f(l) - lf'(l) - \rho + (1/2)\gamma(\gamma - 1)f(l)^2\sigma_y^2}{1 - \gamma} \equiv X(l).$$
$$(10.9a')$$

Likewise, substituting r and w into the definition of ω, we obtain

$$c = f(l) - \omega \quad (10.11)$$

and combining with (10.5′) we obtain

$$\textbf{PP:} \quad \omega = f(l) - \frac{(1-l)f'(l)}{\theta} \equiv Y(l). \tag{10.9b}$$

Equations (10.9a′), (10.9b) describe the analogous tradeoffs between the (mean) growth rate and the fraction of time devoted to labour, to those described previously by (10.9a) and (10.9b). The only difference is that the variance term is introduced into (10.9a′) to reflect the impact of risk in the return to consumption on the one hand, and investment, on the other. The effect of this is to shift the RR curve up or down in figure 10.1, according to whether $\gamma < 0$, or $\gamma > 0$. The tradeoff described by the PP curve remains unchanged.[15] An immediate consequence is that an increase in production risk raises the equilibrium mean growth rate, $\bar{\omega}$, and the fraction of time devoted to labour supply, $\bar{l}$, iff $\gamma < 0$. In addition, the equilibrium volatility of the growth path $\bar{\sigma}_u = f(\bar{l})\sigma_y$, and will respond both directly to an increase in exogenous volatility, σ_y, and indirectly through the response in $\bar{l}$.[16] Substituting (10.9a′) into (10.11), we can solve for the consumption–wealth ratio, C/K, as:

$$\bar{c} = \frac{\rho - \gamma[f(\bar{l}) - \bar{l}f'(\bar{l})] - (1/2)\gamma(\gamma - 1)f(\bar{l})^2\sigma_y^2}{1 - \gamma} + \bar{l}f'(\bar{l}). \tag{10.12′}$$

The parallels between the stochastic equilibrium obtained in this section and the deterministic equilibrium obtained previously are clear and indeed, the two procedures we have adopted are essentially analogous. In both cases we have first obtained the equilibrium growth rate from the evolution of the shadow value and we have then determined the corresponding *equilibrium* C/K residually from the accumulation equation.[17] The advantage of this is that in the stochastic case, we did not need to specify much about the value function. Note that all we specified was that $X(K) = \varepsilon K^\gamma$. But to this point we have not determined ε and we have said nothing about

---

[15] For plausible degrees of risk, σ_y, the shape of the RR curve is subject to only minor changes, so that its intersection with the PP curve in general still jointly determines unique equilibrium values for $\bar{\omega}$ and $\bar{l}$.

[16] An increase in the flexibility of labour, as expressed by an increase in θ, pushes the PP curve up, reducing l, and reducing the volatility of the growth rate. This is a general equilibrium version of the result due to Bodie, Merton and Samuelson (1992), stating that labour supply flexibility helps smooth consumption by buffering risk.

[17] We wish to make it clear that (10.12′) determines the consumption–capital ratio along the equilibrium balanced growth path; it is not a consumption function *per se*.

$H(.)$. This is consistent with the general approach advocated by Chow (1997). There he argues that making efficient use of information about the Lagrange multipliers enables one to economise on information regarding the complete form of the value function.

But this procedure contrasts sharply with how stochastic growth models are typically solved. The usual procedure is first to solve the Bellman equation for the value function and thus obtain the consumption–capital ratio. Having obtained the consumption–capital ratio, the equilibrium (mean) growth rate is then obtained from the product market equilibrium condition, precisely the reverse to the approach we have just discussed; see, e.g., Corsetti (1997), Grinols and Turnovsky (1993, 1998).[18]

3.2 Solving for the value function

But of course the Bellman equation must still be satisfied, so we need to examine it. First, recall the optimality condition (10.19a). Evaluating this for the value function (10.27) implies $C^{\gamma-1}(1-l)^{\theta\gamma} = \varepsilon\gamma K^{\gamma-1}$, so that

$$C = (\varepsilon\gamma)^{1/(\gamma-1)}(1-l)^{-\theta\gamma/(\gamma-1)}K. \qquad (10.32)$$

Combining (10.32) with (10.12′) we obtain

$$\bar{c} = (\bar{\varepsilon}\gamma)^{1/(\gamma-1)}(1-\bar{l})^{-\theta\gamma/(\gamma-1)}$$

$$= \frac{\rho - \gamma\bar{r} + (1-\gamma)\dfrac{\bar{w}\bar{l}}{K} - \dfrac{1}{2}\gamma(\gamma-1)\bar{\sigma}_u^2}{1-\gamma} \qquad (10.33)$$

where $\bar{r} = f(\bar{l}) - \bar{l}f'(\bar{l})$, $\bar{w} = f'(\bar{l})\overline{K}$, and $\bar{\sigma}_u^2 = f(\bar{l})\sigma_y^2$. Having previously obtained $\bar{c}$ and $\bar{l}$, this equation determines $\bar{\varepsilon}$.

Now return to the Bellman equation, (10.22), written as

$$\frac{1}{\gamma}[\bar{C}(1-\bar{l})^\theta]^\gamma - \rho[X(K) + H(t)] + \dot{H}(t) + (\bar{r}K + \bar{w}\bar{l} - \bar{C})X_K(K)$$

$$+ \frac{1}{2}K^2 X_{KK}(K)\bar{\sigma}_u^2 = 0.$$

---

[18] We may contrast these procedures with that adopted by Chang (1988), who begins by assuming a consumption function of a particular form, and then derives the restrictions on the utility function consistent with the assumed form of consumption function.

Substituting for (10.33) and recalling the assumed form of $X(K)$ in (10.27), we can write this in the form

$$
K^\gamma \bar{\varepsilon} \left[(1-\gamma)(\bar{\varepsilon}\gamma)^{1/(\gamma-1)}(1-\bar{l})^{-\theta\gamma/(1-\gamma)} - \rho + \gamma\bar{r} + \gamma \frac{\bar{w}\bar{l}}{K} \right.
$$

$$
\left. + \frac{1}{2}\gamma(\gamma-1)\bar{\sigma}_u^2 \right] + \dot{H}(t) - \rho H(t) = 0. \tag{10.34}
$$

Note that in the standard case where there is no labour income, $l = 0$, the correct conjecture is $H(t) \equiv 0 = \dot{H}(t)$, in which case (10.33) reduces to the standard expression; Eaton (1981), Grinols and Turnovsky (1993) and Corsetti (1997):

$$
\left(\frac{\bar{C}}{K} \right) = (\bar{\varepsilon}\gamma)^{1/(1-\gamma)} = \frac{\rho - \gamma\bar{r} - (1/2)\gamma(\gamma-1)\bar{\sigma}_u^2}{1-\gamma}. \tag{10.33'}
$$

But substituting (10.33) with labour income present into (10.34), the latter reduces to the following differential equation in $H(t)$, namely

$$
\dot{H}(t) - \rho H(t) = -\bar{\varepsilon}K^{\gamma-1}\bar{w}\bar{l}. \tag{10.35}
$$

Since future values of K are not yet known, the bounded solution to this equation is

$$
H(t) = E_t \int_t^\infty \bar{\varepsilon}K(s)^{\gamma-1}\bar{w}\bar{l}e^{-\rho(s-t)}ds. \tag{10.36}
$$

This equation has an intuitive interpretation. It asserts that the (utility) value associated with the labour income stream, that the agent takes as exogenously given, is equal to the discounted expected stream of future wage income evaluated at the marginal utility of income, $\varepsilon K^{\gamma-1}$.

The solution for the value function is thus of the form:

$$
V(K, t) = e^{-\rho t}\frac{1}{\gamma}(1-\bar{l})^{\theta\gamma}\left(\frac{\bar{C}}{K} \right)^{\gamma-1}
$$

$$
\times \left[K^\gamma + E_t \int_t^\infty K(s)^{\gamma-1}\bar{w}\bar{l}e^{-\rho(s-t)}ds \right]. \tag{10.37}
$$

Taking appropriate derivatives and substituting back into (10.22), while noting (10.34), we find that (10.37) does indeed satisfy the Bellman equation. Expressed in this way, we see that the value function at any point of time has a *backward-looking* component, associated with current income earned from assets accumulated in the past, together with a *forward-looking* component, associated with expected future labour income.

But the fact that $w(t) = f'(l)\overline{K}$ and therefore grows stochastically with capital along the equilibrium balanced growth path, enables us to simplify (10.36) substantially. First, we may express $H(t)$ in the form

$$H(t) = \bar{\varepsilon}\bar{l} f'(\bar{l}) E_t \int_t^\infty K(s)^\gamma e^{-\rho(s-t)} ds. \tag{10.38}$$

Next, solving the accumulation equation (10.3b″) implies

$$K(s) = K(t)\exp\{(\bar{\omega} - \bar{\sigma}_u^2)(s - t) + u(s) - u(t)\} \tag{10.39}$$

and using the fact that $u(s) - u(t)$ is log-normal, we see that

$$E_t[K(s)^\gamma e^{-\rho(s-t)}] = K(t)^\gamma \exp\{\{\gamma(\bar{\omega} - (1/2)(1 - \gamma)\bar{\sigma}_u^2) - \rho\}(s - t)\}. \tag{10.40}$$

Combining with (10.31), (10.40) can be written as

$$E_t[K(s)^\gamma e^{-\rho(s-t)}] = K(t)^\gamma \exp\{\bar{\omega} - \bar{r}\}(s - t). \tag{10.41}$$

Setting $t = 0$ in (10.41) we find that the transversality condition,

$$\lim_{s \to \infty} E_0\{X_K K e^{-\rho s}\} = \lim_{s \to \infty} E_0\{\bar{\varepsilon}K(s)^\gamma e^{-\rho s}\} = 0$$

is equivalent to $\bar{r} > \bar{\omega}$ as before, and in turn to $\bar{c} > \bar{w}\bar{l}/\bar{K} \equiv \bar{l} f'(\bar{l})$, which upon combining with (10.5′), again reduces to (10.14), namely $1 > \bar{l}(1 + \theta)$.

Finally, reversing the order of integration and expectation in (10.38), and using (10.33″) and (10.41), yields

$$H(t) = \frac{\bar{\varepsilon}\bar{l}\bar{f}' K(t)^\gamma}{\bar{r} - \bar{\omega}} = \frac{1}{\gamma} \frac{(\bar{c})^{\gamma-1}\bar{l}\bar{f}'(1 - \bar{l})^{\theta\gamma} K(t)^\gamma}{\bar{c} - \bar{l}\bar{f}'}. \tag{10.42}$$

Summing $e^{-\rho t}(\bar{\varepsilon}K^\gamma + H(t))$ yields

$$\begin{aligned}
V(K(t), t) &= e^{-\rho t}\left\{\frac{1}{\gamma}(\bar{c})^{\gamma-1}(1 - \bar{l})^{\theta\gamma} K(t)^\gamma \right. \\
&\quad \left. + \frac{1}{\gamma}\frac{(\bar{c})^{\gamma-1}(1 - \bar{l})^{\theta\gamma}\bar{l} f' K(t)^\gamma}{\bar{c} - \bar{l}\bar{f}'}\right\} \\
&= e^{-\rho t}\frac{1}{\gamma}\frac{(\bar{c})^\gamma(1 - \bar{l})^{\theta\gamma} K(t)^\gamma}{\bar{c} - \bar{l}\bar{f}'}.
\end{aligned} \tag{10.43}$$

Equation (10.43) thus splits the value function into two components. The first, given by the first term on the right-hand side of (10.43) measures the consumption–leisure benefits associated with investment income. The second component measures the consumption–leisure benefits derived from expected future labour income. From (10.43) we see that the fraction of the overall consumption–leisure benefits due to labour income is equal to $\bar{l} f'(\bar{l})/\bar{c}$, which recalling (10.5') equals $\bar{l}\theta/(1 - \bar{l})$. By the transversality condition, this is less than one. This implies that part of consumption–leisure expenditure is financed from asset income. The transversality condition can therefore be interpreted as ensuring that asset income does indeed yield positive consumption–leisure benefits. Nevertheless, evaluating $\bar{l}\theta/(1 - \bar{l})$ for the typical parameterisation, $\bar{l} \approx 0.285, \bar{\theta} \approx 1.75$, implies that nearly 70 per cent of consumption benefits arise from current and expected future labour income, thereby underscoring the importance of the inclusion of labour income.

3.3 Evaluation of welfare along the equilibrium path

A key issue concerns the implications of policy and other shocks on the welfare of the representative agent. This can be evaluated in two ways. The first is by evaluating the optimised value function. Starting from the initial capital stock, K_0, this is given by the expression, $V(K_0, 0)$ and is obtained from (10.43). The evaluation of this expression involves the explicit solution of the value function, as we have done.

Alternatively, it can be obtained by substituting for the equilibrium paths for $\bar{C}, \bar{l}$ into the agent's utility function (10.3a') and then evaluating the intertemporal utility. This does not require the explicit solution for the value function and for that reason is more direct. These two procedures should yield the same value and thus serve as a check on our solution for the value function itself.

Evaluating, (10.3a') we obtain

$$\Omega \equiv E_0 \int_0^\infty \frac{1}{\gamma} (\bar{c}^\gamma (1 - \bar{l})^{\theta\gamma} K(t) e^{-\rho t} dt = K_0 (c(1 - \bar{l})^\theta)^\gamma$$

$$E_0 \int_0^\infty e^{\gamma(\bar{\omega} - (1/2)(1-\gamma)\bar{\sigma}_u^2 - \rho)t} dt = \frac{1}{\gamma} \frac{(\bar{c}(1 - \bar{l})^\theta)^\gamma K_0^\gamma}{\bar{c} - \bar{l} f'(\bar{l})} \quad (10.44)$$

which indeed is identical to (10.43). This confirms our solution for the value function.

Equation (10.44) can be used to evaluate the effects of policy shocks and structural changes on welfare, through their impacts on the equilibrium consumption–capital ratio and the fraction of time allocated to labour supply. Moreover, using the static optimality condition (10.5′), we can express the welfare in terms of $\bar{l}$ alone, namely:[19]

$$\Omega = \frac{(1 - \bar{l})^{\gamma(1+\theta)} f'(\bar{l})^{\gamma-1}}{\gamma\theta^{\gamma-1}(1 - \bar{l}(1 + \theta))} K_0^{\gamma}.$$

4 CONCLUSIONS

The purpose of this chapter has been to show how the introduction of endogenously supplied labour in a stochastic endogenous growth model of the Romer (1986) type can be accomplished in a tractable way. Solving for the macroeconomic equilibrium in a parallel way to the procedure usually adopted to solve the analogous deterministic model enables one to determine the equilibrium without solving completely for the value function. By considering the time derivative of the optimal consumption allocation condition, we can solve for the equilibrium growth rate with only partial knowledge of the value function. And having determined the equilibrium growth rate, we can then solve for the equilibrium consumption–capital ratio residually from the product market equilibrium condition. Finally, having obtained the macroeconomic equilibrium, we can then solve for the value function itself, although any welfare analysis can be conducted by evaluating the intertemporal welfare function directly, and again does not require the explicit solution for the value function. As emphasised by Chow (1997), the approach adopted here, which by exploiting the properties of the shadow values thus avoids the potential intractability of solving for the value function, has a substantial advantage.

One final point should be noted. A key element of our solution procedure is to recognise the impact of the wage rate on the agent's welfare through the function $H(t)$. The rationale here is that the agent perceives the wage rate as evolving exogenously with time, although we recognise that in macroeconomic equilibrium the wage rate is in fact tied to the endogenously growing aggregate capital in the economy. Thus with all agents being identical, a balanced growth equilibrium can be sustained.

---

[19] Finally, we may note that in the case that labour is supplied inelastically, at $l = \hat{l}$ say, the equilibrium growth rate is determined by (10.9a′), with the corresponding consumption–capital ratio being determined by (10.11); the optimality condition, (10.5′) ceases to be applicable. In that case welfare can be assessed through its impact on $\bar{c}$ in the function (10.44).

An alternative approach is to introduce the aggregate capital stock as a second state variable, one that the individual agent does not influence, but one which through the equilibrium wage does impact on the decisions and welfare of the individual. With all agents identical, in equilibrium both the individual and aggregate capital stock move together, so that the macroeconomic equilibrium is in effect driven by a single state variable. This formulation turns out to be equivalent. Instead of solving for the function $H(t)$, as we have done, we have to deal with two state variables, thereby complicating the decision problem for the individual agent, although precisely the same equilibrium is obtained.[20] Upon reflection, with the wage rate being a deterministic function of capital, this is not surprising, since whether the agent views wages as driven by the aggregate capital stock, which he perceives to grow exogenously with time, or directly as an exogenous function of time, makes no difference.[21]

BIBLIOGRAPHY

Adler, M. and Dumas, B. (1983). 'International Portfolio Choice and Corporation Finance', *Journal of Finance*, 38, 925–84

Barro, R. J. (1990). 'Government Spending in a Simple Model of Endogenous Growth', *Journal of Political Economy*, 98, S103–S125

Benhabib, J. and Rustichini, A. (1994). 'A Note on a New Class of Solutions to Dynamic Programming Problems Arising in Economic Growth', *Journal of Economic Dynamics and Control*, 18, 807–13

Bodie, Z., Merton, R. C. and Samuelson, W. F. (1992). 'Labor Supply Flexibility and Portfolio Choice in a Life Cycle Model', *Journal of Economic Dynamics and Control*, 16, 427–49

Bourguignon, F. (1974). 'A Particular Class of Continuous-Time Stochastic Growth Models', *Journal of Economic Theory*, 9, 141–58

Chang, F.-R. (1988). 'The Inverse Optimal Problem: A Dynamic Programming Approach', *Econometrica*, 56, 147–72

Chow, G. C. (1997). *Dynamic Economics*, Oxford: Oxford University Press

---

[20] The proposed value function to solve this problem is specified to be of the form $V(K, \overline{K}, t) \equiv e^{-\rho t} X(K, \overline{K}) = \varepsilon K^{\gamma - \zeta} \overline{K}^{\zeta}$. As in the present approach, we can derive the equilibrium balanced growth path without solving explicitly for ε and ζ. However, we can establish from the Bellman equation that $\zeta = \gamma \bar{l} \theta / (1 - \bar{l})$ so that $\gamma - \zeta = \gamma [1 - \bar{l}(1 + \theta)]/(1 - \bar{l})$. The transversality condition remains $1 > \bar{l}(1 + \theta)$ and ensures that private capital has positive marginal benefits.

[21] Turnovsky (2000b) in his analysis of tax policy in a stochastically growing economy with endogenously supplied labour, summarised in chapter 3, section 3.8, solves the individual agent's problem as a two-state variable problem, with the two state variables moving identically in macroeconomic equilibrium. This procedure can accommodate the more general case where the wage rate incorporates some of the current stochastic fluctuations: see García-Peñalosa and Turnovsky (2001).

Cooley, T. F. (ed.) (1995). *Frontiers of Business Cycle Research*, Princeton: Princeton University Press

Corsetti, G. (1997). 'A Portfolio Approach to Endogenous Growth: Equilibrium and Optimal Policy', *Journal of Economic Dynamics and Control*, 21, 1627–44

Eaton, J. (1981). 'Fiscal Policy, Inflation, and the Accumulation of Risky Capital', *Review of Economic Studies*, 48, 435–45

García-Peñalosa, C. and Turnovsky, S. J. (2001). 'Production Risk and Functional Distribution of Income in a Developing Economy: Tradeoffs and Policy Responses', University of Washington Working Paper, EC-2002–07, November

Gertler, M. and Grinols, E. (1982). 'Monetary Randomness and Investment', *Journal of Monetary Economics*, 10, 239–58

Grinols, E. L. and Turnovsky, S. J. (1993). 'Risk, the Financial Market, and Macroeconomic Equilibrium', *Journal of Economic Dynamics and Control*, 17, 1–36

    (1998). 'Risk, Optimal Government Finance and Monetary Policies in a Growing Economy', *Economica*, 65, 401–27

Ladrón-de-Guevara, A., Ortigueira, S. and Santos, M. S. (1997). 'Equilibrium Dynamics in Two-Sector Models of Endogenous Growth', *Journal of Economic Dynamics and Control*, 21, 115–43

Mankiw, N. G., Rotemberg, J. and Summers, L. H. (1985). 'Intertemporal Substitution in Macroeconomics', *Quarterly Journal of Economics*, 100, 225–51

Merton, R. C. (1969). 'Lifetime Portfolio Selection under Uncertainty: The Continuous-Time Case', *Review of Economics and Statistics*, 51, 247–57

    (1971). 'Optimum Consumption and Portfolio Rules in a Continuous-Time Model', *Journal of Economic Theory*, 3, 373–413

    (1975). 'An Asymptotic Theory of Growth under Uncertainty', *Review of Economic Studies*, 42, 375–93

Obstfeld, M. (1994). 'Risk-Taking, Global Diversification, and Growth', *American Economic Review*, 84, 1310–29

Ogaki, M. and Reinhart, C. M. (1998). 'Measuring Intertemporal Substitution: the Role of Durable Goods', *Journal of Political Economy*, 106, 1078–98

Rebelo, S. (1991). 'Long-Run Policy Analysis and Long-Run Growth', *Journal of Political Economy*, 99, 500–21

Romer, P. M. (1986). 'Increasing Returns and Long-Run Growth', *Journal of Political Economy*, 94, 1002–37

Smith, W. T. (1996). 'Taxes, Uncertainty, and Long-Term Growth', *European Economic Review*, 40, 1647–64

Stulz, R. (1981). 'A Model of International Asset Pricing', *Journal of Financial Economics*, 9, 383–406

    (1983). 'The Demand for Foreign Bonds', *Journal of International Economics*, 15, 225–38

Turnovsky, S. J. (2000a). 'Fiscal Policy, Elastic Labour Supply, and Endogenous Growth', *Journal of Monetary Economics*, 45, 185–210

    (2000b). 'Government Policy in a Stochastic Growth Model with Elastic Labour Supply', *Journal of Public Economic Theory*, 2, 389–433

11

Growth and business cycles

Gabriel Talmain

1 INTRODUCTION

Growth and fluctuations are sometimes referred to as the Twin Horns of Harrod because of two influential essays (see Harrod 1936, 1939). Both Hicks and Solow reacted to the 'knife-edge path' implied by these papers' dynamics. Hicks emphasised the consequences of 'falling off' the edge. Solow gave a rationale, grounded in agents' behaviour, that would keep the economy on this knife-edge path. Yet, the urge to study growth and fluctuations can be traced back, by way of Ricardo, Malthus and numerous other classical authors to the very birth of economics as a field. Given the vastness of the subject matter, one must set clear goals to what one hopes to achieve here.

This chapter is going to visit several schools that have attempted to blend the theory of economic fluctuations with the theory of growth. Both theories are interesting in their own right and are technically difficult. The early non-market approaches of the Hicksian accelerator and of the Goodwin predator–prey model are a good point of departure because of their intuitive nature. Hicks and Goodwin wrote at a time when an author could not rely on mathematical expertise to get published and in a style that borders, at times, on story telling. This chapter will start by reviewing their approaches, in section 2, as they have essentially disappeared from modern textbooks. Therein lies a deep vein of theory that, as we shall see, has influenced more modern approaches and still has the potential to enrich them further. Next, in section 3, we will review both real business cycle (RBC) theory and the deterministic dynamic system approach. RBC has established itself as the leading explanation for economic fluctuations and its paradigm when applied to growth is the model of King, Plosser and Rebelo (KPR) (1988a, 1988b). Anyone interested in working on the

I would like to thank Jagjit Chadha and two anonymous referees for their very useful and constructive comments. All remaining errors are my own.

subject would be well advised to study that model. To help researchers, details of the rather intricate calculations in KPR are provided. Section 4 will evoke the problem of persistence in macroeconomic data. It will point to a convincing source for this phenomenon, namely aggregation. It will argue that persistence fogs our reading of economic relationships. It will call for the development of new tools to deal with the problem of persistence, in the absence of which no theory can be tested properly. Conclusions will be presented in section 5 while proofs will appear in the appendix (p. 560).

2 EARLY NON-MARKET-CLEARING APPROACHES

The two main approaches to growth and business cycles of the 1950s and 1960s are due to Hicks and Goodwin, respectively. They are both steeped in the interaction between an unstable accelerator and a stabilising multiplier.

Hicks portrayed a very vivid picture of entrepreneurs driven to invest by their ever-changing desired level of capital. As there is no inherent dampening mechanism, these oscillations tend to send the economy on an unstable path, either towards total collapse or towards an uncontrolled expansion. When the economy threatens to collapse, the production of physical capital stops, placing a floor under the level of economic activity and ensuring the eventual recovery. In the case of an uncontrolled expansion, the bounded resources hampers the unrestricted accumulation of capital and starts the economy on its way back towards collapse.

Goodwin's approach is more stylised and more analytical. It relies on the competing interest of capital and labour to produce a rich dynamics: while an increase in the share of capital encourages investment, it also produces inflation in wages and carries the seeds of its own reversal.

Both approaches are very intuitive; they are easy to convey to a lay person. Yet, there is something very mechanical about the way the business cycle unfolds. One is tempted to ask why the entrepreneurs of Hicks, or the workers and capitalists of Goodwin, cannot get together and strike a mutually advantageous deal.

2.1 Accelerator à la Hicks

This presentation follows closely Hicks (1950). It essentially relies on the ability of a second-order dynamic equation to admit oscillatory solutions. In that respect, it would not be unfamiliar to a young economist versed in the modern approach to dynamic systems (see, for instance, Azariadis 1993 or Ljungqvist and Sargent 2000). The notion of a self-propagating accelerator made a deep and lasting impression on macroeconomics. Modern business cycle theory still hearkens back to this notion of accelerator as in the classical study of fiscal policy in an RBC context of Baxter and King (1993) (see, for instance, Heijdra and Van der Ploeg 2002).

Let consumption, C_t, and the desired level of capital, K_t, in period t depend on output, Y_{t-1}, at time $t-1$:

$$C_t = c\, Y_{t-1}$$
$$K_t = k\, Y_{t-1},$$

where c and k are fixed parameters. Investment, I_t, at time t is therefore

$$I_t = K_t - K_{t-1} = k(Y_{t-1} - Y_{t-2}).$$

Suppose autonomous expenditure, A_t, increases exponentially at the exogenously given rate g, $A_t = a(1+g)^t$, with $c < 1 + g[1 - (1+g)^{-1}k]$. The national income identity implies

$$Y_t = C_t + I_t + A_t = (c+k)Y_{t-1} - kY_{t-2} + a(1+g)^t.$$

Let us define trend income as $y_t \equiv Y_t / (1+g)^t$; the previous identity can be rewritten as

$$y_t = (1+g)^{-1}(c+k)y_{t-1} - (1+g)^{-2}ky_{t-2} + a.$$

The steady state of this second-order difference equation is

$$\bar{y} = \frac{a}{1 - (1+g)^{-2}[(1+g)c + gk]}.$$

The deviation from trend $\tilde{y}_t \equiv y_t - \bar{y}_t$ satisfies the Samuelson oscillator equation

$$\tilde{y}_t - (1+g)^{-1}(c+k)\tilde{y}_{t-1} + (1+g)^{-2}k\tilde{y}_{t-2} = 0.$$

The associated characteristic equation is

$$x^2 - (1+g)^{-1}(c+k)x + (1+g)^{-2}k = 0$$

with discriminant $\Delta^2 \equiv ((c+k)^2 - 4k)(1+g)^{-2}$.

1. If $c < 2\sqrt{k} - k$, $\Delta^2 < 0$ and the solution is oscillatory with period T

$$T = \frac{2\pi}{\arccos \frac{c+k}{2\sqrt{k}}}$$

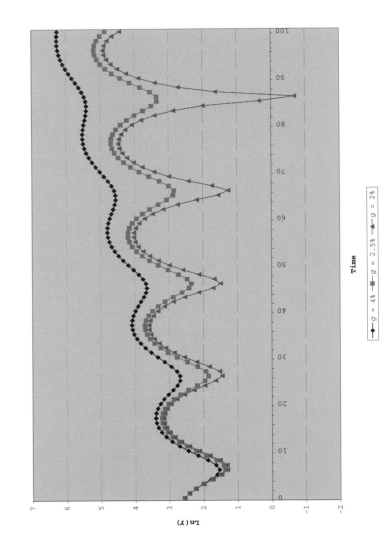

Figure 11.1 Log-level of output in the accelerator model for three growth rates

and modulus ρ

$$\rho = \sqrt{k}/(1 + g).$$

Hence, the cycles are exploding iff $(1 + g)^2 k > 1$.

2. If $c \geq 2\sqrt{k} - k$, $\Delta^2 \geq 0$ and the solution is an exponential decline to the steady state (i.e. the economy is fundamentally stable) or a divergent exponential path (i.e. the economy is fundamentally unstable).

The dynamics depicted by the accelerator model is depicted below for three different growth rates: at $g = 4$ per cent, 2.5 per cent and 2 per cent, the cycles are dampen, stable and explosive, for the chosen values of the parameters.[1]

Summary An increase in g
1. does not affect the presence or the absence of cycles
2. tends to dampen cycles somewhat, i.e. ρ decreases
3. does not affect the frequency of the cycles.

Looking at the first cycle of figure 11.1 , up to $t = 19$, there is not that much interaction between growth and cycles, a feature that we will see time and again. By assumption, the cyclical behaviour of the economy cannot affect the growth trend of GDP g, although actual GDP growth changes with g because this growth rate incorporates the cycle component. The growth rate does affect the dampening of the cycle, although this effect is small for the first cycle. However, even small differences do eventually build up in dynamical systems. This phenomenon is clearly illustrated by the differences between the paths at the end of the fifth cycle, $t = 95$.

Hicks argued that the cyclical behaviour of this oscillator could account for permanent cycles only for $\rho = 1$ and $\Delta^2 < 0$, which imposes a very particular value on the parameters. The path for $g = 2.5$ per cent in figure 11.1, henceforth is unlikely to be generically true. Hicks felt there were two other possibilities:

1. 'Erratic shocks': the motion of $\bar{y}$ is given by Samuelson's oscillator plus a random shock. Hicks states he found this idea in Frisch who attributed it to Wicksell. This approach requires the oscillator to be dampened, see figure 11.2.[2] Hicks argued that, if the oscillator is heavily dampened, the explanatory power of this theory lies mostly with the shock process itself, i.e. the accelerator story is almost redundant. If the oscillator is not

---

[1] Figure 11.1 is drawn using the following values: $k = 1.05$, $c = 0.90$ and $a = 1$. These values were chosen for clarity of illustration rather than for realism.

[2] Different values of the parameters have been used to produce the required dampened shocks.

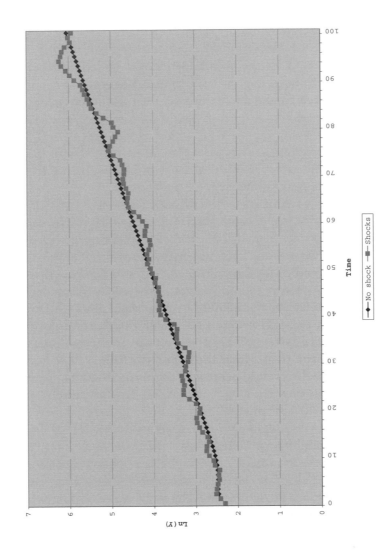

Figure 11.2 The effect of 'erratic shocks'

dampened, then the parameter values must conspire to be close to the degenerate case above. In the former case, one is arguing that economic cycles are produced by shocks which are extraneous to the setup at hand: the explanation for an important economic phenomenon lies outside economics. In the latter case, cycles appear as what should be a rare occurrence; their prevalence argues against this explanation.

2. Supply constraints impose a ceiling on $\bar{y}$ and the impossibility of negative gross investment imposes a floor (see figure 11.3). The presence of these two non-linearities creates a reflective barrier on the oscillator. This preferred explanation requires an explosive path for the economy, either cyclical or exponential. Later work emphasised the importance of non-linearities (see Desai and Ormerod 1998; Goodwin 1951; Matthews 1950).

2.2 Goodwin's Marxian predator–prey model

This presentation follows closely Goodwin (1967). Goodwin assumes a Leontieff technology

$$y_t = \min\left\{\frac{k_t}{\sigma}, a_t l_t\right\}, \text{ with } a_t = a_0 e^{\alpha t}$$

that all labour income is consumed and all capital income is invested, that the labour supply increases exponentially $n_t = n_0 e^{\beta t}$, and that the growth rate of wages, $\dot{w}_t/w_t$, increases with the employment rate, v_t,

$$\frac{\dot{w}_t}{w_t} = -\gamma + \rho v_t, \text{ with } v_t = \frac{l_t}{n_t}.$$

Employment is driven by capital accumulation since $l_t = y_t/a_t = k_t/(\sigma a_t)$. Hence

$$\frac{\dot{l}_t}{l_t} = \frac{\dot{k}_t}{k_t} - \frac{\dot{a}_t}{a_t} = \frac{\dot{k}_t}{k_t} - \alpha.$$

Since $y_t = a_t l_t$ and the wage bill is $w_t l_t$, the share of labour, u_t, is

$$u_t = \frac{w_t l_t}{y_t} = \frac{w_t}{a_t}$$

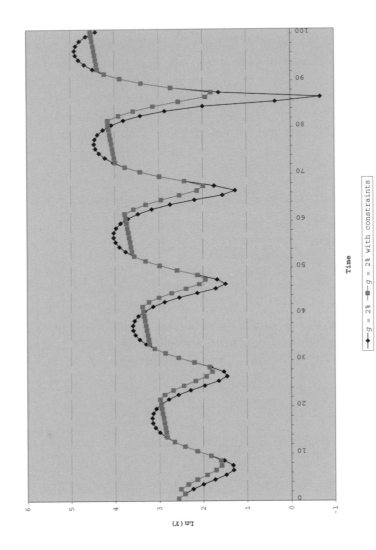

Figure 11.3 The effect of supply and investment constraints

and the share of capital is $1 - u_t$. Since all capital income is invested, we have $\dot{k}_t = (1 - u_t)\, y_t = (1 - u_t)\, k_t/\sigma$, hence

$$\frac{\dot{k}_t}{k_t} = \frac{1 - u_t}{\sigma} \implies \frac{\dot{l}_t}{l_t} = \frac{1 - u_t}{\sigma} - \alpha.$$

The equation of motion for the employment rate is therefore given by

$$\frac{\dot{v}_t}{v_t} = \frac{\dot{l}_t}{l_t} - \frac{\dot{n}_t}{n_t} = \frac{1 - u_t}{\sigma} - (\alpha + \beta). \tag{11.1}$$

An increase in the share of labour u_t squeezes the profit rate which decreases capital accumulation. With lower capital accumulation, the demand for labour increases more slowly while the labour supply increases at the exogenous rate β. Hence, the change in the employment rate depends negatively on the share of labour.

The equation of motion for the share of labour is

$$\frac{\dot{u}_t}{u_t} = \frac{\dot{w}_t}{w_t} - \frac{\dot{a}_t}{a_t} = -\gamma + \rho v_t - \alpha. \tag{11.2}$$

A higher employment rate causes the wage rate to increase faster, which has a positive effect on the share of labour. Together, (11.1) and (11.2) form the Voltera predator–prey dynamic system. Equation (11.2) states that the employment rate, v, the 'prey', attracts the share of labour, u, the 'predator'. Equation (11.1) states that the 'prey' v tries to escape the 'predator' u. The steady state $\bar{u}$ and $\bar{v}$ are

$$\bar{u} = \frac{\eta_1}{\theta_1} \quad \text{and} \quad \bar{v} = \frac{\eta_2}{\theta_2},$$

$$\text{where} \quad \eta_1 \equiv \frac{1}{\sigma} - (\alpha + \beta),$$

$$\eta_2 \equiv \alpha + \gamma, \ \theta_1 \equiv \frac{1}{\sigma}, \ \theta_2 \equiv \rho.$$

A higher rate of technical progress, α, is associated with a lower share of labour $\bar{u}$ and a higher rate of employment $\bar{v}$. Starting away from the steady state, $(u_0, v_0) \neq (\bar{u}, \bar{v})$ will produce a stable cycle given by equating $\varphi(u_t) = K_0 \psi(v_t)$, where

$$\varphi(u) \equiv u^{\eta_1} e^{-\theta_1 u}, \ \psi(v) \equiv v^{-\eta_2} e^{\theta_2 v}, \ K_0 \equiv u_0^{\eta_1} v_0^{\eta_2} e^{-(\theta_1 u_0 + \theta_2 v_0)}.$$

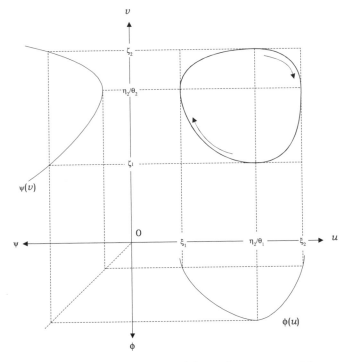

Figure 11.4 The dynamics of the predator–prey model

Unless the economy starts exactly at the steady state, the share of labour u oscillates between ξ_1 and ξ_2, which are the solutions to the equation

$$f^u(\xi) \equiv \eta_1 \ln \xi - \theta_1 \xi = -\eta_2 \ln \bar{v} + \theta_2 \bar{v} + \ln K_0$$

while employment oscillates between ζ_1 and ζ_2, which are the solutions to the equation

$$f^v(\zeta) \equiv -\eta_2 \ln \zeta + \theta_2 \zeta = \eta_1 \ln \bar{u} - \theta_1 \bar{u} - \ln K_0.$$

These dynamics are depicted in figure 11.4.

The effect of an increase in the rate of growth α on the amplitude and on the duration of the cycle is complex. Unlike in the baseline accelerator story, cycles are a generically stable and a permanent phenomenon. As soon as the economy is displaced from its steady state, cycling will take a permanent hold. Once again, there is no reverse effect of fluctuations on the growth trend. Indeed this approach takes a valiant sweep at explaining the persistence of business cycles but has little to say about growth itself.

The idea that the same cycle will endlessly repeat itself is not particularly attractive, but the model can be refined to produce more complex dynamics. There is a large body of literature devoted to developing this paradigm. It has failed so far to produce an impact on mainstream economics, presumably on the grounds of the rigidity and ad hoc nature of its assumptions, and also perhaps due to ideological antagonism. Its legacy lives in the developments of the dynamical system approach to fluctuations.

3 MARKET-CLEARING APPROACHES

Contemporary economics tends to discard the previous approaches as ad hoc theories without microeconomic foundations. There are two modern approaches to fluctuations.[3] The first posits that fluctuations are the expression of an environment that is fundamentally uncertain and subject to elementary shocks. The second views fluctuations as the expression of a deterministic dynamic process which produces a path more complex than a simple monotonic adjustment to a single steady state.

One should point out, however, that researchers have recently started questioning the sharp historical distinction between the purely dynamic and the stochastic approaches to economic fluctuations. Araujo and Maldonado (2000) have argued that even if the economy was essentially deterministic but followed an unknown chaotic process of a certain type, agents could do very well treating their environment as if it were stochastic, i.e. using standard statistical tools.

3.1 Real business cycles and growth

In reaction to the traditional idea that economic fluctuations were the undesirable result of an imperfect market allocation, the RBC literature has explored the hypothesis that economic fluctuations are the result of stochastic productivity shocks. The main challenge for this line of research is to provide a plausible and effective propagation mechanism. From the RBC point of view, the economy can be seen as a 'filter' which transforms the productivity shocks – the input process – into economic fluctuations – the output process. Individual productivity shocks are generally thought to be fairly small, displaying some autocorrelation but dissipating fairly rapidly.

---

[3] One modern line of research on economic fluctuations, that will not be reviewed here, is the so-called 'new Keynesian theory'. The reason is that this research is interested mostly in problems of stabilisation, such as the inflation–unemployment tradeoff, rather than in growth and is the subject of a number of other chapters in this volume.

By contrast, economic fluctuations are thought to be rather persistent and rather larger than the productivity shocks. A successful explanation of business cycles requires an RBC model that can magnify productivity shocks and increase their persistence. The process by which the RBC model translates transitory productivity shocks into persistent changes in output has been labelled the 'transmission mechanism'. There are several strands of research: time-to-build models (Kydland and Prescott 1982), multi-sector models (Long and Plosser 1983), sectoral linkages (Verbrugge 1997 and Horvath 1998) and aggregation to which we will return.

The KPR model of growth presents the best-known extension of the canonical RBC model to a growth environment (see KPR 1988a and 1998b). This is a particularly challenging environment, and the authors resort to a rather unorthodox solution technique as they themselves concede.[4] Nevertheless, the scope of their results is interesting. We are going to study in detail their model as it has become established as one of the leading analyses of growth in the context of business cycles.[5]

On p. 521, we will introduce the framework of the RBC growth model; we show how to transform the problem into a stationary one and we derive the conditions characterising the Euler paths. We then present the KPR approximation approach. First, we introduce the idea behind the approximation in a simplified setting with a fixed labour supply. To the stochastic problem is associated a deterministic one, the certain equivalent, whose equilibrium is easily characterised. The stochastic problem is conceptualised as a perturbation from certainty equivalence, which can be investigated by means of a Taylor expansion. Next, the equilibrium of certain equivalent is calculated for the full deterministic KPR model. The conditions characterising equilibrium in the stochastic case are linearised around this certain equivalent. They are eventually reduced to a system of coupled difference equations. The Blanchard–Khan (1980) method is used to decouple this system. One equation can be solved backward, the other forward. It is then shown how the deterministic equations can be reinterpreted in the stochastic context. Finally, the dynamics of the path of capital (the path of capital per efficiency unit) is shown to depend both on all past and all future expected shocks to productivity. Some examples of the impact of growth on the business cycle are presented. Finally, we mention a few extensions of this RBC framework to demand shocks – monetary and fiscal shocks – and to habit persistence.

[4] See the first two paragraphs of section 4.1 of (1988a).
[5] One should not minimise the amount of scepticism that has greeted the RBC literature, both at its inception (see Summers 1986), and latterly (see Rotemberg and Woodford 1996).

Framework

The basic framework is akin to the RBC specification of Long and Plosser (1983). The representative consumer owns the whole stock of physical capital and supplies all labour. The consumer wants to maximise its intertemporal utility function $U(B_0)$ where B_0 is its financial wealth at the *beginning* of period $t = 0$

$$U(B_0) = E_0 \left[\sum_{t=0}^{\infty} \beta^t u(C_t, L_t) \right], \beta < 1,$$

where C_t and L_t are the consumption of goods and leisure at time t, β is the rate of time preferences. We will mostly be interested in constant relative risk aversion (CRRA) utility functions of the type

$$u(C_t, L_t) \equiv \begin{cases} \dfrac{C_t^{1-\sigma} L_t^{(1-\sigma)\sigma_l}}{(1-\sigma)(1+\sigma_l)}, & \text{for } \sigma \neq 1, \ \sigma > 0, \\ \ln(C_t) + \sigma_l \ln(L_t), & \text{for } \sigma = 1, \end{cases}$$

where σ is the constant relative risk aversion of the consumer, and σ_l measures the elasticity of the labour supply, the limiting case of inelastic labour supply corresponding to $\sigma_l \to 0$. We will sometimes consider the more general case,[6]

$$u(C_t, L_t) = \begin{cases} \dfrac{C_t^{1-\sigma} v(L_t)}{(1-\sigma)}, & \text{for } \sigma \neq 1, \ \sigma > 0, \\ \ln(C_t) + v(L_t), & \text{for } \sigma = 1. \end{cases}$$

Let K_t be the capital stock accumulated by the consumer by the end of period $t - 1$ and which will be used in production at time t. The financial wealth of the consumer at the beginning of period t is $B_t = R_t K_t$, where $R_t \equiv 1 + r_t$ is the return and r_t is the rate of return. Note that, at time t, K_t is predetermined but that B_t is not, as R_t will turn out to be stochastic. As the consumer is a price-taker, its dynamic budget constraint is

$$\begin{aligned} B_t &= R_t(R_{t-1} K_{t-1} + W_{t-1} N_{t-1} - C_{t-1}) \\ &= R_t(B_{t-1} + W_{t-1} N_{t-1} - C_{t-1}) \end{aligned} \tag{11.3}$$

---

[6] Conditions need to be imposed on $v(.)$ to insure that $u(., .)$ is increasing and concave. The function u has the required properties if v is positive and

$$\begin{aligned} \text{when } \sigma = 1, \quad & v \text{ is increasing and concave,} \\ \text{when } \sigma > 1, \quad & v \text{ is decreasing, convex and (*),} \\ \text{when } \sigma < 1, \quad & v \text{ is increasing, concave and (*),} \end{aligned}$$

where the condition (*) is

$$\frac{v'(L)}{v(L)} > \frac{\sigma}{1-\sigma} \frac{v''(L)}{v'(L)}. \tag{*}$$

where W_t is the wage rate, $N_t \equiv 1 - L_t$ is the labour supply and C_t is consumption.

There are a large number of identical firms operating under perfect competition and constant returns to scale, so we can assume one representative firm. We will mostly assume it produces according to the technology

$$Y_t = A_t F(K_t, N_t X_t), \text{ with } F(K_t, N_t X_t) \equiv K_t^{1-\alpha} (N_t X_t)^{\alpha} \quad (11.4)$$

where Y is aggregate output which can be used either for consumption or for investment, K is the capital stock, A is the total factor productivity and X is the labour-augmenting technical progress which we assume to be exogenous and deterministic. It is assumed that technical progress is labour-augmenting as it is a condition for the existence of a balanced growth path.[7] The fundamental cause of uncertainty in the economy are stochastic productivity shocks affecting total factor productivity A. Technical progress X_t is assumed to grow deterministically at the rate γ: $X_t = \gamma^t X_0$, positive growth corresponding to $\gamma > 1$. The capital stock depreciates at the rate δ. It accumulates according to

$$K_{t+1} = (1 - \delta)K_t + I_t \quad (11.5)$$

where I_t is gross investment.

Markets are assumed to be perfectly competitive. Perfect competition ensures that, at an equilibrium, the rental rate is equal to the marginal product of capital and that the wage rate is equal to the marginal product of labour

$$R_t = 1 - \delta + \frac{A_t \partial F(K_t, N_t X_t)}{\partial K_t} \quad \text{and} \quad W_t = \frac{A_t \partial F(K_t, N_t X_t)}{\partial N_t}. \quad (11.6)$$

An intertemporal equilibrium for this economy is a solution, if it exists, to the following consumer problem (CP)

$$\max_{\{C_t, L_t\}} \mathrm{E}_0 \left[\sum_{t=0}^{\infty} \beta^t u(C_t, L_t) \right] \text{ subject to (3)}, \ B_0 = R_0 k_0, \quad (11.7)$$

and a no-Ponzi game transversality condition, together with the production and capital accumulation constraints (11.4) and (11.5), and the factor price equations (11.6). We will assume the existence of such an equilibrium.[8]

Transformation to a stationary problem   Although the previous framework is non-stationary, it can be readily transformed into a stationary one

---

[7] See the appendix p. 560.
[8] The maximum may not exist, say, if the rate of technical progress γ is so high as to accommodate a growth rate of C_t such that $\lim_{t \to \infty} \mathrm{E}_0[\beta^t u(C_t, L_t)]$ is strictly positive and bounded away from zero, making the sum in (11.7) divergent.

by dividing all the non-stationary variables by technical progress X_t. Let $c_t \equiv C_t/X_t$, $y_t \equiv Y_t/X_t$, and so on. Assuming CRRA utility, the consumer problem can be written as maximising

$$E_0 \left[\sum_{t=0}^{\infty} (\beta^*)^t u(c_t, L_t) \right], \text{ where } \beta^* \equiv \beta\gamma^{1-\sigma}, \beta^* < 1,$$

where $E_t[X_{t+\tau}]$ denotes the expected value at time t of the variable $X_{t+\tau}$, the latter condition, $\beta^* < 1$, being imposed to prevent intertemporal utility from diverging to infinity. The Cobb–Douglas production function becomes

$$y_t = A_t F(k_t, N_t) = A_t k_t^{1-\alpha} N_t^{\alpha}, \tag{11.8}$$

and the capital accumulation equation is

$$\gamma k_{t+1} = (1 - \delta)k_t + i_t. \tag{11.9}$$

The factor price equations become

$$R_t = 1 - \delta + \frac{A_t \partial F(K_t, N_t X_t)}{\partial K_t} = 1 - \delta + \frac{A_t \partial F(k_t, N_t)}{\partial k_t}$$

$$\text{and} \quad w_t = \frac{W_t}{X_t} = \frac{A_t \partial F(k_t, N_t)}{\partial N_t}. \tag{11.10}$$

The budget constraint (11.3) becomes

$$\gamma b_t = R_t(b_{t-1} + w_{t-1} N_{t-1} - c_{t-1}), \text{ with } b_t \equiv \frac{B_t}{X_t}. \tag{11.11}$$

Optimum Given the initial endowment of capital k_0, the CP can be written as

$$V(b_0) \equiv \max_{\{c_t, L_t\}} E_0 \left[\sum_{t=0}^{\infty} (\beta^*)^t u(c_t, L_t) \right], \text{ s.t.}(11.11)$$

and subject to a transversality condition, to be specified later, and which states that the discounted value of capital tends zero as $t \to \infty$. Bellman's principle of optimality states that an optimal solution must be optimal at each point in time. Defining $V(b_t)$ to be the CP at time t, Bellman's principle can be written as

$$V(b_t) = \max_{\{c_t, N_t\}} E_t[u(c_t, 1 - N_t) + \beta^* V(b_{t+1})],$$

subject to the production constraint (11.8) and the budget constraint (11.11). To simplify notations, let us denote

$$u_{c_t} \equiv \frac{\partial u(c_t, L_t)}{\partial c_t}, \; u_{L_t} \equiv \frac{\partial u(c_t, L_t)}{\partial L_t},$$

$$F_t \equiv F(k_t, N_t), \; F_{N_t} \equiv \frac{\partial F_t}{\partial N_t}, \; F_{k_{t+1}} \equiv \frac{\partial F_{t+1}}{\partial k_{t+1}}, \; V_t \equiv V(k_t).$$

We can easily reduce the number of controls to one by recasting the problem in terms of the indirect utility. Let $z_t \equiv c_t + w_t L_t$ be the total expenditure on consumption goods, c_t, and on leisure, L_t. In each period, the consumer must make simultaneous decisions on how much to consume/save and on how to divide consumption between expenditure on goods and on leisure. Suppose the consumer knew its optimal total expenditure z_t; the latter problem becomes a purely static one which can be stated as

$$\max_{\{c_t, L_t\}} u(c_t, L_t) \text{ s.t. } z_t \geq c_t + w_t L_t,$$

which implies that

$$u_{c_t} w_t = u_{L_t}. \tag{11.12}$$

Equation (11.12) yields an optimal allocation $(c_t(z_t), L_t(z_t))$. The associated felicity is $u(z_t) \equiv u(c_t(z_t), L_t(z_t))$.[9] The budget constraint (11.11) becomes

$$\gamma b_t = R_t(b_{t-1} + w_{t-1} - z_{t-1}). \tag{11.13}$$

Hence, the CP reduces to finding the optimal path for total expenditure $\{z_t\}_{t=0}^{\infty}$ from which optimal paths of consumption and leisure are easily

---

[9] In the case of the CRRA utility specification

$$u_{c_t} w_t = u_{L_t} \implies c_t(z_t) = \frac{1}{1 + \sigma_l} z_t \quad \text{and} \quad L_t(z_t) = \frac{\sigma_l}{1 + \sigma_l} \frac{z_t}{w_t}.$$

The felicity at time t, $u(z_t) \equiv u(c_t(z_t), L_t(z_t))$, is

$$u(z_t) = \begin{cases} \dfrac{C_1}{(1 - \sigma)(1 + \sigma_l)} \dfrac{z_t^{(1-\sigma)(1+\sigma_l)}}{w_t^{(1-\sigma)\sigma_l}}, & \text{for } \sigma \neq 1, \; \sigma > 0 \\ (1 + \sigma_l) \ln(z_t) - \sigma_l \ln w_t + C_2, & \text{for } \sigma = 1 \end{cases}$$

where

$$C_1 \equiv \begin{cases} \sigma_l^{(1-\sigma)\sigma_l}/(1 + \sigma_l)^{(1-\sigma)(1+\sigma_l)} l, & \text{for } \sigma_l \neq 0, \\ 1, & \text{for } \sigma_l = 0, \end{cases}$$

$$\text{and } C_2 \equiv \begin{cases} \sigma_l \ln \sigma_l - (1 + \sigma_l) \ln 1 + \sigma_l, & \text{for } \sigma_l \neq 0, \\ 0, & \text{for } \sigma_l = 0. \end{cases}$$

derived. The CP can then be stated as

$$V(b_t) = \max_{\{z_t\}} E_t[u(z_t) + \beta^* V(b_{t+1})], \text{ s.t. } (11.13)$$

The first-order condition with respect to z_t is

$$u'_t + \frac{\partial E_t[\beta^* V(b_{t+1})]}{\partial z_t} = 0 \quad \text{where } u'_t \equiv \frac{du(z_t)}{dz_t}.$$

Since

$$\frac{\partial V(b_{t+1})}{\partial z_t} = \frac{dV(b_{t+1})}{db_{t+1}} \frac{\partial b_{t+1}}{\partial z_t} = -\frac{R_t}{\gamma} V'(b_{t+1})$$

$$\text{where } V'(b_{t+1}) \equiv \frac{dV(b_{t+1})}{db_{t+1}},$$

and since, by the envelope theorem, $u'_t = V'(b_t)$, the first-order condition is

$$\gamma u'_t = E_t[\beta^* R_{t+1} u'_{t+1}] = E_t[\beta^*(1 - \delta + A_{t+1} F_{k_{t+1}})u'_{t+1}]. \quad (11.14)$$

No general solutions are known for (11.14). However, a solution is easily obtained for the case of a quadratic utility function and a linear production function.[10]

The KPR approximation approach
The Euler equation (11.14) is typical of the type of stochastic difference equations one encounters in the study of real business cycles. The intertemporal equilibrium of the model, E, depends on the parameters of the utility and of the production functions, on the initial capital stock and on, ϵ, the stochastic process of the shocks on A. Let us use the notation $E(\epsilon)$ to emphasise the dependence of the equilibrium on the shocks. First, consider the case in which, loosely speaking, the variance of the shocks is zero (i.e. the distribution of the stochastic process ϵ is degenerate), which we denote by $\epsilon = 0$. In this case the economy is deterministic and one can generally compute the steady state which we denote by $E(0)$. Next, let the variance of the shocks increase. Under suitable assumptions, the equilibrium still exists and is a continuous function of the distribution of the stochastic process ϵ. A small deviation of ϵ from 0 causes a small departure of the equilibrium E from $E(0)$ and the difference $E(\epsilon) - E(0)$ can be investigated using

[10] See in the appendix, p. 560.

Taylor expansions. This type of procedure falls in the general category of perturbation methods that are presented at great length in Judd (1998).

KPR proposed to perform a first-order approximation of the Euler equation (11.14) around the steady state. Note that a second-order approximation to a function $f(x) \simeq f_0 + f_1 x + f_2 x^2$ corresponds to a first-order approximation of its derivative, $f'(x) \simeq f_1 + 2 f_2 x$. Since only the marginal utility and the marginal productivity of capital appear in that equation, the KPR approximation is essentially equivalent to taking a quadratic approximation of the utility and of the production functions, a procedure that was used by Kydland and Prescott (1982).

Intuition about the KPR approximation   Let us revert to a fixed-labour supply framework in order to get the intuition behind KPR's methodology. In this case, (11.14) becomes

$$\gamma u'(c_t) = E_t[\beta^*(1 - \delta + A_{t+1} f'(k_{t+1})) u'(c_{t+1})]$$
$$\text{where } f(k) \equiv F(k, 1). \tag{11.15}$$

Let us consider the deterministic, stationary framework with $\forall t, A_t = \bar{A}$, and let $\bar{c}$ and $\bar{k}$ be the steady state consumption and capital stock. By definition

$$\gamma \bar{u}' = \beta^*(1 - \delta + \bar{A} \bar{f}') \bar{u}', \text{ where } \bar{u}' \equiv u'(\bar{c}) \text{ and } \bar{f}' \equiv f'(\bar{k}). \tag{11.16}$$

Let the total factor productivity be stochastic, and let $dA_{t+1} \equiv A_{t+1} - \bar{A}$, $dc_t \equiv c_t - \bar{c}$ and $dk_{t+1} \equiv k_{t+1} - \bar{k}$. Taking total derivatives of the first-order condition (11.15), we have

$$(\gamma/\beta^*)(\bar{u}' + \bar{u}'' dc_t + o(dc_t))$$
$$= E_t[(1 - \delta + (\bar{A} + dA_{t+1})[\bar{f}' + \bar{f}'' dk_{t+1} + o(dk_{t+1})])$$
$$\times (\bar{u}' + \bar{u}'' dc_{t+1} + o(dc_{t+1}))],$$

where $\bar{u}'' \equiv u''(\bar{c})$, $\bar{f}'' \equiv f''(\bar{k})$, and $o(x)$ denotes a term that is first-order small with respect to x. At this point, it is tempting to drop all the second-order terms, i.e. terms involving cross-products such as $dA_{t+1} dk_{t+1}$ or that include a $o(.)$. Under assumptions that allow for this simplification, and using (11.16), the first-order condition reduces to

$$(\gamma/\beta^*)\bar{u}'' dc_t = E_t[\bar{A} \bar{f}'' \bar{u}' dk_{t+1} + \bar{f}' \bar{u}' dA_{t+1} + (1 - \delta + \bar{A} \bar{f}') \bar{u}'' dc_{t+1}]$$
$$= \bar{A} \bar{f}'' \bar{u}' E_t[dk_{t+1}] + \bar{f}' \bar{u}' E_t[dA_{t+1}] + 1 - \delta$$
$$+ \bar{A} \bar{f}' \bar{u}'' E_t[dc_{t+1}].$$

In this case, it is legitimate to approximate $E(\epsilon)$ by taking a first-order approximation to (11.15) where A_{t+1} is reinterpreted as $E_t[A_{t+1}]$, k_{t+1} as $E_t[k_{t+1}]$ and c_{t+1} as $E_t[c_{t+1}]$. This is the view taken by KPR which they refer to as the 'certain equivalent perspective'. Note however that disregarding second-order terms cannot always be justified as is clearly demonstrated in standard finance theory. For instance, if the random variable dA has mean zero and a variance $\sigma^2 > 0$, we have $E[dA] = 0 < \sigma^2 = E[dA]$.

A road map to the KPR method To help the reader interested in the original KPR articles, we will follow closely their presentation of impulse responses in the remainder of this section. First, we derive the steady-state solution. Next, we take a first-order approximation of the first-order conditions around this steady-state, ending up with a system of two (non-stochastic) coupled difference equations depicting the motion of the capital stock k_t and of the Lagrange multiplier λ_t. The Blanchard and Khan (1980) method is used to decouple this system and obtain two independent difference equations. The eigenvalue associated with the first one is positive and smaller than 1; this equation can be solved backwards. The eigenvalue associated with the second one is greater than 1; this equation is unstable and must be solved forward. Using these two solutions, we find that the path of capital depends on the contemporaneous, A_t, as well as all future, $\{A_{t+\tau}\}_{\tau=1}^{\infty}$, factor productivities. Lastly, the future values $A_{t+\tau}$ are interpreted as their expected values at time t, $E_t[A_{t+\tau}]$, which can be calculated given the process assumed for A.

Deterministic problem First, we must derive the steady-state equilibrium when there are no shocks. Going back to the problem on p. 521, by the First Theorem of Welfare Economics, the equilibrium of the decentralised economy is identical to the solution of the centrally planned economy. The central planner problem is

$$\max_{\{c_t, L_t\}} \left[\sum_{t=0}^{\infty} (\beta^*)^t u(c_t, L_t) \right], \text{ s.t. } \gamma k_{t+1} = (1 - \delta)k_t + A_t F(k_t, N_t) - c_t.$$

The Lagrangian of this problem at time 0 can be written as

$$\mathcal{L} = \sum_{t=0}^{\infty} (\beta^*)^t \left\{ u(c_t, L_t) + \lambda_t [A_t F(k_t, N_t) - c_t - \gamma k_{t+1} + (1 - \delta)k_t] \right\},$$

where λ_t is the discounted Lagrange multiplier. The first-order conditions are

$$\frac{\partial \mathcal{L}}{\partial c_t} = 0 \implies u_{c_t} = \lambda_t, \tag{11.17}$$

$$\frac{\partial \mathcal{L}}{\partial N_t} = 0 \implies u_{L_t} = \lambda_t A_t F_{N_t}, \tag{11.18}$$

$$\frac{\partial \mathcal{L}}{\partial k_{t+1}} = 0 \implies \beta^* \lambda_{t+1} \big[A_{t+1} F_{k_{t+1}} + (1 - \delta) \big] = \lambda_t \gamma, \tag{11.19}$$

$$\frac{\partial \mathcal{L}}{\partial \lambda_t} = 0 \implies A_t F_t = c_t + \gamma k_{t+1} - (1 - \delta) k_t, \tag{11.20}$$

and the transversality condition is that

$$\lim_{t \to \infty} (\beta^*)^t \lambda_t k_{t+1} = 0.$$

The first two equations (11.17) and (11.18) give us the previous equation $u_{L_t}/u_{c_t} = A_t F_{N_t}$ which governs the allocation of total expenditure between consumption c_t and leisure L_t. The third equation (11.19) depicts the relationship between the return on capital and the tightening of the budget constraint, i.e. governs the choice between consumption and savings. The last equation (11.20) is simply the budget constraint itself. From the producers' optimisation, the wage rate, w_t, is the marginal product of capital, $w_t = A_t F_{N_t}$, and the return at $t + 1$, R_{t+1}, is the marginal product of capital net of depreciation, $R_{t+1} = 1 - \delta + A_{t+1} F_{k_{t+1}}$, while (11.19) implies that

$$\lambda_{t+1} \beta^* R_{t+1} = \lambda_t \gamma \implies R_{t+1} = \frac{\lambda_t \gamma}{\beta^* \lambda_{t+1}}. \tag{11.21}$$

Steady state under a stationary total factor productivity   Let total factor productivity be stationary: $A_t = A_t = A$. At a steady state, we have $\lambda_{t+1} = \lambda_t$, $k_{t+1} = k_t$, $N_{t+1} = N_t$ and $c_{t+1} = c_t$. Hence, from (11.19)

$$\beta^* [AF_k + (1 - \delta)] = \gamma \implies AF_k = \frac{\gamma - (1 - \delta)\beta^*}{\beta^*}.$$

For the Cobb–Douglas production function

$$AF_k = \frac{(1 - \alpha)AF}{k} = (1 - \alpha)\frac{y}{k},$$

the implication is that

$$\frac{y}{k} = \frac{\gamma - (1-\delta)\beta^*}{(1-\alpha)\beta^*}. \tag{11.22}$$

From the capital accumulation equation (11.9), we have

$$\frac{i}{k} = \gamma - (1-\delta). \tag{11.23}$$

Hence, the share of investment and consumption in GDP, s_i and c_i,[11] are

$$s_i \equiv \frac{i}{y} = (1-\alpha)\frac{\gamma - (1-\delta)}{(\gamma/\beta^*) - (1-\delta)} \quad \text{and} \quad s_c \equiv \frac{c}{y} = 1 - s_i. \tag{11.24}$$

Time-varying total factor productivity Next we turn to deriving the equilibrium when A_t is not constant. The time path is still deterministic but A_t moves deterministically around A. We use the method of log-linearisation; c_t denotes the consumption at t under the new path while c denotes the previous consumption when A was constant, and so on for the other variables. Let us denote with a caret the log deviations such as $\hat{c}_t \equiv \ln c_t/c = \ln 1 + ((c_t - c)/c) \simeq ((c_t - c)/c) = dc_t/c$, and so on,

---

[11] In addition, the allocation between consumption and leisure (11.12) implies that

$$\frac{u_{L_t}}{u_{c_t}} = w = \frac{\alpha AF}{N} = \frac{\alpha y}{N}.$$

With the utility function

$$u(c, L) = \frac{c^{1-\sigma} v(L)}{1-\sigma},$$

the steady-state capital satisfies

$$\frac{\alpha y}{N} = \begin{cases} \dfrac{c}{1-\sigma}\dfrac{v'(1-N)}{v(1-N)}, & \text{for } \sigma \neq 1,\ \sigma > 0 \\ c v'(1-N), & \text{for } \sigma = 1, \end{cases} \implies \frac{\alpha}{s_c} = \begin{cases} \dfrac{Nv'(1-N)}{(1-\sigma)v(1-N)}, & \text{for } \sigma \neq 1,\ \sigma > 0 \\ Nv'(1-N), & \text{for } \sigma = 1, \end{cases}.$$

Hence this last equation determines the work effort N. For the CRRA function $v(L) = L^{(1-\sigma)\sigma_l}/(1+\sigma_l)$, we have

$$\frac{\alpha}{s_c} = \sigma_l \frac{N}{1-N} \implies N = \frac{1}{1 + (\sigma_l s_c/\alpha)}.$$

From the steady-state capital ratio (11.22), the steady-state capital stock is

$$\frac{y}{k} = A\left[\frac{N}{k}\right]^\alpha = \frac{\gamma - (1-\delta)\beta^*}{(1-\alpha)\beta^*} \implies k = \left[\frac{A(1-\alpha)\beta^*}{\gamma - (1-\delta)\beta^*}\right]^{1/\alpha} N.$$

and denote elasticities with ξ, in this case that of marginal utility,

$$\xi_{cc} \equiv c\frac{\partial^2 u/\partial c^2}{\partial u/\partial c}, \xi_{cl} \equiv L\frac{\partial^2 u/\partial c\partial L}{\partial u/\partial c},$$

$$\xi_{lc} \equiv c\frac{\partial^2 u/\partial c\partial L}{\partial u/\partial L}, \xi_{ll} \equiv L\frac{\partial^2 u/\partial L^2}{\partial u/\partial L}.$$

For the first equation (11.17), we have the log-linearisation[12]

$$\xi_{cc}\hat{c}_t - \xi_{cl}\frac{N}{1-N}\hat{N}_t = \hat{\lambda}_t. \tag{11.25}$$

For (11.18), we have

$$\xi_{lc}\hat{c}_t - \xi_{ll}\frac{N}{1-N}\hat{N}_t = \hat{\lambda}_t + \hat{A}_t + \xi_{nk}\hat{k}_t + \xi_{nn}\hat{N}_t, \tag{11.26}$$

where ξ denotes elasticities, here of the production function,

$$\xi_{nk} \equiv k\frac{\partial^2 F/\partial N\partial k}{\partial F/\partial N} \quad \text{and } \xi_{nn} \equiv N\frac{\partial^2 F/\partial N^2}{\partial F/\partial N}.$$

For (11.19), we have

$$\eta_a\hat{A}_{t+1} + \eta_k\hat{k}_{t+1} + \eta_n\hat{N}_{t+1} = \hat{\lambda}_t - \hat{\lambda}_{t+1}, \tag{11.27}$$

where η denotes the elasticity of the gross marginal product of capital

$$\eta_a \equiv A\frac{(\partial F/\partial k)}{A(\partial F/\partial k) + (1-\delta)}, \eta_k \equiv k\frac{A(\partial^2 F/\partial k^2)}{A(\partial F/\partial k) + (1-\delta)},$$

$$\eta_n \equiv N\frac{A(\partial^2 F/\partial k\partial N)}{A(\partial F/\partial k) + (1-\delta)}.$$

Finally, the log-linear version of the budget constraint (11.20) is

$$\hat{A}_t + \xi_k\hat{k}_t + \xi_n\hat{N}_t = s_c\hat{c}_t + s_i\left[\varphi\hat{k}_{t+1} - \frac{(1-\delta)\varphi}{\gamma}\hat{k}_t\right] \tag{11.28}$$

where s_c and s_i are the shares of consumption and investment in output, $\varphi \equiv K_{t+1}/I_t$ is a modified capital investment ratio and ξ here are the

---

[12] See appendix (p. 560).

elasticities of production with respect to the factors[13]

$$s_c \equiv \frac{c}{y}, s_i \equiv \frac{i}{y}, \varphi \equiv \frac{\gamma k}{i}, \xi_k \equiv \frac{k \partial F / \partial k}{F} \quad \text{and} \quad \xi_n \equiv \frac{N \partial F / \partial N}{F}.$$

Putting together the first two equations (11.25) and (11.26), we have

$$\hat{c}_t = c_\lambda \hat{\lambda}_t + c_k \hat{k}_t + c_a \hat{A}_t,$$
$$\hat{N}_t = n_\lambda \hat{\lambda}_t + n_k \hat{k}_t + n_a \hat{A}_t,$$

where

$$D_{cn} \equiv \frac{1}{\xi_{lc}\xi_{cl} - \xi_{cc}\left(\xi_{ll} + l\xi_{nn}\right)}, \text{ if } \sigma_l \neq 0 \text{ and where } l \equiv \frac{L}{N}$$

$$c_\lambda \equiv \begin{cases} \left(\xi_{cl} - \xi_{ll} - l\xi_{nn}\right)D_{cn} & \text{if } \sigma_l \neq 0 \\ 1/\xi_{cc} & \text{if } \sigma_l = 0 \end{cases}, c_k \equiv \xi_{cl}\xi_{nk}D_{cn}, c_a \equiv \xi_{cl}D_{cn},$$

$$n_\lambda \equiv \left(\xi_{cc} - \xi_{lc}\right)D_{cn}l, n_k \equiv \xi_{cc}\xi_{nk}D_{cn}l, n_a \equiv \xi_{cc}D_{cn}l,$$

which implies, after substitution into (11.27) and (11.28),

$$\hat{k}_{t+1} = k_k \hat{k}_t + k_\lambda \hat{\lambda}_t + k_a \hat{A}_t, \tag{11.29}$$
$$\hat{\lambda}_{t+1} = \lambda_k \hat{k}_t + \lambda_\lambda \hat{\lambda}_t + \lambda_a \hat{A}_t + \lambda_{a1} \hat{A}_{t+1}, \tag{11.30}$$

---

[13] For the Cobb–Douglas production function, we have

$$\xi_k = (1 - \alpha), \xi_n = \alpha, \xi_{nk} = (1 - \alpha), \xi_{nn} = -(1 - \alpha),$$

$$s_c = 1 - s_i, s_i = (1 - \alpha)\frac{\gamma - (1 - \delta)}{\gamma/\beta^* - (1 - \delta)}, \varphi = \frac{\gamma}{\gamma - (1 - \delta)}, \frac{(1 - \delta)\varphi}{\gamma} = \varphi - 1;$$

from (11.21) and (11.22)

$$\eta_a = \frac{(1 - \alpha)(y/k)}{1 + r} = \frac{(\gamma/\beta^*) - (1 - \delta)}{\gamma/\beta^*},$$

$$\eta_k = -\alpha \frac{A(\partial F/\partial k)}{A(\partial F/\partial k) + (1 - \delta)} = -\alpha\eta_a,$$

$$\eta_n = \alpha \frac{A(\partial F/\partial k)}{A(\partial F/\partial k) + (1 - \delta)} = \alpha\eta_a.$$

For the CRRA utility function, we have

$$\xi_{cc} \equiv -\sigma, \xi_{cl} \equiv L\frac{v'(L)}{v(L)}, \xi_{lc} \equiv 1 - \sigma, \xi_{ll} \equiv L\frac{v''(L)}{v'(L)} \quad \text{for } \sigma \neq 1, \ \sigma > 0,$$

$$\xi_{cc} \equiv -1, \xi_{cl} \equiv 0, \xi_{lc} \equiv 0, \xi_{ll} \equiv L\frac{v''(L)}{v'(L)} \quad \text{for } \sigma = 1.$$

where

$$k_\lambda \equiv \frac{\xi_n n_\lambda - s_c c_\lambda}{s_i \varphi}, \; k_k \equiv \frac{\xi_k + \xi_n n_k + s_i(\varphi - 1) - s_c c_k}{s_i \varphi},$$

$$k_a \equiv \frac{1 + \xi_n n_a - s_c c_a}{s_i \varphi}, \; \lambda_\lambda \equiv \frac{1}{1 + n_\lambda \eta_n} + D_\lambda k_\lambda, \; \lambda_k \equiv D_\lambda k_k,$$

$$\lambda_a \equiv D_\lambda k_a, \; \lambda_{a1} \equiv -\frac{(\eta_a + n_a \eta_n)}{1 + n_\lambda \eta_n}, \; \text{and } D_\lambda \equiv -\frac{\eta_k + n_k \eta_n}{1 + n_\lambda \eta_n}.$$

The two equations (11.29) and (11.30) form a system of coupled difference equations which we can rewrite as

$$\hat{\mathbf{k}}_{t+1} = \mathbf{W}\hat{\mathbf{k}}_t + \mathbf{Q}\hat{A}_t + \mathbf{R}\hat{A}_{t+1}, \tag{11.31}$$

$$\text{with } \hat{\mathbf{k}}_t \equiv \begin{bmatrix} \hat{k}_t \\ \hat{\lambda}_t \end{bmatrix}, \; \mathbf{W} \equiv \begin{bmatrix} k_k & k_\lambda \\ \lambda_k & \lambda_\lambda \end{bmatrix}, \; \mathbf{Q} \equiv \begin{bmatrix} k_a \\ \lambda_a \end{bmatrix}, \; \mathbf{R} \equiv \begin{bmatrix} 0 \\ \lambda_{a1} \end{bmatrix}.$$

By repeated substitutions, it is equivalent to

$$\hat{\mathbf{k}}_t = \mathbf{W}^t \hat{\mathbf{k}}_0 + \sum_{b=1}^{t} \mathbf{W}^{b-1} \mathbf{Q}\hat{A}_{t-b} + \sum_{b=1}^{t} \mathbf{W}^{b-1} \mathbf{R}\hat{A}_{t+1-b}.$$

The characteristic equation of matrix $\mathbf{W}$ is $\mu^2 - (k_\lambda + \lambda_k)\mu + k_\lambda \lambda_k - k_k \lambda_\lambda = 0$, which implies

$$\begin{cases} \mu_1 = \frac{1}{2}[k_\lambda + \lambda_k - \sqrt{(k_k - \lambda_\lambda)^2 + 4k_\lambda \lambda_k}], \\ \mu_2 = \frac{1}{2}[k_\lambda + \lambda_k + \sqrt{(k_k - \lambda_\lambda)^2 + 4k_\lambda \lambda_k}], \end{cases}$$

with $0 < \mu_1 < [\beta^*]^{-1} < \mu_2$. Note that $k_\lambda \lambda_k - k_k \lambda_\lambda = 1/\beta^*$.

A particular set of independent eigenvectors is

$$\mathbf{v}_1 = \begin{bmatrix} k_\lambda \\ \mu_1 - k_k \end{bmatrix}, \; \mathbf{v}_2 = \begin{bmatrix} k_\lambda \\ \mu_2 - k_k \end{bmatrix}.$$

Let

$$\mathbf{P} \equiv \begin{bmatrix} k_\lambda & k_\lambda \\ \mu_1 - k_k & \mu_2 - k_k \end{bmatrix} \text{ and } \mu \equiv \begin{bmatrix} \mu_1 & 0 \\ 0 & \mu_2 \end{bmatrix}.$$

Then

$$\mathbf{W} = \mathbf{P}\mu\mathbf{P}^{-1} \implies \mathbf{W}^b = \mathbf{P}\mu^b\mathbf{P}^{-1}.$$

To decouple the two difference equations, we use the transformation

$$\bar{\mathbf{k}}_t \equiv \begin{bmatrix} \bar{k}_t \\ \bar{\lambda}_t \end{bmatrix} \equiv \mathbf{P}^{-1}\hat{\mathbf{k}}_t, \text{ with } \mathbf{P}^{-1} = \frac{1}{k_\lambda\,(\mu_2 - \mu_1)} \begin{bmatrix} \mu_2 - k_k & -k_\lambda \\ -\mu_1 + k_k & k_\lambda \end{bmatrix}.$$

Pre-multiplying the system (11.31) by $\mathbf{P}^{-1}$, we have

$$\bar{\mathbf{k}}_{t+1} = \mu\bar{\mathbf{k}}_t + \tilde{\mathbf{Q}}\hat{A}_t + \tilde{\mathbf{R}}\hat{A}_{t+1}, \quad \text{with } \tilde{\mathbf{Q}} \equiv \mathbf{P}^{-1}\mathbf{Q} \quad \text{and} \quad \tilde{\mathbf{R}} \equiv \mathbf{P}^{-1}\mathbf{R},$$

which yields the system of decoupled difference equations

$$\bar{k}_{t+1} = \mu_1\bar{k}_t + \bar{q}_k\hat{A}_t + \bar{r}_k\hat{A}_{t+1}, \tag{11.32}$$

$$\bar{\lambda}_{t+1} = \mu_2\bar{\lambda}_t + \bar{q}_\lambda\hat{A}_t + \bar{r}_\lambda\hat{A}_{t+1} \tag{11.33}$$

where

$$\bar{k}_t = D_{k\lambda}[(\mu_2 - k_k)\,\hat{k}_t - k_\lambda\,\hat{\lambda}_t], \bar{\lambda}_t = D_{k\lambda}[(k_k - \mu_1)\,\hat{k}_t + k_\lambda\,\hat{\lambda}_t],$$

$$\bar{q}_k = D_{k\lambda}\,[(\mu_2 - k_k)\,k_a - k_\lambda\lambda_a]\,, \bar{q}_\lambda = D_{k\lambda}\,[(k_k - \mu_1)\,k_a + k_\lambda\lambda_a]\,,$$

$$\bar{r}_k = -k_k\lambda_{a1}D_{k\lambda}, \bar{r}_\lambda = k_k\lambda_{a1}D_{k\lambda}, \text{ and } D_{k\lambda} \equiv \frac{1}{k_\lambda\,(\mu_2 - \mu_1)}.$$

The first equation (11.32) can be solved backwards as $\lim_{h\to\infty}\mu_1^h = 0$, but the second (11.33) cannot as $\lim_{h\to\infty}\mu_2^h = \infty$, and must be solved forward. Solving backward (11.32), we have

$$\bar{k}_t = \mu_1^t\bar{k}_0 + \sum_{h=1}^{t}\mu_1^{h-1}\bar{q}_k\hat{A}_{t-h} + \sum_{h=1}^{t}\mu_1^{h-1}\bar{r}_k\hat{A}_{t+1-h}$$

$$= \mu_1^t\bar{k}_0 + \bar{r}_k\hat{A}_t + \mu_1^{t-1}\bar{q}_k\hat{A}_0 + \sum_{h=1}^{t-1}\mu_1^{h-1}(\bar{q}_k + \mu_1\bar{r}_k)\hat{A}_{t-h}.$$

Solving forward (11.33), we have

$$\bar{\lambda}_t = \frac{1}{\mu_2}\bar{\lambda}_{t+1} - \frac{\bar{q}_\lambda}{\mu_2}\hat{A}_t - \frac{\bar{r}_\lambda}{\mu_2}\hat{A}_{t+1} \implies$$

$$\bar{\lambda}_t = \lim_{h\to\infty}\frac{1}{\mu_2}\bar{\lambda}_{t+h} - \sum_{h=0}^{\infty}\frac{\bar{q}_\lambda}{\mu_2^{h+1}}\hat{A}_{t+h} - \sum_{h=0}^{\infty}\frac{\bar{r}_\lambda}{\mu_2^{h+1}}\hat{A}_{t+h+1}.$$

As the transversality condition implies $\lim_{h \to \infty} \frac{1}{\mu_2} \bar{\lambda}_{t+h} = 0$, the solution for $\bar{\lambda}_t$ is

$$\bar{\lambda}_t = -\frac{\bar{q}_\lambda}{\mu_2} \hat{A}_t - \sum_{h=1}^{\infty} \frac{1}{\mu_2^h} \left[\bar{r}_\lambda + \frac{\bar{q}_\lambda}{\mu_2} \right] \hat{A}_{t+h}.$$

Therefore, the solution for the capital stock and the Lagrange multiplier are

$$\hat{\mathbf{k}}_t = \mathbf{P} \bar{\mathbf{k}}_t \iff \begin{bmatrix} \hat{k}_t \\ \hat{\lambda}_t \end{bmatrix} = \begin{bmatrix} k_\lambda & k_\lambda \\ \mu_1 - k_k & \mu_2 - k_k \end{bmatrix} \begin{bmatrix} \bar{k}_t \\ \bar{\lambda}_t \end{bmatrix},$$

which implies

$$\hat{k}_t = k_\lambda \bar{k}_t + k_\lambda \bar{\lambda}_t \implies \bar{k}_t = \frac{1}{k_\lambda} \hat{k}_t - \bar{\lambda}_t,$$

$$\hat{\lambda}_t = (\mu_1 - k_k) \bar{k}_t + (\mu_2 - k_k) \bar{\lambda}_t = \frac{\mu_1 - k_k}{k_\lambda} \hat{k}_t + [\mu_2 - \mu_1] \bar{\lambda}_t.$$

Substituting into (11.29), we obtain the (forward-looking) difference equation for $\hat{k}_t$:

$$\hat{k}_{t+1} = \mu_1 \hat{k}_t + [\mu_2 - \mu_1] k_\lambda \bar{\lambda}_t + k_a \hat{A}_t,$$

which implies

$$\hat{k}_{t+1} = \mu_1 \hat{k}_t + \psi_1 \hat{A}_t + \psi_2 \sum_{h=0}^{\infty} \frac{1}{\mu_2^h} \hat{A}_{t+h+1}, \qquad (11.34)$$

$$\text{where } \psi_1 \equiv k_a - k_\lambda [\mu_2 - \mu_1] \frac{\bar{q}_\lambda}{\mu_2} \quad \text{and}$$

$$\psi_2 \equiv -\frac{k_\lambda [\mu_2 - \mu_1]}{\mu_2} [\bar{r}_\lambda + \frac{\bar{q}_\lambda}{\mu_2}].$$

'Certain equivalent perspective'   How does the (deterministic) time varying A relate to the stochastic case? Let the sequence of $\{\hat{A}_t\}_{t=0}^{\infty}$ be stochastic, with all the realisations $\hat{A}_t$ 'close' to the steady state $\bar{A}$ (almost surely). By the rationale given on p. 526 above about the intuition, the dynamics of the economy will be given by (11.31) as a first-order approximation once $\hat{A}_{t+1}$ and $\hat{\mathbf{k}}_{t+1}$ are replaced by conditional expectations

$$E_t[\hat{\mathbf{k}}_{t+1} | \hat{A}_t] = \mathbf{W} \hat{\mathbf{k}}_t + \mathbf{Q} \hat{A}_t + \mathbf{R} E_t[\hat{A}_{t+1} | \hat{A}_t], \qquad (11.35)$$

where $E_t[.|\hat{A}_t]$ denotes expectation conditional on $\hat{A}_t$. Taking expectations with respect to A_{t-1}, the rule of iterated expectations implies for the left-hand side of (11.35) that

$$E_{t-1}[E_t[\hat{\mathbf{k}}_{t+1}|\hat{A}_t]|\hat{A}_{t-1}] = E_{t-1}[\hat{\mathbf{k}}_{t+1}|\hat{A}_{t-1}],$$

and since the same holds term-by-term for the right-hand side of (11.35), and by the linearity of the equation, we have

$$E_{t-1}[\hat{\mathbf{k}}_{t+1}|\hat{A}_{t-1}] = \mathbf{W}E_{t-1}[\hat{\mathbf{k}}_t|\hat{A}_{t-1}] + \mathbf{Q}E_{t-1}[\hat{A}_t|\hat{A}_{t-1}]$$
$$+ \mathbf{R}E_{t-1}[\hat{A}_{t+1}|\hat{A}_{t-1}].$$

By backward induction, the dynamics of the stochastic economy at time t are given by

$$E_0[\hat{\mathbf{k}}_{t+1}|\hat{A}_0] = \mathbf{W}E_0[\hat{\mathbf{k}}_t|\hat{A}_0] + \mathbf{Q}E_0[\hat{A}_t|\hat{A}_0] + \mathbf{R}E_0[\hat{A}_{t+1}|\hat{A}_0].$$

Hence, (11.31) describes the dynamics of the stochastic economy for all t once the $\hat{A}$s and $\hat{\mathbf{k}}$s are reinterpreted as conditional expectations with respect to $\hat{A}_0$.

Transition paths   Let us suppose that the economy in the past had been dragged out of the steady state by some shocks, but that all shocks have now subsided: $\forall \tau \geq 0$, $\hat{A}_{t+\tau} = 0$. Assume $\sigma_l = 0$. If the initial value of k_t is not at its steady-state value, we have the following effects

$$\hat{c}_t = \frac{\hat{\lambda}_t}{\xi_{cc}} = \pi_{ck}\hat{k}_t, \text{ where } \pi_{ck} \equiv \frac{\mu_1 - k_k}{k_\lambda \xi_{cc}},$$

$$\hat{y}_t = A_t F_k k_t = \pi_{yk}\hat{k}_t, \text{ where } \pi_{yk} \equiv 1 - \alpha,$$

$$s_c\hat{c}_t + s_i\hat{i}_t = \hat{y}_t \implies \hat{i}_t = \pi_{ik}\hat{k}_t, \text{ where } \pi_{ik} \equiv \frac{\pi_{yk} - s_c\pi_{ck}}{s_i}.$$

Since r_{t+1} is given by (11.21), we have, by (11.27),

$$\hat{r}_{t+1} = \hat{\lambda}_t - \hat{\lambda}_{t+1} = \pi_{rk}\hat{k}_t, \text{ where } \pi_{rk} \equiv \eta_k.$$

Since $w_t = \alpha y_t$ we have

$$\hat{w}_t = \hat{y}_t = \pi_{wk}\hat{k}_t, \text{ where } \pi_{wk} \equiv 1 - \alpha.$$

Table 11.1 *Unit elasticity,* $\sigma = 1$

	$\sigma_l = 0$		$\sigma_l = 2$	
	$g_a = 2.5\%$	$g_a = 5\%$	$g_a = 2.5\%$	$g_a = 5\%$
π_{ka}	0.32	0.37	0.83	0.95
π_{ca}	0.20	0.23	0.47	0.53
π_{ra}	−0.88%	−1.14%	−2.27%	−2.96%
h_f half-life (years)	4.00	3.5	2.9	2.6
s_c	74.1%	72.9%	74.1%	72.9%
k/y	8.29	7.26	8.29	7.26
r (annual)	7.6%	10.2%	7.6%	10.2%

Conclusions

For reasonable values of the underlying parameters,[14] following Rotemberg
and Woodford (1996), growth tends to increase both π_{ka} and π_{ca}, the
elasticities of k and of c with respect to A, i.e. to increase the amplitude
of the business cycle. It also tends to increase the speed of adjustment,
although the last effect is not monotonic, i.e. to shorten the length of
the cycle.

Table 11.1 provides some numerical values for the case of $\sigma = 1$, $\alpha =$
0.64, $\beta = 0.988$, $\delta = 0.025$ and when labour supply is either inelastic
($\sigma_l = 0$) or when it takes a value suggested by Hansen and Wright (1992)
($\sigma_l = 2$). It gives the annual growth rate, $g_a \equiv \gamma - 1$, the elasticities of
capital, consumption and of the interest rate with respect to a change in
productivity; the half-life, i.e. the time it takes for the economy to work
through one-half of the initial deviation: let h_f be the half-life, h_f satisfies
$\mu_1^{h_f} = 1/2$. In addition, the share of consumption, s_c, the capital–output
ratio, k/y, and the annual interest rate, r, are also given.

There is much debate on the measurement of the elasticity of substitution
σ. The effect of σ on the elasticities is depicted in figures 11.5–11.7. In
these graphs, the range of the annual growth rate, g_a, is −4 per cent to
9 per cent, and the values of σ go from $2^{-4} = 1/16$ to $2^4 = 16$ as powers
of 2.[15]

Small values for σ are associated with large elasticities of substitutions
and utility that is nearly linear. A small change in the interest rate will induce
this consumer to switch expenditure across time in order to keep marginal

---

[14] In the papers cited here the parameters have been calibrated on the US economy.
[15] Note that some values in this range violate the restriction $\beta^* < 1$.

Table 11.2 *Effect of a change in σ under zero growth*

	$\sigma = 1/4$	$\sigma = 1$	$\sigma = 4$
π_{ka}	0.50	0.27	0.17
π_{ca}	0.56	0.17	0.06
π_{ra}	-1.17%	-0.64%	-0.39
h_f half-life (years)	2.2	4.7	10.7

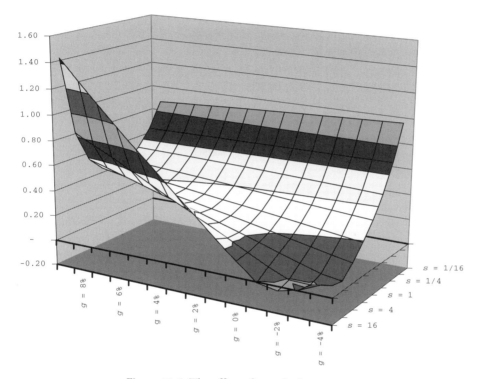

Figure 11.5 The effect of σ and of g_a on π_{ka}

utility nearly constant. A positive shock on A, as it is somewhat persistent, induces a temporary build-up of capital which is reflected in the high π_{ka}: in table 11.2, we see that $\pi_{ka} = 0.50$ for $\sigma = 1/4$ while $\pi_{ka} = 0.17$ for $\sigma = 4$. Consumption and the interest rate also react strongly. The large immediate adjustment means that the effect of the shock is processed through the economy relatively quickly: the half-life is $h_f = 2.2$ years for $\sigma = 1/4$ while $h_f = 10.7$ for $\sigma = 4$.

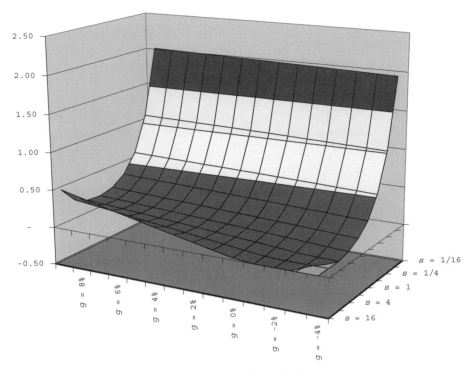

Figure 11.6 The effect of σ and of g_a on π_{ca}

Binder and Pesaran (1999) have started investigating whether the stochastic growth model better represents the data than the traditional growth model. In particular, they found that data from the Summers–Heston data set supported the relationship between the mean and the variance of the capital–output ratio predicted by the stochastic growth model.

The RBC approach to growth analyses how economic growth affects the business cycle but it cannot account for any feedback effect from the business cycle to the rate of growth. It is possible to extend the RBC model to incorporate human capital, however there is a general disaffection for the predictions of an endogenous growth extension, as the predictions that large economies should grow faster than smaller ones are counterfactual, see Jones (1995a, 1995b). However, Chou, Kimura and Talmain (1994) have argued that perhaps this 'theoretical failure' is due to the reliance on the concept of a country as a geographic and political entity. If instead one corrects the size of a country by its degree of integration in the world economy, the picture changes greatly.

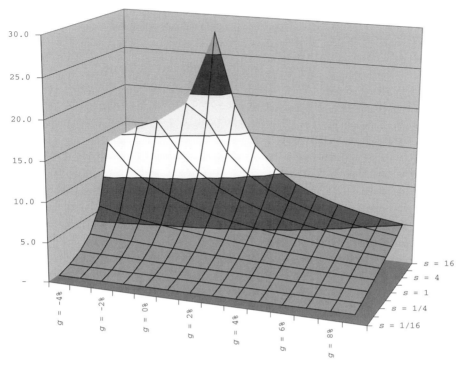

Figure 11.7 The effect of σ and of g_a on h_f (half-life)

Further developments

The RBC model has been developed in a multitude of directions, only a few of which have been investigated in respect to their implications for growth. Perhaps the most obvious missing feature of the baseline model is the lack of aggregate demand shocks. Two traditional sources of demand shocks are the government and the monetary sectors.

Fiscal shocks Effects of fiscal policy in an RBC framework were analysed by Baxter and King (1993). They found that a temporary increase in government expenditure would decrease private consumption and increase the interest rate, thereby inducing an increase in the labour supply and an expansion of output; investment would also fall. These predictions are not so far from the ones from the traditional IS-LM framework. However, calibration of the model delivers small effects, suggesting fiscal policy shocks play a secondary role in the analysis of economic fluctuations. In addition, Perotti (1999) suggested that, for economies experiencing 'fiscal stress', the normal effects were reversed.

Monetary shocks   Monetary shocks have been incorporated in RBC models in several ways.

Early models induced agents to hold money balances by incorporating money in their utility function (see Kydland and Prescott 1982). Money shocks produced effects on output inasmuch as they were unanticipated. While this approach could reproduce some of the stylised facts observed in US and other data, the predicted magnitude of these effects was much smaller than what is required.

Models in which money is held because of a cash-in-advance constraint have been extensively studied (see, for instance Cooley and Hansen 1989; Lucas and Stokey 1983, 1987; and Svensson 1985). These models tend to predict that money growth should be positively correlated with the nominal interest rate, which is counterfactual, and produce only small effects on output and other variables.

Models of limited participation, such as Christiano and Eichenbaum (1992) and Fuerst (1992) can deliver the right sign for the correlation between money growth and interest rates. In these models, new money balances are not distributed equally across agents. Instead, they are obtained, in the first instance, by the financial sector which channels them to firms as loans. As the consumers decide on their allocation of wealth between money (for cash-in-advance purposes) and interest-bearing deposits before new balances are distributed, the issue of new money balances increases the availability of loanable funds at a time when the consumers can no longer rebalance their portfolio, leading to a drop in the nominal interest rate. While this twist delivers the natural effect of money expansion on the interest rate and is intuitively appealing, it still fails to deliver significant effects from monetary shocks. However, Cochrane (1998) argues that allowing, in a VAR analysis, anticipated monetary policy to have real effects leads to more credible estimates of the output response to monetary shocks.

If models without price rigidities fail to deliver significant monetary policy effects, and if these effects are indeed important as Cochrane argues, then one should naturally turn to models with nominal rigidities. These models have become very popular in the last few years.

Some authors study the properties of RBC models under a price rigidity assumption, usually a Taylor or Calvo staggered contract specification. For instance, Ellison and Scott (2000) found that price rigidities improve the performance of the model with respect to inflation but produce unrealistically high-frequency fluctuations in output – a typical finding.

Others investigated the effects of wage rigidities with rather more success, see for instance Cho, Merrigan and Phaneuf (1998). However, the more common view is still that monetary shocks are unlikely to be the most important source of fluctuation (see Cooley and Hansen 1995 and Pesaran, Pierse and Lee 1993).

Habit persistence The contribution of demand shocks to economic fluctuations is still actively debated. The weight of evidence so far seems to favour the notion that demand shocks cannot, by themselves or in conjunction with productivity shocks, explain all of the more salient features of the business cycle.

Although the RBC literature initially developed as a counterweight to demand-dominated Keynesian thinking, the introduction of demand shocks in these models can be seen as a natural development. Since it has, so far, proved unequal to the task of providing a good representation of the observed data, perhaps more radical departures are required. One such departure is to abandon the additive separability property of the consumer's preferences. An interesting type of time-non-separable preferences are preferences that display habit persistence. For instance, Wen (1998) introduces an externality in employment and habit formation in labour. The idea is that the consumer values not only current leisure but also how much more leisure he currently has in comparison with the past. This idea is implemented by assigning negative values to the coefficients of the lagged values of leisure in the utility function. The main success of Wen's paper is in helping represent better the spectral distribution of hours worked. This is important because RBC models have problems accounting for the nearly equal amplitude of movements in labour and in output. However, it has been shown, see Cooley and Prescott (1995), that most of the movement in labour is due to movements between employment/unemployment rather than on the variation of hours worked. Indeed, indivisible employment (Hansen 1985; Hansen and Wright 1992) is one of the most dramatic success stories of the RBC literature.

Furthermore, it is by no means clear that habit persistence necessarily helps explain persistence in the business cycle. For instance, consider the baseline RBC model augmented only with habit persistence in consumption, and let us consider the limiting case in which this habit persistence is so severe as to ensure constancy of consumption over time. Then investment has to accommodate all of the effects of productivity shocks, the 'transmission mechanism' of the RBC model will be weakened, and GDP will display more variability and less persistence than in the baseline model.

Another extension that has aroused considerable interest is the introduction of heterogeneous agents. We will turn to the effect of aggregation on persistence in section 4.

3.2 Deterministic dynamics

In contrast to the RBC approach, the notion that business fluctuations were a purely dynamic phenomena that did not require what Richard Day (1992) has called the machinery of 'shockeries', is still vigorously investigated. In keeping with the new spirit of the time, this effort has been redirected towards equilibrium models. In that respect, the scope for complex dynamics was already present in the seminal paper of Solow (1956). Economists have always thought of the markets as a dynamic environment. In the late 1970s, after a great deal of conceptual work by Samuelson, Morishima, Koopmans, McKenzie and many others (see Wan 1971), theorists were able to reduce macrodynamics to a stylised model amenable to the formidable machinery of dynamical systems. In addition to the long-standing lines of research of the Ramsey model (infinite horizon, representative agent model), Diamond (1965) established Samuelson's overlapping-generations model, Samuelson (1958), as an alternative that emphasised the life cycle and heterogeneity of agents.

Both of these two lines of research remained faithful to the spirit of the traditional growth theory *à la* Solow–Swan–Samuelson, which views technological progress as a serendipitous by-product of scientific inquisitiveness, and therefore makes no attempt at investigating the economic factors that may affect it. With the outbreak of interest in new growth theory following the seminal works of Lucas (1988), Romer (1986) and many others (see Romer 1994 for a survey), these two lines of research were extended to incorporate the feature of interest to endogenous growth. While the traditional growth theory could only look at how growth could affect the business cycle but not the converse, it was possible for an endogenous growth theorist to look at the two-way relationship. However, endogenous growth has been more interested in rehabilitating fluctuations as a positive economic phenomenon than on devising and evaluating stabilisation policies, which is the traditional interest of economists studying economic fluctuations.

Traditional growth models

Solow understood that non-convex technology could create multiple equilibria and unstable steady states. First, it was realised that periodic paths could be generated in that model (see, for instance, Benhabib and Nishimura 1985). These were simple two-period cycles which was a bit restrictive for anyone trying to model the business cycle. Then, it was shown that the Ramsey model placed almost no restrictions on the dynamics of an equilibrium path, and that it could produce even chaotic paths.[16] Given any twice-differentiable function f, Boldrin and Montrucchio (1986) showed how to construct preferences and a production set such that the optimal stock of capital at time $t + 1$, k_{t+1}, be given by $k_{t+1} = f(k_t)$.[17] In essence, these authors showed that a very stylised model could be made to fit exactly economic data, a remarkable *tour de force*! Working with economic data makes one very suspicious of fits that are 'too good to be true'. What can we conclude from this ability to produce miraculous fits? One may have argued that, since in essence the Ramsey model could explain everything, it was not falsifiable as such and it did not qualify as a valid scientific theory according to Popper. However, the Boldrin–Montrucchio result requires the discount rate to become arbitrarily close to zero (see Montrucchio and Sorger 1996), a requirement that cannot be reconciled with standard observations from finance. This result illustrates the weakness of models that seek to represent the data well along one dimension only and typically perform poorly along the others. It also implies that the credibility of the deterministic analysis, in representing the business cycle, must necessarily depend on whether they can produce the right dynamics for the observed value of their parameters.

From an empirical point of view, one would have typically assumed, at least until recently, that the dynamic process of the economy would admit an ARIMA decomposition. Under this assumption, a deterministic cycle would be characterised by the presence of complex roots. The evidence for the presence of such complex roots is weak (see Bierens 2001 for a particularly careful treatment). One may wonder if this weak evidence is not indicative of a lack of adequacy of the ARMA decomposition, a point which we will raise in the next section.

Another idea that became very popular for representing economic fluctuations, pioneered by Azariadis (1981), was to identify expectations as a potential source of economic fluctuations. The workhorse often used in this type of analysis is the overlapping-generations model, a simple version of which we will now describe.

A simple model of expectations-driven fluctuations   Consider a discrete-time, infinite horizon economy that runs in period $t = 0, 1, 1, \ldots$ Two agents live in each period, the old agent who is in his last period of life, and the young agent who is just born and will live for another period. For

---

[16] Chaotic paths are paths that are cyclical and aperiodic, that is no two cycles are the same. For an introduction to the theory of dynamic systems see, for instance, Wiggins (1990).

[17] This result was obtained in a deterministic context. Mitra (1998) showed that it also held in a stochastic environment.

Agents' consumption

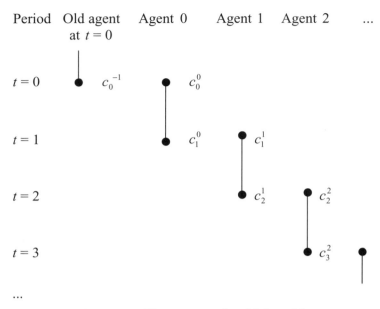

Figure 11.8 The structure of an OLG model

simplicity of exposition, we will assume a distribution economy; it is simple enough to reproduce the results that follow when production is modelled explicitly. In each period of their life, agents receive an endowment of a non-storable[18] homogeneous consumption good; for simplicity, let this endowment $\omega \equiv (\omega^0, \omega^1)$ be stationary, where ω^0 and ω^1 are the endowments when young and old, respectively. Let us denote with a superscript t the variables pertaining to the agent born at time t, e.g. his consumption is $\mathbf{c}^t \equiv (c_t^t, c_{t+1}^t)$, where c_t^t and c_{t+1}^t are his consumption when young and old, respectively. Each agent t tries to maximise his utility from consumption $u(c_t^t, c_{t+1}^t)$, where the utility function u displays the usual properties. This economy can be depicted graphically as in figure 11.8.

One usually interprets the 'young' stage as the working life of the consumer and the 'old' stage as his time in retirement, hence the usual assumption that ω^0 is much larger than ω^1, $\omega^0 >> \omega^1$. Let $\bar{\omega} \equiv \omega^0 + \omega^1$ be the aggregate endowment of the good in each period. Looking only at stationary allocations, i.e. let the consumption when young and old be (c^0, c^1), $\forall t$, $c_t^t = c^0$ and $c_{t+1}^t = c^1$, the aggregate constraint is $c^0 + c^1 \leq \bar{\omega}$. As long as

---

[18] This assumption is not innocuous but it could be relaxed for our purpose. A weaker assumption is that the rate of return on the storage technology never dominates the rate of return on money.

utility u is concave, the consumers will prefer consumption smoothing, i.e. the $\max_{c^0+c^1\leq\bar\omega} u(c^0, c^1)$ obtains for c^0 and c^1 is of the order of $\bar\omega/2$. Hence, the preferred allocation, $(\hat c^0, \hat c^1) = \arg\max_{c^0+c^1\leq\bar\omega} u(c^0, c^1)$, involves saving $\omega^0 - \hat c^0 > 0$ when young for a payoff $\hat c^1 - \omega^1 > 0$ when old.

If all the consumers consume their endowment, the autarkic allocation, each agent $t = 0, 1, \ldots$ achieves the utility $u(\omega^0, \omega^1)$. Next, consider the sequence of reallocations in which each young agent gives $\omega^0 - \hat c^0$ to the old agent and, receives $\hat c^1 - \omega^1$ in the next period from the new young agent. The utility achieved by the agents $t = 0, 1, \ldots$ is $u(\hat c^0, \hat c^1) > u(\omega^0, \omega^1)$. Since the old agent of $t = 0$ also receives more, every one is better off. This redistribution scheme is Pareto-improving. Unfortunately, this scheme cannot be supported in a barter economy as the old agent $t - 1$ has nothing to give in exchange to the young agent t, illustrating the failure of the double coincidence of wants.

However, transactions can be supported at an equilibrium once a medium of transaction is introduced. Let the old consumer of period $t = 0$ be endowed with $\bar M$ units of intrinsically useless fiat money. This consumer can give his stock of money $\bar M$ to the young consumer $t = 0$ in exchange for the quantity of good $\omega^0 - \hat c^0$. In turn, at $t = 1$, consumer $t = 0$ will exchange his stock of money for the goods he wants to purchase from consumer $t = 1$, and so on. Indeed, if a Walrasian auctioneer calls a constant price $p_t = (\bar M/(\omega^0 - \hat c^0))$ for the consumption good, these market exchanges will support the previous allocation as a market equilibrium.

This steady state can always be supported as a market equilibrium, but the market equilibrium is not necessarily unique. To see this, let p_t and p_{t+1} be the price of the good in period t and $t + 1$. The rate of return ρ_{t+1} on holding money from period t to $t + 1$ is: $\rho_{t+1} = p_t/p_{t+1} = 1/(1 + \pi_{t+1})$, where $\pi_{t+1} = (p_{t+1} - p_t)/p_t$ is the rate of inflation. For each possible ρ_{t+1}, one can calculate the optimal savings, s_t, of the consumer and his payoff, $\rho_{t+1}s_t$, in period $t + 1$ as the solution to $\max_{s_t} u(c_t^t, c_{t+1}^t)$ subject to $\{c_t^t \leq \omega^0 - s_t$ and $c_{t+1}^t \leq \omega^1 + \rho_{t+1}s_t\}$. The set of all possible consumption allocations is called the consumer's offer curve. Figure 11.9 depicts the offer curve of an overlapping-generations economy with Cobb–Douglas preferences and such that $\omega^1 = 0$. When the market rate of return is ρ, the consumer's optimum savings are $s(\rho)$ (the time subscript has been suppressed), his consumption when young is $c^0 = \omega^0 - s(\rho)$ and his consumption when old is $c^1 = \rho s$.

Figure 11.10 considers an overlapping-generations model with a backward-bending offer curve. Allocation E_0 is the steady-state allocation. The young consumer's savings, s_0, are the old consumer's retirement

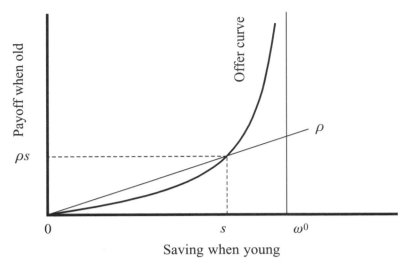

Figure 11.9 The offer curve of the young agent

allocation. However, there is another equilibrium allocation. Suppose generation 1 saves s_h and expects a payoff of s_l when retiring, and generation 2 saves s_l when young and retires with s_h. Graphically, generation 1 has consumption allocation E_l, generation 2 has consumption allocation E_h. By saving s_l when young, generation 2 provides exactly the amount of savings needed for generation 1 to get its expected payoff. Hence, the expectations of generation 1 are fulfilled. Consider the intertemporal allocation in which generations alternate their consumption allocation between E_l and E_h. This allocation is a perfect foresight equilibrium in that agents always get what they expect and markets always clear. It is associated with a two-period cycle in consumption, a rough form of economic fluctuation. Introducing physical capital in the model will also yield fluctuations in production. This model can also produce much more complex dynamics (see Azariadis 1993).

Many also saw this approach as giving substance to Keynes' celebrated animal's spirit intuition (see Grandmont 1985).

Fluctuations and growth So far, expectations have generated fluctuations only. Introducing growth requires substituting a production economy for the previous distribution economy. In such models, agents receive a labour endowment rather than an endowment of goods. A new outlet for aggregate savings is now available to the agents: the accumulation of physical capital. Hence, the model can dispense with the contrivance of

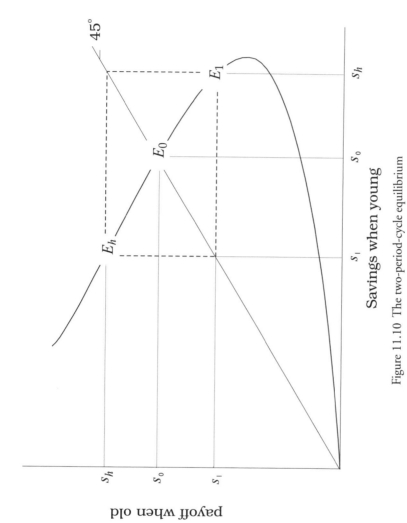

Figure 11.10 The two-period-cycle equilibrium

money. Capital is owned by the old generation who hire the young agents, engage in production using their capital and the labour input they have just hired, pay the wages, collect the capital rental, then sell their capital stock to the young generation at the end of their life. The nature of the relationship between growth and fluctuations depends on whether one assumes the economy operates under constant or increasing returns to scale.

If the economy operates under constant returns to scale, there is minimal interaction between fluctuations and growth. Fluctuations will preclude the economy settling permanently at a steady-state level of capital. Periods of high saving, the counterpart of allocation E_l in figure 11.10, precede accelerated economic expansion, with recessions being preceded by periods of low savings, E_h. However, these fluctuations do not impact the long-run rate of growth. Policies designed to reduce economic fluctuations will not generate permanently higher rates of growth.

If one is prepared to assume that the economy operates under increasing returns to scale, then short-term changes may have lasting effects. However, the nature of the effects will depend on the exact functional form used, and there is as yet no firmly established paradigm. For a more detailed exposition of this literature and its numerous lines of research, see Benhabib and Farmer (1999) and Farmer (1993). Furthermore, recent research has cast doubt on the presence of increasing returns at the aggregate level (see Basu 1996 and Basu and Fernald 1995).

Further developments and impact of expectational models   In the early papers, models that displayed this type of behaviour required agents to operate on the backward-bending part of their offer curve. Also, many economists were unaccustomed to and uncomfortable with the notion of multiple equilibria and reacted to it as a curiosity. Indeed, multiple equilibria can be construed as an attack on the foundations of equilibrium theory. A price equilibrium is self-explanatory when referring to an upward-sloping supply curve and a downward-sloping demand curve: the equilibrium price is the (unique) intersection of the two curves. When there are multiple equilibria, as for instance in the original Solow (1956) paper with non-convex production technologies, the question arises of which equilibrium would in fact prevail. In the case of the Solow model, the notion of equilibrium did at least restrict the set of possible allocation to a few distinct ones. One might have argued that the equilibrium that would prevail was given by the historical conditions of the economy, and that, therefore, history mattered, or one might have remained unconvinced by this argument. In any case, each equilibrium was locally unique and one could make sense of comparative dynamics exercises by looking at the equilibrium only locally. However, it was eventually realised that equilibria need not be locally unique: the allocations could cover a segment of a curve, a section of a surface, and so on. There is no way to isolate one equilibrium from its neighbours, no meaningful comparative dynamic exercise. The concept of equilibrium is still useful in that it can eliminate some feasible allocations, but the concept that demand must be equal to supply is not enough to predict which 'equilibrium price' will prevail: an additional allocation selection mechanism is needed. For a recent example of this line of investigation, see, for instance, Benhabib, Meng and Nishimura (2000).

In light of the exotic nature of these results and their inflammatory implications, it is hardly surprising that their message was not too warmly embraced by mainstream economists. Devotees of dynamical systems were in danger of being ignored and their approach needed to gain respectability fast. At first, proponents of deterministic dynamics tried to establish the genericity of their findings, i.e. to show that their results were not some oddity but would occur in most sensible frameworks; but questions were raised again about the robustness of their results. Sceptics argued that, even if standard models could give rise to multiple equilibria, this would happen only for a restricted set of parameters that would not include their observed values. Consequently, a great deal of effort has been put into writing models that would give rise to multiple equilibria for realistic values of the parameters.

One example is Evans, Honkapohja and Romer (1998), who produced a model of monopolistic competition that relied on the love-for-diversity or complementarity between investment goods to produce multiple equilibria. An additional feature of their model is that the equilibria are stable under some learning rule. This last property is particularly welcome. In economic theory, equilibrium prices are generally assumed to be common knowledge. The simplifying assumption made is that, after some groping, agents are sure to hit the equilibrium price. While of independent interest, the exact process directing the agents to the equilibrium is thought of as a peripheral issue. However, dynamic systems are, as a rule, extremely sensitive to initial conditions. The first generation of multiple equilibria models were driven by agents' expectations and could not accommodate any miss. Any expectational error would send the economy cartwheeling on a bursting expectational bubble. Stability under learning provides a realistic solution to the question of how the agents manage to form, eventually, infallible expectations. Some authors have taken an even more sophisticated approach to modelling agents' behaviour, investigating the implications of bounded rationality. For instance Barucci, Bischi and Gardini (1999) found that relaxing the assumption of strict rationality allowed new cyclical patterns to emerge. Very few economists are prepared to argue that the behaviour of every agent is based on rational decision-making. On the other hand, relaxing the assumption of rationality essentially provides an economic model with more degrees of freedom to match the facts. As there is, as yet, no universally accepted standard of rigour or consistency to apply to models of bounded rationality, one must evaluate departures from rationality on a case-by-case basis.

While researchers are still investigating vigorously the implications of dynamical systems for economics, they have not succeeded yet in making this issue central to the theory of economic fluctuations (see, for instance, Morris and Shin 2000). The problem is that the only clear message from this approach, a central authority can achieve Pareto-improvements by controlling prices, is at variance with most of the experience of policy-makers. Central Banks know that they may lose all of their foreign exchange reserves under a fixed exchange rate, i.e. if they try to fix the price of the foreign currencies. Municipal authorities have learned to their cost that imposing rent control exacerbates housing shortages. Most economists recognise the role played by expectations, say, in determining inflation, but it is not clear yet what insight can be gained from the study of ever-more complex dynamic phenomena.

Endogenous growth and fluctuations

By design, classical growth theory could make predictions on how the growth rate would affect economic fluctuations but it could not entertain the reverse question because it took growth as exogenous. This limitation does not apply to new growth theory as it endogenises growth. However, endogenous growth theory has primarily concerned itself with explaining why economic fluctuations are the price a country must pay in order to continue growing. One notable exception is Fatás (2000), to which we will return in the next section. Readers interested in endogenous growth *per se* are referred to Aghion and Howitt (1998).

Endogenous growth places heavy emphasis on Schumpeterian ideas of 'creative destruction'. While this process is compatible with steady-state growth, the archetypal example being Aghion and Howitt (1992), its nature suggests a far less tame process. There are at least two ways in which economic fluctuations can be seen as a necessary component of the process of growth.

First is the 'cleansing effect of recessions' (see, for instance, Caballero and Hammour 1994). During recessions, less productive firms are more likely to be eliminated. As their resources are released to firms that are more productive, average productivity increases. On the other hand, the hard times of recessions may also discourage the entry of more efficient firms. However, if firm entry is subject to a congestion externality, entrepreneurs will smooth out their entry, balancing the lower cost of entry during recession against the higher discounted payoff of entry during expansions. Therefore, recessions increase the speed at which resource misallocation is dealt with and accelerates growth.

Recessions can also be thought of as yielding beneficial effects with less drama than the previous removal of 'lame duck' firms. Periods of expansion strain the resources of a firm which must concentrate on extracting the utmost from current good times as they are, correctly, seen as a transient phase. Because of this need for haste, activities that are not time-critical may be postponed. These can include restructuring and rationalisation of firms' activities, training, experimental reorganisation, and the like. As these activities compete with directly immediately productive ones, they are best done in periods of recession when they do not crowd-out direct production. These productivity-enhancing activities set the stage for a more vigorous expansion, once a recession has run its course. Examples of this 'opportunity cost' approach to economic fluctuations can be found in Aghion and Saint-Paul (1998) and Saint-Paul (1997).

Secondly is the notion of Schumpeterian waves (see, for instance, Jovanovic and Rob 1990). While technology shocks in RBC models have a direct and simple effect on productivity, technological progress can be seen as a vastly more complex process. First, scientific discovery leads to the development of new 'general purpose technologies' which, in turn, must be adapted to improve, facilitate and enhance the process of production. This latter endeavour is resource-consuming and may require the development and adoption of new capital goods, along the lines of the vintage capital literature (see Greenwood and Jovanovic 1998). Hence, a necessary first phase of a technological revolution is the withdrawal of resources from the productive sector, thereby reducing average productivity and economic growth. This view was particularly popular at the time of the 'dot.com bubble' (see Oliner and Sichel 2000). Hence, like the ebb and the flow of the oceans, one can envision great leaps of growth being

preceded by periods of greatly reduced productivity in which the economy marshals its resources out of the old productive sector, directing them
towards new research, new development and, eventually, new industries.
Indeed, this picture of a dual effect of growth on unemployment is consistent with the notion of a Beveridge curve (see Blanchard and Diamond
1989).

The business cycle inherent in the cleansing of recessions would be easily
recognised as such by, say, a proponent of RBC theory. However, equating
the Schumpeterian waves to business cycles seems akin to attributing wave
action primarily to tidal forces, the gravitational pull of the Moon and of
the Sun, rather than to the build-up of wind action. This remark should
not be taken as belittling in any way the creativity, industriousness and contribution of the numerous gifted contributors to this line of research. They
are responsible for developing and popularising numerous new concepts
of general interest, such as the implementation cycles (see Shleifer 1986),
or a particular notion of social learning in which trailblazing innovative
firms create a template that can be used by other firms wishing to adopt
a new technology (see Kapur 1995). However, their results may be more
germane to structural rather than cyclical considerations (for an example
see, for instance, Violante 2002).

4 AGGREGATION

Traditional Keynesian-type explanations of business cycles are very seduc-
tive as they rely heavily on the economic intuition that economists develop
early on in their study. Their perceived failure in the aftermath of the oil
shock of the mid-1970s convinced economists that a regeneration, from
theoretically sound microeconomic foundations, was needed. This work
is still in progress (see, for instance, Ball, Mankiw and Romer 1988 or
Rotemberg and Woodford 1999). The economics of dynamical systems
has failed to establish itself as a leading explanation of economic fluctuations. Business cycle theories that exploit the properties of dynamic systems
are suspect because the dynamic systems considered are too general. Had we
been living in economies with 1,000-year business cycles, theorists would
be busy, using the same class of dynamic systems, demonstrating that this
should be the length of the cycle for reasonable values of the parameters.
The RBC approach is plagued by two vexing empirical facts: it struggles
to represent the observed amplitude and persistence of the business cycle.
Indeed, some authors have claimed that the time series properties of output
are little different from the time series properties assumed for the process

of productivity shocks (see Rudebush 1993). This problem is referred to as the 'weak transmission mechanism' of the RBC models.

Something is amiss, but what? My contention is that: (i) aggregation across individual producers generates on its own a vast amount of persistence in aggregate data, (ii) no meaningful empirical testing of theory can be done until the problem of persistence is dealt with successfully.

Consequently, aggregation must be considered a central issue for the study of the business cycle and no theory can be complete or be successfully validated, or disproved, unless the effect of aggregation is taken into account.

4.1 Aggregation and persistence

Taking the RBC paradigm as an example, we can think of the shock process in terms of an input process, a signal, that is 'filtered' by the RBC model to produce aggregate output, GDP, as its output process. The 'weak transmission mechanism' is a euphemism that states that the RBC filtering does little to alter the signal's characteristics. This is the case because the signal is thought of as a single aggregate productivity shock process that affects a single aggregate firm. While considering a completely different problem, Robinson (1978) realised that aggregation of simple time series would modify their nature: the aggregate process would not necessarily be of the same type as the component series. Granger (1980) and Granger and Newbold (1986) popularised this idea by pointing out that adding up individual time series with little persistence would yield an aggregate that exhibited long memory, i.e. a lot of persistence. Interpret the individual time series as individual firm's productivity shocks, and the aggregate as aggregate output, and you have an RBC type of model that displays lots of persistence (see, for instance, Chambers 1998). Aggregation modifies the characteristics of the signal; it provides for a 'strong' transmission mechanism. On the empirical side, a number of papers have considered the problem of estimating the 'aggregation bias' (see Lee, Pesaran and Pierse 1990, 1992 and Pesaran, Pierse and Lee 1993, especially with respect to the implication for the contribution of monetary shocks to the business cycle).

The notion that aggregating output across firms creates something essentially different is very intriguing. Some economists (for instance, Forni and Lippi 1997), were so enthralled with the idea that they felt that all macroeconomics could be summarised as a large system of simultaneous linear processes that only needed adding up. Resource allocation, optimisation and the market structure, so central to contemporary economic thinking, all operated unseen in the background. Can economic theory really be disposed of in this way? One problem with this approach is that it assumes that productivity shocks follow some autoregressive (AR) process in their level. Therefore, productivity can take (forbidden) negative values. Macroeconomists usually assume that the *logarithm* of shocks follow an AR process, which is more realistic and guarantees non-negativity of the productivities, but which is much more challenging to analyse. Another problem with this approach is that it does not offer any guidance on the exact specification of the equations to be considered beyond their linearity. One danger, amply demonstrated by earlier Keynesian practitioners, is that small, and apparently insignificant, changes in the specification of the equations lead to totally different properties.

There is no reason to believe that macroeconomics can be summed up by a set of linear equations; only computational convenience. It is therefore not surprising that this linear aggregation produces the wrong kind of persistence, the persistence of fractionally integrated processes. Persistence is the fact that output at time $t + \tau$ is highly correlated with the output at time t, even for long lags τ; let ρ_τ be this correlation coefficient. By definition, $\rho_0 = 1$. In fractionally integrated processes, the correlation coefficient drops precipitously between $\rho_0 = 1$ and ρ_1, then decays very slowly. This slow decay qualifies this process for long memory. However, the actual decay of the empirical data does not exhibit this form at all. The correlation coefficient of aggregate output, at first, declines very slowly from $\rho_0 = 1$, then takes a deep dive: it is as if the memory was lasting almost intact for a while, then departed abruptly.

Where aggregation carried out of computational expediency fails, aggregation combined with even a simple macro model fares much better. When general equilibrium considerations are brought to bear, as in Abadir and Talmain (2002a), one finds an aggregate process which is highly nonlinear, displays long memory yet is mean-reverting. The amplitude of the productivity shocks is amplified by the dispersion of firms, hence small productivity shocks can cause large aggregate fluctuations. Furthermore, the model predicts a functional form for the autocorrelation function, the collection of correlations $\{\rho_\tau\}_{\tau=0}^{\infty}$, which fits well the empirical data (see figure 11.11).

4.2 Persistence and the true nature of economic relationships

Persistence of the business cycle has long been a recognised feature of the business cycle (see Diebold and Rudebusch 1989). What are its implications

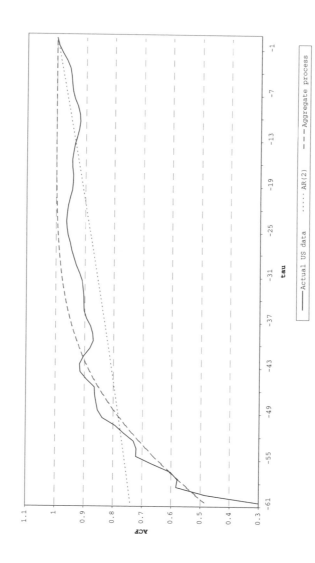

Figure 11.11 The autocorrelation function for for log-level of US *per capita* GDP and the fit for an AR(2) and for the Abadir–Talmain aggregate process

for growth? Fatás (2000) notes that countries with a higher Cochrane variance ratio also display higher growth, but the interpretation of the Cochrane ratio as a measure of persistence is controversial. Perhaps more importantly, persistence obscures the nature of the true relationship between macroeconomic variables. Even AR processes can cause problems if one ignores the autoregressive nature of the process. For example, suppose that our 'dependent variable' y_t depends on an 'independent variable' x_t and on a shock u_t which follow the autoregressive process

$$y_t = \alpha y_{t-1} + \beta x_t + u_t, \tag{11.36}$$

$$\text{with } u_t = \rho u_{t-1} + \varepsilon_t, 0 < \rho < 1, \tag{11.37}$$

$$\text{and } x_t = \theta x_{t-1} + v_t, 0 < \theta < 1. \tag{11.38}$$

Suppose that a researcher, who is unaware of or who chooses to ignore the AR nature of the series u and x given by (11.37) and (11.38), runs a simple OLS regression on (11.36). Also suppose that this researcher either chooses to ignore the warning of his autocorrelation diagnostic tool, or uses an inappropriate test.[19] The OLS regression on the first regression (11.36) yields estimators $\hat{\alpha}$ and $\hat{\beta}$ which are biased and inconsistent, and where the asymptotic bias is given by:[20]

$$\text{asym.bias } (\hat{\alpha}) \equiv \text{plim } \hat{\alpha} - \alpha$$

$$= \frac{\rho \text{Var } x_t \text{Var } u_t}{(1 - \alpha\rho)[\text{Var } y_{t-1}\text{Var } x_t - \text{Covar}^2(x_t, y_{t-1})]},$$

$$\text{asym.bias } (\hat{\beta}) \equiv \text{plim } \hat{\beta} - \beta = -\frac{\beta\theta}{(1 - \alpha\theta)} \text{ asym.bias } (\hat{\alpha}),$$

$$\text{Var } y_{t-1}\text{Var } x_t - \text{Covar}^2(x_t, y_{t-1}) = \frac{(1 - \theta^2)\beta^2\sigma_x^4}{(1 - \alpha^2)(1 - \alpha\theta)^2}$$

$$+ \frac{(1 + \alpha\rho)\sigma_u^2\sigma_x^2}{(1 - \alpha^2)(1 - \alpha\rho)}.$$

For instance, if the parameters are such that $\theta = 0.99, \rho = 0.985, \sigma_x^2 = \sigma_u^2 = 1$, and keeping $\beta = 1$ while varying α from 0 to 1, the probability limits of the OLS coefficients are described in figure 11.12.

The worst bias occurs when $\alpha = 0$ (while $\beta = 1$), in which case the plim $\hat{\alpha}$ is much higher than plim $\hat{\beta}$ when in fact $\alpha = 0$ and $\beta = 1$!

---

[19] Since this model includes a lagged dependent variable, the Durbin–Watson test is not applicable. An alternative is the Breush–Godfrey test (see for instance, Greene 1993, section 15.5).

[20] See Maddala and Rao (1973) who state that this result was first derived by Griliches (1961).

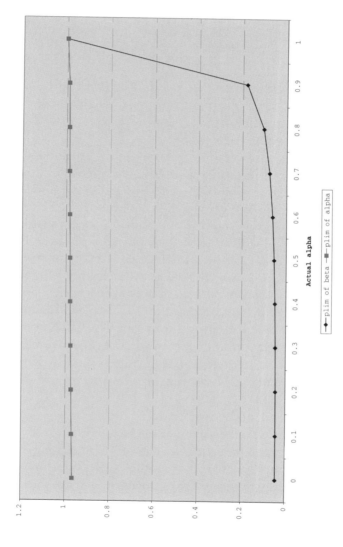

Figure 11.12 The probability limits of the OLS estimators

Table 11.3 *Actual and estimated*
values of the OLS estimator

| | Coefficients | |
	α	β
actual	0	1
plim	0.97	0.044

Indeed, in this case the researcher is led to believe that his dependent variable process y_t follows an 'almost unit root' (AUR) process, which is weakly, if at all, moderated by the independent variable x_t, while, in reality, it is $y_t - x_t$ that follows an AUR process.

No reputable economist would dream of skipping or mishandling a test for autoregression, or disregarding its result. Yet, almost all of the recent macroeconomics literature skips over the salient and recognised feature of a high degree of persistence in macro data. What price has to be paid for this oversight? To someone using standard methods, a process, such as the one hypothesised on p. 556, will make the true nature of the relationship between macroeconomic variables obscure indeed. It is Abadir and Talmain's contention (2002b) that paradoxes such as the well-known uncovered interest parity (UIP) puzzle are purely an artifact of persistence. If even simple contemporaneous relationships become unrecognisable to standard econometric methods, it seems quite optimistic or foolish to attempt to decipher the more demanding relationship between variables characterising the nature of a dynamic process. In particular, what hope is there for a meaningful empirical investigation of the relationship between growth and the business cycle?

The answer is that methods must be developed to cope with the world of long memory in which our economies operate and that is so unlike the merry world of linear processes, the only one comprehensively explored so far. Abadir and Talmain (2002b) did so for the FOREX to show that, once the obvious persistence in the exchange rate is accounted for, the UIP puzzle vanishes. Without the tools to lift the fog of long memory, we cannot test empirically the predictions of our theoretical models. Without aggregation, simulation and calibration exercises are no guide at all. Indeed, a model that would produce the right amount of persistence without taking account of aggregation should be dismissed out of hand because, once aggregation is introduced, it would deliver an unrealistically high level of persistence.

The traditional subjects of interest to macroeconomists, fluctuations and growth, can be studied only with an addition: aggregation.

5 CONCLUSION

Economic growth and business fluctuations are two of the principal areas of interest to macroeconomists. While each topic has generated a vast literature on its own, there has been a comparatively modest effort devoted to understanding the links between growth and fluctuations.

The early non-market-clearing approaches to fluctuations did envisage a relationship in which the growth rate affected economic fluctuations. In the accelerator model, the presence or absence of business cycles and their frequency did not depend on the rate of growth, but the stronger growth tended to dampen the amplitude of economic fluctuations. The effect of growth on the business cycle was more complex in Goodwin's predator–prey model. Yet again, growth influenced the business cycle but there was no feedback mechanism between economic fluctuations and long-run growth. Of course, economic fluctuations have a mechanical effect on growth: the growth rate is lower in recessions than during periods of expansion. However, the message of these models was that this effect is purely transient; over long periods of time, more cyclical economies would not outperform or underperform steadier ones.

General equilibrium approaches to the business cycles suggests a more complex relationship. The RBC model of King, Plosser and Rebelo (KPR) could still only envisage an effect of growth on the business cycle. Its prediction was that growth would increase the amplitude of the cycle and shorten its length, which is at variance with the earlier results of the accelerator model. There are few predictions that could not be supported by some model of deterministic dynamics, but the derived relationships between fluctuations and growth tended to be model-specific.

Endogenous growth shed a new light on business cycles. It suggested that recessions might be a necessary price to pay to obtain growth. It also implied that perhaps this relationship was not simply a linear one. Indeed, Fatás (2001) presented some empirical evidence to that effect.

However, it has been suggested that the presence of long memory in macroeconomic data obscures and hides the true relationships between macroeconomic variables as is arguably the case for the UIP puzzle. As aggregation appears to be the leading candidate for the explanation of these long memory features, the exact nature of the relationship between growth and business cycles may not be elucidated until such feature can be successfully integrated in more general models.

APPENDIX

A.1 PROOF THAT THE EXISTENCE OF A BALANCED GROWTH PATH REQUIRES TECHNICAL PROGRESS TO BE LABOUR-AUGMENTING

The argument is presented in a continuous time setting for expository concision; it readily extends to a discrete time framework. Consider a neo-classical production function F that exhibits constant returns to scale. On a balanced growth path, the saving rate $s \equiv \dot{K}/K$, where $\dot{K}$ is net invest-ment, is constant and labour N and capital K grow at some constant rates γ_N and γ_K. So

$$Y_t = F(e^{z_K t} K_t, e^{z_N t} N_t)$$

where z_K and z_N are the steady-state rate of growth of capital and labour-augmenting technologies. By the homogeneity of function F, we have

$$\frac{Y_t}{K_t} = e^{z_K t} F\left(1, e^{(z_N - z_K)\,t}\,\frac{N_t}{K_t}\right) = e^{z_K t} F\left(1, e^{(\gamma_N + z_N - \gamma_K - z_K)\,t}\,\frac{N_0}{K_0}\right)$$

$$= e^{z_K t} \varphi\left(e^{(\gamma_N + z_N - \gamma_K - z_K)t}\right), \text{ where } \varphi(x) \equiv F\left(1, x\frac{N_0}{K_0}\right).$$

Since capital accumulation proceeds according to

$$\dot{K}_t = s\,Y_t - \delta K_t \implies \gamma_K = \frac{\dot{K}}{K} = s\,\frac{Y_t}{K_t} - \delta \implies \frac{Y_t}{K_t} = \frac{\gamma_K + \delta}{s},$$

we have

$$e^{z_K t} \varphi\left(e^{(\gamma_N + z_N - \gamma_K - z_K)t}\right) = \frac{\gamma_K + \delta}{s}.$$

If $\gamma_N + z_N - \gamma_K - z_K = 0$, this equation implies $z_K = 0$, i.e. technical progress is purely labour-augmenting. If $\gamma_N + z_N - \gamma_K - z_K \neq 0$, the variable $x \equiv e^{(\gamma_N + z_N - \gamma_K - z_K)t}$ is not a constant and this equation implies

$$\varphi(x) = \frac{\gamma_K + \delta}{s} x^{-\frac{z_K}{\gamma_N + z_N - \gamma_K - z_K}} = \frac{\gamma_K + \delta}{s} x^{\alpha},$$

$$\text{where } \alpha \equiv \frac{z_K}{\gamma_K + z_K - (\gamma_N + z_N)},$$

which implies that the production function takes a Cobb–Douglas form (in which case technical progress can be written trivially in a labour-augmenting form)

$$F(K, N) = KF\left(1, \frac{N}{K}\right) = K\varphi\left(\frac{K_0\, N}{N_0\, K}\right) = \frac{\gamma_K + \delta}{s}\left(\frac{K_0}{N_0}\right)^\alpha K^{1-\alpha} N^\alpha.$$

A.2 SOLUTION OF THE STOCHASTIC EULER EQUATION (11.14) UNDER QUADRATIC UTILITY AND PRODUCTION FUNCTIONS

Let us particularise to the case of an inelastic labour supply, i.e. u only depends on consumption and $N = 1$, and of a linear production function F such that

$$u(c, N) = u_0 + u_1 c - \frac{1}{2}c^2 \quad \text{and} \quad F(k, 1) = k;$$

the first-order condition (11.14) becomes

$$\gamma(u_1 - c_t) = \mathrm{E}_t[\beta^*(1 - \delta + A_{t+1})(u_1 - c_{t+1})]$$

$$\implies c_t = \left(1 - \frac{\beta^*}{\gamma}(1 - \delta + \mathrm{E}_t[A_{t+1}])\right) u_1$$

$$+ \mathrm{E}_t\left[\frac{\beta^*}{\gamma}(1 - \delta + A_{t+1})c_{t+1}\right].$$

Let $G_{t+\tau} \equiv \beta^*(1 - \delta + A_{t+\tau})/\gamma$; we have

$$c_t = \mathrm{E}_t[1 - G_{t+1}]u_1 + \mathrm{E}_t[G_{t+1}c_{t+1}]$$
$$= \mathrm{E}_t[1 - G_{t+1}]u_1 + \mathrm{E}_t[G_{t+1}[\mathrm{E}_{t+1}[1 - G_{t+2}]u_1 + \mathrm{E}_{t+1}[G_{t+2}c_{t+2}]]]$$
$$= \mathrm{E}_t[1 - G_{t+1}]u_1 + \mathrm{E}_t[G_{t+1}(1 - G_{t+2})]u_1 + \mathrm{E}_t[G_{t+1}G_{t+2}c_{t+2}]$$
$$= \mathrm{E}_t[1 - G_{t+1}G_{t+2}]u_1 + \mathrm{E}_t[G_{t+1}G_{t+2}c_{t+2}],$$

and by repeated substitutions

$$c_t = \mathrm{E}_t\left[1 - \prod_{\tau=1}^{T} G_{t+\tau}\right] u_1 + \mathrm{E}_t\left[\prod_{\tau=1}^{T} G_{t+\tau} c_{t+T}\right].$$

Hence, if the limit exists, it is clear that the following c_t satisfies (11.14)

$$c_t = u_1\left(1 - \lim_{T\longrightarrow\infty} \mathrm{E}_t\left[\prod_{\tau=1}^{T} G_{t+\tau}\right]\right).$$

For example, suppose that A_t is deterministic and decreases exponentially towards $\bar{A} \equiv \gamma/\beta^* + \delta - 1 \implies \bar{G} \equiv \beta^*(1 - \delta + \bar{A})/\gamma = 1$, that is $A_t - \bar{A} = \lambda^t(A_0 - \bar{A})$, $0 < \lambda < 1 \implies G_t = 1 + \lambda^t((A_0 - \bar{A})\beta^*/\gamma)$, then as a first-order approximation

$$\ln\left[\prod_{t=1}^{\infty} G_t\right] = \sum_{t=1}^{\infty} \ln G_t \simeq \frac{(A_0 - \bar{A})\beta^*}{\gamma} \sum_{t=1}^{\infty} \lambda^t = \frac{\lambda(A_0 - \bar{A})\beta^*}{(1 - \lambda)\gamma},$$

and we have

$$c_0 \simeq u_1\left(1 - e^{\frac{\lambda(A_0 - \bar{A})\beta^*}{(1-\lambda)\gamma}}\right).$$

If we interpret $A_0 > \bar{A}$ as an unanticipated favourable shock at time $t = 0$, the consumer takes advantage of the transitory increased productivity to build up its capital stock.

A.3 DERIVATIONS OF THE LOG-LINEARISED FIRST-ORDER CONDITIONS

For the first equation (11.25), we have

$$\ln \frac{\partial u(c_t, L_t)}{\partial c_t} = \ln \lambda_t \text{ and } \ln \frac{\partial u(c, L)}{\partial c}$$

$$= \ln \lambda \implies \ln \frac{\partial u(c_t, L_t)}{\partial c_t} - \ln \frac{\partial u(c, L)}{\partial c} = \ln \lambda_t - \ln \lambda.$$

Now, as a first-order approximation,

$$\ln \frac{\partial u(c_t, L_t)}{\partial c_t} - \ln \frac{\partial u(c, L)}{\partial c} \simeq \frac{1}{\partial u(c, L)/\partial c}$$
$$\times \left[\frac{\partial^2 u(c, L)}{\partial c^2} dc_t + \frac{\partial^2 u(c, L)}{\partial c \partial L} dL_t\right].$$

Hence

$$\xi_{cc}\hat{c}_t + \xi_{cl}\hat{L}_t = \hat{\lambda}_t,$$

which yields the result since $\hat{L}_t = -(N/(1 - N))\hat{N}_t$.

For the second equation (11.26), let us start from

$$\ln \frac{\partial u(c_t, L_t)}{\partial L_t} = \ln \lambda_t + \ln A_t + \ln \frac{\partial F(k_t, N_t)}{\partial N_t} \quad \text{and}$$

$$\ln \frac{\partial u}{\partial L} = \ln \lambda + \ln A + \ln \frac{\partial F}{\partial N}.$$

Subtracting the left-hand side of both equations, we have

$$\ln \frac{\partial u\,(c_t, L_t)}{\partial L_t} - \frac{\partial u}{\partial L} = \xi_{lc}\hat{c}_t - \xi_{ll}\frac{N}{1-N}\hat{N}_t.$$

Subtracting the right-hand side of both equations, we have

$$\ln \lambda_t \frac{\partial F\,(k_t, N_t)}{\partial N_t} - \ln \lambda A \frac{\partial F}{\partial N} = \hat{\lambda}_t + \hat{A}_t + \xi_{nk}\hat{k}_t + \xi_{nn}\hat{N}_t.$$

For the third equation (11.27), let us start from

$$\ln\left[A_{t+1}\frac{\partial F\,(k_{t+1}, N_{t+1})}{\partial k_{t+1}} + (1-\delta)\right] = \ln \frac{\lambda_t \gamma}{\beta^* \lambda_{t+1}}.$$

Differentiating the left-hand side, we have

$$\ln\left[A_{t+1}\frac{\partial F\,(k_{t+1}, N_{t+1})}{\partial k_{t+1}} + (1-\delta)\right]$$
$$- \ln\left[A\frac{\partial F}{\partial k} + (1-\delta)\right] = \eta_a \hat{A}_{t+1} + \eta_k \hat{k}_{t+1} + \eta_n \hat{N}_{t+1}.$$

Differentiating the right-hand side, we have

$$\ln \frac{\lambda_t \gamma}{\beta^* \lambda_{t+1}} - \ln \frac{\lambda \gamma}{\beta^* \lambda} = \hat{\lambda}_t - \hat{\lambda}_{t+1}.$$

The budget constraint (11.28) and the resource constraint $y_t = c_t + i_t$ implies

$$\hat{y}_t = \frac{dc_t}{y} + \frac{di_t}{y} = s_c \hat{c}_t + s_i \frac{di_t}{i}.$$

From (11.9), we have

$$\frac{di_t}{i} = \frac{\gamma k}{i}\frac{dk_{t+1}}{k} - (1-\delta)\frac{k}{i}\frac{dk_t}{k} = \varphi \hat{k}_{t+1} - \frac{(1-\delta)\,\varphi}{\gamma}\hat{k}_t.$$

The functional form of the production function (11.8) implies also that

$$\hat{y}_t = \hat{A}_t + \xi_k \hat{k}_t + \xi_n \hat{N}_t.$$

BIBLIOGRAPHY

Abadir, K. M. and Talmain, G. (2002a). 'Aggregation, Persistence and Volatility in a Macro Model', *Review of Economic Studies*, 69(4), 749–79
  (2002b). 'Distilling Co-Movements from Macro Dynamics: Uncovering the UIP and other Puzzles', *University of York Discussion Paper*

Aghion, P. and Howitt, P. (1992). 'A Model of Growth through Creative Destruction', *Econometrica*, 60(2), 323–51

(1998). *Endogenous Growth Theory*, Cambridge, MA: MIT Press

Aghion, P. and Saint-Paul, G. (1998). 'Virtues of Bad Times: Interaction between Productivity Growth and Economic Fluctuations', *Macroeconomic Dynamics*, 2(3), 322–34

Araujo, A. P. and Maldonado, W. L. (2000). 'Ergodic Chaos, Learning and Sunspot Equilibrium', *Economic Theory*, 15(1), 163–84

Azariadis, C. (1981). 'Self-Fulfilling Prophecies', *Journal of Economic Theory*, 25(3), 380–96

(1993). *Intertemporal Macroeconomics*, Oxford: Blackwell

Ball, L., Mankiw, N. G. and Romer, D. (1988). 'The New Keynesian Economics and the Output-Inflation Trade-Off', *Brookings Papers on Economic Activity*, 1, 1–65

Barucci, E., Bischi, G. I. and Gardini, L. (1999). 'Endogenous Fluctuations in a Bounded Rationality Economy: Learning Non-Perfect Foresight Equilibria', *Journal of Economic Theory*, 87(1), 243–53

Basu, S. (1996). 'Procyclical Productivity: Increasing Returns or Cyclical Utilization?', *Quarterly Journal of Economics*, 111(3), 719–51

Basu, S. and Fernald, J. G. (1995). 'Aggregate Productivity and the Productivity of Aggregates', *National Bureau of Economic Research Working Paper*, 5382

Baxter, M. and King, R. G. (1993). 'Fiscal Policy in General Equilibrium', *American Economic Review*, 83(3), 315–34

Benhabib, J. and Farmer, R. E. A. (1999). 'Indeterminacy and Sunspots in Macroeconomics', in J. B. Taylor and M. Woodford (eds.), *Handbook of Macroeconomics*, 1A, Amsterdam: Elsevier Science, 387–448

Benhabib, J., Meng, Q. and Nishimura, K. (2000). 'Indeterminacy under Constant Returns to Scale in Multisector Economies', *Econometrica*, 68(6), 1541–8

Benhabib, J. and Nishimura, K. (1985). 'Competitive Equilibrium Cycles', *Journal of Economic Theory*, 35(2), 284–306

Bierens, H. J. (2001). 'Complex Unit Roots and Business Cycles: Are They Real?', *Econometric Theory*, 17(5), 962–83

Binder, M. and Pesaran, M. H. (1999). 'Stochastic Growth Models and Their Econometric Implications', *Journal of Economic Growth*, 4(2), 139–83

Blanchard, O. J. and Khan, C. M. (1980). 'The Solution of Linear Difference Models under Rational Expectations', *Econometrica*, 45(5), 1305–12

Blanchard, O. J. and Diamond, P. (1989). 'The Beveridge Curve', *Brookings Papers on Economic Activity*, 0(1), 1–60

Boldrin, M. and Montrucchio, L. (1986). 'On the Indeterminacy of Capital Accumulation Paths', *Journal of Economic Theory*, 40(1), 26–39

Caballero, R. J. and Hammour, M. (1994). 'The Cleansing Effects of Recessions', *American Economic Review*, 84(5), 1350–68

Chadha, J. S. and Nolan, C. (2001). 'Interest Rate Bounds and Fiscal Policy', mimeo

Chambers, M. J. (1998). 'Long Memory and Aggregation in Macroeconomic Time Series', *International Economic Review*, 39(4), 1053–72

Cho, J. O., Merrigan, P. and Phaneuf, L. (1998). 'Weekly Employee Hours, Weeks Worked and Intertemporal Substitution', *Journal of Monetary Economics*, 41(1), 185–99

Chou, C. F., Kimura, F. and Talmain, G. (1994). 'Scale Effects, Global Market Place Integration, and R&D Effort', *Proceedings of the Fifth Annual Meetings of the American Society for Competitiveness*, ASC, Indiana, PA, 412–24

Christiano, L. J. and Eichenbaum, M. (1992). 'Liquidity Effects and the Monetary Transmission Mechanism', *American Economic Review*, 82(2), 346–53

Cochrane, J. H. (1998). 'What Do the VARs Mean? Measuring the Output Effects of Monetary Policy', *Journal of Monetary Economics*, 41(2), 277–300

Cooley, T. F. and Hansen, G. D. (1989). 'The Inflation Tax in in a Real Business Cycle Model', *American Economic Review*, 79(4), 733–48

(1995). 'Money and the Business Cycle', in T. F. Cooley (ed.), *Frontiers of Business Cycle Research*, Princeton: Princeton University Press, 175–216

Cooley, T. F. and Prescott, E. C. (1995). 'Economic Growth and Business Cycles', in T. F. Cooley (ed.), *Frontiers of Business Cycle Research*, Princeton: Princeton University Press, 1–38

Day, R. H. (1992). 'Models of Business Cycles: A Review Article', *Structural Change and Economic Dynamics*, 3, 177–82

Desai, M. and Ormerod, P. (1998). 'Richard Goodwin: A Short Appreciation', *Economic Journal*, 108(450), 1431–5

Diamond, P. (1965). 'National Debt in a Neoclassical Growth Model', *American Economic Review*, 55(5), 1126–50

Diebold, F. X. and Rudebusch, G. D. (1989). 'Long Memory and Persistence in Aggregate Output', *Journal of Monetary Economics*, 24(2), 189–209

Ellison, M. and Scott, A. (2000). 'Sticky Prices and Volatile Output', *Journal of Monetary Economics*, 46(3), 621–32

Evans, G. E., Honkapohja, S. and Romer, P. (1998). 'Growth Cycles', *American Economic Review*, 88(3), 495–515

Farmer, R. E. A. (1993). *The Macroeconomics of Self-Fulfilling Prophecies*, Cambridge, MA: MIT Press

Fatás, A. (2000). 'Endogenous Growth and Stochastic Trends', *Journal of Monetary Economics*, 45(1), 107–28

(2001). 'The Effects of Business Cycles on Growth', INSEAD, mimeo, http://www.insead.fr/~fatas/

Forni, M. and Lippi, M. (1997). *Aggregation and the Microfoundations of Dynamic Macroeconomics*, Oxford: Oxford University Press

Fuerst, T. S. (1992). 'Liquidity, Loanable Funds and Real Activity', *Journal of Monetary Economics*, 29(1), 3–24

Goodwin, R. M. (1951). 'The Non-linear Accelerator and the Persistence of Business Cycles', *Econometrica*, 19(1), 1–17

(1967). 'A Growth Cycle', in C. H. Feinstein (ed.), *Socialism, Capitalism and Economic Growth*, Cambridge: Cambridge University Press, 54–8

Grandmont, J. M. (1985). 'On Endogenous Competitive Business Cycles', *Econometrica*, 53(5), 995–1045

Granger, C. W. J. (1980). 'Long Memory Relationships and the Aggregation of Dynamic Models', *Journal of Econometrics*, 14(2), 227–38

Granger, C. W. J. and Newbold, P. (1986). *Forecasting Economic Time Series*, San Diego: Academic Press

Greene, W. H. (1993). *Econometric Analysis*, 2nd edn, New York: Macmillan

Greenwood, J. and Jovanovic, B. (1998). 'Accounting for Growth', *National Bureau of Economic Research Working Paper*, 6647

Griliches, Z. (1961). 'A Note on Serial Correlation Bias in Estimates of Distributed Lags', *Econometrica*, 29(1), 65–73

Hansen, G. D. (1985). 'Indivisible Labor and the Business Cycle', *Journal of Monetary Economics*, 16(3), 309–27

Hansen, G. D. and Wright, R. (1992). 'The Labor Market in Real Business Cycle Theory', *Federal Reserve Bank of Minneapolis Quarterly Review*, Spring, 2–12

Harrod, R. F. (1936). *The Trade Cycle: An Essay*, Oxford: Clarendon Press
   (1939). 'An Essay in Dynamic Theory', *Economic Journal*, 49(1), 14–33

Heijdra, B. J. and van der Ploeg, F. (2002). *Foundations of Modern Macroeconomics*, Oxford: Oxford University Press

Hicks, J. R. (1950). *A Contribution to the Theory of the Trade Cycle*, London: Oxford University Press

Horvath, M. (1998). 'Cyclicality and Sectoral Linkages: Aggregate Fluctuations from Independent Sectoral Shocks', *Review of Economic Dynamics*, 1, 781–808

Jones, C. I. (1995a). 'R&D-Based Models of Economic Growth', *Journal of Political Economy*, 103(4), 759–84
   (1995b). 'Time Series Tests of Endogenous Growth Models', *Quarterly Journal of Economics*, 110(2), 495–525

Jovanovic, B. and Rob, R. (1990). 'Long Waves and Short Waves: Growth through Intensive and Extensive Search', *Econometrica*, 58(6), 1391–1409

Judd, K. L. (1998). *Numerical Methods in Economics*, Cambridge, MA: MIT Press

Kapur, S. (1995). 'Technological Diffusion with Social Learning', *Journal of Industrial Economics*, 43(2), 173–95

King, R. G., Plosser, C. I. and Rebelo, S. T. (1988a). 'Production, Growth and Business Cycles: I. The Basic Neoclassical Model', *Journal of Monetary Economics*, 21(2/3), 195–232
   (1988b). 'Production, Growth and Business Cycles: II. New Directions', *Journal of Monetary Economics*, 21(2/3), 309–41

Kydland, F. E. and Prescott, E. C. (1982). 'Time to Build and Aggregate Fluctuations', *Econometrica*, 50(6), 1351–70
   (1987). 'The Workweek of Capital and its Cyclical Implications', *Journal of Monetary Economics*, 21(2/3), 343–60

Lee, K. C., Pesaran, M. H. and Pierse, R. G. (1990). 'Testing for Aggregation Bias in Linear Models', *Economic Journal Conference Papers*, 100(400), 137–50
   (1992). 'Persistence of Shocks and their Sources in a Multisectoral Model of UK Output Growth', *Economic Journal*, 102(410), 342–56

Ljungqvist, L. and Sargent, T. J. (2000). *Recursive Macroeconomic Theory*, Boston, MA: MIT Press

Long, J. B. and Plosser, C. I. (1983). 'Real Business Cycles', *Journal of Political Economy*, 91(1), 39–69

Lucas, R. E. (1988). 'On the Mechanism of Economic Development', *Journal of Monetary Economics*, 22(1), 3–42

(1990). 'Liquidity and Interest Rates', *Journal of Economic Theory*, 50(2), 237–64

Lucas, R. E. and Stokey, N. L. (1983). 'Optimal Fiscal and Monetary Policy in an Economy without Capital', *Journal of Monetary Economics*, 12(1), 55–93

(1987). 'Money and Interest in a Cash-in-Advance Economy', *Econometrica*, 55(3), 491–513

Maddala, G. S. and Rao, A. S. (1973). 'Tests for Serial Correlation in Regression Models with Lagged Dependent Variables and Serially Correlated Errors', *Econometrica*, 41(4), 761–74

Matthews, R. C. O. (1950). *The Trade Cycle*, Cambridge: Cambridge University Press

Mitra, K. (1998). 'On Capital Accumulation Paths in a Neoclassical Stochastic Growth Model', *Economic Theory*, 11(2), 457–64

Montrucchio, L. and Sorger, G. (1996). 'Topological Entropy of Policy Functions in Concave Dynamic Optimization Models', *Journal of Mathematical Economics*, 25(2), 181–94

Morris, S. and Shin, H. S. (2000). 'Rethinking Multiple Equilibria in Macroeconomic Modeling', *NBER Macroeconomics Annual 2000*, Cambridge, MA and London: MIT Press, 141–81

Oliner S. D. and Sichel, D. E. (2000). 'The Resurgence of Growth in the Late 1990s: Is Information Technology the Story?', *Journal of Economic Perspectives*, 14(4), 3–22

Perotti, R. (1999). 'Fiscal Policy in Good Times and Bad', *Quarterly Journal of Economics*, 114(4), 1399–1436

Pesaran, M. H., Pierse, R. G. and Lee, K. C. (1993). 'Persistence, Cointegration and Aggregation: A Disaggregated Analysis of Output Fluctuations in the US Economy', *Journal of Econometrics*, 56(1/2), 57–88

Robinson, P. M. (1978). 'Statistical Inference for a Random Coefficient Autoregressive Model', *Scandinavian Journal of Statistics*, 5, 163–8

Romer, Paul M. (1986). 'Increasing Returns and Long-Run Growth', *Journal of Political Economy*, 94(5), 1002–1037

(1994). 'The Origins of Endogenous Growth', *Journal of Economic Perspectives*, 8(1), 3–22

Rotemberg, J. J. and Woodford, M. (1996). 'Real-Business-Cycle Models and the Forecastable Movements in Output, Hours, and Consumption', *American Economic Review*, 86(1), 71–89

(1999). 'The Cyclical Behavior of Prices and Costs', in J. B. Taylor and M. Woodford (eds.), *Handbook of Macroeconomics*, 1B, Amsterdam: Elsevier Science, 1051–1135

Rudebusch, G. D. (1993). 'The Uncertain Unit Root in Real GNP', *American Economic Review*, 83(1), 265–72

Saint-Paul, G. (1997). 'Business Cycles and Long-Run Growth', *Oxford Review of Economic Policy*, 13(3), 145–53

Samuelson, P. A. (1958). 'An Exact Consumption Loan Model of Interest With and Without the Social Contrivance of Money', *Journal of Political Economy*, 66(6), 467–82

Shleifer, A. (1986). 'Implementation Cycles', *Journal of Political Economy*, 94(6), 1163–90

Solow, R. M. (1956). 'A Contribution to the Theory of Economic Growth', *Quarterly Journal of Economics*, 70(1), 65–94

Sorger, G. (1994). 'On the Structure of Ramsey Equilibrium: Cycles, Indeterminacy, and Sunspots', *Economic Theory*, 4(5), 745–64

Summers, L. H. (1986). 'Some Skeptical Observations on Real Business Cycle Theory', *Federal Reserve Bank of Minneapolis Quarterly Review*, Fall, 23–7

Svensson, L. E. O. (1985). 'Money and Asset Prices in a Cash-in-Advance Economy', *Journal of Political Economy*, 93(5), 919–44

Verbrugge, R. (1997). 'Local Complementarities and Aggregate Fluctuations', *Virginia Tech Working Paper*

Violante, G. L. (2002). 'Technological Acceleration, Skill Transferability, and the Rise in Residual Inequality', *Quarterly Journal of Economics*, 117(1), 297–338

Wan, H. Y. (1971). *Economic Growth*, New York: Harcourt-Brace-Jovanovich

Wen, Y. (1998). 'Can a Real Business Cycle Model Pass the Watson Test?', *Journal of Monetary Economics*, 42(1), 185–203

Wiggins, S. (1990). *Introduction to Applied Nonlinear Dynamical Systems and Chaos*, New York: Springer-Verlag

Author index

Subject index